# Learning
# and the Learner

*A77*

# Learning
# and the Learner

## Janet P. Moursund
*University of Oregon*

*Brooks/Cole Publishing Company*
*Monterey, California*
A Division of Wadsworth Publishing Company, Inc.

61355

*For my parents, with love
and gratitude*

ISBN: 0-8185-0197-9
L.C. Catalog Card No.: 76-7717
Printed in the United States of America

10   9   8   7   6   5   4   3   2   1

Manuscript Editor: *Pamela Fischer*
Production Editor: *Micky Lawler*
Interior & Cover Design: *John Edeen*
Original Cartoons: *Tony Hall*
Cover Photo: *Jim Pinckney*
Technical Illustrations: *L. Donovan Fell III*
Typesetting: *Daybreak Typesetting Services, Albany, New York*
Printing & Binding: *R. R. Donnelley & Sons Co., Crawfordsville, Indiana*

# Preface

*Learning and the Learner* has been written with two purposes in mind. First, it is intended to introduce the teacher-to-be to the essential facts and theories about learning. While taking a basically behaviorist approach, focusing on stimulus-response theory, it also looks at some of the "softer" theoretical positions. The result is, I hope, an amalgam that will acquaint the student with a variety of views and beliefs about learning, allowing—and encouraging—him to choose for himself which position best fits his own style of interacting with students and colleagues.

The second purpose is to hook the student—to make him see the fascination of studying the learning process as it goes on in himself and in others. The interested student does not stop learning at the end of the term or when the final exam is over; he keeps on looking and wondering and forming hypotheses. That is the kind of person I would like to have teaching my children: one who acts on the basis of what he knows now but is never satisfied that that knowledge is complete or closed or unchangeable. I hope that I am that kind of teacher, and I hope that my own curiosity and excitement about how learning takes place will infect the students who read this book.

In format, the book is both traditional and nontraditional. It is traditional in that it covers the basic, time-worn aspects of learning psychology: the laws of conditioning, the factors affecting imitative learning, the role of motivation. It leans heavily on research findings, attempting to relate the "truths" of the psychological laboratory to the real-world hurly-burly of the classroom. It is nontraditional in that it deals with some topics not ordinarily treated at length in an educational psychology textbook: the role of humor, for instance, and the development and consequences of anxiety and conformity and creativity. Moreover, throughout the book, I attempt to bring psychological facts and theories and hypotheses back to the level of what one intuitively believes to be true about people, to weave together sophisticated experimental findings and folk wisdom, and to bring the student to the point where he can say "Oh, yes, that must be true because it feels true to me."

Rather than prepare a list of objective exam questions or an instructor's manual in which "important"concepts are outlined, I have closed each chapter with a set of "Questions for Understanding." These questions explicitly relate the ideas presented in the chapter to actual teaching practice. They are intended to help the student explore and understand the ways in which our theoretical knowledge about learning can affect and shape and improve our professional practice. The questions have no "right" answers. They are designed to be open ended; if they provoke argument and discussion, they will have served their purpose.

In today's climate of movements and liberations and "isms" it is virtually impossible to avoid inadvertently treading on the toes of one group or another. I have tried to deal with issues of race and sex and social class as fairly and as openly as possible. One problem, however, remains insoluble: what to do with personal pronouns. My solution for this book has been to use "he" and "him" as generic pronouns, referring to individuals of either sex. Thus "the teacher," "the student," and "the parent" are "he." This seems to me the least obtrusive way out of a singularly unfortunate linguistic muddle. I wish to state quite unmistakably, though, that I do *not* believe that "he" is in any way better suited for teaching or learning or parenting than "she" is—or vice versa.

I would like to thank a number of people who have helped me in the writing of this book. The reviewers (Peggy Blackwell of the University of New Mexico, Robert Bolus of the University of Windsor, Walter S. Brown of the University of Washington at Seattle, Samuel W. Cochran of East Texas State University, Jeffrey Golland of Bernard Baruch College, Gary Dean Phye of Iowa State University, Thomas Shuell of the State University of New York at Buffalo, and Kinnard P. White of the University of North Carolina at Chapel Hill), who gave so generously of their time and (grrr) their criticisms, contributed more than is usually the case to the final format of the book. The editors who worked with me, Roger Peterson and Todd Lueders, provided Brooks/Cole's usual heady mixture of enthusiasm, encouragement, and realism. My colleagues and students at the University of Oregon have offered so many comments and ideas that it would be impossible to estimate the degree to which they have influenced various chapters; but I would like to offer special thanks to Margaret Wade for her continuing interest and encouragement. My husband and children have been subjected to more spates of ill temper and unreasonable demands than any family should have to endure; were it not for their tolerance, the book would never have been finished. And, finally, a hearty thanks to that unknown hero who helped me gather up some 80 pages of final manuscript after they had slipped from my bike carrier and scattered themselves all over 13th Street—blessings on you, gentleman and scholar, whoever you may be!.

*Janet P. Moursund*

# Contents

61355

# Introduction

It seems to be a characteristic of the English language to pack enormous amounts of meaning into very small words. Indeed, the most important concepts we can think of are packaged in the smallest words: love, work, help, time, and self are a few such words. The word *learn* is another; we use it to refer to a broad range of activities, each with its own special implications and boundaries. To make the situation even more confusing, different people use the same word to refer to quite different things, often without being specific about just what they are talking about.

Few processes are more crucial to the business of being human than the process of learning. No organism that doesn't learn can be thought of as a human being. To be sure, other creatures learn too; but people (we like to believe) do a special kind of learning that sets them apart from lower animals. We are supposed to learn better or faster or more or in different ways or using different equipment than the rest of the animals that we know about. We think of ourselves as intelligent; when we speculate about the possibility of intelligent life on other planets, most of us have in mind a creature that thinks—and learns—rather in the same way that we do.

Our concern with learning affects nearly every aspect of our lives and of our social structure. We are the only species—as far as we know—that sets up formal institutions whose purpose is to facilitate learning. Parents fret over whether Johnny is learning as fast or as well as same-age Susie next door. We can read books or take lessons or participate in group sessions in order to learn to do almost anything, from sailing boats to cooking to making love. And we expect that we and our associates will continue to learn as long as we continue to live, that we will constantly be engaged in the process of observing, assimilating, recalling, and using what goes on around us.

The ways in which we use the word *learn* in our everyday language can perhaps give some insight into just how fundamental the notion of learning is to our human existence. We speak of learning to talk or of learning to read or of learning to balance the accounts. But we also speak of learning to get along with others and of learning to be more graceful and of learning to think ahead. Artists tell us that we can learn to see the world in different ways; preachers advise us to learn to know God; we may even consult a psychiatrist in order to learn to express our feelings. And, perhaps the ultimate in learnings, there is now a whole body of research on the area of learning to learn.

The beginning teacher faces a wilderness of fact and theory about learning with fear and awe. How can he possibly know enough to do his job properly? As he surveys his first classroom, he feels quite inadequate. How can he manage to provide for these young people the conditions each needs for his own individual learnings—whatever those learnings may be? Who are these children anyhow? What goes on behind the face of that boy in the back row, bent over a comic book, or those two girls who are giggling and whispering at the blackboard? What about the one across the room, eyes suspiciously bright, with an angry red welt beginning to show across his cheek? And the freckle-faced redhead, dreaming up at the ceiling, who looks a thousand miles from here? How can the teacher know them? Will they ever let him into their world? How can he ever hope to be wise enough to give each one what he most needs to reach his full potential?

The immediate answer to these questions, of course, is that he can't. Nobody can. No teacher in the world can ever give every child just what that child needs every time. Failures are inevitable; we all blow it occasionally. Just as obviously, though, some teachers seem to do better than others; some seem to have a knack for understanding what is going on inside a child and responding to that process constructively. The question is not so much "How can I do everything right?" as "How can I do things better?" This book is intended to help you in that direction.

The teacher's primary concern, I believe, is with student learning—learning not only the material that is assigned but learning the skills and attitudes and values that shape the person one is to become. This book is about learning in the broadest sense: how people learn, what they learn, and what factors affect their learning.

I have divided the book into two sections. The first deals with the learning process itself, with some of the major ways in which learning takes place and some of the most important variables that influence learning. Learning, though, can never happen all by itself; there must be a learner to do it. The second half of the book focuses on the learner and on the characteristics he brings to (and takes from) the learning situation. In neither section do I claim to have treated the subject exhaustively; there is neither time nor space to do so in an introductory volume of this sort. I have chosen the topics offered here because I think they are important for teachers to know about and (I make no apologies for it) because I find them interesting. I think you will too.

There is no way that you (or anyone else) can make a mental card file of this information and then flip through and find what is needed as you work from moment to moment with your students. Things happen too fast in the real interactions of the classroom; a teacher does what seems best at that instant and wonders later whether he should have done something else. Memorized chunks of unrelated facts about learning will help very little in these interactions; one simply cannot dredge them up fast enough.

Why bother to study a book like this then? Well, it depends on how you intend to study it. If you plan to memorize enough to get you through whatever tests your instructor plans and stop there, you will have wasted your time. The only way that this information can be of use to you in your profession is if it is taken in, chewed up, and thoroughly integrated into your whole set of beliefs about how people behave. I must pause here to point out that nearly all of what psychology offers in the way of facts about human behavior, once it is thoroughly understood, becomes a matter of "Well, of course, everybody knows that." The point here is that everybody doesn't know it; but by making it an integral part of your own knowledge, you feel that it is obvious. And, feeling obvious, it has a chance of being used in the lightning process of deciding what to do with or say to a particular child at a particular instant of time.

Making the material in this book useful to you, then, is a creative process. You cannot simply gulp it up and store it away just as it is given to you; you have to reshape it to fit your own beliefs and needs. In the words of the old Book of Common Prayer, you must "read, mark, learn, and inwardly digest" that which you expect to use in your professional life.

I have tried to write this book in a way that will facilitate this process. I have tried to avoid being stuffy or pedantic and instead to just talk about what I and other psychologists have come to believe about learning. I suspect—I hope—that at times my own ignorance shows through; neither I nor anyone else has all the answers about learning, and we would be pompous fools if we pretended otherwise. Indeed, it is our very ignorance that makes the whole field so exciting; at any moment we may discover something new in our reading or in our research or within ourselves. To learn about learning is to explore the most fascinating area possible: people— you, me, all of us. If there are surprises waiting around the corner, there are also comfortable reaffirmations of what we have always believed or suspected. It should be an interesting trip. I hope you enjoy it.

# PART 1

## Learning

# Chapter 1

# *Conditioning*

All of us are experts in learning because all of us have learned. As teachers and students, you and I devote a significant part of our waking hours to the learning process, trying to encourage it in ourselves and in others. Our expertise in this area stands us in good stead in many ways, for we can introspect about the nature of learning; we can examine our own processes and gain understanding about what happens to us as we move from not knowing to knowing in a given area. But our expertise can also lead us astray. It is all too easy to assume that what happens to me, in my learning, must happen to everyone else. We forget that people differ in what is easy or hard for them to learn, in how fast they acquire concepts or skills, perhaps even in the mechanisms or strategies that they use in their learning.

Too ready a reliance on our personal insights into learning can also tempt us into a kind of snobbishness with regard to experimental data and theory. "Why should I care about all that stuff about rats and eye blinks or about people learning lists of nonsense syllables? I know what real learning is all about, and that's what I'm interested in as a teacher." We do need to be aware of the ideas that have emerged from running rats down mazes or from watching children form concepts based on geometrical designs because these ideas help us to understand our own learning better—and to understand the learning of others better as well. Even learning that a particular theory does not fit what we as teachers are trying to do can help us grasp just what is going on for our students. To be sure, many of the things that are true about the way rats or pigeons learn may not be true about the way people learn, and many of the things that are true about simple human learning situations may be untrue or only partially true about more complex learnings. But even though human learning may be complicated and may involve factors that can never come into play in the learning of lower animals, humans do engage in more basic kinds of learning too. When a human being enters a sophisticated learning process, one that involves all the complex mental machinery and the vast array of learning techniques that he has acquired over the years, he does not leave the older, simpler kinds of learning behind. Rather, he adds to them and builds upon them.

Psychologists have been arguing for years about the differences between human and animal learning. Are there qualitative differences between the way a man and a rat learn something, or is the difference simply one of quantity? Later in this book, we take a look at some of the arguments on both sides. For now, however, it suffices to say that, whatever unique learnings man is capable of, he also does a great deal of "simple" learning. We need to understand some of the principles involved in simple learning before we can deal with the more complex varieties. In this chapter we shall examine the learning process stripped to its bare essentials—a learning skeleton, if you will—and shall look at some of the ways in which theories based on these essentials bear directly upon classroom techniques.

Unfortunately, in talking about bare essentials and skeletons and simple learning, I may already have created a false impression. No learning is really simple. Indeed, the closer we come to isolating the basic elements of the learning process—the building blocks—the more we realize that we don't understand much at all. Learning—the ability to adapt and change—is part of the very stuff of life itself. Psychologists deal with only one aspect of the mystery of learning. Theirs is the task of describing, ordering, and predicting the learning behavior of individuals and groups over relatively short time periods; as they dig into smaller and smaller details or expand to more and more molar phenomena, they must turn to their sister sciences: neurology and biochemistry on the one hand, and sociology and anthropology on the other. Yet our own task is quite large enough to keep us busy. In fact, it may be too large; over the last few decades, so much has been learned about the psychology of learning that it is virtually impossible for any one individual to keep up with all of it. Estes wrote in 1971: "Technological and economic developments have enormously accelerated the volume of research on human learning, and the consequent cascade of data is overloading our capacities for organization and interpretation" (pp. 16-17). We cannot hope to understand it all. But we can understand the basic assumptions, the underlying theories, of learning. Thus armed, we can begin to attack the specific problems of the classroom teacher.

In order to follow the line of reasoning of many of the scientists whom we shall meet in the next few pages, we must accept (at least temporarily) a new kind of mental discipline. This is the discipline of *behaviorism,* and it may seem stringent to those of us who enjoy playing with words and ideas. In its simplest form, behaviorism demands that nothing be assumed or taken for granted about human behavior; only those behaviors that can be observed by an outside witness may be used as explanations or cited as results. Internal events, like thinking about or figuring out or forgetting or wanting, have no place in a behavioristic theory. "Perhaps what character-izes all behaviorists is their use of experimental methods, their reliance on empirical data based on careful observation, their concern for objectivity and replication of results, their focus on the environment and what the organism is doing currently, and their rejection of inner causes or entities as the sole or most important determinant of human action. To the behav-iorist, the 'here and now' contemporary environment is a prime focus of concern because much of what a person does is a function of environmental events" (Thoresen, 1972, p. 390).

To the behaviorists belong the theories dealing with conditioning, the simplest form of learning that we know of. Some psychologists insist that all learning can be explained in terms of complex combinations of condi-tioned responses. All would agree that conditioning is woven into the fab-ric of even the most complex human behaviors. To understand the princi-ples of conditioning is to build a foundation for the understanding of other, more complicated learning patterns. A useful theory of educational psy-chology should provide principles from which one can derive optimal pro-grams and teacher behavior. Such a theory is partly a theory of learning, specifically adapted to the conditions arising in an educational setting (Logan, 1971). And such a theory of learning logically begins with simple conditioning. As we begin to understand more and more the underlying rules that govern how people learn, we can also begin to arrange the learning environment of students to take advantage of these relationships. The art of teaching must, if it is to be maximally effective, be built upon the science of learning. Let us turn now to that science, as it is reflected in our understanding of basic stimulus-response patterns.

## CLASSICAL AND OPERANT CONDITIONING

*Conditioning* is a general term that refers to the attachment of a par-ticular response to a particular stimulus. Obviously, this stimulus-response connection must be one that is new to the individual; learning implies that something different has happened. The response itself need not be new, however; an old response may be conditioned to a new or a different stimu-lus. A child may be quite adept at waving his hand in the air, for instance, so that the waving response is not a new one. If we teach the child to wave whenever we say "bye-bye," however, learning has occurred. The waving has been conditioned to the stimulus word *bye-bye*.

The Russian scientist Ivan Pavlov did more than anyone else to work out the basic principles of *classical conditioning*. In this form of condi-tioning, an innate response—a reflex such as salivating at the smell of food or jerking away from an electric shock—is paired with a new stimulus. Pavlov presented dogs with a food stimulus and a sound stimulus (a bell or a buzzer) at the same time. After repeated pairings of food smell and bell,

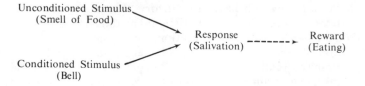

*Figure 1-1.* Schematic representation of classical conditioning.

the bell alone came to elicit the salivation response. The original stimulus (food smell) is the *unconditioned stimulus,* and salivation is the *unconditioned response.* When the *conditioned stimulus* (bell) replaces the unconditioned stimulus in producing the response, we call the response a *conditioned response.* Figure 1-1 shows in diagram form what happens in such conditioning. In classical conditioning, the response does not change (or changes only slightly). The unconditioned response and the conditioned response look the same; but the conditioned response is made to a stimulus that did not cause (elicit) that response before.

In *operant conditioning,* the picture is somewhat different. Instead of pairing an old response with a new stimulus, operant conditioning reinforces (rewards) a particular response that originally occurs more or less randomly. The learning animal is placed in a total stimulus situation, and when it emits a designated response, it is rewarded (it is allowed to eat, drink, or engage in another desired behavior). Each time the response is rewarded, it is strengthened—that is, its occurrence becomes more likely the next time the animal finds itself in that stimulus situation (see Figure 1-2). A rat, for instance, is placed in a cage with a lever built into the corner. As it explores the cage, it accidentally depresses the lever; immediately a bit of food (reward) is put into the cage. The rat explores some more and pushes the lever again—another reward. In a relatively short time, the rat learns to push the lever whenever it is hungry; the stimulus situation—cage with lever plus hunger—produces the response "press lever."

There are some "obvious" similarities and differences in these two forms of conditioning. I place quotation marks around obvious because, as learning theorists dig deeper and deeper into conditioning, arguments arise

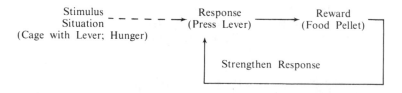

*Figure 1-2.* Schematic representation of operant conditioning.

as to just what the relationship is between the two. We are on firm ground when we note that, in each, a response becomes associated with a stimulus that originally did not elicit that response. But when we try to go further, we must step carefully, for our footing becomes a bit shaky. One of the common distinctions between classical and operant conditioning lies in the nature of the response. Typically, classical conditioning deals with *respondents*—responses that are "naturally" elicited by an unconditioned stimulus. You don't have to teach a dog to salivate at the smell of food or a human to blink his eye when you direct a puff of air at it. *Operants*, the responses of operant conditioning, are more often learned patterns and are not reflexively connected to a certain stimulus. No known stimulus elicits a bar-press reflex. Gagné (1965, p. 35) characterizes the classical-conditioned response as "general, diffuse, and emotional" and says that such learning "has a truly 'involuntary' character, and applies to responses that are not typically under voluntary control." This description seems right and reasonable—but is it? Work goes forward in the Soviet Union and elsewhere in using classical-conditioning techniques with learned, voluntary responses; and studies of biofeedback suggest that operant conditioning can be effective in the control of involuntary responses such as blood pressure and brain-wave production.

As we compare the diagrams of conditioning, another difference seems immediately apparent: operant conditioning involves selective reinforcement, while no reinforcement is necessary in classical conditioning. Again, though, more thought may make us hesitate. If the conditioned stimulus is presented over and over to a dog that has learned to salivate at the sound of a bell, in the absence of the unconditioned stimulus, the conditioned response may begin to fade. The dog will not continue to salivate when the bell sounds unless it is occasionally refreshed by a re-pairing of bell with food smell. However, without such re-pairing the salivation response can still be strengthened by rewarding it (by placing a bit of odorless meat powder in the dog's mouth, for instance). Classical and operant techniques can be used together to obtain and then strengthen a desired response.

Whether we believe, with Gagné, that classical and operant conditioning are two fundamentally different kinds of learning or whether we see them as different forms of a basic, not-yet-completely-understood process, one thing is clear: both work. Each method can be used to facilitate one's own learning; each can be used to aid or manipulate or control the learning of others. In the Western world, and particularly in North America, attention has tended to focus on operant rather than on classical models of learning. Particularly in the world of education, an emphasis on reflexive or involuntary responses has not been as immediately applicable as the notion of selectively rewarding voluntary behaviors. Operant conditioning goes on all the time in the classroom and has done so since the first teacher praised the good work of the first student. One reason operant theories are so persuasive is that they describe, with elegant simplicity, what we all do.

We reward and punish our children, our students, our colleagues, and ourselves. We do not have a choice as to whether operant conditioning will be a part of our classroom behavior; it is already there. We can choose only whether we ourselves will be effective dispensers of reinforcement and to what ends.

## OPERANT CONDITIONING: A CLOSER LOOK

Although most of us associate operant conditioning with the work of B. F. Skinner (in fact, it is often called Skinnerian conditioning), the notion of shaping behavior through selective reinforcement did not begin in Skinner's Harvard laboratory. Like most other "big ideas" of psychology, operant conditioning is rooted so far back that it is hard to say where it started. A convenient bench mark, though, is the research of Thorndike in the early 1930s. Thorndike, more than anyone else, pulled scattered data, ill-tested ideas, and folk wisdom into a coherent theory. Until his time, psychologists and philosophers alike stumbled over the notion that a future state of affairs could work backward in time upon a present situation. How can a reward that will occur later affect what I am doing right now? Thorndike attempted to explain, in physiological terms, just how this could happen. A satisfying state of affairs, he said, is registered in an organism's nervous system; it is these physiological changes that cause us to describe the state as satisfying. But such satisfaction is not limited to the stimulus situation that caused it; rather, it spreads to those stimuli that preceded and will follow it. The effect of this spreading satisfaction is to strengthen the connections made before and after the satisfaction is experienced. By a connection, Thorndike meant a stimulus-response connection. The greatest strengthening, his data indicated, occurred in the connection immediately preceding the satisfying state; lesser degrees of strengthening showed up in earlier connections and in later connections. Connectionism, as Thorndike's ideas came to be designated, was greeted with cries of joy by psychologists; at last, here was an acceptable explanation of what every parent knew and used daily. Thorndike's Law of Effect summed it up neatly and cleared the way for new and productive lines of research. Here it is, in his own words: "the after-effects of a modifiable condition work back upon it, . . . in particular, a satisfying state of affairs accompanying or directly following a connection strengthens it" (1933, p. 1).

If behaviorism, and with it the whole set of theories about operant conditioning, can be thought of as a structure, then Thorndike cleared and prepared the site on which that structure was to be built. Skinner laid the foundation and erected the framework. And swarms of psychologists are busy today shingling and painting and adding on rooms. Nowhere in all the history of psychology has there been an idea that led to more research, that stimulated more creative thought, or that carried with it more implications for real life outside the laboratory. In order to understand some of these implications, we shall have to chop things up a bit; the whole picture is too complicated to grasp all at once, so let's look at some of the individual components.

## Stimulus

Unlike the stimulus in classical conditioning, which is a relatively short-duration, well-specified event, the stimulus in operant conditioning is a total situation. The learning organism may be responding to this part of the whole or to that part; we, as observers, can only specify the overall situation. We can neither know nor control which parts of the whole will come to be primarily responsible for the response we are conditioning. "The experimenter does not ask whether a stimulus looks the same to the organism as it does to him. . . . To guess what an organism sees when a stimulus is presented would be to abandon all that physics has to offer by way of specifying environmental events" (Skinner, 1969, p. 79).

In classical conditioning, the stimulus is under the control of the experimenter (teacher). He decides what it will be, how long it will last, when it will start and stop. In operant conditioning, although the experimenter can specify what the total stimulus situation will be, he cannot control (or can control only through the conditioning process itself) which parts the learner will attend to. In fact, some aspects of the stimulus situation are quite out of his control: the stimulus situation includes all the sensory impressions impinging on the learner, even internal sensations. Muscle tension, excitement, hormonal balance—all may play their part in defining for the learner the nature of the stimulus to which he is responding. I am a part of each stimulus situation in which I find myself, and any definition of that stimulus must include me, the learner. If the behavior of an intelligent organism at any instant results from the total stimulus situation, including internal stimuli, it follows that responses can never be exactly alike because the total stimulus situation is never repeated. The more factors we can be aware of and take into account, the more we can make two similar stimulus situations resemble each other—the more overlap there will be—but our control can never be complete.

An annoying question—annoying because as yet we have no definite answer—in this context is whether one must be consciously aware of a part of the stimulus situation in order for that part to affect learning. Clearly, an effective stimulus must be within our capacity to perceive it; we cannot be conditioned to respond to a tone too soft to hear or a light wave outside our visual spectrum. But what about the high shrill that we aren't conscious of hearing? The change in light intensity that we pay no attention to? Or the children-at-play noises that we don't notice until they stop? A few decades ago, there was great interest in a phenomenon called subliminal perception. Images were flashed on a screen for just a fraction of a second—too

short a time for conscious recognition to take place—and the subjects were then tested to see whether some sort of subconscious recognition had occurred. The phenomenon was especially interesting to advertising specialists, who envisioned conditioning people to buy products by the subliminal flash of a message on a movie or TV screen. The efforts eventually faded out, largely because the data were ambiguous; nobody knows to this day whether subliminal conditioning is possible. We do know that awareness is an important factor in conditioning—even in classical conditioning (Dawson & Biferno, 1973)—and that conditioning generally takes place much more readily if the learner is aware of and is cooperating in what is happening to him. But we don't know the extent to which awareness is necessary.

The question of awareness of the stimulus is particularly important when we try to place it in the context of our educational philosophy. Most of us react with horror to the idea of a society of robotlike individuals, conditioned to respond mechanically and helplessly to a series of stimuli of which they are not even aware. We are much happier with a model of learning in which students and teachers work together to create and select stimuli that enhance learning. Awareness of the nature of the stimuli to which we are responding is the key to freedom, according to Thoresen (1972, p. 400): "awareness is the basis of freedom and self-control because it provides the individual with the information he needs to change his own sources of stimulation, both internal and external." Whether or not unconscious conditioning of humans is theoretically possible, it would seem that a major goal of education must be that of helping each individual become aware of and alert to those stimuli that affect his own behavior.

## Cues and Thresholds

I said earlier that an individual may react to various parts of the total stimulus situation. We call these salient parts of a situation *cues*. To a child playing in a neighbor's yard, the sound of his mother's voice calling his name is only one part of a complex situation, but that single aspect is a cue for him to run home to dinner. Learning to discriminate and respond to appropriate cues is an important part of the child's educational task: only when he can pick out the relevant cue or cues can he begin to respond efficiently. In this sense, most if not all operant-learning situations involve two major phases, that of *cue recognition* and that of *response learning*. Again, the question of whether we must be aware of the cues we are using in order to respond to them is not yet answered, though it does seem likely that we learn to respond to configurations of cues without knowing exactly what the individual components are. This is particularly true in social learnings; we can know that someone is in a good mood or is down without knowing exactly which stimulus cues gave us that impression.

The mention of cues leads us to the concept of thresholds. We have already noted that only those parts of a stimulus situation that the individual is physically able to perceive can serve as cues: I cannot learn to respond to a figure too dim to make out or a tone too faint to discriminate from background noise. The lowest level of intensity at which an organism can discriminate a stimulus cue is called its *threshold;* below-threshold stimuli cannot be cues because they are not received by the learner. That seems like a simple and obvious statement; but the situation is complicated by the fact that not all people have the same threshold levels, nor is the threshold level for a given person always the same. Many factors can influence stimulus thresholds; a few of the more common ones are general sensory acuity, fatigue, attention or alertness, and the presence of competing stimuli. In the case of a learning failure—that is, a situation in which learning might be expected to occur but does not—it is wise to ask first about the learner's threshold for the cue to which a particular response is to be conditioned. The first phase of learning, cue recognition, must begin before the second, response learning, can take place. The conditioning of a particular response to a particular cue may be initiated before the cue is clearly and completely differentiated, but it cannot be initiated if the cue is not perceived at all.

One other factor is an important determinant of stimulus threshold: the learner's emotional state. Anxiety, elation, depression—all have their effect on the sensitivity with which he interacts with his environment. Emotion, as a physiological state, plays two major roles in the learning process:

it helps to determine which cues one will receive, and it is itself a part of the stimulus situation and thus may serve as a cue. The overanxious child who forgets his lines in a school play may not hear the prompter's whisper because anxiety has raised his perceptual threshold. And the feeling of anxiety itself may serve as a cue for a variety of previously learned responses.

To sum up: Anything in the learner's perceptual environment, internal or external, may serve as a stimulus cue to which a response may be conditioned. The experimenter/teacher does not always know which facets of the total situation have been isolated by the learner as relevant cues for a response. Below-threshold cues cannot serve as response-eliciting stimuli, although cue configurations may sometimes be utilized without awareness of their individual components. Finally, failure to learn or to perform a previously learned response may often be due to nonreception of a cue to which we are trying to condition a response.

*Response*

The stimulus-response-reward paradigm can be misleading in that it tends to suggest that a response is an easily identified unit that follows a stimulus and that may or may not lead to a reward. To be sure, this can be (and, in the experimental situation, often is) the case. But when we look at behavior in the natural setting, we realize that responses occur continuously and that it is sometimes difficult to say when one response leaves off and another begins. A basic assumption of operant theory is that the organism is always responding; we emit responses in a continuous stream. Moreover, we may make quite a number of responses simultaneously.

The definition of a response depends on the focus of the person doing the defining. As I sit here right now, I am pressing my fingers against a specific sequence of typewriter keys. I am also smoking a cigarette and drinking (at intervals) a cup of coffee, and I am occasionally blinking my eyes and moving my feet. I am composing sentences, writing a book, working for my university, and trying to earn tenure. I am also not doing some things, and specifically choosing not to do something can also be a response. I am not eating lunch today, and I am not grading an exam paper that lies on my desk. If I am to be reinforced for these activities, exactly what is it that is being reinforced? One reason awareness is so important in working with human subjects is that one's own perception of what one is doing helps to determine the stimulus-response sequence that will be learned in a given situation.

Researchers frequently work with lower animals because the "what am I doing now" problem can be simplified with them. While a dog or a rat may also do a number of things simultaneously, it is easier to *operationalize*—to define unambiguously—the behavioral alternatives open to it in a given time segment. The dog may move toward or away from a goal object or remain in one place. The rat may press a lever or not press a lever. The behaviorist does not ask why the animal makes a response or what it "thinks" it is doing, but merely indicates which of a number of nonoverlapping categories the behavior falls into. Hypotheses or rules or laws about learning established in this way may not transfer perfectly to human behavior, but they do at least give us jumping-off places—they help us to formulate more clearly the variables with which we are working. And, surprisingly often, the "simple" rules of animal learning predict human behavior very well indeed.

One such simple rule has to do with the production of nonrewarded (or not obviously rewarded) responses: "When faced with a number of equally attractive alternatives, an organism tends to *alternate* between responses. . . . This tendency to vary responses rather than to repeat them produces more rapid exploration of the environment than would occur by chance" (Walker, 1968, p. 19). The tendency to emit a varied sequence of responses makes it possible for the teacher to select desired responses to reinforce. If the rat did not explore its cage, it might never accidentally press the bar that releases the food reinforcement. If the school child sat all day in one place scribbling on a piece of paper, we would never have the chance to reward him for writing his name or asking a question or showing interest in a friend's work. Without the organism's inherent tendency to vary its responses, operant conditioning would not be possible.

The converse of the response-alternation rule can also help us to understand and use effectively the learning environment: when an organism does not vary its responses, but rather continues to make the same response or response sequence again and again, we must assume that that response is being rewarded in some way. We shall discuss rewards in more detail later. Here it should be pointed out that many rewards are the natural consequences of responses, without any intervention at all by a teacher/experimenter. Operants—the responses of operant conditioning—are so named because they operate on the environment in some manner (Skinner, 1969). They are an organism's way of interacting with the world around (and internal to) it. As such, they usually affect the world in some way and thus result in a change in the environment. These changes may be pleasing or displeasing to the organism; they may be rewards or punishments. The child may like the feel of scribbling on his paper and may be pleased with the way the scribbles look. If so, the scribbling behavior is automatically rewarded.

Responses that carry with them automatic or inevitable rewards are called *consummatory* responses. Consummatory responses were originally thought of as those that involved the consumption of food or water; for the hungry or thirsty animal, such consumption is in and of itself reinforcing. But other behaviors can satisfy basic or learned drives: a cautious child stands close and rubs against his mother, or a monkey plays with a simple puzzle, or I settle down to read a murder mystery. These behaviors do not need to be externally rewarded. They are self-reinforcing.

Some students of human learning have suggested that simply repeating or recalling a learned behavior may well be a consummatory response—that there is a basic pleasure in doing that which one has learned to do. Black is one such theorist. He speculates "It seems possible that the act of retrieving or recalling an association constitutes the analogue of a 'consummatory response' in learning; each time it is recalled, it is inherently reinforced by the very act of recall" (Black, 1973, p. 64). Black goes on to point out that if this is indeed the case, simply providing the learner with the opportunity to rehearse what he has learned creates a reinforcement situation; and, conversely, little retention or learning can be expected when such opportunities are not provided.

## Reward

Throughout all the foregoing discussion, I have been referring to rewards and reinforcements; it is impossible to discuss operant conditioning in the absence of such concepts. But now it's time to take a closer look at them. Just what is a reward, and how does it work? Thorndike, as we have seen, said that rewards act on the organism in a physical way, changing the state of its nervous system. He defined a *satisfier* as something that the animal does nothing to avoid and that the animal often attempts to maintain or renew. In other words, if an organism makes no move to avoid something or if it seems to actively seek it out, then we can assume that the something is satisfying or rewarding. Skinner, building on Thorndike's theories (or at least taking them as a starting point), recognized that this definition was not wholly operational; it still required the observer to make an assumption about what was going on internally in the learning organism. He recognized that any account of an interaction between the learner and the learner's environment had to include what happened to the learner after (or as a consequence of) its action, but he wanted to describe those consequences without making an assumption about what the learner wanted or liked or enjoyed. His solution essentially turned Thorndike's definition around upon itself: anything that strengthens (or makes more likely in the future) a particular behavior is a reward. In fact, Skinner objected to the word *reward* because it connotes internal, nonobservable reaction. He suggested that we use instead the term *reinforcement*. Any state of affairs that, following a particular behavior, makes that behavior more likely in the future can be said to reinforce that behavior. *Positive reinforcers* are those occurrences that increase the likelihood (or rate) of a response when they appear, and *negative reinforcers* increase the likelihood (or rate) of a response when they disappear. Food is a positive reinforcer; noxious stimuli like extremely loud noise or confinement in a small, empty room are negative reinforcers (Skinner, 1969).

Critics of Skinner's brand of behaviorism have pointed out that this definition is a circular one: reinforcement has the effect of strengthening a behavior, and that which strengthens a behavior is a reinforcement. Skinner contends that this apparent circularity doesn't matter since it is anchored in observable behavior. By watching an animal (including man), we can determine whether a given state of affairs reinforces behavior, and once we have determined that, we can predict the animal's future behavior with some accuracy.

## Schedules of Reinforcement

Some of the most interesting findings that have emerged from the work of Skinner and his students have to do with the relationship between learning behavior and the timing of reinforcements. We can provide reinforcement immediately following (or even during) a behavior that we want to condition, or we can wait some length of time and then provide the reinforcement. We can reinforce the behavior every time it occurs, or only some of the time. The effects of various *reinforcement schedules* tend to be remarkably consistent across different kinds of learned behavior, among different individuals, and even across species.

One consistent result is that the more immediate a reinforcement is—that is, the less time that elapses between the behavior to be conditioned and the reinforcement—the greater the effect of the reinforcement. Praising Stevie for a neat paper as soon as he has finished with it is much more reinforcing than praising him a day later when the paper is handed back. With immediate reinforcement, learning tends to proceed rather quickly. Learning also is most rapid when reinforcement occurs every time the behavior occurs, rather than only some of the time.

In the real-life situations of home or school, however, it is unreasonable to assume that an external reinforcement can always be administered every time a desired behavior occurs. When we remove the reinforcement for a particular response, the response ordinarily will recur less and less frequently. Ultimately, it will disappear completely—it will be *extinguished.* As teachers, though, we certainly hope that some learned behaviors will continue to occur even when we aren't around to reinforce them. The kind of reinforcement schedule that was in effect when a behavior was first learned has an important influence on what happens to that behavior when the original reinforcement is no longer given. In general, behaviors acquired under a partial or intermittent reinforcement schedule last longer (are more *resistant to extinction)* than those acquired under a constant reinforcement schedule. Although Stevie may learn more quickly to turn in neat papers if we praise him every time he does so, he will tend to revert back to his original sloppiness as soon as we stop praising him. If we praise him only once in a while for an especially neat paper, the neatness habit will be more likely to persist in the absence of praise.

Partial reinforcement comes in a number of different varieties. We can, for instance, reward every third or fifth or *n*th occurrence of the behavior to be conditioned; or if the behavior is a continuous one (like sitting still and listening or doing a series of push-ups), we can reward it after it has been occurring for *n* seconds and on every *n*th second thereafter. Such schedules are called *fixed-ratio* schedules; the learner comes to anticipate when the reward will occur next, and his production of the learned activity often speeds up just before reinforcement time and slows down again until just before the next reward is due. Reinforcing on a *variable-ratio* schedule involves determining ahead of time how often a behavior will be rewarded on the average, but varying the between-reinforcement intervals. For instance, a behavior might go unrewarded two times, then be rewarded twice in a row, then go unrewarded five times, and so forth; over the whole reinforcement period, the learner could average one reward for every three behaviors, but he would not be able to predict just when these rewards would happen. Performance during the learning period and resistance to extinction are both improved by a variable-ratio schedule; subjects tend to learn faster on variable- than on fixed-ratio schedules (Walker, 1968) and to extinguish learnings more slowly. Indeed, the reinforcement schedule may be the single most important factor in determining how long a particular behavior will continue after explicit reinforcement stops (Ackerman, 1973). It is our good fortune as teachers that the kind of schedule that seems to be most effective in the long run is exactly the kind that seems most natural to provide in the classroom.

## Learning as a Reinforcer

We have already pointed out that in Skinner's definition of reinforcement, it is unnecessary to try to say why a particular situation is reinforcing or to predict ahead of time whether an organism will be reinforced by this thing or that event. If it works (if it reinforces a behavior), it is a reinforcer; if it doesn't, it isn't. A number of students, however, have been dissatisfied with this position; they are concerned about why things are reinforcing, about whether the ability to be reinforced by this thing or that is innate or learned. We shall discuss these questions in some detail in the chapter on motivation, but one special class of possible reinforcers should be mentioned here. This class can be roughly described as things that satisfy curiosity or as novel situations or as situations that provide the organism an opportunity to learn. (We might suspect that the lack of precision of these definitions would be enough to make Skinner turn away in disgust!) Interest in the reinforcing effect of novel stimuli began in the late 1950s and has continued to the present time. It is now possible to state a general relationship: a novel stimulus presented following a specific behavior has the effect of facilitating that behavior (Fowler, 1973). In other words, just being exposed to a novel stimulus can be reinforcing. Pushing this notion a bit further, we might say that organisms take innate pleasure in seeing (sensing, experiencing) something new. Since something new is, by definition, something about which one has not learned before, it seems reasonable to hypothesize that the feeling of pleasure may be connected with learning about the new thing. Taking in a novel stimulus situation—learning about it—is a kind of consummatory response in which the situation's novelty is "consumed."

If such a hypothesis is valid, it has enormous implications for educators. We no longer need to try to find ways of rewarding students for learning; we need only provide situations in which they can learn, and the reinforcement will take care of itself. Logan (1971, p. 59) takes this position: "The student is motivated to learn something, somewhere, somehow. If the educational program is one in which his efforts to learn are highly successful, the resulting drive reduction will directly reward those efforts and generate incentive motivation to repeat them in future states of learning-drive motivation." What we must remember here, though, is that the student must experience the learning if it is to be reinforcing. To try to learn and fail, to tackle a problem too difficult to master (or too easy to be a challenge), is not reinforcing. The reinforcement schedule, whether intrinsic to the learning or provided extrinsically, must be geared to the student's capacities; he must be allowed to succeed before success can be reinforcing. "The one rule we can state confidently," says Logan (1971), "is that the correlation in reward must make contact with the individual's performance. That is to say, variations in reward must occur within the range of variation in performance of which the learner is then capable. In effect, the standards should not be absolute but should be relative to the student's current level of proficiency" (p. 57).

The concepts of stimulus, response, and reward, as they are used in operant conditioning, provide a rich field for speculation. They offer a new viewpoint from which to examine our behavior as learning facilitators—a new game plan from which we can evolve fresh strategies for dealing with both the ongoing needs of students in general and the puzzling problem cases that so often frustrate and defeat us.

## ADDITIONAL CONCEPTS

While stimulus, response, and reward alone provide us with a great deal of food for thought, these three concepts by no means exhaust the vocabulary of behaviorism. Students of operant conditioning have come up with a wealth of terminology, hypotheses, and possible applications, many of which have important implications for the educator. While we cannot hope to deal with all the operant-learning concepts relevant to teaching, in the next few pages we shall discuss a number of the more interesting and/or immediately applicable ones.

*Generalization/Discrimination*

Distinguishing one stimulus from a similar stimulus—psychologists call it *discrimination*—is a central concept in learning theory. Discrimination is the act of responding differently to different aspects of the environment. Its converse, *generalization,* is the treatment of two different things as if they were the same. Usually, we speak of generalization as an ability—the ability to see and respond to important similarities and to deal with classes of things.

Generalization and discrimination are both necessary skills (for lower animals as well as humans). We must be able to discriminate one thing from another in order for our responses to be appropriate. And, conversely, we could not possibly come up with separate appropriate responses for each of the millions of percepts in our environment, so we must be able to generalize. In fact, the human brain can keep track of a surprisingly small number of isolated and unrelated concepts; evidence from the Wechsler Adult Intelligence Scale, for instance, suggests that, even in short-term recall, adults can hold in mind only 12 or so nonrelated digits. Clearly we couldn't function well if we had to treat each new percept as if it were unique. Our world becomes livable as we give it order by classifying its contents: these are chairs; these kinds of things are food; those are people; and so on.

A useful distinction can be made between *primary* and *secondary* generalization. Primary generalization occurs when a person treats two things as if they were the same because he can't discriminate between them. Secondary generalization is based on the perceived similarity of stimulus patterns; the individual knows that two things are different but also sees them as similar enough to be assigned to the same class. Primary generalization tends to be maladaptive, for it cannot help the organism to learn; indeed, it often hinders learning. Secondary generalization, however, is necessary for meaningful learning.

Watching a person or an animal function, one can see that discrimination and generalization processes are essentially cyclical. The organism sees differences, then similarities; it classifies, separates, reclassifies. Discrimination leads to generalization, and generalization leads to further discrimination. The importance of this interaction cannot be overestimated. It lies at the root of all kinds of learning, from the simplest stimulus-response bond to the most complex acquisition of social-interaction patterns.

Of course, there is nothing startling in the idea that we discriminate one thing from another or that we generalize objects and concepts into classes. However, the statement of the obvious, the calling of attention to what "everyone has always known," often has made a great contribution to our understanding of human behavior. The *generalization gradient*—the possible amount of similarity between two stimulus objects—is a good example. The more alike two stimulus objects are, the closer together they are on the generalization gradient. And the closer they are on the generalization gradient, the more likely an observer will be to generalize them—that is, to say they are the same. It sounds somewhat simple minded to point out that the more similar two things are, the more likely that they will be mistaken for each other. Yet this observation has led to many advances in our understanding of learning. Researchers have been able to predict the shape of the learning curve (that is, the speed of learning at different times during the learning process) on the basis of how similar the stimulus materials are (Bahrick, Clark, & Bahrick, 1967). If the student is working with unfamiliar place names in a foreign country, for instance, ones that all sound the same to him, learning will proceed much more slowly than if he needs to discriminate only among cities or states that are already familiar to him.

Let's reexamine our earlier statement that the discrimination-generalization cycle lies at the root of all learning by going back to the simplest possible learning schema:

$$\text{Stimulus} \longrightarrow \text{Response} \longrightarrow \text{Reward}$$

Stimulus should really be called Stimulus$_1$, for the response is learned to one particular stimulus (or class of stimuli). In order for the learning to occur, the individual must be able to discriminate Stimulus$_1$ from Stimulus$_2$, Stimulus$_3$, and so on. Also, he must be able to generalize successfully to all the different specific cases of Stimulus$_1$. For example, a child learning to respond to the sound of his own name must learn to recognize and classify as "my name" that name spoken by many different kinds of voices as well as a number of different pronunciations of that name and possibly a whole group of nicknames. He has to learn to respond similarly to "Johnny" in a high, female voice, to "Son" in a bass voice, and perhaps to "Jah-Jah" in a child's voice. His response is also one of a large group of possible responses, some appropriate and some inappropriate. The major discrimination he makes, of course, is between those responses that are positively reinforced and those that are not; and here we see an inherent generalization of possible responses into two classes. But, to add to the complexity of the problem, some responses are more appropriate to one particular subclass of "my name" than are others. Thus, the learning proceeds with both stimulus and response becoming refined, classified, redefined, and reassigned through perpetual cycles of discrimination and generalization.

## Punishment

If some stimulus situations following a behavior tend to make that behavior more likely in the future, it seems only reasonable to assume that other sorts of situations following a behavior might make it less likely in the future. Such stimuli are called *punishments*. A behavior that is consistently punished should eventually drop out of the learner's repertoire.

We might pause here to take note of an interesting phenomenon: a behavior that has been "unlearned" or extinguished by punishment may often return after a rest period during which the original stimulus for the response does not occur. A nursery school child, for instance, amuses himself on Monday by making squeaking noises during the afternoon rest period. Using appropriate positive and negative reinforcements, his teacher manages to extinguish the response; by Friday afternoon, the behavior no longer occurs. But, to the teacher's dismay, the squeaks are back again the next Monday. This phenomenon is known as *spontaneous recovery,* and it is a common occurrence. We cannot assume that a response, extinguished once, will stay extinguished; responses can and do recover. The recovered response, however, is usually not as strong as it was originally. Extinguishing it a second time is easier, and its subsequent recovery is weaker still. Parents and teachers, take heart! Getting David not to slam the door or breaking Sarah Jean of throwing her coat on the floor may seem a hopeless task because it must be redone so often. But each spontaneous recovery of the old pattern, provided it is not rewarded again, is easier to get rid of than the last.

Punishment effects are considerably less predictable than reward effects. One source of confusion is the relationship between punishments and negative reinforcements. You will recall that a negative reinforcement is reinforcing when it stops, as in the case of a loud, unpleasant noise. Most punishments are also negative reinforcements; the organism "wants" them to stop. In administering a punishment, then, we inevitably terminate it with a (negative) reinforcement. The interaction of these two contradictory events determines future behavior, and we don't always know just what that interaction is.

Another way of looking at punishment is to recognize that a learner cannot just not do something. Since he is always producing behaviors, not doing one thing implies doing something else. When we punish a particular behavior with the expectation that it will die out, we are expecting that it will be replaced by another behavior. In this sense, punishment can be looked at as a special case of reinforcement in which "something other than what I was doing" is the reinforced behavior. But "something other than what I was doing" is rather broad and vague; if our intent is to reward an alternative behavior, why not do it directly? Homme makes exactly that suggestion in his plea for contingency management. In *contingency management,* behaviors are controlled by positive reinforcement: getting desired rewards is made *contingent* upon producing desired behaviors. Contingency management does not concern itself with doing away with the nondesired behaviors. "Contingency management in general has no technology for 'getting rid of' a response. [It] has only a technology for strengthening a behavior which is incompatible with the response to be eliminated" (Homme, 1965, p. 505). Strengthening an incompatible response serves the same function as a punishment in that it reinforces "something other than what I was doing," and it has the added effect of focusing the reinforcement on a specifically desired alternative.

At times, however, reinforcing an alternative behavior is not a viable technique; when the undesired behavior is so extreme or so persistent that it must be dealt with here and now, punishment may be the only alterna-

tive.[1] Punishment serves one purpose just as well as reward: it supplies information. Just as reinforcement tells the learner "You did the right thing," so punishment tells him "You made a mistake." The information-providing function of rewards and punishments has nothing to do with their "satisfyingness," to borrow Thorndike's terminology. "Since the earliest experimental studies of human learning, it has been recognized that, for the adult learner, rewards and punishments serve to an important extent as carriers of information quite independently of any effects they

[1]We should note, though, that our labeling some behaviors as undesirable often reflects our own needs rather than those of the learner—and that's not necessarily bad. It's all right for a teacher or a parent to demand that some of his needs be met by the learner; what can confuse everybody is when the parent or teacher tries to hide his own needs behind a false "this is for your own good" facade.

may have as satisfiers or arousers of drives or motives" (Estes, 1971, p. 19). The more specific the information conveyed by a punishment, the more effective that punishment is.

Rewards can occur only when the learner emits a rewardable behavior. But sometimes an undesirable behavior has become so well learned that it takes the place of and precludes the occurrence of a more desirable one. The child who always whines at bedtime can't be rewarded for going to bed cheerfully because that behavior never occurs. In such situations, punishment may be the only way to jolt the learner out of his established pattern; it's about as controlled and precise as kicking the TV set, but (like kicking the TV set) it sometimes works. It is extremely important that the learner understand what behavior is being punished (maximizing the informational value of the punishment) and that alternative behavior be rewarded immediately; all too frequently, punishment is not directly connected to a specific transgression, or the transgressor doesn't know what he should do instead of the thing he was punished for.

Another difficulty in using punishment effectively is that determining the situations that are punishing for a particular child can be difficult. One of the most frequently used punishments in the classroom is teacher disapproval; yet teacher disapproval can and often does reinforce the very behaviors that the teacher is trying to eliminate. Becker (1973) describes the plight of a kindergarten teacher trying to deal with a group of unruly children. She tells them to "sit down" and they do—for a short while. As they begin to move about, she again says "sit down." Again the rowdiness subsides for a time. The teacher believes that by saying "sit down" in a disapproving tone, she is punishing the children's rowdy behavior. And she believes it works; after all, they do sit down and behave when she scolds them. In fact, the rowdiness may be a bid for attention, and the teacher's scolding is exactly that—attention. From the point of view of the children, the relationship is "Ask her to notice me" (response)⟶ "She notices me" (reward). Just because I, the teacher, think a situation is punishing does not guarantee that it is punishing to the students. And what is a punishment for one child may be a reward for another. If we are convinced that punishment is necessary, we had better make sure that what we intend to do will, in fact, weaken rather than strengthen the unwanted behavior.

Becker points out still another reason why punishment should be used sparingly if at all. Frequently the response to punishment is to escape from the entire punishment situation rather than to change the specifically punished behavior. Punishment is aversive; people want to avoid it. The child punished for classroom misbehavior is likely to learn to stay away from school. The consequence of such avoidance behavior is, of course, restraint: the child is forced to be in the very place he most wants to avoid. And restraint is in itself punishing, so the whole state of "me in school" becomes a punishment. The vicious cycle is begun; it usually ends only when the child leaves school for good.

If the teacher must punish as a last resort, the following four rules will help make the punishment effective. First, give reinforcement for behavior incompatible with the punished response. Second, make sure that the undesired behavior is no longer reinforced. (After all, it was learned in the first place because it was reinforced in some way; it makes little sense to punish it if the original reinforcement is not removed.) Third, punish by removing reinforcers, and provide a clear-cut method for earning them back. And, finally, always precede the punishment by a warning.

## Shaping

We have said repeatedly that, in order for a response to be conditioned, it must first be emitted by the learning organism. Only after the learner does something can the teacher reward it. But what about responses that the organism doesn't know how to make or never makes on its own? How do we get the learner to make that first response? The techniques of shaping have been developed to deal with this problem.

In shaping a behavior, we begin by rewarding a response in the learner's repertoire that is close to the desired response. Because of an organism's natural tendency to vary its responses, the initial rewarded behavior is sometimes closer to (more like) and sometimes further from (less like) the final behavior we are interested in. Gradually, we restrict our rewards to those behaviors that are more and more similar to that desired end product. And the behavior changes: because of our selective reinforcement, it approaches and finally conforms to the desired response. This gradual formation of a desired response is called *shaping*.

A favorite way of demonstrating response shaping in the laboratory is to tell a subject that he is working for points, which will be indicated by the experimenter's tapping his pencil on a table. The subject has no idea how to earn these points, yet the experimenter has decided on a specific behavior—say, touching the tip of the nose with the finger. At first the subject just sits, waiting to be told how to proceed. Perhaps he shifts uneasily in his chair—tap, one point earned. Another body movement—tap. He crosses his legs—no tap. He moves his arm—tap. He begins moving his arm in different ways, trying to discover how to earn another point. The skillful experimenter awards taps for movements that bring the subject's hand closer to his face, gradually making the reward contingent on responses closer and closer to nose touching, the final result of the sequence. In a surprisingly short time, this nonverbal, now-warmer–now-colder procedure succeeds in eliciting the exact behavior that was specified at the beginning of the experiment, even though the likelihood of its having occurred by chance was almost zero.

In this experiment, of course, we are working with a subject who is actively aware of the conditioning going on and who cooperates with the experimenter in producing the desired response. Shaping works in the same way with lower animals or with human subjects who are unaware of the conditioning procedure; it just takes longer. The more the subject can be induced to cooperate with the experimenter/teacher, however, the more quickly the desired behavior will be learned. It is not hard to find examples of classroom behavior in which shaping techniques can be quite effective. For instance, the child who is trying to learn cursive writing can be shaped. The teacher begins by rewarding very awkward and straggling letters and then gradually confines the rewards to smooth, legible handwriting. Shaping in the absence of learner cooperation may also occur. Through selective reinforcement, a bright student who pokes fun at the efforts of his slower classmates can be led through stages of attending quietly to others, of showing interest in them, and finally of offering encouragement and constructive help.

Shaping seems to work best when the rewards are not in the form of immediate consumables (jelly beans or free time) but rather in the form of *secondary reinforcers*—points or credits that can be traded in later for the primary reinforcer. Walker (1968, p. 107) explains why this is so: "Shaping proceeds most rapidly and effectively when a reinforcement precisely coincides with the response. Most primary reinforcers, such as food for a hungry animal, require some time for delivery and consumption. Furthermore, a secondary reinforcer can be used many times without producing satiation, as would food, for instance. Thus, training can be extended much longer with a secondary reinforcer than with a food reward."

Usually, as teachers, we are interested in shaping fairly complex behavior sequences: cooperating with peers, solving math problems, learning to read. In such cases, it is important to identify the individual components of the behavior goal because these components must be reinforced. Bloom (1973) discusses this problem in some detail in the context of teaching reading. He begins with such basic components as keeping attention on the printed page; you can't learn to read a book unless you look at it. It is easy to lose sight of such basic components in our eagerness to see the end behavior emerging, and the teacher must be firm with himself so as not to try to go too fast or to tackle too-large chunks all at once.

Shaping, then, requires a number of skills on the part of the teacher: identifying the behaviors that must precede and/or accompany that which is to be learned, finding and establishing an effective unit of secondary reinforcement, and administering those reinforcements in such a way as to mold the learner's behavior into the desired pattern.

### Critical Periods and Imprinting

The concepts we have discussed thus far have to do primarily with things external to the learner—things more or less under the teacher/experimenter's control. We can choose a critical stimulus or decide what sorts of responses to reinforce or vary the timing or amount of reward to be earned. But what about the learner himself? Are there factors or characteristics about him, not under our control, that affect the learning process? We have already mentioned motivation and postponed its discussion until a later chapter; in fact, the entire second half of this book is devoted to a consideration of such learner factors. But there is one factor that needs to be looked at now: the readiness of the learner.

*Readiness* can refer to several different things, and many of these are not yet well understood. In general, though, readiness seems to be part of an individual's overall developmental pattern. Depending on the response (or response sequence) to be learned, we may be concerned with muscle development, with neural structure, with previous social-interaction experience, or with other aspects of the learner's development that can affect his ability to learn. Learning to read, for example, requires a certain degree of visual accuracy (depending on the size of print we use) and a certain degree of motor coordination. The child who has not acquired these skills will have a hard time learning to read; he is not physically ready for that kind of learning.

It is relatively easy to identify the physical components of a response and then to say that an individual who has not acquired these components (either through physical development or through previous learning) is not yet ready to learn the response. But there is more to the readiness notion than this rather common-sense approach. For some kinds of learning, there seems to be a period of psychological readiness, not tied to any known physical characteristics, during which the learning takes place much more readily than at any other time. These *critical periods,* although probably occurring among all species, are most easily recognized in certain infrahuman groups. Let's look, therefore, at some interesting behaviors common to geese and chickens (recognizing that to dwell too long on such materials would be for the birds).

Baby chicks are not hatched knowing how to peck at food. They must learn how during their first few hours of life. If they are prevented from learning how to peck right away after hatching (for instance, by being kept in the dark), they will never be able to learn. In other words, there is a critical period for this learning; if it doesn't occur during the critical period, it never will. If it does occur at the proper time, it is never forgotten. It becomes a permanent part of the organism's behavior repertoire; it is *imprinted* onto the learner's behavioral circuits.

True imprinted behavior often appears to be an all-or-nothing, one-trial-only learning. At first, the organism doesn't make a certain response. Then the critical period occurs, the necessary stimulus for the behavior (sometimes called a releasing stimulus) is there, and the behavior is emitted —pop!—there it is, learned from then on. Greylag goslings, for example, follow their mother around. They don't follow other geese around, so they must have to learn who their mother is. Ethologists (those who study animal behavior in natural settings) have determined that learning the mother–not-mother discrimination is an imprinting behavior and occurs almost immediately after hatching: the first large, moving object that the gosling sees is "mother" from then on. Konrad Lorenz, a famous etholo-gist, has been "mother" to a number of goslings; he simply arranged to be the first large moving object in their visual world. No subsequent exposures to their real parent had any effect on these goslings; they followed Lorenz whenever he appeared, until they grew into adult goosehood (it is not recorded whether their own child-rearing techniques were affected by this early confusion).

Imprinting can occur at different times during an animal's life, though examples of very early imprinting are most common. One instance of later imprinting occurs among species of birds that mate for life; such mate selection, occurring once and once only and resulting in permanent behav-ior change, falls within the definition of imprinting. Ardrey, in the fasci-nating book *African Genesis* (1961), tells of another experience that Lorenz had with his feathered friends. This time one of them (a jackdaw, to be precise) wanted more from Lorenz than a platonic relationship. He wanted Lorenz to be his mate and demonstrated this desire by repeatedly depositing beakfuls of minced worms in Lorenz's ear. One might expect that Lorenz would react rather strenuously to this token of affection, and we are told that he did; the fact that the amorous jackdaw remained undis-couraged speaks to the strength of an imprinted response pattern.

True imprinting can occur only during an appropriate critical period. The imprinted behavior cannot be acquired before the onset of the critical period, and if the critical period passes without acquisition of the desig-nated behavior, it cannot be acquired afterward. It is difficult to think of any human response or response sequence that is learned in such a rigidly circumscribed period. In fact, true imprinting seems to occur most com-monly among those species in which complex instinctual patterns make up much of the behavioral repertoire. In such species, imprinting often more resembles the release of an instinctive set of responses than the acquisition of something new. As we move up the phylogenetic scale, from bugs to birds to beasts, we see more and more behaviors that are learned rather than inherited; we see the rigid either-or of imprinting give way to a more flexible relationship. Instead of all or nothing, we must speak of the likeli-hood of a behavior being learned or of the ease with which it is acquired. So it is with humans and critical periods. As far as is now known, nothing in human behavior is imprinted in the same sense as a chick's pecking behav-ior or a gosling's attachment to its mother. But there are critical periods for learning various responses, periods during which the learning is much faster and proceeds much more smoothly than it could either before or after the critical period.

Much remains to be learned about readiness periods in human learning. Are they more or less the same for different people, or are some individuals ready for a given learning earlier than others? Can a readiness period be made to occur sooner by changing the environment in some way —by enriching it or by drilling the learner in some of the necessary prerequisite skills? Can a learner be made to reenter a critical period by regressing him in other ways? Will reteaching a 7-year-old to crawl, for instance, help him learn what he missed learning during the normal crawling stage? These and many other questions are currently under study by specialists in learning and in child development; hopefully, it will not be too many years until useful ground rules begin to emerge. In the meantime, we facilitators of learning must try to sensitize ourselves to the readiness level of students —to be aware of when a child is ripe for a certain kind of learning and to provide opportunities for that learning to occur before the readiness period has passed.

## Inhibition

A particular response or response sequence is learned not in a vacuum but rather in a context of other responses. Sometimes this network of responses tends to support the acquisition of a given behavior, and sometimes it interferes with it. When such interference occurs, we generally refer to the effect as *inhibition*. There are several different kinds of inhibition, and most have immediate implications for educators.

One of the earliest distinctions among kinds of response inhibition was made on the basis of the time sequence of the responses being studied. If response A interferes with response B, which is to be learned after A, we speak of *proactive inhibition*. If response B interferes with the production of previously learned A, we call it *retroactive inhibition*. For example, if a student learns a list of foreign vocabulary words only to find that in doing so he has managed to wipe out the list he learned yesterday, retroactive inhibition has occurred. The new list has interfered with or inhibited the previously learned responses. If the old list—the one the student learned yesterday—interferes with the learning of the new one (if the student persistently gives the previously learned responses when presented with the new stimuli), proactive inhibition is occurring. Proactive inhibition is also present when a previously learned incorrect response persists, so that learning the correct response is especially difficult. This often happens to me in learning the names of a new class of students: if I mislearn a name and call Judy Jones "Jane Jones," it is exceedingly (and embarrassingly) difficult to learn to call Judy by her right name, no matter how often she may correct me.

You may have noticed that in each of these examples the inhibiting response is quite similar to the inhibited response. This similarity illustrates a general rule about inhibition: the more similar two responses are, the more likely one is to inhibit the other. Also, the closer together the two sets of learnings take place, the more likely it is that inhibition will occur. Putting these two facts together, we can come up with a rule of thumb for scheduling learning activities so as to minimize inhibition: when similar responses are to be learned, practice periods should be spaced as far apart as possible. It also seems to be a general rule that an intervening activity that is unlike the two potentially inhibiting sets of responses reduces inhibition. If you are studying for a French exam, the inhibiting effect of your responses on one another can be kept to a minimum if you break up your total study time into small units and space them out with totally unrelated activities in between. You might memorize ten verbs, for instance, and then go out for a cup of coffee with a friend; then memorize ten more, and stop to straighten a desk drawer or iron a shirt. Sleep is a good intervening activity for minimizing inhibition; most students find that learning that occurs just before going to bed at night is retained well and tends not to interfere with subsequent learning the next day.

Stimuli, too, can have inhibiting effects on certain classes of responses. The most obvious examples are those situations in which we are taught specifically not to make a certain response under given conditions: not to touch the stove burner when it is turned on, not to cross the street when the light is red, not to talk to our neighbor after the bell has rung. In these examples, inhibition of a specific response is a learned response itself and follows the same stimulus-response-reward rules as any other response.

More interesting—and usually more difficult to analyze—are situations in which the effect of a stimulus (that is, the kind of response it elicits) changes over time. "Stimuli which tend to call out a response may lose that tendency, or *if they occur without the response, go further and acquire inhibiting effects*" (Guthrie, 1930/1953, p. 32; italics added). Consider the case of Garvin, who has developed the habit of biting his fingernails down to the quick during spelling tests. Here the spelling test is the stimulus, and nail biting is the response. If Guthrie's formulation is correct, one way to break up this pattern is to prevent the occurrence of the response while continuing to present the stimulus. In other words, we must figure out some way to (physically) keep Garvin from biting his nails while continuing to give the spelling tests. Let's try providing him with chewing gum during the tests; for most people, chewing gum and nail biting are incompatible responses. If Garvin chews the gum (and does not bite his nails) during the tests, eventually the test should have an inhibiting effect on the response it originally called forth; being exposed to a spelling test should make Garvin less likely to bite his nails than he would be under other conditions. I wish I could report to you that I had actually used this procedure successfully and that Garvin now has nice long fingernails. Unfortunately, I can't; the example was purely theoretical, and I must leave it to you to discover whether it works in the cold and complicated world.

Before we leave this topic, we must look at one more type of inhibition. *Latent inhibition* is a phenomenon usually associated with classical rather than with operant conditioning, but it too has implications for the classroom. You will remember that in classical conditioning a conditioned stimulus is paired with an unconditioned stimulus until the conditioned stimulus alone comes to elicit the same response that the unconditioned stimulus elicited originally. If, however, the conditioned stimulus is presented alone for a series of trials before it is paired with the unconditioned stimulus, the conditioning process is inhibited; it is more difficult to get the individual to respond to the conditioned stimulus with the desired conditioned response. This sounds rather complicated; perhaps an example will help make it clearer. Let's say we are working with a group of preschoolers, and we want them to quiet down for a rest period when we turn down the lighting in the room. We know that soft music accompanied by the recorded rhythm of a heartbeat tends to lower children's activity level, so we use that as our unconditioned stimulus. We lower the lights and play the music and heartbeat; eventually, the lowered lights alone should produce the reduced-activity-level response. But—and here is where the latent inhibition comes in—if we have been trying to get them to quiet down when the room gets dim for days or weeks before we hit on the idea of using a conditioning technique, the association of the response (quiet down) with the conditioned stimulus (dim room) is inhibited.

Lubow (1973), in a review of the literature dealing with latent inhibition, says that to date no adequate theory has been developed to explain this phenomenon. He then puts forward his own explanation, which sounds (to me) remarkably like common sense: during the early nonreinforced exposure to the conditioned stimulus, a decrease in the attention paid to that stimulus occurs, and this lessened attention is responsible for the subsequent latent-inhibition effect. In other words, after the first few times the room gets dim and nothing much happens, the children learn not to notice the illumination level. This formulation may well carry over to operant situations; if a stimulus is presented but is followed by no consistent response-reward pattern, the individual soon comes to disregard it. Consider the plight of the poor teacher who used to walk into a study hall (it was my study hall, more years ago than I like to admit) and shout "Shut up!"—with no effect at all on the general noise level. Originally, this stimulus might have been a good one for eliciting *orienting responses* (talking stopped, heads turned, eyes focused on the source of the stimulus). But because it had been presented day after day with no discernible response-reward pattern following it, latent inhibition had occured. The students came to ignore it; and it is safe to assume that, by the time I was aware of the situation, it would have been difficult indeed to condition any sort of response to that stimulus.

## Aversion

Aversion behavior is somewhat related (at least superficially) to latent inhibition. In latent inhibition, the stimulus comes to be ignored, and its effectiveness in calling forth a desired response is lessened. In aversion, the stimulus comes to be associated with an unpleasant situation (a punishment), and it is actively avoided. The relationship between aversive stimuli and the more common sorts of inhibitory stimuli is also fairly straightforward: an inhibitory stimulus causes the learner to not make a response that he might otherwise have made, while an aversive stimulus causes him to actively avoid the stimulus situation itself. Aversive stimuli are punishers, and they have the effect of extinguishing the behaviors that immediately precede them.

As I mentioned in the discussion of punishment, aversive stimuli can occasionally be used with good effect by learning facilitators, though such techniques have definite risks. The aversive-stimulus situation can be especially destructive when it is not recognized as such by the experimenter/teacher. Sadly, this state of affairs is not nearly as infrequent as we might like to believe.

Stimuli can acquire aversive properties in a number of ways. One of the most common of these (in classrooms) is the situation in which a training program fails to provide sufficient reinforcement for the learner. Traditional classroom methods often place the student in a relatively structured activity sequence, with rewards contingent upon the student's meeting a set of teacher expectations. If the reward is in fact not rewarding to the student or if the student cannot meet the expectations and thus is not rewarded at all, the absence of a reward can have the same effect on the child as punishment. Moreover, since there is no way in which he can be rewarded (as far as he can see), the whole pattern of "me in this situation" comes to be associated with punishment and thus becomes an aversive stimulus. Bloom (1973) points out that this kind of learning happens particularly often in early reading instruction, so that "me trying to read" becomes a task to be avoided by the child. Not only does this state of affairs interfere with the acquisition of reading skills, but it tends to color subsequent reading activities and may interfere with the establishment of an intrinsic reinforcement system for reading, by which reading would gain positive attractiveness. The activity of reading can acquire so many negative connotations—become so intrinsically aversive—that the child may never be able to learn to enjoy it.

It is not hard to think of ways to prevent this sort of situation from developing; we need only make certain that what we think of as reinforcers are rewarding to the child (teacher praise may embarrass rather than please him) and then ensure that some response of his will in fact be rewarded during the learning period. The problem, viewed in this way, becomes one of designing a behavior-shaping program.

But what of the child who is already trapped in this pattern and has come to hate reading or math or school in general? Riccio and Silvestri (1973) suggest that a *two-process theory* can help in understanding both how a stimulus situation can come to be aversive and how such a problem can be dealt with. According to their research, both classical and operant conditioning are present in a learned aversive response. The learning situation is the conditioned stimulus that is paired with punishment (the unconditioned stimulus), with fear as the conditioned response. Through classical conditioning, the learning situation by itself comes to elicit the fear response. As the child moves to escape the situation, his efforts are rewarded with fear reduction; he draws airplanes instead of doing his math problems or skips school altogether, and thus he succeeds in avoiding those unpleasant fear feelings. And his success reinforces, in an operant-conditioning sense, his aversive responses (see Figure 1-3).

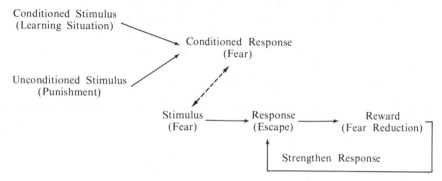

*Figure 1-3*. Both classical and operant conditioning contribute to the learning situation ⟶ escape behavior pattern.

Riccio and Silvestri point out that both the learnings involved in this two-process event must be dealt with if the avoidance response is to be extinguished. The fear response to the conditioned stimulus (the learning situation) must be eliminated, as well as the reinforcement of avoidance behaviors. Providing strong and immediate rewards at the onset of the learning situation may eliminate the fear response, since these rewards elicit a pleasurable response that is incompatible with the old response. And rewarding alternative behaviors, incompatible with avoidance, helps to extinguish the avoidance responses.

In all this discussion of avoidance behavior and aversive stimuli, I have said little that is new: I have merely pointed out specific implications and applications of learning theory to a common classroom problem. The important thing to remember is that these techniques can be used only after we recognize the various stimuli, responses, and rewards that are operating in the learning situation. In dealing with avoidance behavior, as with other learned responses, our first job is accurate analysis of the learning pattern that has occurred or is occurring. Only after such analysis can we make effective changes in the ongoing stimulus-response-reward patterns.

## Premack's Principle

In 1965, Premack proposed a way of looking at operant conditioning that turned a number of previous assumptions upside down and has far-reaching implications for everyone who intends to use operant principles in real-life situations. Premack essentially challenged the notion that some behaviors are natural reinforcers and reinforce all sorts of different responses (eating food is the most commonly used example of such reinforcers), while some behaviors are just responses and can never themselves serve as rewards. Actually, said Premack, any response can be a reinforcer provided it is a more likely (more frequent) response than the one being reinforced. "Reinforcement involves a *relation*, typically between two responses, one that is being reinforced and another that is responsible for the reinforcement. This leads to the following generalization: of any two responses, the more probable response will reinforce the less probable one" (Premack, 1965, p. 132).

Premack's statement invites one obvious question: what do we mean by a more probable response? In his experiments with lower animals, Premack determined response probability very simply, by allowing the animal to wander freely in the experimental (stimulus) situation and keeping track of how often and how long each sort of response occurred. The percentage of total time spent on any response defined the probability that that response would occur during some time period in the future. With rats, for instance, Premack determined the relative probability of licking a drinking tube, of running in an activity wheel, of eating, and so on. The relative probability, rather than the absolute probability, is important here; the reinforcing property of any response depends on whether it is more or less probable than the response to be reinforced. A mildly improbable response can reinforce an extremely improbable response, even though there are other probable responses that would be more strongly reinforcing.

Let's pause for a moment here and look at one of Premack's experiments to see just how these relationships work in practice. Premack wanted to have a startling demonstration of how his theory differed from traditional approaches, and so he decided to let running in an activity wheel be the reinforcer for drinking (his subjects were white rats). Ordinarily, in operant conditioning, the relationship is just the opposite: the thirsty rat learns to run in the wheel in order to get a drink. Now, under these standard conditions, drinking (the reinforcing response) is in fact the more probable response; the thirsty rat is more likely to take a drink of water than to run in a wheel, given equal opportunity to do either. To reverse these response probabilities, Premack made water continuously available in the rats' cages but locked the activity wheel so that the rats couldn't run in it. Then, during the training sessions, the apparatus was arranged so that each five licks at the drinking tube freed the activity wheel for 10 seconds. In learning-theory terminology, running was made contingent upon licking;

I USED TO RUN IN ORDER TO LICK...THEN I USED TO LICK IN ORDER TO RUN...AND NOW I'M SO MIXED UP I RUN TO SWEAT OFF MY FRUSTRATION...

the rat had to lick in order to earn a chance to run. And Premack's predictions were borne out. Under these conditions, licking occurred more frequently than it did when no such contingency relationship was established. The chance to run did act as a reinforcer of the drinking response.

Later, after much more extensive research, Premack extended his principle to include punishments as well as rewards. Just as making a more probable response contingent upon a less probable one causes the less probable response to be reinforced, so making a less probable response contingent on a more probable one decreases the frequency of the more probable response (Premack, 1973). Suppose, for instance, that we have an individual for whom playing with puzzles is a highly probable response and washing his hands a less probable response. That is, the individual likes to play with puzzles more than he likes to wash his hands; given a free choice, he is more likely to turn to the puzzle box than to the soap and water. We can predict that if we make that individual "earn" a chance to play with the puzzle by washing his hands (making the more probable behavior contingent upon the less probable), the frequency of hand washing will increase. But if we turn the relationship around and force the individual to wash his hands after he plays with the puzzle, the frequency of puzzle playing will decrease.

Premack's theory was extremely useful to learning theorists because it forced them to look at the nature of reinforcement in a different way. It tends to be impressive—and often confusing—to students because of the technical terminology Premack uses. We can gain insight into just what Premack is saying if we allow ourselves to continue the line of thought we used a moment ago. The essence of Premack's insight is that letting an organism do something it "wants" to do can be used to reinforce something that it doesn't "want" to do. Similarly, forcing it to do something it doesn't "want" to do can be an effective punishment for something it does "want" to do. Most people have an intuitive understanding of these relationships, as reflected in such commonly used phrases as "work before play" and "saving the best for last." Premack's principle does not tell us something new but rather gives us a rule for understanding, quantifying, and predicting relationships that are already familiar to us.

Understanding and using Premack's principle frees the experimenter/ teacher from having to rely on a predetermined class of reinforcing events. It also frees him to tailor reinforcements to the needs of the individual learner. Some behaviors are highly improbable for most learners (few children would choose to be deprived of dessert or to sit in the corner) and so serve as nearly universal punishments. Likewise, some behaviors are highly probable for nearly all learners (most children will eat candy, given the chance to do so). In between, though, are a host of behaviors whose probability varies from learner to learner and whose reinforcement value also varies. Some children love to clean erasers, while others hate to. Some are acutely uncomfortable listening to a scolding, while others crave attention so much that they gladly submit to scolding in order to be in the limelight. As Fowler (1973) points out, we must determine what is reinforcing for each learner on the basis of what he approaches and avoids—that is, the sorts of responses he chooses and the sorts he does not choose to make. Only in this way can we be sure that what we think is a reward will be a reward for the particular learner we are working with.

*Coverants*

An *operant* is a response that operates in some way on the environment. Operants are distinguished from reflexes in that they are not called forth automatically by a specific stimulus but rather are emitted by the organism as it goes about interacting with its universe. If we accept the kind of operational behaviorism that Skinner advocates, we must further specify that a response, in order to qualify as an operant, must be unambiguously observable by someone other than the behaving organism—that is, it must be an external, overt response. In the years following Skinner's original operant-learning formulations, however, some theorists began to be dissatisfied with this restriction. After all, they argued, nonvisible important events do occur in learners: people think about things, make decisions, notice cues, set goals. Since we know, on the basis of our own experience, that these things happen in learners (at least in human learners) and that they do make a difference in the way learning proceeds, does it make sense to ignore them? Homme (1965) maintained that it made no sense at all, and he coined the term *covert operant,* or *coverant,* to describe operant responses that are made internally and hence cannot be observed by an outsider. Coverants are not reflexes—they do not always occur in connection with a particular stimulus—and they are not simply states in which an organism finds itself. They are true operant responses, with all the characteristics of operant responses, but they operate on an organism's internal environment rather than on its external environment.

Extending our definition of operants to include covert behaviors allows us to explain and make use of many kinds of behavior that fit awkwardly (at best) into a rigorously operational framework. Look at Henry's Sunday evening activities, for instance. Henry is 17 and plans to go out for basketball; he has a slight weight problem and has decided to lose five pounds. He has been watching TV, and during a commercial he wanders out to the kitchen and opens the refrigerator door. Right in front of him is a large slab of lemon meringue pie left over from supper. He reaches for it, stops with his hand in mid-air, pauses for a full second, and then shuts the refrigerator and returns to the living room and the TV. A purely behavioristic theory would have to stretch rather far to explain Henry's behavior; a theory that takes coverant responses into account can handle it easily. The sight of the pie was a stimulus for a coverant response that might be described as "remembering my diet" (coverants are difficult to describe precisely because they are private and often nonverbal responses); this coverant, in turn, served as an inhibitory stimulus for the eating behavior.

Recognizing and reinforcing coverants that lead to external behaviors can be a more effective technique of behavior shaping than reinforcing the external behaviors themselves. This is particularly true for self-reinforcement, whereby an individual wants to train himself to make (or not to make) a particular response. "If there should be any reason for strengthening [a particular] coverant, it can easily be done," says Homme. "All that is required is that [the subject], to whom it is private, demand that it occur immediately prior to the execution of some momentarily high probability behavior" (pp. 503-504). Homme is, of course, applying Premack's principle to coverant responses. Reward the coverant you want to strengthen by doing something you like (emitting a high-probability response) every time you make that coverant. Our friend Henry might have strengthened the coverant response "remember my diet" had he followed it with a phone call to his girl friend or a trip to buy a magazine he had been wanting.

Homme points out that the sequence desired coverant ⟶ probable response does not always occur naturally; often we have to engineer such sequences by means of careful planning. I may have to write a paper for a sociology class, for instance; I know I should think about that paper, but I've been putting it off. "Thinking about my paper" is a desired covarant response. Now I've just finished a class, it's the middle of the morning, and it's time to get to that paper. Well, I tell myself, I'll just have a cup of coffee and then I'll really get to it. No! That's the wrong order; that's making the less probable (desirable) response contingent on the more probable (desirable) one. If I think about the paper for a while and then reward myself with coffee, I'll have strengthened the think-about-paper covarant—and, incidentally, I'll have accomplished part of my task as well.

Coverant responses, says Ackerman (1973), are reinforced by subsequent consummatory behavior. "Thinking about my paper" followed by "drinking coffee" reinforces "thinking about my paper"; "remembering my diet" followed by "talking to my girl friend" reinforces "remembering my diet" (assuming that I enjoy talking to my girl friend). However, subsequent behaviors can also reinforce nondesired behaviors; if Henry goes ahead and eats the pie, we have the sequence shown in Figure 1-4.

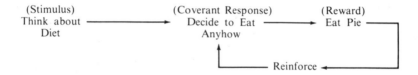

*Figure 1-4.* Subsequent overt (probable) behavior reinforces a previous (less probable) coverant.

Ackerman discusses how partial coverant reinforcement can interfere with an attempt to give up smoking. The (consummatory) response of smoking a cigarette is usually preceded by the coverant "I want a smoke," and the smoking response reinforces that coverant. The successful habit kicker may try to insert a new response, so that "I want a smoke" is followed by (and punished by) "I am going to quit," which is in turn followed by a (rewarding) response incompatible with smoking, such as chewing a stick of gum or sucking a mint. But if the habit kicker breaks down occasionally and responds to a particularly strong "I want a smoke" coverant by smoking, "I am going to quit" is followed by the coverant "I'll smoke anyhow," which is reinforced by smoking. This consummatory behavior reinforces "I want to smoke" and "I'll smoke in spite of wanting to quit" on a variable-ratio schedule, which, as we saw earlier, leads to response learnings that are especially hard to extinguish. Under the influence of this reinforcement schedule, "I want to smoke" and "I will smoke" occur more and more frequently, with greater and greater strength. And any of your friends who have "quit smoking" but are now smoking again can tell you the end result of such a sequence.

## PUTTING IT TOGETHER

In this chapter I have introduced a great deal of terminology and a number of quite important concepts. Unless you have already been exposed to this material in another class, you are probably feeling confused and overwhelmed about now. Don't give up! Give yourself a rest period (remember proactive and retroactive inhibition) and then go back and reread just the section labeled Classical and Operant Conditioning. Everything in the rest of the chapter—every single thing— is based on this section, so read it until you understand it. Then quit for the night—go to a movie or make love or eat a hot fudge sundae. Tomorrow, go after the rest of the chapter. If you don't understand something, try to relate it to that original basic section (you may have to trace it back through some new terminology that was introduced in a later section).

Be sure to reward yourself when you finally feel you've mastered a particularly difficult bit—or even when you've just managed to keep at it for a while in spite of wanting to do something else. Remember, every principle, every effect, every application that is introduced in the later sections is based on the few simple rules that were stated at the beginning. And all of them apply to your own learning behavior as well as to the learning behavior of your future students.

## QUESTIONS FOR UNDERSTANDING

1. Describe a classroom learning situation that might involve (primarily) operant conditioning and another that might involve (primarily) classical conditioning.
2. What are three kinds of reinforcement frequently used by teachers? What kind of reinforcement schedule usually governs the way each is used?
3. Discuss the major (psychological) drawbacks in using punishment as a classroom technique.
4. The students in a particular gym class have gradually become more and more rowdy, and now they almost completely ignore what the gym teacher says and does. On advice from the principal, the gym teacher decides to crack down, but he finds that he can't really control the class. Relate this situation to the phenomenon of latent inhibition.
5. Think of a coverant response that you would like to make more often. How could you use Premack's principle in setting up a reinforcement scheme that would encourage you to emit this desired coverant?

# Chapter 2

# Imitation

When we talk about conditioning, particularly operant conditioning, it seems to be a very logical and complete model of learning. After all, what could be simpler? We learn to do (and think and say) the things that get us good results, and the things that get us bad results don't get learned or drop out of our repertoire. Unfortunately (from the point of view of simplicity), operant conditioning doesn't take care of all the kinds of learnings that animals—particularly human animals—engage in. More specifically, it doesn't adequately answer the question of how such a great variety of behaviors gets into our repertoire in the first place. If one were to take operant conditioning as the only model for human learning, one would have to assume that everything is learned on a trial-and-error basis; we have to make a mistake before we learn not to make it again, and we have to accidentally stumble over a useful behavior before it can be reinforced and thus added to our repertoire. A brief consideration of the way people act will convince you that this simply isn't so. We learn from other people, from what they do and say and have written down for us. Life is just too hazardous and too complex for each person to have to try for himself every dangerous or maladaptive behavior before finding out that it won't work.

The operant-conditioning model has an appearance of completeness, and many of its adherents seem to talk as if it were complete—as if it could indeed cover all aspects of human behavior. Bandura, one of the chief architects of social-learning theory, suggests that this misleading aura of completeness may be due to the artificiality of the laboratory set-ups in which parts of the theory are traditionally tested. "Had experimental situations been made more realistic so that animals toiling in Skinner boxes and various mazes were drowned, electrocuted, dismembered, or extensively bruised for the errors that invariably occur during early phases of unguided learning, the limitations of [operant] conditioning would have been forcefully revealed" (1971a, p. 3).

Much—most—human learning takes place in a social context. Children learn by imitating what other people do and by carrying out symbolic imitations—that is, by doing what other people tell them to do. Would an infant ever learn to talk if he did not have human speech patterns to imitate? I think it highly unlikely. And imitation is a factor in all sorts of other behaviors as well. Experiments have shown that many kinds of verbal and motor patterns can be learned or modified through imitation. We imitate relatively simple motor behaviors, like a golf swing or the curve of a finger on a piano key; we imitate complex social and verbal interactions, as when a child at play mimics the way his parents talk to each other and to him; modifications of aggressive behavior (Kniveton, 1973), of altruistic behavior (Elliott & Vasta, 1970), of physical expressions of affection (Acker, Acker, & Pearson, 1973), of question-asking patterns (Henderson & Garcia, 1973), and even of creativity (Zimmerman & Dialessi, 1973) have been achieved by offering subjects an opportunity to imitate. Classroom behavior is clearly shot through with imitation, both of teacher and of peer models. Clearly, if our understanding of learning is to be complete, we must include in it the phenomena of imitation.

Bandura says that the term *social learning* or *modeling* is more appropriate to use than *imitation* since we learn from others in a variety of ways and not all these ways involve true imitation. First, there is what he calls the *observational learning effect,* which is what we usually mean by imitation —one person learning a new behavior pattern by watching the performance of someone else. Second, there are *inhibitory effects,* in which an observer learns not to do something (that he already knows how to do) through watching a model. Inhibitory effects can come from watching a model do something differently (and better), so that the observer too discards the older and less useful behavior, or they can come from watching a model be punished for a behavior.

Third on the list of modeling behaviors are *disinhibitory effects,* in which the observer increases the performance of a behavior he already knows but didn't engage in (often) before. "Disinhibitory effects are evident when observers increase performance of formerly inhibited behavior after observing models engage in threatening or prohibited activities without adverse consequences" (Bandura, 1971a, p. 6). Finally, Bandura speaks of *facilitation effects,* in which the behavior of others is a cue for the observer—as when one member of an audience begins to clap and everyone else follows suit.

Once we recognize that modeling occurs and that it plays an important role in classroom learning, the next questions are of the how and why sort. Just what goes on when I learn from watching what you do? Why do I learn some of your behaviors but not all of them? Why do I imitate you but not someone else? Bandura, reviewing a number of modeling studies, points out that just seeing someone do something does not ensure that modeling will take place. "Mere exposure to modeling stimuli does not provide sufficient conditions for imitative or observational learning" (1971b, p. 122). Even when children are instructed to imitate a model's behavior and even when they are generously rewarded for doing so, they do not reproduce all that the model does. Modeling is selective and creative; we select out of a total stream of behavior those elements that we wish to imitate, and we weave those elements into our own behavior in such a way as to create a new and unique behavior pattern of our own.

## PROCESSES IN MODELING

As we begin to investigate the phenomena of modeling, we find ourselves awash in a sea of information. Modeling has been studied in literally hundreds of contexts, with attention focused on scores of variables. We need a plan of attack, an organizational scheme that will help us relate all this information to our own behavior as teachers and learners. Bandura (1971a) has devised such a scheme, and (with a few modifications) we shall follow it in this chapter. There are, he says, four major processes involved in modeling. The first of these is *attention:* modeling does not occur unless the observer is attending to what the model is doing. Many variables affect observer attention, and we shall discuss them in some detail. Second, the observer must *retain* what the model does: he must remember it (at some level, not necessarily a conscious one), or he can't repeat it. The third process is *reproduction:* the observer must be physically capable and motivated to reproduce the modeled behavior. It has been amply demonstrated that observers remember much more of models' behavior than they are likely to repeat themselves. Finally, *reinforcement* affects whether the observed behavior will be reproduced many times, only once, or never.

As we shall see, these processes are interrelated in real-world behavior. Nevertheless, pulling them apart artificially does give us some handles that we can use to come to grips with this complex subject. Figure 2-1 is a chart that Bandura uses to break down still further these four major processes in observational learning; you may find it helpful to refer back to the chart occasionally as we proceed. We will not be able to discuss in detail all the things on Bandura's list; we will, however, deal with those items most directly relevant to learning in the school setting.

### Attention

We have all had the experience of being asked what someone has just done or said—someone who was clearly visible and/or audible to us—and being unable to say because we weren't paying attention. In order to model someone's behavior, the observer must know what that behavior is; in order to know what it is, he must attend to it. Moreover, if the model's behavior involves manipulation of objects or materials, the observer must be able to attend to them (Sarason, Pederson, & Nyman, 1968). Put simply, we don't imitate what we don't notice. But let's go a bit further with that

| Attention Processes | Retention Processes | Reproduction Processes | Reinforcement Processes |
|---|---|---|---|
| *Modeling Stimuli* | Symbolic Coding | Physical Capabilities | External Reinforcement |
| Distinctiveness | Cognitive Organization | Availability of | Vicarious Reinforcement |
| Affective Valence | Symbolic Rehearsal | Component | Self-Reinforcement |
| Complexity | Motor Rehearsal | Responses | |
| Prevalence | | Self-Observation | |
| Functional Value | | of Reproductions | |
| *Observer Characteristics* | | Accuracy Feedback | |
| Sensory Capacities | | | |
| Arousal Level | | | |
| Motivation | | | |
| Perceptual Set | | | |
| Past Reinforcement | | | |

*Figure 2-1.* Processes in the social-learning view of observational learning. (From "A Comparative Test of Status Envy, Social Power, and Secondary Reinforcement Theories of Identificatory Learning," by A. Bandura, D. Ross, and S. A. Ross. In A. Bandura (Ed.), *Psychological Modeling: Conflicting Theories.* Copyright 1971 by Lieber-Atherton, Inc. Reprinted by permission.)

notion. Why do we notice some things and not others? What are the variables that affect the attention of observers?

According to Bandura's scheme, the first factors that have an effect on attention are certain characteristics of both model and observer. Many characteristics have been shown to affect modeling behavior—age, race,

competence, and friendliness are only a few; indeed, observer and model characteristics are probably the most extensively researched variables in the whole area of observational learning. Many of the findings that have emerged from this research, however, do not apply specifically to attention but rather to the occurrence of modeling as a unitary phenomenon. For example, it has been shown that the age of the model affects the likelihood of imitation. Part of this influence is due to differences in the amount of attention we pay to older and younger people. But part is also due to differences in retention, in reproduction, and in reinforcement; and nobody knows how to separate out these different causes. All we really know is that the model's age has a bearing on the overall outcome—on whether his behavior is, in fact, reproduced by the observer. For this reason, we are going to defer our discussion of model characteristics and observer characteristics until we have had a chance to look at some of the other variables that clearly do relate more to one aspect of modeling than to another.

*Arousal.* Arousal is a general term that refers to overall activity level. At the low end of the arousal continuum, we describe an individual as being asleep or in a coma or—the final extreme—dead. At the other end, he is alert, attentive, active, "hyper." Obviously, arousal level must be somewhat related to attention and imitation; we do little attending to others while we are sleeping. But the relationship goes beyond this rather trivial observation: among awake and interacting individuals, the more alert and aroused one is, the more likely he is to imitate or model the behavior of other people around him (Akamatsu & Thelen, 1974). Part of the difference in modeling behavior may be due to a generalized arousal effect on performance; overall, performance under conditions of moderate arousal is usually superior to performance under nonarousal conditions. In addition, however, there is probably a more specific relationship between arousal and imitation. The aroused individual frequently seeks an outlet, a focus on which to discharge his energy; the behavior of a model provides such a focus. In other words, a model can act as a sort of behavioral lightning rod, drawing the attention of an aroused observer and providing him with cues as to what to do.

Additionally, imitation may interact with arousal by means of anxiety reduction. Arousal, while it can be experienced as pleasant or exhilarating, is often experienced as anxiety, particularly when the aroused individual finds himself in unfamiliar surroundings or circumstances. The anxiety that you feel when you are not sure of yourself, when you don't know what the appropriate behavior may be, is uncomfortable; in such a situation you are especially likely to imitate the behavior of a model who seems to know the ropes. For that matter, just being able to watch someone else, whether one imitates him or not, can reduce anxiety. "Observing others in a novel situation may serve, through increased familiarity, to reduce the apprehension of an observer when he enters that situation" (Sarason et al., 1968, p.

509). The observer may not acquire new behaviors from the model; but he is likely to inhibit or disinhibit previously acquired responses on the basis of the model's behavior and the consequences of that behavior.

Arousal, then, facilitates modeling in a general way; it also facilitates the more specific processes of attention. The aroused person is more likely than the nonaroused person to notice what others are doing, particularly if those model behaviors relate in some way to the arousal state of the observer. If I'm angry with my boss, I pay attention to what he says that might relate to my anger. If I'm afraid of someone, I certainly pay attention to what he says and does, for my own protection. And most of us know (or remember) how closely we attend to every word or gesture of the loved one when we are in that high-arousal state called infatuation. While the relationship does not carry through to the highest levels of arousal—a person can be so aroused that he is in a "blind rage" or "paralyzed with fear"—in general, it seems true that to raise an observer's level of arousal is to raise the likelihood that he will attend to modeled behavior.

*Discrimination.* In order to imitate someone's behavior, you must be able to discriminate what he does from what other people are doing. In order to imitate his successful behavior, you must be able to tell which of the things he does usually lead to wanted consequences and which to unwanted consequences. Thus two sets of discriminations are involved in modeling, and each affects imitative behavior in different ways.

The more distinctive a model is—that is, the more easily his behavior can be discriminated from the behavior of others—the more likely it is that he will be imitated, particularly when his behavior is being rewarded. Rewarding a model for what he does helps to make him distinctive because it calls attention to him. People tend to notice who gets the goodies and what they do in order to get them. But even when few or no rewards are being dispensed, the easily differentiated individual, doing easily differentiated things, is most likely to be imitated (Durrell & Weisberg, 1973).

Nobody ever imitates everything that a model does; imitation is selective. Discrimination helps to determine which of a model's many behaviors will be imitated. Logically enough, the more distinctive a behavior is, the more likelihood there is of its being imitated by an observer. This is true whether the (distinctive) behavior of the model is specifically rewarded or not. When we see someone who is successful (who gets lots of rewards), we often don't know which of his individual behaviors lead to those rewards. All we know is that he's doing something right. Under those circumstances, we pay attention to him; we want to find out what he's doing, so we can do it too. Which behaviors are we most likely to imitate? The ones we notice, the ones that are most easily discriminated from the ongoing behavior stream. But it may well be that those easily noticeable behaviors are not the ones that lead to our model's rewards. The less clear it is to the observer why a model is being rewarded, the more likely it is that the observer will imitate the model's unusual or outstanding behaviors—and that he will continue to imitate them even though he himself is not rewarded for that imitation. Bandura (1971a, p. 53) calls this the *discrimination hypothesis* and states it as follows: "according to the discrimination hypothesis, nonrewarded imitations persist in the absence of extraneous social controls because individuals fail to discriminate the basis on which diverse modeled behaviors are reinforced." A child (or an adult!) may imitate nonadaptive behaviors as well as adaptive ones and may continue to produce these behaviors even when they don't work for him simply because he doesn't know which of his model's activities are successful. He can't discriminate the rewarded from the nonrewarded model behaviors, so he continues to imitate on a hit-or-miss basis, hoping that eventually he will stumble upon the magic combination that will produce the desired rewards or reactions from others.

The combination of arousal and discrimination can help to explain some of the puzzling imitative behavior that we often see in the classroom. Mickey, for instance, is a child who is popular with his classmates, but who tends to be a trouble maker. He's very bright, and (when he is so inclined) can be cooperative, industrious—all those things that make teachers feel good. But he can also be loud, disruptive, and downright devilish. And it is those disruptive behaviors that many of his classmates tend to imitate. Why? Let's take the sequence apart. Disruptive behaviors often occur during high-arousal times. And, when arousal isn't already high, the disruption probably raises it. Thus, arousal conditions are optimal for imitation during and just following Mickey's "bad" behavior. As for discrimination, clearly, disruptive acts are more noticeable—more easily discriminated—than cooperative ones; cooperation tends to just blend into everything else that's going on in the room. The student whose overall aim is to be like Mickey tends to imitate Mickey's most noticeable behaviors—not because they are "bad," but just because he's most immediately aware of them. Finally, we have to consider our own attention processes; we are likely to notice when someone imitates Mickey's spitball throwing or dirty-picture passing and pinpoint Mickey as the source; we are much less likely to notice when a student imitates Mickey's other, more conventional, behaviors.

## Retention

A number of theorists have pointed out that successful imitation involves both learning what the model has done and deciding to do the same thing oneself. Cook and Smothergill (1973), for instance, talk about imitative behavior as contrasted with imitative knowledge. They suggest that researchers look at a person's behavior under conditions of minimal reinforcement; the amount of imitation that occurs here is a measure of how much of the model's behavior the person accepts and decides to incorporate—a measure of *imitative behavior*. Later, he can be asked to recall and reproduce as much of the model's behavior as he can, with rewards for success; the amount of successful reproduction here is a measure of *imitative knowledge,* of how much he has learned.

According to Flanders (1968), imitation involves knowledge and acceptance. Acquiring knowledge of the behavior to be imitated follows, in general, the rules that govern other kinds of learning, while acceptance is determined by those variables that yield information about the appropriateness of the modeled behavior. Whether the model explains what he is doing and why affects the observer's *knowledge* of the behavior to be imitated; whether the model is rewarded for that behavior affects the observer's *acceptance.* Walters and Parke (1971) emphasize the same relationships: "imitative responses are *learned* on the basis of contiguous association of sensory events (classical conditioning), and . . . vicariously experienced reinforcements are determinants only of *performance"* (p. 153). We are concerned in this section with learning the modeled response; performance will be considered later.

*Rehearsal.* If simple knowledge—recall—of what a model has done is an important element in imitation, we might expect that the person who practices the model's behavior will be a more successful imitator than the one who does not engage in such rehearsal. Up to a point, this seems to be true. Observational learning can be enhanced if the learner is encouraged to practice, especially if the entire modeled sequence can be broken down into natural subunits and the practice can take place immediately following each of these. In teaching someone how to hit a golf ball, for instance, a model might demonstrate approaching the ball, the backswing, the swing, and the follow-through, giving the observer an opportunity to practice each one separately.

Even more important than overt rehearsal however, says Bandura, is covert, or internal, rehearsal of a model's behavior. Covert rehearsal can be engaged in when overt practice or participation is impractical, and it too may help the learner to remember what he has seen. The observer may say to himself "First he did this; he held his hand in thus-and-such a way; he tried to make the ball (or the pencil or the test tube) do that." Such covert (verbal) rehearsal improves imitative knowledge, though it has little effect on imitative acceptance (that is, the likelihood that the observer will try the new behavior on his own).

A word of caution is necessary, however, with regard to rehearsal: the timing of the rehearsal is important. As was mentioned previously, rehearsing logical segments of an overall sequence immediately after each has been performed by the model is the best way to practice a new behavior. The longer the interval between observing a behavior and rehearsing it, the more likely it is that mistakes will creep in; the observer will remember wrong and will practice things that the model didn't do. Rehearsing can come too soon, too. If the observer begins to practice while the model is still finishing the activity to be learned, practice can interfere with imitation, particularly when the behavior to be learned is a motor activity (Zimmerman & Rosenthal, 1974). Every teacher knows the frustration of trying to demonstrate a technique only to have students begin to try it themselves before the demonstration is finished. The first part of the sequence is fine, but the last part disintegrates because the students don't pay attention to what they are being shown. Here, then, is a second advantage of breaking up a long sequence into shorter units: it allows students to rehearse early segments without interfering with their attending to later ones.

*Coding.* Perhaps the most important factor involved in the retention processes of imitative learning is coding. The exact imitation of a specific bit of behavior is relatively unimportant in learning, both in and out of the classroom; in most modeling, a general form of behavior is acquired through imitation, but the specific ways in which that form is exhibited or used are created by the observer according to his particular situation. "What is most often being learned in modeling appears to be rules or rule structures. These rule structures can then be applied to a wide sample of particular stimulus instances" (Zimmerman & Rosenthal, 1974, p. 39). The important thing is that training helps the learner to arrange and consolidate the things he knows and is learning. The observer abstracts out of the model's behavior a *behavior rule,* or *code,* which he then uses to generate behaviors of his own.

An example may help to clarify this point. Consider a small child playing with dolls. If you watch him closely, you can identify bits of behavior that he has clearly learned from watching his mother caring for a small sibling or from TV ads showing other children playing with similar toys. But he does not go through an entire sequence of mother's behavior or TV child model's behavior; instead, he abstracts out small chunks of those behaviors and strings them together according to a pattern. It is the pattern that is of most interest to us, the general behavior code, as it were, that he is working with. It is as if he has, through watching several models, developed a blueprint of child-care behaviors. The blueprint might include such general rules as sing to the baby, change the baby's clothes, and put the baby to bed. The child's behavior is thus a creative amalgam of activities, some borrowed from one place and some from another (and many originating in areas having nothing to do with child care at all), put together under the direction of this code. The formation of the code and the way in which it is retained are the essence of healthy imitation.

The importance of the coding process becomes more clear when we consider what happens to a learned imitative sequence over time. Gradually, the behavior of the observer deviates more and more from the original behavior of the model; the observer learns to express the code (or blue-

print or pattern) in a variety of ways. Moreover, the learner tends to interpret subsequent model behavior in the context of the original coding. "The
model's initial performance," say Zimmerman and Rosenthal, "appeared
to act as a [pattern] which children maintained even when the model failed
to precisely adhere to it. Apparently, as the subject acquires the rule underlying the model's behavior, he becomes less dependent on the model as an
environmental influence" (p. 31). George, who began imitating Mickey's
behavior in fourth grade, may still be passing dirty pictures around (or the
verbal equivalent of that behavior, telling not-very-funny dirty stories)
long after Mickey—and other models—have gone on to more mature
forms of social interaction. Or, to take a more positive view, George may
encode Mickey's behavior as "make people laugh and feel good" and may
be doing so in highly appropriate ways, while Mickey is still busy with
clumsy, fourth-grade humor. This sort of adaptation of learnings to new
situations is called *transfer of training;* it is obviously essential if classroom
learnings are to have significant effects later in life.

Looking at imitative learning as a coding process helps us to understand, at another level, how rehearsal of a modeled behavior can sometimes interfere with learning. If the observer is so busy trying to copy the
individual bits and pieces of the model's behavior that the effort interferes
with his coding process—that he loses the flow of what is happening or
fails to abstract from it—he does not learn much from the model. "It is not
the fact of responding actively itself that improves performance; unless
overt response leads to terser coding, it may interfere with observational
learning" (Zimmerman & Rosenthal, 1974, p. 38). Inaccurate or incomplete coding interferes with imitative learning; in order to learn from a
model, I need to have a fairly good idea of what the model is trying to do,
and I need to schematize his behavior in a way that is useful to me. If my
blueprint is wrong or if it is so sketchy that I can't reconstruct much from it,
then I won't have learned from watching the model.

In a number of studies rule structures have been provided along with
modeled behavior to discover whether such a procedure facilitates the
coding process. That is, the reasons for the model's actions were explicitly given, along with the behavior to be imitated. In one such study, children watched a model reacting to moral-dilemma stories—stories in which
the listener must provide a solution to a moral problem. One group of children heard the model responding to the stories in a "morally sophisticated"
way, while another group heard the responses along with an explanation of
why the model answered that way. Only the latter group—the group provided with both the behavior to be modeled and a rule structure—exhibited significant imitative learning (Crane & Ballif, 1973). In another study,
using a different learning situation, children watched an adult model work
on an object-sorting task. While all the children benefited from watching
the model, the children who did best on that and similar tasks were those
who had both watched the model and heard him explain what he was

doing. Again, the verbal explanation apparently helped the observers to abstract and code what they were seeing.

Adequate coding not only helps the observer to understand what the model is doing but also makes possible more efficient storage in memory. A student watching a teacher demonstrate, say, a desk calculator, is certainly not going to be able to remember every single move that the teacher makes. He must abstract from all the things that the teacher is doing those that are relevant and generalizable: the use of the arithmetic symbols, the operation of the "clear" button, the correct order for performing various operations, and so on. His task is to understand what the teacher is doing and to build out of that understanding a code that will allow him to solve similar problems. Note especially that word *similar*. Because it is unlikely that the student will ever (or very often) want to solve the exact same problem that the teacher demonstrated, it would do him little good to copy the exact sequence of motions. Rather, the student must generalize—he must build a code that allows him to apply what the teacher has done to the new sets of specifics that he will encounter in the future. The teacher can facilitate this process by providing explicit codes: "You must do this whenever you want to add a sequence of numbers." "Using this key will always transfer the number displayed into a memory location." "Be careful about hitting this button accidentally, for it will wipe out everything and leave the machine completely cleared."

It is also helpful to encourage the learner to produce his own relevant coding. A code (generalization) that I have constructed myself is more memorable for me simply because it is mine; in the process of building it, I have already stored it in memory. However, the teacher must be careful to check on the adequacy of such self-produced codes. Asking students to take notes on a demonstration may only crystallize the inadequate or inaccurate coding of some of the observers. A safer technique is to stop the demonstration at intervals to ask "What is being done now?" or "Why did I do that?" This procedure builds a reality check into the sequence. And (as an added benefit) it exposes the less able students to the coding processes of their quicker peers; thus, a secondary set of imitative learnings can take place.

After reviewing the literature dealing with modeling as a way of acquiring abstract principles—that is, codes—Zimmerman and Rosenthal concluded that people can and do learn abstractions through watching models, that concepts so learned can be generalized both immediately after training and also after long delays, that the kinds of codes that are learned are relatively independent of the particular stimuli and experimenters involved in the original training, and that the instructions, rules, and explanations given during the course of observation are important not only in acquiring the concepts but in retaining them and generalizing them to new situations. What these findings mean to us as teachers is that we must be aware not only of the possibilities for providing models in the classroom but also of the ways in which model behavior may be coded (or miscoded) by students. When imitative learning fails to occur, it is probably due not so much to poor modeling as to poor monitoring of the coding process.

## Reproduction

Having acquired and coded a model's behavior, an observer may or may not reproduce it. Reproduction depends on two major factors, capability and acceptance.

*Capability.* No matter how well I understand what someone else is doing and why he is doing it, there can still be limits to the degree to which I am able to reproduce his behavior. The most obvious of these limitations involves simple physical ability. Reproducing a behavior involving motor coordination requires a similar degree of coordination on the part of the observer: I can't learn to play the piano just by watching a skilled pianist or to play basketball by going to all the Milwaukee Bucks games. Reproduction of physical or intellectual performance requires that the reproducer have some skills and capabilities to start with. Some of these can be acquired through practice; some probably cannot. If I am only 5 feet tall, I will never be a professional basketball player; and if I have, by the time I am an 18-year-old, reached a mental age of only 7, I almost certainly cannot become a neurosurgeon.

We must be careful, though, in considering limitations on imitative-learning ability, not to close doors too soon. Practice, determination, and skilled use of models in the teaching process can create surprising effects. The stumbling, uncoordinated child may become a fine dancer, or the stutterer an orator, or the (apparently) dull or dim child a philosopher or theoretician. Physical and mental handicaps can be overcome to a degree that most of us cannot appreciate. What is important for the teacher, in using modeling techniques effectively, is not that he excuse (or, worse, discourage) a child from effort on the grounds that "he'll never be able to do it anyhow," but rather that he help the child to set realistic goals for gradual performance improvement over time.

*Acceptance.* The observer who sees a model perform and understands exactly what he is doing and is physically capable of reproducing that behavior still may not imitate. Thank goodness! Imagine what our schools would be like if all students faithfully imitated every bit of peer behavior they noticed and remembered. People choose what and whom they will imitate. They make their choices on the basis of what they think the new behavior will do for them—what it will bring in the way of rewards and how it will make them feel about themselves. Here again we find ourselves edging toward the area of model characteristics; in many instances, acceptance of a modeled behavior is a function of the perceived characteristics of the model or of the interaction between model and observer characteristics. We shall be dealing with this topic shortly.

In some situations the acceptance or nonacceptance of a model's behavior is not a matter of conscious choice. We often act "without thinking" (and what is meant by that phrase, of course, is "without conscious awareness of thinking"), and a common pattern for such actions is "do what everyone else is doing." I'm sitting at a concert, for example, daydreaming about a vacation I'd like to take. Suddenly I become aware that the people around me are clapping. Automatically—without conscious thought—I begin to clap too. Or, I'm at a football game and the officials call a particularly unfair penalty against my team; the fans begin to boo, and I realize that I'm doing the same thing. These are examples of *behavioral contagion:* the activity of the model (or, in these cases, many models) disinhibits or triggers my own behavior. I have not learned anything new from the models—I already knew how to clap or to boo—but their doing it made it all right for me to do it as well.

Observer behavior can be inhibited by models as well as disinhibited. I speak more softly in a quiet group than in a loud group, and I am likely to refrain from sitting on the floor (even though I might be more comfortable there) if everyone else is in a chair. One of the major differences between inhibition and disinhibition, in the context of modeling, is the number of models needed to produce the effect. In general, it takes several people, behaving differently than I might like to behave, to inhibit my behavior; but a single model may be a disinhibitor for a whole group of observers. In a classroom at the end of a dull, rainy day, one spitball can set off a war. When the group is tense or anxious, one child starting to cry virtually guarantees that half a dozen others will follow suit; but if the first outburst is a giggle, rather than tears, the group might well convulse itself with laughter.

### Reinforcement

*Vicarious Reinforcement.* In discussions of imitative learning, the term *vicarious reinforcement* refers to the rewards given to the model—that is, the rewards the observer sees the model getting as a result of his (the model's) behavior. Common sense suggests that an observer is more likely to imitate behavior that has been rewarded than behavior that has been punished or ignored, and in general the research bears this intuition out (Bandura, 1971a; Flanders, 1968). However, some qualifications must be placed on this apparently simple relationship.

"It is interesting to note," says Bandura (1971b, p. 125), "that the performance by a model of socially disapproved or prohibited responses (for example, kicking, striking with objects) without the occurrence of any aversive consequences may produce disinhibitory effects analogous to a positive reinforcement operation." In other words, the absence of punishment may in itself act like a reward. If I see behaviors that I would expect punishment for exhibited by a model with no subsequent punishment, I am likely to imitate them. This fact often poses a dilemma for the teacher or parent. We may be quite convinced that the best way to deal with Linda's or Tommy's obstreperous behavior is just to ignore it; but to do so creates a modeling situation in which other children are likely to learn and display the very behavior we would like to get rid of in Linda or Tommy.

Another problem with vicarious reinforcement is that of definition. How do we determine what sorts of consequences are reinforcers? It is all too easy to assume that what would be reinforcing to me will also be reinforcing to an observer or that what is reinforcing to the model will be seen by the observer as a reward. And, of course, this is not necessarily true. As was pointed out in Chapter 1, rewards are individual things, and a successful reinforcement must be planned with the learner, rather than the teacher or the model, in mind. A study carried out by Dubner (1973) illustrates this idea. He showed fourth-grade girls a videotape of a girl drawing; later, the girls were given the opportunity to draw (as well as to do other things). Girls who saw the model drawing were more likely than girls who were not exposed to the model to draw rather than work with other things. So far, no surprises. But some of the videotapes ended with a teacher coming in and praising the model for what she had done (vicarious reinforcement), and some omitted the adult-child interaction. The addition of vicarious reinforcement had no effect at all on the likelihood of observer imitation. While Dubner did not attempt to determine the reasons for this result, we may speculate a bit. Quite possibly the apparent satisfaction that the model got out of just doing the drawing was sufficient vicarious reward to facilitate imitation all by itself. Moreover, the praise of the teacher might have elicited self-critical comparisons from some observers ("She must have done really well; I could never do that well"), and these comparisons might easily inhibit imitation. Whatever the reason, the message is clear: vicarious reinforcement is effective in enhancing imitative learning only if it is perceived as reinforcement—and as reinforcement to a noticeably greater degree than exists in its absence—by the observer.

With all this discussion of reinforcers and perceived reinforcers, though, we have not said just what reinforcing a model does to an observer. How is it that learning in one person can be helped or hindered by consequences to someone else? First, of course, vicarious reinforcement serves an informative function: the observer may simply learn what the consequences of a behavior are likely to be, or he may learn when (in what environment, under what conditions) a behavior is or is not acceptable. Some theorists, in fact, believe that when the nonessentials are pared away, vicarious reinforcement influences learning only through information transmission. Walters and Parke (1971), for instance, insist that what happens to a social model serves only to help the observer discriminate between permissible and nonpermissible actions within a given social context. Bandura (1971b), however, suggests a second mechanism. There may be *incentive motivational effects,* in which the observer's expectations of similar treatment are aroused. This is the "I didn't want a lollipop until I saw Jerry get one" phenomenon, with which all parents are quite familiar. A third category of effects has to do with attitudes toward the model or toward the reinforcing agent or both. As a result of the interchange between the model and the rewarding (or punishing) person, the observer may feel good or bad about what has happened to the model, he may like or dislike the reinforcing agent, or his evaluation of the model's status may change. Any of these results can affect the likelihood of imitation, as we shall see when we discuss model characteristics.

*Direct Reinforcement.* Whatever unique characteristics imitative learning may have, it is still learning. The laws of reinforcement that govern all kinds of operant learning also govern imitative learning. It seems fairly clear that, of all the factors that may influence whether a particular behavior is learned, the consequences of that behavior to the learner are the most important. In comparing direct with vicarious reinforcement, for instance, Bandura found that direct reinforcement was far more effective in facilitating learning. "The introduction of positive incentives completely wiped out the previously observed performance differences, revealing an equivalent amount of imitative learning among the children in the model-rewarded, model-punished, and the no-consequences treatment group" (1971b, p. 121). Similarly, the rewards (or punishments) that follow an observer's imitation of a model's behavior will be more influential in determining whether that imitation is repeated than will any characteristics of the model himself. A prestigious or attractive model may induce a person to try a new behavior, but if the behavior doesn't work, it will be discarded and the model will be less influential in the future. We should notice two important implications of these statements. First, reinforcement to the observer, by its very nature, cannot directly affect the likelihood of the first occurrence of the imitative behavior. That must depend upon other factors, a number of which we have already discussed. Second, the effects of direct reinforcement are not confined to the particular behavior being reinforced. Depending on the nature of the reinforcement and the way in which the imitated behavior is coded by the observer, the observer's perception of (attitude toward, opinion of) the model may change. These changes, in turn, may influence the model's effectiveness in future learning situations.

*Self-Reinforcement.* In many situations one person wants to be like someone else. We emulate the behavior of people we like, admire, and respect. We do so partly in the expectation that acting as they do will bring us some of the rewards we believe they get. But there is another aspect of acting like an admired person: by imitating his behavior, I can make myself feel like him. That is, when I do as I think my model would do, I see myself as more similar to him than I was before. And this feels good—it is self-reinforcing behavior.

Self-reinforcement of modeled behavior can be a powerful force. Not infrequently, it can outweigh the effects of externally administered punishments to both model and observer. A teen-ager who imitates a friend's burglarizing of a gas station, for example, may be caught and sent to jail (as was his friend). But the self-reinforcement of seeing himself be like his friend can be more important to him than the threat—or even the actuality—of a jail sentence; if so, he will probably be back into criminal activities as soon as he is released.

Related to the modeler's desire to be like the model is the finding that modeling seems to be more likely to occur when the modeler sees himself as somewhat similar to the model (Rosekrans, 1967). One reason might be that when a modeler sees the model as more and more distant from him, he begins to see the model as increasingly unattainable on the one hand, or unworthy of imitation on the other. Also, when the potential modeler feels himself to be closer and closer to the model, the consequences of his (the model's) actions are more likely to apply to the modeler as well.

While reinforcement of any kind cannot directly affect the first instance of imitative behavior, it can have an indirect effect. If an observer, because of a history of reinforcement, comes to believe that imitating a particular model will lead to reward, he will be increasingly likely to imitate future behaviors of that model. This is true partly because of expectation of reward; the observer comes to believe that if he adopts (learns) a general imitation rule of "do whatever he does," he will usually be rewarded. Expectations of this sort also affect attentiveness; if I expect to be rewarded for copying someone's behavior, I watch him rather closely in order to learn what he does.

Reinforcement, by itself, is a powerful factor in learning; so is imitation. But in their combination we can see their full force. Providing a good model and reinforcing the resulting imitation—this is, indeed, a one-two punch in facilitating learning. And, when we think about it, this is the prototype for an enormous amount of "natural" or unplanned learning. Babies learn to walk, to talk, to feed themselves through a combination of imitation and direct reinforcement. School children are explicitly directed to copy teacher behaviors and are then rewarded for complying. Social learnings nearly always follow the same pattern: try out a behavior that you saw somebody else using, and then either keep or discard it according to the consequences that follow. Teachers and other learning facilitators cannot avoid being a part of these imitation-reinforcement patterns; our only choice is the degree to which we try to plan or control how they happen.

## MODEL AND OBSERVER CHARACTERISTICS

Having looked now at Bandura's four major social-learning processes, we are ready to turn to the characteristics of model and of observer that have been shown to affect imitative learning. As we think about these characteristics, it may be helpful to remind ourselves occasionally that they do relate in rather specific ways to the processes we have been discussing. The perceived characteristics of the model affect the *attention* given his behavior by the observer, the degree to which his behavior is *remembered,* and the likelihood that it will be *accepted* (believed, respected, emulated). Observer characteristics affect those same processes; in addition, they often influence the likelihood of *reinforcement* of a socially learned behavior. It will not be possible (and, even if possible, it would soon become repetitious) to call your attention to the relationship of each characteristic to each process. But, in reading through this section, you should stop at intervals and run through the list, tying the ties and building the bridges for yourself.

### Characteristics of the Model

*Competence.* A major characteristic that determines social learning is the perceived competence of the model. Again, common sense would suggest this to be the case: it seems only natural that we imitate those people whom we believe to be more expert than ourselves. "People are inclined to pay little attention to models who have proved ineffectual," says Bandura (1971a, p. 48), "but to observe closely models whose actions have been successful in the past." Some caution must be exercised here, however, in our understanding of what "successful" means. Behaviors that are highly unsuccessful from a teacher's point of view may seem wonderfully successful to an observer/student. The teacher may see Shirley's giggling and note passing as seriously interfering with her studies (as well as disrupting the class); but to Jane, Shirley is an expert in making friends and being attractive to boys. A competent model, in social-learning terms, is one who is competent in ways that are valued by the observer who is to do the imitating. We may also note that observers tend to be able to differentiate areas of competence and to use different models for learning different kinds of behavior. Jane may imitate Shirley's giggly behavior in an attempt to gain social status with her peers, but she is unlikely to use Shirley as a model if her goal is to produce a good math paper. Inappropriate generalization of model competence seldom occurs more than once; after the first occurrence, the direct consequences of the modeled behavior tend to become the main influence. If we think that Roger is being unduly influenced by Fred, that he is copying everything Fred does in every area, we are probably seeing the situation through our own biases. Roger copies those behaviors of Fred's that seem to work—that is, in which Fred appears competent—in terms of getting what Roger would like to have; but Roger won't copy those behaviors that (in his perception) don't work.

*Status.* Somewhat related to competence is the variable of model status or power. The higher a model's status, the more likely it is that his behavior will be imitated. Putting it in a different perspective, a low-status individual is more likely to imitate a high-status individual than a high-status person is to imitate a low-status one. Walters and Parke (1971) cite a study in which models were dressed as high-status persons while others wore low-status clothes. Even though the models all behaved in the same ways, subjects who saw a well-dressed model imitated more than subjects who saw a poorly dressed model. The authors speculate that the difference may have to do with *inferred vicarious reinforcement:* we tend to assume that high-status people receive more rewards for their behavior than do low-status people and thus that imitating high-status models may bring similar rewards to us.

Another possible interpretation has to do with the perceived power of the model. In general, higher-status individuals have more power; that is, they are able to dispense or withhold rewards. Experiments have shown that people imitate powerful models, even when there is no direct or even implied promise that such imitation will cause the model to reward them (Bandura, Ross, & Ross, 1971). This fact provides the teacher with a built-in head start in being a model for students. Unfortunately, it also gives an advantage to the class bullies and snobs. To the extent that we can provide status and rewarding power to students whose behavior is productive and creative, we enhance their ability to be behavior models for their peers.

*Friendliness.* Does the model's apparent friendliness and openness affect how much people learn from him? In trying to answer this question, we can begin to appreciate some of the complexities of research into model characteristics. A model displays not just one characteristic but a whole composite of characteristics, and the observer reacts to that total picture. We can hold everything else constant and vary one quality (such as friendliness) systematically, but can we say what relevance our findings may have in the real learning situation? For example, with regard to friendliness, one research team allowed 4- and 7-year-old children to watch either friendly or neutral models (adults) play with toys. The children were then asked to recall what the model did. For the older children, the friendly model's behavior was better remembered; for the younger children, friendliness seemed to make no difference (Joslin, Coates, & McKown, 1973). But what does this mean? Did the younger children simply fail to notice the difference in friendliness ("All grownups are alike")? Were they keyed in to another variable that the experimenters weren't aware of? Might not friendliness, for some observers, interact with power or status—that is, be interpreted as indicating an equality of power or status—and might not nonfriendliness or neutrality be a cue that the model has higher status or greater power than the observer? While it is useful to have working hypotheses about the effects of model characteristics on imitative learning, we must be careful to use these hypotheses tentatively. We must keep in mind that any characteristic exists in the context of a total behavior pattern as it is interpreted by the observer and that any single element may either enhance or negate the general impact of another.

*Demographic Variables.* When we turn to the demographic variables —sex, age, race—the situation is somewhat clearer. With regard to age, children are much more likely to learn from children older than themselves. This, of course, is but a variation on the status (or power) characteristic; older children have both status and power in the eyes of their juniors. Children tend to imitate same-sex peer models more readily than opposite-sex peer models, and this imitation extends even to learning sex-inappropriate behaviors (Wolf, 1973). That is, girls may learn "boyish" behaviors from other girls when they would not imitate boys engaging in those same behaviors and vice versa. When the model is an adult, however, specific sex differences begin to appear: boys are still reluctant to imitate female models, but girls imitate adult males (Bandura et al., 1971). Bandura and his co-workers attribute this difference to the fact that girls have more role ambivalence than do boys. Most boys prefer a masculine role, while many girls have not yet chosen a role or may even have rejected roles they consider to be feminine. Social training has a bearing on this pattern, of course; in our society it is still somewhat unacceptable for boys to do "sissy" things, while many "masculine" behaviors are quite acceptable in girls. In fact, a good many adult social rewards (prestige, authority, power) are reserved in large part for success in "masculine" roles and occupations. While the general social movement seems to be in the direction of more equality in roles for men and women, there is still a great deal of covert pressure toward supportive, "helpless," admiring behaviors for women and authoritative, competent, leadership roles for men. Under such conditions, it is hardly surprising that boys tend to avoid female model behaviors and that girls are often attracted to masculine roles.

Most of the studies of the effects of race on modeling have compared black and white models and observers. The general finding is that both black and white children tend to imitate white models more than black models (Cook & Smothergill, 1973). Here again we may hypothesize a power or status variable underlying the obvious possibilities of prejudice and bias. In the United States, at least, white people do usually have more power than black people, and children are certainly aware of this difference. A particularly interesting study of race differences in modeling was carried out by Thelen and Fryrear (1971). They asked white and black teenagers to watch models performing on a pursuit rotor (a manual-dexterity task in which a subject attempts to keep a metal wand in contact with a small spot on a rotating disc). Some of the models were white and some black; in addition, the models differed in the degree to which they rewarded themselves for either good or moderate performance. Thelen and Fryrear found that the "liberal" (that is, the more self-rewarding) white was imitated more than the "liberal" black model, by both black and white observers; but there were no differences in the amounts of imitation of black and white "stringent" self-rewarders. It is likely that differential imitation of a white model and of a black model depends on the behavior being modeled. For example, greater imitation of the self-rewarding behavior of the white "liberal" model may have occurred because both black adolescents and white adolescents believe that a white adult generally has more power and resources to liberalize standards than does a black adult. Again, power and status would seem to be important variables; but we must be very careful about equating race with power/status. In some situations race-difference effects may be quite independent of power or status.

*Models as Symbols.* Before leaving the question of model characteristics, we must consider one further extension of the notion of modeling: the model as a symbol. Symbolic modeling takes place in two ways. In one case, the observer himself transforms the model behavior into symbols. Much imitative learning is not put into practice until some time after the original modeling has occurred; even with preschool children, modeling can occur after delays of as long as four months (Kniveton, 1973). It seems reasonable to assume that the observer does not hold an exact reproduction of the model's behavior in his memory during such an interval—a mental movie, as it were—but rather translates that behavior into meaningful symbolism. Kniveton's subjects, for example, watched an adult model behave aggressively with toys; they may have incorporated some such notion as "hit doll" or "throw toy," but they almost surely could not have replicated every detail of the model's performance.

We have already discussed this symbolization process as the coding of a model's behavior. What is important here is that the characteristics of the model are bound to have an effect on the way in which his behavior is symbolized. What a model does is remembered in terms of what the observer thinks the model is. Consider, for instance, a child watching a violent action scene on TV. Two men are fighting, and one knocks the other down. If the winner of the fight is a "bad guy," his behavior may be remembered as a sneak attack on the hero, and his victory the result of dirty fighting. If he is Superman, the symbolization is likely to involve the triumph of good over evil, in spite of the fact that Superman is portrayed as having extraordinary powers that give him a highly unfair advantage in a fist fight. Thus the perceived qualities of the model affect not only how much is learned from him but also what is learned—which aspects of his behavior are abstracted by the observer and to what degree they are distorted.

The second kind of symbolic modeling that is important to us is that in which the model has already been transformed into a symbol. When we read biographies or novels, we are not observing live models or even pictures of models, but rather written descriptions of people's behavior. Even more abstract are the directions found in how-to manuals, where we never see the model as a person at all, but only (at most) as a pair of hands holding knitting needles or a series of words giving advice on study habits. Bandura (1971b) points out that modeling verbal symbols is gradually substituted for modeling observed behaviors as children grow older and gain linguistic competence; by the time we are adults, a major part of our social learning comes from verbal modeling. Relatively little is known about the role of model characteristics in verbal modeling. Variables such as tone of voice or rate of speech are probably less important in and of themselves than are the imagined characteristics of the speaker, which may be conjured up as we listen to (or read) the words. But what contributes to this image or how the spoken or written word can be made to suggest a learn-from-able model are questions yet to be answered.

### Characteristics of the Observer

In order for a characteristic of a model to affect imitative learning, that characteristic must be externally observable. The observer—the one who is to do the learning—must be able to notice or respond to the characteristic if it is to affect his behavior. This is not true of observer characteristics; one's private, internal, unobservable condition can affect one's learning. I can be anxious, excited, stupid, bored, sleepy, hyperthyroid, in love—and all of these may hinder or facilitate my imitative skills and/or inclinations without being immediately apparent to anyone else (or even to myself). For this reason, we include in the list of observer characteristics a number of states that we did not consider when talking about model characteristics.

*States and Traits.* The use of the word *states* brings us to another way of categorizing the things that seem to be important in models and observers. In talking about models and how their characteristics affect imitative learning, we tend to concentrate on *traits*—that is, relatively stable and long-lasting characteristics. With observers, however, the *states* seem to affect learning most immediately. Unlike a trait, a state is moved into and out of easily, over a relatively short period of time. Hunger is a state; in the course of a single day I may move into or out of a hunger state five or six times. The same is true of many other common states: fear, boredom, restlessness, amusement.

States are usually more difficult to study experimentally than are traits because they do change so readily; and there is relatively little information as to the exact relationship between this or that state and one's ability to or likelihood of learning through imitation. In general, though, the relationship seems to be most directly determined by two factors, arousal and state relevance of modeled behavior. We have already discussed arousal and modeling; an observer state that increases arousal level usually enhances social learning. As for state relevance, it is generally true that entering a state that relates specifically to a model behavior enhances attention to and learning (if not acceptance) of that behavior. Conversely, being in a state not relevant to a particular model's behavior makes learning that behavior less likely. A hungry person may find himself unable to concentrate on a calculus assignment, for example; but let him watch a Julia Child episode on TV, and he remembers every step involved in making a crepe or roasting a leg of lamb!

We shall not attempt to discuss here all the states and traits of the learner that may influence the learning process. The latter part of this book discusses a number of these in some detail. What we shall do here is look at a few such characteristics that seem to be especially relevant to social learning—to modeling. We must bear in mind, though, that observer states and traits are more or less important depending on the kind of imitation situation the observer is in. Akamatsu and Thelen (1974), after their comprehensive review of observer-state research, concluded that observer states and traits have the greatest effect on imitation when little information is provided by the situation. As the amount of information increases, the effects of observer states and traits decreases. The more ambiguous a social situation is, the more a learner's performance is affected by his own feelings and characteristics. Akamatsu and Thelen go on to suggest that, in an ambiguous situation, the observer's state influences his learning by changing his ability or motivation to use the cues available. In other words, when it is not clear what I should do or say or try to remember, my own characteristics tend to determine whether I become superattentive to the few cues that are available (in the form of models' behavior) or whether I tend to close out those cues altogether.

*Physical Characteristics.* Just to clear away the obvious, we should say at the outset that an observer's sensory capacities do influence his social learning. I cannot imitate behaviors that I cannot see or words that I cannot hear. Other physical and mental limitations may come into play as well; social learning is faster and smoother for those behaviors that our bodies and minds are developmentally ready for and in which we have already acquired partial training or skill. One's mental set in a given situation also surely affects his social learning. We tend to see and hear what we expect to see and hear, so our expectations affect both our inclination to learn from others and our perceptions of what they are showing us.

We have already seen that age is a factor in imitative learning, in that younger children tend to learn from older ones. Is there, though, a more direct relationship between observer age and modeling? The answer seems, on the surface, to be yes: in general, younger children imitate more than older children, given adult models (Fein, 1973). This generalization, however, is not an altogether straightforward one. Forehand and Gardner (1973) have looked at two different kinds of imitative learning in children, mimical and conceptual. *Mimical imitation,* as might be expected, is direct copying of the exact behavior of a model. *Conceptual imitation* involves the sort of coding we have talked about several times; the conceptual modeler reconstructs the behavior in such a way as to learn a general rule that will serve him in a variety of situations similar but not identical to the original one in which the model performed. Forehand and Gardner found that a shift from mimical to conceptual modeling occurs around the middle of the sixth year. "Young" 5-year-olds use mimical imitation significantly more than do "older" 5-year-olds, while the older 5-year-olds do significantly more conceptual imitation than the younger group. It may be that the apparent decrease in imitative learning among older children reflects merely a more sophisticated (and harder to detect) style of imitation, in which slavish copying of a model's behavior is replaced by the acquisition and storage of behavior suggestions that can be sorted through and applied when needed.

*Personality Characteristics.* It has long been supposed that imitating someone's behavior can be a strategy for gaining his approval. "Imitation," we say, "is the sincerest form of flattery." If this is true, then we might expect that people who, in general, experience strong needs for the approval of others might be more likely to imitate. And, in fact, need for approval, as measured by means of personality tests, has been shown to relate to one's tendency to imitate (Akamatsu & Thelen, 1974). However, the relationship is a weak one and disappears almost entirely when variables such as model competence or direct reinforcement are introduced.

A much stronger relationship exists between a person's tendency to imitate and his perception of his own competence in the situation. The more self-confident we are, the less likely we are to imitate the behavior of someone else. A corollary of this relationship relates to failure experiences: people who experience failure frequently are more likely to imitate than people who experience success (Akamatsu & Thelen, 1974). A word of caution, though: the effects of perceived self-competence on imitation are situation specific. A fallen soufflé or a muffed passage in a violin solo is not likely to affect my tendency to imitate the way someone else ties flies. But if I've been fishing all day and haven't caught a thing, while you've been sitting beside me hauling them in, I'm quite likely to watch what you're using for bait or how you hold your rod, and try to do the same myself.

Experiences of failure, however, can be either specific or generalized. A relatively self-confident child can turn in a miserable paper and react with "I had a bad day yesterday" or "I just wasn't interested in that topic." A child whose entire school experience has been shot through with failure, on the other hand, may see each new failure as further evidence of his general stupidity or worthlessness. For this child, incompetence is a way of life, and he is likely to imitate in nearly every situation simply because he assumes that any model is probably more competent than he is. Research with retarded children bears out this hypothesis; retardates imitate more than "normals" because their own failures have taught them to rely less on their own abilities and more on cues from others (Zigler, 1966).

One last observer characteristic should be mentioned before we move on, and this is negativism. The negativistic individual imitates, but in a reverse direction: he does exactly what the model does not do. Negativism seems to be a function of an observer's set; a person who is set to respond negatively does so even in the face of strong reinforcement to the contrary. A negative set can be intensified or perhaps even elicited by characteristics of the task and/or model; it does not always have to be inherent in the modeler. Highly structured tasks are most likely to elicit negativism, as are tasks that the observer has already decided not to like. Consider the child who wanders into the kitchen to comment "I never tasted that before and I hate it!" No amount of lip-smacking or tummy-rubbing on the part of other family members or dire threats of no dessert can persuade him to take one bite of the dish that the others are eating with relish. Models most likely to meet with negative response tend to be coercive or hostile. Also, negativism occurs frequently with certain patterns of relationship between model and observer. Age, sex, and status relationships are most related to negativism, with negative sets occurring frequently in patterns opposite to those associated with constructive social learning: boys don't want to "act like girls," and older children regard the behavior of younger ones as "little kid stuff."

## IMITATION IN THE CLASSROOM

It is hard to know where to begin in considering the practical implications of social-learning theory for teachers. Social learning—imitation—in its many forms is so pervasive that we frequently take it for granted, hardly noticing that it is occurring. Yet it does occur, and it occurs in ways that can be predicted and directed so as to maximize the child's learning potential.

As an example of the planned use of social learning in a classroom situation, consider an experiment carried out by Randolph and Wallin (1973). They asked fifth- and sixth-grade teachers to identify children in their classrooms who were consistently off task—that is, who consistently became distracted or disruptive in work situations. The group of students identified by the teachers became the subjects for the experiment. They were exposed to a number of treatments, but the one we are most interested in here combined behavior management with model reinforcement group counseling. *Behavior management* is simply the application of operant-learning theory to classroom practice—most specifically, the principle of rewarding desired behaviors rather than punishing (and thus rewarding with attention) undesired ones. *Model reinforcement group counseling* involved meeting with groups of subjects for regular sessions in which a model demonstrated a desirable classroom behavior and then the group imitated him. Successful imitations were followed by rewards. The combination of behavior management with model reinforcement group counseling improved on-task behavior significantly in this group of subjects and was significantly more effective than behavior management alone. In other words, the planned use of social-learning principles (imitation principles) had a significant effect on overall classroom behavior in this group of difficult-to-manage children.

Lest we conclude that imitation training is effective only in training students to be good little robots, following instructions and never getting out of line, let's look at another study of imitative learning. In this study, by Elliott and Vasta (1970), 5- to 7-year-old children watched a film of a same-age peer sharing his candy with another child who had none. Later in the study, each child was given an opportunity to share his own candy (given to him by the experimenter) with children who had none; the situation was structured so that the child was not aware that anyone would ever know whether he shared or not. Significantly more sharing was done by children who saw the film than by children who did not, and (surprisingly?) the older children shared more than the younger. Another research team (Acker et al., 1973) studied social learning of the physical expression of affection among children and concluded that children do indeed learn social demonstrativeness from observing the behavior of others. Just how much of our social behavior—our attitudes toward others, our sense of belonging or isolation, our concern and caring for the well-being of our fellows—is learned through imitation? Nobody knows for sure, but it seems safe to assume that imitation accounts for a great deal of it. How much can be done, through the use of planned imitative learning, to make children more socially responsive and responsible? Again, the research suggests that the possibilities are great indeed.

The role of imitation in learning and using language is an area that has interested many investigators. We shall deal with this subject in considerable detail in Chapter 3; here, though, we should note that teachers and peers, as well as parents, play important roles in the imitative learning of language. Language, as we know and use it, could hardly be learned without imitation. Throughout our formal educational system, adult models are explicitly involved in teaching language skills. (I have just finished marking a stack of college term papers, and even at this level I find myself correcting grammatical errors.) Most of the grammatical training provided by parents and teachers is done by what Whitehurst and Novak (1973) call the *expansion method:* the model provides an example of correct usage, and the child is expected to expand and apply this example to other sets of words as well. The notion that the observer constructs a template, based on the model's behavior, seems particularly valid for verbal learning. It is hardly likely that any child stores and remembers each of the thousands of grammatical constructions he uses; nor is it likely that he stops and consciously applies the rules of grammar taught in an English class. Rather, he hears an adult or older child say "I play, but you don't play." That construction forms a template, which in turn allows him to construct for himself "I want, you don't want" or "I like, you don't like." And, quite frequently, it leads to errors such as "I got, you don't got," which must be corrected by additions or revisions of the original basic pattern.

Imitation can affect general language habits as well as simple grammatical habits; it can help children to develop major patterns of verbal interaction. Children learn through observation that talking is appropriate in some situations but not in others or that different people respond differently to humor, to question-asking, or to argument. The deliberate use of modeling can be highly effective in encouraging appropriate communication habits, as was demonstrated in a study by Zimmerman and Pike (1972). They worked with second-grade Chicano children from Spanish-speaking homes, children who tended to be quite silent in the classroom. Using a combination of modeling and praise for successful imitation, the experimenters were able to increase the amount of question-asking behavior that these children engaged in. The implications are obvious: since so many other kinds of learning depend upon adequate two-way communication, improving communication habits can have an enormous impact on the overall learning process of the child.

Another team of researchers also worked with question-asking behavior among Chicano children, but they trained the children's mothers as models. "Parents who were given training and who were instructed to use procedures of modeling, cueing, and reinforcement in interaction sessions with their children had a significant effect on the target behavior of asking causal questions" (Henderson & Garcia, 1973, p. 198). The authors go on to suggest that what has in the past been labeled as a problem in achievement motivation may—especially among children from other cultural backgrounds—relate more directly to home instruction in and support of question-asking behavior. Again, it is easy to relate problems in this area (and the consequent labeling of the child as difficult or as slow) to a whole host of other educational experiences. Particularly interesting in the Henderson and Garcia study, however, was the use of parents as explicit models for in-school behavior. Parents and teachers, working together, can reinforce each other's imitation training. Here again the education potential of such teamwork is just beginning to be explored.

A number of specific findings have relevance for the teacher who wants to begin using imitation training systematically in the classroom. I shall close this chapter with a list of some of the more important or immediately applicable of these findings; the reader should bear in mind, however, that any list of this sort is necessarily only partial.

*Model Present versus Model Absent.* Landers and Landers (1973) allowed 10- to 12-year-old girls to watch a model performing a motor task. The girls then tried their own skill at the task. Their performance was significantly better when the model was still present than when she was absent. The presence of the model seems to motivate observers to try harder for successful imitation. In classroom situations involving demonstration of a skill, with subsequent practice on the part of the students, it is best to keep the model in the room during the practice period. His presence is particularly important at the beginning of the practice, in order to maximize the possibility of rewarding successful imitation. Later on, some students will have gained enough skill to be more nearly self-rewarding and also to serve as interim models for the slower students, and at this point the presence of the original model is less critical.

*Other Students as Models.* Using students as models leads us to an extremely important topic: peer modeling techniques. As Dubner points out, "The teacher need not constantly be involved in dispensing reinforcements; the students themselves serve as behavior models from which other students learn, and this can be done in a very structured, refined way" (1973, p. 137). The teacher should be alert to opportunities for letting children watch each other work constructively and for dispensing rewards for appropriate peer imitation.

*The Copy-Cat Problem.* In some situations imitation is inappropriate —for example, in wholesale copying of another person's behavior. Children are well aware of the social pressures against being a copy cat and may resist invitations to imitate because of such pressures (Fein, 1973). The teacher must repeatedly clarify the distinction between being a copy cat and imitating creatively.

*Unanticipated Modeling Effects.* The flip side of peer modeling is the possibility that children will imitate undesired or inappropriate peer behaviors. Indeed, it seems to many a harried mother or teacher that these are the only peer behaviors a child imitates! In working with children, we must try to be sensitive to all the possibilities for imitation that may arise within the group and be ready to reward selectively those imitative behaviors that lead to growth. We must remember, too, that some peer imitation can be helpful and even necessary for social growth and well-being, even though it irritates, distracts, or annoys the teacher. The child who is never naughty should concern us at least as much as the one who is always that way; the child who never goes along with the subversive activities of his peer group may have serious gaps in his interpersonal skills.

*Sequencing of Modeled Behaviors.* A study by Wilcox, Meddock, and Steinman (1973) emphasizes the importance of planning the order of

events in a learning process. Wilcox and his co-workers found that, with young children, learning a discrimination task was facilitated greatly by watching an adult model before they had worked on the task themselves. Once they had established their own solution pattern, though—whether it worked or not—they were virtually unaffected by seeing the model perform. In providing imitative opportunities in the classroom, observation of a model should precede individual practice whenever possible. Ideally, observation and practice should be alternated in a kind of sandwich, so that the student can see the behavior to be learned, then try it himself, then watch again in order to compare and refresh his memory, then practice again, and so on.

*Modeling and Self-Evaluation.* If the model appears to be too competent, too skillful, he may discourage observers from even trying to imitate. Zimmerman and Dialessi (1973), in their study of modeling influences on creativity, found that observers were more fluent (that is, gave more responses) after listening to a fluent model. But listening to a highly flexible model (that is, one who gave many different kinds of responses) tended to inhibit the flexibility of observers. The authors speculate that hearing the flexible model may have created a tendency for self-evaluation, an "Oh, I could never manage to be that clever" expectation among the observers. Along with the opportunity to imitate, observers need to learn to set reasonable, reachable performance goals for themselves. The model himself can help in this process, by discussing the steps by which he reached his present level of proficiency and by being open and comfortable about the mistakes he may still continue to make.

It is difficult, if not impossible, to overestimate the importance of imitative learning, both in and out of the classroom. When paired with techniques of selective reinforcement, imitative learning becomes perhaps the single most influential factor in a child's educational experience. Moreover, techniques of imitative learning can be introduced in the classroom at any level; they interfere little, if at all, with whatever other instructional techniques may be in use. The ease with which imitation can become a part of the classroom routine, however, is a two-edged sword: it can equally easily be misused or overused. Also, failure to anticipate the effects of some important variables (model or observer characteristics, sequencing of observation, direct or indirect reinforcement of modeled behavior) can cause an imitative-learning plan to go awry in quite mystifying ways. Like any other powerful tool, imitation training should be used with care and only after thinking through the various effects that it may have on the group as a whole and on the individual students (and teachers) who compose the group.

## QUESTIONS FOR UNDERSTANDING

1. You are planning a classroom demonstration of first-aid techniques. Relate your plans to the four processes of modeling: attention, retention, reproduction, and reinforcement.
2. Using the same plan, give an example of how a failure in any of the four processes would be likely to affect what is learned by a student.
3. Think of a person in your present environment whom you imitate or who is a potential model for you. What characteristics of yours and of his are most relevant to this model-observer relationship?
4. Think of another person whom you are extremely unlikely to imitate. Again, what characteristics of yours and his make him an unacceptable model for you?
5. Amy is a quiet seventh grader who has exceptional artistic abilities. Recently, the class was invited to decorate one panel of a board fence that conceals a construction project in the downtown area. What (if anything) can you do to maximize the peer-modeling potential in this situation?

# Chapter 3

# *Language*

Of all the facets of human behavior that one might wonder about, none is more fascinating, more influential, or more mysterious than language. Man uses words almost constantly, either out loud in verbal speech or silently in thought. Indeed, language has been one of the traditional characteristics used to differentiate man from the other animals. Yet we know so little about language: it seems as if every linguistic discovery leads us further into a twisting maze of questions and paradoxes. In this chapter we shall explore that maze, trying to sort out what is known (or generally believed) about language. We shall pose some of the more interesting as-yet-unanswered questions and highlight some of the major controversies that have developed among students of linguistic behavior (oh, yes, we argue among ourselves here too!). And, finally, we shall attempt to use what is now known or suspected about the nature of language to draw some conclusions about education.

I said a moment ago that the presence or absence of language has been considered one of the major differentiating characteristics between man and the nonhuman species: people talk, but nothing else does. This assumption, however, is currently being challenged by a number of research programs. The work done by John Lilly with porpoises and by David Premack and by Allen and Beatrice Gardner with chimpanzees casts into doubt the idea that only humans can use language. (For an introduction to this provocative work, read Fleming, 1974.) Does man use symbols—language—in a way that is qualitatively different from what other creatures do with them? Or is it merely that man has gone further, is simply more advanced than his linguistically primitive brothers? Attneave suggests that the latter point of view is correct, that the higher mammals "have concepts and concept structures that are not ridiculously different from ours, and that when these concept structures reach a certain level of evolution, they are ready to have language grafted onto them" (1974, p. 496).

The question of whether nonhuman species do or can use language has implications extending far beyond the academic curiosity of the anthropologist or linguist; it touches upon the very nature of language and perhaps of man himself. As the Russian psycholinguist Luria (Luria & Yudovich, 1959) points out, man's use of language allows him to acquire information from others in a unique way. All other creatures must learn through their own experience—or, at best, from watching somebody's behavior—but man can transmit facts and ideas abstractly. It is interesting to note, in this context, that neither of the chimps that have been trained to "speak" (the Gardners' Washoe, who uses sign-language symbols, or Premack's Sarah, who uses variously colored and shaped chips as symbols) seems able or willing to discuss abstractions.[1] Their "conversations" concern the immediate, here-and-now world. Does man have a special conceptual structuring that allows him to use his symbols in a qualitatively different way? Or has man's use of abstract symbols allowed him to learn to think abstractly? These questions lie at the heart of the Great Linguistic Controversy, and we shall return to it a bit later.

That we do use words to denote abstract concepts is undeniable. But how much easier would be the job of the linguist if each word always meant only one thing and always the same thing. Instead, "everything has many names and every name 'has' many things" (Olson, 1970, p. 262). A chair can be a soft, plump, chintz-covered thing or an instrument of torture in the dean's office. And, conversely, a particular object may be referred to as a chair, a recliner, a seat, "my place." As we begin to consider the diversity, the complexity, the seeming perverseness of language, we wonder how anyone ever learns to talk at all! Yet, in spite of multiple names for things and multiple meanings for names, words do become firmly attached to clusters of related notions. In fact, that attachment is often so strong that the word in some sense becomes part of the thing—that is, the word is no longer just a sound that stands for something but *is* that something and seems to share its characteristics. "The word *glass* sounds brittle but it is not. . . . If you do not believe that the word *glass* is transformed, repeat it aloud fifty times. Like Cinderella at midnight, it will lose its transformation and revert to what it was, a drab little vocable" (Percy, 1972, p. 7).

But language involves much more than attaching meanings to words; it involves the ways in which we string those words together. The pattern of our words is at least as important as the words themselves. Consider, for instance, the two sentences "John hit his mother" and "His mother hit John." Or Lewis Carroll's famous question, does "I mean what I say" mean the same as "I say what I mean"? And, as a final twist, what do we do with the ambiguous constructions so easy to find in English, like "The duck is

---

[1]Since this section was first written, several more chimps have been taught to "talk." It is still true, however, that none of them uses abstract concepts.

ready to eat"? There is not space here to go into the work of linguists who are trying to unravel the relationship between a thought, as it occurs to us, and what comes out of our mouths when we try to express that thought. Suffice it to say that the field is as fascinating as it is complex.

In fact, it seems safe to say that nothing about language is simple. Even if we understood perfectly the rules of structure of a language—the grammar, the semantics—we would still have to reckon with its social rules, which are even more difficult to specify precisely. "Every language exists in many styles. . . . These many styles, for all their communicative richness, contain many pitfalls. For woe to him who uses a style that does not fit the occasion" (Moulton, 1973, p. 17). We don't say to the bank manager "Hi, fella, how'sa 'bout a loan?" And your girl friend would probably wonder what was wrong if, in the middle of a movie, you turned and said to her "Excuse me, Miss, but would you mind moving down one seat so I don't have to be behind this very-tall person in the next row?" Of course, if the two of you had been joking about being formal with each other, and she had just asked whether you would "care for some popcorn, Sir," your statement would probably have been both appropriate and (moderately) funny. Which brings up another complicating factor about language: not just the speaker, but also the listener, contributes to the meaning of what is being said. As Bateson (1972) points out, communication can be "magically modified" by accompanying communication.

Language not only has different styles for different social occasions, but also has different forms for various kinds of content. Engineers, business executives, society editors, and educators each have their own *jargon*, their own highly specialized sublanguages with which they communicate efficiently to each other but that are virtually incomprehensible to outsiders. As society becomes increasingly complex, the number of such sublanguages grows, and the ability to communicate meaningfully across disciplines or interest areas decreases. This state of affairs is—or should be—of grave concern to those of us who are committed to the need for generalists, for people who can think creatively about relationships among widely varying sets of facts, and to the education of young people along these lines.

All languages—the language of everyday social intercourse, the stylized jargon of the specialist, the "foreign" languages that can enrich our perceptions in unexpected ways—should be tools for clearer and more creative thinking. Perhaps teaching students to use languages in this way is what education is all about.

## THE GREAT LINGUISTIC CONTROVERSY

Do we think as we do because of the way we talk? Or do we talk as we do because of the way we think? If our thinking is determined by our language, then it follows (or would seem to follow) that by teaching children more adequate verbal techniques, we should be able to speed up their cognitive development. If, however, language is simply the natural outgrowth of the kind of mental processes that humans are innately equipped to engage in, then trying to improve cognitive ability by improving language is akin to trying to make the tail wag the dog. Let's examine the arguments, and see what educational implications may emerge.

## All Humans Talk

There are, to begin with, a number of observations about language that nearly everyone agrees with. For instance, all normal children learn to talk. Hardly a profound statement, that—or is it? When we consider the difficulty that children often have in learning to read and the fact that many individuals never master the conversion of visual symbols (written language) into ideas, the near universality of spoken language becomes impressive. Why should auditory symbols be more readily understood than visual ones? Certainly there is at least as much ambiguity in oral as in written speech, and probably more; oral speech tends to contain more grammatical sloppiness, more idiomatic and slang expressions, than does written speech, not to mention wide variations in pronunciation. The universality of spoken language alone provides support for the notion that some kind of ear-to-brain channels may be wired in genetically, or at least that those nerve pathways that link auditory receptors with cognitive centers in the brain have special suitability for that role.

Not only does nearly everyone learn to talk, but students of child language are discovering that the early speech of children follows universal patterns regardless of the language they speak. The Finnish child, the American child, and the Mandarin child all begin to speak using a common grammatical structure. They begin with single words, used to designate gestalts—that is, unitary percepts. For the American child, "ma-ma" may refer to any adult female, "go" may mean "being outside in my stroller," "Boo" is the family cat; each of these is, for the child, a whole, indivisible concept. He soon graduates to two-word sentences that use a pivot word and a modifier word. The form of these sentences is also universal across languages; it is roughly the same regardless of whether the child is speaking in French, Arabic, or Urdu. Does this mean that at the deepest, most primitive levels, language and/or thought patterns are genetically preprogrammed?

## Thought Leads to Language

Jean Piaget, one of the most influential of modern psychologists, believes that there is preprogramming of thought patterns in that certain cognitive skills always appear in a given order and always around a certain age, regardless of the kind of training or environmental stimulation that a child may have. Language, he believes, follows and is shaped by the logical development of the individual. We learn to think in certain genetically determined ways, and our language patterns grow out of those patterns of thought.

One of the best known of Piaget's "tests" for logical functions has to do with children's perception of conservation of mass. Small children, watching you roll a lump of clay from a ball into a long snake, will tell you that there is more clay in the snake than in the ball; or, seeing water poured from a short, fat glass into a tall, thin one, they will say that there is more water in the tall, thin glass. They do not yet understand that the quantity can be unchanged even though the form is different. They do not yet *conserve* matter. If Piaget is right about the relationship between thought and language—that language emerges out of our thought patterns—then teaching a child better language skills should not make any difference in his logical thinking. The concept of conservation will come when the child is ready, and learning more words won't speed it up. DeStefano (1973) attempted to test this notion by teaching "nonconserving" children the verbal symbols they would need if they were to describe a Piaget-type experiment from a "conserving" point of view. He found that the children were not helped by the new words—exactly the result that would be expected if language grows out of thought, rather than the other way around.

## Language Leads to Thought

The opposite point of view was perhaps most tersely expressed by the Russian psychologist L. S. Vigotski, who said that "thought is not merely expressed in words, it comes into existence through them" (quoted in D. E. Day, 1974, p. 67). Those who follow Vigotski's position hold that we are able to think only through words and that our linguistic structure shapes the way in which we think. Benjamin Whorf, a linguist, maintains that thoughts do not exist unless there is a verbal form for their expression. It certainly does seem to be the case that cultures in which particular concepts are useful have words to express them, and if a concept does not have a convenient verbal label in our own language, it is often quite hard to grasp. Kinship terms provide a good example. Many groups have a kinship label for mother's sister that is the same as the label for mother. For these groups, mother and mother's sister are precisely the same; they are difficult —if not impossible—to differentiate. In our own culture, cousin refers to any child of our mother's or father's siblings; we hold the same relationship to all our cousins. The Tlingit people of Alaska, among others, do not, however, see all cousins as the same. For them, a cross cousin is the child of a mother's brother or a father's sister, while a parallel cousin is the child of a mother's sister or a father's brother. Parallel cousins and cross cousins stand in different relationships to one, and those relationships would never be mixed up; but an elder male parallel cousin and an elder brother are both referred to by the same kinship term and might easily be confused. The terminology calls attention to—if indeed it does not create—the concept to which it refers.

The relationship between early language and early thought, then, is a kind of chicken-and-egg problem; it is further confused by the fact that those who study it must do so according to their own linguistic structures. What is certain is that however thought and language begin, they continue to interact as the person grows and develops. The way I have learned to think has been and is affected by the language I use. And the way in which I use language is shaped by the kinds of thinking I engage in. Speech patterns in the child can serve as clues to the level of development of certain logical processes: most probably, the absence or late maturation of a given cognitive ability is signaled by a language habit—if we are sensitive enough to pick it up.

## Language and Time

One of the clearest examples of the speech-thought relationship is found in the area of time binding—that is, the use of time-oriented concepts. Research with primates (man's closest relatives), with normal children, and with deaf children strongly suggests that language is necessary for understanding temporal relationships. A chimpanzee (or a prelanguage child) can solve problems involving spatial relationships: it can learn to choose the larger of two objects or the circle (instead of the square or the triangle) in order to win a prize. But it cannot learn to respond differentially to a series of five clicks or tones (as opposed to a shorter or longer series). Spatial relationships can be dealt with immediately, in the here and now. But relationships over time require storage in memory, and such storage can be done only by using abstractions—by using language. Blank (1974) suggests that the ability to deal with temporal concepts continues to be closely related to language development well into the early school years. Retarded readers, for instance, do poorly on problems dealing with time sequences. Language itself is a sequence in time; in order to understand a spoken sentence, we must hold the first part of it in memory until we hear the end. Memory (as we shall see in Chapter 5) involves symbol storage; and as soon as we talk about making and using symbols, we are talking about language.

All behavior is sequenced in time. We do things in some order, and to the extent that the order of our behavior is "sensible," we are better able to accomplish what we want to. Thinking does not always feel as though it goes on in a logical, orderly sequence—we often have flashes of insight or understanding—but planning and problem solving are more efficient if they can make use of orderly sequences of thought. When we are especially upset or anxious, we may lose the ability to order our thinking; we say that our thoughts "go 'round and 'round in circles" or that we can't "think straight." It seems reasonable to suppose that such jumbled thinking represents a temporary loss of the ability to symbolize, to express concepts and feelings in an orderly sequence of words. The child who has not yet developed language must be involved in this kind of thinking all the time; he doesn't know about any other kind. As he begins to symbolize and to organize his symbols into language strings, he also begins to be able to order his thoughts. Luria and Yudovich (1959) maintain that the ordering of concepts through language is the basic process through which the child's consciousness is formed. As language develops, thoughts no longer are translated into words—they are words. Luria and Yudovich go on to say that complex behavior patterns are possible only as language and thought develop. As he acquires word symbols for things and for actions, the child can play through behavior sequences in his mind and choose those that will work best. Thus language allows him to plan ahead, to develop new and elaborated behaviors, to problem solve with increasing skill and accuracy.

## Language as a Way of Experiencing

Piaget tells us that "the line of development of language, as of perception, is from the whole to the part" (1926, p. 133). For Piaget, the primitive concept comes first, and its name comes later. Luria would qualify this, I think, only by pointing out that as we learn to use various names for a concept and for different parts or aspects of that concept, we come to experience the concept in a different way. The more completely symbolized an idea is—the more ways we have of looking at it and talking about it and seeing it in relationship to other ideas—the more richness it has for us.

Language, then, allows us to sort out what is happening to us, to make sense out of the myriad of stimuli that constantly bombard us from within and without. It helps us to select what we will attend to by providing us with a sort of road map of what is important or relevant at any given moment. When we are able to use abstract symbols, we can say to ourselves (or to someone else) "I am doing this, not that or that. If I do this, then that will probably happen." In this sense, words are more than just symbols for real-world things; words shape our very experiencing of the real world by determining which aspects of that world we attend to and which we ignore. "Words," says Olson, "neither symbolize, stand for, nor represent referents, objects, or events. They serve rather to differentiate some perceived event from some set of alternatives" (1970, p. 265). Language is the bridge by means of which one person can share his experiences with another person. But it is also, in a very real sense, the way in which I share my experiences with myself—the way in which I can tell myself what it is I am experiencing and how I shall understand and use that experience.

## LANGUAGE AND BEHAVIOR

We have now introduced, at a philosophical level, the notion that language somehow influences, shapes, and directs human behavior. Let's look more directly at that idea, at the specific ways in which speech and behavior interact. Again, we shall have to go back to that early and (to us) confusing period in which language is just beginning to become a part of the child's experiencing. The prelanguage child does not see the world as a mass of confused and unrelated stimuli; even small infants are capable of responding to visual patterns. The ability to respond to regularities in the perceptual field, to organize and categorize stimulus experiences, thus seems to be an innate human characteristic (and this ability is also found in species that never develop language). But, for the prelanguage child, the categories are shifting, amorphous, and often unpredictable. One of the first functions of language is nailing down categories, clarifying the differences between "this" and "not this." All languages have in common the fundamental assumption that the outside world can be separated into things that maintain their identity—that are stable over time—and so can be held in thought and communicated about.

In the nailing-down process, though, some characteristics of a concept must be emphasized and some ignored. To say that a cow is a four-legged animal that gives milk is to omit the fact that all cows also have hooves, chew their cud, and attract flies; it further ignores details about this particular cow (it is brown and white, it has had one calf, it likes blueberry muffins). As we build up a language about things, we underscore our perception of the generally agreed-upon qualities of those things; further, we learn to attend to those agreed-upon qualities that the language consensus designates as important or useful. All cows get up back legs first (as contrasted with horses, which get up first with their front legs), but this is not one of the first things that we think of as we say what the word *cow* means. Words allow us to think in shorthand, to deal with the idea of cow without having to think about all the characteristics of every cow we have ever seen or heard about.

## Perception

Words not only highlight the socially agreed-upon abstract symbol of a concept, though; they also carry highly individualized meanings and can call forth other concepts according to relationships unique to the individual. "Cow" may suggest a particular week on a farm to one person; it may call to mind a distinctive smell or texture to another; it may be a pleasant, bucolic concept for me and a terrifying one for my small daughter. Thus the language symbols that we use give us access to those symbols and symbol qualities held in common with all members of our language group, to other qualities and associations shared with smaller groups, and to perceptions and relationships unique to our own mental processes. At all these levels, the way we learn to talk about things inevitably affects the ways in which we perceive them. "Language structure is like a lattice or screen through which we see the world of our experience. This lattice, as it were, may obscure little bits of our experience, but it lets through the rest in larger or smaller chunks, perhaps, clarifying some parts, clouding other parts, and suggesting a larger pattern for still another. All the while, however, we see the pattern of the whole and are as little bothered by the lattice as if it were a screen installed on our front porch" (Cazden, 1972, p. 227).

It is important to note, in discussing the effect of language on perception, that it is a double-edged sword. Language calls attention to important attributes of our percepts and makes it possible for us to think about them efficiently and to communicate about them with other people. But it also makes it difficult (if not impossible) for us to notice other attributes, to differentiate things we have learned to call by the same name, or to see as one class a set of things we have learned to think of as different. Says Moulton: "In one sense, then, a language liberates us: it permits us to send an unlimited number of messages and thus serves as a vehicle for our endless thoughts. But in another sense it enslaves us: it forces us to communicate our thoughts in strictly regulated ways" (1973, p. 19). Only the poet, as he frees himself from the conventions of language, can reintroduce us to the realms of prelanguage perception. It is up to each of us to try to conserve the poet in us even as we develop our consensual, efficient, practical language skills.

## Problem Solving

Language not only shapes our perceptions but also is a vital element in planning and problem solving. While we may not go as far as Luria, who maintains that "a word *gives rise* to new temporary connections in the brain" (1971, p. 185; italics added), we must agree that the words we use in our thoughts relate directly to the patterns those thoughts tend to form. Because we use language, we can think about doing things instead of actually doing them. We can think about doing them in several different ways and select the easiest or the quickest or the most enjoyable way to enact them in actual behavior. We can imagine possible consequences without having to experience them. In other words, we can engage in symbolic trial-and-error sequences. Such symbolic activity has at least two major advantages over real-world behavior. In the first place, obviously, just thinking about a problem allows us to discard poor solutions without having to mess up our reality. We can consider whether we have any eggs before we begin to stir up the rest of the ingredients for the cake; and we don't have to burn our hand in order to decide to use a pot holder to take the pan out of the oven. A second and not-so-obvious advantage is that we can break off symbolic solutions when it becomes obvious that they aren't going to work. We don't have to take the time to follow them through to the end and then try to salvage something from the ruins. Symbolic trial-and-error is considerably more efficient than the real thing.

In naming things, we divide the world into categories; we manipulate the category names instead of trying to manipulate the objects themselves. In symbol manipulation (thought) we attempt to make predictions; we try to decide ahead of time what the consequences of a behavior will be. Attneave (1974) calls these predictions *SRS linkages:* the prediction that a certain response (R) to a certain set of stimuli (S) will lead to a new set of stimuli (S). Some SRS linkages are determinate—they allow quite accurate predictions of the consequences of behavior—while some are more ambiguous. Attneave suggests that one's use of language affects how determinate the SRS linkages are and, further, that language patterns that lead to determinate linkages are most helpful to an individual. "Good organization in the representational system is organization that makes for relatively determinate SRS linkages; poor organization is that which makes for more indeterminate linkages" (p. 495). Language habits that help us to predict consequences accurately make for effective problem solving; language habits that don't lead to accurate predictions won't help us much and may even get in our way.

SRS linkages lead to behavior. I act as I do because of my expectations of the consequences of my action. The more determinate an SRS linkage is, the better I can predict those consequences, and the more effective or adaptive my behavior is likely to be. What all this means, then, is that language, in affecting and directing thought, inevitably must also affect behavior. The kinds of words we use and the ways in which we string those words together shape and direct what we do. Behavior is determined largely by our perceptions and our beliefs; both of these are molded by language. "To say that we believe a proposition implies that, under appropriate circumstances, we would take action or make decisions based on it. In its most general form, therefore, belief is what gives language its powerful control over our behavior" (Miller, 1966, p. 101).

## Verbal Self-Control

The kinds of propositions Miller is talking about come not only from other people but from ourselves. We literally tell ourselves what to do every day. Small children do this quite overtly: a 2- or 3-year-old, for example, may reach for a forbidden object, pause, shake his head, say "no-no," and then move on to something else. But adults, too, may do the same sort of thing: the would-be nonsmoker reaches for his pocket and then mumbles "I will not smoke a cigarette," or the hostess sits at the kitchen table (all by herself) saying "I have to stop at the market for some cream, and I'll pick up the bridge tallies at the drug store."

Luria studied the development of this kind of verbal self-control and found that the ability to use speech to control overt behavior begins to be effective only at about age 4. His small subjects were told to press a bulb when a green light flashed but not when a red light flashed. If the spoken words "press" or "don't press" accompanied the stimulus, the children followed the instructions quite well. At around age 4, they begin to be able to say "press" or "don't press" themselves when the light flashes and thus control their own behavior. Later, the need to say the words out loud diminishes; the response becomes internalized, and "external speech becomes superfluous.The directive role is taken over by those inner connections which lie behind the word, and they now begin to display their selective effect in directing the further motor responses of the child"(Luria, 1971, p. 192). In other words, the speech of a child whose language development is still at a relatively primitive stage is not an effective determinant of behavior. As the child's language capacity matures, he begins to be able to use his own words to direct what he does. At first the words must be said aloud to be effective, but later the whole process is internalized. (Does this relate to the need that beginning readers have to read aloud in order to understand the text? Is it perhaps hearing the words, rather than saying them, that makes the difference?)

That egocentric speech (that is, speech directed to oneself rather than to someone else) is more common in younger than in older children has been known for a long time. As early as 1929, Vigotski commented on the way in which small children talk out problems as they attempt to solve them. "The child states the situation that has arisen, takes from it 'verbal copy,' and then reproduces those connections of his past experience which may help him out of present difficulties" (quoted in Luria & Yudovich, 1959, p. 19). Piaget, too, has maintained for years that children's speech "accompanies and reinforces individual activity" before it is used to communicate ideas to other people (1926, p. 39). Most students of language development assume that as the child grows older, he gradually internalizes verbal problem solving; instead of having to say the words out loud in order to use them, he can simply think with them. D. E. Day (1974), plotting the incidence of egocentric speech, reports that it appears at around age 3 and increases until it reaches a peak sometime between 4 and 6; after that it declines rapidly until it disappears.

There are two problems with Day's finding, however. First, it is intuitively apparent that people become more self-conscious about egocentric speech as they grow older. The 4-year-old is not bothered by the fact that he is talking to himself; for him, such behavior is natural. The 12-year-old, in contrast, has learned that you are "supposed to" talk to other people and think to yourself. He is therefore likely to inhibit his out-loud thinking when there are other people within earshot, even though he may still do a lot of it in private. In other words, the researcher, simply by being in the same room with the person he is observing, may well have a significant effect on the very behavior he is most interested in. A second problem has to do with the fact that we learn to use speech for more than one purpose at the same time. I may decide to tell you about a problem I am working on. As I talk to you, I am communicating—I am not engaging in egocentric speech—but I am also thinking out loud about the problem, and my own communication may clarify the problem for me much more than just thinking quietly about it would have done. Indeed, the frequency with

which people seek out others to "talk things over" with and then ignore the suggestions made by the other tends to support such a notion.

I am not convinced, in fact, that most adults have given up or grown out of talking to themselves. I know I do a lot of it myself; I plan menus in the car on the way home or rehearse lectures while walking across campus or argue with myself about the interpretation of a research result while I'm in the shower. I suspect that many other adults do the same—covertly, almost guiltily, because we have been taught by our culture that such behavior is childish or even "crazy." But we do it anyway because it helps us to think. Cazden says that his own thought "is frequently clarified and even changed by the act of giving it form in words, whether in conversation or teaching or writing" (1972, p. 224). Might we, perhaps, do ourselves—and our students—a service by encouraging more thinking out loud as a technique of problem solving? Piaget tells us that "as we pass from early childhood to the adult stage, we shall naturally see the gradual disappearance of the monologue, for it is a primitive and infantile function of language" (1926, p. 17). I think—I'm not sure, but I think—I disagree. I shall have to talk it over with myself and decide.

## LISTENING

In thinking about language, we often overlook or take for granted the fact that speech is a reciprocal process—that, in order for speech to be useful, there must be someone to listen to it. Sometimes, to be sure, that someone is the speaker himself; but often it is someone else. In any case, speakers are also listeners (or, more accurately, we might say that transmitters of speech also function as receivers of speech). It is the reciprocal nature of speech that makes it such a powerful factor in human behavior: speech as a medium of interaction (with myself or with someone else) is the molder and shaper of behavior. Bateson (1972), who has spent many years studying communication behavior in humans and nonhumans, points out that most of what we can say about personality is a function of communication (and therefore, indirectly, of speech): "No man is 'resourceful' or 'dependent' or 'fatalistic' in a vacuum. His characteristic, whatever it be, is not his but is rather a characteristic of what goes on between him and something (or somebody) else" (p. 298). Since "what goes on" between two communicators involves as much receiving as it does sending of messages, it seems highly appropriate that we consider—for a moment, at least—the special problems involved in listening to speech.

## Decoding

Producing speech involves a coding process: the coding of ideas into distinctive sounds, connected by agreed-upon rules into meaningful units. By the same token, listening is a decoding process, in which the packages of sounds are transformed into ideas again. Listener and sender both must deal with individual sounds (phonemes), with stringing-together rules, and with the overall rhythmic pattern of the final product. If we think of speech as the result of packaging ideas into manageable chunks by encoding, the other side of this process is that the listener, using the same coding scheme, must decode these chunks. And the listener needs all the help he can get, considering the details of his task (Dittman, 1972).

As difficult as this decoding process may be, though, it is not the whole of the listener's decoding task. The listener is not a passive machine, carrying on a running translation of sound into ideas. Listening is an active process, in which every message and message fragment is screened and either rejected or accepted (and often highlighted) so as to fit with whatever else is going on in the listener's thoughts and feelings. "Everything that comes into the brain is processed through a filter—the word is not quite appropriate—rather, an active mechanism programs the signals occurring in the input systems. By the time the signals arrive in the parts of the brain that are coordinate with consciousness they have been altered, changed, broken in, and made ready for the individual to accept" (Pribram, 1973b, p. 154). We are all familiar with the notion that, under many circumstances, people hear what they want to; my son will swear that I told him he could have a cookie when I know I said no such thing, and I am equally sure that my husband said he would go shopping with me this afternoon, even though he now denies it. These are common examples of mis-hearing, and they obviously involve activity on the part of the listener. But even accurate listening demands more than passive translation. I must compare the sound stimuli that I receive with some kind of phoneme dictionary to see what word the sound represents; otherwise I would have to treat each variation in pronunciation as a separate word. I must decide where one word ends and the next begins, and make the same kind of decision for phrases, sentences, and perhaps even longer units. I must recognize ambiguities ("The duck is ready to eat") and assign them a meaning appropriate to the context. And I must carry out all these activities repeatedly, in a fraction of a second, while at the same time continuing to receive the next set of signals from the speaker. When we stop to consider all that is involved in understanding spoken language (as well as in speaking it), it seems to be something of a miracle that we can do it at all!

We said earlier that our language shapes the way we think; this is as true for the person listening to a message as it is for the person framing it. My understanding of a message is influenced by my perception of its context; but my perception of the context is equally influenced by the message I receive. Indeed, to refer to "the context" is misleading: communication is a series of contexts, each one leading into the next. The communication process, a sequence of messages-in-contexts flowing between two or more individuals, affects and structures future messages, future perceived contexts, and the general ways in which each participant views his world. "Listening to an utterance provides information about both the intended referent and the alternatives from which it must be differentiated. There is, therefore, considerable information to the listener in an utterance; the utterance restructures his perception" (Olson, 1970, p. 272). When I tell a student that "logging is one of the most important industries of the Pacific Northwest," he is moved toward differentiating between the Pacific Northwest and other areas of the country, toward recognizing that some places have a logging industry and others do not, toward seeing the harvesting of trees as a business, toward noticing a log truck speeding down a highway. The listener is affected by a message in many ways, ways of which neither he nor the speaker is usually aware.

### Listening Responses

Another task is involved in listening (as well as in speaking) effectively: that of role playing. Neither listener nor speaker can do his job well unless he knows something about the person he is communicating with. Each must know the frame of reference of the other, must know the contextual setting in which communication occurs. Every message may mean a host of different things; the listener has to decide which of these possible meanings is intended. He makes this decision, in large part, on the basis of his knowledge of the message sender. Additionally, he must find a way of informing the sender that the message is being received, that he does understand or at least is attending to it. Most adult listeners emit a constant stream of responses as they listen, responses that facilitate communication by signaling the message sender that he is being attended to, that it is all right to continue sending. These listening responses may be verbal ("uh-huh," "fine," "really!") or nonverbal (nodding, smiling, leaning forward, looking surprised); they all reassure the sender that he is not talking into a vacuum. A knowledge of how much of this sort of feedback a particular sender needs is essential to good listening. The listener must be able to put himself in the role of the speaker and emit signals that inform the speaker how he is doing. Dittman (1972) maintains that this aspect of the listener's role is more difficult than the complementary task of the speaker (that is, taking the role of the listener to decide how well the message is being understood). The listener's job requires that he understand the needs of the speaker and respond to those needs. Young children cannot do this with any regularity, and good listener feedback is unusual during the early school years.

It is more difficult for an observer to know what is happening to a listener (during and as a result of a communication) than to know what is happening to a speaker. After all, we can use the speaker's subsequent words as a basis for our suppositions. In observing the listener, we must rely on his listening responses, and these are not nearly as extensive or as objectively analyzable as is the speaker's message. Nevertheless, we can make some reasonable inferences from a listener's listening responses. For one thing, the presence or absence of listening responses helps us to determine whether a message was received. Bateson suggests that "to discriminate accurately what people are really expressing, we must be able to comment directly or indirectly on that expression" (1972, pp. 215–216). In other words, if a normal adult listener is receiving a message, he must be able to make listening responses; if there are no listening responses, it is reasonable to assume that the message is not being received. (In some unusual cases, listening responses may be deliberately suppressed; but in such cases there is usually an artificial stiffness of expression or posture that in itself may be considered a listening response.)

If listening responses are present, indicating that a message is being received, we may also make inferences about the accuracy of reception by assessing the appropriateness of the listening responses—that is, how well the responses correspond to the speaker's expectations for listener reaction. This correspondence may be assessed not only by the content of the listening response but also by its timing. Listening responses, as Dittman points out, follow the rhythmic pattern of the message and tend to occur during the pauses that usually punctuate meaningful segments of speech (at the ends of sentences or long phrases, for example). Among adults, listening responses at other than these final junctures may mean not "Yes, I'm listening," but "Please stop talking and let me have a turn" or "I'm bored and want to do something else."

Children, as has been pointed out, do not make nearly as many listening responses as do adults, nor do they time them as well. There is "a perseverative characteristic in children's talk: having an idea to communicate, a child is likely to try to get it into the conversation whether the other person has come to the end of a speech unit or not" (Dittman, 1972, pp. 415–416). This is true for listening responses as well as for actual communication interchanges; the child's listening response is likely to be popped into the conversational stream too early or too late, so that it has the quality of an interruption rather than a facilitator of communication. As the child matures, both the quality and the quantity of his listening responses improve. He uses more of them, and he fits them into the speaker's pattern more smoothly.

In summary, then, listening is far from a passive taking-in of information. It is a complex activity, involving screening and adapting messages to fit the listener's expectations and providing ongoing feedback to the speaker. As teachers, we tend to agree that learning to communicate well is a primary goal for students, but we often interpret "communication" to mean the transmission of messages. We must recognize that students also need to learn to be good receivers—to be good and accurate listeners.

## THE DEVELOPMENT OF SPEECH

There is no question that the use of language, either by speakers or by listeners, is an exceedingly complex phenomenon. Yet nearly all humans acquire this ability. How does language acquisition come about? What are the factors that govern its appearance? In this section we shall attempt to trace the development of language as an individual grows to maturity and to assess the importance of some of the environmental factors that may affect that development.

Before we begin, however, we must consider again the growing belief among students of child language that humans are genetically programmed to use language. That is, many linguists believe that nothing in the child's learning experiences can wholly account for the acquisition of language; there must be an innate propensity to use verbal symbols (and to use them in rule-governed ways) in all humans. Chomsky, perhaps the best-known proponent of this point of view, says "If there were not an innate restriction on the form of grammar, then the child could employ innumerable theories to account for his linguistic experience, and no one system, or even small class of systems, would be found exclusively acceptable or even preferable. The child could not possibly acquire knowledge of a language" (1971, pp. 429–430). Chomsky and his colleagues point out that the child hears a wide variety of correct and incorrect grammatical forms as he grows up. Adults, both in speaking to him and in speaking to one another, probably use fragments more often than they use complete forms; and his peers can hardly be expected to provide better language models than the adults in his environment. Yet, in spite of this confusing babel of inconsistent rule usage, children do learn to speak properly. They learn to produce sentences that follow grammatical rules. More curious still is the fact that, having learned to speak grammatically, most people are quite unable to say why they construct sentences as they do. "It is generally the case that people who can follow the rules with amazing skill are often completely unable to provide any explicit statement of the rules they are following" (Miller, 1966, p. 98). Knowledge of the rules of grammar must be present in most people; otherwise we could not account for the way in which they follow those rules. But it is an implicit, unconscious knowledge rather than a consciously learned and applied knowledge. Chomsky and others, then, suggest that this knowledge is never learned at all; it is built in, present at birth, and ready to be used as other structures and abilities mature or are acquired. We have come back, full circle, to the Great Linguistic Controversy and now see the other side of the coin: just as language inevitably influences thought, so must our linguistic programming, a part of our genetic equipment, structure the language we come to use.

## The Growth of Speech

The first evidence of language behavior in the child occurs during the first few months of life: he produces gurgling or cooing sounds that are clearly distinguishable from crying. These sounds are the precursors of babbling, which usually begins at around 4 or 5 months. Babbling involves repetition of sounds, of distinct phonemes. It is important because the phonemes of babbling provide the pool from which the child will later begin to form his first words. The child does not learn to make new sounds—or words—by imitation; rather, adults imitate him and thus call attention to those sounds in his repertoire that most closely resemble words. Picture a tranquil domestic scene. Baby is sitting in his play pen, waving a toy about and drooling down his chin, while Mother stands at the ironing board. Is Mother likely to lean over and—out of the blue—say "Come on, Charlie, say 'ma-ma' "? No, it happens just the other way. Charlie babbles on and accidentally produces something that Mother (fondly, and by using just a *little* imagination) hears as "ma-ma." Then she leans over and says " 'Ma-ma'—that's right—'ma-ma.' Say it again, Charlie—'ma-ma.' "

By the time Charlie is 8 or 10 months old, he will probably recognize a number of words and gestures and phrases, and may well be spontaneously using a few himself. Understanding of and responding to commands ("Open your mouth, Charlie." "Don't touch!") usually start at about 10 to 12 months (Carroll, 1971). By this time Charlie may be saying quite a few words himself—or he may not. He should, however, be using some vocalizations in a systematic way: it doesn't matter so much whether he says "water" or "wah-wah" or "guk" as he tugs at his mother's skirt and points to the sink, but he should be verbalizing something. Using sounds as if they were speech—producing the intonations of spoken language—is an important sign that language development is proceeding normally. Children appear to pick up patterns of rhythm and intonation first and fit actual words into these patterns later.

Although a great deal of preparatory language learning occurs during the first two years of life, the most dramatically apparent language development comes between ages 2 and 5. During this period, children begin to engage in true reciprocal communication. They acquire a large vocabulary (the average 5-year-old knows upward of 1500 words) and are able to use, or at least understand, most basic grammatical structures. And all of this happens, we must again emphasize, with little direct teaching on the part of the parents. The child's earliest "true" words usually designate things, specific chunks of his environment. He does not use many descriptors at first, and even adjectives or adverbs tend to designate objects (as when he points to the stove and says "hot"). Nearly all early words "serve as nouns that refer to the total object because that is what the child perceives" (Blank, 1974, p. 240). Moreover, speech during the 2- to 5-year period focuses on and acquires meaning in concrete-active situations. Children of this age talk about what is here and now; they are not yet able to use language to refer to abstract ideas or to things and activities with which they are not immediately involved.

As words become familiar parts of the child's vocabulary, they begin to be strung together. By age 2, most children are able to construct two-word sentences (and even these sentences, as we mentioned earlier, follow consistent grammatical rules). Gradually, more words are added, and the sentences begin to lose their telegraphic quality and take on the elaborated form of adult speech. The child's cognitive ability and his speech seem to develop along parallel tracks. A new idea, a new way of thinking about something, is expressed in words and grammatical structures that are familiar to the child, while new language structures are used to express familiar concepts in a new way. As Slobin puts it, "New forms first express old functions, and new functions are first expressed by old forms" (1972, p. 200). It is as if the child uses the form or function he is comfortable with, the one he has mastered, as a tool to explore the new and the unfamiliar. This process results in a blending of older and semiautomatic combinations with highly creative and innovative constructions in the child's speech. Voluntary and automatic activities are closely interlaced, innovative construction alternating with ready-made phrases. The child sometimes chooses new sets of words for a particular meaning and sometimes submits to the routine use of learned sequences; in short, the results of conditioning alternate with spontaneous creation. And all of this within the short span of three years! Compare what we think of as typical speech behavior of the 2-year-old and of the 4-year-old—"Mommy go" and "big dog" on the one hand, and, on the other, such productions as that which my youngest managed last week, "I would have did it but Rusty was in the way"—and we can only be awed by the speed with which this complex skill is acquired.

## Errors in Speech

You will have noticed, of course, the grammatical error in my 4-year-old's comment: "I would have *did* it." According to Cazden, this sort of error is often an indication of linguistic progress. The child who says "foots" for "feet" or "goed" for "went" is applying a rule that is appropriate for most of his speech behavior; we tend to notice the mistake rather than the correct application. The fact that he makes the mistake, though, tells us that he has acquired the underlying rule; he is not merely parroting a phrase spoken by someone else. Moreover, such rule-governed errors tend to drop out of the child's speech quite naturally as he develops further linguistic competence. They are, says Cazden, "open to shedding when the child is in some sense 'ready' to move on, no matter how well practiced they may be" (1972, p. 111).

There is some disagreement among linguists as to just how well the 4- or 5-year-old child knows his language. Superficially, it would seem that most children by this age have all but completely mastered basic grammar. One study (Gardner, 1974) indicates that even preschoolers can understand metaphoric speech ("Her voice was as cold as ice." "My love is like a red, red rose."), though they cannot usually explain why a particular metaphoric choice is correct. Other studies, however, suggest that mastery of complex linguistic forms at this early age may be more apparent than real. Three- to 5-year-old children have been shown to have trouble understanding negative instances of concepts (Miller, 1966), negative comparison words such as "less than" and "shorter than" (Baron, 1973), and common function words like "rather," "unless," and "while" (Rystrom, 1972); and they have trouble detecting ambiguity in various kinds of sentences (Shultz & Pilon, 1973). In summary, as Dittman (1972) says, current research is showing that language structure takes much more time to learn, that the small child's grasp of language is far less complete than we had supposed. By the time he is ready for school, the child has usually mastered the basics of simple, everyday speech; but he may very well misunderstand or misuse more complex or unusual forms and may also have unexpected and unpredictable gaps in his understanding of even simple structures.

## Egocentric and Interactive Speech

The kindergartener or first grader is still very much involved in egocentric speech: he talks to himself at least as much as to anyone else. Piaget and his co-workers took detailed records of the speech behavior of two 6½-year-olds and found that nearly half their total spontaneous speech was egocentric (1926, p. 37). "True," says Piaget, "when they are together they seem to talk to each other a great deal more than we do about what they are doing, but for the most part they are only talking to themselves. We, on the contrary, keep silent far longer about our action, but our talk is almost always socialized" (p. 38). At this age, Piaget maintains, virtually all thought is carried on out loud. The child says whatever comes into his mind, whether anyone is listening—or is there to listen—or not. Moreover, the question of whether the listener can understand what the child is saying does not arise because the child does not yet realize that other people may perceive (or understand) differently than he does. What the 5-year-old understands is, by definition, understandable; he understands it, and there simply is no other point of view. It follows, then, as Piaget points out, that "if children fail to understand one another, it is because they think that they *do* understand one another" (p. 101). The perception checks, the "let me see if I get your meaning" comments so common in adult speech, are absent in childhood speech. Children probably misunderstand each other as often as they understand each other; but things tend to balance out in that each is much more interested in his own speech than in that of his friend, so misunderstandings don't often matter very much.

By about age 7, egocentric speech begins to taper off and be replaced by attempts at true communication. Piaget notes that at this age children begin to be concerned with getting things in the right order. Until this point, stories are related in whatever order the bits happen to come to mind; after all, order doesn't matter when you're sure the other fellow will understand anyhow. But as the egocentric stance is abandoned, the child begins to realize that some sort of ordering is necessary if his idea is to be communicated accurately. Houston (1973), who studied children's story telling in some detail, lists the characteristics of the child's communication at this age: the child reproduces the content most important to the story, omitting many details; he preserves the order of the story in its original version; and he tends to leave out whatever he didn't understand rather than make an overt error (p. 111).

We can see here the beginning of that most important aspect of adult language behavior, the ability to role play the listener even as one is speaking. As the child loses his egocentric orientation, he begins to be able to think about what the listener needs in order to understand a message and to alter the message accordingly. Until this role playing begins, children simply do not communicate verbally—not as adults do, at any rate. "It is only from the age of 7 or 8 that there can be any talk of genuine understanding between children. Till then, the ego-centric factors of verbal expression (elliptical style, indeterminate pronouns, etc.) and of understanding itself, as well as the derivative factors (such as lack of order in the accounts given, juxtaposition, etc.), are all too important to allow of any genuine understanding between children" (Piaget, 1926, p. 125).

During the early school years, then, children are making the transition to true communication and mutual understanding. One means of accomplishing this transition is through interactive speech about easily checkable, presently occurring activity. Before adolescence, children are likely to engage in activities, not conversation. They do talk a great deal, but usually by way of commenting about the activity at hand (Dittman, 1972). This orientation is hardly surprising; until good communication skills have been acquired—including sensitivity to feedback and its listener complement, appropriate listening-response emission—there is little use in trying to talk about anything more abstract or remote than "what we are doing right now." The activity talk of the 7- to 10-year-old, with its built-in checks on accuracy of both sending and receiving, is a natural training arena for later, more abstract interactions.

## Parent Influence

What are the factors that most strongly influence the development of language skills, as we have described them in these pages? We shall discuss the teacher's role more specifically in the next section; for now, let us focus on the influence of the adults with whom the child associates most frequently during the early, preschool years: the parents.

"All the available evidence," says Carroll, "supports the general prediction that the quality of a child's early linguistic environment is the most important external factor affecting the rate of language development" (1971, p. 208). The parents and other adults in the home are the primary providers of that linguistic environment. The child tends to speak as do his parents (and other significant adults). But how does this parental influence make itself felt?

One thing seems clear: parental influence does not come from the overt, deliberate teaching of language and language structure. No evidence suggests that parents either correct improper language usage or reward proper language usage often enough to have any significant effect (Cazden, 1972). This is not to say that such corrections and rewards are ineffective; rather, they just don't happen often enough or with enough regularity in most families to make much difference. What we are left with, then, must be imitation: the child follows a natural imitative process in picking up the speech forms of his parents. But even here there are problems. First, there is no marked relationship between the frequency of a form in parental speech and its time of acquisition in the child (Slobin, 1972). Apparently, whatever imitation the child may do, he does on his own terms and in his own good time. Parents cannot increase the speech complexity of their child appreciably by using more complex speech themselves. (By using a lot of speech, however, and taking care that it is "good" speech, they can both encourage the child's quantity of speech production and broaden the pool of examples from which he can draw when he is ready to acquire a new form.)

Second, and more puzzling, imitation alone simply cannot explain how the child learns grammatical structure. Not only do adults use a large proportion of incorrect or fragmented forms in the presence of the child, but even their correct usages are not presented in any systematic manner. In the case of "a" and "the," for example, the child can learn the words themselves by imitation, but he must learn what they mean and how they differ and when to use each one by other means. It is simply not reasonable that a child should be able to sort out, from the welter of words that surround him from hour to hour and day to day, a rule that tells him when to say "the cat" and when to say "a cat." But, beyond all reason or logic, most English-speaking children do exactly that.

Our best guess about how children learn speech from their parents is that it is a two-part process. The parent's speech behavior shapes and directs the development of the child's cognitive processes, and the cognition is expressed in speech. Once speech begins to be produced, there is a back-and-forth effect, as we have seen: thought does affect language, but language has a reciprocal effect on thought. Through it all, however, most parents focus much more strongly on what the child is trying to say—what he means—than on how he is trying to say it. They "concentrate on the inner meaning of their child's speech, sure in the conviction that as the child's capacity and need to express more complex ideas grows, so the forms in his language will change accordingly" (Cazden, 1972, p. 137). And that conviction is usually borne out. The child is encouraged to think and to communicate his thoughts. Adults provide many of the verbal building blocks of thought; they demonstrate by example the relationships between words and ideas. "By naming objects and so defining their connections and relations, the adult creates new forms of reflection of reality in the child, incomparably deeper and more complex than those which he could have formed through individual experience. This whole process of the transmission of knowledge and the formation of concepts, which is the basic way the adult influences the child, constitutes the central process of the child's intellectual development" (Luria & Yudovich, 1959, p. 11).

To be sure, adults do modify their speech habits to accommodate to the language level of children. Houston (1973) describes adult-to-child speech as characterized by shortened sentences, slower rate, more intonation and stress peaks, and simplified content. In other words, adults, when speaking to children, often talk more like children themselves (or, more accurately, like they think children talk). This adaptation is seen in exaggerated form in the affected "baby talk" of some adults when addressing small children: "Couldn't him get him's sockkies on? Poor widdle boysie!" Mercifully, such atrocities seem to be becoming rarer as more and more adults come to appreciate the value of early and consistent exposure to correct speech. A more reasonable approach is that the adult try to use forms that are marginally more complex than those used by the child, speaking slowly and clearly enough so that the child can hear the words easily. This approach allows the child to gain understanding of the meaning of the new

form from its context, and he is gradually encouraged to broaden his own grammatical usage. Again, we must remember that children tend to pick up more complex structures at their own rate, regardless of how hard they may be pushed; nevertheless, marginal leading ensures that the forms are there for imitation when he is ready for them and at the same time ensures that the adult's messages are not too complicated for him to understand.

## SPECIFICALLY FOR TEACHERS

"Language poses multiple problems for education because it is both curriculum content and learning environment, both the object of knowledge and a medium through which other knowledge is acquired" (Cazden, 1973, p. 135). All too often, the teacher feels himself to be between a rock and a hard place: if he pushes for high standards in language usage, he may stifle creative expression; but if he focuses on creativity at the expense of grammar, punctuation, and the like, he may give tacit approval to potentially harmful language behavior. He cannot turn his back on the problem, for it is an important one. Indeed, many educators believe that learning how to use language constructively may be the single most important goal for students. According to Pribram, learning *is* language: when we learn something, we are setting it into coded form and storing it in memory. Language is the code that most of us use for such storage, and so all learning hinges on how adequate our language—our coding system—is.

"Proper coding is what education is all about, or ought to be" (Pribram, 1973a, p. 141). What can we, as psychologists, say about language that will help the teacher to do his job better? How can students be helped to develop language skills? What language habits are important, and which can be ignored? In this section, we shall try to find some answers to questions like these.

### Talking versus Silence

Language skills are developed through practice. Children learn to think in words by thinking out loud; silent thought follows oral thought. Few things can be worse for language development—especially in the younger child—than preventing him from talking. Yet not to talk is often the first lesson a child learns in school. "Sit quietly in your seats." "Don't whisper, Tommy, you're supposed to be working." "I won't start to read the story until everyone is quiet." A certain amount of structure, including restrictions on verbal behavior, is necessary in the classroom—necessary for optimal learning on the part of the students and also for the teacher's sanity! It is sometimes easy, however, to overestimate the need for quiet and discipline. When such rules are overstressed, children soon learn that the kinds of talking they are used to outside school are inappropriate in school, and they are likely to turn off their interest, their excitement, and their joy along with their noise. The important concept here is balance: between quiet and noisy time, between individual work and interaction with others. The child must learn that it is good to talk some of the time, good to listen some of the time, and good to work quietly some of the time.

It is important, I think, that teachers begin to ask themselves "Am I enforcing silence now because of the students' needs or because of my own?" If the answer is "my own" too often, then the students' language development may be getting shortchanged. Creber (1972, p. 97) gives us an extreme (I hope) example, taken from an elementary school he visited in England. The teacher gave the students a short lecture on the geography of a particular area and then set them to drawing and labeling maps. As he watched, Creber says, "the conviction grew that this was an exercise whose sole value—like the teacher's talk—was as part of a conditioning process designed to render pupils quiescent." Now, I don't believe that many teachers start out with the conscious goal of teaching children not to talk, but how many of our actions in the classroom have that effect? The first step toward improving language teaching is to examine what one is already doing, to dig out of the camouflage of "routine" those unnecessary habits and rules and customs that are costing more than they are worth.

We must remember, too, that different children are likely to respond to a language environment in different ways. Depending on the language habits the child brings with him to the classroom—the styles used at home or among his peer group—he may or may not find it easy to adapt to the demands of school. All too often, a teacher creates rules for language behavior that are compatible to himself and (more or less) to most of the students; those who "don't fit," being a minority, are expected to adjust to those rules. While a certain amount of such adjustment is probably necessary in any classroom (and, in fact, being able to make adjustments to one's social environment is a useful skill and should perhaps be taught as such), it should neither be taken for granted nor be laid exclusively on a minority of the students. Addressed explicitly as a skill to learn and set as a goal for all students, the ability to work within an unfamiliar behavior framework can become a task like any other task. The middle-class majority (including the teacher) can try working in a language-rule setting more comfortable to some of the other children in the room; both groups can benefit from this kind of role switching. More importantly, every child can have some chance to participate on his own linguistic home ground.

Throughout all this, it is the teacher's job to continue to engage each child in verbal communication and to do so in ways that stretch the child's imagination, that introduce him to the excitement of words as tools. Carroll (1971) points out that, at least in the primary grades, new or unfamiliar language patterns should always be introduced in spoken language before they are introduced in reading. The teacher who enjoys words himself and feels comfortable about using complex grammatical structures can do a great deal of this introducing of new patterns in everyday interactions with students. Reading aloud, followed by group discussion of the material, is another way to introduce more complex patterns verbally. Cazden (1972, p. 139) sums it up well:

> First, teachers must provide a school environment rich in both language the child hears (from people and from books) and in provocations to self-expression and communication. Such an environment seems to happen very naturally in many homes. But in schools—preschool and beyond— the language environment can be woefully meager without the teacher's deliberate attention. She needs to be self-conscious about her own language—both what she says and how she distributes her talking attention during the day. Second, teachers need to be able to listen diagnostically to the children's language and track their progress toward increasingly adequate oral and written forms, giving help as needed without imposing an arbitrary instructional sequence on a learning process we don't fully understand. Paradoxically, such diagnostic listening must not interfere with responding at the moment, fully and intently, to the ideas the child is trying to express.

## Teacher-Student Interactions

Cazden's comments underline the necessity that the teacher be aware of where the student is and what he is trying to say or do; the teacher must listen. The most accurate criticism, the most creative example, is not likely to be effective if it interferes with the child's own train of thought. It is an often-ignored truism that a child (or an adult, for that matter) who is not paying attention to you does not understand what you are saying to him. Rule One for teacher speech, then, is to make sure that someone will listen when you intend to say something. And a corollary of this rule is to make equally sure that what you have to say is more important than what the child would have been doing if you had kept still. "How often, when we seek a child's attention, are we responding to him, and how often are we intruding on his mental life with some interest of our own?" (Cazden, 1972, p. 207). It may be that this question is seldom considered by educators simply because the answer is too uncomfortable.

Of course, interruption—or at least redirection—of a student's mental life is often appropriate teacher behavior. After all, we are paid to participate in the child's learning process, not just to observe from the sidelines. Cazden goes on to point out that the best way to command attention is by the introduction of novel stimuli. A stimulus, either verbal or nonverbal, that has just the right amount of novelty captures and engages the child's attention naturally, with no need of threats or rewards from the teacher. Too-familiar stimuli tend to be boring, and too-strange ones threatening; by finding a happy in-between, the teacher can enhance the amount of attention that children pay both to what he is saying and to the way in which he is saying it.

Just listening is not enough. To make a skill one's own, one must practice it. To use Pribram's term, new knowledge must be "enacted." Students at all levels must be given the opportunity to talk, with adults and with one another—to try out new verbal forms, to experience the exhilaration of good communication. "The child's prime need," says Creber, "is for 'compensation' which provides not merely experiences, but situations in which he is led to use language to make experience meaningful, experience expressed being experience possessed. Only by articulating can he improve his articulation and, as he does so, gain the insight and the motivation that make further learning increasingly possible. Through language he makes the present comprehensible, the past available, the future conceivable" (1972, p. 31). Encouraged to discuss ideas or projects in small groups—or to think about them out loud—the child puts language learning into practice. He begins, in Creber's words, to "grope his way towards thought." Provision of a nonthreatening, actively encouraging environment for this sort of activity is essential.

## Teaching Language Skills

At this point, I am sure that many of you are beginning to wonder where the active teaching of language skills comes in. What happens to English grammar, to the parts of speech, to spelling and punctuation, and to all those things that we had to learn in school? Cazden (1973) answers that question with painful bluntness: all the available evidence shows that teaching grammatical rules in school has *no* effect on students' performance in speech or writing. In other words, grammatical performance seems to be based on implicit grammatical knowledge, which is not touched by explicit teaching. This does not mean that we should give up trying to teach grammar—on the contrary! But we should move to teaching by example, by using words and phrases correctly ourselves, and by expanding rather than correcting student mistakes. Consider the primary child who, asked to describe a picture, replies "The boy gots a glass of milk." If the teacher says "No, Terry, the boy *has* a glass of milk," the child is negatively reinforced. He is less likely to respond at all the next time he is called on. But if the teacher says "Yes, Terry, the boy has a *glass* of *milk,*" he rewards the correct parts of the sentence, corrects the error, and makes the child feel good about his participation.

In the upper grades, demands can be more specific and more rigorous. Students can be expected to rewrite and polish written work; they can be given group exercises to improve the fluency of oral speech. Sensitivity to what sounds right can be encouraged without resort to learning rules about why this form and not that one is used; rules can then be given when requested. In this way, the rules can facilitate rather than interfere with the whole thought-to-speech process; they can provide an "aha!" that ties together what the child already knows, rather than an irritating restriction on how he is allowed to talk.

That children learn naturally to follow a set of grammatical rules is evident: all children do it. Many children, however, learn to conform to rules not consistent with standard English. Our task is not to teach children to follow *a* set of grammatical rules in their speech, but rather to teach them to follow a *certain* set of rules—and to do so comfortably, naturally, in a way that does not interfere with their freedom and creativity.

## Verbal-Deprivation Theory

Among linguists and language teachers, one group may disagree rather vigorously with these last few paragraphs. A number of educators have become interested in the effects of black speech, or Negro Nonstandard English, on those who speak it, as well as in the effects of trying to teach the black child to speak standard English. The controversy began with the statement of the *verbal-deprivation theory* by such students as Bernstein (1971) and Bereiter and Engleman (1966). This theory posits that ghetto children's poor school performance is caused by their inability to think abstractly (or to do so as well as nonghetto children), and that this inability results, in turn, from the language that they use. Negro Nonstandard English, it is hypothesized, simply does not have a conceptual structure that facilitates the kind of thought needed to do well in school—and, by extension, in the mainstream culture of the United States.

Predictably, the statement of the verbal-deprivation theory created a flurry of argument among theorists and practitioners in education. Researchers tested various aspects of the theory, while philosophers eagerly took sides and raged at each other from their armchairs. Now, after several years of furious activity, the air seems to have cleared a bit, and two facts have emerged:

First, speakers of Negro Nonstandard English are not handicapped in their abstract conceptual ability. Black English, as a tool, can handle ideas as well as standard English. It is not a more primitive language, though it is structurally different from standard English. Moreover, black children are not, as a group, linguistically inferior to white children. "When valid reconstructions from standard English to Negro Nonstandard English are considered correct, black inner-city children's language performance is nonsignificantly different from [that of] their white middle-class counterparts" (Anastasiow & Hanes, 1974, p. 708).

Second, speakers of Negro Nonstandard English are not handicapped in their understanding of standard English. Black children seem to understand English as well as Negro Nonstandard English, but they may be unable (or unwilling) to speak it. In one typical study (Hall & Turner, 1974), the Stanford-Binet intelligence test was translated into Negro Nonstandard English and administered to a group of lower-class black children; a matched group took the standard English version of the test. There were no significant score differences between the two groups.

In summary, then, the verbal-deprivation theory appears to be misleading at best. The black child's language habits are a handicap only insofar as he is less able to produce written or oral speech that conforms with the middle-class teacher's expectations; his language is quite adequate for handling conceptual thought. "Given its totally fraudulent basis," writes Newmayer, "it is indefensible that anybody who is in the business of teaching the English language (or any other language, for that matter) should be gullible enough to accept the verbal-deprivation theory at face value" (1973, p. 407).

Why, if the verbal-deprivation theory has been so thoroughly discredited, do we bother to mention it at all? There are two reasons for doing so. First, as a teacher you may encounter references to it in your professional reading or among your colleagues; you should know enough to avoid being unduly influenced by it. Second, even though the basic claim of the theory has been discredited, some spin-offs from this line of reasoning cannot be ignored. We shall look at a few of these.

Because the lower-class black child speaks a dialect different from that of his white counterpart, he is likely to be misunderstood, even though he may understand standard English perfectly. It is important that the white teacher, in his desire to be fair or unprejudiced, not try to deny that differences do exist between standard English and Negro Nonstandard English;

in communicating with the black child, the white teacher may have to take special pains to be sure that he understands what the child is saying.

In addition to whatever specific grammatical differences may exist between black speech and standard English, there may be more far-reaching differences in communication style. Houston (1973), studying story-telling patterns among black and white children, noted that the black children prompted each other much more often than did the whites and in general operated in a cooperative mode more than in a competitive mode throughout the experiment. Also, the black children tended to embellish their stories creatively, while the white children were more interested in giving a precise and accurate copy of the original narrative. In other words, an excellent performance by a white child's standards was poor by black standards, and vice versa. The black child's language does not force him to think in a manner inferior to the white child; but black speech may signal the existence of cultural norms quite different from those of the white teacher. The good teacher will take pains to sensitize himself to these norms —not, by the way, in order to socialize the black child to white standards, but rather to enrich the creative and evaluative framework of both white and black participants in the classroom interaction.

Even though the black child is not conceptually handicapped by Negro Nonstandard English, it would be naïve to deny that he is often socially handicapped if he does not speak standard English. The social handicap may well begin to show up in the classroom; it is sad but true that white teachers make evaluations of a child's academic competence and potential according to the dialect that the child speaks. When a child speaks Negro Nonstandard English, "there is empirical evidence of an indirect adverse effect—the effect of a child's speech on his teacher's attitudes toward him, and thereby on the learning environment that she creates" (Cazden, 1973, p. 140).

The social effects of speaking Negro Nonstandard English do not, of course, stop at the classroom door. Rather, they tend to intensify in the competitive, commercial mainstream of our culture. Just because we can pooh-pooh the suggestion that black speech is primitive does not allow us to ignore the negative social consequences of speaking it. Whether we like it or not, the person who does not speak "good" English is at a disadvantage in getting a job, in succeeding in higher education, in the great majority of arenas where he may want to compete. These negative consequences may reflect both intellectual laziness and cultural snobbery on the part of most Americans; but they still occur. We do the black student no favor if, in respecting and valuing his linguistic heritage, we fail to teach him the language skills that will be most useful to him. And, at this juncture of history, useful language skills are standard English skills.

This does not mean that we must force feed black students white grammar. Any child, of any cultural background, will learn to use standard

English easily and naturally if two conditions are present: the language environment is stimulating and nonthreatening, and the child wants to speak standard English. The problem is not how to teach good language usage but how to motivate students to learn it.

Children are busy, almost from birth, learning how to communicate. There seems to be, among humans at least, a strong pull to share ideas, to compare notes, to talk about. Similarly, children seem intuitively to be bent on understanding. They want to hear what others are saying, to make sense out of other people's messages (unless the message is asking them to dry the dishes or do their math). I believe the teacher's first responsibility is to maintain and enhance this natural inclination toward language use. Whatever else we do or don't do, we must at all costs keep the stream of communication flowing and growing. Creber describes a child who feels completely stifled by the rigid communication rules of his classroom and who says that the teacher might as well be talking in Spanish for all he is able or inclined to understand. "Every experience which leads the child to conclude that the teacher is 'talking in Spanish' is in effect teaching him when listening is unnecessary and is imposing a restriction upon the range of situations in which he will be willing to *trust words*. Such a trust is a prerequisite of effective learning in school; the damage caused by a teacher's incomprehensibility is to be measured not in terms of particular meaning lost, but of the cumulative effect of such experiences on the child's attitude to learning. The real danger is that we may so condition him that he learns to *accept his incomprehension*" (Creber, 1972, p. 30). Teachers must understand and be understood. If we strive toward those goals, reaching always a little higher toward linguistic clarity, everything else will fall into place.

## QUESTIONS FOR UNDERSTANDING

1. Most college students have studied or will study a foreign language. What are the main differences between the way you learn a foreign language as an adult and the way you learned to speak English? Are there any conditions under which an adult might learn a new language just as he learned his native language?
2. Larry is a voluble, active fourth grader who seldom stops talking. Les is shy and withdrawn; he speaks only when directly urged to and then in short, terse sentences. What classroom activities could be planned to help each of these children develop better communication habits?
3. It was suggested that students (and teachers) be given the opportunity to interact occasionally in the linguistic environment more familiar to some of the other (minority) class members. How might such an opportunity be provided, and what might be the result?

4.  Try to examine and analyze your own thought patterns. Do you ever think without words? Can you block all words out of your mind by making a conscious effort to do so? How much do you think your verbal habits affect the way you see and interact with the world?

5.  What effects do you think television has had on the language patterns of high school students in North America today?

# Chapter 4

# *Thinking*

In all of education, there is perhaps no stranger fact than this: the thing we most want to teach our students to do is the thing we are least able to define for ourselves. We are interested, to be sure, in the storage and retrieval of facts; we want to help students to form appropriate stimulus-response bonds and to learn from observing the behavior of others; we recognize the importance of that marvelous tool called language. But we want to go beyond; we want students to solve problems, to formulate and test theories, to understand what it is they are learning.

Education has as its highest target a number of related activities: concept formation, problem solving, rule generalization, learning to learn. These are not different words for the same thing; there are important differences among them. But there is also a great deal of overlap. For our purposes, the overlap is more important than the differences; the similarities and relationships among all the higher cognitive processes make it possible for us to look at those processes as a general pool of mental activity that we refer to loosely as thinking.

But thinking is an extremely hard notion to nail down, to get a handle on. We can't see a thought or measure it directly. We can't (usually) trace the steps a student goes through on the way to a constructive problem solution. Cognitive activity is, by its nature, hidden; we can only infer it from other behaviors. Thinking is, nevertheless, a kind of behavior. "Cognitive events arise as responses to other cognitive events or to frankly motoric responses" (K. Smith, 1974). Our task in this chapter is to try to understand what happens as a child learns to think and to identify some of the ways in which we can facilitate that process.

One of the reasons cognition or thinking or problem solving or concept formation is so hard to understand is that each of these notions does overlap the others. And each builds upon other, simpler kinds of learnings.

Problems are solved and concepts are formed on the basis of stored information. Some of that information has been learned by rote or acquired through imitation or has resulted from previous cognitive activity; much is coded in a language structure that also influences the cognitive process. These various activities not only borrow from each other but blend together in ways that make it hard to say where one leaves off and another begins. What, for instance, is the major difference between conceptual learning and rote learning? Nolan (1973) suggests that the difference is primarily one of organization: in rote learning, we chunk things together because we have experienced them at the same time or in the same place (three of the principal industries of Oregon are timber, grass seed, and tourism); while in conceptual learning we group things on the basis of shared attributes or logical relationships (Oregon is on the northern Pacific coast of the United States, and this location implies scenic and climate features that draw tourists and that provide good growing conditions for trees and grass). But one cannot choose the relevant attributes or understand the logic without drawing upon stored information, which, in turn, may have been categorized or chunked. Moreover, in order to use that stored information, one must have acquired guidelines for forming categories or for making inferences: one must have stored rules, and rules about rules.

Where do such rules come from? Does what we call logic arise naturally from our interactions with the world, from repeated exposure to the kinds of deductions and inferences made by others? Is it—in part, at least—

built in as part of our biological heritage? And, even if it is, what determines when it is called into play? When do we accept a fact, a situation, a relationship, and simply store it away, and when do we begin to process it, to try to fit it into a whole cognitive structure? Some theorists believe that cognition, as an active process, is triggered by apparent inconsistencies; when something doesn't seem to fit, we begin to think about it. "An act of concept learning may be seen as being triggered by the confrontation and delineation of puzzling, disturbing, curious, or problematical situations. Similarly, conceptualizing may be viewed as the conferring of significant meaning upon previously meaningless stimuli" (Martorella, 1972, p. 12). But if all our experience consisted of "previously meaningless stimuli," we would never be able to confirm any of our understandings or hypotheses. Surely another important part of cognition must be repetition: meeting new things along with familiar ones and discovering that they can be fitted into our overall world view. A giraffe is indeed an impossible creature, until I see it in the context of what I already know about animals and their environment. The new affects the old as it becomes a part of that structure; the old affects the new since we experience all new stimuli through the screen of what we knew before. Both are needed if we are to grow and learn.

If, having acquired a new concept, we could only cast ourselves back into the state of not knowing and then follow our own thinking as we moved toward knowing, we would surely gain valuable insights into what happens in conceptual thought. Unfortunately, it is virtually impossible to do that. Bruner, Goodnow, and Austin, in their classic book, *A Study of Thinking* (1956), comment on the curious "quantal nature" of concepts. Once we have learned to notice a certain characteristic, to categorize on the basis of an aspect of the thing we are dealing with, we can't will ourselves to be unaware of that characteristic. The categorization, or conceptualization, becomes an integral part of the perceptual process. "Having learned a new language, it is almost impossible to recapture the undifferentiated flow of voiced sounds that one heard before one learned to sort the flow into words and phrases. Having mastered the distinction between odd and even numbers, it is a feat to remember what it was like in a mental world where there was no such distinction" (p. 50). In order to keep track of what I do to reach a certain conceptual goal, I have to know the end point; but once I know the end point, I can no longer remember how I got there.

Fortunately, the situation is not nearly as hopeless as these comments might lead us to believe. While I cannot recapture my own conceptual innocence, I can still observe other problem solvers on their way to solutions. Most of the experimental and theoretical work on cognition has been based on such observation, frequently bolstered by whatever introspective checks are possible. One of the most insightful—and prolific—students in this area is Jean Piaget; his detailed observation of thousands of hours of problem-solving activity among children led him to formulate the best-known modern theory of cognitive development. Piaget's ideas form a foundation on which each of us can build our own notions of how to facilitate constructive thinking among our students. For this reason, I devote the next few pages to an overview of Piagetian theory. Later, we shall look at other approaches to the overall study of higher thought processes; I believe we will find that most of these are quite compatible with Piaget's theory of how thought develops as the child matures. Finally, I shall end the chapter with some rather specific suggestions for the teacher who wants to help his students to "learn to think."

## PIAGET AND THE DEVELOPMENT OF THOUGHT

Piaget was born in 1896 in Switzerland. Throughout his academic years he was interested in the relationships between psychology, philosophy, biology, and religion. After receiving his Ph.D. in 1918 (Switzerland, you will recall, maintained neutrality during both World Wars, so army service did not interrupt his academic career), he began to search for opportunities to use and to test in practice some of the psychological theory he had acquired in school. He worked in an experimental psychology laboratory, in a psychiatric clinic, and, finally, with Alfred Binet in developing a method for testing children's intellectual ability (see Chapter 6). The work with Binet was a kind of turning point for Piaget; he became fascinated with the wrong answers that children gave to Binet's questions and began to believe that by studying the kinds of mistakes children make in thinking, he could begin to understand the way in which logical thought develops. From then on, there was no turning back. On the strength of a paper written about these early observations, he was offered a job at the Institut J.-J. Rousseau in Geneva. He took the position and began a series of studies of children's language and thought that made him world famous before he was 30 years old.

Better known in Europe than in North America, Piaget, because of his naturalistic observation (as opposed to carefully controlled experiments) and his armchair philosophizing, made many psychologists in the United States uncomfortable. Only since the mid-1960s have psychologists come to appreciate the importance of the Piagetian model, and even now most students in the United States find Piaget's work difficult to understand and to relate to the contributions of others in the field. One reason for this difficulty is Piaget's writing style: he is at once chatty and technical. He rambles on, describing an interaction in loving (and seemingly endless) detail; but on the next page he uses jaw-breaking words and phrases to explain the significance of the previous description. In short, to understand Piaget we must first understand his terminology, which, in itself, accounts for no small part of the theory! We shall turn now, therefore, to a few terms that are crucially important in Piaget's view of the development of thought; later we shall look at the major stages through which he believes children move as they approach adult modes of thinking.

## Major Concepts

*Accommodation and Assimilation.* Piaget is convinced of the essential unity of all aspects of human functioning; he maintains that each of the various systems and subsystems in an individual operate according to one underlying set of rules. That Piaget frequently uses biological analogies to describe and elaborate on psychological processes is, given this philosophy, perfectly consistent. One of the best examples is his description of the way the individual adapts to his ongoing internal and external environment. Adaptation, says Piaget, involves two complementary processes: accommodation and assimilation. This is as true for the individual's biological adaptation as for his psychological adaptation. The organism assimilates new material, changing it so as to make it more usable or manageable for itself. And it accommodates itself to the new material, changing itself so as to use and integrate the new. For example, consider the way we interact with food: we accommodate our bodies to food by opening our mouths and chewing and secreting digestive enzymes and so forth; we also change (assimilate) the food so that our bodies can utilize it. Just so with information, says Piaget. We modify information in perceiving it and processing it in order to make it usable (understandable, acceptable). At the same time, new information affects our cognitive structure; old ideas must shift and adjust themselves and make room for the new. Flavell (1963, p. 17), describing the accommodation-assimilation relationship, says "Intelligent activity is always an active, organized process of assimilating the new ideas to the old and of accommodating the old to the new. Intellectual content will vary enormously from age to age in ontogenetic development, yet the general functional properties of the adaptational process remain the same."*

There are two major implications here. One is the obvious: every encounter with the environment involves (from the point of view of the person doing the encountering) a change in the environment so that the person can take it in (assimilation), and it involves a change in himself as a result of taking it in (accommodation). And yet even that statement implies a sequential relationship, which is misleading; assimilation does not precede accommodation any more than accommodation precedes assimilation. They are simultaneous processes, both necessary aspects of the interaction between intelligence and experiencing.

The second implication of Piaget's notion of assimilation and accommodation is that these two aspects of the adaptive process occur throughout life. They are not a unique characteristic of one or another developmental stage; rather, they are characteristic of all mental life. A strange

*From *The Development Psychology of Jean Piaget,* by J. H. Flavell. Copyright © 1963 by Litton Educational Publishing, Inc. This and all other quotations from this source are reprinted by permission of D. Van Nostrand Company.

kind of tension or polarity seems to be implied in this view of cognitive functioning. As we accommodate to the world, we move out into it—we experience more and more of external reality. Simultaneously, assimilation involves bringing the world inside, representing it intellectually and gaining skill at this kind of symbolic manipulation. Piaget says "By virtue of the very fact that all knowledge is simultaneously accommodation to the object and assimilation to the subject, the progress of intelligence works in the dual direction of externalization and internalization, and its two poles will be the acquisition of physical experience and the acquisition of consciousness of the intellectual operation itself" (1954, p. 356).

Notice, too, that the assimilation-accommodation process provides a constant bridge over which the individual moves from past to future. Old concepts, organizational structures, habit patterns *(schemas,* Piaget would call them) are not simply replaced by newer ones; they are modified by gradual degrees, just as they themselves exert a modifying influence on the new ideas coming in. Flavell (1963, p. 50) describes this process well: "There can never be a radical rupture between the new and the old; events whose interpretation requires a complete extension or reorganization of the existing structure simply cannot be accommodated to and thence assimilated. . . . Assimilation is by its very nature conservative, in the sense that its primary function is to make the unfamiliar familiar, to reduce the new to the old. A new assimilatory structure must always be some variate of the last one acquired, and it is this which insures both the gradualness and continuity of intellectual development." Thus each individual is in a constant process of reinterpreting the world and of revising his old interpretations; yet the changes are gradual, ensuring that when I talk with John Doe today, he is essentially the same as when I talked with him yesterday and (almost) the same as when I talked with him last week or last month.

*Egocentrism.* One of the major changes that come about through the assimilation-accommodation process is a broadening of perspective—a realization that there are other people in the world, that they are, like me, unique. The infant knows only what his sense receptors tell him about his immediate surroundings. He does not discriminate between "me" and "not me"; all he knows is "is." Gradually, as his cognitive structure adapts, he learns to categorize some perceptions as belonging to himself and others as belonging to an out-there. The out-there becomes further differentiated into alive and not alive, and the alive into people and not people. But even here there is no awareness that the other people in the world live inside their own skins, just as he lives inside his own. He assumes that everyone else sees the world just as he sees it, thinks in the same way he thinks, feels just as he does. He is the center of his universe—he is, in Piaget's term, *egocentric.* We met egocentrism in Chapter 3 when we looked at the language world of the small child, But, for Piaget, egocentrism goes beyond language. The egocentric individual not only sees the world from one point of view (his own) and expects everyone else to see it the same way but is quite unaware that there is any other way to see it. His viewpoint is the only one there is, so of course it must be the viewpoint of everyone.

Egocentrism can manifest itself in various ways. It is most frequently tested for in the form of perceptual egocentrism. A child is shown a three-dimensional model of a town or a countryside and is asked to describe it. "Is the tree in front of the house or behind it?" "Is the car to the left or to the right of the gas pump?" Then the experimenter, who is seated on the opposite side of the model, asks the child what it looks like from *his* point of view: "From where I'm sitting, is the car to the left or to the right of the gas pump?" "Does the tree look like it is behind the house or in front of the house to me?" The egocentric child indicates that the model looks the same to the experimenter as it does to him, for he is incapable of imagining that someone else could look at what he is looking at and (correctly) see something different.

As we have seen, linguistic egocentrism is common among preschool children. Sentence fragments are tossed out with perfect confidence that they will be understood. Four-year-old Jimmy runs into the house and demands of his mother "Why won't she do it?" It just doesn't occur to him that his mother might not share his knowledge of who "she" is or what it is she "won't do." Conceptual and attitudinal egocentrism is also common at this age, and patches of such egocentrism tend to linger late into development. Most of us have had the experience of being surprised that someone we know could believe something that is "obviously" untrue (that is, we are surprised that there is another belief than our own) or could feel so differently from the way we do about something. Like every other aspect of cognitive functioning, egocentrism does not simply disappear; as a result of accommodation and assimilation, our egocentric perceptions and beliefs are gradually modified. The world of people and things who are "just like me" gradually constricts until it includes only myself—leaving occasional small islands of unaccommodated egocentrism where we least expect to find them.

*Conservation.* Another Piagetian concept that we met in Chapter 3 is conservation. Conservation—of mass, of volume, of energy—is a physical concept and refers to the fact that matter (and energy) have measurable, quantifiable attributes that remain stable. A given volume of water has the same weight and the same volume, no matter what shape container it is poured into. Ten beads are ten beads, whether they are pushed together or spread apart. A lump of clay does not change in quantity when it is mashed into a ball or rolled out into a long snake. Adults (in our culture, at least) tend to take these facts for granted and don't question how they came to believe or understand them. Piaget and his students have determined, however, that young children do not understand the principles of conservation and that the acquisition of these principles marks a turning point in the child's mental development. We shall discuss the way in which children come to acquire the principles of conservation at a later point in this chapter; for now, we can simply say that the young child seems to be greatly influenced by the more superficial characteristics of an object, such as shape or spread-out-ness, and allows his estimates of quantity to be overly determined by such characteristics. He has not yet developed a logical system with which he can relate seemingly contradictory information systematically.

Closely related to the notion of conservation is that of *reversibility* of operations. The 4-year-old, watching a pint of water poured from a short, fat container into a tall, thin one, is not bothered by the apparent inconsistency in his statement that "now there is more." One reason he senses no inconsistency is that he does not symbolize the operation in reverse; it does not occur to him to wonder what would happen if the water were poured back into the wider container. The older child knows (without consciously having to think it through) that operations are potentially reversible: the clay, stretched out, can be rolled back into a ball, and the heaped-up beads can be set far apart again. The adolescent carries reversibility still further, into a symbolic realm. He extends it to what-if situations—what if the egg shell could be glued back together?—and to even more abstract chains of logical reasoning. Reversibility implies a certain quickness of thought, a flexibility, a willingness to play with the symbols that we use in cognition. Nonreversible (and nonconserving) thought, in contrast, is slower, more bound to physical reality. And again, it should be emphasized that it is not the conservation or the reversibility, as such, that is important in Piagetian theory, but rather the fact that they are characteristic of certain periods of mental development. They are observable mileposts, signaling the child's arrival at a particular level of cognitive functioning.

### Stages of Development

Piaget is perhaps best known for his delineation of four major stages of cognitive development; they begin at birth and extend through adolescence. An understanding of developmental stages is useful to the teacher in at least two ways: It helps us to set our teaching behavior at the level best fitted to the student's capabilities. And it gives us guidelines for determining when a child is performing at a higher-than-age or lower-than-age level and may thus need special attention. We must be careful to remember, however, that the stages described by Piaget do not provide neat, global pigeonholes into which each child may be fitted. The boundaries between stages are often fuzzy and unclear, and a child may be operating at one stage in one activity and at a quite different stage in another activity. In other words, while progression from stage to stage is a general trend and average ages for the various stage behaviors are known, any individual child is bound to vary back and forth a great deal as he goes about his daily activities.

We must also remember that the behaviors and cognitions of each stage are not simply superseded by the behaviors and cognitions of the next. As our earlier discussion might lead us to expect, old behaviors and structures are modified by new learnings, so that the resulting patterns are an amalgam of the old and the new. Says Piaget, "The fact should be emphasized that the behavior patterns characteristic of the different stages do not succeed each other in a linear way (those of a given stage disappearing at the time when those of the following one take form) but in the manner of the layers of a pyramid (upright or upside down), the new behavior patterns simply being added to the old ones to complete, correct, or combine with them" (1952, p. 329).

With these cautions in mind, then, we are ready to take a look at the specific characteristics of Piaget's major stages. As I said, there are four. First is the relatively short stage of infancy and babyhood, extending roughly through the second year, which Piaget calls the *sensory-motor* stage. From ages 2 to 7 the child progresses through the *preoperational* period; this is the stage of development in which nonconservation is most typical. During the early school years, from 7 to 11, the child is at the stage of *concrete operations;* and in early adolescence he begins to move into the final, adult phase of *formal operations.*

*Sensory-Motor Stage.* The sensory-motor stage is a period of exploration and differentiation. The infant, a stranger in a strange land (and a stranger to himself), is involved in discovering who and what he and his environment may be. At first the two basic functions of assimilation and accommodation are not even differentiated from each other, since the me and the not me are not experienced as two different things. Sorting out these two functions is perhaps the greatest task of the sensory-motor stage. "With increasing differentiation and equilibration of the two functions," says Flavell (1963, p. 61), "comes a development of great significance for intelligence: there is simultaneously a centrifugal process of gradual objectification of external reality and a centripetal process of burgeoning self-awareness—the self comes to be seen as an object among objects." Having achieved a rudimentary understanding of the self-environment relationship, the child is ready to move into the next stage, that of preoperational thought.

*Preoperational Stage.* During the early part of the preoperational stage, the child first becomes truly testable. He can focus on a task and use his intelligence in trying to solve a problem rather than simply making his surroundings a part of some egocentric play activity. (The lower age limit in most of Piaget's experiments is about 4 years; before this, nearly all the data come from simple observation of children at play.) We cannot infer from this that the preoperational child is not egocentric—he is, profoundly so—but rather that he has at least learned to relate to other people and things as external to himself. He is still unable, however, to see his own viewpoint as one of many possible ones and to take those other possible viewpoints into account in dealing with other people. He cannot yet justify his reasoning to others; indeed, he does not believe his thought processes are susceptible to questioning or examination. What he thinks *is*. He cannot yet think about his own thoughts.

One of the major characteristics of preoperational thought is its tendency to focus on a single, striking feature of an object or situation. The preschool child, having noted that something is tall or red, seems unable to take into account any other qualities. This fact goes a long way in explaining why conservation is absent at this stage. Tall things, the child has learned, are bigger than short things. Therefore a higher water level in a container means more water, regardless of the width of the container. Reasoning is distorted in various directions, depending on which characteristic of the situation first captures the child's attention. The child looks at one thing at a time; he cannot hold factor A in mind while he relates to factor B. "Preoperational thought . . . is static and immobile. It is a kind of thought which can focus impressionistically and sporadically on this or that momentary, static condition but cannot adequately link a whole set of successive conditions into an integrated totality by taking account of the transformations which unify them and render them logically coherent" (Flavell, 1963, p. 157). The difference between preoperational thought and operational thought is analogous to the difference between a slide show and a moving picture: the preoperational child moves jerkily from one idea to the next and is relatively unable to deal with or reconcile the contradictions that occur along the way.

*Concrete-Operational Stage.* As with each of the stage transitions in Piaget's model, the transition from preoperational to concrete-operational thought seems to begin with a settling-in, a kind of developed competence in dealing with ideas at the previous level, and then a gradual facing-up to the inconsistencies and gaps left by that kind of logic. As preoperational thought becomes easier for the (approximately) 6-year-old, he becomes more and more aware that it doesn't quite work sometimes. Nigl and Fishbein (1974) describe this as a "growth following consolidation," in which the consolidation of one mode of thought frees the child to move on to more sophisticated cognitive activity.

As the child progresses into concrete-operational thought, he begins to be able to consider more than one idea at a time. His cognitive structures begin to become related and systematic. He acquires the notion of reversibility—a key characteristic of this stage. It is important to realize that children do not pass into this stage overnight, like walking from one room into another. There is always a confused transitional phase, in which the child exhibits preoperational characteristics in one task and concrete-operational characteristics in another. There may be plateaus and even setbacks, during which the child falls back on older, more primitive modes of thought. But always the general trend is forward, toward greater organization, system, and logic. In learning to hold in mind one characteristic, so as to relate it to another, the child improves his ability to represent things symbolically. At the height of the concrete-operational stage, the child is adept at the symbolic representation and manipulation of physical objects. He can imagine what a thing would look or act like *if.* He can manipulate concrete objects in his mind. This ability gives the concrete-operational stage its name: the child can now represent and carry out concrete operations mentally. Flavell (1963, p. 203) describes it this way: "The structures of concrete operations are, to use a homely analogy, rather like parking lots whose individual parking spaces are now occupied and now empty; the spaces themselves endure, however, and lead their owner to look beyond the cars actually present towards potential, future occupants of the vacant and to-be-vacant spaces."

Yet the mental organization of the concrete-operational child is not complete; it is still chunked. The procedures and logic of one organized subsystem do not carry over into another. It is as if each of Flavell's parking spaces had high walls around it; the child can operate perfectly consistently within one parking space, but those operations have little or no effect on the operations carried out once he enters another. This disjunction inevitably leads, as the child becomes more acute, to a sense that something is missing, something is wrong. There are gaps; things sometimes do not fit. Again, we see the phenomenon of consolidation leading to confusion. The child has mastered concrete operations, and that very mastery pushes him on into the next stage of cognitive activity.

*Formal-Operational Stage.* We must approach an examination of Piaget's final developmental stage—that of formal operations—with great care because it is our own. Formal-operational thought is the "adult" mode of thinking, the last stop on the line. It stands to reason that most of us do not function at that level all the time, that many of us fluctuate between formal operations and concrete operations depending on the kind of task we are involved in. Formal-operational thought is hard to understand because it is often difficult to engage in, much less to examine and analyze. Nevertheless, we are committed to the effort; let's plunge in!

There are two major differences between formal-operational and concrete-operational thought. One has to do with the degree of organization, of systematization, in the overall thought structure; the other with the degree of abstraction the child is capable of. We said earlier that the logical subsystems of the concrete-operational child are isolated from each other; this isolation breaks down as he moves into the formal-operational stage. More and more bridges are built between subsystems; gradually the barriers fall and the systems merge. As he is able to carry more and more facts and incorporate more and more perspectives simultaneously, the adolescent tends to be aware of both the whole and its separate parts. The intricate structures of formal logic and of set theory are attempts to describe and catalog the kind of thinking that is natural at the stage of formal operations. (One reason many of us find set theory and formal logic difficult to master is that we have become so accustomed to thinking in these ways that we can't take them apart and analyze them any more. We are like the centipede that fell on its back in a ditch when it tried to figure out how its legs worked when it walked.)

Even more important than systematic and organizational gains, however, is the gradual breaking of the adolescent's ties to concrete operations. Increasingly, he is able to consider chains of possible (and even impossible) events. In considering what might be, he is better able to isolate and understand the dimensions of what is. "Much of the difference between the everyday behavior of the child and the adolescent can be expressed in this way: the adolescent, like the child, lives in the present, but also, unlike the child, he lives very much in the nonpresent, i.e., in the future and in the domain of the hypothetical. His conceptual world is full of informal theories about self and life, full of plans for his and society's future, in short, full of ideation which goes far beyond his immediate situation" (Flavell, 1963, p. 223).

It is important for us to realize, in dealing with adolescents, that they are our conceptual equals. We may have acquired experience and (one hopes) wisdom; but the teacher and the teen-ager have essentially the same tool kits for dealing with facts and ideas. In fact, to the extent that the adult comes to rely more and more on crystallizations of his past learnings and less and less upon his analytic and deductive processes, the tools of the adolescent may be a good deal sharper and better oiled than his own! We can share our experience and ideas with an adolescent and encourage him to use and expand his developing abilities, but we can no longer assume that we are somehow ahead of him developmentally.

Thus Piaget's four major stages. We have touched only briefly on some of the important concepts that Piaget has developed, but this overview should give us a framework for understanding some of the specific findings and theories in the area of cognition and problem solving.

## HOW DO WE THINK?

### Concept Formation

While philosophers have been intrigued by the question "How do we think?" for thousands of years, experimental study of the problem is much more recent. The classic pioneer study of concept formation was carried out by Clark L. Hull in 1920; it was the model for work in that area for many years. Hull showed his subjects sets of Chinese characters, each set being based on a common element embedded in the characters. Subjects had to learn a class name (a nonsense word) for each set of characters. Hull found that subjects could learn the classes correctly and could generalize that learning so as to categorize a new stimulus character they hadn't seen before; but, in many cases, subjects who could do so were unable to verbalize their reason for assigning the new stimulus to the proper category. They knew what the symbol was called, but they didn't know why. Hull concluded that concepts can be learned before they are defined—that people can recognize and use attributes of a stimulus object without realizing what they are doing.

*Concept Attributes.* While Hull's finding was interesting in and of itself, even more important was the attention that his work brought to the area of concept formation. Researchers began to elaborate and expand on Hull's design and to identify the variables that make a particular concept problem easy or hard to solve. Let's look at a typical concept-formation exercise, and see what some of these variables are.

The subject is presented with a series of drawings; for each drawing, he must say whether it is or is not a "ying." The first drawing is a large red circle and a small green triangle. Our subject hasn't the faintest idea what a ying is, so he just guesses—yes, it is. "Wrong," he is told. "Here's the next one." The next one is a large green triangle and a small red triangle. "Okay," says the subject, "that's not a ying either." "Wrong," says the experimenter, "that *is* a ying. How about this one?"—showing the third picture, a small green circle and a large red triangle. And so it continues, with the subject guessing and being told "right" or "wrong" until he finally learns that yings are drawings containing only triangles—that the size and the color have nothing to do with it.

Now, "triangles" is a relatively simple concept; in the language of psychologists, we may say that it is a concept based on a single attribute, that of shape. In our experiment we might have defined a ying as a green triangle or a small green triangle or one-and-only-one small green triangle; in other words, we could have used only shape, or shape and color, or shape and color and size, or shape and color and size and number as defining criteria. The number of relevant attributes and the kind of attributes that are relevant are important factors in determining the difficulty of a concept problem. Even more important, though, is the number of irrelevant attributes that are varied. Consider the ying experiment again. If the subject had simply been presented with line drawings of triangles and circles, all the same size, he would have been able to determine rather quickly that yings were always triangles. Adding the variables of color and size had a masking effect on the importance of the shape; it distracted him and kept him from focusing immediately on the important part of the stimulus. We have rediscovered one of the early findings of concept-formation research: the more irrelevant attributes that are varied, the more difficult the concept is.

*Salience.* Let's go back for a moment to those relevant attributes. We said that both the number and the kind of relevant attributes contributed to the difficulty level of a concept. But the relationship, unfortunately, is not as simple as was the case with irrelevant attributes. To some extent, increasing the number of relevant attributes does increase the difficulty of the concept. But some attributes are more *salient* than others—that is, they are more readily focused upon. And the more salient the relevant attributes, the easier the concept is (Odom & Corbin, 1973). This, of course, is only logical: nonsalient attributes tend not to be attended to, and it's hard to take into account an attribute that you haven't even noticed! With regard to the number of relevant attributes, then, we have to hedge a bit: the difficulty of the concept is a joint function of the number and the salience of the relevant attributes.

Somewhat related to the notion of attribute salience is Rao's (1971) finding that abstract materials are easier to work with in concept formation than are thematic materials—that is, pictures of people, landscapes, or other familiar objects. Rao concluded from his research that when thematic material is used, subjects attend to and evaluate attributes on the basis of how relevant those attributes have been in past experience. In an experimental situation we often overlook aspects of the stimulus that have not been particularly relevant to us in forming discriminations in the past—they are nonsalient—and concept problems involving them as relevant attributes are harder to solve. In solving abstract-stimulus problems, however, we have fewer past experiences to draw upon in deciding which attributes are likely to be relevant: the size, shape, and color of an abstract figure are, for most people, more or less equally salient. Therefore, the abstract problems tend to be solved more easily. The lesson here for teachers, I think, is not that we should try to deal more with abstract problems, but rather that we should help students to be flexible in the way in which they draw upon past experience in problem solving.

Salience of an attribute is also related to its intensity: a particularly bright color or loud noise is more readily attended to than a less intense stimulus. Not surprisingly, the relative intensity of relevant and irrelevant attributes is a factor in determining the difficulty of a concept problem. According to Melnick (1973), one reason younger children have trouble dealing with abstract relationships is that they are perceptually trapped by the intensity of the more concrete attributes of stimulus materials. As children grow older, both learning and maturation help to lessen the impact that concrete stimuli have on perception, and they are free to attend to other aspects of the situation. This formulation, we might note, provides another possible criterion for movement from one to another of Piaget's developmental stages.

*Kinds of Concepts.* As we move away from the characteristics of the stimulus material from which the concept must be extracted, we find another factor that contributes to the difficulty of a concept problem: the *kind* of concept we are dealing with. According to Bruner and his colleagues (1956), there are three main kinds of concepts. *Conjunctive* concepts involve the joint appearance of relevant attributes (a red triangle) and tend to be the easiest concepts to work with. *Disjunctive* concepts involve either-or relationships (a ying is anything that is red or triangular) and present somewhat harder problems to solve. *Relational* concepts are the hardest of all; they involve relationships among the various attributes (red things are yings if they are triangular, and green things are yings if they are circular). Applying these principles to the problems of a third-grade teacher struggling with a geography unit, we might predict that it will be easier for his students to master the concept of an island as a body of land surrounded by water (a conjunctive concept) than of precipitation as either rain or snow or hail (a disjunctive concept). And relational concepts, such as the relationship between annual rainfall and closeness to mountains (high rainfall if you are on the west side in the northern hemisphere and low rainfall if you are on the east side), will be most difficult of all.

*Cognitive Strain.* The number of attributes, both relevant and irrelevant, and the kind of relationship among them contribute to what has been called cognitive strain. The more things we have to attend to at once and the more complicated the way in which we must relate them to each other, the greater the cognitive strain and the more difficult it is to solve the problem. Dominowski (1974) relates cognitive strain to an overload of the information-processing system—something like increasing the number of balls a juggler must keep in the air at once or making more intricate the pattern in which he is juggling them. Cognitive strain is a strange variable in that it is at once both cause and effect of problem difficulty: the more difficult the problem, the more cognitive strain it will create; and the more cognitive strain that exists, the more difficult it will be to solve the problem. Obviously, the amount of cognitive strain experienced at any given time is a function not just of the immediate problem but of all the things that are going on in a person's life; his problem-solving ability is decreased to the extent that his information processor is trying to deal with other sorts of things at the same time.

With the introduction of the notion of cognitive strain and its relationship to factors outside the immediate problem-solving situation, we have opened the door to consideration of other *nonprocessing variables*—characteristics of the learner as opposed to characteristics of the problem. Such factors as intelligence, attitudes, and motivation might affect the success and speed with which a student can solve a problem or master a concept. These learner variables, though, can lead us far astray from the main concern of this chapter, namely, the nature of problem-solving and cognitive processes in general. We shall, therefore, defer their consideration to the latter part of this book and move on now to the notion of hierarchies of processes in thinking and problem solving.

## Levels of Thinking

*Kinds of Symbolizing.* As we saw in Chapter 3, the acquisition of language skills is a tremendously important factor in problem-solving ability. Piaget emphasizes the growing ability of the child to symbolize his experience, and language is one of the primary means of achieving such symbolization. Bruner (1966a), too, says that language makes a qualitative difference in the way cognition occurs. But language is not the only way in which people symbolize experience. According to Bruner, the first knowledge a child has of the world is through the habitual actions he uses for interacting with it. This knowledge is not true imagery, but is rather a sort of reciprocal imagery in that each facet of the environment is known and recognized by the way the individual responds to it. A chair is to sit on; food is to eat; a ball is to throw. In time, this motoric representation is supplemented and then gradually replaced by representation through imagery—through pictures of and symbols for the thing represented. The third layer of the hierarchy is representation through language, in which the symbols become linguistic abstractions rather than pictures of the various aspects of the environment. Being able to use linguistic representations adds mightily to the child's formal problem-solving ability. But there is a loss, too, for as language comes to the fore, other kinds of imagery fall back. "For the child who still searches for the vivid perceptual cue the task of attaining conceptual meanings is necessarily made more difficult. Yet for the child who uses the newly acquired conceptual categories and the language that goes with them there is also a cost. Language becomes the preferred mode of grouping, and as time goes on imagery is used less and less and 'decays with disuse' " (Bruner, 1966a, p. 27). And with decay of imagery comes a decay of some of the vivid, holistic, intuitionlike insights of childhood.

*Kinds of Learning.* Bruner's notion of different levels of representation is not the only hierarchical scheme with which we, as educators, should be familiar. Gagné (1974) has developed a model of learning in which each level builds upon, or requires as a prerequisite, the earlier, simpler forms. At the base of the structure are simple stimulus-response or rote learnings. Having acquired a set of such building blocks, an individual can begin to form basic discriminations. He can use these to build up simple concepts and can formulate rules from the concepts. At the apex of Gagné's pyramid are higher-order rules, the sorts of rules that are used to generate and test and evaluate hypotheses. Gagné's formulation, while it doesn't correspond exactly to Bruner's, is certainly compatible. A child, for instance, learns not to touch a hot radiator. He can learn this at a purely motoric level (in Bruner's terms), and can respond to the radiator according to the pain he felt when he touched it or according to a jerk-away response to it. He may learn to discriminate between hot objects and non-hot objects, and this kind of generalization-discrimination learning is likely to require some visual imagery. Moving to the level of concepts, the child begins to formulate notions about what sorts of objects are likely to be hot and what sorts are not; this level seems to be a transition between visual and verbal imagery. Rules imply some sense of causality, of why things are hot or how they get hot or when they are likely to become hot. In other words, rule learning involves moving from the concrete here and now into the abstractions of past and future and "what if"; and these sorts of abstractions require language.

*Organization of Thought.* Another source of information about learning hierarchies—and a fertile source—is the work being done in computer simulation of learning. In trying to program a sophisticated computer so as to make it think and learn (and there have been some successful efforts along these lines), researchers have found it useful to build upon the computer's past learnings and levels of learning. Newell, Shaw, and Simon (1958), who pioneered in this area, report results that argue strongly that human as well as machine problem solving does indeed rest on a hierarchical structure.

If there is any single practical lesson for teachers to be derived from these theoretical notions, it would seem to be that we must make haste slowly—that we must be sure the student has acquired the foundation facts and skills before we push him into higher-level learning. "The kind of learning outcome that supports creative problem solving . . . is acquired by embedding the problem-solving rule in a bank of the appropriate propositional knowledge" (Mayer, 1974, p. 656). Facts and definitions and concrete experiences are the basic ingredients of concept formation and rule building, just as flour and sugar and milk are needed to bake a cake.

Of these basic ingredients, it may be that the concrete experiences are the most critical. In the models of each of the theorists we have looked at—Piaget with his sensory-motor and preoperational stages, Bruner with his motoric representation, and Gagné with his basic simple learnings—it is the hands-on, physical interaction with the environment that provides the floor on which later learning is built. Berzonsky (1975), who observed children working at conceptual tasks, supports this notion. His results suggest that experiences with familiar objects and phenomena may be necessary before a child can appreciate the role of coincidental or chance factors. Concrete experiences appear to influence the ability to distinguish a causal relationship from a chance concurrence; perhaps they help the child to make a rudimentary distinction between causation and correlation. Both these notions, in turn, seem to be used before the child is able to explain remote, unattainable objects. We appear to go from what we can feel and manipulate, to what we can see and hear, to what we can only think about.

All these levels are interrelated, just as the concepts and rules of Piaget's formal-operational stage are interrelated. Concepts grow and develop; solutions become elaborated; ideas are never "finished" but rather flourish and merge and intertwine with each other. In other words, the relationships are both vertical and horizontal: among various concepts and ideas, at a given level, and up and down the hierarchy. The truly productive thinker does not think on a single level, any more than he considers a single idea in isolation. He involves himself, rather, in the full spectrum of ideation and imagination and experiencing available to him, across a wide variety of concepts, rules, and hypotheses.

## Hypothesis Testing

To understand thinking as a hierarchical activity, although helpful in analyzing different levels of cognition, still does not explain exactly what goes on at the higher levels. To gain insights here, we must turn to another set of ideas, those that relate higher-level thought to hypothesis testing. An early notion of Bruner and his colleagues, that problem solving involves the active construction and testing of various hypotheses, has proved useful indeed, though it in turn has generated a whole new set of questions. As we look at some of the work done in this area, though, let's remember that we are talking now about the higher levels of Bruner's, Piaget's, and Gagné's models. Young children and less experienced problem solvers are much less likely to use hypotheses; and if they do use them, they do so less efficiently (R. T. White, 1974; Olson, 1966). Effective use of hypotheses presupposes that the individual has successfully passed through the earlier and simpler modes of representation and that he has learned to think in terms of related sets of verbal symbols.

*Feedback.* When we solve a problem by means of hypothesis testing, we begin with a set of possible solutions and gradually eliminate all but the correct one. One of the first questions to ask, then, in trying to understand this kind of thinking, is just how people go about eliminating incorrect hypotheses. In traditional concept-formation research, a subject may be "right" or "wrong" on any trial; and any trial may or may not be a positive instance of the concept. We can best understand what is going on here if we think of the possible occurrences in this learning situation as a table (see Figure 4-1). The stimulus presented to the subject may or may not be a

Subject's Perception

|  | | *Yes,* it is an instance. | *No,* it is not an instance. |
|---|---|---|---|
| Objective Reality | *Yes,* it is an instance of the concept. | Right | Wrong |
|  | *No,* it is not an instance of the concept. | Wrong | Right |

*Figure 4-1.* Varieties of "right" and "wrong" hypotheses in concept formation.

ying; these two possibilities are shown along the vertical dimension. Also, the subject may guess that the concept is or is not a ying; this choice is shown across the top of the table. There are, then, two different ways that the subject can be right (he can say "no" when the stimulus is not an instance of the concept, or he can say "yes" when the stimulus is an instance of the concept), and, similarly, there are two different ways that he can be wrong. If he says "yes" and is right or if he says "no" and is right, he is likely to stay with the same hypothesis; we tend to switch to another hypothesis only when we find that the one we're using causes us to make mistakes (Rao, 1971). What this means is that unless we happen to accidentally hit upon the right hypothesis at the beginning (which probably doesn't happen often), we have to be told "wrong" several times in order to work our way around to the right one. Now, look at the two ways in which a subject can earn a "wrong" feedback. If he says "yes" and is told that he is wrong, all he knows is that he has seen something that is not what he is looking for. But if he says "no" and is told that he is wrong, he knows that he is looking at a positive instance of the concept—that the stimulus before him is an example of what he is after. It seems reasonable that this latter situation would, in the long run, be more helpful to the learner, and research generally supports this conclusion. Seeing positive instances of a concept—seeing true yings—usually helps the learner more than seeing non-yings. And wrong guesses—mistakes—frequently facilitate learning more than accidental right answers.

Of course, there are different kinds of negative examples of concepts, and even positive instances can be more or less helpful depending on the sequence in which they are presented. Moore, Hauck, Biddle, and Houtz (1973) define a *good negative* as a negative instance of a concept in which only one attribute is "wrong"; they argue that it is easier to learn from good negatives than from instances in which several characteristics of the stimulus do not fit the definition of the concept that is being learned. Using good negatives, as well as using a series of positives that call attention (by repetition) to one relevant attribute at a time, may be expected to facilitate learning.

*Learning Strategies.* Knowing what kind of strategy a learner is likely to use in shifting hypotheses makes it possible to design sequences of examples that make for optimal learning. Two major kinds of shifts can be made in changing hypotheses: one involves changing the *value* of a dimension (from red things to blue things) and the other involves changing the *dimension* itself (from red things to triangles). In general, adults tend to make the dimension shift, while children tend to make the value shift (Offenbach, 1974). Shifting only the value of a dimension tends to be limiting in that it prevents the learner from attending to other dimensions that may be relevant; in helping a child to acquire a concept, then, the teacher should be alert to this strategy and ready to break in with a suggestion that other attributes may be important.

Children also are more likely than adults to switch hypotheses after positive feedback—that is, after being told that an answer is right. While it is possible to obtain positive feedback when using an incorrect hypothesis, such switching tends to be self-defeating in that it prevents a systematic check of alternative possibilities. Again, the teacher who is alert to this learning pattern can intervene with suggestions for more efficient strategies; it has been clearly demonstrated that learners can benefit from such intervention and can learn to adopt better strategies for solving this kind of problem (R. T. White, 1974).

The notion of different strategies used in hypothesis testing brings us to another major question about this kind of learning: given that learners do reject incorrect hypotheses on the basis of feedback, where do the new hypotheses come from? How do we generate the series of hypotheses that will be rejected, one by one, until we finally hit upon the right one? White suggests that, at least early in our work on a problem, hypotheses are generated only on the basis of the positive examples we see. If we are shown a picture of a zebra, for instance, and are told that this is an example of a "wug," we may hypothesize that wugs have four legs or that they have stripes. Later, when we have more experience, we can begin to use negative examples as sources of hypotheses; told that a picture of a bird is not a wug, we may hypothesize that a wug is any nonflying creature.

While this thesis is interesting in that it helps to explain why positive examples are more helpful than negative examples, especially for inexperienced learners, it is even more useful in pointing out a general characteristic of hypothesis testing: the older and more experienced a learner is, the more his selection of strategies tends to be systematic. Older learners can use a sort of mental checklist, in which they keep track of "eliminated" and "still possible" solutions. This kind of categorization makes negative examples more useful to the more experienced learner. Mosher and Hornsby (1966, p. 100), who studied the kinds of questions children ask in problem-solving situations, sum it up this way: "Six-year-olds seek information directly by testing specific hypotheses, eight-year-olds establish some constraints before leaping to hypotheses, while eleven-year-olds postpone specific hypotheses until they have narrowed the possibilities beyond a first set of constraints. The development of strategies for seeking information is toward increasingly connected acts designed to locate relevance by more economical but less direct means." All learners select hypotheses as they are suggested by the examples and the feedback they are exposed to. But as the learner grows more skillful, he begins to be selective: he doesn't try just any old hypothesis or skip back and forth from one idea to another, but rather tries to set up a pattern that will lead him to a solution as quickly and efficiently as possible.

According to Bruner and his colleagues (1956), three major objectives must be met by an overall hypothesis-testing strategy. The first is that the hypotheses selected must be *testable*—that is, hypotheses must relate the information (stimuli) in such a way that the learner can decide whether to stay with a given hypothesis or to shift to another one. Second, a good strategy makes as easy as possible the task of assimilating and keeping track of information. It is systematic, working through various sets or categories of hypotheses in an orderly fashion, so that each discarded hypothesis need not be memorized as an isolated fact. Finally, a good strategy is a compromise between gambling for a quick solution, on the one hand, and making sure that no possibilities are missed, on the other. That is, it regulates the amount of risk that one takes. Good problem solvers (and concept formation is a kind of problem solving) are able to set up strategies that meet all three of these objectives; indeed, the ability to do so is the major difference between experienced and inexperienced problem solvers.

*Doodles and Hill Climbs.* There is just one thing wrong with this emphasis on the systematic nature of good problem-solving strategy: it doesn't always happen that way. While in many situations the learner can set up an overall plan for learning what he wants or for solving a particular problem, other situations just don't seem to lend themselves to that kind of organization. The more complex a problem is, the harder it is to see ahead

of time what sorts of hypothesis testing are going to be most useful. In complex situations like this, we often *doodle* with the problem, trying first this and then that, without any clear idea of where we want to end up. "There probably are situations in which a person neatly charts his way through a problem before taking any operational steps in what he hopes is the correct direction. But more often, an idea of what seems like a potentially useful direction is followed up and calculations are actually carried out, even though the subject does not yet know that those calculations are going to produce anything helpful toward solving the problem" (Greeno, 1974, p. 106).

Even doodling, however, seems to have a basic organization. Usually it goes something like this: doodle around with it, see if you are any closer to a solution; if you are, keep on the same track, and if not, go back to where you were before the last doodle. Computer scientists call this kind of strategy a *hill climb*. In a hill climb, getting to the solution of a problem is analogous to getting to the top of the hill. You take a step and then assess whether you are higher or lower than you were before. If you are higher, you continue in the same direction; if you are lower, you go back to where you were and try a different direction. As long as the hill is fairly simple in contour, this procedure eventually gets you to the top. Visualizing a problem-solving or concept-formation task as a hill climb can be useful if you know where you want to be when you are done. If you don't have some idea of what the solution ought to be like, though, a hill climb won't work because you won't be able to tell whether a given step has taken you toward it or away from it.

*TOTEs and Plans.* The notion of problem solving as a hill climb bears a close resemblance to Miller, Galanter, and Pribram's (1960) description of a TOTE as the basic problem-solving unit. TOTE stands for Test-Operate-Test-Exit. All behavior, according to these theorists, can be broken down into sets of TOTEs. First, we *test* to see what is needed or missing in a situation. Then we *operate* on the situation, to change it in the desired direction. Next, we *test* again to see whether it is now the way we want it. If not, we go back to the operate phase; if it is okay, we *exit* from that particular TOTE unit and move on to another (see Figure 4-2a). If we expand the

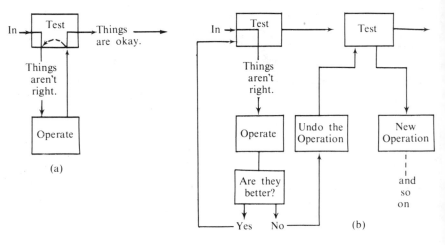

*Figure 4-2.* (a) The TOTE unit as described by Miller, Galanter, and Pribram (1960). (b) The TOTE unit modified to describe a hill-climb process.

diagram of Miller and his colleagues so that the second test allows us to decide that the operation took us in a wrong direction, then we have something that looks like Figure 4-2b—and this is a hill climb.

The TOTE unit is intriguing because it allows us to relate a lot of different notions about problem solving and thinking in general. It fits nicely into the general notion of hypothesis testing, and as the learner works up from simple to complex TOTEs, the theory encompasses many of the hierarchical notions about learning. However, it too begs one important question: how does the learner set up new TOTEs? Where do they come from? Do we store all the TOTEs we have used in the past and retrieve and modify them as the occasion demands? Storage seems unlikely simply because there are too many TOTEs; the storage load would be enormous. Miller and his colleagues suggest that there are hierarchies of TOTEs; at the highest levels, TOTEs are organized into *plans*. A plan is simply a series of TOTEs, set up so as to reach a given goal or solve a certain kind of problem. And the hierarchy goes a step further: "In the more complex kinds of problem-solving, . . . we must have some way to generate alternative plans and then to operate on them, test them, evaluate them. These [ways of generating new plans are] metaplans—plans for forming other plans" (1960, p. 169). The difference between remembering a plan and generating a plan can be small indeed. Let's say, for example, that I have stored (remembered) the information that a bird has feathers, lays eggs, and has no teeth. My plan for determining whether a particular creature is a member of the bird family, then, looks something like Figure 4-3. Now I certainly have not

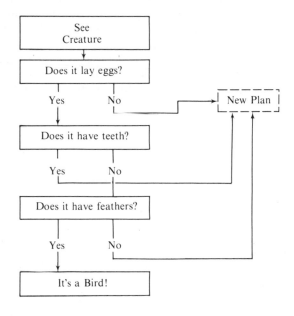

*Figure 4-3.* Plan for determining whether a particular creature is a bird.

stored anything that detailed; I have simply stored the information that allows me to construct the plan, together with some basic rules for putting that information together in plan form. Say Miller and colleagues "When we say that most plans are remembered, not created, we do not mean that the plan is stored in memory ready for execution down to the very last muscle twitch. Often it is a metaplan that is stored—a metaplan from which a large number of different plans can be generated as they are needed" (p. 178).

A bit earlier we talked about the amount of risk involved in choosing a particular strategy (or plan) for solving a problem. In many kinds of problems, we may choose a solution plan that is sure but slow, or we may gamble on the possibility of a quick solution with the risk of not finding any solution at all. Consider the familiar (for me, at least) situation of having misplaced the car keys or a pair of sunglasses. How do you go about finding them? A gambling solution is to look in likely places; those places have the best chance of success. Using this strategy, you may reach your goal quickly. But if a child has been playing with your lost object and has carefully stored it under the cat's blanket, your gambling solution will never win. You need a different kind of strategy, the slow-but-sure kind; you start in one room and look in every single place large enough to hold the keys or sunglasses, and you proceed that way through the house until you find them. Such strategies may be called *systematic,* in contrast with gambling, or *heuristic,* strategies. People seldom if ever use systematic plans to solve cognitive problems; "for most problems the only plans we have are heuristic, and much of the study of thinking can be reduced rather generally to the study of the heuristic plans people use for generating proposed solutions that are worth testing" (Miller et al., 1960, p. 167).

The heuristic process has essentially four parts. First, we must understand the problem clearly—the kinds of information available, the restrictions on the way that information can be used, and the kind of solution we are looking for. When we have completed this part of the process, we have formed an image of the problem and are ready to look for a solution. Second, we devise our plan; we generate a way to move from the data (which we know) to the solution (the unknown). The third step is to carry out the plan, checking each step as we go along. Each step, of course, is a TOTE unit (and may include a number of simpler sub-TOTEs), which may lead us forward to the next step or back to a previous one; the outcome of a given step may even cause us to discard the whole plan and begin again at the second stage by generating a new one. The final aspect of problem solving (and one that is all too often overlooked) is to evaluate the solution we have found and decide whether it is good enough. In a relatively simple problem, like finding the car keys, the "goodness" of the solution is obvious —either we find them or we don't. In other problems, though, there are different qualities of solutions; some solutions do the job well, and others may just get by or may turn out, in the long run, to be no solutions at all.

Although we nearly always use heuristic rather than systematic plans when dealing with cognitive problems, there are ways in which we can systematize a heuristic—that is, there are different degrees of risk taking. We choose a particular plan on the basis of many different considerations: how quickly a solution is needed, how serious the consequences of failure are, how many second chances we get, how much we enjoy risk taking, whether the problem lends itself more readily to a gambling or to a systematic approach. Most of us, in choosing problem-solving strategies, don't consciously think through our reasons for using one approach rather than another. Yet it is often true that if we did think them through, we would choose a more appropriate strategy—in the phraseology of Miller and his colleagues, a more systematic metaplan would generate a better plan.

### Learning to Learn

One implication of what we have been saying in the last section will have occurred to you a number of times by now: experience in solving one problem (building and utilizing a metaplan) affects the way we approach subsequent problems. This fact is of fundamental importance to teachers. Whether students do well in classroom activities is of negligible interest to us; what counts is how classroom learning is carried into the activities of later life. Psychologists have studied this phenomenon under a number of rather forbidding titles: learning set, transfer of training, generalization, and learning to learn. Each of these phrases refers to a slightly different tack that researchers have taken, but, as we shall see, they all have to do with the same kinds of behaviors.

One of the earliest—and the most delightful—research efforts in the learning-to-learn area was that carried out by Harlow in the late 1940s. Harlow was at that time deeply interested in teaching monkeys to solve simple discrimination problems (one is not quite sure why), and he took the trouble to pay attention to a fact that everyone had known all along: the monkeys got better at solving problems as they went along. Harlow summed it up like this: "Before the formation of a discrimination learning set, a single training trial produces negligible gain; after the formation of a discrimination learning set, *a single training trial constitutes problem solution.* These data clearly show that *animals can gradually learn insight"* (1949, p. 56).

If monkeys, of course, then people as well. Harlow stimulated a great interest in just how an animal of any species learns to learn. And, far from dying down, that interest is still as high as it ever was. The language has gotten more complicated, the list of variables more extensive, but the problem is essentially unchanged: how do we learn to improve our problem-solving skills? How do we transfer what we have learned from one setting to another? For part of the answer, we can turn back to the theorists who talk about hierarchies of learning. Transfer comes most readily within a given level, and it is least likely from a lower to a higher level. That is, the more similar a new problem is to one I can already solve, the more readily I can apply my old techniques in the new situation. Sometimes a higher-level learning allows me to go back to a lower level with new perspectives and thus allows me to generate better solutions; but I am not likely to make many direct applications of lower-level skills to new high-level problems. Similarly, the more sophisticated the level of representation that an individual uses, the more he is able to pull out similarities between old and new situations and thus apply old learnings to new problems. "With development, the child builds a more constrained strategy for using information. He is increasingly able to guide his inquiries by what he has found out earlier and to eliminate possibilities by ruling out whole classes of objects or events" (Mosher & Hornsby, 1966, p. 101). But such a strategy is typical of the child who represents his world symbolically; the child who can use only ikonic (or motor) representation simply has not developed the cognitive structure needed for such an approach. The very young child can generalize motor learnings, and the ikonic-level child can improve at the level of simple discrimination learning (the level at which Harlow's monkeys operated); but logical, systematic cognitive activity requires something more.

At least part of the learning-to-learn phenomenon can be understood in terms of fairly straightforward stimulus-response principles. As we test and discard hypotheses in search of a solution to a given problem, eventually we find one that turns out to be right—our choice of that hypothesis is rewarded. Rewarded responses are more likely than nonrewarded ones to be repeated under similar circumstances; so the next time we are faced with a similar problem, we are likely to try out first those hypotheses that worked in the past. If we are working a series of problems, all having similar solutions, we begin by trying out a wide variety of approaches. Gradually we learn that one approach seems to work best, and we discard the others and concentrate on the one that has worked before. It follows that we solve the problems faster and faster since we are eliminating much of the time we used to spend on testing wrong hypotheses (M. Levine, 1974; Brown, 1974). We gradually come to expect that a certain solution will work and we go directly to it, instead of fiddling around with other possibilities.

*Backlash.* Learning to learn, or establishing a learning set, helps us to be efficient problem-solvers as long as the type of problem doesn't change. When it does change, there is a possibility of a backlash effect, in which the individual who has formed a strong learning set is at a disadvantage. He expects to be able to use one solution, and it takes a good bit of negative feedback to get him to cancel that expectation and try another solution. Luchins, who developed the water-jar tests,[1] found this behavior clearly evident with his subjects. People who learned to solve difficult water-jar problems using particular operations had a hard time solving a simpler problem that required a different initial approach; but naïve subjects, who hadn't worked first on the more complicated problems, had little trouble with the simple one (Luchins, 1942). Duncker (1945) found this same *set effect* in other sorts of problem-solving tasks. People get in a rut in the

---

[1]A typical water-jar problem is as follows: You have two jars, one holding 9 quarts of water and one holding 4 quarts. Your task is to take the jars down to the river and bring back exactly 6 quarts of water. (A solution is given on page 135.)

approaches they use to a problem situation—or, to use M. Levine's (1974) terms, they have been so strongly reinforced on one kind of hypothesis that they tend to use that kind exclusively, even when it doesn't work very well.

The learning-to-learn effect, then, can be either helpful or harmful. It is helpful when the approaches—hypotheses—one has learned to test do in fact apply to the new situation. And it is harmful when they don't, when the new problem is not solvable by the old methods. Students need to find ways of generalizing old learnings to new situations, but they must also be sensitive to the possibility that such generalizations may not work. They (and we teachers, too, for we are surely not immune to the same sorts of behavior) need to develop a flexibility that allows them to shift strategies when the hypotheses they are trying to use do not yield useful results. How can we facilitate this optimal performance? It seems to me that there are two major factors involved, factors that we can use to our advantage.

*Making Transfer Work.* First, the kind of training—the sequence of problem-solving experiences—is a major factor in the degree to which a strategy is generalized to other situations. Mayer (1974) points out that a learning set is developed quite early in a learning sequence, and that the content learned is structured within that set over the entire course of learning. We cannot afford to think of any learning experience in isolation; it is part of a total pattern and is understood and used by the student in the context of that pattern. Moreover, there are subpatterns within the larger learning experience, and we can manipulate the subpattern arrangement to maximize development of learning sets. We can design a given series of experiences to point up the way in which a certain hypothesis (or hypothesis type) can be generalized across problems. When the student has mastered that kind of problem, we can introduce a new series in which the old methods don't work. The student must switch hypotheses, must get out of his rut. But—and this is critical—the new kind of hypothesis must also be used on a series of problems. It too generalizes. Working through a whole group of subpatterns of this sort, with plenty of opportunities to go back and reuse old techniques, gives the student working experience in both generalization and hypothesis switching. He develops an overall style—a metaplan—of trying out hypotheses that worked before and switching to another approach when the old way doesn't work.

Second, we should remember that all these experiences need not be discovery events for the student. The teacher can introduce problem sets and point out ways in which one looks for those differences and similarities that help determine the strategy most likely to work. In the classroom, unlike the laboratory, we are not interested in watching the student struggle through on his own; we are free to give him whatever information will most help his learning. Well-thought-out instructions can heighten a learner's sensitivity to the generalization and switching process and make him aware of the degree to which he may be restricting himself in his choice of strategies.

We are trying to strike a difficult balance here among a number of important factors. We want to make the subseries of similar problems long enough so that the student does get the idea of generalization, but not so long that he is unnecessarily hooked into a single process. We want the instructions to be clear enough to sensitize him to the notion of generalization and switching, but not so explicit as to deny him the chance to discover, experience, and internalize the process for himself. And we want to intervene with the individual student often enough to prevent him from snarling himself hopelessly in a single pattern, but not so often that he comes to depend on us to tell him when it is time to switch.

*Piaget Again.* It would be a shame to leave this section without going back and tying up at least one loose end. The whole process of generalization, of transfer of learning skills, relates quite closely to Piaget's description of accommodation and assimilation. You will recall that the learning organism accommodates itself to the environment; and simultaneously it restructures that environment to fit in with what it already knows and understands. In the same way, we restructure new problems to maximize their similarity to problems that we already know how to solve—we assimilate them into our problem-solving scheme. And, at the same time, we accommodate our old techniques to make them work better with the new problem. In problem solving, as in other areas of functioning, the line between these two processes is not clear: they occur simultaneously, and each is constantly affected by the other.

Piaget maintains firmly that accommodation and assimilation are not uniquely typical of a certain stage; they are typical of mental life at every stage. Just so with generalization, with the formation of learning sets, with transfer of training. The research is clear on this point: children of any age (and adults of any age) do form learning sets (Wickens, 1974). Yet the kind of set changes with development, as the child learns to attend to different aspects of the situation and becomes more and more adept at symbolic manipulation. While a preoperational child can utilize transfer effects, we cannot expect him to generalize at a symbolic level. Accommodation and assimilation go on within the level a child is operating on (and that includes the accommodated residual of all previous levels).

It cannot be stressed too strongly that, in all cognitive processes, the learner is engaged in interaction with his environment. He is not simply manipulating objects, nor is he simply acted on by external stimuli. Rather, in the dynamic tension between accommodation and assimilation, both learner and what he learns are affected. "Concept development is a process, an interplay of old and new generalizations, a changing of concepts in varying conditions and contexts, a participation by the pupil in the concepts as well as with them as tools; . . . concepts are highly personal" (Henry

& Brown, n.d.). When I am truly and personally involved in learning, I cannot help changing as I learn; my new learning becomes a part of me. And the things I am learning about are changed, too; they will never look the same to me as they did before I learned about (and with) them. It is this quality of irreversible change, of going ahead with no chance of ever going back again, that makes learning—and teaching—so frustrating, scary, and exhilarating.

## IMPLICATIONS FOR THE CLASSROOM

We have now expended a great deal of time and used a large number of words describing some theoretical and research approaches to the nature of concept formation, problem solving, and cognition in general. Along the way, we have occasionally paused to point out a particular implication for teaching behavior. Now it is time to look at a number of specific applications and to construct guidelines for the teacher who wants to facilitate higher-level conceptual behavior among his students.

### Building on Natural Processes

It is important to realize, at the outset, that we are building upon a natural process of development rather than forcing strange or alien tasks on the child. We want to encourage the child to develop his own thinking abilities; it is our job to ensure that such development takes place in an orderly fashion, that the child's cognitive systems come to be as interrelated as possible, and that he be provided with experiences that encourage him to stretch toward new levels of understanding. "The classroom problem is one of how to internalize strategies of the highest kind, representing the best cognitive endeavor. What the classroom must be interested in is the continuous refinement of native strategy" (Henry & Brown, n.d., p. 35).

As the child goes about this process of refinement, he frequently deals with old material but uses new methods. He finds that situations that seemed trivial, problems that were solved long ago, have unexpected aspects or implications. Often, that which he could deal with at an earlier level seems new and puzzling when first encountered in the context of higher-level thinking. Bruner (1966c) calls attention to this phenomenon when he talks about growth errors, pointing out that a child often becomes more mistaken about a situation as he grows older. "A growth error is precisely the first unsuccessful stage of trying to achieve correspondence or concordance between systems of representation. It may well be that a certain tolerance is needed in an educational system to appreciate the benign nature of such errors!" (p. 322). Far from being discouraged when a child who "knew" something last month now seems puzzled by it, the teacher should realize that such apparent regression may be the outward sign of real cognitive growth. When the teacher can accept errors as signs of and potential for growth, the student is free to explore questions and confusions openly rather than to try to give the "right" answer whether he understands the problem or not.

Children are able to deal with concrete objects and manipulations before they can handle abstractions. Presentation of a new concept in concrete form facilitates the child's learning to deal with it abstractly later on (Kodroff & Roberge, 1975). Similarly, students do best in abstract reasoning tasks when they are thoroughly familiar and comfortable with the factual knowledge needed for that reasoning. Just as the mason knows about different kinds of stone and the dressmaker is familiar with various kinds of fabric, so the conceptualizer must have well-understood facts—raw materials—with which to conceptualize. "Discovery teaching to subjects who lack the appropriate [factual] knowledge will not result in discovery learning or creative problem solving and may result in no learning at all" (Mayer, 1974, p. 656). I can't understand the relationship between Fahrenheit and Centigrade until I know how to count; and the notion of a food chain won't be meaningful to me unless I understand that different kinds of creatures require different kinds of nourishment. Like it or not, good conceptualizing requires quite a lot of rote learning (just as rote learning can be enhanced by categorizing and conceptualizing the material). Nolan (1973) points out that younger and older children may deal with the same material in different ways, the older at a conceptual level and the younger through rote memorization. And, he goes on, encouraging the young child to memorize is not poor teaching—quite the contrary, for when the child is developmentally ready to work at a conceptual level, he will have the raw materials ready and organized in a way well suited to be dealt with at that higher level.

### Providing Information

The young child, who must work at a level involving much memorization, is processing more information than the older, conceptual child. The older child sorts through the new input, checking off that which he already knows and storing only what he has not acquired before. For the younger child, in contrast, it is all relatively new; it must all be symbolized and stored in some way. Because of this difference in information processing, it is particularly important that material be presented to younger children in a well-organized manner and that the presentation be slow and often repetitious. All these things—organization, speed, and repetition—affect the symbolization and storage of new information.

Inevitably, students find themselves dealing with problem situations in which they do not know all the relevant facts. Information was not properly symbolized or stored when it was first encountered (or was never encountered at all) or, although stored, cannot be readily retrieved. Students therefore need to know how to seek additional data; they should be encouraged to use all sorts of mechanical storage devices and memory aids, from scratch pads to libraries and computers. Martorella (1972), describing a typical concept-formation problem, indicates that subjects tend to do best when all the previous stimuli, both positive and negative instances, are available on every trial. The learner can then refer back to them, noting similarities and contrasts, and reviewing the hypotheses he has tested and discarded. Other sorts of cognitive activity work the same way: the less energy one must expend in holding complicated information in memory, the more energy left for the conceptualizing process. This is not to deny the importance of propositional knowledge—of solid, hands-on familiarity with the data—but rather to stress that cognitive strain is decreased markedly by lessening the burden on the short-term memory system.

## Explicit Teaching

How much guidance, how much showing how, is best for concept learning? Do children learn to solve problems better when allowed to figure things out for themselves (discovery method) or when given rules for solution? Which method leads to the most appropriate generalizations? In trying to answer these kinds of questions, we must first realize that they pose an artificial dichotomy. We do not have to choose between discovery and rule learning, between observation and practice. Rather, we have to decide what combination of experiences best facilitates conceptual growth. To insist that the child learn exclusively from watching and listening to others would be foolish; it would deny that very hands-on experience that we have already seen to be essential. But there is some evidence that pressure to respond directly in a problem situation can interfere with the process of problem solving; sometimes observation does result in better learning than does working with the problem oneself (Rosenthal & Zimmerman, 1973). The child needs to participate in a variety of learning experiences; he needs to learn to move from one to another, using the special insights he gains in one setting to enrich the further learnings of the next. Any single teaching method, used exclusively, is wrong; children need to see the same kind of strategy used and demonstrated in different ways and to practice with that strategy themselves in order to master it.

One reason why practice, leading to individual discovery, is not sufficient by itself in facilitating conceptual development is that it doesn't push the student to the limits of his capabilities. Children often tend to use those techniques they have already mastered rather than trying new ones of which they aren't sure. They try strategies that have worked in the past, rather than venturing out with untested ideas. By demonstrating or explaining new (and possibly higher-level) ways of proceeding, the teacher can speed up the pace at which the child explores new and more advanced problem-solving techniques. Even when the child is engaged in individual practice or is set the task of exploring a problem for himself, some guidance can be helpful. Nolan (1973) found, for instance, that forcing children to organize their data semantically—that is, by using abstract verbal symbols—increased the amount they were able to recall; clearly, this organization facilitated their later use of information in problem situations. The children in Nolan's study showed distinct developmental differences. Kindergarten children, forced to organize on one task, went back to an unorganized approach when left on their own in later tasks. Third graders did show some transfer of organization on subsequent tasks, but not a great deal. And even ninth graders, "though they spontaneously organize much better than younger children, profit from being forced to organize; there is a transfer of organizing to similar learning situations" (p. 255). What Nolan's data suggest is that when the child is guided in his approach, his experience is more useful to him. The teacher must again strike a difficult balance between too few demands (thus failing to push the child into demonstrating to himself what he can do) and too many demands (which run the risk of overstructuring or of forcing the child into repeated failures).

Information giving, we are fond of saying, should be clear and unambiguous. When we try to teach a child a new concept or technique, we should explain it in the most understandable way we can. But is this always true? Rosenthal and Zimmerman (1973) suggest that while clear explanations are most useful to the child in the immediate problem situation, they may not always be the best facilitators of transfer. When the presentation is a bit fuzzy, the student (if he is to benefit from it) is forced to become more active; he has to sharpen his own perceptions and pick out for himself what the essential elements are. In so doing, he puts himself in a much better position to generalize his learning appropriately to other situations. There is probably, these authors speculate, an optimal range of fuzziness. Too fuzzy and the student gets lost or tunes out; too clear (!) and the student becomes a passive receiver of a specific how-to-get-through-this-immediate-problem method. Good learning lies somewhere in between.

## Strategies

While some amount of fumbling may be helpful in dealing with specific problem solutions, another kind of information giving should be handled as clearly as possible. This is the general area of setting up heuristic strategies, of constructing metaplans. Because these general problem-solving strategies can be adapted to a wide range of problem situations, students can be taught them quite explicitly and then be given opportunities to put them to use. Miller and his colleagues (1960) list four such strategies, all of which can aid problem solving in quite varied situations. The first is perhaps the most obvious: look at the new problem and then try to think of other, more familiar problems that are similar. The strategy that worked with the old problem may be applicable to the new, or perhaps the new problem can be redefined or restated in some way to increase the similarity and thereby increase the possibility that the old strategy will work.

The second strategy suggested by Miller and his colleagues is to start with the desired end point and then work back to the beginning. You might try this method with the water-jar problem given on page 128. You want to end up with 6 quarts of water, and you have a 9- and a 4-quart jar. How can you get 6 quarts? By pouring exactly 3 quarts out of the full 9-quart jar. How could you do that? Well, if the 4-quart jar already had 1 quart in it, and you filled it up from the full 9-quart jar, that would do it. So how do you get the 4-quart jar to have exactly 1 quart in it? One way is to get just 1 quart in the larger container and then transfer it to the smaller one. Is there any way to subtract 4 or a multiple of 4 from 9 and end up with 1? Of course —and the problem is solved.

The third problem-solving strategy bears a distinct resemblance to our old friend the hill climb: you break the overall problem down into subproblems and try to set up a strategy for dealing with each subproblem in such a way that solving it brings you closer to the ultimate solution or goal. This kind of analysis is particularly helpful in complex situations where many variables must be taken into account. Writing a term paper, for instance, can be a complicated problem. But break it down into subtasks (and maybe even sub-subtasks) and it begins to look do-able:

1. Choose a topic
   a. List the topics I already know something about
   b. List the topics that I can readily find out more about
   c. List the topics I would enjoy knowing more about
   d. Select one topic that appears on all three lists
2. Gather information
   a. Outline what I know about the topic
   b. Identify areas where more data are needed

—and so on. Each subtask, when carried out, moves the overall problem a little closer to solution. The method has two advantages: it allows one to see the overall strategy more clearly and thus plan better, and it also allows one to work on small chunks rather than being overwhelmed by the problem as a whole.

Finally, Miller and his colleagues describe a strategy known as the *planning method*. In this method, one first identifies as many of the relevant variables as possible. One then simplifies the problem by deciding to ignore one or more of the variables. The plan generated to solve the simpler problem can be used as a base for developing a plan for the original problem.

Each of these methods—these metaplans—may or may not be appropriate in a particular problem situation. But chances are that one of them will fit or at least provide insight into most of the problems one may need to solve. Teaching them as overall strategies and giving students ample opportunity to experiment with how to apply them and to decide whether they will work can be a useful technique.

We have moved from a consideration of simple stimulus-response learning through more complex patterns of interaction up to a discussion of highly abstract levels of conceptualization. Before we shift our focus from acquiring information to storing and retrieving that information, we would do well to remind ourselves of the process quality of all learning, simple or complex. We, as organisms, are in a constant state of interchange with our environment; we affect our surroundings, and our surroundings affect us. The process is never complete, and learning is never complete. We do not learn fixed, finished things so much as we learn to see, to use, to do, and to be—fitting all those learnings into the ongoing stream of our existence.

Henry and Brown, in the course of their research, developed a series of propositions about concepts that can be a model for learning in general and especially for higher-level learning. Henry and Brown capture, in these propositions, some of the quality of process and interrelatedness that is so important and yet so easy to lose sight of. I can think of no better way to close this chapter than to quote Henry and Brown's (n.d.) list. Take it seriously. It nearly says it all.

1.  A concept is best learned through the progressive development of meaning rather than as products or finished definitions.
2.  The strategy of concept development is best acquired by exploration (heuristics) rather than by step-by-step direction (algorithmics).
3.  A concept is best developed as it serves to harmonize more and more cases and discriminates among these cases. A concept is not a storing up of many cases.
4.  A concept is best developed within a stated or explicit frame or situation.
5.  A concept becomes better "understood" as it is used as a tool in the analysis of successive situations or sets or as a hypothesis to guide strategy in a series of varying situations or events or cases or other concepts.
6.  A concept can be said to be "understood" when it can be engaged in the interpretation of situations more and more unlike the situation in which it was first learned.
7.  A concept becomes still further "understood" as it can be a means of incorporating other concepts into it, or other concepts be distinguished from it.
8.  A concept is best "understood" when it is sought within, or a place is discovered for it in, a pattern or structure, when it itself becomes an element in a structure.
9.  A concept can be said to be attained when it emerges from an inquiry

as a principle that fulfills certain stated conditions set down beforehand; but it is never closed, never fully learned [pp. 121–122].

## QUESTIONS FOR UNDERSTANDING

1.  Many children discover, sometime during their first year in school,
    that the letters of the alphabet combine in different ways to form
    words. Relate this discovery process to Piaget's ideas about assimila-
    tion and accommodation.
2.  Throughout their public school careers, children interact with each
    other. How would two preoperational children differ (in peer relation-
    ships) from two concrete-operational children? From two formal-
    operational children?
3.  A small Indiana high school offers a course called Knowing Nature, in
    which a major objective is that students learn to recognize local plants,
    animals, insects, and birds. How might what you have learned about
    positive and negative instances of concepts be used in teaching such a
    course?
4.  History, civics, and geography classes should be designed to prepare
    students to understand current world events and to formulate their
    own opinions about national policy. How can the teacher best facili-
    tate such transfer from classroom to real-world affairs?
5.  In the latter part of the chapter, four general heuristics (problem-
    solving strategies) are presented. Discuss how each of these might or
    might not be applicable in (a) solving a story problem in math, (b) fig-
    uring out how to change a typewriter ribbon, (c) designing the set for a
    stage production of a musical comedy, or (d) writing a series of lesson
    plans for a junior high school health unit.

# Chapter 5

# Memory

In one sense, we have been studying memory throughout the first part of this book. Learning something, whether the something is simple or complex, implies remembering it; after all, if you don't remember, then you can hardly be said to have learned. But our study of memory thus far has been only by implication; we have not addressed ourselves to just what is involved in remembering, or what happens when we forget or remember incorrectly, or how our memory capacities can be enhanced. These sorts of concerns form the basis for the present chapter.

As you have read through the preceding chapters, you have noticed the progression from the more simple and outwardly observable learning behaviors through the more complex ones, in which the observer must infer what is going on in the learner's head. With memory, this sort of inference becomes even more necessary. No one has ever "seen" a memory (though, as we shall discover, physiologists have tried hard to discover the physical basis of memory and are, in some cases, close to doing so); we must infer the mental structures and processes involved in memory from the individual's external behavior. The strict behaviorist deplores this kind of inference and would have us deal only with what can be observed and recorded. Yet, if we are to have a useful understanding of how people remember, we have to deal with ideas about what goes on inside the mind. Paivio (1971) points out that this inside-outside conflict has been a theme in psychological research for many years: "Mental variables have been repeatedly thrown out because there was no place for them in stimulus-response psychology, but they repeatedly find their way in again in one form or another because they are necessary to a full account of behavior" (p. 6). We must be careful, though, to distinguish the observable from the hypothetical and to remember that descriptions and hypotheses about memories do not (at this point, at least) refer to physical structures; they are merely descriptions of processes that we find easier to talk about if we use concrete analogies.

Just as we find it easier to talk about mental processes as if they related to actual structures or locations, so also we find it easier to chop up the various things our brains do and talk about them one at a time: thus we have looked at stimulus-response learning, at imitation, at talking, at problem solving, and now at memory. But we certainly don't do these things separately. In our day-to-day functioning we are busy with all of them simultaneously, and each kind of activity influences all the others. Memory, as Jenkins (1974) points out, involves all the other processes— perception, comprehension, problem solving, and stimulus-response learning. The simple act of reading a word on this page is in fact a highly complex synthesis of looking at a stimulus, converting it to meaningful form, comparing it with other similar forms that you have encountered before, deciding whether and how it relates to those other forms, dealing with it accordingly—and carrying on a host of other activities (holding the book, sitting in a chair, deciding when to break for lunch, noticing that someone else has just walked into the room) at the same time. These activities are all important; they all form the context within which memories are laid down. There is simply no way that we can talk about them all at once; we have to tear them apart, artificially, and deal with them as if they were separate processes. Let's try to remind ourselves occasionally, though, that memory—like any other psychological function—doesn't happen by itself; it is in reality an intertwined and indissociable part of the whole complex miracle of thought.

## THE PHYSICAL BASES OF MEMORY

Although most of what I shall have to say about memory involves processes and analogies rather than physical structures, a great deal of research is being conducted to find the true physical basis for memory. This interest is certainly understandable: after all, when we remember something we store it in the brain, and a physical change somewhere in the brain must cause or result from or be concomitant with that storage. Research in this area has been carried out for many years; to date the findings are exciting but tantalizing; one has a so-near-but-yet-so-far feeling that researchers are just on the edge of breaking through the mystery.

### Electrical and Chemical Changes

While it is certainly beyond the scope of this book to deal in any comprehensive way with the physiology of learning and memory, I can at least mention a few of the major areas of interest and research. One of the most long standing of such areas is the patterns of electrical activity in the brain.

It has been known for more than a hundred years that the nervous impulse is electrical, that messages travel to and from the brain along the nerves in the form of an electrical current. It was only natural to extend this knowledge to thoughts and memory, to look for electrical charges or patterns of charges that would correspond to mental activity. But electrical phenomena are evanescent, quickly changing, while a memory can last for years; how then could long-term memories be stored electrically? Out of such reasoning gradually grew the notion that there may be two forms of memory, one short term and quickly changing, and the other more permanent. A number of researchers came to think of short-term memory as a transitory process, perhaps mediated by reverberating circuits, which give rise ultimately to unidentified long-term physical structures (Iversen, 1973).

While the reverberating-circuits notion is still considered by many to be a reasonable hypothesis about how short-term memory works, it has received less attention in recent years than have other notions about brain functioning. One such newer notion has to do with the *synapse*—the point at which a nervous impulse transfers itself from one nerve to another on its way to or from or within the brain. The nerve cells do not actually touch each other, and so the electrical current has to jump across a tiny gap when it reaches a synapse. Recent research has suggested that as a result of learning the receiving fibers in the synapse change so as to be more sensitive to incoming impulses. The result is that the nervous impulse traverses the synapse more quickly and easily. Receiver sensitivity increases for a while after the initial learning and then goes down again; the rate at which it increases depends on the amount of initial learning (Deutsch, 1973). What we have here, then, is another bit of evidence for a short-term, temporary physical change that corresponds to the initial laying down of a new idea or behavior.

The synapse is essentially bathed in liquids, through which the nervous impulse travels as it jumps from sending nerve to receiving nerve. Since it is well known that some liquids conduct electricity more readily than others, it seems reasonable to ask whether the variable sensitivity we have just described might not be—at least in part—related to the chemical composition of these liquids. From here it is only a step to ask about the overall chemistry of the brain: are there ongoing chemical changes that relate to memory and learning? Unfortunately, in order to look at patterns of chemical activity in the brain, it is usually necessary to kill the experimental subject—which makes it exceedingly difficult to study subsequent brain activity! A somewhat easier method is to look at the effects of introducing known chemicals into the brain or bloodstream. That is, instead of allowing the subject to learn something and then looking for changes in brain chemistry, researchers change the brain chemistry and look for the effects of those changes on memory. And here, too, has been found evidence for more than one kind of memory. Learning can be interfered with chemically, and it can be stimulated chemically. If we chemically disrupt a memory shortly after it has been formed, that memory is lost; but it can be regained if we chemically stimulate the nervous system soon enough. If we wait too long, no amount of stimulation can bring back what was lost. These results suggest that some form of *template,* which can accomplish retrieval, survives after disruption and decays over approximately a 6-hour period. It can be reactivated, however, if the central nervous system is stimulated during this period (Dawson & McGaugh, 1973). We can only assume that this template is somehow, in the normal course of things, transferred to more permanent form before it decays.

## Protein Changes

But what could be the nature of this more permanent form? The most likely answer at this point seems to be that long-term memory depends on a change in the protein structure of the cells. A few years ago there was a wave of excitement and enthusiasm when researchers reported the "cannibal" transfer of memory. Flatworms (a primitive sort of research subject) were trained to respond to a light signal. They were then killed, ground up, and fed to untrained flatworms, who proceeded to display the same learned response to the light as had been taught to their recent dinner. This result, if it held up, would be nearly indisputable proof that learning—memory— is laid down in the cell structure; the worms that ingested the changed cells

THE HAM WAS DELICIOUS DARLING.......AND IT'S LEFT ME SOME REMARKABLE MEMORIES OF LIFE IN A PIG-STY......!

of their colleagues incorporated those cells into their own physiology and thus acquired the same learning. Unfortunately, other researchers have been unable to duplicate these original results, so the evidence is not nearly as straightforward as one would have hoped (and there are no immediate plans underway to chop up old professors and serve them in sandwiches at the Student Union).

There is, however, little doubt now that long-term memory does involve protein formation. Minute amounts of new protein are formed, probably within minutes of a new learning or perception. This new protein has been shown to be critical in the retention of the new information but much less important in the retrieval or use of older learnings. *Bioassay methods,* in which cells of trained animals are extracted and treated, and then injected into naïve animals, allow more control over which parts of the cell are to be studied than do the cannibal studies. So far, these studies have supported the relationship between brain proteins and memory; more specifically, they relate learning to RNA and DNA—the very compounds that are now known to be responsible for passing on genetic information from one generation to the next.

Again, one has that breath-holding feeling, that sense of being at the edge of discovering what makes our memory work. And yet, we are still so ignorant: the processes to be studied are incredibly complex; the physical changes are minute; and as soon as researchers learn to control one part of the problem, they discover two or three new things that might be interfering with or influencing their work. It is terribly exciting, and frustratingly slow; and it will probably be years or decades before we can begin to build the bridge between this area of research and the tasks of teachers and learners.

## HOW DO MEMORY PROCESSES WORK?

### The Flow of Memory

With at least a general picture of what may be happening physically as the brain receives and stores a memory pattern or trace, let's turn now to a more functional description. It is thought that there are three major memory processes: the sensory register, the short-term memory, and the long-term memory. Each of these, in turn, may have several different parts or subprocesses. The sensory register is the place or point (it's difficult to find a word to use here since we don't know the location of the sensory register) at which information is first received by the nervous system. Information stays in the sensory register for less than a second, and the individual may not ever know that the information has been there. It is as if the sensory register were a kind of dumping bin, into which is poured all the stimulus information that a given sense modality (vision, hearing, and so forth) is capable of receiving. Only the small portion of information that is attended to is retained, and the rest spills out again almost as fast as it is poured in.

Even in that fraction of a second, however, a great deal of processing of information takes place. In the case of visual information, pattern analysis occurs: the contours of an object may be enhanced, lines and movement detected, and different colors separated and categorized. All this activity is preattentional; it goes on in the bin, before the individual attends to the percept and thereby transfers it from the sensory register into short-term memory.

Attending to a percept—taking it out of the bin—is equivalent to transforming it from a physical image to a psychological one (Norman, 1973). Instead of being a collection of lines and colors and movements, the percept becomes a thing, more or less similar to other things that I have attended to in the past. Consider again the example of reading a word on a page in a book. "A word (e.g., *plant)* is first of all a physical code which uniquely represents details of the structure of the print or accent in which it is presented. A hundred milliseconds or so later it is also represented as part of a 'name' which is in itself indifferent to mode of presentation. Still later it may be related to semantic structures having to do with flowers and vegetables or with labor unions and factories" (Posner & Warren, 1972, p. 25).

The transfer of a memory trace from short-term to long-term memory is even less clear cut than is the transition from sensory register to short-term memory. Indeed, as we shall see later, some workers (in spite of the physiological evidence) question whether there are really two qualitatively different kinds of memory. It should suffice to say that after the memory trace enters long-term memory, it becomes stronger and more resistant to interference, and it seems to settle into a relatively complex interrelationship with other memories. In this more settled form, a memory may be retained for many years with little change or loss of information. There is some evidence, according to J. H. Johnson (1974), for two different kinds of long-term memory. One form, which he calls *episodic,* refers to one's own personal past—the things I remember having happened to me—and is organized according to when and where they happened. The other, the *semantic,* is a more formal, cognitive kind of store—these are the things I know about the world. A given event may result in traces being laid down in both stores: if someone calls me an iconoclast and I go home and look up the word in a dictionary to find out whether I've been insulted, I may remember both the incident (episodic memory) and the meaning of the word (semantic memory). I retrieve and use information from the semantic memory constantly, as I talk or listen or react to my environment according to its known (by me) properties. And I'm not aware of dipping into that store for the information I need. The act of retrieval from semantic memory is not usually entered into episodic memory and is never entered into semantic memory. Episodic memory is clearly a more fluid and flexible system; things drop in and drop out, recollections ebb and flow. The semantic memory, in contrast, is more like a constantly used and efficient filing system in which an item may occasionally be misplaced but in which, for the most part, everything is kept right where it is needed.

My description so far shows information flowing into the organism through three major stages, as shown in the upper part of Figure 5-1. But

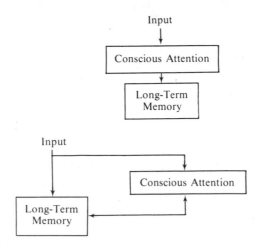

*Figure 5-1.* Two representations of the flow of information between input and long-term memory. (From "Traces, Concepts, and Conscious Constructions," by M. I. Posner and R. E. Warren. In A. W. Melton and E. Martin (Eds.), *Coding Processes in Human Memory.* Copyright 1972 by V. H. Winston & Sons, Inc. Reprinted by permission of the publisher, Hemisphere Publishing Corporation, Washington, D.C.)

(as usual) the process is not quite that simple. Not only does new information flow into and affect the old, but the old also affects the ways in which the new is coded and perceived. The lower part of Figure 5-1 is a more accurate representation of the flow of memory. This is the Piagetian accommodation-assimilation idea again, in a new context. Short-term and long-term memory interact with each other, and both interact with the sensory register. These interactions are affected, in turn, by situational factors: how fast the information is coming in and at what intensity, how similar it is to other information being received or already in storage, and so forth.

When new information is stored in long-term memory, it must also be cross-referenced. Stored information does no good at all unless it can be retrieved later; the storage location must be capable of being reached by various pathways, so that one idea reminds us of another. The cross-referencing process also involves interaction between the new information and the old: "The memory system is tightly interconnected with itself. Stored concepts, images, and ideas are all associated with one another. The acquisition of new information requires that the new be inserted properly into the cross-referencing of the old" (Norman, 1973, p. 411). The old memories are needed to decide what the new percept is and what shall be done with it; the new memory readjusts our understanding of older ones and requires that new pathways for association and retrieval of ideas be set up.

The raw stimulus data that enter the sensory register are worked over, digested, transformed, and (sometimes) stored in their new form in long-term memory. From that single statement we can begin to understand why there is no such thing as "just memory," any more than there is "just perception" or "just concept formation." The three processes are parts of one activity, and the activity cannot be carried out in the absence of any of its parts. To perceive is to conceptualize and to store (for however short a time); to remember is to have perceived and conceptualized; conceptualization draws upon and is a part of both perception and memory. Let's move on now to look at some of the more specific aspects of the memory system, but let's keep reminding ourselves that the separation of memory from other cognitive processes is only an artificial one.

## Questions about Memory

As in so many areas of psychology, research on memory has tended to focus on a number of rather specific questions. We shall look at three of these questions now, both because they may shed light on the nature of the memory process itself and because they have particular relevance for teaching.

*Short-Term versus Long-Term Memory.* As I mentioned, there has been a continuing discussion about the differences (if any) between long-term and short-term memory. We have already looked briefly at some of the physiological evidence that would seem to point at two different processes—one electrochemical and the other involving the creation of (protein) substances in the brain—that may account for or at least accompany the laying down of memory traces. Studies of amnesia—forgetting—also seem to indicate two different kinds of memory. More recent memories seem to be considerably more fragile than older ones, in that they can be disrupted more easily. A blow on the head may produce *retrograde amnesia,* in which recent memory is disrupted while older patterns are unaffected. (This phenomenon has enriched the plots of mystery novels for years.) Conversely, in other forms of amnesia a person is quite unable to retrieve information from long-term episodic memory but can remember recent events normally. This is the pattern seen in the *classic-amnesia* victim who is discovered wandering around with no knowledge of who he is or what he has been doing prior to a specific event. Both retrograde- and classic-amnesia victims may recover spontaneously, although there may be permanent loss of memory for short time periods (in retrograde amnesia, the period of time immediately preceding the blow is least likely to be recovered) or particular events. The fact that one kind of memory can be seriously impaired while the other continues to function normally, however, does suggest that we are dealing with two different systems (Warrington & Weiskrantz, 1973).

However, some theorists are increasingly inclined to consider short-term and long-term memory as simply two end points on a continuum of memory processing—that is, to believe that a memory trace enters the brain and is gradually changed over a period of time. These theorists argue that a two-memory theory would require two memory traces, one for short- and one for long-term memory. This model seems cumbersome and unnecessary; the data "are equally consistent with a single-trace hypothesis, though this single trace must be viewed as undergoing a consolidation process that progressively reduces its rate of forgetting and its susceptibility to amnestic agents with increasing age" (Wickelgren, 1974, p. 775). In other words, a percept is not entered into a short-term store, processed, and then transferred to a different kind of storage; rather, each memory trace is gradually changed into a more integrated and durable form.

Both schools of thought here agree on one point: that new (recent) memories are more fragile, more easily lost, than old. The concern of the teacher lies in finding ways to facilitate the processing of important material through this early stage and of integrating it into the more durable storage characteristic of long-term memory. We do know that items not processed in some way are lost rather quickly. That telephone number you look up and remember just long enough to dial is a good example. Losing this kind of information is extremely functional; you would certainly not want to clutter up your memory with every phone number you ever called, every face you had ever seen, every conversation you had ever heard. Indeed, on some occasions the ability to *forget*—to destroy a memory trace —is quite valuable (and forgetting is something that we do not know how to do in a conscious and directed way). At any rate, whether we think of it as transfer into long-term memory or as a consolidation process, selective and efficient storage of appropriate information is one large part of what school learning is all about.

*Recognition versus Recall.* Once information has been stored—no matter how that storage is accomplished—it is of use only if it can be retrieved. The name that you know but just can't quite remember is of no more use to you than the pot of jam that you can't find in your kitchen cupboard. Retrieval, then, is an essential aspect of memory and one that has received a great deal of research attention.

More or less by accident, two major techniques have been developed for the study of memory in general and retrieval in particular. One of these is the *recognition* technique: the subject is exposed to stimulus material, is allowed to rest for an interval (the interval may or may not be filled with specific activity), and is then shown a new set of material. Some of the material in the new set is identical to the original, and some is not; the subject must indicate which material he has seen before. In other words, he is asked to recognize the things he learned in the first session. The other major technique is *recall;* here a subject is exposed to information and, after a time interval, is asked to reproduce it as accurately as he can. Most of the studies using both recognition and recall techniques have involved words as the stimulus materials; they are easily quantifiable and may be varied in meaningfulness and familiarity—two characteristics that seem to be quite important in determining how easy a thing is to remember.

A list of words can have many other attributes as well—length, speed of presentation, number of repetitions, physical manner of presentation. Some of these attributes seem to be particularly important in recognition memory and others in recall memory; some are important for both. Underwood (1969) argues that some stimulus characteristics are used primarily for discrimination—to distinguish between one thing and another (similar) thing—and that others are used primarily for retrieval. Retrieval characteristics serve as hooks (or addresses) that allow us to fish up an item of information that has been stored away in memory. Recognition (discrimination) characteristics, however, do not locate the information; they are merely cues for differentiating among items in the perceptual field or in conscious imagination. Temporal cues (how fast a list was presented), spatial cues (how large the type was or what color the background was), and frequency cues (how often it was presented) are thought to be used in recognition but not recall. If you show a subject a list of words printed in various-sized type and in different-colored letters and later ask him to pick out of another list those words you showed him before, his performance will be much better if the recognition items on the new list are in the same color and type size as they were in the original. If you use a recall technique, however, he will remember many of the words without being able to tell you the color or size of type in which he first saw them (Underwood, 1972).

It would seem that the characteristics of the stimulus most important for recognition have to do with its physical appearance rather than its abstract meaning. Paivio (1971) has taken this reasoning a step further and proposes that the more concrete a stimulus item is, the more readily it will be recognized later. His research bears this proposal out: "Recognition increases from abstract words, to concrete words, to pictures. These findings are generally consistent with the interpretation that concreteness is related somehow to distinctiveness, or differentiation" (p. 184). In a recall situation, however, the most important variable is how meaningful or familiar the item is to the subject. It is as if the more meaningful items fit more easily into the established associations already in memory; they can be located (addressed) via a number of different pathways. Unfamiliar items (and unfamiliarity, in most instances, implies meaninglessness) do not have these multiple associations all ready for them; they may be stored (and recognized, in a recognition test), but they are not easily recalled.

Before we decide that recognition and recall are two different kinds of activities, though, let's examine that notion more closely. When I am presented with a list of words and asked to learn them, am I learning them for the first time? Of course not, if they are common words. Rather, I am supposed to tag words that are already in my vocabulary with a symbol that means "this word was on the list in that silly experiment" or something to that effect. If the test involves recognition, I will be shown a new list of words; I can look at each of them in my own memory store and determine whether it has been tagged. If, however, I am asked to reproduce the list, I must search around until I find a tagged word and hope that that first word will suggest other tagged words. Recall requires the building up of associative paths among items on a list, while recognition does not. But both processes require that we access the storage location of each item on the list. In recognition, we are given a set of individual cues in the form of a new list; for each cue word, we merely access the appropriate storage location and look for a tag. But in free recall there must be some way for one item to suggest another, for we haven't time to search through all the words we know.

Looked at in this way, recognition and recall can be seen as differing mainly in the amount of external cueing or help given the rememberer in finding the addresses of list items. In recognition, he is given the maximum possible help; he is told where (what) the item is and must determine only whether it has been tagged. In free recall, he is given no help at all; he must establish his own system of associations to get from one item to the next. There are ways of providing tasks intermediate on this continuum. We can pair each item to be learned with a cue word and, at test time, present the cue word and ask the subject to recall the associated item. *Paired-associate learning,* as this technique has come to be called, may be the most widely used of all the verbal learning methods. Tulving and Watkins (1973) have demonstrated the continuum notion in an even more direct way. They asked groups of subjects to learn the words on a list and then asked them to recall the lists under varying cue conditions. One group got no help at all, another was provided with the first letter of each word on the list, another with the first two letters of each word, and so on. As you would predict, performance steadily improved as the number of cue letters increased. In both recall and recognition, Tulving and Watkins point out, the rememberer has to access memory and look at what is in the appropriate storage location. The difference lies in how much help he has in getting there.

Most of our real-life memory tasks are intermediate on the recall-recognition continuum. We seldom are called upon to decide whether we have seen an item on some previous list, and neither do we often have to reproduce a list with no cues at all. Rather, we find ourselves trying to access memory locations on the basis of one or a few externally provided associations: "What is the capital of Florida?" "What is the name that goes with that face?" "How can I find the best word to fit in this sentence?" It would seem that one of the most important jobs of teacher and learner alike is building retrieval systems, establishing pathways or address indexes that allow us to get at the information we store away.

*Pictures versus Words.* Thus far, we have been dealing almost exclusively with ways in which we remember and retrieve verbal information. But what about nonlanguage inputs? Do we code all stimuli into words and then remember the words, or do we sometimes store both an image and the words describing it? A growing body of evidence (Salthouse, 1974; Paivio, 1974) suggests that the latter is closer to the truth: when we see an object or a picture of an object, we process and store both the visual image and a word code for that image; moreover, the storage systems are separate and partially independent of each other. Paivio showed subjects three different information sets: a list of words, with each one presented twice; a set of pictures, with each picture presented twice; a set of words and matched pictures (for example, the word *dog* and a picture of a dog). Seeing the words or the pictures twice increased the amount of recall over that of a control group who saw them only once; when the items were spaced—that is, with intervening material between the first and second presentation of a word or picture—the amount of recall doubled over that of the control group. But with the word-picture list, the amount of recall doubled even without spacing. Paivio concludes "Pictures and their printed names set up quite different memory traces, either of which can be decoded to yield the same nominal response during recall" (p. 509).

On the basis of this sort of evidence, Paivio has developed a *dual-coding hypothesis.* This hypothesis assumes not only that verbal information and imaginal (picture) information are stored differently, but that they are also differentially available for retrieval. Images are more easily retrieved as they become more concrete. If we are trying to remember the word *dog,* we store both the word and an image of a dog. Later, both the word and the image can be accessed in trying to retrieve the image. If the word is *freedom,* the image is fuzzy at best, and recall is not as good for such abstract words. We have already seen that concreteness is important in recognition memory; apparently it is also important for recall. Among meaningful stimuli, "the meaning attribute that most consistently and strongly predicts recall is abstractness-concreteness, or imagery value: Objects and pictures are better remembered than concrete nouns, which in turn are superior to abstract nouns" (Paivio, 1971, p. 178).

We tend to think of much of what students are expected to remember as being essentially verbal information. The dual-coding hypothesis may well lead us to reexamine that assumption. Much information that is reported verbally may be stored in image form. Consider, for example, the number of times we resort to a chart or a diagram or even an informal squiggle to explain an idea or relationship. Is the diagram a new construction of the verbal idea, or are our words a (partially successful) way of communicating what was originally stored in image form? If information is naturally stored in memory in visual form and if (as Paivio and others suggest) such imaginal codes are often more easily accessed and retrieved, then perhaps we should begin to develop techniques for building more accurate visual images. The student who can conceptualize a relationship (the relationship between energy and mass, for instance, in physics) as a concrete image of some sort may be better able to remember and use it at a later date than the student who can conceptualize it only verbally. Verbal coding, Paivio suggests, is used effectively when the codes are readily available (that is, when the ideas are already familiar ones in verbal form) and when the information is not easily stored nonverbally. But verbal coding need not be used if the subject has good visual memory, if the stimuli are simple shapes or familiar objects that can be stored as uncoded images, or if the verbal code is not readily available in the subject's response repertoire. Improving visual memory through practice and encouraging students to develop their imagery skills would appear to have considerable potential as means of facilitating recall of complex information.

## FACTORS IN MEMORY

### Encoding

In the preceding section, I frequently used the term *processing* to refer in a deliberately vague way to whatever is done to an input to get it into a form in which it can be stored. It is time now to look at this processing idea more closely. To begin, I'm going to exchange the vague "processing" for the more precise term *encoding*. The encoding process has at least four major aspects, and different workers have chosen to emphasize one or another of these in their research. But all four are important and, indeed, almost inseparable. Encoding involves *selection* of important aspects of a stimulus, *rewriting* those stimulus parts so that they form a knowable whole, *categorizing* the information according to its attributes or characteristics, and *elaborating* or exaggerating key characteristics (Bower, 1972). Let's use an example to see how all these fit together. I'm sitting at my desk, typing; a few moments ago I looked at my notes to check a reference. I encoded that information, and now I can remember it—I know what the notes said. But I don't have a line-by-line, detail-for-detail picture of that particular page of my notebook. Something has happened to the information; it is not now stored in the same form as I received it. How did I encode it for storage? For one thing, I *selected* the parts that were important to me; I didn't try to remember the state of my handwriting or the color of the paper or even the order in which the words were strung together. I *rewrote* the information into a kind of personal code, only partly verbal, in such a way that the code would allow me to reconstruct the general idea when I needed it. I assigned the information to *categories:* research study, carried out after 1970, dealing with visual memory, and so forth. There are probably a large number of other categories too, of which I'm only partly aware, like interesting research design or used human subjects or even complicated and took up a lot of room on the page. The important thing here is that each of these categories can be an *access path;* that is, later on the cue "recent research" or "interesting information about visual imagery" may be all I need to fish out my encoding of this particular set of information. To facilitate the process of retrieval from memory even more, I have *elaborated* on some of these characteristics: my memory code has heightened or even embroidered some at the expense of others, so that I now have a kind of caricature of the original information.

The encoding process probably takes place at a number of different levels. As we have seen, a certain amount of selection and elaboration takes place in the sensory register before the stimulus even enters conscious awareness. This is almost certainly true for all sense modalities, not just for vision; and there is strong evidence to suggest that each sense modality has its own short-term storage and processing area, in which information is further refined as it enters consciousness (Nilsson, 1974; Warrington & Weiskrantz, 1973). Just when this entrance into consciousness occurs is difficult to say; it is probably a gradual rather than an all-or-nothing phenomenon, and its timing appears to vary depending on the intensity of the stimulus and the degree of alertness of the individual. The highly alert individual, who expects to be presented with important information, becomes aware of a stimulus quickly and does a lot of encoding at a conscious level. The less alert individual is not consciously aware of the stimulus as quickly, and more of his encoding is done automatically and without conscious awareness.

*Encoding and Meaning.* When a verbal stimulus—a given word—is presented to a subject, he may attend to it in two different ways: he may look at it as an image, a pattern, having certain physical characteristics such as size or shape or color; or he may see it according to its meaning for him. Other things being equal, literate subjects are more likely to react on the basis of personal meaning. Look at the word *ball.* Was your immediate impression that of a shape that was tall on both ends and dipped down in the middle, or of two more or less rounded shapes followed by two skinny ones? More likely, your response was to the meaning of the word, as a round object that is thrown or kicked or caught. When we code a word for memory, we prime one or more of its features to give us a handle for retrieving it the next time we need it; the way in which you encoded the word *ball* determined which of its features are now primed in your memory trace of that stimulus event.

We differentiate items in memory to the degree that we encode them or group them differently (Bjork, 1972). How many times did the word *ball* appear in the preceding paragraph? If you can't remember, you probably threw each successive occurrence of the word into the same storage location. If you did remember, chances are you did so by reconstructing the paragraph in some way; you encoded the word *ball* differently according to the sentence context in which it occurred each time.

Trying to remember how many times the word *ball* appeared in a paragraph is much easier than trying to remember which words were the first in each line or which prepositions were used. We are particularly sensitive to (that is, we encode on the basis of) semantic aspects of words—to their meaning—and are much less sensitive to their physical or grammatical characteristics (Wickens, 1972).

Whatever the characteristics upon which you base your encoding of a stimulus, those are the pathways by means of which you later retrieve it. It stands to reason, then, that the more characteristics that are encoded (or primed), the easier it is to retrieve the information later. If I want to remember that Salem is the capital of Oregon, I will do better to encode Salem as the name of a city, as the home of Abraham Lincoln (in another state, of course), as a kind of cigarette, and as a location halfway between Eugene and Portland than to just try to remember it as the capital of Oregon. The more characteristics I can encode, the better my chances for later retrieval. Underwood (1969, p. 570) uses a familiar experience to further illustrate this *alternative-coding* notion: "Multiple attributes always allow more than one route to a target memory. Most have had the experience of being unable to recall a name, or a term, only to have it suddenly 'pop into mind' at a later time. It may be presumed that an attribute, not previously present, was elicited by the changed situation and that this attribute was responsible for the recall."

*Chunking.* Earlier, I used as an example the way in which I encoded a segment of information from my notes; more recently, I've been talking about remembering a single word or fact. Intuitively, there would seem to be important differences in these two processes. Miller (1956) has amassed a great deal of data from different kinds of experiments, all suggesting that humans can hold in memory only a small number of unrelated items of information. The number differs slightly depending upon the kind of information we are dealing with, but in general it is well below ten; people can seldom repeat a string of more than ten numbers or remember more than ten pictures of unrelated items or differentiate more than ten different tones. The key word here is *unrelated.* Most of the things that we try to remember are not unrelated; on the contrary, they are closely interrelated. By building relationships, we organize bits of information into larger

chunks; later, these chunks can be retrieved and broken down again into their component parts. "Since the memory span is a fixed number of chunks, we can increase the number of bits of information that it contains simply by building larger and larger chunks, each chunk containing more information than before" (Miller, 1956, p. 93). In remembering the information from my notebook, I do not recall a set of isolated facts; I remember a system of chunks and subchunks, organized into a superchunk, which is hooked to the various attributes I mentioned earlier.

You can easily test this notion for yourself. Look around the room you are in right now, and write down the names of 20 or 30 things you see. Then take a few minutes to read the list over several times, but don't make any effort to organize the items on it. Tomorrow, see how many of those names you remember. Then make a new list, but this time organize the names of the objects into groups, each containing about five names. Use any kind of organizational scheme you want—color, size, location in the room. You will find that when you test your memory this time, you will recall first the categories you used—far left corner, yellow things, things that begin with the letter *r*—and then you will decode each one into the items that composed it. N. F. Johnson (1973) refers to these kinds of chunks as opaque codes and maintains that even though each chunk is composed of definite parts (and can be decomposed into those parts), they are maintained in memory as a single, whole unit. The decoding process requires an active effort after the opaque chunk has been retrieved from memory.

The notions of alternative codes and of chunking have important implications for school learning. Memory increases directly with the number of alternative memory codes available for an item (Paivio, 1971), and it is also directly related to the skill with which we can chunk information and to the degree of interrelatedness of those chunks. Teachers can present material in such a way as to maximize these factors and can help students develop their own ability to process information accordingly. We have seen that spacing the presentations of an item is important for good recall. Paivio (1974) suggests that when the second occurrence of a bit of information closely follows the first presentation, the learner/observer fails to encode it separately; he just dumps it into the same memory bin as the first one went into. No alternative codes are developed, and the repetition is useless. Appropriate spacing, then, is an aspect of teaching that should be given a great deal of attention in classroom activities and in study assignments. Similarly, alternative coding depends upon attending to a number of different characteristics or qualities or association potentials of a stimulus, and the teacher can emphasize these characteristics in presenting material. Ultimately the goal must be to train the student to do this sort of priming for himself; such training can be accomplished both by example and by direct teaching. Students should be encouraged to look at ideas and relationships in as many different ways as possible and to build conceptual bridges between apparently unrelated sets of information. In this way, both the number of alternative codes and the amount of interrelationship between chunks and superchunks can be increased.

## Levels of Encoding

If long-term memory depends on the number of categories or associations or alternative codes that an item acquires and on the degree of association it has with other items, then it would seem that the more thoroughly one encodes new information, the better it will be recalled. Craik and Lockhart (1972, p. 675) studied levels of processing and concluded that new information is normally processed, or encoded, in a relatively predictable pattern: "After the stimulus has been recognized, it may undergo further processing by enrichment or elaboration. . . . Similar levels of processing exist in the perceptual analysis of sounds, sights, smells and so on. Analysis proceeds through a series of sensory stages to levels associated with matching or pattern recognition and finally to semantic-associative stages of stimulus enrichment." Other workers, too, have noted the progression from physical characteristics of a stimulus to deeper levels of meaning and association (Nelson, Wheeler, Borden, & Brooks, 1974; Paivio, 1971). Paivio, in particular, has been interested in the relationship between early, concrete kinds of coding and later, more abstract imagery. He points out that there is a parallel between the rapid encoding of an item of information by an individual, on the one hand, and the development of encoding techniques over one's entire lifetime, on the other. In both instances, encoding moves from the concrete to the abstract, from emphasis on physical characteristics of stimuli to emphasis on meaning, usually verbally mediated. It is important, though, to remember that one kind of symbolization does not replace another. "Instead, it may be assumed that new modes are added to the symbolic repertoire of the individual and that their utilization is a function of situational demands, just as their original development presumably occurred in the interests of utility. Furthermore, it is likely that the modes continually interact in their functioning" (Paivio, 1971, p. 27).

*Familiarity.* The more familiar and meaningful a stimulus is, the more compatible it is with existing cognitive structures and the more readily it can be encoded to a deep level. Try yourself out on the following sentences:

1. The most striking illustration of information provided by confidence intervals is shown in the charts of confidence limits for a binomial parameter.
2. John Adams recognized that laws rather than changeable emotions must be the foundation for the establishment of justice in the United States.
3. Teaching in an elementary or secondary school setting is a demanding and difficult task if it is done so as to maximize the potential of each child.

Having read them over once or twice, which do you think you will remember best? For most readers of this book, the last sentence will be the easiest to remember, and the first sentence the most difficult. You may argue that any differences in recall of these sentences is due simply to differences in difficulty—the last sentence is easy to understand, while the first sounds like gibberish. But that is precisely the point—the last sentence is "easy" because it is familiar and meaningful. To a statistician, the first sentence would seem simple and obvious and would be easily recalled, while the last sentence might strike him as typical education-ese and would not be remembered. Familiar material is easy to encode because it matches information that has already been encoded; it fits neatly into our chunk structure. Unfamiliar material has to be worked on harder; we either spend more time on it or let it slide by and thus fail to retain it as well.

Degree of familiarity also affects the way in which information is rehearsed. Rehearsal involves both bringing the stored items back into consciousness and constructing new association pathways for them—in other words, it is a form of encoding. Recall, depending as it does on depth of encoding, is greatly affected by the amount of rehearsal given an item. New and unfamiliar material requires a great deal of initial encoding, and the learner must concentrate rather exclusively on that information. More familiar material, in contrast, can be encoded more easily, so there is opportunity to simultaneously rehearse older, related information when processing familiar material. Thus not only is the familiar information fitted into existing structures, but the association paths among those structures are also strengthened (Nolan, 1973).

Incidentally, rehearsal frequency is probably responsible for a phenomenon of learning known as the primacy effect. In learning a list or a written passage, subjects generally tend to remember the first part *(primacy effect)* and the last part *(recency effect)* better than the middle section. The recency effect is probably caused by differences in stored-image intensity—that is, the most recently stored information has not had as much time to fade or decay—and in opportunity for subsequent stimuli to interfere with the information stored. (We shall discuss interference at greater length later in this chapter.) Using this kind of logic, though, we would expect the first items on a list to be the least well remembered—and just the opposite is often true. To explain this result, we must look at the rehearsal possibilities for the different items. The first items in a list or a written passage are stored, and there is opportunity to rehearse them while the rest of the material is being dealt with. "The primacy effect seems to be due entirely to the fact that the initial serial positions provide a convenient and near universally used basis for serial rehearsal" (Underwood, 1972, p. 12).

*Implications for Teaching.* If encoding and rehearsal (which involves encoding) are so fundamental in determining how well information is recalled, it seems obvious that the teacher must structure activities so as to encourage as much deep encoding as possible. One way to do this is to encourage students to form associations to information. Forming associations not only assists in establishing alternate encodings but also encourages one to deal with an item or a concept on increasingly deeper levels of meaning. Hall and Pierce (1974) found that both children and adults performed better on a memory test when they were told to form associations to the words on the list than when they were told just to repeat the words over and over again. Forming associations leads to organization. As I discover or create ways in which one bit of information reminds me of another, I am gradually constructing a system, an organizational pattern, among those bits of information. The more systematized the associations are—that is, the more they fall into an orderly pattern—the more they facilitate recall. Indeed, at least one group of researchers maintain that recall is almost completely dependent on organization. "To organize is, to a considerable extent, to remember. Active and consistent categorization is sufficient to yield a relatively high level of recall, and additional instructions to recall do not facilitate performance further" (Ornstein, Trabasso, & Johnson-Laird, 1974, p. 1017).

One way to get a student to organize material is to insist that he understand it. Understanding requires that new material be fitted into one's cognitive scheme, that it be made to relate to other things one knows or believes. Jenkins (1974) points out that, in any learning situation, if the task requires comprehension, the information is readily recalled. If we look at information that a child has "learned" and later "forgotten," it is likely that we will find that he did not understand the material but rather attempted to store it away in some sort of undigested and undifferentiated block. Well-understood material is seldom forgotten; and when it is lost, it is relatively easy to reacquire since it can be put back into a ready-made cognitive framework.

## Changes over Time

The organization and encoding of information is not a one-time-only process that ends when the information is placed in storage. Rather, it is ongoing. We have seen that processing occurs at all levels, from the sensory register through long-term memory. I have also mentioned that acquisition of new material affects the way in which the old is organized. Memory, then, is dynamic, constantly in a state of flux. Everything that I know (remember) at this instant is, to some degree, influenced by everything else I know; and what I know tomorrow won't be exactly the same as what I know now because it will have been affected by the new things I have learned.

*Adding to Memory.* As we acquire and store new information, we integrate it into the ongoing memory system. Sometimes a new fact is entered as an event in the episodic memory (I remember, for instance, reading the book by Paivio to which I have referred so often in this chapter), but often the event is not recorded; the new information is merely integrated into the old, and the resulting system continues as before. Over time, then, we tend to lose track of where a memory item has come from; all we have is one memory, which may have been built up from a number of sources over a long period (Loftus & Palmer, 1974). A study by Sulin and Dooling (1974) illustrates this phenomenon quite nicely. Subjects in this research were asked to read a biographical passage about either a famous person or a fictional character. Later, they were asked to identify information that came from the material they had read. Subjects who read about famous people (about whom they already had stored some information) had a higher false-recognition score than subjects who read about fictional characters. The real-people subjects thought they recognized information that had not, in fact, been included in the stories they had read. They had simply integrated the new material in the stories into what they already knew; when asked to indicate which material came from their recent reading, they were unable to differentiate the more recent information from that which they had stored before.

The memory process, then, is a kind of ongoing fusion that seems to occur over all sorts of memory stores. Words and their definitions fuse together; pictures melt and blend into one another; events widely separated in time merge into a single happening in memory. Jenkins (1974) asked subjects to listen to sentences describing various parts of a series of events. Their later recall of what they had heard indicated that the memory of the individual events had blurred; they recalled a composite of the entire sequence. "Once the fusion of strands into events has occurred . . . the subject cannot perform an analysis to recover the exact pattern of input that furnished support for the construction that he made" (p. 790).

As fusion, reorganization, and selective rehearsal continue, some aspects of a memory trace are emphasized more than others are. Information that relates most comfortably to the rest of one's cognitive system is likely to be enhanced and remembered; awkward or unnecessary details tend to drop out. The early research of Bartlett (1932) demonstrated this effect. Over time, his subjects tended to reconstruct a story that they had read into a kind of skeleton of the original. Like a skeleton, the details of this reconstruction became quite rigid; the retellings of the story came to assume a set, stereotyped form that changed less and less with each telling.

*Proactive Inhibition.* Memory traces not only are reorganized and stereotyped as a result of subsequent information but may also be interfered with and sometimes wiped out altogether. This kind of interference is known as *inhibition* and has been the subject of a great deal of psychological investigation. We discussed inhibition briefly in Chapter 1, in the context of simple stimulus-response learning; let's look at it now a bit more closely. Students of memory have been most interested in *proactive inhibition,* the form of memory interference in which a past learning or memory interferes with one's ability to learn (to lay down a memory trace) in the present. In one type of design for studying proactive inhibition, a group of subjects is asked to learn a list of words, while another group spends the same amount of time in a nonlearning activity such as stacking blocks or sorting cards. Next, both groups learn a second list (more or less similar to the original list learned by the first group). Both groups are then tested for their recall of the second list. Subjects who fill the first time block with a non-memory-related activity perform better on the recall test than subjects who have learned two sets of materials; and the more similar the original material is to the test list, the greater the differences between the two groups' performances.

Wickens (1970) explains the proactive-inhibition phenomenon in this way: "The process of perceiving a word involves encoding that word into positions within many categories; if a series of items comes from the same set of categories, they will interfere with each other and depress retention performance" (p. 3). In other words, when we try to retrieve a word from the test list, we may be able to find only items from the original list. It stands to reason that the more thoroughly the new material is learned, the less pro-

active interference there ought to be; and this is in fact the case. Also, interference tends to increase as the interval between test-list learning and the
effort to recall is increased (Keppel & Underwood, 1962).

The fact that interference increases as the interfering material becomes
more and more similar to the newly learned material supports the notion
that we fish out the wrong item because we enter the wrong associative
pathway. The more similar two items are, the more associations they share.
It would be fairly easy for the previously learned word *sofa* to interfere with
a newly learned *couch* since many of the associations you use to get to
couch will lead you to sofa just as easily. In contrast, *cathedral* will interfere very little with *couch* because they share few if any associations.

In order to investigate the relationships between different characteristics of memory traces, Wickens and his students carried out a series of
release-from-proactive-inhibition experiments. In these studies, subjects
learn a series of lists; over time, the amount of interference builds up and
performance gets worse and worse on each new list. At some point, a new
kind of list is introduced, one that differs from all the others on some characteristic. The subjects may have been learning lists of animal names, for
instance, and then be switched to kinds of furniture or names of famous
people. As expected, the more extreme the shift in list content, the greater
the amount of release from proactive inhibition—that is, the better one's
performance on the different list is. By varying the ways in which the lists of
words were similar, Wickens and others were able to determine the most
important characteristics by which memory items are coded. Our primary
codings (those that are later most easily retrieved) appear to be those that
relate to what the stimulus is—that is, the meaning of the categories we fit
it into. Also important is the evaluation we give it: "good" words like *true*
and *kindness* interfere with each other, but the interference disappears
when a list of words like *danger* and *evil* is learned. Similarly, interference
is reduced when the potency, or strength value, of the materials is switched;
"hard," "strong" words interfere with each other, as do "soft" words like
*moon* and *sweet;* but there is less interference between strong and soft
words.

What is now known about proactive inhibition has important implications for educational practice. First, we can minimize proactive interference in general—and thus facilitate retention—by spacing materials to be
learned. We should avoid asking students to perform several learning
tasks in a row, especially when the materials to be learned are at all similar.
Second, we must realize that similarity—and thus potential interference—
can be based on a number of different characteristics. Learning about the
Battle of Bunker Hill and learning about coal mining are conceptually different, but they are similar in that both are "strong" concepts. Recall is
best when to-be-learned information is varied not only in content but in
evaluative quality, strength, and "quickness" as well. (Compare learning
about tap dancing with learning about turtles, or compare practicing

speed-typing exercises with practicing an adagio passage in a piano concerto.) Finally, the poor recall performance of several students can be a diagnostic tool for the teacher: when a class does surprisingly poorly on a test, the teacher should look for possible proactive-inhibition effects in his classroom schedule and take steps to arrange activities differently.

*Other Effects.* Information does drop out of memory for reasons other than interference. There seems to be a simple decay process in memory storage; information that is not used or rehearsed gradually weakens over time. Little is known about how this process occurs. It is likely, though, that the decay has to do with association paths rather than with the memory trace itself, for things we haven't thought of for years can suddenly pop into mind with extraordinary vividness and clarity. What dissolves with disuse is the organization, the system that allows us to locate those things we have stored away. Thus active rehearsal of information does not serve as much to strengthen the memory itself as to clear out the pathway to that memory.

We have seen that two (partially) contradictory processes occur in memory over time. One involves the weakening of one's ability to recall; the less vivid the initial memory trace, and the less subsequent rehearsal and reorganization, the more rapidly the memory weakens or decays. There is also, however, a process of consolidation that occurs in memory. As memory traces become better organized and integrated, they become less vulnerable to interference—they become less fragile. Our overall memory store loses on the one hand, and gains on the other. And both the loss (gradual weakening over time) and the gain (more independence from interference effects) can be affected by our active, conscious efforts to rehearse and organize that which we particularly want to retain.

## Retrieval

No matter how strongly a memory trace is established in storage, it must be retrievable if it is to do us any good. We have all experienced the frustration of "knowing" something but being unable to bring that information out of storage. The ability to retrieve a bit of information is a function of the way in which that information was originally stored and of the conditions present at the time one tries to retrieve it. And in both those factors, organization seems to be the key: the organization and integration of the original memory trace, and the way in which the present situation calls forth or facilitates reconstruction of the original organization. As I mentioned in the previous section, most memory failures are failures of retrieval rather than storage; they occur because we cannot access stored information rather than because that information is no longer in memory (Thompson, 1972). It follows, then, that memory performance can be best improved by improving the ways in which we search for and locate what we want to remember.

Some of the best rememberers that psychologists know of are master chess players; they are able to remember dozens of chessboard arrangements and to play numbers of games simultaneously without ever having to look at the pieces. For those of us who are not chess experts, trying to remember the sequence of even one such game would set up enormous amounts of inhibition; the access pathways to one picture of the chessboard would become hopelessly confused with the pathways to other similar pictures. For the master, though, the subtle differences between one arrangement and another (differences that you or I might not even notice) are so important and so salient that each new set-up is qualitatively different from the previous one; there is no more confusion of access than there would be for us in trying to remember what we had for dinner last night and how we got to the restaurant where we ate it.

The chess master primes his mental organization of a particular board set-up according to its implications for further play. When called upon to remember that set-up, he need only remember those (relatively few) details that make it unique; he then uses his general knowledge of chess to reconstruct the rest of the board. In a study of chess players reported by Posner and Warren (1972), the chess masters invariably paused several seconds after being exposed to the stimulus before starting to recall. Less skilled players began to reproduce the board immediately, before losing the little they could retain. For the master, the pause provided time to access his memory and to reconstruct those extraneous details that he hadn't bothered to store away. The less skilled player, in contrast, tried to store everything; he had to get everything out again quickly before the inhibition process had time to muddy up the pathways. Underwood (1972, p. 13) reports a similar kind of behavior in people trying to remember long lists of unrelated words: "It is as if there is a busload of people all trying to get out the door at the same time, and the number involved for long lists (or a big bus?) is far greater than could occupy the theoretical short-term memory." Poorly organized information must be recalled in a burst (if at all), and a time interval between the request for recall and actual recall performance will decrease the amount that is remembered; well-organized information, in contrast, can be recalled (or reconstructed) in bits and pieces, and an intervening time interval may facilitate that reconstruction.

The most impressive facet of memory is perhaps not what we remember but rather what we don't; we are amazingly good at not bringing out of storage the wrong information. Occasionally, to be sure, we sift through a number of "wrong" chunks in an effort to find what we want. "What *was* his name? Robertson? Robinson? Rassmussen?" More often, though, our response is all or none: either we know something, or we know that we don't know it. This is particularly true with new stimulus information; we are able to say almost immediately that we have never seen that thing or person before, without having to sift through hundreds of stored memories to make sure. "How do you know that a situation is novel?" asks Norman (1973, p. 404). "How do you know so quickly with mantiness that you do not know the meaning of the word 'mantiness'? You could not have scanned all of memory to discover that the new experience or word was not there. No, presumably you looked where the sensory image said that the information ought to be, and found nothing there."

Given an item of information that has meaning for us, be it a word, a picture, a gesture, or what have you, access to that meaning is almost instantaneous. Such items are part of the semantic memory; access must be fast here, or communication would break down rather quickly. Indeed, man as a species had to have immediate access to this kind of memory; he couldn't afford time to search for the meaning of a particular kind of rustle in the grass or of a low growling sound behind him. Access to episodic memory is often slower. Here are the things we search for slowly enough to be aware of the search process: "Where have I seen that face before?" "What did I do with that notebook?" In both kinds of memory, though, access is based on the meaning of the stored information. The more meaningful a word or an event is to us, the more readily we are able to recall it. And the more closely related in meaning one word or event is to another word or event, the more likely it is that recalling one brings about— whether we want it or not—the recall of the other.

Ritter and Burche (1974) point out that items are not recalled independently but are recalled through use of retrieval schemes in which the retrieval of each item is integrated with the retrieval of other items. And so we return to the notion of chunking. Items close to each other in meaning are chunked in memory; access to one implies access to the other. The closeness may be based on semantic meaning or it may be an episodic closeness: for my son, "going barefoot" is part of a meaning chunk that also includes "broken glass" and "blood" and "emergency room." Small chunks, in turn, are organized (and can be accessed) according to their relationship to other chunks. "Going barefoot" is part of a superchunk called "summer," which also includes other chunks having to do with such things as day camp and backyard picnics. An individual chunk may be—and nearly always is—integrated into more than one superchunk. These complex organizations account for retrieval; we wind our way from one organizational structure to the next, until we find what we need. The incredible part is how we manage to do it so quickly and efficiently.

We have made only a beginning in understanding how memory retrieval works. But even that beginning yields some important suggestions for improving the retrieval process. In storing information for future retrieval, we should make that information as meaningful as possible. The better we understand something and the more important it is to us, the more likely we are to be able to find our way back to it later on. We should enhance the meaningfulness of information in more than one way—that is, we should try to build multiple access routes to it. The spelling of a particular word, for instance, might be connected to the visual image of the printed word, to an exaggerated pronunciation of all the letters in the word, and to a rhyme or joke that calls attention to the usually misspelled part. It is best if the learner himself builds these pathways, for the things one makes oneself are more meaningful than the things one borrows from others. But the teacher can facilitate the process by providing examples and generally encouraging students to construct meaning networks.

## TEACHING FOR MEMORY

Throughout this chapter, I have mentioned a number of specific implications for teaching of the various theories and hypotheses about the nature of memory. Now we shall turn to a more direct approach to teacher behaviors. Much of what I shall say in these paragraphs will be a review of what has gone before, but all of it will (I hope) have immediate implications for what the teacher does with students in and out of the classroom—and how he does it.

### Organization and Meaningfulness

One of the major jobs of the teacher is to present information; the better the presentation, the better it is remembered by students. Just what kind of presentation is good in the sense of being memorable? Most obviously, it is understandable. There is a direct relationship between how well information is understood and how well it is remembered. But beyond this, the data suggest rather strongly that the more different ways information can be understood, the more easily it is recalled later. Understanding and organization are, as we have seen, intimately related; and the organizational scheme seems to be the most fundamental element in providing access to stored information. The more such schemes there are, the more likely one (or several) will prove useful in accessing needed information. The teacher must be careful though, in presenting several organizational schemes, that the different patterns do not interfere with each other. Multiple retrieval paths are helpful only as long as safeguards are provided to maintain the first path during acquisition of the second path (Nelson & Hill, 1974). Such safeguarding can be accomplished through appropriate spacing of presentations (see the discussion of spacing later in this chapter) and through review and rehearsal of previously learned patterns.

A common error made by students in learning new material is trying to learn everything—every detail—as if it all were of equal importance. This procedure not only hinders organization but also clutters up the memory with information that could more easily be dealt with by means of reconstruction rather than recall. For this reason, it is often helpful to tell the student directly "This is the most important part of what you are learning." As he concentrates on this important part, he develops an organizational scheme that allows him to reconstruct or access the details only as they are needed (Gieselman, 1974). Again, the meaning of information is what is important. Learning that tooth decay is caused by bacterial activity and that this activity occurs most rapidly when there are plenty of nutrients for the bacteria and when they are allowed to build up large undisturbed colonies leads to better understanding (and organization and recall) than learning a lot of rules about daily flossing, brushing after every meal, and cutting down on sweets.

When presenting a number of different ways of organizing or understanding information, a teacher should make some of these schemes verbal-logical and some visual-spatial. In the dental-care example, the teacher can explain what goes on in the mouth as food bacteria multiply; he can also show photographs and diagrams and cartoon pictures of bacteria "fortresses" or teeth yelling for help. Visualization, used as a means of organizing and retrieving information, is a powerful tool, but it tends to confuse the order in which things happen and to allow the introduction of extraneous information. Verbal-logical analysis may not set up such strong access pathways, but it favors classification of material and also works in abstract situations, where visual imagery is difficult (Bartlett, 1932; Paivio, 1971). Combining the two allows us to use the strengths of one to make up for the deficiencies of the other. The visual image can provide access to the chunk, while verbal processes allow reconstruction, elaboration, and organization of the stored information within the chunk. Moreover, in presenting new information, teachers should probably begin with concrete, visual examples and then move to generalizations and abstractions. This sequence establishes access routes before organizational details must be stored away.

We must remember too that every event takes place in a context—no information is learned in isolation—and that this context is an important part of the organization of material. If you would like to experience a vivid demonstration of contextual effects, go back to your old high school some late afternoon when nearly everyone has gone home. Step inside the door, close your eyes, and take a deep breath: if you are like most people, the smell of the building will bring back a flood of memories of people and events. Yet, at the time you were experiencing those events and interacting with those people, you were probably quite unaware of the odor context. Since contextual effects are so strong, we should try to take advantage of them in our teaching. We should make our presentations as rich as possible in all modalities; the students should see and smell and taste and touch ideas, not just talk about them. We should try to plan information contexts so that similar contexts touch off associations and trigger recall at the time the learned information is needed. This can be as trivial a matter as planning for students to study and discuss material in the same room they will

later be tested in (not a bad suggestion, by the way, any time you are anticipating a tough exam) or as far ranging as setting up a voting booth in class
on the day you talk about elections or tape recording the sounds of a field
trip to play back later as a part of a discussion of what the group learned.

## Spacing

As I pointed out earlier, the timing of new information presentation
and of rehearsals of old information is critically important. "One of the
more persistent findings in the literature of long-term memory is that a
word that is presented twice in succession will be retained more poorly in
long-term memory than if the repetitions were distributed" (Posner &
Warren, 1972, p. 38). The more similar two bits of information are, the
more important it is to space them if both are to be remembered. Rehearsal
of information (which amounts to repeated internal presentations) must be
spaced if it is to be useful—unless the rehearsal can emphasize new organizations and associations, so that one is not merely repeating but also elaborating on the information. Rehearsal of this latter sort, in which the stored
information is enhanced with new associations during the rehearsal process, is in fact a kind of treatment of memory. If it is truly immediate (with
no spacing at all between original learning and rehearsal), it can be thought
of as a means of transferring information from short- to long-term memory
or of facilitating the deep encoding necessary for laying down a lasting
memory trace. A certain amount of this kind of treatment seems to be
facilitative—if not necessary—for good long-term recall, and this fact
probably accounts for some of the effects of new-information spacing.
That is, spacing new information allows time for the learner to rehearse,
elaborate, and organize each chunk before having to deal with the next
one. Gieselman (1974) suggests that the information presenter incorporate
this notion specifically into his presentation technique, pausing appreciably after each significant input to allow the listener time to rehearse and
organize it before moving on.

Related to the need for spacing information to allow selective rehearsal
and organization is the phenomenon of inhibition. When material is presented too quickly, both backward and forward inhibition tend to occur;
new items disrupt retrieval of previously learned ones, and old learnings
interfere with retrieval of new items. And again, the more similar the material, the greater the likelihood of interference. Spacing the material to be
learned greatly reduces interference effects. The best kind of spacing is an
interval filled with a non-memory-involving activity; next best is an activity
involving memory of entirely different sorts of material, used in different
ways.

In developing individual study habits, students should be encouraged
to make optimal use of spacing. Cramming for an exam is the antithesis of
well-spaced learning and virtually never results in significant long-term

retention. Students can be shown that studying hard for a specific (short) length of time or number of pages or problems, then becoming involved in a different activity for a while, and then going back to studying, is much more efficient than long, unbroken study stints. The optimal length of a study period and of its related rest space probably differs from person to person and may even vary for a given individual depending on such factors as previous knowledge of the subject, motivational level, and fatigue. What is certain is that some spacing is helpful; each person must work out for himself his own most efficient study pattern.

## Retrieval Aids

The teacher is involved not only in presenting new information to students but also in helping them develop ways of retrieving that information. Evaluation of learning always depends (at least in part) on how well students recall information. Both in setting up such formal evaluations and in preparing the student for real-world experiences in which he will need to retrieve and use stored information, the teacher must be aware of the kinds of cues available for getting at what has been learned. Retrieval cues determine at least the initial pathways searched for stored items, and recall may be trivially easy or nearly impossible depending on the cues given. "Who was President of the United States during the Civil War?" will be easier for most students to answer than "Who was President of the United States in 1862?" even though they may "know" (have stored) when the Civil War was fought. Test questions, even "objective" ones, probably do not test whether an item was learned as much as they test the adequacy of the organizational scheme according to which it was stored.

Two techniques stand out as useful to the student (or anyone else, for that matter) in making the best possible use of retrieval cues. One has to do with expectation based on cue plus context. Ordinarily, the combination of a cue (or set of cues) and its context sets up an expectation about the nature of the information to be retrieved or about the place where it is probably stored or both. If I see a young person standing at the door of my office, I may reasonably expect that he is a student; I then search my memory for names of students in my classes or students I advise in order to remember who he is. But sometimes these expectations lead us astray; the young man at my door may be a friend's son who has come by to deliver a book his mother promised to lend me. In this case, the only chance I have of identifying him correctly is to give up my initial expectations, to shift gears and look in other memory locations. Such gear shifting can be difficult, but it is a technique that can be developed through conscious practice and is a significant aid in recall.

Deliberately running through alternative association pathways is another recall technique that can be consciously developed. I'm trying to remember where I saw an article on, say, Carl Jung, that I want to go back and reread. I know I saw it somewhere a couple of weeks ago, but where could it have been? Instead of going around and around on a treadmill of "where did I see it?" I can try to get at the information along a different pathway. What was I doing just before or just after I saw the article? Can I trace it back that way? What kind of print was it in, with what size pages, and how many pictures? By trying to recapture the visual image, I may be able to recover the entire incident. What was I doing physically when I saw it—standing up, sitting down, bending over a table, or what? While we don't often notice the kinesthetic messages that tell us what our body is doing, those messages are nevertheless part of a stimulus context and may be quite useful in retrieving information. The more alternative pathways I can try, the more likely I am to finally get the information I need. And, if all else fails, I should try to involve myself in an entirely different train of thought, to stop working on the problem. Often, after we have activated access pathways at a conscious level, a subconscious working through of associations occurs; later, as a result of a stimulus that we would never consciously connect with the needed item, a whole new association comes into play, and the thing we were struggling for suddenly pops into consciousness.

## Age Differences

One of the things that we, as teachers, need to be sensitive to is developmental changes in various skills and abilities. Throughout this book, when talking about different kinds of learning and, later, in discussing various personal characteristics that the learner brings to his task, I try to take into account the ways in which children of different ages are likely to function. Unfortunately, when we consider memory, data on age differences are sparse and contradictory. Fajnsztejn-Pollack (1973) reports that the rate of forgetting is independent of age from 5 to 16 years, but that acquisition of information increases with age. One reason age differences in memory are so hard to isolate is that, again, we are dealing with two interacting processes: storage and retrieval. Younger children are probably as good at storage as older ones—perhaps better— but they have not had opportunities to develop the complex organizational schemes so important in retrieval. In Western cultures, the organization patterns that develop with age and experience are mostly verbal; we tend to lose much of our spatial- and visual-imagery ability through simple disuse (Underwood, 1969). The ability to rehearse items verbally also increases with age, and this ability too facilitates recall.

Another advantage that the older student has over the younger is in the use of indirect, alternative retrieval pathways. There is an increase, at least during early childhood, in the individual's ability to think of indirect retrieval strategies (Ritter, Kaprove, Fitch, & Flavell, 1973). We have already discussed some of the ways in which students can be encouraged to develop such strategies; the teacher should be aware, though, that this kind of mnemonic process may be developmentally out of reach for the primary student.

### Mnemonics

Speaking of mnemonic processes leads us neatly into the last major topic of this chapter, the use of mnemonic devices. There are many such schemes and systems for improving memory, and they can be loosely divided into true organizers and false organizers. *True organizers* are those organizational schemes that are logical developments of the material to be remembered; we have discussed the use of such organizational schemes earlier. True organizers may be particularly helpful when they are presented in advance of the material to be learned. Used in this way, not only do they provide organizational foundations that can be recalled and used as a basis for reconstruction, but they also draw upon whatever the learner already knows about the material and facilitate integration of the old with the new (Ausubel, 1960).

More generally recognized as mnemonics are the *false organizers*— verbal or visual mediators that provide an extra associative pathway to get to the learned information. There are many such devices, and they are used by many people in a variety of memory situations. Often they have a rhyme form, in which both rhythm and rhyming words aid recall of hard-to-organize material; the familiar "I before E, except after C" and "Thirty days has September" are examples of rhyming mnemonics.

Another frequently used mnemonic device for recalling a list of items is to construct a sentence, each word of which begins with the initial letter of one item in the list. In an old music-hall routine a man tells about a great way he has found to remember all the states and capitals. He has a long sen-

tence (one of 96 words, in those days) that provides first-letter cues for each state and its capital. His friend listens to him in silence, and then asks mildly whether the sentence isn't a little hard to remember. "Yes," the first man replies, "it is, but I've got that all figured out too. I just memorize all the states and their capitals, and that gives me the first letter of each word in the sentence." The point, of course, is that mnemonics can get so long and cumbersome that they are no longer useful.

There is also some question as to how much long-term memory is facilitated by mnemonic tricks. As we have seen, long-term memory depends most strongly upon organization, understanding, and the development of alternative access pathways to stored material. While the mnemonic device does set up one new organization or association, it fails to set up multiple pathways; indeed, it may hinder the development of true organizers by giving the learner a sense of false confidence, a feeling of "now I've got it, and I don't have to try to understand it very well." When used in this way, mnemonics can assist short-term memory (for that test on Friday or the speech that has to be delivered without notes next week) but are likely to be useless or worse in the long run.

Mnemonics that are helpful over longer periods of time, like the "thirty days" jingle, are recalled because they are frequently used and rehearsed. Also, the more visual imagery a mnemonic device uses, the better it is likely to work: the words plus the image automatically provide two pathways to the stored items. One such scheme that has been used for literally thousands of years is that of associating to-be-learned material with points along a trip, where the route is well known and can be easily visualized, or with rooms or locations in a familiar building. Let's assume, for instance, that you've gone to a party where you heard four jokes that you want to be sure to remember. To do so, you can put together two memory devices, chunking and a visual mnemonic. You can chunk the jokes by trying to remember just the punch line and reconstructing the rest from your understanding of how the joke hangs together. But how to remember four unrelated punch lines? Here's where the visual mnemonic comes in. Visualize the room in which the party took place, and choose four places in the room. Then create an image of a concrete part of each punch line, actually located in each place. The punch line that has to do with memorizing all the states and capitals in order to remember the 96-word sentence (this is just an example; I can't imagine anyone wanting to remember *that* joke!) might conjure up a mental picture of a person sitting cross-legged under a lamp in the corner, studying a United States map. Later, trying to remember the jokes, one "looks around the room" in memory and "sees" the various images associated with the different places in it.

Another well-worn visual mnemonic is the one-bun system. Here one memorizes (and rehearses, so that the list itself is not forgotten) a set of ten words that rhyme with the numbers from one to ten: one-bun, two-shoe, three-tree, four-door, five-hive, six-sticks, seven-heaven, eight-gate, nine-wine, ten-hen. The items on the list to be remembered are then visually associated with the concrete rhyming words. If I need to remember to buy catsup, paper towels, frozen corn, and a green pepper the next time I go to the store, I may visualize a bun covered with catsup, paper towels stuffed into a shoe, a tree with kernels of corn dangling from its branches, and a door with a green pepper instead of a door knob. If my visual imagery is vivid enough, simply thinking of bun, shoe, tree, and door will conjure up these images, and I'll be able to remember my shopping list.

Lowry (1974) suggests that mnemonics work insofar as they make previously learned material more resistant to interference from other learned material. They do so by providing alternative pathways to the stored memories, pathways that are likely to be quite different from the logical pathways utilized by true organizers. They can be quite helpful in the recall of specific information over relatively short periods, but again I must emphasize that they cannot take the place of the good organization and understanding necessary for long-term memory.


We have now reviewed a rather large body of information about memory, from the physical and chemical basis for information storage to the use of psychological devices to facilitate recall. If any theme has emerged from our discussion, it must be the fundamental role of organization, categorization, and the building of associations. To organize (and to understand) is indeed to remember. Moreover, no memory exists in a vacuum; everything that we store away is interconnected to a host of other information. As we store it, we automatically (and often without conscious knowledge) build pathways to other, previously stored information; we also store with it or near it data about what else was occurring during the learning event—the context. Finally, our understanding—our perception —of the learned information is determined in part by what has already been stored in memory. Jenkins (1974, p. 793) warns us of the dangers of oversimplifying our notions of how memory operates: "We should shun any notion that memory consists of a specific system that operates with one set of rules on one kind of unit. What is remembered in a given situation depends on the physical and psychological context in which the event was experienced, the knowledge and skills that the subject brings to the context, the situation in which we ask for evidence for remembering, and the relation of what the subject remembers to what the experimenter demands." What is true for the psychological experiment is doubly true for the classroom: storage of information in memory can never be an isolated event, but rather takes place in the context of what has occurred before and what is occurring now. To make information vivid and meaningful within its contexts is to make it memorable.

## QUESTIONS FOR UNDERSTANDING

1. Choose one bit of information that you remember from this chapter. Trace how that information came into your memory store through the sensory register and short-term memory. What was there about it that made you choose it for this example rather than something else?
2. Think of one or two examples of school learning in which recognition memory, rather than recall, is sufficient. How might a teacher best facilitate recognition in these instances?
3. A mixed-age group of students are watching a film about the life cycle of moths and butterflies. Discuss the different ways in which older and younger children might *select, rewrite, categorize,* and *elaborate* information from the film.
4. How might a physical education teacher use spacing to help a group of children remember the rules used in playing basketball or soccer? How does spacing occur naturally in the child's experience with such formal games?
5. In chemistry, it is necessary (or at least desirable) to memorize the atomic numbers of the more common elements. Devise a mnemonic scheme to aid in this memory task.

# PART 2

## The Learner

# Chapter 6

# *Intelligence*

It is hard to imagine any characteristic more valued in our culture today than that of intelligence. To be stupid or dumb is to be condemned to second-class citizenship. Indeed, in our everyday language we tend to use "dumb" as a generally negative descriptor; kids talk about "my dumb old teacher" or complain about having to wash the "dumb dishes." And among adults the reference to somebody as a "stupid pig" has little more to do with his intelligence than to his possible future as a ham sandwich; it simply indicates that the speaker doesn't like him very much. For us, "stupid" equals "not good."

Because this equation of lack of intelligence with lack of value is so ingrained in our culture, and especially in our language, it tends to be accepted without question—indeed, like most values, it is not usually a matter for conscious concern or imagination. Every child "knows" that it is good to be smart and that he will be evaluated over and over again on the basis of how smart (good) he is. And most children have a good idea of where they stand in this evaluation process and accept those evaluations as valid indicators of their worth as persons. Moreover, most people (children and adults) believe that the quality of smartness or dumbness is fixed, that the smart kid stays smart and the dumb kid stays dumb for the rest of their lives. In this chapter, we shall take a look at this notion, as well as a number of other notions about intelligence. I cannot promise that we will emerge with many firm and indisputable facts about the subject—for it is one of the many controversial areas in psychology and education—but we will surely have a better idea of just what is not known as well as some interesting theories about what may be true.

## DEFINING INTELLIGENCE

In talking about intelligence, perhaps the most difficult thing to do is to say exactly what we mean by the word. Scientists and philosophers have been trying to define intelligence for hundreds of years. Obviously, since people keep trying to define it, nobody has been able to come up with a definition that has satisfied very many people for very long. Yet we all seem to be able to use the concept, and we all think we know fairly much what we mean by it. "Intelligent? Why, sure, that's, uh, that's how smart you are." Okay, now what does that mean? "Well, smart people can think better than dumb ones." Fine; and what does it mean to think better? "Well, like figure things out. You know, understand things and stuff." That short conversation took place not long ago between me and myself, and I think it's typical of most thinking about the nature of intelligence.

### Intelligence as a Quality of Thought

The first assumption that people tend to make (and that was made in the internal dialog that I just quoted) is that intelligence has to do with thinking. Some believe that the speed of thinking or problem solving or learning is the factor most related to intelligence, that the intelligent person is the one who can think or learn faster than other people. Others focus on the amount that can be learned or the difficulty of the problems that can be solved as the differentiating factor. But the common thread seems to be the ability to use abstract thought, to conceptualize, to do whatever one is trying to do inside one's head.

This view of intelligence is not new; St. Thomas Aquinas talked about "the ability to combine and separate" concepts, and, some 700 years later, we find Charles Spearman trying to measure "the ability to educe relations and correlates." Surely both are struggling with the problem of pinning down in words the way in which humans deal with abstractions. To the degree that a person can acquire (that is, understand), associate, construct, and evaluate concepts, he is generally judged to be intelligent. If he cannot do these things—no matter what else he can do—he is judged to be less intelligent. Consider, for example, two learning tasks: learning to type and learning to solve mathematical problems. Person A has mastered the typing but not the math, while person B has mastered the math but not the typing. Now, if the only information you had about these two people was their relative mastery of these two tasks, how would you rank them in intelligence? Of course, you know that the question is rigged; you are being led to say that the typist is less intelligent. Most people would make that choice —even though nothing at all was said about how difficult the math problems were. Solving math problems is a conceptual task, while typing "merely" involves physical coordination.

But is conceptual ability all that is involved in intelligent behavior? Notice, I said *behavior*. There is another underlying assumption about intelligence here, that it must be reflected in some sort of behavior if it is to count. I can claim to think deep and profound thoughts, but if I can't demonstrate that ability, nobody is going to give me much credit or point to me as an example of an intelligent person. Moreover, I must demonstrate my intelligence in ways that are appropriate to the situation: I must show good judgment, some sensitivity to the realistic demands of my environment. The vacant-eyed professor who goes about losing his lecture notes and answering every question with a quotation from the Greek may be an "intellectual," but he is not demonstrating much intelligence as we commonly use the word. David Wechsler, author of one of the most widely used tests of intelligence, insists that intelligence must include more than cognitive ability. Many people make a false assumption, Wechsler says, that intelligence is a "quality of the mind." To be clever or inventive or alert is, to be sure, indicative of intelligence, but just having those characteristics is not enough. "Actually, intelligence is an aspect of behavior; it has to do primarily with the appropriateness, effectiveness, and worthwhileness of what human beings do or want to do" (Wechsler, 1975, p. 135).

Interestingly, this concern with the practical, behavioral aspects of intelligence was also voiced more than 60 years ago by the authors of the first and most well-known tests of intellectual ability, Alfred Binet and Theodore Simon: "It seems to us that in the intelligence there is a fundamental faculty, the alteration or lack of which is of utmost importance in practical life. This faculty is judgement, otherwise called good sense, practical sense, initiative, the faculty of adapting oneself to circumstances. To judge well, to comprehend well, to read well, these are the essential activities of the intelligence. . . . Indeed, the rest of the intellectual faculties seem to be of little importance in comparison with the intelligence." Binet and Simon seem to be implying that a number of strands, taken together, make up one's intellectual ability. The most important of these is some kind of pragmatic "can do it," some quality of understanding, communicating, interacting with the world effectively and efficiently.

However many strands contribute to intellectual ability, Binet and Simon seem to have been quite content to view "the intelligence" as a single, unitary characteristic. Spearman, too, as we noted earlier, was trying to quantify a single ability; but he too suggested that other, lesser abilities might also contribute to the overall picture of intellectual competence that a person presents to the world. Spearman's viewpoint is particularly important in that he laid the groundwork for a whole new approach to the definition and measurement of intelligence. According to Spearman, many independent abilities may contribute to how well a person performs a particular task; and different abilities come into play as we try to do different things. But the major ability that the student of intellectual ability should try to measure is the general, pervasive quality that is fundamental to all intelligent behavior. Spearman called this quality the *g*, or *general,* factor and devoted the better part of his professional life to devising ways to measure *g,* to tease it apart from all the other, shifting abilities that affect our behavior.

Spearman used a mathematical tool called factor analysis in his study of intelligence. Factor analysis is a complicated statistical technique, and we shall not spend much time discussing it here. Suffice it to say that a number of factor analysts, using similar techniques, have found evidence that intelligence is indeed the product of several separate abilities or factors. These abilities vary independently from person to person—that is, Jane Jones may be high on factor A and low on factors B and C, while Bill Baker is low on A and B and high on C.

Some researchers still subscribe to the Spearman model; they believe that there is a *g* factor that influences all tasks involving mental activity, while other abilities may or may not be called upon, depending on the nature of the tasks. Other workers argue that the notion of a *g* factor is misleading—that one possesses a host of separate and partially independent abilities, and the pattern of these abilities accounts for intelligent performance, much as the chips of glass in a kaleidoscope come together to form a picture or design. Such factors are *task specific:* they have to do with fragments of one's overall performance, rather than being generalized skills useful in a variety of situations. Still other factor analysts support some combination of general and specific factors, seeing intelligence as composed of both general and specific factors or of a single *g* factor plus some group factors (each affecting performance within a more limited range of tasks) plus some other specific factors (see Figure 6-1).

In contrast to the hierarchical tree of factors typical of most factor theories of intelligence, Guilford (1959) developed a three-dimensional model of the "structure of the intellect." The three major dimensions are *operations* (such as cognition and memory), *contents* (such as images and symbols), and *products* (which range from units and classes to implications). The easiest way to understand a three-dimensional model like this one is to imagine it mapped onto a big cube (Figure 6-2). Each face of the

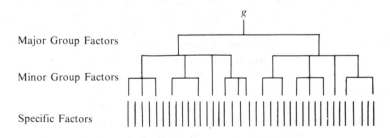

*Figure 6-1.* A hierarchical theory of mental organization. (From *The Structure of Human Abilities,* by P. E. Vernon. Copyright 1950 by Eyre Methuen Ltd. Reprinted by permission.)

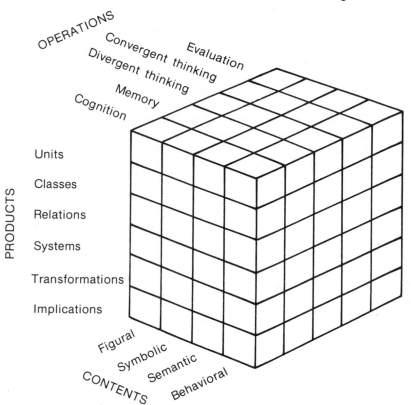

*Figure 6-2.* Model of the structure of the intellect. (From "Three Faces of Intellect" by J. P. Guilford, *American Psychologist,* 1959, *14,* 469–479. Copyright 1959 by the American Psychological Association. Reprinted by permission.)

cube contains a map of the relationship between two of the three dimensions: the way that operations and contents interact may be shown on the top, contents and products on one side, and products and operations on another. The squares on the sides, in turn, mark off smaller cubes, and each smaller cube is the coming together of one element from each major dimension. In Figure 6-2, for instance, the small cube in the top front corner represents the part of the intellect that deals with *evaluation* at a *behavioral* level in single *units.* An example of this particular intellectual function is the quick, nonverbal check we sometimes make of another person's words and facial expression before we respond to him, in order to decide whether he is joking or serious.

As you can see from the figure, Guilford's model yields a large number of tasks, each one an intersection of elements of the three major dimensions. Guilford believes that any intellectual activity can be identified by these intersections and that breaking a task down into its major intellectual components is useful in that it helps us to diagnose and treat task failures. Moreover, it is possible—even probable—that different aspects of intelligence develop at different speeds or to different degrees in an individual; analyzing what a person can and cannot do in Guilford's model can tell us not only how intelligent he is but in what ways he is intelligent.

Piaget takes a still different approach to intelligence. As we saw in Chapter 4, he sees intelligence as a kind of organic relationship between an individual and his environment. According to this view, intelligence is not a body of acquired content, but an internalization of the operations one performs on objects and the transformations involved in those operations (Gaudia, 1972). The child, as he matures, develops different ways of understanding and relating to the world around him; these different interactive modes characterize the stages of cognitive development that Piaget describes. Piaget does not seem to be particularly interested in measuring the intelligence of any one person or in determining whether this child is brighter or duller than that one; his concern is to discover the developmental path along which all people travel as their intelligence grows. And, like Wechsler, Piaget looks to practical, efficient, in-the-world behavior as the essence of intelligence.

## Intelligence and IQ

It is valuable to grapple with definitions, to armchair-theorize, in order to get a notion of just how difficult and slippery the concept of intelligence is. But just talking about intelligence isn't enough: we want to see it, work with it, find out how it grows and changes. Sooner or later, nearly every psychologist who has been seriously involved in unraveling the mystery of intelligence has tried to measure it, to test for it. The mental-testing movement has had its ups and downs; it is currently in a state of some disrepute. The California legislature has voted twice to prohibit group mental testing in schools on the grounds that the effect of such testing is to limit the education black children receive. Nevertheless, tests of intelligence have been and are of great value, both in research and in the assessment of the intellectual strengths and weaknesses of individuals moving through the educational system. Mental tests are harmful when they are misused; they are most often misused when they are misunderstood. And one of the most common misunderstandings has to do with the meaning of the IQ and the use of the IQ score.

The concept of IQ, or Intelligence Quotient, grew out of the notion that the normal child's mental growth is somehow analogous to his physical growth: just as older children are bigger and stronger than younger ones, so their intellects should be bigger and stronger. Binet, commissioned in 1904 by the French government to find better ways of dealing with dull children in the schools, tested thousands of school-age children on a variety of tasks and found general support for this notion: the older children could indeed do more difficult tasks than the younger ones could. Binet determined the number and kind of tests that an average child of each age group could complete; using these standards, he could then categorize any child as having a certain *mental age*. Underlying the notion of mental age is the assumption that a person's mental age and his chronological age should be roughly the same: most 9-year-olds have a mental age of 9 as well. If we write a fraction using mental age as the numerator and chronological age as the denominator, the value of that fraction should usually be 1: a child with a mental age of 5 is usually about 5 years old, and a 12-year-old usually has a mental age of 12. Sometimes there are slight variations; a 5 $^2/_{12}$-year old may have a mental age of 5 $^3/_{12}$. These variations make for awkward decimals when we try to figure out the mental-age/chronological-age ratio. To get rid of the decimals, though, all we have to do is multiply the fraction by 100. Voila! Every child who is tested can be given a number —a nice, whole number—that tells us just how he is doing mentally according to his chronological age. Children who are just where they "ought" to be have a score of about 100; children whose mental development is relatively slow have lower scores, while bright children score higher. And thus the IQ was born.

Knowing the origins of the IQ concept, we can immediately explode two of the more prevalent myths about IQs. First, a person's IQ is not his intelligence. It is an estimate of his intellectual ability, based on his performance on a particular test. If the test fails to tap the areas he is good in, that estimate is wrong. Likewise, if (for whatever reason) he doesn't happen to be functioning well on the day the test is given, the IQ is an underestimate of his true ability level. An IQ is accurate only to the degree that the test on which it is based is good (comprehensive, relevant, fair) and is administered properly and to the degree that the person being tested has done as well as he can on it. Second, a person's test score is not his IQ. His test score is simply a number indicating how many items he completed correctly; that score must be compared with those of a normative group in order to get an IQ score. It must be converted first to a mental age (based on how well other children do on that test) and then to a fraction. If the comparison group is different from the group to which our testee belongs (if they are from a different cultural background or have gotten a different kind or amount of education or even have taken the test under different conditions), then the IQ score isn't particularly meaningful.

There is another, more fundamental problem with IQ as it is described in these paragraphs: it is based on the notion that a person's intellectual abilities continue to grow as he continues to age. And this simply is not true; mental ability, as measured by most tests, doesn't usually increase much beyond the late teens. You can easily see that this poses a serious problem for assigning IQ scores to adults. (If I were to take a mental-ability test and come up with a mental age of 18, my IQ would be about 45.) For this reason, IQ is now generally calculated as a statistical concept, with the average score for each age group on a particular test arbitrarily set at 100, and individual scores adjusted accordingly. This mathematical tinkering, though, doesn't change the underlying nature of the IQ score: it is simply an estimate of the ability of one person compared with the average ability of others in his age group. And it is still valid only to the extent that the test on which it is based is a good one, administered correctly, and scored on the basis of an adequate and truly comparable normative group.

One last word about IQs before we move on: to the degree that the IQ concept does have meaning and that IQ tests are indeed measuring something of interest to students of human functioning, it would seem that human IQs are changing over time. Comparative studies of mental-age scores from previous large testing groups and from large groups tested more recently show a consistent trend for the later groups to score higher. This trend has been noticed in rural as well as urban communities. The data, according to Koppen-Thulesius and Teichmann (1972), indicate that the development rate of intellectual ability is accelerating in both verbal and nonverbal areas. Moreover, the trend exists not only among older children; infant and preschooler scores on developmental schedules also suggest that today's children are developing faster than their grandparents did. Whatever the IQ tests measure, it seems likely that people are improving over time in those areas—or are at least improving in their ability to perform well on the tests.

### Intelligence and Cultural Competence

Most intelligence tests measure one's ability to solve problems and to answer questions. They deal, to a greater or lesser degree, with abstractions —with shapes, with numbers, with logical relationships. Yet we have seen that at least some testing specialists maintain that this ability to deal with abstractions is only a part—a facet—of what we mean by intelligence. Why, then, do we continue to use tests that measure primarily one kind of ability as indicators of something that we suspect to be much broader and perhaps even quite different altogether? Part of the answer to that question has to do with the surprising consistency of most IQ tests. These tests, despite wide variability in the specific tasks they include (stacking blocks, defining words, solving math problems, drawing pictures) are measuring something—there is too much agreement among them to deny that fact. Moreover, the characteristic or quality being measured seems to correlate rather well with the kinds of how-to, cultural-competence things that people like Wechsler point at as involving "real" intelligence—things like academic ability, job success, and even socioeconomic status. We don't know that there is a causal relationship here—that being able to do well in the abstract sorts of things measured by most IQ tests helps one to succeed in school or on the job. It is quite possible that high IQ and high achievement both relate to another factor or ability in an individual, and that this X factor is responsible for both sorts of high performance. Even so, it is hard to deny that IQ tests can be used successfully as at least a partial measure of the presence or absence of such an X factor. And the X factor makes for cultural competence—the ability to do and get and hold on to the kinds of things that our culture says are important. "Our society values highly the abilities measured by IQ tests; our educational system is such that those who score highly are also found to do best, on the whole, in their examinations, and those who are successful in the more complex and difficult jobs are usually those who score well on IQ tests. This is not only true in England and the U.S.A.; it was also found to be true in the U.S.S.R." (Eysenck, 1971b, p. 55).

Just because the abilities measured by IQ tests appear to relate to competence in Western culture, however, does not mean that they do so in other cultures. In North America and in Europe, abstract conceptual ability relates to cultural success, and people who have such abilities are generally labeled intelligent. If abstract conceptual abilities were not related to cultural success, we would not see them as indicators of intelligence. We don't believe that many other abilities varying from person to person have anything to do with intelligence simply because they don't relate to cultural competence. Take whistling, for example: some people can whistle, and some can't; and it's easy to tell a whistler from a nonwhistler. Why do we not consider people who can whistle to be more intelligent than people who can't? Because the ability to whistle has no (known) relationship to the kinds of competence valued in this culture. If all whistlers could design electrical circuits or make money on the stock market, we might well have come to use whistling as an index of intelligence. In some cultures, whistling is an important means of communication; whole conversations are carried on across long distances by using different tones and patterns of whistles. People who can't whistle in that culture are handicapped; and they are most probably considered somewhat less bright than those who can.

There are two points to be made here, and both of them, I think, are quite important. First, our own ethnocentrism makes us value the skills of the West more highly than the skills of other cultures. No intrinsic quality makes our "civilized" intelligence any better than the "uncivilized" intelligence of a peasant or a tribal hunter. We are, fortunately, becoming considerably more aware of our cultural tunnel vision than we have been in the past; particularly when comparing Western and Eastern values, we are beginning to understand that our own way of viewing the world is not the only way and perhaps not even the best way. But we still tend to apply Western standards when evaluating intellectual competence, asking (either through formal tests or in more subjective evaluation processes) how well a person would do in tasks valued in the West: solving abstract problems, handling time pressures, and competing.

The second important point is, in a sense, the flip side of the first: if we are concerned with how well an individual can or will function in Western society, then it is highly appropriate to evaluate him on Western skills. No matter how well a person might be able to get along in rural China or how bright he would be considered in the jungles of Brazil, if he plans to settle down in Akron, Ohio, then he needs the abilities valued by most people in the United States. And these are, in large part, the very abilities that tend to be measured by conventional IQ tests and to be referred to when most Westerners talk about intelligence. In other words, while we must take care not to be too culture bound in thinking about the nature of intelligence, we must at the same time not become so abstract that we lose sight of the realities of the situation. Most of the people with whom you and I will deal professionally—whose education we will be involved with—will spend their lives in our cultural context. To the degree that we concern ourselves with intelligence at all, it makes sense for us to be most interested in the kind of intelligence that works for these people here and now.

In summary, intelligence is whatever allows one to survive and excel in his own cultural milieu. The intelligent Englishman might make a dull Bantu; the bright Apache child is often thought to be backward by his white teacher. In Western culture, cultural competence appears to be closely related to abstract conceptual ability. While we should not equate the two, we can and do use the one (somewhat measurable) ability to estimate the other (amorphous and nonmeasurable) one. An IQ score is an estimate of an estimate: we use a specific, one-time-only performance on a set of test items as an estimate of an individual's ability to deal with abstractions and/or language and/or spatial relationships, and we then take that estimate as an indicator of his intelligence—his cultural competence.

## DEVELOPMENT OF INTELLIGENCE

Psychologists used to believe that the human infant was born with virtually no intellectual abilities; he was a blank tablet upon which was to be imprinted the accumulation of life's wisdom. William James, the father of American psychology, spoke of the "blooming, buzzing confusion" that was the baby's sensory impression of the world. Present-day students of human development have discarded most of these notions; we now believe that a baby comes into independent life with a number of pre-set patterns that he uses to make sense of his surroundings. Very young infants, for instance, show a clear preference for some kinds of visual patterns—in particular, they seem to prefer patterns that suggest human faces. They can differentiate colors and shapes and usually prefer to look at symmetrical rather than at asymmetrical designs. It is very difficult to determine the extent of these perceptual abilities in the infant since he may be able to see a great deal that he cannot tell us about; also, the kinds of things we can think of to test him on are severely limited by our own acquired ways of understanding the world. The very small infant may be able to make distinctions or perform other operations that never occur to us adults simply because we have lost those abilities in the course of our growing up.

### The Role of Heredity

If we are to understand how intelligence develops among human beings, it is helpful to know something about the starting point: just what do people bring with them at birth in the way of intellectual equipment? And even more important than the abilities present in the newborn are his potentials for growth. Psychologists and educators have long been concerned with the question of whether (and to what degree) a child's future development is fixed or limited by his genetic endowment—that is, whether one's heredity determines how bright or dull one will eventually become.

In recent years, the heredity issue has stirred considerable controversy. The way in which many of the experts have fought it out has been unfortunate in two respects: First, many of the participants have failed to define their terms clearly enough so that we on the sidelines can be sure that they are talking about the same things. Second (and this is truly one of the scientific shames of our generation), emotional arguments and name calling have been too frequently substituted for hard evidence. In spite of the confusion, however, the issue is a serious one; the implications are extremely important. If smart children are born smart and dumb children are born dumb, then any attempt to improve the level of a child's performance is, for the most part, a waste of time. If, however, one's environment and early experiences are responsible for one's later intellectual performance, we must find out how to make those early experiences as growth producing as possible. Environmental influences such as diet, the language structure in the home, or the expectations and labeling practices of school teachers can be changed; a child's genetic make-up cannot. Environmentalists maintain that most dull children (and adults) are dull because those early conditions have made them so, and our first priority is to change that situation. Hereditarians claim that to treat all children as if they had the same potential for the same kind of intellectual functioning is to close our eyes to biological reality.

One of the standard measures used by the hereditarians is called the *heritability index*. In order to arrive at this index, IQ data are collected from groups of individuals who are related to each other in varying ways— identical twins, fraternal twins, siblings, parents and children, nonrelated but of the same racial stock, and so on. From these data is determined the degree to which intelligence (as measured by IQ tests) correlates with genetic similarity. According to Eysenck (1971b), the best available estimates suggest a ratio of 4 to 1 for the relative importance of the contributions of heredity and environment. In other words, genetic factors can be argued to be responsible for something like 80% of all the variation we find in IQs within a given population such as that living in England or the United States at the present time.

There is little doubt that estimates of heritability are getting at a real relationship between genetic potential and actual functioning. The question is not whether such a relationship exists, but rather how strong it is and whether it can be modified by other factors. Says Cronbach (1975b, p. 2) "The evidence is that differences among American or British whites in the past generation have been due in part to genetic differences. The precise proportion, but not the principle, of hereditary influence can be debated." He further points out that the heritability index is an index of sociocultural conditions, not a biological inevitability. Change nutrition, home experience, and schooling in the next generation, and the heritability index will change. The heritability index simply tells us that two things go together: an individual's intelligence and the intelligence of his family. This does not mean that the one causes the other. People who have less intelligent parents (again, defining intelligence as whatever is measured by IQ tests) also tend to come from certain kinds of home environments, to be exposed to similar schooling opportunities, and to share a number of negative expectations placed on them by other members of the society.

The heritability index has come under fire from statisticians as well. A number of scientists contend that because intellectual functioning involves so many different structures and characteristics of the human organism—structures and characteristics that have their roots in many different genes and combinations of genes—it doesn't make sense to talk about a single heritability factor. "The plain facts are that in the study of man a heritability estimate turns out to be a piece of 'knowledge' that is both deceptive and trivial" (Hirsch, 1972, p. 23). Heritability, argue the environmentalists, assumes that a person's level of functioning is fixed—unchangeable—as a result of his genetic structure; but we know that in fact one's early experiences do play a crucial role in determining what one will be able to do as an adult. Hirsch points out that paying too much attention to genetic factors may blind us to more important causal factors in intellectual performance; heritability tells us absolutely nothing about how a given individual might have developed under conditions different from those in which he did develop.

## Racial Differences

The argument about whether intelligence is inherited might well have continued as a quiet discussion among scholars had it not been for the emergence of a new factor: the possibility of racial differences in intelligence. If intellectual ability is inherited—carried genetically—then it would seem reasonable to at least inquire whether different racial groups, which differ in other genetically determined characteristics, might also differ in this one. At first glance, the data would tend to support such a conclusion. "It is a known and uncontested fact," says Jensen, one of the more outspoken contenders in this argument, "that blacks in the United States score on average about one standard deviation below whites on most tests of intelligence" (1973, p. 80). This is a statistical statement; it deals with averages and is relatively useless in making predictions about individuals. Nevertheless, if we interpret the data as indicating that black people are, as a group, less intelligent than white people, we have clearly taken a position that has far-reaching social implications. And these implications would be extremely distasteful to most people.

Jensen, Eysenck, and others have pulled together from many studies evidence that tends to support the idea that blacks consistently do less well on tests of intellectual performance than do whites and that a part of the difference is hereditary. They have not claimed that all the differences are based on heredity—such a claim would be foolish—but rather that explanations that involve only environmental influences do not cover all the observed differences among racial groups. In almost any other area of human behavior, such a claim would be considered relatively mild—but not so in the case of racial differences. Our social history has created for us an emotional potpourri of guilt, anger, and fear that simply does not allow us to be calm or objective about racial issues. The hereditarians were quickly branded as racists (and worse); and they seem to have become, in turn, more defensive and strident as the battle wears on.

But where does all this battling leave us foot soldiers, who have to make day-to-day decisions about what to do in the classroom? Let's see whether we can clear away some of the rubble and reach a few (at least tentative) conclusions. To begin, intellectual performance is a joint function of both heredity and environment. Cronbach points out that "even the most hereditarian position does not hold that ranks in performance will remain stable when the initially low-ranking children are treated specially" (1975b, p. 5). Similarly, no environmentalist would deny that some children are born with intellectual handicaps, that there is, in some cases, a ceiling on what a child can hope to accomplish. The important point is that we don't know—especially when dealing with individuals—what that ceiling is. Heredity may—probably does—put a top limit on what a person can accomplish intellectually. But nobody knows ahead of time what that limit is. I suspect that few of us reach our limit, that for the great majority of people environmental factors slow and (all too often) eventually halt growth long before one's potential is realized. For a teacher to assume that a black child or a child from a nonachieving family or a child with retarded parents is not going to be able to do well in school or society is to ensure that the environment will work against rather than for that child.

Researchers, I believe, must change their focus. Rather than fighting over how much of intelligence is genetically determined, we need to know about the kinds of differences that exist in the way groups tend to function best. There is no reason that I know of why some particular brain or neural structure might not be more characteristic of one race than of another; all sorts of physical and physiological differences have been shown to be racially linked. If such differences do in fact exist, then blacks and whites and reds and yellows may indeed also approach specific tasks in different ways—different, not better or worse. And if such differences exist, then we need to know about them. We need to structure our teaching so that we can build on the strengths and teach to the weaknesses of each child. Playing ostrich won't help us, any more than it will help us solve our racial problems in other areas. The teacher who believes blacks (or any other group) to be biologically inferior is a bigot, but so is the teacher who refuses to consider any possibility of racial differences. We must keep open minds, remembering always that we work with individual children, not statistical groups; and we must have the courage to learn, along with each child, to deal honestly with whatever strengths and weaknesses he brings to his own learning and growth.

## The First Few Years

Knowledge and ability increase explosively during the first few years of a child's life. Again, both our own adult blinders and the young child's difficulty in communicating with us (and us with him) make it hard to tell just what and how much he knows. Most of the so-called infant intelligence tests deal with perceptual discrimination and coordination; the tester determines whether the baby can grab a rubber ring or stack one block on another or put together a simple puzzle. Few of these kinds of skills are tested for in adult intelligence tests, and one suspects that the main reason they are used with infants is that they are about the only skills we can test babies on. Given this kind of discontinuity between what is called intelligence in infants and in adults, it is hardly surprising that attempts to predict later intelligence scores on the basis of infant performance have ended largely in failure.

Many scientists contend that it is not only the difficulty in getting accurate measurements from a young child or the difficulty in knowing exactly what to try to measure that is responsible for these failures in prediction. More important is the fact that we don't know what is going to happen to that child in the years ahead. No matter how skilled we might become at measuring an infant's potential, they argue, the degree to which that potential will be realized is largely a function of the experiences he has as he matures. "In fact, trying to predict what the IQ of an individual child will be at age 18 from a DQ [a developmental quotient, the term given to scores analogous to IQ scores but obtained from early-age tests] obtained during his first or second year is much like trying to predict how fast a feather might fall in a hurricane. . . . Any laws concerning the rate of intellectual growth must take into account the series of environmental encounters which constitute the conditions of that growth" (Hunt, 1969, p. 6).

That the problem is one of potential functioning versus actual behavior, rather than just the IQ-DQ discontinuity, is shown by the fact that prediction is poor even for older children. Klonoff (1972), for instance, beginning with children during the preschool years, found that 12% of his subjects' IQ scores changed more than ten points over a single year. And—sadly—these changes were not all in the desired direction. Children with initially high scores changed just as much and as often as the initially low scorers, and both groups had children whose scores went up and went down.

A great deal of imaginative research has been carried out in the effort to understand child intelligence. As an example of the studies that have been done, consider the work of Willerman and Stafford (1972). These researchers wanted to know whether the intellectual level of one parent was more influential than that of the other in determining the intelligence of a child. They looked for families in which there were clear differences in the test scores of father and mother and tried to determine which parent the children would most resemble in their own test performance. One serious problem in the research had to do with prevailing cultural patterns in the United States: there were few families available for study in which the wife had clearly higher IQ scores than the husband. (We might note that this kind of problem is often the bugaboo of natural, as opposed to laboratory, research; people simply don't arrange themselves into all the nice, balanced groups that we would like to study and compare.) Even with this gap in the sample, however, Willerman and Stafford found support for the notion that children's IQ scores tend to match the IQ of their mothers rather than that of their fathers.

Apart from its usefulness in illustrating the kind of research that is going on in the development of intelligence, this study has some bearing on the nature-nurture controversy that we discussed earlier. If intelligence is determined largely by heredity, then we might (as a first hypothesis) expect both parents to contribute equally to the intellectual ability of their child. If, however, intelligence is a matter of environmental influence, then we might expect the mother (who usually spends more time with the small child) to have more impact than the father.

The Willerman and Stafford study exemplifies the kind of research that fills the child-development journals: each study focuses on one or a few important variables and usually finds some support for its hypothesis. We can now safely conclude that children's intellectual growth is (partly) a function of the parenting they get, the environmental stimulation to which they are exposed, and the adequacy of their physical care. As my own children would say, big deal. That's just common sense; why did we have to do high-powered research to find it out? We are no closer now than we were a decade ago to predicting what an individual child will be able to do as an adult, and most of the environmental-influence research sounds suspiciously like what grandma knew long ago.

These two discouraging statements are not at all unrelated; they are part and parcel of the same problem. If we knew more specifically the role environment plays in the development of intelligence, we could predict individual growth much more accurately. And accurate measures of early IQ, measures that do tend to predict long-range ability, could be useful in attempts to sort out the influences that affect intellectual growth. If we could measure the intellectual potential of young children, then watch (or even manipulate) what happens to them as they grow up, and then measure their intelligence again, the amount of change would indicate the helpfulness or harmfulness of their intervening experiences. Without accurate change scores of this sort, we can only compare groups of children or young adults who have been reared under different circumstances and make rough guesses as to which factors contributed most strongly to differences between those groups. While this procedure gives us some hints about what goes on during the early development of intellect, it doesn't provide the accuracy that would be possible if we could trace what happens to individual children.

It might be nice, at this point, if I could provide you with a cookbook of intellectual growth—a "he should do this at 5 years, that at 6" kind of list. But such a list will not be found on these pages for several reasons. First, to provide such information here would be time consuming and redundant. The intelligence-testing literature is replete with information about age norms for all sorts of behaviors; if one is interested in pursuing the subject, that is the place to go. Second, too much reliance on age norms of this sort tempts the teacher to overlook the individual child. Age norms are statistical, based on large groups of children; within any such group, there is wide individual variation in skill or ability. To expect every child to perform at a given normative level is as foolish as to expect all children to be exactly average in height or weight. Yet the existence of a specific norm tends to make us place that kind of expectation on children: if Kathy can't work up to norm then something must be wrong with Kathy. This thinking is not only foolish, it can be downright harmful to the child.

Finally, even if one treats norms in the right way—as fuzzy guidelines rather than specific points that each child should reach at a set age—they still can be misleading. Intelligence of the sort we as teachers should be interested in fostering is not simply performance on a test; it is potential actualized, working and developing and fermenting in the child's social and educational environment. Test scores tell only a small part of the story, no matter how wisely they are used. The best all-round measure of a child's ability is what he does and how he does it. The teacher who needs to know more than that about a child should probably request testing by experts; we foot soldiers have more important business to be about.

### Crystallized and Fluid Intelligence

In determining the way intelligence develops in an individual, just as in understanding the heredity-environment argument, the problem of definition is crucial. Are we talking about the development of intelligence as a unitary ability, which manifests itself in a large number of ways? Or must we think rather about tracing the growth of several independent abilities, each of which develops in its own way and at its own speed, and look at the interaction patterns that evolve as these separate abilities grow and change? We have already discussed the notion of a *g* factor of intelligence, as contrasted with group-factor theories, and we have looked at Guilford's three-dimensional model of the intellect. Another way of cutting the pie is to think of intelligence as being of two major kinds, fluid and crystallized. *Fluid intelligence* is closely related to creativity; it is a flexible, adaptive, bubbling-out ability that appears to have little to do with the specifics of what one has already learned. *Crystallized intelligence* is directly related to previous learning; it is the "what I can do, now and in the future, as a result of what I have already learned." Horn (1972, pp. 53-54) puts it this way: "Fluid intelligence . . . is relatively independent of education and experience; and it can 'flow into' a wide variety of intellectual activities. Crystallized intelligence, on the other hand, is a precipitate out of experience. It results when fluid intelligence is 'mixed' with what can be called 'the intelligence of the culture.' "

To gain a better idea of the differences between these two kinds of intelligence, let's go back to the concept-formation experiment that we discussed in Chapter 4. In this experiment, the subject is presented with a series of geometrical patterns; it is his task to determine which of the patterns are yings. Each time he sees a pattern, he says whether or not he thinks it is a ying, and the experimenter tells him whether or not he is right. The experimenter has decided that a ying will be defined as any triangular figure; he is interested in the logical processes that the child uses to arrive at that definition for himself. If the type of problem is a new one for the child, he will begin by making guesses that seem to follow no particular logical pattern. Gradually he will begin to eliminate individual figures as possible yings, and he may eventually sort the figures into classes on the basis of their major characteristics. If he begins relatively early to use a systematic process of elimination to determine which groups may be yings and which are not, this process must be a function of high fluid intelligence: he has no past experience with this sort of problem on which he could be drawing. If, however, he has worked with this sort of problem before, he may know right away what sort of strategy to use. He has learned how to learn in this situation. He may, for instance, decide to test the hypothesis that all blue things or all things with more than one figure are "yings"; or that no small figures or no yellow round ones are. He moves confidently into the problem, using a plan of attack that he has worked out during his previous experience with similar problems. Such a child is displaying high crystallized intelligence; his behavior is a blend of intrinsic ability and previous learning.

The importance of the fluid-crystallized distinction for our present discussion is that these two kinds of intelligence appear to follow quite different developmental courses through the life of the human organism. Both fluid and crystallized intelligence increase through childhood; maturing neural structures undoubtedly have an influence here, as well as perceptual and motor experiences. Fluid intelligence tends to peak sometime during late adolescence, and from then on it can be expected to decline slightly. Crystallized intelligence, in contrast, doesn't show this sort of decline. Although its growth slows down considerably in late adolescence or early adulthood, it tends to level off or even continue to increase slightly throughout life.

It seems clear that we are talking about two distinct sorts of phenomena here. We do not know enough about them, though, to be able to say whether they are truly independent or whether the development of crystallized intelligence is limited somehow by the amount of fluid intelligence one possesses. Neither do we know with any confidence what specific experiences are most beneficial for the development of one or the other—if, indeed, to speak of experience benefiting the growth of fluid intelligence is not a contradiction in terms. We do know some general rules about not inhibiting the growth—or the use— of fluid intelligence; and, as we have seen, we have some ideas about the kinds of factual tool kits that make for efficient building on past knowledge. We shall turn to these rules and ideas in a later section and shall also deal with them in Chapter 7. For now, let's just bear in mind that the fluid-crystallized distinction may not be the only meaningful way to distinguish aspects of mental ability, aspects that may be relatively independent of each other. Again, every child needs to be encouraged to use what he does well—and to feel good about it—as well as to work on those skills that he may have neglected in the past.

## Stages of Intellectual Growth

We have already discussed Piaget's model of cognitive growth: that children move through definite, traceable stages, each stage representing a more mature mode of interaction with the physical world. If this view is correct, then the qualitative nature of the child's thought processes does change as he grows up; it is not simply a matter of getting better at problem solving or memory or whatever but of doing these things in a different way. Moreover, the changes are not random or haphazard but rather take place in an orderly and predictable pattern. There is no particular reason to expect, given Piaget's model, that a child's performance at the sensory-motor stage should bear any specific relationship to how well he will do later on in the preoperational phase or still later during the period of conceptual thought; the child is doing something quite different at each of these points or periods in time.

One question that has been asked within the Piagetian framework, though, is how closely the child's speed in progressing through Piaget's various stages relates to more traditional measures of intelligence. That is, does the bright child (as we have ordinarily understood the term) develop more quickly and thus reach the preoperational stage or the stage of formal operations sooner than the dull child? There is not a great deal of evidence as yet; but what there is suggests a slight relationship. A study by Dudek (1972), for instance, showed a correlation of .62 between IQ and Piagetian stage development. While this is clearly higher than would have been expected just by chance, it still leaves a lot unaccounted for: more than half of the variability in stage development is not correlated with IQ.

Another measure that may have promise for future research is that of stage instability. As Piaget points out, children don't slide smoothly out of one stage and into another, as if a switch had been thrown. There is a transitional period, during which the child flip-flops back and forth between the two modes of thinking. "Thinking at intermediate stages is fluid and unstable. Until terminal stages are achieved there is no equilibrium, and lapses into primitive thinking may be expected" (Dudek, 1972, p. 468). Studying more closely the nature of such lapses may give us greater insight into just what the qualitative differences are between the different Piagetian levels and how the child may be helped to make the transitions into more mature thinking styles.

Shifting from one style to another involves a certain amount of conflict for the learner; a person can be expected to discard a learned pattern of dealing with the world only as a result of discovering that it doesn't work so well for him any more. Indeed, this sort of conflict—the tug of war between what I usually do and what I might try out—is probably the basic proto-type of learning. Bruner proposes that all learning patterns—thinking styles—arise out of just such conflicts. The child's developing perceptual ability and his growing ability to apprehend and evaluate what he perceives lead to mismatches, situations in which the input and the learned means of dealing with it just don't fit. Out of these mismatches come new learning strategies, new models for handling similar situations in the future as well as future nonfit situations. "There develops a range of 'devices' and 'prepa-rations' that have to do with dealing with mismatch on the next encounter: trust in one's body image or strong reliance on a visual framework and the world of objects, etc." (Bruner, 1966b, p. 49). Different children, then, are likely to develop different ways of handling mismatch problems; again, the teacher needs to look at the individual child, at his particular mismatch strategy, in order to create an optimal situation for consolidating growth within a stage or for moving into the next stage of intellectual development.

*Memory*

Flavell (1971) points out yet another way in which children's cognitive processes seem to change qualitatively as they grow older. Extensive studies of memory in children suggest that while young children obviously do remember things, they don't seem to do so deliberately. Young children do perceive and otherwise assimilate present data. Also, they do recall past data, but they do not consciously and deliberately try to process present data in such a way as to facilitate its future recall. The older child learns deliberately; that is, he deals with new data in such a way as to consciously facilitate his being able to remember and use it later. The younger child seems not to have learned yet that he may need to use a particular fact later on—perhaps the concept of "later on" is not yet a clear one to him—and so he does not engage in a deliberate storage and addressing process. Again, the information and insights we have in this area are slight com-pared with what we don't yet know: we don't know, for instance, just what deliberate processing for recall is or how the child acquires such an ability. We do know—or at least suspect—that the presence or absence of such an ability has far-reaching implications for other cognitive activities engaged in by the child. For example, storing information away for future use (or even, for that matter, the very idea of thinking in terms of past and future rather than being trapped in the endless instant of now) can be an extremely important tool in the development of mismatch strategies. As Flavell points out, individuals should exhibit a wide variety of interesting and important changes in all sorts of memory behaviors as their conceptual knowledge and their cognitive abilities evolve during childhood.

One such change that has been verified experimentally is the use of *mediation*. Mediation occurs when a person uses one idea or concept as a bridge to the recall of another; we have already discussed some of the ways in which familiarity and meaningfulness provide mediating links that make for easy retrieval of information. An obvious example is the use of a mnemonic technique to remember proper names. I may be introduced to a lady named Marion Waters, who wears large, horn-rimmed glasses. I form a mental picture of this lady standing in strong wind with her glasses off and her eyes watering; I hope that when I see her next, I'll be reminded of this image and then be able to remember her name. Mediation by means of mnemonics is a deliberate, conscious process. Many students of memory have also used the notion of unconscious mediating processes to explain how we remember and understand. That is, a particular word or idea or context within which an idea is embedded creates a response in us—a response determined by our past experiences with that word or idea or context. And the response serves as a cue as to how to react or respond further to the word or context: how to understand it or fit it in with other ideas or dredge it out into consciousness. A study by Kendler, Kendler, and Ward (1972) indicates that this kind of mediating process occurs more frequently in older than in younger children. That is, the older child has learned to make greater use of his own responses in dealing with new input rather than being limited to the new input all by itself. The older child has more such responses just by virtue of having been exposed to more experiences. But he also seems to use these responses differently, more appropriately, than he did when he was younger. This age difference probably holds for both conscious and unconscious mediating processes. "It seems very likely that, as children grow older, they become more aware of and more knowledgeable about their own mnemonic processes, capabilities, and contents" (Flavell, 1971, p. 227).

In summary, we have many reasons to believe that intellectual functioning changes qualitatively as well as quantitatively over time. An IQ test, no matter how carefully thought out and validated, cannot hope to tap all these qualitative differences—much less deal with the changing blends of abilities and stages that the child goes through. Nor can any teacher possibly be aware of all the factors that enter into a child's intellectual performance at a given point in time. What we can be aware of, though, is the fact that intelligence is not fixed for a given individual, either in quantity or quality. By making ourselves sensitive to the processes a child is using, we can better understand both his strengths and his weaknesses.

## FACILITATING INTELLECTUAL GROWTH

Being, for the most part, practical folk, young people tend to have a common response to situations or problems. Okay, they say, now what can we do about it? We have spent a great deal of time in these last few pages describing the growth and development of intelligence as we understand it.

Now it is time to address ourselves to the practical question: what can we, as teachers, do to help each child come as close as possible to developing his full potential?

## Hunt's Work with Infants

Much of what can be done to facilitate intellectual growth is (fortunately or unfortunately, depending on your point of view) long past by the time a child reaches the classroom. Increasingly, experts are recognizing the crucial importance of early experience in the development of intellectual ability. One such researcher is J. McV. Hunt. (For those readers who are interested in pursuing this subject further, Hunt's book *The Challenge of Incompetence and Poverty,* published in 1969, would be an excellent place to start.) Hunt points out two major effects of infant experience. One seems to be primarily an emotional or motivational effect, in which early painful experiences tend to make the individual less sensitive to or bothered by later painful or strange circumstances. Such desensitization must have an effect on learning, changing or blunting the effectiveness of punishments or negative reinforcers as well as making the individual less aware of his own emotional responses to all sorts of potential learning situations. If the infant's experiences can be varied without making them painful, though, later learning is facilitated. "The other kind of effect is one increasing the capacity of an organism to learn. . . . It looks very much as if any increase in the variation of circumstances encountered during [the] first three weeks of life will facilitate later learning, not only in the avoidance situation but also in . . . problem-solving situations" (Hunt, 1969, p. 23). If Hunt is right, the implications for parents and for educators are enormous. Essentially, he is proposing that a child will be skilled in problem solving and other thinking activities (other things being equal) to the degree that he has experienced, early in life, a wide variety of sensory input. Hunt's experiments with nonhuman species have led him to believe that this effect holds for other animals as well, but to a lesser degree than with humans.

In past years, early experience was thought to affect emotional development almost exclusively; its possible effect on cognitive behavior was quite ignored. It is possible that this emphasis was due to the fact that the earlier experimenters carried out most of their studies on lower animals. As we move up the phylogenetic scale (that is, from the lower animals like birds and reptiles to the higher animals like apes and men), a larger and larger portion of the front brain, or cerebrum, is devoted to learned capacities. At the same time, less and less of the cerebrum seems to be involved primarily with instinctual functions, with emotion, and with temperament. The early experimenters in the field of infant experience, working with nonhuman subjects (the ubiquitous white rat, for instance) may have come to place too much emphasis on the emotional effects of handling or cage decorations in infancy simply because their four-legged subjects did not have the physiological capacity for large-scale intellectual changes. Freud, too, helped focus on emotional effects, as he formulated his theories of infant sexuality and of the early genesis of lasting emotional problems. Hunt suggests that the emphasis on emotionality is misplaced—that early experience, for humans at least, probably has much more influence on perceptual, cognitive, and problem-solving functions than on feelings and emotions.

One experiment that Hunt and his associates carried out to demonstrate this effect involved placing various brightly colored and "interesting" patterns over the cribs of very young (5-week-old) infants. The babies were from middle-class families (in which we would not expect to find massive deprivation under ordinary circumstances) and were reared in their own homes. The effect of this simple intervention was startling: the blink response, which usually appears in infants around 10.4 weeks, appeared in these babies at an average age of 7 weeks—a highly significant change. Further research certainly needs to be done here—we cannot afford to place too much faith in the early appearance of an eye blink—but this finding is both suggestive and encouraging.

Hunt has an interesting explanation of how such early stimulation influences later intellectual functioning. He posits the existence of two intrinsic systems, each of which is of central importance in the thinking process. One of these systems is in the outer layer of the front part of the brain (the frontal cortex), and it is critically important in making and exe-

cuting plans; it is the higher administration of the cognitive process. The other system is not (as yet) as specifically located because it involves several different anatomical areas within the brain; its function is information processing. We might think of these two systems working together like a computer programmer and a computer: although neither can get anything done without the other, together they form an extremely powerful problem-solving unit. Hunt believes that early experience conditions these systems so that they can function effectively with each other later on. Carrying the computer analogy a bit further, it is as if the early experience provides the language with which the programmer interacts with the computer as well as many of the programs that will be used later on as parts of more complicated sets of directions.

This explanation aids us in understanding why helpful early experiences may seem quite unrelated to the kinds of skills they will enhance later in life. Preprogramming the two intrinsic systems to work efficiently together does not necessarily mean that they must learn to function on scaled-down versions of later problems, any more than the warm-up exercises of an athlete have to resemble the kinds of body movements he will make during the game. "Thus antecedent practice at tower-building and buttoning may be relatively unimportant for the development of skill in these activities; but an unhampered antecedent opportunity to throw objects and to manipulate them in a variety of situations, and an even earlier opportunity to have seen a variety of sights and to have heard a variety of sounds, may be of tremendous importance in determining both the age at which tower-building and buttoning will occur and the degree of skill that the child will manifest" (Hunt, 1969, p. 13).

### Other Experiments in Improvement of Intelligence

Many experiments have been carried out in which young children were exposed to special learning situations in an attempt to raise their level of intellectual functioning; these have met with varied success. Levinson (1971), for instance, taught 5-year-old children how to classify objects ("something you wear," "animal") and found that they scored significantly higher on verbal parts of an IQ test after such training. A control group, who worked on drawing, beads, puzzles, and so forth, while the other children were learning classification, showed no similar increase in either the verbal or the nonverbal parts of the test, in spite of the fact that the nonverbal parts involved tasks similar to the control-group activities. It would seem that, for these children, it was possible to improve conceptual and abstract processes by providing specific training in those processes.

Another study that tends to support this conclusion was done by Jacobson, Berger, Bergman, Millham, and Greeson (1971), using as subjects children from a day-care program in a large-city poverty area. Children in the experimental group were given about 20 hours of training in concept formation, while the control-group children continued in their regular daily activities. Both groups were tested at the beginning and at the end of the experiment; the experimentals, but not the controls, showed a significant increase in IQ scores.

We must bear in mind that studies of this sort, using standardized tests for small children and involving variations on real-life rather than strictly controlled laboratory situations, are subject to a number of experimental flaws. We know only the short-term and not the long-term effects of the treatment; moreover, we know only that the treatment was effective in changing test performance and not whether the children's day-to-day learning and thinking activities changed. Nevertheless, the findings are suggestive. It may well be that by the time a child reaches preschool age, he is ready to benefit from experiences specifically designed to enhance and sharpen his abstract-thinking abilities. If so, researchers must move on to discover which experiences are most beneficial to which children, which will have the greatest long-term influence, and which will have the most rapid influence on intellectual functioning in other skill areas than the specific one being dealt with during training.

## Intervention Strategies

I think it likely that these studies and others like them illustrate a trend in what might be called intervention strategy. That is, the older the child, the more specific the intervention may be to conceptual functioning. For infants and toddlers, Hunt's preprogramming model works well, while older children benefit more from direct training in conceptual skills. Young children need to acquire basic coordination and the perceptual raw materials that are used in thinking. Older children are less flexible and to a greater degree must learn to use optimally the raw materials they already possess. The kinds of skills that should be taught vary both with the sorts of things the child is able to do currently and with the amount of preprogramming that has already occurred and is already shaping his cognitive abilities. By the time a child reaches junior high or high school age, much if not all of his preprogramming has already taken place. In Piagetian terms, he is already on the brink of formal-operational thought. At this level, he can profitably work with conceptual patterns as such, without having to go back to the basic perceptual processes that underlie such patterns. Meehl addressed this notion with reference to college students. He contrasted the "bubble-headed" and the "hard-nosed" approach to problem solving. He was concerned with the need to teach students to be rigorous and critical, while not destroying their innovative and creative tendencies. After noting that too great an emphasis on rigor may foster a dreary, know-more-and-more-about-less-and-less sort of person, he continues "It does not follow that there is no such thing as training a person into certain habits of thought, or perhaps I should better say habits-cum-attitudes of thought, by combining emphases on methodological generalization *and* diversified substantive content, producing a kind of 'disciplined mind' " (Meehl, 1972, p. 933).

Even after one's formal education is over, the intellectual processes are still being shaped. As was mentioned earlier, fluid intelligence begins to decrease, while (for most people) crystallized intelligence continues to grow. People can and do learn to substitute previously acquired problem-solving patterns for the kind of bubbling creativity that characterizes the younger problem solver. Unfortunately, this kind of learning is not auto-matic; the amount of overall intellectual gain or loss that occurs in an adult seems to be directly related to the degree of stimulation and challenge he encounters throughout life. The more interesting and varied a person's job is, for instance, the less likely he is to decline in intellectual ability. This fact tends to create a vicious double-jeopardy situation in our culture. The more able a young person is, the more likely he is to find himself in an envi-ronment that enhances his abilities. The less able youth may easily find himself spending many of his waking hours in a job that tends to push him even farther down on the scale of cognitive competence. The system tends to be particularly unfair to women: a study done by Lunnenborg and Lunnenborg (1972) showed that while men who do not go to college tend, on average, to continue to improve slightly over the years in IQ scores, non-college women's scores decline.

### Guidelines

If our discussion thus far has done nothing else, it has underscored the importance of considering intellectual functioning in the context of the cul-ture or subculture in which it takes place. It makes no more sense to talk about how to educate a child to use his intellect in a cultural vacuum than it does to talk about the nature of intelligence apart from one's culture. One cannot prescribe experiences for children unless one specifies the environ-ment they must adapt to. The first dictum for the teacher, then, is to be aware of and to take into consideration the child's environment, both past and future. His past environment has had much to do with shaping that which he now is, and his future environment will help to determine whether that which he is will be adequate for that which he wants to become.

More especially, the teacher must be careful not to assume that the child or young adult in his care will necessarily go into—or have come from —the same cultural milieu as he himself. My model of the world and myself in it has been shaped by my surroundings and is not necessarily the same as yours; if it is different, it is not necessarily more valid than yours. The skills and abilities that I value—and have therefore chosen to call intelligence—are useful to me in my particular surroundings. I must not assume blindly that they will be equally useful to you; I must rather try to shed my cultural and personal biases and assess your needs and your strengths in the context of your world.

The late-20th-century school system in the United States is an environment in and of itself. Most children must learn to cope with this environment; to fail to do so is to risk suffering serious handicaps in later life. Schools vary, of course; they are rigid and flexible, large and small, orderly and chaotic, permissive and autocratic—and good and bad. The important point is that they constitute a cultural context within which most children must learn to function for a significant period of their lives. Quite apart from how well he is "educated" or "prepared for future life," the child's experiences of success and failure in school can be critical for his functioning in other environments later on. We need, therefore, to be sensitive to the intellectual skills that a child needs in the school environment—an issue that is more complex than might appear on the surface. Different schools and different levels within a single school require different skills on the part of the student. "Apparently, adequate functioning in each grade calls not for stability of skills from one grade to another, if success is to be obtained, but rather demands are made upon the subject to be flexible. What cognitive skills are important in the first grade are not necessarily crucial for adequate functioning in later grades" (Duffy, Clair, Egeland, & Dinello, 1972, p. 362). To convey to the child that he must develop a battery of skills, rather than selecting and perfecting one skill area, and to convince him that success today no more guarantees success tomorrow than failure today ensures failure tomorrow are two of the most important goals for a teacher to have.

In spite of the need for flexibility and the changing demands of various environments, a few skill areas seem to thread their way through nearly all intellectual functioning. One of these is language. As we have seen, language not only helps us communicate with others, but also is an internal problem-solving tool. It allows us to conceptualize, categorize, and manipulate; it gives us a means of dealing with reality through weightless symbols instead of heavily consequenced real-world trials and errors. Language, according to Bruner, tends to shape reality just as reality shapes language. The child's vocabulary reflects the world as he sees it and limits his interactions with the world; at the same time his experience of the world is molded by the words he has learned to use to describe it. Both words and grammatical structures, then, play an important role in the whole developing experience of self-in-world. As the availability of words and structures increases, so do the number and variety of intellectual activities accessible to the developing person. "If it should turn out to be the case that mastery of the culture depends on one's capacity to perform well on the basis of competence one has stored up, and to perform well in particular settings and in particular ways, then plainly the question of differences in the way language enters the problem-solving process cannot be dismissed" (Cole & Bruner, 1971, p. 871). Duffy and his colleagues (1972) remind us again that different levels of school (and, we might surmise by extension, different environments outside the school) require different kinds and combinations of linguistic abilities. We must continue to guard against a premature settling on one skill area as *the* thing to be polished and perfected, but there is little doubt that language competence is a major factor in the application of intellectual ability, if not intelligence itself.

The child needs not only to possess the intelligence to cope successfully with his environment but also to have faith in his own ability to do so. Intelligence, however defined, is nothing by itself; it needs to be applied, to be used. The child who experiences only failure in situations involving thinking or problem solving comes to think of himself as stupid and soon cuts himself off from chances to learn that he is not. Every child needs to experience situations in which he can succeed, to be given problems that he can solve—and to somehow find the courage to risk himself in those situations. For most children, this is not difficult; they have been succeeding at one thing or another all their lives. For some, however, the experience of failure has been so pervasive that they can hardly imagine success. A wise and sensitive teacher can provide enough security and enough faith to encourage these children to try—and risk failure—one more time. There is a delicate balance point, different for each child, between too much failure (and consequent despair) and too much success (which means few mismatches, little real learning, and unrealistic expectations for the future).

Cole and Bruner warn that the teacher may easily fall into the trap of perceiving the nonsuccessful, failure-oriented child as deficient, lacking some essential intellectual ability. While the child may indeed be deficient in some areas, and these areas are often ones that are important in the school setting, he is probably quite competent in others. Recognition of a child's educational difficulties as a difference rather than a special kind of educational disease should change his status in the eyes of the teacher. Once the beam has been removed from the teacher's eyes, he can proceed to work on the mote that is bothering the student. And the best way to do this is to find out which areas the student can perform in. "The teacher should stop laboring under the impression that he must create new intellectual structures and start concentrating on how to get the child to *transfer* skills that he already possesses to the task at hand" (Cole & Bruner, 1971, p. 874).

Intelligence is a difficult concept—difficult to define, difficult to understand, difficult to measure. But, however murky the area may be, our culture has decided that it is important (indeed, as we have seen, that importance itself is one definition of intelligence), and those of us who have as our goal the facilitation of learning are probably stuck with it. I think it fitting to close this chapter, in which we have struggled so hard with the inadequacies of our conceptualizations of intelligence, with the words of Binet, the father of intelligence testing: "A child's mind is like a field for which an expert farmer has advised a change in the methods of cultivation, with the result that in the place of a desert land, we now have a harvest" (quoted by Hunt, 1972, p. 33). To whatever degree we can increase the harvest, we have succeeded as teachers. We may not be able to change a student's potential ability, but we can have a profound effect on the way in which that potential is expressed and actualized. Perhaps that expression, that actualization, is what the learning process is all about.

## QUESTIONS FOR UNDERSTANDING

1. Into which (three-dimensional) cell(s) of Guilford's structure-of-the-intellect model would each of the following activities fit: (a) finding the action words in a set of sentences, (b) preparing a rebuttal of the "con" argument in a formal debate, (c) translating a paragraph of a German story into English, (d) teaching a group of first-grade children to play hopscotch.
2. Many schools routinely administer group IQ tests to students during each school year. How can the classroom teacher use the information yielded by such testing? What are some of the dangers involved?
3. In what ways might you be considered to be unintelligent if you were suddenly and magically transformed into a novice priest in a Tibetan monastery? What intellectual skills might the Tibetan lama need in Western culture that he would probably not need in his own cultural milieu?
4. How can you, as a classroom teacher, best utilize student errors to facilitate mismatch experiences that will lead to intellectual growth?
5. Meehl encourages teachers to combine emphases "on methodological generalization *and* diversified substantive content, producing a kind of 'disciplined mind.' " How might this dictum be translated into classroom practice? Give an example that would be appropriate for a third-grade class, for a seventh-grade class, and for a high school civics class.

# Chapter 7

# Creativity

If you had a dime for every word that has been written about creativity and the creative process in the last ten years, you would not need to be preparing for a career in teaching; you would be independently wealthy. Creativity is a topic that has fascinated scientists and philosophers in many branches of human thought; and, as in most areas of great interest, some of what has been written is sheer garbage, much is trivial and obvious, and some is quite useful and thought provoking—in a word, creative! In this chapter, we will try to sort through some of the ideas that various people have had about creativity. Some of the major questions that we will be addressing are the following: What is creativity, and what are we talking about when we try to relate creativity to other aspects of the person? What are the specific abilities or characteristics that contribute to overall creativity? Can we, as teachers, encourage or increase creativity in those with whom we work? Let's begin by trying to get a working idea of just what we are talking about when we use the word *creative*.

## WHAT IS CREATIVITY?

One of the most interesting (and most difficult to unscramble) relationships in the creativity literature is that between creativity and intelligence. A number of researchers have worked diligently to show that creativity and intelligence are unrelated, that the highly creative person may score quite low on standard tests of intelligence and the high scorer on intelligence tests may not be creative. Having already acquired some sophistication (and a highly suspicious attitude) about the nature of intelligence, you may raise your eyebrows a bit at that last statement; since when can we glibly equate intelligence with IQ scores? And is it possible that an equally suspect relationship may exist between creativity and creativity scores? The answer is, of course, yes; there is a great deal of well-founded skepticism about what many of the so-called tests of creativity are measuring. We shall deal with that issue in more detail a bit later; for now, let's stay with a more intuitive notion of what a creative thing looks like.

## The Creative Product

Jackson and Messick (1965) draw some useful comparisons between intelligent and creative products; they suggest that one of the first places to look in differentiating between the two is in the way we react to them. In deciding whether a particular response is intelligent, we ask ourselves if it is right or wrong, true or false—in other words, we use logical, objective criteria to evaluate how well the response corresponds to reality. In evaluating a response for its creativity, however, the distinction between right and wrong is of less importance; the operative concern here is whether the response is "good" or not. Good responses, say Jackson and Messick, "satisfy subjective criteria; although they may not necessarily be limited by the demands of logic and reality, they are responsive . . . to a wide variety of judgemental standards" (p. 310).

The very subjectivity of our evaluation of a creative response makes it extraordinarily difficult to pin down just what it is we are looking for. Jackson and Messick go on to suggest four major criteria. The first of these is *unusualness:* does the response being evaluated strike us as different from the ordinary, run-of-the-mill response that most people would make? For example, consider two answers to the question "What can you use a paper clip for?" One answer is "To hold sheets of paper together." A perfectly correct answer, practical, down to earth—but not particularly creative, primarily because it is not an unusual answer. Another response might be "You can unbend it and use the end to scratch designs in the frost on a windowpane." Now here is an unusual answer, and we would be much more likely to call it creative.

If unusualness or uniqueness alone were the criterion for creativity, however, we would have to include in that category all sorts of responses that are merely bizarre or strange. "What can you use a paper clip for?" "I carry my lunch in a sack." That response is certainly unusual; we would not expect many people to answer in that way. But it doesn't strike us as particularly creative; rather, it is just inappropriate. *Appropriateness,* then, is Jackson and Messick's second criterion for a creative response.

Outstanding examples of creativity, though, seem to go beyond even the two criteria of uniqueness and appropriateness. They are special somehow; they make us see things in a new light. We find ourselves wishing that we had thought of them and wondering why we didn't. Jackson and

Messick describe this quality as "the power to transform the constraints of reality." They elaborate: "Some objects combine elements in ways that defy tradition and that yield a new perspective. They literally force us to see reality in a new way. These products involve a *transformation* of material or ideas to overcome conventional constraints" (p. 318). This quality of transformation, then, is a third criterion for the creative product.

Finally, there is a quality of elegant simplicity in the truly memorable creative product: whatever it says or does, it says it or does it so smoothly or simply that one must look again to verify or capture or appreciate what has been done. Picasso's famous dove symbol is a good example; any child could draw it, having once seen it, but it took a truly creative mind to bring those elements together for the first time. There is a kind of *condensation* of many subtle factors into one smooth and harmonious whole; this quality is hard to define or describe, but easy to recognize.

Jackson and Messick emphasize again that the locus of these criteria is not in the product being evaluated as much as in the evaluator himself; it is our feelings about the product that we use to decide whether it is creative. A feeling of surprise leads us to describe a product as unusual; a feeling of comfort with it leads us to say that it is appropriate; and the qualities of transformation and condensation make us feel stimulated and aesthetically satisfied. Creativity cannot be separated from emotion either in the creator or in the receiver; it is precisely the emotional quality of our reaction to a creative product that leads us to say that it is not merely correct or intelligent, but something more.

## Product versus Process

Jackson and Messick's description of the creative response, particularly with regard to its qualities of transformation and condensation, clearly applies to a mature, finished product. Most ordinary people do not produce responses that possess such characteristics. Ausubel (1964) is quite explicit on this point; he says that a truly creative person must discover something original in human experience, not merely something unique in his own experience. When an individual performs in a novel way insofar as his own past experience is concerned, but his discovery is just a common rediscovery or his degree of originality is merely ordinary, he cannot be considered creative. The child who discovers that four fingers on one hand plus two fingers on the other add up to the same thing as three fingers on each hand, according to Ausubel's point of view, has not engaged in a creative act, regardless of the uniqueness or appropriateness or transforming force of that discovery in his own experience. To be truly creative, the product must be special—unique, transforming, what have you—in all human experience.

This viewpoint brings us to the heart of one of the great controversies about creativity. Is it a rare quality, held by a few individuals in an all-or-nothing way, or is it a characteristic that is distributed among all people, with some individuals possessing more of it and some less? Is the child proudly working out the rhyme "One, one, one is fun" creative in the same way as (but to a lesser degree than) a Shakespeare writing "But, soft! what light through yonder window breaks?" Ausubel would say no, that there is a qualitative difference between the two performances. Many others would disagree.

Part of the problem here, it seems to me, is a failure to distinguish between the creative product and the creative process. In looking at a *product,* we may apply whatever standards of creativity seem appropriate; and, in an ultimate sense, a truly creative product must be judged in the light of the sum of human experience as understood by the evaluator. If we go back to Jackson and Messick's comments, this requirement makes perfect sense; if the response of the evaluator is to be the final criterion and that emotional response is shaped by his past experiences, then surely it is his comparison of a particular product with other examples of responses in the same category on which his decision rests. We are here begging the question of who shall do the evaluating; and this is a fundamental flaw in such definitions: whether a particular product is seen as uniquely original in all human experience will surely depend upon the evaluator's own acquaintance with that human experience.

If we focus on the process, rather than on the product, the nature of the problem changes. The *process* of creativity is contained within the creating individual; it is his evaluation, and his alone, that tells us whether that process is a creative one. Proving a mathematical theorem, with all the frustration and excitement and satisfaction that such an exercise can entail, can be a highly creative process even though the product (given that the theorem has been proven before by someone else) is not unique. To me, as a teacher, it makes more sense to focus on the process of creativity than on the product as we attempt to define and understand creativity. I tend to believe that the characteristics and skills that enter into the process of creative discovery are the same, regardless of whether the end product is uniquely creative. I have no evidence to support such a belief; indeed, gathering such evidence might well be a great contribution in this area. However, the idea makes intuitive sense; and it is not unsupported by the theorizing of others. Even Ausubel, contradictory as it may seem, tends to move in this direction in his discussion of general creative abilities. While everyone cannot be a creator, he says, everyone may possess, to a greater or lesser extent, some of these creative abilities. "Typically, when teachers or school psychologists refer to pupils as being creative, what they really mean is that they exhibit a high degree of the general creative abilities" (Ausubel, 1964, p. 346). Whether it is the across-the-board sum of these abilities or their sum plus the pattern in which they are distributed or their sum and pattern plus an as-yet-undefined quality that differentiates between one who can be truly creative and one who merely performs "in a novel way insofar as his own past experience is concerned," Ausubel does not make clear. What does seem clear is that we must start with these abilities, whatever they are; they form the foundation, at least, if not the entire structure, of the creative act.

It is important to notice that the phrase *general creative abilities* is plural; there are more than one of these abilities. One of the major flaws in much creativity research to date has been that workers select one ability that has been associated with creativity and use it to stand for creativity as a whole process. This "all chickens have feathers; therefore anything with feathers must be a chicken" logic has been at the root of much of the erroneous thinking about creativity; we should try hard to avoid it. It is the aggregate, and perhaps the patterning as well, of a number of abilities that leads to creativity. We cannot identify an ability that we find to characterize the work of, say, both Thomas Edison and J. S. Bach and assume that it must therefore be prominent in every creative person. Nor may we deduce that any person who possesses this ability is necessarily creative. "We can neither assume that any personal characteristic has the same psychological significance in eminent and ordinary men nor arbitrarily select one of the distinguishing characteristics of eminent creatives as the index of creativity in all men" (Nicholls, 1972, p. 718). Rather, we must try to identify the various abilities that contribute to creativity, teasing them apart like strands of a rope, but remembering all the time that it is ultimately the rope that is important and not the strands themselves.

## IDENTIFYING THE STRANDS

A number of investigators have attempted to list the specific abilities that go into the creative process. Ausubel's (1964) list of general creative abilities is a good example; he includes such intellectual problem-solving traits as sensitivity to the existence of problems; facility in formulating, testing, and reformulating hypotheses; skill in improvising solutions; openness to new experience; and spontaneity and flexibility in approach to problems. Also involved are personality traits bearing on problem solving, such as perseverance and venturesomeness. Let's look more closely at some of these abilities (not necessarily in the order that Ausubel lists them), and see what other researchers have to say about their importance.

### The F Ability

Guilford and his students, beginning around 1950, set off what was probably the first major flurry of interest in measuring creative behavior or creative potential. They developed a number of tests that were intended to measure such things as uncommonness of responses, the ability to make remote associations, and "cleverness." In the early 1960s came the Torrance tests (Torrance, 1961), generally thought of as measures of "divergent thinking." We can lump together what both these tests were reaching for and call it cognitive flexibility or fluidity—the quality of being able to throw off lots of ideas, quickly and easily. Cronbach (1968) labeled this ability the $F$ factor (for fluidity and flexibility), and it is safe to say that most of the research on creativity has centered around this mysterious $F$. As an example of the studies that have been carried out, we might look at one done by Torrance himself, in which he followed up a group of high-$F$ high school students 12 years after they had originally been tested. He found that the old $F$ score, the one they earned in high school, correlated quite significantly with measures of their creative production—that is, things they had written, painted, or what have you as adults—and that many more of the high-$F$ students tended to be in unconventional occupations than was true for the low-$F$ students (Torrance, 1972).

Educators have long been interested in identifying and measuring creativity among their students; it is not surprising that tests of the $F$ ability quickly found enthusiastic adherents among teachers and educational psychologists. To the disappointment of many, however, research with such tests soon began to yield conflicting and confusing conclusions. Creativity, as measured by tests of the $F$ ability, sometimes was and sometimes was not linked to excellence in other areas. Worse still, people who were highly creative according to one sort of testing procedure looked only moderately so when tested under different conditions. Most of the $F$ tests had rather low reliability (that is, people did not score at the same level when they were tested again on the same criteria); and it proved to be difficult, if not impossible, to check their validity by comparing them with other measures of creative ability. A study by Thacker and Rosenbluth (1972) illustrates this validity problem. They asked teachers to identify the highly creative and the noncreative students in their classes and then administered the Torrance tests to all the students. The results suggested that teachers were able to pick out the students in their classrooms who were low scorers on the Torrance tests, but could not identify the very high-scoring students. In other words, the quality of thought that enabled students to do well on these tests did not influence their school behavior enough to allow teachers to differentiate between the excellent and the merely average.

This sort of research result has led a number of investigators to question the use of $F$ tests as indices of creativity. Nobody disagrees with the notion that cognitive flexibility is an important part of the creative-ability pattern, but there is growing reluctance to assume that the ability to score well on the Guilford or Torrance tests is, by itself, evidence of true creativity. Thus Dellas and Gaier (1970, p. 56), in a comprehensive review of creativity research, conclude that the results "have been contradictory and far from conclusive"; and Nicholls (1972, p. 723), in another survey of the literature, goes even further when he sums up: "the evidence suggests that divergent thinking tests do not provide a meaningful index of creativity." Cronbach rounds off the chorus of disillusionment with Torrance- and Guilford-type tests; after a most thorough discussion of the evidence, he concludes "My final impression is that the $F$ variable has disappointingly limited psychological significance. It can scarcely be considered a measure of ability or creativity; there is no evidence that high $F$ children produce responses of superior quality in any situation" (1968, p. 509).

At this point you, the reader, may well be growing quite confused. "First you suggested that these tests do measure something worthwhile, and then you haul in all sorts of experts to say they're no good at all," you may be saying. "What am I supposed to believe?" I have a reason for bringing in all this contradictory evidence. The study of creative behavior is a good model of the way scientific discovery in psychology proceeds, and it is probably a good example for us to bear in mind as we cover a number of different areas later in this book. As in other fields, the study of creativity has gone through a number of distinct phases. Phase 1 is marked by the first Guilford publication, in 1950; this was the beginning, when bits of interesting research and speculation began to catch the eye of a number of researchers across the country. Phase 1 gradually evolved into phase 2: a period of intense enthusiasm with great quantities of research rolling out. The Torrance tests were developed during this phase and were greeted with cries of delight—hooray, now we have a quantified instrument for measuring this thing we've been working with! Then, in the early 1970s, came the beginnings of phase 3: the sober, critical assessment of the products of all that earlier enthusiasm. Phase 3 is always a period of controversy, a time when the loyal defenders and the eager attackers go at it tooth and nail; the fur flies, bits and pieces of theory come apart and are furiously kicked about, and a wonderful time is had by all. Eventually (one hopes) everyone moves into a phase 4, in which there is some agreement about what should be retained as valid and useful, and what should be thrown out. And then a whole new cycle can begin again, building on the phase-4 agreement as its foundation.

While we have not yet reached phase 4 in creativity research, I believe we are almost there; and I will predict one of the general outcomes. It will be decided that divergent thinking, or the *F* ability, is necessary for creative thinking, but that other things are equally necessary. Indeed, some researchers have already said this very thing: Jackson and Messick (1965), for instance, comment that the identification of the unusual is, at best, a first step in trying to understand the good. In other words, while a creative product must indeed be unusual, it must also possess other important characteristics, characteristics that are not assured by the fact of its unusualness. Nicholls (1972) points out that not only the amount of several different abilities may enter into creative productivity but also the way they are patterned. That is, the way in which a whole array of abilities are arranged in relationship to one another may be at least as important as the separately measured level of any one of them or of the overall sum of their separate levels. And Dellas and Gaier (1970) pull us back to an earlier problem, that of finding an appropriate criterion for creative behavior. How can we decide whether or to what degree any group of abilities constitute "it" when we aren't sure what "it" is? Different kinds of people may be creative in different ways; different individual personalities may require different optimal patterns or amounts of the various individual abilities involved in creativity.

In sum, it would seem that in the first rush of enthusiasm over creativity research, many scientists oversimplified the problem. We are now gradually becoming aware that there is not one creativity that people may or may not possess, but rather a number of abilities that interrelate in some as-yet-unknown way(s), with some relatively ill-defined product as the result of that interrelation. Nicholls (1972, p. 724), talking about how confused the whole area of creativity research is, comments that one researcher compares those who study creativity to the proverbial blind men who tried to describe the elephant. Well and good, says Nicholls, but the simile doesn't go far enough: "There are, in fact, a variety of genuine elephants, and the blind men have in many cases coped with this pretty well. A major source of confusion, however, is the unacknowledged collection of domestic pets that accompany the blind men into the elephant compound." Now, I think, we must go even further and realize that neither the elephants nor the domestic pets by themselves will satisfy us; it is the whole collection of creatures and how they arrange themselves in the compound that we need to look at. One of the elephants is surely the *F* ability—the compound wouldn't be the same without it—yet it by itself cannot be equated with the whole thing. It is time to move on and see what other sorts of animals may inhabit our zoo.

## Intelligence

Guilford (1959), in his early studies of thinking, identified five intellectual operations, among which was divergent production—our old friend the $F$ ability. Listing this ability as part of intelligence gave impetus to a number of studies that attempted to pin down the relationship between creativity (whatever that is) and intellectual ability. As might be expected, many conflicting findings have been published; depending on how we choose to define creativity, we can point to studies showing a significant positive relationship, little or no relationship, or even an inverse relationship between the two. One of the larger studies, involving more than 400 high school seniors (Olive, 1972), found correlations of .13 to .50 between measures of divergent thinking and IQ scores. This kind of relationship— slight correlation, but better than one would expect just by chance—is fairly typical of the majority of studies in which divergent-thinking scores are compared with IQs.

One problem with studies of this sort is that they frequently utilize a restricted sample; a group of "highly creative" individuals is identified by one means or another, and the measures of both divergent thinking and IQ are obtained from this group. Any time you restrict the range—that is, the amount of variability—in one or both of the abilities you are interested in, you automatically decrease the correlation between them. McNemar (1964), who is regarded as an authority on the use of statistics in social science, has pointed out that we should not be surprised at the fact that so-called creativity tests do not yield high correlations with IQ tests; the correlations are, in fact, generally far higher than those found in typical studies with range restrictions. In other words, even though the correlations may look low, they probably reflect a rather substantial degree of relationship between the two variables.

McNemar goes on to describe what he believes to be the true nature of this relationship. At very high levels of IQ, there is a wide range of creative ability. High IQ scorers may be creative, or they may not be creative at all; simply being able to score high on an IQ test does not guarantee that one is a creative person. However, as we move down the IQ scale and look at people who appear to be only moderately intelligent, we find a smaller percentage of them to be creative, and among low-IQ individuals there are few creatives indeed. "Having a high IQ is not a guarantee of being creative; having a low IQ means creativity is impossible" (McNemar, 1964, p. 879). It begins to look as though we have a situation similar to the old analogy of the chain with many links: the weaker any individual link, the weaker the whole chain. Divergent-thinking ability and intelligence may be two of the links in the chain that we call creativity.

Before we leave the subject of intelligence, we might mention briefly the work of H. Day (1968), who has tried to bring together what is known about intelligence, curiosity, and creativity. According to Day, intelligence and curiosity are independent characteristics—that is, a person may be high or low on either without affecting his position or score on the other. The person who is high on both intelligence and curiosity is the creative person, while the person who is low on both is characterized by Day as "going nowhere." The high-IQ/low-curiosity person never reaches his full creative potential because he isn't pushed by his own curiosity into further exploration. Day comments that the schools are full of such students; they are the ones who are often used as examples of the stultifying effects of a too-structured educational environment. The high-curiosity/low-IQ child, however, is one for whom exploration is often not rewarding; he simply hasn't the intellectual ability to capitalize on his own curiosity and soon

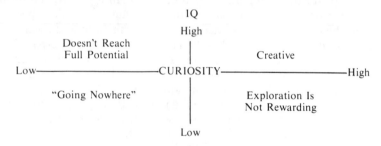

*Figure 7-1.* The relationship of IQ, curiosity, and creativity.

learns that it doesn't pay to explore very much. Figure 7-1 shows Day's hypothesized relationships among these three characteristics.

## Personality

Having opened the door to considerations of personality, we can find a number of other traits or characteristics that have been related to creativity and that may form links in the chain. One such characteristic is cognitive style. We shall deal with cognitive style in some detail in Chapter 9, but it seems appropriate to give it at least passing attention in this context. Cognitive style is a sort of wastebasket term that covers a number of dimensions relating to the way in which people think. One such dimension has to do with one's preference for complexity as opposed to simplicity. Some individuals seem to be more comfortable with relatively complex stimulus patterns, while others prefer simpler, cleaner stimuli. Several studies, according to Dellas and Gaier (1970), indicate that creative people in general prefer more complex, rather than simpler, stimuli. We don't know which way the causal relationship (if any) goes: do people prefer complexity because of their creative bent, or does the preference for complexity tend to enhance creativity? Renner and Renner (1971) attempted to shed light on this question. They gave college students a six-session course in creative problem solving, in which they emphasized such skills as sensing and recognizing problems, idea finding, and "making unusual ideas useful." The course had two major effects on the students: it made them more fluid and flexible in their thinking (the $F$ ability), and it also increased their preference for stimulus complexity. Thus we have again the chicken-egg problem: which caused which, or were they both similarly affected by other experiences or characteristics of the individual? Whatever the answer (and it would be a highly interesting research avenue to pursue), one thing does seem clear: the creative person is more comfortable with, and tends to prefer, cognitive complexity.

Both in problem solving and in problem recognition, the person who has access to more information has a head start. Thus, we would expect the creative problem solver to be someone who is sensitive to and aware of a broader range of data—of stimuli—than his less creative counterpart. This expectation tends to be borne out in research: creative individuals tend to take note of things that happen to them and around them, to be less defensive about their own feelings, and generally to be more open in their relationships with the world. Notice that I did not say that they are more open in their relationships with other people; while this may be the case with some creatives, it is not necessarily so with all of them. What does seem to be characteristic is an overall sensitivity and awareness: it's as if the creative person were some sort of giant vacuum cleaner trained on all the world, internal and external, scooping up and storing away impressions for future reference. This receptiveness is considered to be one aspect of cognitive style, just as cognitive complexity is, and we may add it to our list of characteristics of the creative individual.

By definition, the creative individual brings forth—says, makes, writes, paints, invents—something new and different. Were his product not new and different, we wouldn't label it creative. But any departure from the old and tried involves risk: risk of failure, risk of personal loss, risk of ridicule. In order to bring his creative impulse and ability to fruition, the creative individual must be willing to take these risks. He must be willing to expose himself to the criticism—or worse—of others. It may be that for a few creatives the risk is minimal, that they are so sure of the internal validity of their creative productions that the criticisms of others carry little or no threat. Many others, though, have a terrible vulnerability. The newly hatched product is often fragile; exposed to the cold winds of indifference or scorn, both it and its author can wither painfully. Remember, the creative product is not right or wrong; it is good or bad; and the definition of good depends on who is doing the judging. The painter, the playwright, the inventor all may be aware of this; they know that no matter how convinced they are of the goodness of their product, still the goodness may not be apparent to their audience. The risk, then, is a double one: that the product may not in fact be good, and that the critics may not use the same definition of goodness as the creator.

There is a third kind of risk taking as well; it lies in the area of problem selection. In choosing a problem on which to work, we can usually choose to take either an easy, safe, low-payoff problem or a difficult, risky, high-payoff one. The easy problem won't win us any laurels, but we won't lose our jobs over it either. It's the high-payoff, risky problem that allows the exercise of creativity. In order to give one's creative abilities full scope, one must be willing to choose problems that challenge those abilities. Such willingness to take on a difficult problem or to indulge in high risk differs from one individual to the next, and when present at a high level, it is a basic personality characteristic of the creative person.

Motivation is an important element of personality. What sorts of drives impel us to do what we do? What sorts of drives impel the creative to produce? Scientists wonder about the motives of creative people; I suppose the creative people occasionally wonder about themselves. To the extent that writing this book is a creative enterprise, I might ask myself what causes me to do it. I certainly don't enjoy the actual writing; it is for the most part a difficult, grinding process, and I would always rather be doing many other things. What I do enjoy, and what makes it worthwhile for me, is the feeling I get when I've finished a part of it, and I can look at my own work and believe that it is good. Perhaps this is a part of what Carl Rogers means when he talks about the drive for self-actualization, or what R. W. White (1959) calls the need for "competence"; perhaps all of us are driven to do those things that we can do best and to keep on trying to do better. But that doesn't explain the motives that are particularly and specifically important in the creative process. Matti (1965) speaks to this issue when he suggests that two needs are involved in creative activity, a need for novelty and a need for quality. Creativity is born out of the tension that results when both these needs are strong. The person who feels a strong need for novelty but not necessarily for quality is an innovator, an idea man, who seldom follows up or works out the implications of his ideas. The high-quality, low-novelty person tends to be a craftsman rather than a creator. The creative person demands of himself and his work both novelty and quality; he wants clear evidence that he is doing things, functioning, in ways that he himself believes to be excellent. Nothing less than excellence, in both quality and novelty, will do; the creative individual is literally driven by this need.

The creative person, then, tends to be one who prefers complexity to simplicity in his sensory inputs, who is highly sensitive to such inputs, who is willing to take risks, and who is driven by a need for novelty and for quality. Dellas and Gaier (1970, p. 65) list a number of other characteristics that researchers have associated with creativity: "Independence, manifested not only in attitudes but also in social behaviors, consistently emerged as being relevant to creativity, as did dominance, introversion, openness to stimuli, and wide interests. Self-acceptance, intuitiveness, and flexibility also appeared to characterize the creatives, and though they had social presence and poise, they exhibited an asocial attitude and an unconcern for social norms." That's quite a portrait; we might reasonably expect that the true creative would often be quite difficult to live with. I suspect that it is as hard for him to live with himself as it is for others to live with him. The demands of creativity—the very tensions out of which the creative product emerges—must make his life a kind of pressure-cooker, maelstrom experience. Let's move on to take a closer look at that experience, at the things that this sensitive, risk-taking, self-accepting individual does with his abilities.

## THE CREATIVE PROCESS

It is important to realize, as we consider the nature of the creative process, that there are many different kinds of creativity. Producing an elegant mathematical proof may well involve a quite different sort of activity than does painting a portrait or building a better mousetrap. As Shouksmith (1970, p. 199) points out, "A thinking mode which 'pays off' or is productive in one situation may not be effective in another. It would seem better, therefore, to speak not of a unitary trait or process called 'creativity,' but of a creation, or a creative act. A creative cognitive act may well occur in more than one way, the circumstances and the material involved determining in part which thinking mode will lead to discovery or creation." Mednick (1962), too, suggests that different cognitive styles may be optimal for different areas of creativity; a visualizer, for instance, may be highly creative in the plastic arts, while a verbalizer may be useless with a paintbrush but highly creative at the typewriter. Creativity seems to narrow in scope as the individual matures. The small child, to the extent that he is able to be creative (here defining creativity as the $F$ ability), is so in many areas of his life. As he grows older, he tends to begin to specialize; and the truly creative adult (now identified by the excellence of his productions) is likely to exercise his creativity in only a few selected areas (Ausubel, 1964). We might speculate, using Matti's notion of the drives for quality and novelty, that as the individual matures, the drive for quality strengthens; he begins to specialize in those areas in which he can meet both the need for quality and the need for novelty, and productions in other areas (which earlier might have been used to satisfy the need for novelty), not meeting the quality need, are now suppressed.

## Trial and Error

Realizing, then, that there are different kinds and styles of creative behavior, can we find any common denominator—any characteristic that seems to be true of all creative processes? Campbell (1960) suggests that there is such a common denominator, and that it is neither unusual nor mysterious. Creativity is, in the last analysis, problem solving; and problems are solved by the application of trial-and-error thinking. Creativity is a streamlined and highly efficient form of trial-and-error behavior, in which the trials are performed by manipulation of mental images rather than of real physical objects, but it is still trial and error. The difference between the creative and the noncreative lies primarily in the "accuracy and detail of their representations of the external world, of possible locomotions in it or manipulations of its elements" (Campbell, 1960, p. 391). In other words, the creative thinker is performing his trials—and making his errors—symbolically, inside his head. The creative individual is able to do this better than most people because the raw material he is using is more detailed, more accurate, and covers more than the raw material of his less-creative counterpart. A creative poet, for instance, wishing to write a poem about the sea, can call upon a great range of ideas, images, and perceptions of the sea from which to construct trial chunks of his finished product.

Campbell points to another difference between creatives and noncreatives: the creative produces a larger number of trials and varies these over a wider range than does the noncreative. Moreover, the creative has greater editing talent, which he uses in weeding out the good from the bad (is this an echo of Matti's need for quality?). While the creative process does not differ from other sorts of learning, in that all may involve trial and error, creativity works from a wider range of possibilities in selecting trials and involves stricter criteria for products that are not deemed errors.

A similar view of creativity has been taken by Mednick (1962); he sees the creative process as essentially the forming of new combinations of associative bonds out of the thought elements available to us. These new combinations are evaluated as to whether they meet some set of requirements or are useful in some way; the further apart the elements are in most people's ordinary way of thinking and the less likely they would seem to go together, the more creative the process of putting them together usefully is seen to be. This view is highly compatible with that of Campbell; in order to form new associative bonds, the creative thinker must have a wide range of elements from which to choose. The wider the selection, the more likely he is to hit on a creative solution. And it almost goes without saying that he will be involved in a trial-and-error process, as he sets this element over against that one, compares, evaluates, discards, tries another combination, and so on. Again it is not so much the nature of the process that seems to distinguish the creative thinker, but rather the raw materials that go into that process and the degree of selectivity involved in deciding when an acceptable solution has been reached.

If these views of creativity are correct, then one characteristic of the creative is apparent: he must be able to hold in his mind (or have readily available in some way) a large array of thoughts, ideas, perceptions—his store of raw materials—from which he constructs his trials or attempts to pair off elements. And as he engages in this process, it is quite likely that he will, on the way to one particular solution, hit on new juxtapositions that are relevant and useful in other problem areas. "Much of creative thought is opportunistic in the sense of having a wide number of selective criteria available at all times, against which the thought trials are judged. The more creative thinker may be able to keep in mind more such criteria and therefore increase his likelihood of achieving a serendipitous advance on a problem tangential to his initial main line of endeavor" (Campbell, 1960, p. 392). Interestingly enough, the creative himself is often unaware that this process is going on. He speaks of lucky accidents, of things just popping into his head, of stumbling across a necessary fact at just the right instant. And in a sense he is right; the creative does have many more such lucky accidents than do most people. He has them for two reasons: he carries with him a great spinning kaleidoscope of ideas, which presents multiple opportunities for a new thought to bounce into the pattern in a useful way, and he is highly sensitive to such "accidents" when they occur.

## Commitment

Another characteristic of the creative process that seems to hold true across widely varying fields of creativity is the consuming interest and commitment that it evokes in its practitioners. The true creative is not only dedicated to but virtually enslaved by his creativity. I have talked with artists, with mathematicians, with writers, and they all tell the same story: when they are truly involved with an idea, they are simply unable to let go of it. The creative process dominates their lives. "No one has identified task commitment as an index of creativity in normal subjects, presumably because it is so obvious that the characteristic can have widely different meanings in outstanding creators and people in general" comments Nicholls (1972, p. 718). Nevertheless, it is a common, if not universal, characteristic. I suspect that this commitment is not as much a characteristic of the people as it is a characteristic of the process. It is the thing that is being done, the experience of creative activity, that has such compelling power. Significantly, we find the element of commitment to creativity only when we define creativity by the product—not when we look simply at high-$F$ individuals. Anastasi and Schaefer (1969), for example, studied 400 high school girls who were categorized as creative or noncreative on the basis of teacher evaluations of their creative products. The most conspicuous characteristic of the creatives was a "pervasive and continuing interest" in their chosen field. The high-$F$ idea spinner is not so absorbed; he seems to abandon interest in the idea once it has been voiced. It is in the interactive process between novelty and quality that the creator becomes enmeshed; it is this process that has the ability to captivate, intrigue, and consume the creator.

Nicholls goes even further in discussing task commitment and creativity; he suggests that such commitment may be the single most critical criterion by which creative process may be identified. "If research evidence on eminent creators is taken as a guide, there is more justification for calling the tendency to become intrinsically involved in tasks creativity than there is for labeling divergent thinking as creativity. Perhaps the identification of divergent thinking rather than task commitment with creativity reflects the popular view of creativity that emphasizes freedom of impulse and absence of constraints" (Nicholls, 1972, p. 723). It is not the absence of constraint that allows creativity; it is rather the presence of a self-imposed constraint that makes for creative process.

True creativity is not playful; it is not even fun in the ordinary sense of the word. It is work—hard, demanding, and exhilarating. This is no new insight; creatives are characterized throughout literature as demanding and self-critical to the point of appearing driven. Some early psychological thinkers made the same observation. Alexander Bain, an early Scottish psychologist, is quoted as saying "The number of trials necessary to arrive at a new construction is commonly so great that without something of a fascination for the subject one grows weary of the task. This is the emotional condition of originality of mind in any department" (Nicholls, 1972, p. 720). There is no way, save by the unlikeliest of chances, that even the highly original thinker can sustain creative excellence without long, hard work. The original idea must be developed, evaluated, and elaborated; new ideas may be woven in. This process demands time and effort.

More than the hard work, exercising the self-criticism necessary for creative excellence is often quite painful. The creator exposes his tender and tentative parts in the creative act; he must then be willing to chop away at the very thing he has given birth to in the never-ending attempt to make it better. To criticize, modify, or even destroy that which has evolved out of oneself is indeed painful; it is only the strong motivation of the creator and the compelling force of the process itself that make it possible. Matti (1965, p. 334) speaks of the "positive, purposeful surging that leads in the direction of creative acts," and goes on to say that this motivation is probably the most important reason why people functioning creatively are not vulnerable to the snares of restrictive, evaluative environments and states of torment and frustration. I would amend Matti's observation somewhat: creatives are vulnerable to their environments—most painfully so—but they continue in the creative process in spite of that vulnerability. They continue, often, not because they want to, but because, enmeshed in their own creative drive and in the dynamic tension of the process itself, they must.

## The Creative Cycle

The picture I have painted here is a bleak one: the creative seems doomed to a life of continual despair, locked in a hopeless struggle to meet unmeetable expectations. And, like most one-sided pictures, it is incomplete. To be sure, the pain of self-criticism is a part of the creative experience; but it is only one part. "There is an alternate blending of working style, a cyclical pattern of patience and passion, of reflection and spontaneity, a continual shifting from total acceptance of one's ideas and actions to a critical rejection of them" (Jackson & Messick, 1965, p. 326). The cyclical pattern seems to be another almost universal characteristic of the creative process. In order for ideas to flow, there must be openness and an absence of criticism; later, during the winnowing and elaboration stage, come criteria, restrictions, and a ruthless weeding out of that which is not acceptable. Shouksmith (1970) suggests that this cycle relates to the cognitive style of the creative individual (see Chapter 9). In order for him to function as both an open acceptor of new and unlikely ideas and a critical demander of excellence, he must be able to shift from an open to a restricted style of thinking.

Whether we see it as a cycling between openness and restrictiveness or between disintegration and reorganization or between reflection and spontaneity, the cycling pattern itself seems unmistakable. And it is truly a cycle, rather than a once-around pass through a series of modes of approach. The restricted and elaborated product is opened up to a flow of still newer ideas and associations; the new organization in turn is demolished; the fruits of a period of spontaneity are subjected to further reflection. Thesis leads to antithesis leads to synthesis, and the round begins again. Where does it stop? Perhaps that is the greatest mystery of all. The creative becomes aware, somehow, that his product is complete (or as complete as he can make it), but neither he nor we can tell just how he knows.

## ORIGINS OF CREATIVITY

I have been trying so far to describe the creative individual and the process by which he exercises his creativity. In so doing, I have almost taken the *person* for granted: he is there, functioning, and our job is to understand what he is like and what it is he is doing. But our job includes more than that: we need to know, too, how he came to be that way. Where do creatives come from? What makes some people creative and others less so? Do people pass through steps or stages on the road to creativity? These are some of the questions we shall attempt to answer in this section.

### Unusual Experiences

A number of researchers have commented on the occurrences of atypical experiences in the life history of creative individuals. Torrance (1972), for instance, noticed that highly creative young people tend to develop careers that involve detours for relevant but unusual combinations of training and/or experience. More of them, he says, include study or work in a foreign country as a part of their career development than do their less creative peers. Unusual experiences must be subjectively defined: what is unusual to me may be commonplace to you. Torrance seems to be pointing at experiences that are either unusual for most young people of this generation in this culture or unusual in their combination with each other. Such experiences and combinations of experiences seem to help in breaking up our taken-for-granted patterns of perceptions; they facilitate seeing and feeling in new ways and asking questions about that which most of us, through long familiarity, don't even notice.

The same sort of thing seems to be true of adult creatives: "persons who have been uprooted from traditional cultures, or who have been thoroughly exposed to two or more cultures, seem to have the advantage in the range of hypotheses they are apt to consider, and through this means, in the frequency of creative innovation" (Campbell, 1960, p. 391). New hypotheses are possible only when the validity of the old ones is questioned. The culture-bound individual is less likely to question those hypotheses accepted by his culture; being uprooted from a culture often means the overturning of values and assumptions. It is likely, too, that there is a spread of effect from this sort of experience: if this thing, which I have taken for granted all my life, can be questioned, why not other things as well? And again the cycle emerges; confusion and questioning lead to new answers and ideas, which in turn must be questioned and examined and evaluated.

Another aspect of the unusual experience is the effect it may have on the personality of the experiencer. Anastasi and Schaefer (1969) speculate that the youngster who experiences a number of atypical events in his early life is less likely to be a conventional or conforming person, and that this lack of conformity is a necessary characteristic of the creative. We have seen, too, that creativity demands a certain amount of risk taking; the young person who has survived a variety of contrasting experiences may feel less threatened by risk than those who have had a more safe and sheltered childhood.

## Emotion

Among the experiences that creative individuals—and all the rest of us, for that matter—have are those that are highly emotional. Meyer (quoted in Grimberg, 1972) hypothesizes that two sorts of emotional experience are of particular significance for creatives. One is the intimate relationship with a colleague or friend, which involves a deep sharing of feelings, and the other is the experience of bereavement or other deep grief. Both of these experiences might be expected to increase one's emotional sensitivity and one's capacity for feeling. I mentioned earlier that many creatives seem to be highly sensitive both to sensory input from external sources and to their own feelings, and that this sensitivity tends to increase the amount of raw data available to their creative process. Quite possibly, any experience that tends to heighten one's emotional sensitivity—as long as that sensitivity can be kept under some control—enhances one's creativity.

### Parental Influences

One of the most common procedures used in searching for the antecedents of any particular trait or characteristic is to look at the characteristics of the parents. Creativity research provides no exception; numbers of studies have been made of the parents of creative individuals. Anastasi and Schaefer's (1969) study is fairly typical: they found that the parents of creative adolescents were better educated and came from a higher socioeconomic level than the parents of the noncreatives. (I must hasten to point out that this finding, like most of the others discussed in this section, is a statistical one. That is, it merely indicates that more of the creatives had well-educated, high-socioeconomic-level parents than did the noncreatives. It does not imply that all creatives come from well-educated families or that the child of a low-socioeconomic family cannot be creative.)

Anastasi and Schaefer's finding is not particularly surprising for at least two reasons: first, the well-educated and well-to-do parent is probably more likely to provide his child with the unusual experiences we have been discussing; and, second, the child who is a product of this relatively well-off subculture is more likely to have an opportunity to utilize his creative abilities—and to have them recognized—than is his less fortunate peer. What may be more interesting to us is a further finding of Anastasi and Schaefer, that the opposite-sex parent seems to be more influential in the lives of creatives than of noncreatives. This finding is highly speculative and certainly needs to be replicated before it can be taken as fact, but it still provides food for thought. Does the influence of the opposite-sex parent make for greater sensitivity to all people, male and female, in later life? Does it perhaps create sex-role conflicts in the creative? And, if so, how might such conflicts enhance his creativity? Or is it rather a matter of learning, early on, to see things from a point of view different from one's own?

MacKinnon (1965), using life-history data from groups of highly creative and less creative architects, found support for the importance of a number of early interpersonal experiences in the development of creativity. Among these were respect of the parents for the child and willingness to grant him the freedom to explore and make decisions; parental expectations that the child would act both independently and responsibly; acceptance of the child for what he was; provision of models for ego identification; clear standards of moral conduct in the family; and an emphasis on the development of one's own moral code. We can see in this list a dual message: be your own person and do your own thing, but be a good person and make sure that your thing is a responsible thing. And again the reciprocality comes through, the elements of the cycle—try out, experiment, innovate, be independent; but evaluate, seek quality, make sure it's right for you.

Otto Rank has described three stages through which the creative person must pass as he matures, and here too we can see intimations of the cyclical conflict of creativity. The first stage is that of the adapted man, who has accepted and internalized society's demands. There is no conflict between what he wills and what he must do because they are one and the same. This, says Rank, is where most people stay, primarily because it's comfortable. Some go beyond adaptation, however; the self demands something other than what society will allow, and these demands are too strong to be ignored. Yet the demands of society cannot be ignored either, and so the person in this stage is trapped and miserable: "He remains stuck there plagued by self-criticism and feelings of guilt and inferiority." The truly creative individual must go one step further, into a synthesis of what Rank calls will and counterwill; he reaches his full creative potential when he learns to turn the conflict between self and society to his own advantage (quoted in MacKinnon, 1965, p. 277). The child who is led early into responsible independence and self-exploration, who is told by word and example to be himself but to be sure that that self is good, would seem to be getting some taste of the possibility of harmony emerging out of the demands of self and society. To be sure, no amount of parental influence can teach such a synthesis—each individual must create his own harmony out of the needs and strains of his individuality and his surroundings—but the experiences of childhood and the parental models available must certainly have their influence upon the adult that is to be.

## FACILITATING CREATIVE GROWTH

We have finally come around, I think, to the question that we as teachers must inevitably ask ourselves: what can we do to facilitate the growth of creativity in those with whom we work? There are many answers to this question, some simple and some complicated indeed. One of the simplest comes from Ausubel. He says, flatly, that to teach for creativity is impossible. Either a person is creative or he isn't, and no amount or kind of educational influence will change that fact (1964, p. 346). Ausubel does soften his position a bit, however, in saying that while few people are truly creative, most of us possess some creative abilities. We shall return in a moment to his recommendations for the enhancement of these abilities.

Before that, though, I want to go back to a distinction that was made at the beginning of this chapter: the distinction between the creative product and the creative process. When we talk about the enhancement of creativity, are we referring to something that makes for a better product or a better

process? Obviously, we would most like to enhance both. But it may be that most of us will never create a truly distinctive product, and I submit that this does not mean that we cannot participate in the creative process. To improve the process means to strengthen the creative abilities and increase the skill with which those abilities are employed. This kind of facilitation is possible for anyone, regardless of whether he is to be a "true creative." Here we come to a third important aspect of creativity: the creative experience. We have defined the creative product by its excellence and its novelty, and we have described the process by means of which such products emerge. But we have said little about the feeling of being a creator. This feeling is one of the most exhilarating experiences available to us humans, and it too is possible for people who will never be recognized as eminent creators. It comes as a result of participating in the creative process, and it is reward enough in itself for the rigors of that participation. The teacher should and must be aware of the potential for truly creative contributions on the part of a few of his students, but he must also realize that experiencing the creative process is a worthwhile goal for the many who will never make such a contribution. With this goal in mind, let us turn to some more or less specific notions about enhancing the creative abilities.

### Building a Store of Ideas

According to Mednick (1962), one can achieve a creative solution in three ways: serendipity, similarity, and mediation. Serendipity is the happy-accident method, the solution that we just happen to stumble over at just the right moment. Similarity involves putting together two ideas because they are in fact similar; by inference, it means searching for a solution on the basis of similar responses that have worked before in similar situations. Mediation goes a step farther: it involves thinking of one idea because something about another idea reminded you of it. For example, you might be trying to decide what to wear to a costume party next weekend, and in the course of your cogitation you realize that you would really rather skip the party and go off exploring the countryside on your bike. You think with pleasure of a small trail on a hiker's map you bought a few days ago, and that gives you the idea for your costume—you can ink a complicated pattern of lines on a white shirt and jeans and go as a road map. The example is rather simple minded (it's amazing how hard it is to think of a creative solution when you have to figure out a problem as well), but it gives the general idea: the road-map costume was mediated by the thought of taking a trip. There is no particular similarity between the ideas of costume and trip, but the one suggested the other. Now, what is important about all three of Mednick's creative methods is that each depends on the availability of a wide range of possibilities and on a kind of sensitivity to associations. One of the most obvious ways to facilitate creativity in any of these modes, then, is to increase the store of ideas, of percepts, available to a person. Everything is grist for the creative mill; no notion is too foolish or trivial to store away for future reference. We should encourage our students—and ourselves—to be scavengers of ideas. The more things we can expose ourselves to, whether or not they seem related to our chosen field of creativity, the greater the number of possible associations we can make.

Notice, too, that these three modes all imply the juxtaposition of two or more ideas. Even the serendipitous solution, happy accident though it may be, requires that we notice the relationship between the solution that we have stumbled over and the problem that it relates to. The ability to relate seemingly isolated facts or ideas comes more naturally to some than to others, but it can be cultivated by anyone. The Red Queen in *Alice in Wonderland* set herself the task of believing three impossible things every morning before breakfast; similarly, we might regularly try to relate three unrelated things every day. How might a comb and a piece of typing paper be related? A telephone and a bit of dental floss? The theory of relativity and a candy cane? Doing exercises like these is like playing scales on the piano: the tasks are relatively useless in and of themselves, but they develop skills that are useful elsewhere.

*Pressure*

One of the common misconceptions about creativity is that it is best exercised in an atmosphere of complete freedom from pressure. Different people do, to be sure, work best under varying degrees of pressure; but it seems likely that everybody needs a certain amount of pressure or strain to spur him to his best level of creativity. Students should be encouraged to discover for themselves what their optimum pressure level is and then to structure their time in such a way as to take advantage of this optimum level. Andrews and Farris (1972), in a study of NASA scientists and engineers, found that a sense of time pressure could enhance several qualities of scientific performance, including innovation. In addition to experiencing the most time pressure, the highest-performing scientists also tended to *want* relatively large amounts of pressure. When the pressure experienced was markedly out of line with the pressure desired—in being either too low or too high—performance was likely to suffer. Pressure can come from sources other than schedules and deadlines. It can come, for instance, from one's own needs and desires and can act as either a spur or a stopper to one's creative flow. We all know people who perform at their highest level when the stakes are high, and we know others who clutch up and are unable to perform at all under conditions of tension or risk. Again, it is important for each individual to recognize the need state under which he functions optimally. Once we know what is best for us, it is often possible to set the gauge on our own personal pressure cooker so as to maximize our creative output.

We might note in passing that there are probably more pressure-full situations in the modern world than there are pressure-free ones, and that the person whose creativity cannot tolerate much pressure tends to be at a disadvantage. Learning theory suggests that tolerance to, and even enjoyment of, pressure can be acquired through gradual exposure coupled with reinforcement. It would not be difficult, I suspect, to work out a program of experiences and exercises that would increase one's optimal pressure level; such a program might be helpful to someone who tends to be inhibited by high stakes or imminent deadlines.

*Teaching the Cycle*

The practice of brainstorming, in which participants are encouraged to produce as many ideas as possible, regardless of quality, and in which criticism or evaluation of any kind is strictly forbidden, has received a great deal of publicity in recent years. It has been hailed as a means of encouraging flexibility and openness to new ideas and thus as an enhancer of creativity. There is little doubt that, for many people, brainstorming does facilitate the exercise of the $F$ ability. Buchanan and Lindgren (1973) carried out an interesting study of brainstorming with children. They allowed fourth-grade students to participate in a group brainstorming session and then gave them a similar task to work on individually. A control group of students participated in two individual sessions and had no group experience. As expected, the youngsters who had had the group experience did better in the later session (based on judges' ratings of their productions as "original, clever, and interesting") than those who had just worked alone. At the very least, we may assume that the group session relaxed some of the standards about how good a response ought to be before it is worth expressing. Open to question, however, is the effect of such sessions on the overall creative quality of productions. "However successful [techniques such as brainstorming] are in producing unrestricting, permissive social environments, there is currently little clear evidence that they increase *individual* creativity" (Matti, 1965, p. 331). As an exercise designed specifically for the enhancement of one aspect of creativity—the *F* abilities—brainstorming may be quite useful; but we must be careful to convey to students that this is only one part of creativity.

Again and again, in our examination of creativity, we have come across evidence of the cyclical nature of the process. It is as if there are two distinct sides of the same coin: one involving flexibility, freedom, innovation, absence of judgment; and the other involving reflection, self-criticism, and the exercise of quality control. The true creative process involves both these aspects, and the would-be enhancer of creativity must be careful lest in improving the one he inadvertently detracts from the other. Flexibility must not be acquired at the cost of losing the ability to be critical, but the critical ability must not stifle one's flexibility. Why not, then, attempt to teach both? Stratton and Brown (1972), working with university undergraduates, did just that: they worked with three groups of subjects, giving one group training in productivity, one group training in evaluation, and a third group training in both productivity and evaluation. They found that the students trained in productivity increased the number of problem solutions, but not the quality; in addition, these students were unable to evaluate the quality of their own responses. The judgment-trained subjects produced fewer responses, but those that they did produce were of high quality. Combined training produced higher-quality solutions than production training alone, and more solutions than judgment training alone. The implication seems clear: for these subjects, at least, specific training in both phases of the creativity cycle enhanced the overall process. The authors go on to point out that further training is needed to enable subjects to apply what they have learned to activities other than the ones used in the experiment. What is most needed is for training programs in creative problem solving to demonstrate transfer from training activities to classroom activities. This kind of transfer would be enhanced if students were taught how to set up criteria for solution evaluation—criteria such as question asking and library search—as well as how to derive techniques for generating ideas. Knowing how to generate and use such criteria would give problem solvers a well-defined goal and a means by which to evaluate their own ideas rather than relying on someone else for evaluation.

Creativity—the ability to bring into being something new, something useful, something excellent—may well be a gift, granted to the few but denied to the many. But it is also a skill, and like other skills it can be improved through practice and instruction. We have looked at some suggestions as to how such instruction might be carried out; as you consider the various ability strands involved in the creative process, you doubtless will be able to think of others. Instruction for creativity is important for two reasons. First, it is useful in helping to develop the (statistically rare) creative abilities of the true creators; and, second, it can help the rest of us to experience whatever creative process we are capable of. Ausubel (1964, p. 347) lays this responsibility at the door of the schools, maintaining that they are best suited to contribute to the creativity development of young people. "They can help pupils possessing unique creative potentialities actualize them by providing adequate opportunities for spontaneity and individuality, by setting suitably challenging tasks, by rewarding creative accomplishments, and by providing appropriate guidance and encouragement. These same techniques can also be used to further the actualization of more limited and less unique degrees of creative potentiality as well as to foster the development of the general creative abilities." Not only in the classroom, but in the many other settings in which teachers function, creativity should be encouraged and actively trained for. And this means all sides of creativity, both the innovative, flexible aspects and the evaluative, quality-demanding aspects. As we learn to facilitate creative development in a balanced fashion, with appropriate emphasis on all its facets, we may be pleasantly surprised at the number of creative individuals we find among our students.

## QUESTIONS FOR UNDERSTANDING

1. Think of the last time you created something that you felt really good about. What was there about either the product or the process that made it special for you?
2. According to Jackson and Messick, the truly creative product is unusual, appropriate, transforming, and condensed. Think of examples of things that you have done or seen other people do that have seemed to you to be creative; apply Jackson and Messick's criteria to those products.
3. Design a classroom exercise that would help facilitate the growth of the F ability among a group of second graders. How would this exercise have to be modified in order to use it with junior high school students?
4. Indiscriminate praise can discourage the development of a student's self-evaluative ability; not enough praise or encouragement can stifle flexibility and production, especially in a low-risk-taking child. How can a teacher strike a reasonable balance between these two extremes?
5. A group of highly talented high school students, identified by their classroom teachers, have been encouraged to participate in a creativity seminar. One of the tasks of the seminar is to find ways of encouraging creative activity among all the students in the school. How can you, the seminar leader, help the students with this task?

# Chapter 8

# *Motivation*

Educators have traditionally regarded motivation as the wellspring of the learning process. Once a person is motivated, we say, the battle is all but won; the teacher's job from then on is almost that of an interested and helpful observer rather than a teacher. In this chapter we shall examine some of the ways in which psychologists and educators have looked at the phenomenon of motivation; I suspect that we shall discover it to be considerably more complex than we may have expected. There are many facets to motivation, many ways of describing and defining it, and many implications for the teacher inherent in those descriptions. Because the topic is so complex, we shall begin with two statements that may be helpful in making sense of all of it. The first is a simple outline. Hunt pointed out in 1960 that we typically ask three questions about motivation: Why does a person become active? Why does he act one way rather than another? How can we get him to change? Almost two decades have gone by since then, but the outline still holds; and those are the major questions that we shall be dealing with in these next pages.

The second statement is a caution, a here-there-be-dragons warning against oversimplification. It was written about the same time by Raymond Cattell, a personality theorist: "If we have fallen into the intellectual immaturity of assuming that wherever there is one word there is one thing, we are doomed to failure and confusion" (1958, p. 200). *Motivation* is a single word. It does not refer to a nice, simple concept, or even to an ugly, complicated concept, but rather to a whole family of interrelated ideas and observations. It is this family, with all its interrelationships and overlappings, that we are about to explore.

## DRIVE THEORY

*Primary Drives.* The simplest, and certainly one of the oldest, ways of looking at motivation is commonly known as drive theory. According to drive theory, animals (including humans) are born with certain innate needs that must be met if the animal or his species is to survive. The most widely accepted of these needs are hunger, thirst, and sex. The animal is so constructed that failure to meet its basic needs sets up a *drive:* an internal compulsion that forces it to seek whatever substance or activity will meet the need. When it has been met, the drive is reduced. "The common denominator of most definitions of need is the belief that it results from deficiencies in the organism. These deficiencies cause tensions which, in turn, initiate processes. The inherent aim of these processes is to relieve the pressures of the need and/or to satisfy it" (Buhler & Massarik, 1968, p. 4).

Psychologists have spent many hundreds of hours exploring the behavioral implications of these simple primary drives. Rats have run down thousands of feet of runways, pigeons have pecked at hundreds of bars, and all sorts of animals have been deprived of all sorts of substances in an effort to discover a constant set of relationships that would at least describe, if not explain, how drives work. Out of all this experimentation have emerged a number of formidable-looking mathematical equations. These equations tend to raise more questions than they answer, and—in the minds of many students—suggest that the notion of drive reduction or need meeting is too simple. Clearly, thirsty animals seek water and hungry animals seek food, but that is only a small part of the (apparently) motivated behavior of even the subhuman species that have been studied.

While the rat runners are trying to set up equations relating things like speed of running to length of food deprivation, another group of scientists are attacking the problem of motivation from a different angle. These are the physiological psychologists; they are interested in physically locating the motivational centers of the behaving animal. Behavior is directed by the brain, so their reasoning goes, and therefore something must make the brain direct the animal to do whatever it does. Where in the brain do the signals originate—what part of the brain is the starter mechanism? Find that, and you have found the seat of motivation. And these researchers have been, to some degree, successful. They have managed to isolate certain areas of the brain that do seem to be of central importance in the motivational process. If an electrode is implanted into one of these areas in the brain of, say, a monkey, and is wired so that every time the monkey presses a certain lever in its cage an electrical current passes through the electrode into its brain tissues, the monkey will work constantly to stimulate itself in this fashion. It will ignore the demands of hunger and thirst and will do nothing but press the lever until it is too exhausted to continue.

Researchers involved in these experiments believe that they have found a parent motivational area in the brain: that other basic motivators

SINCE HE HAD THAT ELECTRODE PUT IN HE DOES NOTHING BUT THIS UNTIL HE'S TOO EXHAUSTED TO CONTINUE.........

like hunger and thirst work through this parent center. "Our conclusion from these preliminary experiments is that we are stimulating genuine reward systems in the brain. We believe that the effect derives from no mere compulsion or automatism, but from stimulation of cells actually involved in food, sexual, or other reward processes" (Olds, 1971, p. 257).

Yet even here, in what is unquestionably an exciting breakthrough, there is still the feeling of something missing, of masses of questions yet to be answered. In one corner we see a monkey with an electrode implanted in his brain; in another is an artist sweating and cursing over his work; in still another is a Hitler planning to take over the world or a Joan of Arc martyred for her beliefs. How can we make the jump from simple, isolated animal responses to the splendid complexity of human activity?

*Learned Drives.* It seems clear that if we are to find a bridge from primary-drive activity to complex, real-world motives, we must look to learning processes. Man, like every other animal, is a learner; his behavior is affected by the learnings he acquires throughout his life. Is it not reasonable to assume that the primary-drive motivations of the infant—the instinctive need structure with which he is born—will be molded, shaped, and elaborated by his life experiences? This is no new notion in the study of human behavior; here again a whole body of definitions and hypothesized relationships has grown up as psychologists have attempted to trace the ways in which motivations shift and change and grow. One of the earliest terms to find its way into general usage in this area was *functional autonomy*. Functional autonomy, as described by Gordon Allport in the 1930s, refers to the tendency of intermediate steps in the chain of need-meeting activities to take on need-meeting characteristics of their own. As a child grows older, he builds increasingly long and complicated sets of "I do this in order to get that" kinds of behaviors, where the "that" at the end of the chain is a primary reinforcer—something that reduces a primary drive. But eventually the reinforcement value of "that" spreads back to the "I do this," and "doing this" is sought in its own right. A child may learn, for example, to climb up on a stool and get a glass down from a cupboard in order to get a drink of water when he is thirsty. If he does this often enough and the end result—the drink of water—is rewarding, he may learn to enjoy the activity of climbing up on the stool and getting the glass in and of itself. Climbing and getting will acquire functional autonomy; he will be motivated to do this even when he isn't thirsty.

Dollard and Miller (1971), looking at this same phenomenon from a different point of view, use the expressions *learned reinforcements* and *learned drives*. Climbing and getting, having acquired functional autonomy, is now rewarding; the child will work in order to climb and get just as he would previously work in order to drink water when he was thirsty. Various stimuli, either in the external environment or internal to the child (such as the sight of the stool or a kinesthetic sensation in the muscles), set off the desire to climb and get. These stimuli have learned-drive value in the same sense that thirst had value as the original drive setting off the drink-getting activity. "When, as the result of learning, previously neutral cues gain the capacity to play the same functional role in the learning and performance of new responses as do primary drives, such as hunger and thirst, these cues are said to have *learned-drive value*" (Dollard & Miller, 1971, p. 97). Such a formulation is useful in that it allows us to hypothesize about a specific individual's motivations according to what he appears to be trying to do. No two people have the same learning history, so no two people can be expected to be motivated by exactly the same set of learned drives. The notions of learned drives and of functional autonomy give us a scientific rationale for the great diversity of motivated behavior— a logical explanation for the confusions and conflicts in human activity that all students of human behavior notice and puzzle over.

One of the more important implications of the learned-drive notion is that it opens the way to consideration of environmental influences on motivation. As long as psychologists were locked into a primary-drive approach, with motivation rising and falling as a function of tensions caused by deficiencies, cues or stimuli from the environment were relatively unimportant. But riding in on the coat tails of learned drives came the assumption that stimulus cues could set off or elicit motivational patterns. A child may not particularly want to read or draw until he sees another child engrossed in his book or his crayons; a stimulus from outside an individual can trigger a learned drive. As the number of functionally autonomous motives increases through learning, so does the number of stimulus situations that can trigger those motives. And again, diversity and individuality are the rule: the sight of Sammy drawing may send Tom to get his own crayons, while it motivates Joan to move over and joggle Sammy's arm.

*Relationships among Drives.* To complicate matters still further, we must recognize that all drives, both primary and learned, may be interrelated. Some of these interrelations may be acquired (learned) and are thus different in different individuals; some of them may be innate and may thus be a common dimension of all human behavior. One possible example of a common dimension is the relationship between sexual arousal and aggression. A number of researchers have speculated that these two drives (if there is such a thing as an innate aggressive drive, which other scientists have questioned) are biologically related. Berkowitz (1970) reports a study in which two groups of adult males were provoked (frustrated) by a partner. One group then watched a brief sex movie. In the last part of the experiment, men in both groups were allowed to "punish" the provoking partner by giving him electric shocks; consistently, the sexually aroused men gave stronger punishments than did the nonaroused ones.

Berkowitz suggests that part of the relationship among drives may come about through one drive's acting as a releaser, or disinhibitor, for another. In the case of aggressiveness, most of us have learned that overt aggression is disapproved and often punished in our culture. We have learned to stifle our aggressive responses or to convert open aggression into less obvious (and dangerous to ourselves) forms: dirty looks, mumblings under the breath, and the like. The motivation toward the aggressive act is present, but the act itself is inhibited. The presence of another strong drive—in the study described above, sexual arousal—even though it has little or no direct relationship to aggression, may nevertheless act as a releaser. By lifting the inhibitions against aggressive behavior, it allows that behavior to become overt; and to the outside observer it appears that the sexual arousal "caused" the aggression.

*Habit.* Another factor that tends to complicate our understanding of how complex drives are acquired and how they operate is that of habit. Habit is a familiar notion: we can all think of examples of habitual behavior. A psychology professor of mine, in my undergraduate days, as he sat in conversation with his students, would fill and light his pipe. When the pipe was well lit, he held the still-burning match in front of the student sitting nearest him (still carrying on the conversation, of course). The student invariably blew out the match. "Aha!" my professor would shout triumphantly, *"now* tell me I can't control your behavior!" This used to annoy us students no end, but it did illustrate the force of habit and the way in which a would-be controller of behavior can set off a habitual response pattern by supplying the appropriate stimulus. Why did the student always blow out the match? Simply because that is a habitual response, strengthened by the very act of repeating it. In other words, every time I blow out a match, it becomes more likely that I will do the same thing the next time I am presented with a similar stimulus. "An acquired mode of activity becomes by repetition habitual, and the more frequently it is repeated the more powerful becomes the habit as a source of impulse or motive power" (McDougal, 1971, p. 19). That statement was originally written in 1908, and we have learned nothing since then that contradicts it.

Habits, to an outside observer, may look very much like motivated behavior, like behavior in the service of primary or learned drives. In each case the sequence of activities is likely to be directed toward a specific end, and the behaver is likely to express discomfort if he is interrupted before he reaches that end. And, indeed, habits are often established as a part of motivated behavior and may still serve those same drives even after they have become established as habits. The important difference is that the habit becomes self-reinforcing; it tends to perpetuate itself even in the absence of the drive on which it was originally based. Drive-activated behavior, in contrast, occurs only when that drive is present. A person will not try to get a drink of water if he is not thirsty—unless he has made a habit of taking a drink every time he passes the water fountain.

*Drive Reduction and Drive Enhancement.* Drive theories, as I said at the beginning of this section, are among the earliest explanations of motivation, and they are among the simplest. To be sure, when we add to the notion of primary drives the idea that new drives can be learned and try to explain the rules that govern such learnings, the concept of drive becomes more complex. But the basic simplicity is still there: a drive is activated, and the organism behaves in such a way as to reduce it. But is this, in fact, the way it always works? Do we really seek a static situation in which no drives are operating and in which our motivational system is quiescent? A number of psychologists have taken the position that even expanded drive-reduction theories do not account for this aspect of human—and lower-animal—behavior.

One of the best-known studies bearing on this question was done in the mid-1950s by a group of Canadian psychologists at McGill University. These researchers tried to put human subjects into a minimal state of drive arousal to see how they would respond. They paid college students to lie on comfortable beds in a darkened room, with no stimulation at all. Even though the pay was relatively high—more than most students would have been able to earn by working an 8-hour day—the subjects were unable to continue the experiment for more than a few days. While specific individual reactions differed, all reported that they needed more stimulation, that they were unable to tolerate the quiescent situation (Heron, 1957). It is generally assumed that increases in stimulation tend to increase the arousal level of an organism; the drive-reduction theory would predict, therefore, that organisms would be reinforced (provided their primary needs were met) by a reduced level of stimulation. Yet, in line with Heron's studies, numerous researchers have found quite the opposite effect. "In fact, much behavior serves the function of bringing the animal into conditions of increased stimulation" (Hinde, 1971, p. 43). And when we stop to think about it, this makes intuitive sense: one of the most uncomfortable states to find oneself in is that of boredom. We do, indeed, try to escape from over-stimulation; we are refreshed by peace and quiet when we have been assaulted by noise and confusion for a while, or we may walk gratefully into a dimly lit room after spending several hours at an exhibit of modern art. But we also grow tired of peace and quiet; we were, after all, motivated to expose ourselves to that modern-art exhibit in the first place. When animals or human beings have been living under conditions of low and unchanging stimulation for a time, increases of stimulation become reinforcing. If you don't believe this, try sitting quietly in a back corner of the library sometime, looking at nothing in particular. In only a few minutes you will find yourself listening for any footstep that suggests someone may be coming by. We crave stimulation, and the need for it is an exceedingly strong motivator.

If increased stimulation leads to increased arousal and increased stimulation can be reinforcing, does it then follow that increased arousal is itself the reinforcing event? Studies of novelty-seeking behavior in lower animals suggest that this is indeed the case. In observing the exploratory behavior of rats, for instance, researchers can easily tell when an animal is aroused. And rats, under a variety of conditions, seek out a level of stimulation that maintains them in an aroused state. R. W. White (1959), discussing a study in which rats were allowed to explore a maze (with no extrinsic reward for exploration), comments that in the laboratory, as in their natural habitat, the animals did not wait to have novelty thrust on them, nor did they avoid situations in which novelty might be found. Such behavior can be most readily understood by admitting that under certain circumstances an increase in arousal or excitement can be reinforcing. Humans, no less than rats, exhibit the same kind of behavior. We like to be excited (but not too excited), to be frightened (but not too frightened), to experience the spice of just a little bit of frustration. "It is nothing short of extraordinary what trouble people will go to in order to get into more trouble at the bridge table or on the golf course; and the fascination of the murder story or thriller and the newspaper accounts of real-life adventure or tragedy is no less extraordinary. This taste for excitement *must* not be forgotten when we are dealing with human motivation. It appears that, up to a certain point, threat and puzzle have positive motivating value, beyond that point negative value" (Hebb, 1971, p. 130).

   This formulation of motivation seems to suggest, then, that people seek some middle ground of arousal. But here, too, there are problems, for we do not seem to want to stay at that middle point. The trouble at the bridge table or on the golf course is irritating and unpleasant if it is not resolved; we don't read the thriller most of the way through and then take it back to the library (unless it has failed to arouse our interest, puzzlement, or what have you). In fact, if we consider the whole sequence of activities from the initial seeking after stimulation or arousal to what seems to be a terminus or logical end point, we find that the satisfying sequences do end with a resolution, a decrease in arousal. Is it not possible, then, that the satisfaction lies not in the state of being either nonaroused (that is, drive satisfied) or moderately aroused, but rather in the process of drive reduction? We seek moderate arousal in order to be able to experience drive reduction. Animal psychologists have noted this possibility and have designed experiments to test it: hungry rats, for instance, will work to be allowed to drink saccharine solutions even though such solutions have no nutritive value at all. Tinbergen, one of the best known observers of animal behavior, points out that "strictly speaking, it is not the litter or the food the animal is striving towards, but the performance itself of the maternal activities or eating" (1971, p. 31). If we couple the notion of the process of drive reduction as reward with Allport's notion of functional autonomy, we may have an explanation of much of human arousal-seeking behavior. We know that we have to become aroused in order to experience arousal (drive) reduction, so the initial quest for arousal is a means to that end. As we learn that sequence (seek arousal, become aroused, experience arousal reduction), the intermediate steps take on reward value of their own. It is not inconsistent at all, then, to say that one's basic motivation involves arousal reduction as a process, but also that the state of being aroused can have reward value in and of itself.

   Hebb (1971) tells us that at low levels an increase of drive intensity may be rewarding, whereas at high levels it is a decrease that rewards. Again, this view is consistent with the inclusion of functional autonomy in our system: we come to enjoy those situations that lead to pleasurable reductions in arousal. At low levels of drive, there can be little or no further reduction, so the organism seeks arousal; we skip lunch (arousal of hunger drive) in order to be able to enjoy a special dinner party (hunger reduction), or we go to a sad movie knowing that it will make us cry. At a high level of drive, we are ready for the drive-reduction process to begin, and any further increase has the effect of postponing that process and is therefore negatively reinforcing. The key concept is that satisfaction comes not from having reached any particular level of arousal or nonarousal (except insofar as those intermediate stages have acquired reward characteristics through functional autonomy) but rather from the process of change from one level of arousal to another. "Satisfaction has to be seen as lying in a considerable series of transactions, in a trend of behavior rather than a goal that is achieved" (R. W. White, 1959, p. 322).

## "SOFTER APPROACHES"

To say that we seek the experience of drive reduction or to say that the process of a need being met rather than a low-drive or no-need state is satisfying to us is useful in that it helps to explain behaviors that appear to be tension raising. The explanation broadens our understanding of the ways in which motivation affects behavior. But in another sense it simply postpones answering the main question: if we have decided that people enjoy the process of meeting their needs, how do we specify just what those needs are? We have seen that the early theorists were most interested in the so-called primary drives, those physiologically based and presumably innate motivations shared by all humans (and many nonhuman species as well). Later researchers developed models that showed how, as a result of learning, an individual's original set of drives could be elaborated into a complex and unique set of motivations. These two points of view, that of primary drives and that of learned drives, do help us to understand much of our own and others' behavior. Many students, however, believe that something—and a very important something—is still left out.

### Interaction and Exploration

R. W. White, writing in 1959 (p. 297), declared "We need a different kind of motivational idea to account fully for the fact that man and the higher mammals develop a competence in dealing with the environment which they certainly do not have at birth and certainly do not arrive at simply through maturation. Such an idea, I believe, is essential for any biologically sound view of human nature." White, in company with most if not all the Third Force school of psychology, believes that the mechanistic models of learned drives cannot possibly explain the vigor and persistence with which people engage their environments; these psychologists are convinced that the very acts of such engagement must in themselves be satisfying. Not just people, but other animals as well, appear to enjoy exercising their abilities. Problems are solved for the joy of problem solving, not for the other rewards that a solution might bring. To attempt to explain the complex sets of behavior involved in the exercise of competence by means of a conglomerate of separate and specific offshoots from primary drives, these theorists contend, is futile. Harlow, who gained fame for his creative work with monkey behavior, believes that simple behavior patterns may help us to understand behaviors that are still simpler, but they are seldom if ever useful in explaining more complex patterns. "I do not want to discourage anyone from the pursuit of the psychological Holy Grail by the use of the Skinner box," he concludes, "but as far as I am concerned, there will be no moaning of farewell when we have passed the pressing of the bar" (1971, p. 110).

As we begin to explore the notion that interacting competently with one's environment may be motivating in and of itself, we must be alert for hard, objective evidence that relates to our hypothesis. Researchers in more traditional studies of motivation have collected enormous amounts of data to support primary- and learned-drive theories; we shall need more than armchair philosophizing to alter or refute their conclusions. Fortunately, such evidence is not difficult to find. We can begin with a commonsense observation of the everyday behavior of people, particularly of children. "Can anyone seriously believe," asks Harlow, "that the insatiable curiosity-investigatory motivation of the child is a second-order or derived drive conditioned upon hunger or sex or any other internal drive?" (1971, p. 111). The small child is intensely interested in his surroundings. He explores the movement of a plastic toy in the bathtub or the patterns made by poking a stick into a sandbox with a patience and persistence that amazes (and frequently exasperates) his parents. Older children and adolescents can be turned on by an idea and spend long hours reading, studying, talking about it. Even very small babies exhibit a fascination with their own interactions with their surroundings; Piaget's many descriptions of the behavior of his young son, Laurent, provide beautifully detailed examples of how rewarding such interactions can be to the infant.

R. W. White points out that most animals tend to share this need to interact with and manipulate the things that surround them. Nearly all animals attempt to explore whatever environment they are placed in; indeed, the absence of such exploratory behavior is often interpreted as an indicator that something is wrong with the animal. Moreover, the opportunity to explore can serve as a reward in the conditioning of other kinds of behaviors. This is an important point: learning theory tells us that if a particular behavior is followed by a reward, that behavior will be more likely to occur again in the future. We can turn this statement around and say that if a behavior is consistently followed by something, and that behavior is then exhibited more and more often (it is learned), the "something" must be a reward. Rewards are rewarding because they meet needs; they relate directly to the motives of the behaving organism. Therefore, if a something (a stimulus or another behavior or the opportunity to behave in some way) acts as a reward in such a learning paradigm, that something must be related to a need or motive in the learner. The opportunity to explore is just such a something for many animals, and this fact has been experimentally verified. "Monkeys—and presumably all primates—have a strong motive toward visual exploration of their environment, and . . . learning may be established on the basis of this motive just as it may be established on the basis of any motive that regularly and reliably elicits responses" (Butler, quoted in R. W. White, 1959, p. 298).

The exercise of one's ability to interact with the environment does differ from the primary drives and from many learned drives in one important respect. Ordinarily, satisfaction of one set of needs does not interfere with our attempts to satisfy other needs. If an animal is both hungry and thirsty, and I offer it a drink of water, it will still work to satisfy its hunger even after its thirst is slaked. Offering an animal a primary reward for behaving in an exploratory fashion, however, can detract from the reward value of the exploratory behavior itself. In a study of problem solving in primates, Harlow (1971) rewarded one group of monkeys with food every time they solved a puzzle; another group received no such reward when they came up with a solution. When the food-rewarded monkeys had solved a puzzle, they abandoned it. When the non-food-rewarded animals had solved the puzzle, they frequently continued their explorations and manipulations. Indeed, one reason the non-food-rewarded monkeys sometimes failed to "solve" the problems was that they became so interested in exploring and manipulating the puzzles that they no longer worked for a solution. From this point of view, the hunger-reduction incentives were motivation destroying, not motivation supporting. The primary rewards can be too important; they can prevent the individual from being caught up in the reward possibilities of the interaction itself. This finding has exceedingly important implications for teachers: by offering extrinsic rewards for learning activities, we may be inadvertently destroying the child's own healthy, innate motivation to learn for the fun of learning. We shall return to this topic later in the chapter.

In a sense, successful interaction with one's environment may be thought of as a primary drive. Different theorists have proposed different specific mechanisms to explain or describe this behavior more completely. Let's look at a few of them in more detail now; each contributes a slightly different perspective of the phenomenon we are trying to understand.

## Competence

I have already quoted some of R. W. White's observations in the preceding paragraphs. His 1959 paper, perhaps more than anything else, made psychologists begin to think seriously about adding *competence* to the list of primary motivators. White believes that the process of exercising competence in dealing with one's environment, however that may be done, is a primary satisfier. Shooting a gun, skipping rope, writing a theme, tying one's shoes, playing a violin concerto—any of these is satisfying if it is experienced as competent behavior. "The behavior that leads to the building up of effective grasping, handling, and letting go of objects, to take one example, is not random behavior produced by a general overflow of energy. It is directed, selective, and persistent, and it is continued not because it serves primary drives, which indeed it cannot serve until it is almost perfected, but because it satisfies an intrinsic need to deal with the environment" (R. W. White, 1959, p. 318).

Carl Rogers (best known as a psychotherapist) and Abraham Maslow (best known as a personality theorist) have taken complementary positions with regard to motivation. Whereas White concentrates primarily on the here-and-now rewarding aspects of the exercise of competence, Rogers and Maslow have been more interested in long-term directions in human behavior. Both these men use the expression *self-actualization* to describe the ultimate human goal. Man strives, they believe, to be the best possible self he can be—to be fully functioning in the sense that he realizes all his potential. Self-actualizing behaviors are intrinsically rewarding because they lead toward this ultimate goal. And it is the process of becoming self-actualizing, of functioning in this manner, that is rewarding, rather than the external goodies that may be acquired along the way.

## Curiosity

A somewhat different, but still compatible, view is held by theorists Harry Harlow (whom we've already met) and David Berlyne. "Berlyne maintains that incongruity, uncertainty, surprise, and incompatibility tend to attract rather than repel infants. These features set up competing tendencies or conflicts which demand resolution by the infant, and it is this drive for resolution or selection among stimuli that constitutes the basis of learning and discrimination" (Eiduson, 1968, p. 109). Harlow puts it more simply: people (and monkeys and rats) are curious. Eiduson's rather complicated statement is one way of explaining curiosity in the more traditional language of drive and conflict and thus serves as a partial bridge between the competence and curiosity people and their more behavior-oriented colleagues. Berlyne's "drive for resolution or selection among stimuli" suggests that higher organisms are intrinsically motivated to categorize, to set in order, to relate new and unusual things to things that they already know about. His is essentially a tension-reduction theory; that is, he sees curiosity behavior as an attempt to reduce discomfort rather than an attempt to increase pleasure. In this respect his ideas differ from those of Harlow, who describes exploratory behavior as a joyful movement toward the new and unusual. But despite this difference, both regard exploration of the novel and unusual as basically satisfying. If we relate their view to White's ideas about competence, it seems reasonable that curiosity behavior—exploration of the novel—allows the exercise of known competence and always carries a potential opportunity to develop new areas of competence. The individual (child, adult, or white rat) who has been able to deal competently with new situations in the past and who has found in such situations new ways to develop and exercise his abilities delights in novelty. In contrast, the individual who has experienced shifts from the known to the unknown as failures, who sees himself as able to be competent only in familiar settings, may exhibit little curiosity behavior. His drive to explore has been reduced because exploration in the past has led to pain in the form of experiencing incompetence.

## The Open System

Another shift in perspective, now: another view, slightly different, but one that still portrays man as competent initiator rather than driven reactor. Traditional drive theorists tacitly assume that all behavior—all activity

—must be explained in terms of something the behaver is trying to get away from. The competence and curiosity people we have been looking at tend to disagree; behavior can be explained in terms of what the behaver is trying to get or accomplish. Both views seem to imply that somehow a "natural" life state is one of no activity at all, that activity must therefore be explained by something else. But what if activity—behavior—is seen simply as a natural and intrinsic characteristic of living organisms? We then need not worry about why an individual behaves; he behaves because he is alive. Our question becomes "Why does he choose to behave in this way rather than in those other ways?" Kelly (1958) argues from this point of view. It is easy to observe that people are not inert as long as they are alive, he points out. "Should we not follow up our observation with a basic assumption that any person is motivated, motivated for no other reason than that he is alive? Life itself could be defined as a form of process or movement. Thus, in designating man as our object of psychological inquiry, we should be taking it for granted that movement is an essential property of his being, not something that has to be accounted for separately" (pp. 49-50). The living organism can be thought of as an *open system,* a series of interrelated processes of interaction. These processes go on simultaneously at various levels: on a molecular level, with the exchange of oxygen and carbon dioxide in the cells; on a molar-mechanical level, as we manipulate and are manipulated by objects in our environment; on a symbolic level, as information flows between system and surroundings. Adherents of parapsychology, as well as of religious orthodoxy, would probably agree that there are even more abstract levels of exchange, levels that are not (as yet) amenable to the kinds of measurements that science knows how to use. Be that as it may, the open-system model allows us to look at behavior and motivation in a qualitatively different way. Stimuli modulate behavior, but they do not initiate it. An individual behaves because behavior is a necessary part of life—perhaps even a definition of life. He neither drives toward nor is driven from; rather, he interacts with. Both reinforcement and motivation are intrinsic to the organism's relations with its environment, intrinsic to the organism's information processing. It is as if the organism operated like a feedback system in which errors, derived from the discrepancy between receptor inputs of the present and residues of past experience, activate and modify ongoing behavior (Hunt, 1960).

### Buhler's Bipolar Model

The open-system model is for me a useful tool for examining my assumptions. It helps me to think critically, forces me to crawl up and around and under and look at things in ways I hadn't before. But it is not, for me, a sufficient explanation of human motivation; the open system is a little too mechanical to account for human hope and grief, boredom and ecstasy. Curiosity, competence, self-actualization—these are better, but they too feel a bit one sided. They all have a feeling of busyness, of striving. Man is a striving sort of creature; but he is also a cuddling creature, a seeker of warmth and comfort. Sometimes he likes to just lean back and go with the flow. Buhler recognized this other side and posited a two-way tension in motivation. We all seek fulfillment, she says, but fulfillment means different things to different people. For some, it means achievement and accomplishment; for others, it is comfort and ease. "A predominant tendency toward need satisfaction plays a role in the one case, and a predominant tendency toward creative expansion in the other. However, environmental factors also exert their influence in both cases. The polarity between comfort and accomplishment seems to me most decisive as far as life goals are concerned" (Buhler, 1968b, p. 24). She goes on to speculate that the tendency toward one or the other of these two poles may well be genetically determined, although environmental influences are important in determining the means one uses to try to accomplish one or the other.

Buhler has expanded this bipolar model into four *motivational parameters:* need satisfaction, self-limiting adaptation, creative expansion, and upholding internal order. Creative expansion has to do with the same sorts of things Maslow and Rogers mean by self-actualization. Self-limiting adaptation refers to the growing and changing that come about through interacting with the environment and is thus clearly related to the interaction and exploration model we discussed previously. Need satisfaction ties in with the notion of drives and drive reduction. And the idea of upholding internal order rests on an assumption that man needs to—is driven to, is satisfied by trying to—set objects and percepts and stimuli into consistent patterns that make them understandable, an assumption that Berlyne's explanation of curiosity surely shares. Buhler, then, seems to have captured essential elements of all the models we have been looking at. But rather than trying to make them all fit together, to make them predict or explain human behavior in a unitary way, she allows them to interact, to support each other some of the time and to conflict at other times. Unconsciously or consciously, the individual decides which of the various directions is to predominate at a given time and then selects the goal that will most effectively satisfy the corresponding need structure.

It is not necessary that we decide which of these models is most likely to be the "right" one or even that we conclude with Buhler that people are motivated in all these ways. As Boring (1957) points out, models by their very nature are incomplete representations of behavior; a model is "right" if it aids our understanding, but we may have many different "right" models of the same behavior. Observation and introspection tell us that man is active and that he tries to approach some things and to avoid others. Any or all of the models we have discussed may be helpful in understanding the approaching and avoiding behavior of a particular learner in a particular learning situation.

## DEVELOPMENT OF MOTIVATION

From what I said in the preceding section, the phrase *development of motivation* seems to make little or no sense. Man is by nature motivated; motivation doesn't need to develop because it just is. Yet man's behaviors do change; his goals shift and fade; his interests ebb and flow over time. In the next few paragraphs, we shall try to discover some of the factors involved in these changes. We are interested not so much in why man behaves, but rather in why he behaves as he does. Buhler points out that values, as they influence behavior, are changing in time and are determined by age; motivation does develop in the sense that as an individual grows and matures his motivational pattern changes too. Some of these changes may be determined by physical changes in the organism; others are surely the result of learning, of interacting with the environment. We may inherit predispositions to react to these experiences, both internal and external, in particular ways. "It seems to me that we know far too little about people's inner organization, how they arrive at decisions between preferences, and what ultimate needs they have other than the more visible or pressing ones. Few people know themselves in this respect" (Buhler, 1968a, p. 39).

As we discuss the development of motivational patterns, particularly as they affect and are affected by learning, we shall inevitably be talking about man's interactions with his environment. Yet this distinction—between man, on the one hand, and the environment, on the other—is sometimes misleading. As the open-system model suggests, man is so inextricably involved with his environment that it may not make sense to try to separate the two. Biological studies have made it quite evident that environment can no longer be defined as something outside the organism that affects or becomes part of the organism by internalization. Environment must include internal factors as well, for the nature-nurture interaction is so meshed and interdependent, even on the prenatal level, that it is impossible to determine what is heredity and what is environment, or what is "inside" or "outside" (Eiduson, 1968). We must learn to look at man, at any moment in time, according to what he is. We can then trace the ways in which that is-ness grows and changes and look at some of the specific factors that influence those changes. But we must continue to remind ourselves that teasing out this factor or that is an artificial device, a way of distorting reality so as to see parts of it more clearly. Ultimately, it must all be put back together again and seen as a whole. Man is his heredity and is his environment, just as he is his hopes and his fears and his dreams.

### Birth—Before and After

The logical place to begin, in looking at how all this complexity comes to be, is at the beginning—at birth. Unfortunately (for those who like neat, simple starting points) the moment of birth isn't the beginning. The embryo is alive; it interacts with its limited environment; and it is capable of learning. For both practical and ethical reasons, data on embryo behavior are rather scarce; the data we do have suggest that the embryo interacts with its surroundings in a relatively simple, need-satisfying way. Its senses are severely limited: it can see nothing, and auditory stimulation is usually muffled. There is little or no variation in temperature. It responds primarily to kinesthetic and tactile stimuli, by moving about, flexing and relaxing various muscle combinations, and experiencing the resulting changes in sensation.

Birth, then, is a great upheaval—for some theorists, *the* great upheaval to which all later experience is unconsciously related. There is pressure, new kinds and intensities of movement, the sensation of light and vision, the (possibly painful?) sensation of breathing, a whole host of sharper, more acute sensory inputs. Surely nowhere in all man's extrauterine life does he experience such an enormous and abrupt transition; we may well wonder that he survives at all! And we cannot help speculating whether it may be here, in a primitive and unformed consciousness of "I have survived," that the first germs of curiosity and self-actualization may be found.

It does not take long to begin to observe behaviors in the neonate (newborn) that tend to support such a notion. Within a few hours of birth, the infant is trying to raise his head (heavy flower on fragile, yielding stalk) and is showing interest in his surroundings. Exploratory behavior is at first far overshadowed by the difficult business of staying alive: eating, eliminating, resting. Yet even here, the basic needs include more than simple, observable tissue needs. Human infants are born with social needs as well; without cuddling, holding, and social interaction (the pediatricians call it TLC, for Tender Loving Care), the baby will die just as surely as he will starve without food. With TLC, he will continue to expand, to extend himself more and more into his environment. "While I cannot agree with the theory that the mother's care is the *sine qua non* for the baby's finding his way into the world of objects," says Buhler, "I do agree that to establish contacts with responding persons is part of the infant's most basic needs and goals" (1968a, p. 32). Whether with mother, father, or the big kid down the hall, dependable and comfortable human interaction is a basic need and thus a primary motivator for the infant. And, I believe, for the adult. While the ways in which we meet that need may change almost beyond recognition, the need itself remains with us throughout our lives.

### Childhood

As the child matures, his behavior becomes more complex. His muscular and nervous systems grow, making him capable of greater physical and cognitive activity. And he learns—incredible, enormous amounts; great insatiable gulps of experience/interaction/I can–I do–I am. To the casual observer, a baby waving a rattle or chug-chugging a toy car over the floor is a quiet, peaceful sight. Viewed more closely, that behavior is a dynamic, emotional, intensely complex pattern of learning and testing and exploring of self-in-world. The child is occupied with the agreeable task of developing an effective familiarity with his environment. This task involves discovering the effects he can have on the environment and the effects the environment can have on him. To the extent that these results are preserved by learning, they build up an increased competence in dealing with the environment. The child's play is serious business, though to him it seems merely interesting and fun (R. W. White, 1959).

Exactly what learnings occur, what varieties of motivation are strengthened, during these early years is impossible to say. Surely basic concepts of the world as trustworthy or threatening and of the self as competent or incompetent must be formed; and such hypotheses inevitably are the foundation of adult motivational patterns. Hoffman (1972) suggests that the period between the ages of 1 and 3 or 4 is a critical stage for developing a sense of independence and competence. The child who does not acquire such a sense of self then will have difficulty acquiring it at a later age. Curiosity, exploration, a joy in affecting objects (both animate and inanimate) around him—all of these can be seen clearly throughout infancy and early childhood. The success with which these motivations are experienced and satisfied not only teaches the child need-meeting techniques but also helps him to form expectations about what kinds of needs will be met (and, as a necessary adjunct, what kind of person he will be) in the future.

## Reinforcement

When we talk about experiencing and satisfying motivations we are talking in part about reinforcement. Positive reinforcement comes as the child experiences success; he gets what he is trying to get (extrinsic reward) and/or he is rewarded simply by the process of manipulating his internal or external environment (intrinsic reward). A healthy mix of positive and negative reinforcement allows the child to develop expectations of success and techniques for moving toward success, as well as an ability to tolerate occasional failure. Parents and teachers can facilitate this process both by providing appropriate rewards and reward recognition (that is, calling to the child's attention the intrinsic-reward value of his activities: "I bet it was fun to do that" or "Did that make you feel good?") and by helping the child to set reasonable goals, goals that are neither too easy nor too difficult to attain. The child's interactions with the environment (and again, remember that he himself is part of that environment) can and should provide most of his reinforcements; adults, as part of the environment, can try to shape the reinforcement pattern so as to encourage the development of curiosity, courage, and creativity.

All reinforcement is not positive; punishments (meted out, again, by both animate and inanimate parts of the environment) are an inevitable part of life. A certain amount of unpleasant stimulation is growth producing; such punishments help us to discriminate between effective and ineffective interaction techniques and to build up as well a tolerance for future lack of success. At some point, however, punishment becomes destructive of motivation. That point is reached when the experience of punishment, of lack of success or incompetence, begins to create an expectation of future failure and a sense of self-as-failure. The child who is encouraged to set goals beyond his abilities, to "try just a little harder for Mommy," is an easy victim to this failure pattern, as is the child whose parents and teachers ignore or belittle his efforts. Inconsistency of reward—a behavior rewarded one day, punished the next, and ignored the third—creates not so much expectation of punishment as fear of punishment, and fear of punishment is also a motivation destroyer. The speed with which fear extinguishes exploratory, curious behavior can be easily demonstrated, in rats (R. W. White, 1959) and monkeys (Harlow, 1958) as well as in man.

We have spoken of reinforcement as it occurs through getting what one was after, through the experience of interacting competently, and through social interaction. Another important source of reinforcement is the learned or internalized reward. Earlier in the chapter I discussed the notion of learned rewards, in which those behaviors associated with primary rewards come to have reward value themselves. Verbal behavior is particularly interesting in this context: words, sentences, and tones of voice from other people and even from oneself can come to have strong reinforcing value. "After a child has learned to respond to promises, promises may be used in a similar way [as reinforcements], provided the learned reinforcement value of the promises is maintained by regular enough association with primary reinforcement. After sufficient training, words that the child says *to himself* may function in the same way. . . . This is a part of the mechanism of 'hope' and plays an important role in the response to remote goals" (Dollard & Miller, 1971, p. 100; italics added). The often distressing thing about symbolic learned reinforcements (such as verbal behavior) is that they are learned whether such learning was intended or not. And (as I have discovered, in trying to cure myself of swearing at other cars while driving in traffic) they are hard indeed to unlearn. Part of the reason one's own verbal reinforcers are so tenacious may be their intimate relationship to one's sense of self and self-worth. As I learn to control my own behavior by my words (either spoken or unspoken), I build my sense of competence and efficacy. I am in control of myself. Buhler (1968a) points this relationship out in the behavior of small children: In his first "I want to" behavior, the child is quite arbitrary regarding his objective and may say "yes" one time and "no" another, in answer to the same offer or request. He is trying to see how it feels to make choices and decisions of his own and, if his environment permits, to discover himself as a person in his own right. As his sense of self becomes more certain and as he learns better how to play the game of social interaction, his self-defining verbal behaviors are more subtle; but they are still present.

## Symbolization and Time Binding

It is characteristic of small children that they are here-and-now oriented. The very small child is unable to conceptualize the existence of something he cannot see; the game of peek-a-boo is fascinating to him because in it familiar objects literally move in and out of existence. Events of the past are quickly forgotten or blend into a vague haze of "once we went to the zoo and once I fell down and scraped my knee"; possible events of the future are seldom if ever a part of the small child's conceptual framework. Somehow, through the learning and maturation process, the child gradually begins to develop the capacity for representing symbolically that which is not present in time and space. This capacity adds a whole new dimension to motivation; as he learns to time bind and to take into account people and things not in his immediate visual field, he can begin to work toward longer range and more complex goals. Perhaps the first evidence of such expansion is in the development of what has been called ego strength, or socially approved behavior constraints. As ego strength grows, the child gains in self-control; he becomes able to delay gratification in order to receive a better reward (or to avoid a punishment) later on. The relationship between "I will not hit my sister with a rock because then she will cry and then Mother may punish me" and "I will learn the periodic table instead of going to a movie because I hope to be a doctor some day" may not be immediately apparent, but such a relationship exists. Both statements are time binding in that they compare immediate reward with later consequences; and both involve the internalization of socially approved values.

The child's parents and teachers play an important part in the process of motivational expansion. Both in direct teaching and in the roles that they model for the child, they help him to understand and bring some organization into his ever-widening field of awareness. Ordering goals and priorities is a critical aspect of motivation. An individual has to learn when and for how long to focus on one particular goal. He has to learn to recognize goal hierarchies, to work for subgoals. He has to learn that one kind of activity may satisfy several different kinds of motivation—may bring him closer to several goals—or that, conversely, working toward one goal may defeat his efforts in another direction. "The child, flooded by many stimuli around him, recognizes that by establishing a hierarchy of importance of the stimuli and an ordered manner of responding, he is likely to achieve greater effectiveness and greater satisfaction. Such recognition is accomplished in simple ways. The child is encouraged to complete one task before beginning another, thereby helping him to see the advantage and pleasure of one completed task over two incomplete ones" (M. M. Meyer, 1968, p. 193). Here too the element of ego strength is apparent. To continue to work on one task, even though a new one would be more fun, is a matter of delay of gratification. The only way a child can discover the benefits of such delays is to try them; the only reason for trying them in the absence of knowledge of their benefits is some sort of social pressure: immediate approval from parents or teacher or the knowledge that such approval will be forthcoming. As the habits of goal ordering and task persistence become stronger, they are reinforced in two ways, through the internalized values acquired from adults and by the extrinsic rewards that come with successful effort.

As I said, the development of time binding and motivational expansion is a gradual process. It continues throughout childhood; and a number of theorists have suggested that moving into an adult way of dealing with time is one of the critical tasks of adolescence. Buhler takes this position, asserting that, developmentally speaking, children usually live in the present. As he approaches adolescence, the child begins to take the future into account. If his childhood was unhappy or did not allow him to develop a sufficient zest for living, he may fall prey to "brooding over the past," which is a characteristic of neurotic development. The healthy adult considers both the past and the future, trying to "learn from the past in order to decide in the present what will benefit his future, regardless of the direction in which his goals lie" (Buhler, 1968b, p. 25).

## Goals

In all this discussion of interaction and striving and time binding, I have frequently used the word *goals*. How do goals fit in with what we are saying about motivation? Goals are the end points of motivated behavior; they are the things (or processes) we are motivated to reach (or avoid). Different individuals may choose different goals as a way of satisfying the same general motive; my need for affection and respect, for instance, may lead me to strive toward a goal of having a closely knit family, while another person with the same need may work to be a successful student or a competent secretary. The development of goals, like the development of all personality characteristics, cannot be attributed to any single factor. Goals are the result of the interaction of a number of factors; M. M. Meyer (1968) suggests that the two most crucial are the inherent characteristics of the child and the attitudes and the actions of the parents. Meyer goes on to point out the importance of cultural attitudes and also the influence of special talents that a child may possess in determining the goals he will choose to work for.

The phrase "choose to work for" is perhaps not a good one in that it suggests that one's choice of goals is a conscious process. Sometimes it is, to be sure: career decisions, for example, are often thought out and carefully weighed. Other goals, though, don't "feel" as if they were consciously chosen; even some career goals have this quality. "I don't know when I decided to be a teacher; it seems like I've always wanted to"; or "I heard that professor talking, and I knew that was what I wanted to spend the rest of my life working on." (That, incidentally, was more or less the nature of my own career "choice.") Still other goals are so far from being consciously chosen that the individual may not even be clearly aware of what he is working for; psychotherapists' offices are full of such people.

R. W. White suggests a more or less steady progression, as a child grows up, from an undifferentiated need (motive) to interact competently with the environment toward a clearly hierarchical and compartmentalized set of goals. "Later in life it becomes profitable to distinguish various motives such as cognizance, construction, mastery, and achievement. It is my view that all such motives have a root in motivation for competence. They are differentiated from it through life experiences which emphasize one or another aspect of the cycle of transaction with environment. Of course, the motives of later childhood and of adult life are no longer simple and can almost never be referred to a single root" (1959, p. 323). Goals are selected—nobody is born wanting to get A's in school or wanting to get even with his father or wanting to be a computer scientist—but the process through which these choices come about is still unclear.

Buhler (1968a) suggests five major phases through which people move regarding the major goals and motives with which they are occupied. In the first, which extends roughly through middle adolescence, the goals for self-determination are still hazy. The child is, for the most part, still present oriented, and it is difficult for him to think about future accomplishments or rewards. Later adolescence, from about 15 to 20 years, is a period of "tentative, programmatic self-determination." The young person is trying out ideas about goals, just as he is experimenting with his whole sense of self. In young adulthood and well into middle age (Buhler suggests age 45 as a rough end point of this period), the individual operates on the basis of specific and definite self-determination. He is relatively sure of who he is and what he wants of himself. At around 45, however, he frequently becomes aware of the fact that most of his life choices are behind him. The possibility of major changes in long-range goals is severely limited. This realization ushers in a period of self-assessment and review of past activities, with a concurrent reorientation for the future. The final stage in goal behavior begins around the time of retirement, in the sixties. Here the person tends to become concerned with experiencing his life as he lives it (in a sense, returning to the here-and-now orientation of the child) and may do so with a sense of resignation, failure, or fulfillment.

Throughout the whole process of goal development, of the expansion and delineation of one's personal structure of motives, one builds a pattern of expectations. One learns not only that certain activities can lead to satisfaction, but also that other activities lead to failure. These learnings, in turn, affect motivation: one learns not to strive in certain directions or to work for a sure and certain X rather than for a doubtful Y. As Kelly (1958) points out, man forms a bridge between his past and his future, using the learnings of the one to set up restrictions upon the other. He organizes his constructs into a personal system that is both conscious and unconscious, both intellectual and emotional. This personal construct system provides him with both freedom of decision and limitation of action—freedom because it permits him to deal with the meanings of events rather than forcing him to be helplessly pushed about by them, and limitation because he can never make choices outside the world of alternatives he has erected for himself. Whatever we may decide upon as primary motivator(s), the process of learning and experiencing self-in-environment guarantees that every individual, at every moment of his existence, is operating on the basis of a highly personalized structure of felt or perceived needs and goals. Understanding someone's past history can help the teacher to understand his present motivation, but the key word is *present:* what I do today is based on how I think and feel now about both past experience and future consequences.

## SPECIFIC MOTIVATORS

Buhler's stages are a broad-stroke outline of human goal development. Obviously, within each phase are many finer processes and detailed interrelationships. Equally obviously, she is talking about goals as a single category when in fact we all respond to a great complex of goals and motives. Several of the (more nearly) individual goals and motives are of particular interest to educators. Three of these, the need for creative expression, the need for social involvement, and the need to achieve, deserve special mention here.

### Creative Expression and Social Involvement

Buhler suggests that curiosity and exploration, as motivational forces clearly apparent in infants, may relate directly to creative behavior later in life. We aren't sure, she says, how close the relationship may be between curiosity, on the one hand, and a later preference for adventure and novelty, on the other. Creative expression, seen in this light, may represent an individual's need to interact with and explore something new—in this case, the something new being provided by his own mind and hands. The experiences of life also affect the ways in which the child deals with this need to explore and to experience novelty. According to Buhler, the individual's innate tendencies to be either creative and independent or noncreative and dependent are determined by both the goals and the values of his environment. "These enhance the 'openness to experiences' and the willingness to

I KNOW IT'S DANGEROUS BUT ON THE OTHER HAND, IF WE PUNISH HER IT **MAY** WELL DISCOURAGE HER CREATIVITY......

take risks which were found in the creative child as, on the other hand, they encourage the orientation toward security and success which were found in the noncreative child" (Buhler, 1968a, p. 35). Thus the drive to explore and interact with new surroundings, satisfied, may be the wellspring of creativity, while the same drive leading to behaviors that are punished (either directly or indirectly through the experience of failure) may be the source of safety seeking and fearfulness.

The need for social involvement is satisfied in early life primarily through interactions with parents, especially the mother. Gradually, social involvement reaches out to include siblings, extended-family members, and others with whom the child interacts regularly. During childhood and early adolescence, there is not as much a seeking of such relationships as an acceptance of them as part of the normal course of events. Yet the need for social contact is present, and the process of meeting this need makes possible the later growth of more adult social motivations. During his teens, the youngster typically becomes involved in a conflict of motives, in which a growing need for freedom and independence can make it difficult for him to satisfy his (still growing and changing) needs for love, protection, and nurturance. The adolescent discovers and aspires to two new goals of human relationship: intimacy and commitment. Healthy intimacy and commitment may be defined as voluntarily chosen bonds. Although they represent a voluntary reduction of independence, the free-choice element distinguishes them from involuntary dependency (Buhler, 1968a). Here we can see an example of the paradoxical need combinations that frequently characterize self-actualization in the Maslow and Rogers sense: the fully aware and experiencing person must come to function in a kind of tension that allows him to be at once free and committed, autonomous yet intimately involved with others.

## Need Achievement

Aside from the so-called primary needs, the one area of motivation that has probably received more attention than any other is achievement motivation. Henry Murray coined the term *nAch* (need achievement) to refer to this kind of motivation and was instrumental in stimulating research on its strength and its effects on both children and adults. Murray was not, however, the first to single out the need to achieve as a common human motive. Alfred Adler, famous as the founder of Individual Psychology, made striving for superiority a fundamental part of his whole theory of personality. According to Adler, man's primary social and psychological need is to feel superior to others; inferiority feelings that result from failure to meet this need are the cause of neurosis.

The notion of nAch, as described by Murray, is not as central to human functioning as is Adler's striving for superiority; it is one of a whole constellation of needs that Murray believes are shared to a greater or lesser degree by all people. The individual's uniqueness results from the particular mix of need strengths characteristic of him: one person, for instance, might be high in nAch and low in needs for nurturance or dependency or dominance or affiliation, while another might have a quite different pattern of high- and low-need areas.

Need achievement, like the other needs discussed by Murray, is considered relatively stable; that is, a person tends to be either high or low or intermediate in strength of nAch over a long period of time. This is not to say that a high-nAch person goes about constantly bent on achievement to the exclusion of anything else; rather, the drive is latent unless it is "aroused by situational cues which indicate that performance on a task will be instrumental to achievement" (Roberts, 1972, p. 37). In other words, it is the stimulus situation that elicits nAch behavior. Placed in similar situations, situations that suggest that a particular activity may lead to achievement, the high-nAch person will engage in that activity while the low-nAch person may not. Telling a high-nAch child that there will be a spelling test tomorrow afternoon may elicit achievement-related behavior (studying), but it may have little or no effect on the low-nAch child.

Weiner (1972) has studied the growth of achievement motivation in children and concludes that it is directly linked to the child's understanding of the effects of his own efforts to succeed. That is, a child may see success (or lack of success) as related to effort or to ability; he may succeed because he works hard or because he is just good at whatever he is doing. A child's pride is highest, according to Weiner, when he believes that he has succeeded through hard work; conversely, shame is greatest when his failure is attributed to not working hard enough. Achievement motivation and morality are linked so closely in our culture that some people believe that failure, given ability but no effort, is immoral—as though it were against a prevailing moral ethic not to utilize one's capacities. Thus our society places a kind of moral pressure on the child to try harder—that is, to act in achievement-oriented ways. But only the child for whom such behavior leads to success sees any payoff in doing so; and, conversely, the child for whom success comes with little or no effort is not likely to see achievement striving as particularly necessary or desirable. We shall discuss these ideas more fully in Chapter 11 when we consider the development of *locus of control*—a person's sense of who or what is responsible for the things that happen to him.

The experience of success with little striving and of failure with much striving, then, can contribute to an overall low level of need achievement. According to Buhler (1968a), the perception of oneself as an achiever or a nonachiever tends to crystallize somewhere between the 8th and the 12th year. During this time, all a child's foregoing experiences of being able to master things and situations and to overcome failures converge to generate an attitude toward achievement. The child who has learned that goals can often be attained by means of hard work is likely to be a high-nAch individual; conversely, the child who has learned to expect failure in spite of effort or to expect success with little or no effort will probably have a lower level of achievement motivation.

It has also been hypothesized that nAch is related to ego identity—to the strength of one's sense of self. Bauer and Snyder (1972), reasoning that resolution of one's attitudes toward achievement and one's self-image tend to solidify at about the same age, suggest that a deficiency in motivation to achieve is accompanied by low self-image. A study of male college students supported this hypothesis: students who scored high in nAch tended to have more positive ego-identity scores that did those who scored low in nAch. This finding is quite consistent with at least part of Buhler's reasoning: we would expect the child who experiences success through effort to think more highly of himself than the child who experiences failure. As for the child who usually succeeds with little effort, Weiner's comments on pride and shame in achievement suggest that little pride or value is assigned to personal success when no effort has been involved in attaining it; in this child, ego identity or ego strength might be low because he has never had to prove what he can do when challenged.

One of the continuing problems in studies of nAch has been a confusion in determining just what is meant by a low nAch score. Some theorists see such scores as indicators that an individual is motivated to avoid success—the polar opposite of a motivation to achieve it—while others are concerned with differentiating between trying to achieve success, on the one hand, and trying to avoid failure, on the other. The difference between striving to achieve success and striving to avoid failure is reflected most clearly in goal-setting behavior. The person who is motivated to achieve success is likely to set goals of moderate difficulty, goals that he is likely to be able to reach with effort and from which he thus can experience—and feel good about—success. The failure avoider, in contrast, more often sets easily reached goals (with which he is almost sure to succeed, even though he may not realize a sense of accomplishment) or extremely difficult goals (since reaching the goal is nearly impossible, not doing so cannot be seen as failure).

Motivation to avoid success presents an altogether different picture. Both the success achiever and the failure avoider welcome success when it comes, even though the failure avoider may not actively strive for it. The success avoider, in contrast, is fearful of success. In our culture, such fears are most commonly found in women and usually have to do with concern over the "nonfeminine" connotations of competition and goal striving. "Femininity and competitive achievement continue in American society, even today, to be viewed as two desirable but mutually exclusive ends. . . . Many achievement-oriented American women, especially those high in the motive to avoid success, when faced with the conflict between their feminine image and developing their abilities and interests, disguise their ability and abdicate from competition in the outside world" (Horner, 1972, p. 171). Other individuals, both male and female, may fear that being successful will lead to higher expectations for future behavior, expectations that they will not be able to meet. Whatever the roots of success avoidance, it must be dealt with in a way different from the way in which one might deal with failure avoidance. Providing the failure avoider with opportunities to succeed on the basis of his own efforts—to experience gradually increasing degrees of achievement striving followed by success—may well wean him into a more achievement-oriented mode. Providing such opportunities to the success avoider is likely to increase his anxiety and thus to further strengthen the success-avoidance pattern. Discussion of conflicts about success and its implications and, for girls, exposure to role models of women who are both successful strivers and are comfortable with their femininity are more likely to have an impact on the success-avoidance problem.

## IMPLICATIONS FOR LEARNING

At a general level, the implications of motivational level for learning activities are quite clear and straightforward. Weiner states it well: "Individuals high in achievement needs perceive that outcome and effort covary. That is, they perceive that hard work leads to success, and that a lack of effort results in failure. This perceived relationship is greatly modulated among persons low in achievement needs. Therefore, if it may be presumed that beliefs influence action, then we would expect individuals high in achievement needs to expend greater effort in achievement-related contexts than individuals low in achievement concerns" (1972, p. 209). For practical solutions, however, such a statement doesn't help us much. It is too broad, too general. Students who think they can succeed will work hard, while students who think they can't won't—so what? We need a way of breaking down that equation, of looking at specific aspects of the overall motivation picture.

Murray (1958) provides us with one such breakdown. He suggests that motivational activity can be seen in phases, the most important of which are the *prospective,* or decision-making, phase and the phase of *actuation,* or endeavor. The prospective phase is concerned with goal setting, with deciding what I shall try to do. The actuation phase is the working-toward phase, in which the goal-directed activity is carried out. In addition, we must also be concerned with an evaluative phase, in which the individual decides whether his activities were indeed successful and makes a judgment as to whether the payoff was worth the effort.

## Goal Setting

The choice of a goal is obviously a major determinant of the amount of striving behavior a person engages in. I am not going to work hard to reach an objective if I know beforehand that the objective can be reached with little or no effort; similarly, I am not likely to invest a great deal of effort in a task if I believe that I have little or no chance of success. In this cause-and-effect relationship, then, motivation level can be seen as (in part) an effect of goal setting.

But, as we have seen, motivation is also a causal factor in goal setting. The highly achievement-oriented person tends to set difficult but do-able tasks for himself, while the non-achievement-oriented person tends to set himself tasks that are either very easy (trivial) or very difficult (impossible). Moreover, these patterns tend to be self-sustaining: the high achiever who succeeds in his difficult task is reinforced in this behavior and will therefore be inclined to continue setting difficult but reachable goals; while the low achiever continues to be reinforced in his nonstriving patterns. Low-achievement individuals initiate fewer achievement activities (so they have less opportunity to be rewarded for such activity), and they don't work as hard or as long on the activities they do initiate (thus further reducing their opportunities for success).

If we believe that achievement-oriented behavior is desirable in the learning process, it seems clear that one necessary part of our task as teachers is to encourage the choice of goals that make for successful achievement striving. Here, however, we must make an important distinction: we must differentiate between the success avoiders, the low-goal-setting failure avoiders, and the impossible-goal-setting failure avoiders (see Table 8-1). Success avoiders don't like to set any goals at all; if a goal is

*Table 8-1.* The relationship of goal-setting behavior to approach and avoidance of success and failure

| Avoidance Behavior | Approach Behavior | Goal Difficulty |
|---|---|---|
| Avoid failure | | Low |
| | Approach success | Intermediate |
| Avoid failure | | High |
| Avoid success | | No goal setting |

set, then the success avoider is in conflict about whether he wants to work toward it. This conflict is at the roots of the success avoider's motivational difficulties, and recognizing the conflict is the first step in dealing with it. In the other two typical patterns, goals are set but they are often inappropriate. The teacher must recognize the too-low goal and the too-high goal and encourage the learners to shift to more appropriate tasks. Thus two individuals, both with motivational difficulties, may be encouraged to move in exactly opposite directions: one should be encouraged to work toward more difficult goals, while the other should be encouraged to set his sights lower. In both these instances it is the expectation of an unpleasant outcome—specifically, of failure—that has prevented appropriate goal setting in the past. A person's processes are psychologically channeled by the ways in which he anticipates events, Kelly (1958) reminds us. In the case of the student who fears failure, it is misleading to speak about low motivational level: such people are strongly motivated to avoid failing. Depending on the individual, either helping him to recognize the nature of those fears or providing him with the experience of successful striving through helping him set more appropriate goals—or both!—can be instrumental in breaking the cycle of behavior.

## Actuation

It is a truism that people who are highly motivated toward success (whether in academic or other areas) work harder to obtain such success than those who are not so highly motivated. Yet we might look at that notion a bit more analytically: why do some people work harder than others? One factor is, undoubtedly, that those who work harder do so because they believe they have a chance to succeed. A failure may be temporarily discouraging, but they can still hope to succeed the next time around. "On the other hand, individuals low in achievement motivation ascribe failure to a lack of ability. Ability is a relatively stable attribute, not under personal control, that cannot immediately be increased. Hence, among individuals low in achievement motivation, continued failure is anticipated following nonattainment of a goal, and goal striving ceases" (Weiner, 1972, p. 208). In order for goal striving to continue, at least one of two conditions must exist: either the individual must experience some success, or the striving itself must provide some rewards. Cohen (1971) explored some of the implications of the latter possibility. He studied kindergarten children who were trying to solve visual puzzles under three different motivational conditions. In the first condition, children were encouraged to work on the task simply because "it's fun to do." The second condition was the "social" condition; here children were told that the experimenter "would like you to have fun with it." And, in the third condition, primary reinforcement was added: "here is some candy to help you have fun with it." The ten children in the social condition tended to persist longer in working on the puzzles, while the ten children in the first condition achieved the most correct solutions. On no measure did the primary-reinforcement group look best. It seems reasonable to assume that providing a primary reward tended to detract from the intrinsic reward value of the process itself and thus reduced overall task motivation. But calling attention to the fact that the puzzle was "fun" (which was more specifically the case in the first two conditions than in the third) tended to improve both performance level and persistence.

*Competition*

Competition is a factor that often is present in motivation behavior. Striving to achieve academically or athletically or socially is in our culture frequently a matter of winning, and winning most usually implies that someone has to lose. Not surprisingly, there is a fairly stable relationship between achievement motivation and competitive behavior. Not only do high achievers tend to be more successful competitors, but people whose anxiety levels are high relative to their motivation level tend to outperform their more relaxed but high-nAch friends in noncompetitive situations (Ryan & Lakie, 1965). Let's look at that rather complicated relationship more closely. When achievement level is high and anxiety is low, competition is relished. It's fun to win and to try to win, especially when you aren't worried about the outcome. So far, no surprises. The unexpected fact is that low-motivation, high-anxiety people do better than high achievers in a noncompetitive situation. Either the low achievers do not see a chance for failure (which they would have to avoid, characteristically, by not trying to succeed) in the noncompetitive situation, or the high achievers are not challenged enough to exert themselves. Whatever the reason (and it poses a fascinating research question), the implication for teachers is clear: provision should be made for both competitive and noncompetitive activities, and students should be encouraged to move into the situation where they are most comfortable.

For the highly achievement-motivated child, competition would seem to be a useful means of stimulating effort. Unfortunately, the thrill of competing and (frequently) winning can become such an important part of a child's life that he loses sight of what the competition is all about. "Where the drive for achievement as a means of competition has become the end in itself, the child is likely to lose sight of the values in the achievement and to be busy with his competitiveness as a means of surpassing instead of learning" (M. M. Meyer, 1968, p. 196). As an alternative to competition with others, Bandura and Perloff (1967) investigated using competition with oneself to stimulate performance. Working with 7- to 10-year-old boys and girls, they asked them to set a criterion for their own performance on a wheel-cranking task. Some of the children were rewarded when they reached the criterion they had set for themselves; others were not. Bandura and Perloff found that, on this kind of task, the children did not maintain their performance in the absence of an external reward.

## Intrinsic and Extrinsic Rewards

One implication of the studies of competition with self and others is that there must be some reward for the child if he is to continue behaving in "desirable" ways, either in or out of the classroom. For some children the reward may be winning or at least having an opportunity to try to win; the danger here is that the desire to win may quite eclipse the fun of learning or the satisfaction inherent in the task being performed. Extrinsic rewards, like candy or extra free-play time, can also help to maintain children's behaviors, but again the child is likely to focus on the reward to such an extent that he loses sight of any intrinsic value in the behavior itself. One of the effects of extrinsically motivated activity on task performance, notes Cohen (1971), is to shift attention from the requirements of the task to that of its reward value or rewarding agent. The ideal solution would be to make it possible for the child to focus on the value of the task to himself, so that the reward is automatically a part of task performance.

Such a strategy imposes rather difficult decisions on the teacher; we may discover that a number of the things we have been asking Johnny and Susie to do simply have no reward value for them. The typical classroom imposes a good many rules on a child not so much for the benefit of the child as for the benefit of his classmates and of the teacher(s). Not working on an arithmetic assignment out loud, for example, may be difficult and may slow down a child's learning process, but he is expected to work quietly so that others in the room can go about their business. It is important for the teacher in this or any other learning situation to make quite clear to the child which of the rules are for his (the teacher's) benefit. There is nothing wrong with expecting someone with whom you are to spend a good deal of time to conform to some of your needs—as long as you are willing to reciprocate and bend a little for him and as long as you are open about just why you want him to do whatever you have asked him to. Even though this "social" rule or task may have no intrinsic first-order rewards, it certainly has second-order rewards in that behaving in the expected way carries social approval (or the cessation of disapproval) from peers and adults.

Looking at our relationships with students and clients from the point of view of the intrinsic-reward value of the things they do—or are expected to do—often involves us in a learning experience of our own. It is easy to fall into the habit of making suggestions or prescriptions or assignments on the basis of general expectations about people, without realizing that such suggestions have little or no value at all for the specific individual with whom we are interacting. Kelly (1958), working as a consultant in the public schools, found that this happened frequently with teachers. The teacher who asked for help in getting a particular child or group of children motivated was usually asking the children to do something that was simply not rewarding. In general, Kelly found that the most practical approach to "motivational problems" was to try to reorient the people who thought in such terms. Complaints about motivation seemed to tell more about the complainant than they did about his pupils.

## Open Classrooms

The open-classroom concept currently attracting so much interest in our public schools is a direct consequence of the notion of the intrinsic-reward value in learning. In the open classroom, the child (theoretically) works on tasks because he is interested in them, not because he has to complete an assignment. Hebb (1971, p. 123) reports on a particularly drastic and inclusive shift to an open-classroom model in one school: "All of the six hundred-odd pupils in a city school, ranging from six to fifteen years of age, were suddenly informed that they need do no work whatever unless they wanted to, that the punishment for being noisy and interrupting others' work was to be sent to the playground to play, and that the reward for being good was to be allowed to do more work. In these circumstances, *all* of the pupils discovered within a day or two that, within limits, they preferred work to no work (and incidentally learned more arithmetic and so forth than in previous years)."

While I am quite in agreement with the principles on which the open classroom is based, I am concerned about the fadlike way in which it is being seized on in many schools. The open classroom is not a situation in which the minimally competent teacher may sit back and take it easy because, after all, the students are just doing whatever they want to anyhow. Managing a good open classroom is, I suspect, considerably more difficult than more traditional teaching. The teacher must be continually alert to opportunities for pointing out the intrinsic value of this task or that in order to guide (but not coerce) the child into new areas of learning. He must be aware of problems in appropriate goal setting, including fear of failure and distaste for competition, and he must be sensitive to the ability of the child to anticipate where rewards may lie. He must learn to say "try it, you'll like it" to one child, while gently suggesting a different course for another child. And, at the same time, he must attend to the social dimensions of the classroom, helping the children to be alert to the second-order rewards inherent in kindness and cooperation. Finally, he must have the judgment to know when to step in and use his adult authority; he must not allow freedom to become license. He must give over control to the students while retaining responsibility for their learning—a most difficult charge indeed.

In spite of all the difficulties, however, I believe the open concept to be the key to understanding and working with motivational patterns—not only in the open classroom, but in open families, open counseling, open "welfare" structures. Openness in this sense means the willingness to face squarely the question of why—why do you want to do this, why do I want you to do that, why does society make these demands on you, and so on. The teacher can help the student to recognize his own motivations and those of others and to work constructively in the dynamic interaction of those changing motivational patterns. Above all, we must recognize that people are different—that they are rewarded (and punished) by different things. "Different strokes for different folks" is a shorthand phrase for an important concept: each of us has learned to be rewarded by different things, and each of us has learned to fear and avoid different things. The ways in which we behave today, the things we work toward and shrink from and are indifferent to, are determined largely by those learning patterns of the past. Just as each of us has experienced different yesterdays, so the motivation of our todays and the goals of our tomorrows are different. To be an effective teacher, one must consider all three—the yesterday, the today, and the tomorrow—in dealing with each individual child.

## QUESTIONS FOR UNDERSTANDING

1. How many of your classroom or school-related behaviors do you think are habits, continued for no reason other than that you have learned to perform them and now they are self-rewarding? If you should decide to change such a habit or behavior, how might you go about it?
2. If Harlow, White, and others are right, and the exercise of competence and the satisfaction of curiosity are in fact basic motivators, how might you utilize this fact in working with a group of ninth graders?
3. I have asserted that the need for warm, affectionate interactions with others is present throughout an individual's life span. How is this need likely to manifest itself in a first-grade classroom? A sixth-grade classroom? Among high school students?
4. Your fourth-grade class is beginning a unit on the Soviet Union; you hope to integrate learning of communication skills, economics, math, history, and geography in this unit. How, specifically, can you help individual students set appropriate goals for their own achievements as they work on this material?
5. Within an open classroom, how might a high-nAch student, a failure-avoiding student, and success-avoiding student be expected to behave differently?

*Chapter 9*

# Cognitive Style

Thinking, feeling, and sensing have long been identified as the "great triad" of mental functions. These three areas represent the major tasks of the mind—the things people do inside their heads. Thinking: manipulating symbols, solving problems, forming ideas and associations. Feeling: experiencing emotion and responding accordingly. Sensing: receiving input from the outside world, perceiving, being aware of the inputs from our sensory organs. Psychologists down through the years have tried to understand and describe how these functions are carried out and how they relate to one another, but only in relatively recent times have we come to believe that people develop consistent patterns of mental functioning, individual styles or habits that tend to persist throughout their lives. A person's cognitive style is determined by the way he takes note of his total surroundings—how he seeks meaning, how he becomes informed. Clearly, such a definition involves all three of the major functions. It is perhaps this cross-cutting of traditional divisions that has made cognitive style such a slippery concept to study and analyze. In this chapter we shall try to determine just what is meant by cognitive style; we'll look at a number of cognitive-style dimensions that have been identified and consider some of the implications for learning of various cognitive styles.

## WHAT DOES COGNITIVE STYLE INVOLVE?

### Creating Reality

Most of us tend to believe that the worlds of today, of yesterday, and of tomorrow are fairly much the same places and that they are the same because of some sort of objective consistency in the out there. We know that things change, but we also know that change usually takes time; if the world changes significantly, we expect that the change will occur slowly enough so that we can see it happening. We expect the same kind of consistency in our social relationships. In the social world, as in the physical world, things tend to stay the same or to change rather slowly: if John is my friend today, I expect him to be my friend tomorrow; and if I was respected by my peers yesterday, I have no reason to believe that respect will have evaporated by today. We attribute this social consistency too to external rather than to internal factors; we say that these "things" tend to stay the same, implying that we are passive spectators of events over which we have little or no control.

But the world in which we live is not composed of objective realities that we react to and interact with. In fact, it is even misleading to assume that we all deal with the same realities. Each of us builds our own world, subtly different from anyone else's. The building materials are our sensory impressions, and the building process occurs as we deal with those impressions through categorizing, storing, discarding, and augmenting. As we continue to build an increasingly detailed set of beliefs and expectations about the world, those beliefs and expectations further color our perceptions; to an ever-increasing degree, we see what we expect to see and respond to what we expect to find. Both our perceptions and our behavior, then, are built around a highly idiosyncratic world view. Each of us inhabits a universe unique to himself. The world I live in is influenced not only by my beliefs and expectations about it but also by the ways in which I form those beliefs and expectations—the moment-to-moment flow of my thinking processes. What I perceive at any given time is a function as much of how I process information as of the information available to me (Katz, 1972).

One of the ways in which we restructure our world is to give it the kind of consistency I described a moment ago. We want things to be predictable, to stay the same from one day to the next. "The consistency evident in the lives of most human beings is not due to an overriding static structure which operates as in a vacuum, without regard to changes in the situation; it is due rather to our considerable ability to recreate the same situation over and over again" (Wachtel, 1972a, p. 784). In other words, far from being passive observers, we are active participants in creating—even forcing—consistency within our world.

Perception, according to this view, involves shaping and processing data as well as merely receiving them. When we see an apple, we not only receive a set of sensory impulses in the form of electrical patterns in our brain cells but must also create an image out of those patterns. The process is a complex one when applied to the perception of an inanimate object; it is vastly more so when we deal with social perceptions and interactions. The notion of cognitive style has emerged as one way of dealing with this complexity—a way of bringing some order to the process, of formulating some rules that help us to understand and predict how individuals differ in their perceptions of and dealings with their worlds.

## Personality

According to Wachtel (1972a), the cognitive-style approach views perception as an active process whose final product is determined by the characteristics of the perceiver—both long and short term—as well as by external stimulus conditions. In order to understand perception, then, we must identify those characteristics of the perceiver that play such an important part in the process, and we must try to understand what those characteristics do as they interact with each other and with the world of external reality.

What we have here is a never-ending circle: the perceiver affects the perceived, and the perceived affects the perceiver. In order to understand why a given individual structures a particular situation in some way, we need to know about that situation as well as about the person. We need to know what the person wants or intends in the situation and what choices he thinks he has in how he will deal with it. We need to know how he has dealt with similar situations in the past and whether those dealings have led to successful outcomes.

Gradually, as we consider all these things we need to know, we begin to get a feeling for the nature of the concept we are dealing with. Stable, enduring, cutting across most if not all of a person's cognitive functioning —surely we are talking about personality, about the nature of the self. Personality covers a lot of ground; it has long been a sort of wastebasket into which were tossed all traits and characteristics that didn't seem to fit anywhere else. Yet there is a consensual meaning inherent in the term, a feeling that here, if anywhere, are to be found those elements that most truly define the nature of the individual as he constructs his world. "One may consider the current stable features of personality as a residue of a long process of interaction between individual and environment" (Wachtel, 1972a, p. 780). Personality, Wachtel seems to be saying, is a sort of stalagmite that is constantly being built up over the years out of the interactive processes of perception and reaction to perception. As such, it must be affected by one's cognitive style since that style determines the way one perceives things. But even more important, one's cognitive style is part of one's personality; it is one of those enduring characteristics that define the nature of the self. Shouksmith (1970), who had a number of things to say in our discussion of creativity in Chapter 7, comments that people who adopt particular cognitive styles tend to have related self-concepts. Students who adopt a non-conforming style, for example, evaluate themselves more highly than their conforming colleagues. My cognitive style directly affects my view of myself, as it does others' views of me; it enters directly into my perceptions and probably plays a subtle part in most of the other learning, growing, and interacting activities that I engage in.

## A Variety of Styles

Before we become too firmly entrenched in thinking of a person's cognitive style, *singular,* I should hasten to point out that we all have many different cognitive styles. There are at least two bases for this belief. First, researchers have identified a number of dimensions along which cognitive style can be measured; some of these dimensions may be independent of each other, while others almost certainly overlap. Assessed over a wide range of situations, an individual's cognitive style is a pattern of strategies that he typically adopts in his attempts to solve problems that face him. Evidence from studies cited by Shouksmith (1970) suggests that an individual's cognitive style is not necessarily unitary; a hierarchical model of cognitive style seems to offer the best starting point for understanding. Second, and perhaps more important to bear in mind, a person's cognitive style on any one dimension need not always be exactly the same; we bring into play different aspects of our styles—different areas of competence, if you will—depending on what we are trying to do. Davis (1971, p. 1457) puts it this way: "each person is a complex with the differing probabilities of approaching tasks from one point of view or another depending on varying personal and situational conditions." We cannot predict a person's behavior unless we know the situation in which that behavior will occur; and, even then, we can talk only of more or less probable behavior alternatives. So it is with cognitive styles: given a specific task or situation or problem, we may be able to say that a particular stylistic approach is likely or unlikely for a given individual, but it would be misleading to say that he will always adopt this or that particular style. Even this limited understanding, though, can be helpful, both in understanding the why of a person's behavior and in predicting what he may do next. Through these kinds of groping approaches come hypotheses about facilitating new behaviors, new learnings, and new growth.

Research in cognitive style has brought us a long way toward being able to make and test such hypotheses. This research has tended to focus on two major questions: whether it is possible to characterize people by their habits of thinking and perceiving, and what may be the adaptive significance of such habits for an individual. On the basis of the data now in, it seems clear that the answer to the first question is yes. As we look at some of the different kinds of behaviors that have been identified as more or less separate styles, we can begin to decide for ourselves the answer to the second.

## FIELD DEPENDENCE/INDEPENDENCE

Probably the best-known and most thoroughly investigated of all the cognitive-style dimensions is that of field dependence/independence. First studied by Witkin and his associates in the mid-1950s, field independence involves being able to see one part of a total stimulus situation independently of the rest—to attend and respond to the figure without being influenced by the ground. It is the ability to overcome an embedded context—to experience an item independently of the organized field or configuration. The field-dependent person tends to experience his surroundings in a relatively global fashion, passively conforming to the influence of whatever context he finds himself in (Fleck, 1972).

The apparatus most commonly used to test for field independence is a movable wooden frame, within which a movable rod is placed. As the rod and the frame are moved into different positions relative to each other, the subject is asked to indicate whether the rod is vertical. Field-independent subjects are expected to be able to make more accurate judgments because they are less likely to be influenced by the position of the frame; that is, they are more able to overcome the influence of the background part of the stimulus. Another frequently used test is the Hidden Figures Test, in which line drawings of familiar objects or geometric figures are camouflaged by other lines running through or around them; subjects are asked to pick out the hidden figure from the background of lines.

Witkin suggested that performance on tasks of this sort is strongly affected by the degree to which the person experiences the world in a differentiated or separated fashion, the degree to which he experiences aspects of his life space as discrete from the context in which they appear. In other words, Witkin assumed that perceptual habits of teasing apart or differentiating immediately relevant aspects are characteristic of thinking processes as well, that the person who easily distinguishes figure from ground

or who can focus on the relevant aspect of a stimulus situation and ignore the other, irrelevant parts is similarly able to differentiate and deal with his personal experiences apart from the context in which those experiences take place. This step from a relatively easily measured perceptual phenomenon to internal modes of thinking and experiencing is a very large step indeed. Research provides some tentative support for linking the two, but the relationship is still far from completely understood or established.

One instrument used in efforts to confirm the perception-cognition relationship is the Stroop test, a series of tasks involving identification of colors of ink on a card. This is ordinarily a fairly easy task, but in the Stroop the inks are used to print color names, and the color names do not correspond to the color of the ink. To respond "red" to the word *green* printed in red ink requires a good deal of concentration—and, theoretically, calls into play the ability to attend to relevant information while ignoring the rest. A study by Eisner (1972), using subjects ranging in age from 10 to 83 years, demonstrated a significant relationship between Stroop scores and field-independence scores—that is, people who performed in a highly field-independent manner on more traditional tests of field independence tended also to do well on the Stroop.

In another study, Hochman (1971) showed that Stroop scores are related to compulsiveness and general restriction of attention and suggested that these characteristics may also be more common among field-independent than field-dependent individuals. It can be argued that the Stroop, while involving perception, calls on cognitive processes more specifically than do the rod-and-frame test and the Hidden Figures Test. If we accept this argument, then studies demonstrating a correlation between performance on other field-independence measures and performance on the Stroop can be seen as evidence that these perceptual habits do indeed carry over into cognitive functioning; studies such as Hochman's and Eisner's may lead to an even better understanding of the bridge between seeing and thinking.

### Piaget's Stages

It would seem that field independence may well be a two-edged sword: after all, most of us want to be able to deal with relevant data and not be cluttered up in our thinking processes by masses of useless information; but few of us would like to be thought of as compulsive or as suffering from restriction of attention. We need to look further, to determine if we can the implications of one's position on the field-dependence/field-independence continuum for functioning in other areas. A number of researchers have attempted to do just that. Fleck, for instance, is interested in the relationship between field independence and the child's progress through Piaget's stages of cognitive development. Working with first- and second-grade boys, he found that children who showed a high ability to operate in a field-independent manner tended to be further advanced (in the Piagetian sense) than those who were able to behave in only a field-dependent way. Fleck explains this relationship rather convincingly: "Piaget sees the decentering of perception as the development from the passive, best form dominated perception of the young child to the active, operation-directed perception of the older child and adult. It seems as though the field-dependent child's perception is passive and is centered on what is to him the dominant configuration of the visual field. On the other hand, the field-independent child's perception seems to be more active, spontaneously restructuring the visual field into many possible organizations. This enables him to attend to relevant stimuli and correctly analyze the conservation problem" (Fleck, 1972, p. 754).

We must bear in mind that Fleck's experiment is designed to test for the ability to behave in a field-independent way rather than the preference for doing so. He assumes that the person who is able to behave field independently (that is, to perform well on a rod-and-frame test or the Hidden Figures Test) could also be field dependent if he so chose, but that the reverse is not true—that field independence grows out of field dependence. For children, this assumption does seem to hold; developmentally, a field-dependent style seems to precede field independence. It is less certain that adults or children can easily change their established style, whatever it may be. Once one has become habituated to a field-independent style, it may be extremely difficult to slip back to more field-dependent perceptual operations.

*Social Behavior*

The field-dependent person, I have said, has difficulty separating and attending to the relevant parts of a stimulus situation while ignoring the irrelevant parts. We might expect that field dependence would have some effect on social behavior since social interactions involve a highly complex stimulus situation from which each participant chooses those parts he must attend to and those that may be relatively ignored. At least two studies support this conjecture. In one, second- and third-grade children were tested to see how much their performance on a problem-solving task would be affected by social cues—that is, verbal and nonverbal hints from their peers. True to expectations, the field-dependent children were much more responsive to such cues than the field-independent children (Ruble & Nakamura, 1972). Field-independent children apparently focused on the task at hand and paid scant attention to the rest of their environment, while the field-dependent children tended to consider the whole situation a part of the problem to be solved and thus were more receptive to social help. Again, we see here that field independence can be both a positive and a negative characteristic. In this experimental situation, the "extraneous" parts of the stimulus situation were helpful and allowed the field-dependent child to perform at a higher level. But it is easy to think of situations, both in and out of the classroom, in which the extraneous aspects of the problem would be distracting and nonhelpful and in which the field-independent child would be at a distinct advantage.

The second bit of social-influence research to which I referred also has a sometimes good, sometimes bad flavor. Thomas (1972) attempted to measure the effects of TV watching on field-dependent and field-independent children; he reports two major findings. Field-dependent children are in general more easily influenced by TV viewing: the less cognitively organized and differentiated a child is, the more vulnerable he is to the influence of stimulation such as TV provides. But there is more aggressive behavior as a result of TV watching among field-independent children than among field-dependent children. Thomas speculates that the field-dependent children are less able to manufacture for themselves a fantasy outlet for their aggressive impulses, so TV aggression provides such an outlet for them. The field-independent children are more likely to have constructed their own individual fantasies to deal with aggression, and TV cannot help them much in this way. For such children, TV violence merely provides a model for actual aggressive behavior.

One last word of caution before we move on: in reading the research reports and attempting to formulate our educated hunches about cognitive style, we must be careful not to invest the data with more generality than they possess. Test results are useful and instructive, but they seldom tell us more than the test was intended to measure. This caution is especially important in the case of field-independence research, in which nearly all the existing tests have been designed to measure how field independent a person is able to be when he is pushed in that direction. Such tests do not measure a person's preference for a field-dependent as contrasted with a field-independent mode, nor do they tell us much about a person's habitual style of behavior. Most of the field-independence tests have loaded the dice against the field-dependent individual; they seem to be built with the assumption that it is good to be field independent and bad to be field dependent. As Wachtel (1972b) points out, field dependence is too often designated by a lack and assessed (almost by definition) in situations well suited to the adaptive capacities of all but field-dependent persons. If all we know about a person is what he can't do well, we generally have little basis for predicting what he can do, given the variety of possible alternative outlets for his talents. Certainly field-dependent people aren't simply inferior individuals, but studies that overestimate the value of the rod-and-frame test and similar instruments, and attempt to characterize people on the basis of such measures alone, provide few clues to the positive abilities of such people.

## Global/Analytic Styles

The terms *field dependent* and *field independent* are value loaded: in our culture, at least, independence seems to be more desirable than dependence. A number of theorists have abandoned the dependent-independent terminology for a new pair of descriptors, *global* and *analytic;* these terms have the advantage of being relatively value free, as well as being brief. However, as is too often the case, controversy seems to have arisen as to whether global and field dependent, and analytic and field independent, really do have the same meanings and implications. Let's take a quick look at the problem.

Witkin, Dyk, Faterson, Goodenough, and Karp (1962) are quite explicit about the interchangeability of the two sets of terms. An analytic style of perceiving, they say, involves a tendency to experience items as discrete from their backgrounds and reflects an ability to overcome the influence of context. Notice, though, that we have moved subtly from a nonevaluative description of style or preference to a highly evaluative notion of what the analytic person can—and the global person cannot—do. For Witkin and his colleagues, not only is analytic equivalent to field independent, but there is also a clear assumption that if one were able, one would always choose to be analytic rather than global.

Denney (1971) takes a slightly different tack, and one that seems somewhat more objective. He distinguishes between people who use a visible element shared by all class members as a preferred way of sorting out a perceptual situation and people who use a functional relationship among the class members. For example, imagine that you have a set of six drawings: an apple, a dog, a doll's bed, a ball, a hamburger, and a pig. A functional arrangement of these drawings would put the apple, the hamburger, and the pig together (as things that can be eaten), and the doll's bed, ball, and dog together (as things that can be played with). An analytic grouping might set the dog, pig, and doll's bed on one side (they all have four legs), while the apple, hamburger, and ball would go together because they are all round.

Denney has thrown us another curve by introducing a fifth term, *functional.* Can we assume that functional and global mean the same thing? I am inclined to believe that we can, just on the basis of Denney's operational description. The functional grouping of objects uses the whole object rather than abstracting out a particular characteristic. In this sense, it carries the same flavor as the global style, the attention to the totality of the stimulus rather than a narrowing in on one or two parts. Another aspect of Denney's definition should be noticed too: the value judgment is absent. There is no intrinsic reason to believe that a functional approach is better or worse than an analytic one.

A certain amount of value judgment, or preference, does seem to pervade even the global/analytic research, however. For children, at any rate, there seem to be distinct advantages in having an analytic conceptual style. Kagan, Rosman, Day, Albert, and Phillips (1964), for instance, found a relationship between analytic responses and performance on one of the subscales of the Wechsler Intelligence Scale for Children. In trying to explain this relationship, Kagan and his colleagues concluded that the analytic child seems to be able to take longer to respond to a task, and that this longer response time allows him to sort through possible answers, inhibiting the wrong ones and waiting until he can find the right one. In contrast, the global child tends to use the first solution that occurs to him, even though it may be incorrect or of poor quality. Kagan and colleagues support this explanation with data that suggest that when children are encouraged to slow down, to not answer questions so quickly, their responses become more analytic.

Tarrance and Davis (1971) attempted to explore an even more practical implication of the analytic/global continuum. They were interested in how these cognitive styles related to classroom learning—more specifically, whether children with differing styles learned geography better when offered one kind of learning experience than when offered another. Choosing to work with expository and discovery teaching methods, they found that there were no across-the-board differences in how well analytic and global children learned under the two methods. But when they looked just at the extreme scorers, the children who were either very global or very analytic, they did find differences: the very global children did better when they were taught by a discovery method, and the very analytic children thrived in an expository setting. They also found that, regardless of teaching method, analytic children tended to be more able to apply their knowledge of geography to new situations than were the global children. So much for neutrality: in ability to generalize (an ability highly prized in the academic setting), the analytic children had a distinct advantage.

Even Denney, who provided us with that nicely objective definition toward the beginning of this subsection, concludes with a clear evaluative preference: "This investigator was continually impressed with the greater self-assuredness, comfort and openness of analytic children during testing. In contrast, [functional] children showed more concern over their performance in the testing situation and were generally more cautious and less responsive" (Denney, 1971, p. 154). For children, at least, the conclusion seems inescapable: there are clear advantages in moving to an analytic style earlier rather than later in the developmental sequence. At what point in time the adult finally settles on the style that will characterize him and whether there are similar value implications about that choice are not yet known.

## COGNITIVE COMPLEXITY

Another related, but not quite identical, dimension of cognitive style is that of cognitive complexity. Witkin and colleagues (1962, p. 15) write "Our analysis of the growth of experience of the self and world led us to postulate that progress toward differentiation would be expressed in increasing articulation (that is, analysis and structuring) of experience.

Included in this is a more articulated way of experiencing the world; also included are a more clearly defined body concept and a growing sense of separate identity, which together reflect particularly the development of self-differentiation." As the infant's perceptual abilities grow, he becomes increasingly aware of differences in the world around him. He learns that this is not the same as that, that stimuli may be divided into increasingly complex sets of categories. While this growing ability clearly relates to his analytic skills, it may also be thought of as a dimension in and of itself: this dimension has been labeled *cognitive complexity.* Barron did the original work in isolating and defining cognitive complexity in the early 1950s; he, unlike most other workers in the field of cognitive style, specified that he was looking for stylistic preference rather than ability. That is, the cognitively complex person is one who prefers a complex stimulus situation to a simple one and who tends to seek out such complexity.

We have already encountered cognitive complexity in Chapter 7, you will recall; creative individuals show a greater preference for stimulus complexity than do the less creative. Researchers have reported that people with a preference for complexity also tend to be flexible, independent, impulsive, nonconforming, and mentally quick. Here again we can detect a value judgment, with socially desirable traits tending to be associated with a preference for the complex, rather than the simple. A few studies have even examined cognitive complexity in non-Western cultures and found it to be related to other desirable characteristics: Anwar and Child (1972), for instance, found that among Japanese, Pakistani, and American subjects, cognitive complexity was related to aesthetic judgment.

In contrast with this general trend, a study of underachieving school children (Altmann & Conklin, 1972) found them to be more cognitively complex than their normally achieving peers. In view of all the evidence favoring complexity, however, we must view the underachiever-complexity relationship with some suspicion. Most data seem to indicate that complexity is associated with a variety of desirable characteristics. Renner (1970), working with college students, concluded with almost a paean of praise: he said that people who have developed complex cognitive styles have been found to be more self-sufficient, achievement oriented, introspective, perceptually and cognitively independent, tolerant of ambiguity, and risk taking than are those whose cognitive styles are simpler.

But suspicion may be appropriate here too; such a catalog of undiluted virtue, whether it comes from a psychologist or a car salesman, usually makes me wonder what is being left out. In this case, it seems possible that one likely outcome of a preference for cognitive complexity might be an interest in social science research; after all, one can hardly find a more complex field to explore. If so, we might logically expect that most of the researchers whose work we have been reviewing are themselves at the complex end of the continuum, and their position there might help to explain in part why they tend to be more sensitive to the advantages of complexity than to the advantages of cognitive simplicity. It is much easier to understand and be sympathetic toward those cognitive habits that resemble our own than to those that are foreign to us. Undeniably, certain aspects of a complex cognitive style are helpful to the individual; but I think we should be very careful about ruling out other and possibly equally useful concomitants of cognitive simplicity.

## IMPULSIVITY/REFLECTIVITY

I commented earlier on the apparent relationship between an analytic style and the ability to inhibit wrong responses or to generally slow down the whole responding process. Kagan and his associates (1964) have been interested in this relationship and have concluded that the tendency to respond quickly or slowly is in itself an element of cognitive style. They label this dimension *impulsivity/reflectivity* and maintain that it, like other cognitive-style aspects, tends to be a relatively stable characteristic of an individual's functioning and to affect a wide variety of behaviors. Moreover, as with the analytic/global continuum, there is a clearly observable developmental pattern: both analytic scores and indexes of reflectivity increase with age during the school years. That is, just as older children tend to be more field independent or analytic, they also tend to be more reflective and less impulsive.

Impulsivity is easier to observe directly than most other cognitive-style dimensions, and researchers have been able to find its origins (or at least to speculate about it origins) in infancy and very early childhood. Zelniker, Jeffrey, Ault, and Parsons (1972) point out that a short attention span is part of the total impulsivity pattern. Since attention-span differences are observable very early in life, and may therefore be inherited, at least the tendency toward impulsivity or reflectivity may be genetic in origin. Kagan and his associates (1964) also suspect that heredity may play a large part in determining one's impulsivity or reflectivity; they say that the older child's or the adult's behavior on this dimension of cognitive style can be previewed in the activity and attentiveness of the infant. They also believe, however, that the amount of impulsivity one displays in a situation may be affected by the nature of the task and by how much one is interested in or motivated to perform well on that task. As one becomes more and more involved, one's standards for an adequate performance tend to go up; this escalation would be expected to result in longer response time (and thus less impulsivity) as one rejects substandard responses and continues the internal search for better ones.

Also, Kagan and colleagues have been concerned with the effects of anxiety on impulsivity. They hypothesize that the highly anxious person is less able to tolerate the wait—the silence—while he searches for a good solution. He is more likely to verbalize the first response that comes to mind, thus increasing the likelihood that his verbalized response will not be good and will be rejected or punished. And when the rejection or punishment does occur, his anxiety level is raised even more, and so the cycle goes.

At least one researcher has suggested that cognitive style and particularly impulsivity/reflectivity may relate to a person's whole way of experiencing time (Botterberg, 1971). We are all familiar with the fact that time travels at different subjective speeds: when we are enjoying ourselves it fairly flies past, but when we are bored or engaged in a distasteful task it drags. Quite possibly, the average rate of experiencing the passage of time differs from person to person. Botterberg found three kinds of time experiencing among his subjects: some experienced "rapid consuming time," some a "quiet continuous pace of time," and some were relatively indifferent to time experiences. It is quite likely that one's tendency to be either impulsive or reflective, whether genetically determined or acquired through experience, may shape one's time perception. If so, this dimension of cognitive style may indeed have broad implications in many other areas of functioning.

As far as school behavior is concerned, the evidence leaves little room for doubt: impulsivity does relate to a number of important behaviors, and it is clearly less desirable (in terms of these other behaviors) to be impulsive than to be reflective. In general, reflective children have been found to perform better on visual discrimination, serial recall, inductive reasoning, and reading in the primary grades than do those identified as impulsive (Zelnicker et al., 1972). We can easily conclude that reflectives are better off than impulsives in the classroom. We must also remember, however, that the primary characteristic—perhaps even the defining characteristic—of the impulsive is that he tends to spit out the first response that comes to mind rather than casting about for the best possible answer. The analytic child has statistics on his side; he is able to think of several possible responses and then verbalize only the best one. The impulsive child may be quite capable of thinking of better responses than he gives. Katz's (1972) data tend to support this notion. Working with preschoolers, he found that impulsive children did less well than reflectives on a form-sorting task, but that when he slowed the children down and probed for a correct response, all the children, reflectives and impulsives alike, were able to handle the task.

Katz's study is especially interesting in that he allowed the children to respond in an object-sorting task to either the form or the color of the objects. The number of form responses differentiated the two groups: impulsive children were more likely to sort the materials on the basis of color (defined by the experimenter as an incorrect response) instead of shape. Psychologists who use the Rorschach test (the ink-blot test) tell us that the choice of color rather than form as a determinant of a response may be an indicator of emotional arousal. If this is true, it lends some support to the hypothesis of Kagan and his associates that anxiety is involved in the quick response of the impulsive child: it was the impulsives who tended to choose color as the basis for their responses. Katz, though, relates the impulsive children's performance to their use of information: impulsive children make fewer form responses than reflectives do because they respond quickly and do not process all the available information. In Katz's study, such children did not discriminate even between large figures presented repeatedly and with no time restrictions. The need to respond quickly inclines the impulsive child to speed up his data-processing activities. He doesn't notice form similarities because he doesn't take the time to look for them. Color, being a "hit you in the eye all at once" quality, doesn't have to be looked for, so this immediately apparent characteristic becomes the basis for the impulsive child's categorizations. The fact that sorting tasks and gross-discrimination tasks differentiate impulsive and reflective subjects indicates how pervasive tempo effects may be.

Whatever the reason, the impulsive child is at a distinct disadvantage academically—and quite possibly in other ways as well. Not only does his typical mode of functioning handicap him in his performance, but it also tends to set up a negative spiral: every wrong response makes him more anxious, less tolerant of pauses, more inclined to respond quickly the next time—and more likely to give still another wrong response. Surely here is one style area in which the teacher might try to intervene; we will discuss the possibility of such intervention in a later section.

## OTHER DIMENSIONS

With an area as broadly defined as cognitive style, it is quite possible to leap in and carve off almost any set of behaviors to define a mode of functioning. Many researchers have done this kind of leaping in, and the result is rather fragmented research, with each person convinced that the dimension he has defined is the one everyone else should take a look at. Before moving on to some of the more general implications of cognitive-style research, let's explore a few of these less widely accepted dimensions.

### Open/Restricted Styles

Shouksmith (1970), in his book on cognitive style and creativity, describes the use of the Osgood semantic-differential test as a determinant of cognitive style. This test asks subjects to rate concepts on a series of continua, the ends of which are opposite adjectives. For example, a subject might be asked to indicate whether the concept *home* is more nearly black or white, cold or hot, bright or dark, strong or weak, and so on. Shouksmith noticed that some subjects consistently rated concepts at the extremes of the adjective continua, while others made nearly all their ratings more or less in the middle, regardless of the concept being rated. Hypothesizing that this verbal behavior was typical of a broad range of other behaviors, he described the extreme raters as cognitively open, and the middle-ground raters as cognitively restricted. Moving on to tests of general cognitive ability, with college students as his subjects, he discovered that the open/restricted dimension correlated with test performance, but only under certain conditions. With a restricted answer format (such as true-false or multiple-choice questions), restricted and open students did about equally well. But with an open-ended format, where students constructed their own responses, the open students tended to score in the middle ranges, while the restricted students did either very well or very poorly. Students who appear to be cognitively restricted on Shouksmith's test may fall into two rather distinct groups. For some, a middle response (home is neither very black nor very white) reflects a careful consideration of all the alternatives and factors, with the middle-ground response chosen because it best represents the final decision made on the basis of those factors. For others, a middle response may be a rather sloppy or careless "oh, just say something"; or it may be symptomatic of an inability to even consider an extreme position. In this case, it tends to lock one away from considering relevant data. The open/restricted dimension appears to have some interesting relationships to academic behaviors; we need considerably more data, however, before we can be sure exactly what we are dealing with or how the knowledge can best be used.

### Leveling/Sharpening Styles

A quite different dimension of cognitive style has been identified by Klein (1958) as leveling/sharpening. This dimension is identified primarily by visual behavior: sharpeners tend to notice and enhance contrasts in the visual field, while levelers are more sensitive to similarities. Shown a series of squares that gradually change in size, for instance, sharpeners notice the changes more quickly than levelers. Klein relates this sensitivity to the ability to change sets—that is, to expect that the next stimulus may be different from what came before. Sharpeners are more flexible than levelers; they can shift easily from one framework to another. Levelers tend to see each successive stimulus as just the same as the previous one, so that the new stimulus tends to lose its identity. Levelers are also more likely to be affected by an extra, irrelevant stimulus in a stimulus-judgment situation; the irrelevant stimulus requires that they shift expectations, and they find it difficult to shift back again when they resume their task.

The leveling/sharpening dimension is, you will notice, similar to field independence/field dependence or the analytic/global style. Levelers tend to be more global, more field dependent. But the leveling/sharpening distinction has a different quality: while the global or field-dependent individual sees a given stimulus as an organized unit, the leveler tends to reduce differences, to overgeneralize. Similarly, the sharpener does not so much analyze a percept and attend to its relevant parts (like the analytic person), but rather is captured by contrasts, by differences—whether they are particularly relevant or not.

Closely related to leveling and sharpening is the scanning/nonscanning continuum. Scanners attend to the total perceptual field, but in a sequential fashion. "Attention is broadly and intensively deployed. The scanner is aware of a broad array of background qualities of a stimulus field. His investment is intensely incorporative, characterized by a constant, close look" (Klein, 1958, p. 109). Scanners are usually sharpeners, but not all sharpeners are scanners. Those who are, according to Klein, have a number of general personality traits in common: they tend to be highly controlled and inhibited, distrustful, and generally pessimistic. They regard the world as a dangerous place: it is as if their scanning were a defense mechanism, a surveying of the horizon to be constantly alert to potential danger or hurt.

Notice that in each of these three descriptions—open/restricted, sharpening/leveling, scanning/nonscanning—there is a value judgment. Shouksmith is perhaps the least evaluative, pointing out that his restricteds may do either very well or very badly on a cognitive task. Klein seems to regard leveling as much less desirable than sharpening and to associate scanning with a number of painful and generally undesirable traits. It is important to remember that the evidence on these characteristics and their concomitants is scant indeed. While there is no particular reason to deny the advantages that one trait or another may imply, it would be a mistake to assume that there may not be other, equally valuable advantages in its opposite. The leveler may, for instance, be quite good at relating concepts, at finding conceptual bridges between one idea and another. Or he may not. We just don't know. The scanner, defensive though he may seem, may also be much more sensitive to all sorts of stimulus input and thus have an augmented store of information on which to base his cognitive processes. Or, again, he may not. The data aren't in.

## A "BEST" COGNITIVE STYLE?

In spite of my efforts to remain neutral, to look at potential advantages and disadvantages of both ends of each cognitive-style continuum that we have considered, there is still a strong pull toward labeling one style, or set of styles, best. I have made protestations to the contrary, to be sure, but the tendency is still there. Perhaps the thing to do now is to face the issue head on: what firm evidence is there that, in fact, one cognitive style is more useful or leads to better performance or adjustment than another?

To begin, let's clear the air by getting rid of a misconception: just because cognitive styles tend to be a stable element in one's dealings with the world, with implications for a wide variety of behaviors, does not mean that one always behaves in ways consistent with a single position on a given style continuum. That is, a person who is generally disposed toward cognitive complexity or toward impulsivity may (depending on the circumstances) sometimes behave in a reflective or a cognitively simple manner. Witkin and his colleagues elaborate: "It is possible for a person to operate at different levels of differentiation at different times, or even at the same time. It is true, however, that a more differentiated person is *capable* of functioning at a relatively high level if required and motivated to do so in a particular situation" (1962, p. 17). In other words, Witkin believes that there is a "better" end of most continua in that the person who is able to function in the more differentiated or developmentally more advanced way is also able to choose to function in the simpler way when the situation calls for such behavior. But the person who can behave only in the simpler way—in a field-dependent or global style, for instance—doesn't have that freedom of choice; his options are limited.

*General Trends*

The literature contains a number of reports that claim to relate one cognitive style or another to intellectual ability. (This orientation should come as no surprise, as researchers seem determined to relate everything to intellectual ability!) The most commonly reported relationship is between field independence and intelligence; high scores on various measures of field independence have been shown to correlate with high IQ scores. Again, it is important to note that the tests of field independence are, for the most part, tests of ability rather than of preference; and it would probably be more accurate to say that the data support the notion that the more intelligent individual is able to function in a field-independent manner when asked to do so. We should also note that most of the commonly used IQ tests have a large proportion of items that seem to call for some sort of analysis, some mental separation of relevant from irrelevant information. Without again becoming embroiled in a discussion of the nature of intelligence, we have to wonder whether the tests themselves are so constructed as to favor the field-independent individual and whether a differently constructed test might show a quite different relationship. "The significant relation frequently reported between measures of field dependence and total standard intelligence test scores is 'carried' largely by those portions of intelligence tests which require analytical functioning. In other words, the relation is based on the expression of a particular style of field approach in both" (Witkin et al., 1962, p. 80). Whether the reliance on an analytic, or field-independent, style is an artifact of the test construction or an integral element of intelligent performance is not yet known.

In contrast with the field-independence findings, Richardson and Soucar (1971) were unable to establish a relationship between IQ and cognitive complexity. They concluded that two nonrelated characteristics were involved in their measures of complexity. Complexity involved not

only a preference for complex rather than simple stimuli but also the ability to understand that one's perceptions are not always valid—that there is a difference between a perception and external reality. It is almost as if the cognitively complex individual's ability to notice and deal with discrepancies between "what I see" and "what is" allows him to relish the whole process of perception, to enjoy seeing for the sake of seeing. For the cognitively simple person, in contrast, seeing is a means to an end; the more simple the stimulus, the more quickly he can get on with whatever he is trying to do. Notice that here again we are finding elements of what a person is able to do interacting with what he prefers to do. Moreover, the question of a "better" style must be answered in the context of what the overall task is; to be cognitively complex may be a great advantage for a sculptor, but not so useful for an auto mechanic.

When we turn to impulsivity/reflectivity, we find a good deal of evidence that (at least during the elementary school years) the reflective child has the advantage. We have already mentioned some of the evidence for this point of view. The hypotheses of Kagan and his associates about the relationship between impulsivity and anxiety, for instance, clearly show the impulsive child as the victim of his own emotional reactions. The data, however, still leave some questions unanswered. A study by Harrison and Nadelman (1972) is typical: they looked at the performance of black preschool children and found that reflectivity and IQ scores were significantly related for boys but not for girls. On the basis of the data now available, it seems reasonable to conclude that a child's reflectivity or impulsivity probably does affect his ability to perform in intellectual tasks, but that a number of other relevant variables act in such a way as to make the reflectivity-IQ relationship something other than a simple, linear correlation.

Logically, it would seem obvious that if different situations call for different stylistic approaches, it is the person who can switch from one style to another rather than the person who always approaches a task in the same way who will do best in the long run. This ability to switch from style to style has in itself been identified as a cognitive style (or perhaps we should call it a superstyle), and there is some spotty evidence that cognitive flexibility, as it is called, correlates positively with general ability (Goldberg, 1972). If it is true that one end of a given continuum is the more developmentally mature position, so that a child must move through, for instance, a field-dependent stage or phase and then into field independence, we might expect that tests of ability to perform in the more mature way would correlate with cognitive flexibility. The child who cannot be field independent cannot, by definition, be flexible in that dimension. There is an untested assumption here: that the highly field-independent person is able to switch back to a field-dependent mode when appropriate. Eisner (1972) reports some partial support for that assumption: in a study of males ranging in age from 10 to 83 years, he found that people who had high field-independence scores tended to be mobile in response to situational demands and that with a decrease in the level of field independence there was a tendency toward fixity of response. While there are some serious methodological problems in Eisner's study, the findings are at least consistent with the notion that the individual who can choose which cognitive style he wishes to use has an advantage over the one who is locked into a particular mode of functioning.

## The Importance of Pattern

The problem of trying to relate a particular cognitive style to optimum performance on an IQ test or a learning task or what have you is complicated by the large number of factors involved in such performance. Not only do performances differ depending on their context—the configuration of situational demands—but also the configuration of abilities brought to the task must be taken into account. A high field-independence score may have vastly different implications for personality when seen in the context of one pattern of cognitive styles rather than another. From this point of view, the search for even relatively stable personality traits that accompany a particular cognitive-style dimension is likely to be a rather risky business. Field independence may have quite different functions for a field-independent, extensive-scanning sharpener than for a field-independent, minimal-scanning leveler (Wachtel, 1972b). Human performance is a complex orchestration of individual elements. It is difficult to say whether a particular violin passage will sound right in the middle of a symphony without knowing what the rest of the instruments are doing; similarly, it is difficult to determine whether a particular cognitive-style approach is appropriate without knowing the pattern within which that style appears.

Research in this area is further hampered by the fact that so many externally similar behaviors may be based on a whole range of different internal arrangements. Different styles and patterns of styles in different individuals may result in the same performance in the classroom or on an ability test. If our analysis of the implications and effects of cognitive style is to be more than introspective philosophizing, we must pin our assumptions to observable and measurable phenomena; yet the specific relationships of human behaviors take on an almost uncanny perversity when we try to observe and measure them. We think we have one element tied down neatly, only to discover that several other factors have shifted or changed, and we can no longer be sure of just what we are looking at. Hertzig sums up the problem neatly: "Similar levels of achievement can result from very different stylistic responses to cognitive demands. . . . Similarities in style may be associated with widely varying levels of performance" (1971, p. 155).

If researchers have been less than successful in associating a particular style or styles with optimal performance, perhaps we should approach the problem from the other side. Are there styles that are clearly maladaptive? Can we identify any cognitive style or style pattern that is associated with poor learning skills, with low intellectual ability, with anxiety or defensiveness or other undesirable personality traits? Here, too, the answer seems to be the same: it is not the specific style but rather the configuration of styles in the context of the situational demands that spells success or failure. While defenses may be grounded in a particular cognitive style, the degree of defensiveness or pathology is relatively independent of the particular direction of development one takes (Wachtel, 1972b). Any style clung to too strongly and rigidly can become the foundation for maladaptive behavior.

Pluralism—cognitive flexibility—would seem to be the only "best" choice. The individual with the highest potential for learning and growth and mastery is the individual whose cognitive pattern is relatively fluid—who, within a framework of stable style preferences, can shift to meet the shifting demands of his environment. It follows that future research must ascertain when and how such shifts occur; we need to be less concerned with what single style an individual is able to use or usually uses and more concerned with the variety of styles available to him. "To know the adaptive implications of a particular dimension of cognitive control, it is necessary to know when the person functions in a way *not* typical for him, how readily he can make such shifts when the situation calls for it, and precisely what the consequences of either persisting in or changing his typical mode of functioning might be in any situation he might face" (Wachtel, 1972a, p. 782).

## FACTORS AFFECTING COGNITIVE STYLE

We have come now to recognize that cognitive styles differ, not only from person to person but also within an individual from time to time and from situation to situation. We need to know more about the ways in which such differences occur—about the variables that tend to be associated with the expression of one or another stylistic approach. Several such variables have been investigated with regard to cognitive style. We shall look at three of them, age, sex, and social class. The choice of these three variables is dictated partly by the interest that cognitive-style researchers have shown in them and partly by their appearance as causal factors in so many other areas of human performance.

### Age

For the most part, studies of changes in cognitive style as a function of age have been carried out only with children. Age-related changes through adulthood may occur but are not at all well documented. One of the few studies that did attempt to look at cognitive style throughout adulthood was that of Eisner, which I referred to earlier. Eisner (1972) studied males ranging in age from 10 to 83 years and found a significant relationship between age and measures of field independence. In general, field independence increased during childhood (a finding consistent with those of a number of other studies), with a possible temporary reversal in late adolescence. In late adulthood and old age, the trend was reversed, with field independence tending to decrease with age. Remember, again, that Eisner tested for the ability to perform in a field-independent manner; he did not test for preference for field independence, nor did he attempt to find out whether his field-independent individuals could, when they wanted to, switch to a field-dependent mode. Yet Eisner's conclusions assume that such switching is possible for the field-independent person. In one situation, he says, a person may respond to a perceptual task globally, and yet in another situation the same person may respond analytically. A child, though, can respond only in the ways he has achieved or developed, so his switching capacity is limited. Eisner assumes that because the child appears to pass through a field-dependent stage on his way to field independence, he can move back into such a mode at will. While some individuals are clearly able to make this switch, the assumption that all can or do has not been experimentally supported.

Kagan and his associates (1964) also found a tendency for the analytic, as contrasted with the global, style to be more common as children grow older; they point out too that stable individual differences can be found within any single age group. Baird and Bee (1969), following up the Kagan results, attempted to determine whether the increase in analytic responses is caused by reinforcements over time—that is, whether those responses are learned as a result of the environment in which a child finds himself or whether they are simply a part of his physical and neurological development. Using first- and second-grade children as subjects, they succeeded in producing both more analytic and less analytic test scores by using appropriate reinforcements. They also found that changes in the direction of more analytic scores (that is, less field-dependent scores) tended to be more lasting. The interpretation would seem to be that while the environment—reinforcement of behavior—does contribute to the growth of analytic behavior, there is also a "natural" developmental trend in that direction. Rewarding analytic responses works with developmental changes and thus has relatively long-lasting effects; rewarding global responses works against the grain, and effects here are rather quickly washed out as the child goes about his daily business.

Performance on sorting tasks of one kind or another has been used as a criterion for a number of different style assessments: children have been judged to be either global or analytic, or impulsive or reflective, or functional or descriptive, depending on how they perform on such a task. We have seen that analytic styles tend to become more common as the child grows older; but K. M. White (1971) presents evidence that attending to functional rather than descriptive determinants in a sorting task increases with age. We should not be too surprised to find conflicting evidence here, though; the uncertainty of definitions and the lack of clear understanding of similarities and differences among concepts like global, functional, and descriptive simply mean that we are dealing with a complex pattern. As more data come in, we will be in a better position to sort out just what we are trying to trace. For now, the best generalization possible is that children seem to be able to do more kinds of things (and perhaps use a greater variety of styles) as they grow older and that the particular pattern "discovered" in any single bit of research may be a function of the research design rather than of the style being looked at.

Children do seem to become increasingly able to deal actively with a stimulus situation and react to its individual elements as they grow older. Part of this ability may be due to an increase in reflectiveness—that is, the willingness to think longer about a response before committing oneself to it. It seems reasonable to assume that a response involving analysis of a stimulus and responding to its parts would require more time than responding simply to the whole. "It may be concluded," says Denney (1972a, p. 821), "that younger children are more responsive to less sophisticated conceptual-strategy models and older children are more responsive to more sophisticated conceptual-strategy models." A statement like this may sound so obvious as to be useless—of course older children can be expected to be more sophisticated than younger ones; but we must be aware of our adult biases here. In making a "more sophisticated" response, a child does indeed demonstrate analytic ability; but he also fails to demonstrate the kind of integration needed for a more global response. It is quite possible that there are two sorts of field-dependent or global styles, one that occurs at an early time in the child's development and is due to his inability to operate analytically, and another that occurs much later and represents a resynthesis of the analyzed and differentiated stimulus pattern.

## Sex

It is to be expected that researchers should look for sex differences in cognitive style. After all, it is a tenet of our culture that boys are "supposed to be" analytic, logical, and reflective, while girls are stereotyped as intuitive, emotional, and impulsive. Witkin and associates (1962, p. 227) maintain that the stereotype is essentially accurate: "Both in perceptual and intellectual situations men tend to be relatively more analytical than women. . . . Developmental studies have demonstrated that sex differences are present down to the 8-year level, but they may not exist in children below that age or in geriatric groups." Boismer's (1971) results suggest too that sex differences in cognitive style (if any) do not emerge until middle childhood; he found no differences between boys and girls in any element of cognitive style among preschoolers or first, third, and fourth graders.

If sex differences do not appear until relatively late in childhood, their late development may suggest that such differences must be learned. Perhaps it just takes six to ten years for the child to assimilate his appropriate sex role regarding cognitive style. If so, may we conclude that observed differences between the sexes are purely a learned characteristic and that there are no biological or genetic reasons why men should tend to adopt one style pattern and women another? The work of Dawson (1972) suggests that this is not entirely the case. Dawson studied the cognitive styles of men and women who had been deprived, for one reason or another, of their normal androgen level (androgen is one of the primary male hormones). He concluded that while cultural patterning is undoubtedly partly responsible for the adoption of cognitive style, there are also biologically based differences: normal male cognitive style (higher spatial, numerical, and field-independence scores) is in part influenced by prenatal androgen levels in the brain.

Studies of sex-related cognitive-style differences in adults are frequently plagued by small samples, inadequate definitions, and uncontrolled variables. Apter (1971), for example, studied "productivity, flexibility, and complexity" among college students and concluded that the women were more flexible and complex, and less productive, than the men. Subjects in Apter's study arranged pictures of objects into various patterns; the number of different sorting rules (sort into groups of things, arrange so as to tell a story, and so forth) used by a person was taken as an index of flexibility, while the ratio of his flexibility to the total number of different arrangements he used was his complexity score. While Apter's flexibility seems logically related to the cognitive flexibility we have discussed on these pages, his complexity does not link so clearly to any particular cognitive style; that lack and the small sample used make Apter's study less useful than one might wish.

Another search for cognitive-style differences among college men and women was carried out by DeRussy and Futch (1971), and here again we find methodological problems. DeRussy and Futch's males were more field independent than females, and their science majors were more field independent than liberal arts majors. Since there are usually more men than women majoring in science and more women than men majoring in liberal arts, we must wonder whether the observed differences were associated with the sex of the subjects or with their choice of major—that is, if we compared male science majors with female science majors or male liberal arts majors with female liberal arts majors, would we still find sex differences? Or we could take the argument in the opposite direction: the differences found between the science majors and liberal arts majors might be due to the disproportionate number of women in liberal arts and of men in science. The two major variables in this study, college major and sex, are *confounded;* there is no way to tell whether one or the other or both are responsible for the observed differences in the data.

A final note on sex differences: it is quite possible that the same cognitive style may have different implications for boys (or men) and for girls (or women). That is, a style preference or pattern that is useful or adaptive or facilitates learning among males might have the opposite effect among females either for cultural reasons or by virtue of the interactive effects of other sex-associated variables. Either in or out of school, girls may be rewarded for behaving in ways that boys would be punished for, and vice versa. Or, at a more subtle level, a given cognitive style may be useful in doing some "masculine" thing, but less useful in doing a "feminine" one, while another style works in the opposite way. A result that lends tentative support to such a possibility was reported in a study by Lewis; in that study impulsivity among grade school boys was associated with test-taking errors, while among girls the relationship between impulsivity and errors was less strong (1971). Apparently, among these children at least, another sex-associated behavior or characteristic interacted with impulsivity in such a way as to make it less of an academic handicap for girls than for boys.

## Socioeconomic Class

A number of researchers have suggested a possible relationship between socioeconomic class and cognitive style. Such a relationship, if it exists, would be important for at least two reasons. Practically speaking, if teachers and other learning facilitators in lower socioeconomic neighbor-hoods could assume that their children were working within the framework of a style range different from the range among other groups, they could begin to develop teaching techniques specifically designed for those children. And, at a more theoretical level, the identification of a particular cognitive style or styles as typical of a socially distinguishable group might well provide a beginning step in sorting out the environmental—as opposed to the hereditary—factors that influence cognitive-style development.

Hertzig has reviewed the literature on cognitive-style differences among various social classes and concludes that, indeed, rather strong evidence suggests that such differences exist. "In general the view has been advanced that lower-class children have an orientation and a style of response to demands for cognitive functioning which are fundamentally different from and less efficient than [those] possessed by middle class children. More specifically it has been suggested that lower-class children possess fewer language skills and are less well able to use such skills in the course of cognitive work, have difficulties in organizing and responding to temporal sequences, and are less capable of advanced planning and delaying immediate gratification than are middle class children" (Hertzig, 1971, p. 151). We should note that this description carries with it the traditional biases of the middle-class teacher: all differences are described as handicaps for the lower-class child trying to function in the middle-class school environment. In more objective terms, Hertzig seems to be saying that the lower-class children are more global than analytic, more cognitively simple than complex, and more impulsive than reflective.

Assuming that these differences—or a significant part of them—are real and are not just artifacts of a testing situation or a particular research design, where do we go from here? One question that immediately springs to mind is whether the differences may be genetically influenced. After all, many lower-class children are non-Caucasian, while most middle-class children are Caucasian, and so there are some observable genetic differences. Moreover, marriage within one's social class is (even in the United States) still more common than marriage outside one's social class, so it is quite possible that genetic differences may be accumulating along class lines. The counterargument is that the environmental differences between the lower-class child and the middle-class child are so great, and their effects so clearly observable, that it is foolish to even speculate about genetic effects at this time. To do so is like worrying about a pimple on the face of a man who is bleeding to death. This view has tended to prevail among investigators of cognitive style; except for one study in which the researchers were unable to find any evidence of style differences among very young children of different social classes (Golden & Birns, 1971), little has been done in the way of isolating the effects of environment and heredity in this area.

The practical question does remain: given that style differences do seem to appear among children of various social classes at some time before or during their early school years, what implications do these differences have? Hertzig (1971) carried out a fairly extensive study of Puerto Rican working-class and middle-class children and found that the effects of cognitive-style differences tended to multiply over time. That is, given slight differences at an early age, the effect of the less adaptive style (in the context of middle-class demands), interacting with the home conditions that tended to produce those styles in the first place, was to steadily lessen the lower-class child's ability to compete with his middle-class peers. Hertzig's subjects were 3 years old at the time of their first testing and 6 when they were tested again, and in that three-year period the increasing spread between middle- and lower-class children was apparent. The differences at age 6, Hertzig concludes, may have been caused by the earlier and much slighter 3-year-old differences. The greater tendency of the middle-class children to work at problem solving, to establish and express relations between what was already known and what was new, as well as their overall greater verbal ability, may well have contributed to the easy and rapid acquisition of both the information and the skills that formed a base for their superior performance at the later age.

Hertzig goes on to hypothesize differences in family patterns that may be a primary factor in creating these differences in cognitive style. The lower-class families put much more emphasis on social interaction than on task completion. In the middle-class families, in contrast, the mothers were very concerned about the age at which their children could assume responsibility for and exhibit skill in carrying out activities of daily living and self-care. Rather than presenting the child with a global task, they broke down the requirements into part processes, thus facilitating a stepwise, analytic approach to mastery. From this description it seems likely that the lower-class mothers were themselves more global than analytic, and that this pattern may be transmitted from generation to generation through traditional infant-care patterns.

It would appear, from these few paragraphs, that the question of the origin of cognitive-style preferences is still very much a mystery—that, like intelligence, these patterns arise out of a complex blend of biology and environment. An individual's sex, his visual acuity, his intellectual ability —all of these probably play a part in determining the cognitive-style pattern he adopts. But each of these biologically based or influenced characteristics interact with social factors to create an environment tailored to the needs of and expectations for a given individual. Those aspects of cognitive style that seem to be typically "female," for example, are associated not simply with biological femaleness, but also with the whole complex of social constraints and influences that go with being a girl in our culture. And research efforts to separate the effects of one particular environmental or physiological factor from all the others or to determine which aspect of environment or physiology is responsible for a specific cognitive-style characteristic have not yet met with a great deal of success.

## CHANGING A COGNITIVE STYLE

If we cannot figure out what causes cognitive-style patterns to arise by looking into a person's background, we have still another research possibility open to us: we can expose a subject to a variety of environments and measure the effects of these exposures on his current cognitive-style preferences. Here again we find two major research implications, that of discovering the significant factors that can alter cognitive style, and that of changing—and, one hopes, improving—an individual's cognitive behavior. "Cognitive style is not immutable. It can be augmented. Missing strengths . . . can be built on a student's existing strengths" (Nunney & Hill, 1972, p. 12). Clearly, the intent of Nunney and Hill and of others working in this area is benevolent. They want to help the student reach his full potential. Causing changes in someone's behavior, however, is a touchy business—especially when the changes have to do with something as far reaching and basic as one's cognitive style. We must be alert, in discussing results and hypotheses, to the potential for abuse, both in the treatment of experimental subjects and in the imposition of one professional's biases on his (relatively helpless) clients.

### Methods

Kagan and associates (1964) have shown that some changes in cognitive-style behavior can be brought about by the simple expedient of asking for them. That is, a request to grade school children to respond more slowly results in a significant increase in analytic responses. You will recall that global responses and impulsivity were correlated in the studies of Kagan and his associates; when the children were asked to behave in a less impulsive fashion, they apparently had time to construct and verbalize the analytic responses that had been displaced before by the quicker and easier global responses.

Asking a child to respond more slowly is a form of influence that does not seem particularly offensive or coercive to most of us, probably because we are so familiar with it. "Take your time, Andrea," or "Now *think* about it before you answer, Jennifer" are common phrases in the teacher's repertoire. Yet even here the teacher would be well advised to tread carefully. We do not know how lasting the changes in habit pattern may be when the initially impulsive child is consistently urged to slow his responses, nor do we know whether the length of time spent in the (apparently) developmentally earlier impulsive stage is somehow related to his readiness to move into an analytic mode.

Selective reinforcement has also been shown to be effective in changing a child's preferred cognitive style. Denney (1972b) found that children could be changed from global to analytic, from analytic to global, from impulsive to reflective, or from reflective to impulsive by giving them the appropriate reinforcements. Exposure to models was effective too in changing a child's cognitive style; children tended to imitate the style of the model they watched. Such findings take us a long way toward being able to say that cognitive styles are learned rather than innate; if artificially imposed reinforcements can bring about major changes, it seems reasonable to suppose that the reinforcements that the child encounters in his natural environment have the same effect. And, similarly, if seeing a model behave in one consistent way tends to make the child behave that way too, then we can probably assume that many of the style patterns he exhibits have been acquired from models in his natural environment. Hertzig suggests that this is indeed the case and also that we must take into account more than a child's home situation: "The growing child is exposed not only to the manner in which his parents approach demands for cognitive functioning, but to the ways in which other children do so as well. Thus stylistic patterns are transmitted and reinforced by his peer group as well as by the adults with whom he comes in contact" (1971, p. 163).

Agreeing that much of cognitive-style behavior is learned through exposure to various models and through having one's early attempts selectively reinforced forces the teacher into a rather uncomfortable position. If cognitive styles are learned, they can be unlearned. If selective reinforcement can teach one cognitive-style pattern, it can reteach another. We are close to knowing how to remodel a child's cognitive-style pattern and to do it without his permission—indeed, without his knowledge. Denney's work (1972a, 1972b) underlines the enormous power over human behavior that behavior-modification techniques give us. I seriously question whether we are ready for such power—whether we, as teachers or parents or just plain human beings, have the wisdom to use it constructively. The ethical questions that must be raised are as difficult as they are numerous: When does one human have the right to impose his values upon another? Who shall decide which cognitive patterns are best? What may be the long-term consequences—to the individual and to society—of imposing some "optimal" cognitive pattern on children? To be sure, as long as there have been teachers there have been attempts to mold children to the teacher's idea of what they ought to be. Provision of models and selective reinforcement are nothing new; they have been with us for millennia. What is new is our ability to use them systematically and to be reasonably certain of their efficacy. It is not the purpose of this volume to delineate the techniques of behavior modification: those who choose to travel that road need far more intensive training than can be provided here. What we all must be aware of, though, is that these techniques do exist and that there are those who use them. Whether they are to be used for good or for ill, wisely or foolishly, is the responsibility of all of us to determine.

## The Teacher's Role

Philosophical speculations are all very well, but the professional educator is going to be out in the thick of things, dealing with children who want (or don't want) to learn a variety of knowledges and skills. Can we say anything about cognitive style that has immediate, practical relevance to our day-to-day activities? I believe we can.

It seems clear that there is indeed an optimal cognitive-style pattern for the child in a typical middle-class school. The child who does best in that traditional setting is probably analytic, cognitively complex, and reflective. He is an obedient problem solver, gulping in chunks of information and setting them up in orderly relationships in his memory. Such a child is easy to work with—but how dull a school would be if it were filled exclusively with them! And, indeed, I suspect that these children (as well as their adult counterparts) would fare rather badly if they didn't have global or cognitively simple or impulsive people to react to. We must realize that while the public schools are, in general, so structured as to make it easiest for the analytic, reflective child to succeed, the school environment is nevertheless heterogeneous. Depending on what is going on in a particular room or group at a particular time, the analytic child may or may not be best fitted for the learning task. As Kagan and his colleagues (1964) point out, it seems reasonable to assume that efficient learning and performance on varied intellectual tasks will sometimes be facilitated by a reflective or analytic approach, sometimes by a more impulsive or less analytic orientation.

Schools, by the very nature of things, tend to be organized and run by people who like schools, and these people in turn are most likely to be people who have done well themselves in school. Carrying the logic one step further, we can reasonably suppose that most of these runners of schools are analytic, cognitively complex, and reflective. Moreover, we can suppose that, try as we may, it will often be difficult for us to get away from the idea that one function of education is to train children to be more analytic, complex, and reflective (just like us). After all, it's this sort of child who goes on and does well in college—thus further perpetuating the pattern. Most of the research on cognitive style has addressed itself to problems of succeeding within this rather narrowly defined setting. But what of the innovators, the artists, the child rearers of the next generation? Is the analytic individual any better than his global friend at getting along with people, at being concerned about his environment, at giving and receiving love? As long as the people operating the schools, as well as the people doing research and trying to determine which style is best, have in common a tendency toward reflectivity and analysis, they are likely to create a self-fulfilling prophecy: we are analytic, it is good to be analytic, we set up schools to enhance analytic qualities—and we prove the validity of our position by showing that analytic children do better in this setting.

Educational programs that are geared to one particular cognitive style or cognitive pattern do not provide convincing proof that that pattern is indeed best for all individuals. Nor do they take advantage of the individual child's unique methods and techniques for acquiring knowledge. "We must stop using individual differences as a means of determining who succeeds or who fails in group competition and instead adapt to differences in cognitive styles as a means of varying teaching techniques to ensure the individual's success in his educational program" Nunney and Hill conclude (1972, p. 10). Instead of trying to show the global child how to be analytic or persuading the impulsive child to adopt a reflective style, we should be looking for ways to take advantage of that globalness or that impulsiveness. What are the strengths of a global approach? We can conjecture that a global individual may be better at integrating the parts of a situation or may make better use of what we (for lack of a better word) call intuition. As for impulsivity, can quickness of response be somehow wedded to standards of quality? Focusing on the strengths inherent in whatever styles the child brings to his learning situation, rather than on somehow shaping him to a predetermined pattern, seems to me a much better strategy.

Both within and among people, our society has need of pluralism. If we are to meet the complex and changing demands of today's world, we need a variety of strategies: we need the strength and the insights that arise out of the interplay of many styles of thinking and problem solving. And, similarly, the individual who is most able to cope with the demands of his particular microcosm of the world is that person who can draw on a number of styles within himself. If there is a best style toward which teachers should aim their students, it is the superstyle of cognitive flexibility: the ability to move from one point on the continuum to another as the situation changes. A child is most likely to attain such flexibility if he is allowed to experience the consequences of trying out a variety of styles and if he is allowed to interact with role models (teachers, among others) who themselves are flexible. Once the trend is begun, it grows naturally: greater flexibility leads to greater realization of potential, which reinforces the flexibility. The teacher who is aware of his own style preferences and makes a conscious effort to break those habits occasionally can help to begin the cycle. The teacher who imposes his own idea of a proper mode of functioning on the child may create an efficient learning machine but is not likely to facilitate the growth of a creative, adaptable, flexible human being.

## QUESTIONS FOR UNDERSTANDING

1. Different children enter school with different expectations of what school will be like and of how they will react to it. How do these expectations help to shape the reality of a child's school experience?

2. Consider your own cognitive-style pattern. Where do you think you fall on each of the dimensions we have discussed? What are the major advantages and disadvantages of your cognitive style?

3. Other things being equal, what sorts of classroom tasks might you expect a global 10-year-old to do better on than an analytic 10-year-old? A leveler than a sharpener? An impulsive than a reflective?

4. The question of race, sex, or class differences in cognitive style is, because of our own social values, difficult for most of us to deal with. Should you, as a classroom teacher, take such differences into account in dealing with children? If so, how? If not, why not?

5. On page 289 a number of ethical questions are raised regarding the use of behavior-modification techniques to change children's cognitive styles. How would you answer these questions?

# Chapter 10

# Anxiety

"Anxiety," wrote Freud, "needs no description; everyone has personally experienced this sensation, or to speak more correctly this affective condition, at some time or other. . . . One thing is certain, that the problem of anxiety is a nodal point, linking up all kinds of most important questions: a riddle of which the solution must cast a flood of light upon our whole mental life" (1917/1969, p. 341). Throughout the history of clinical psychology, a great many people must have disagreed with the first part of that statement and agreed with the second part. More has probably been written about anxiety than about any other human condition, and a great deal of what has been written has been concerned with description and definition. In this chapter, we shall attempt to wade through some of the description, and we shall consider suggestions about why anxiety arises in people, what its consequences may be, and what can be done about it.

With so many descriptions and definitions of anxiety floating about, it is hardly surprising that confusion has arisen as to just what the word means. Or perhaps we should say, what we shall allow it to mean; with Humpty Dumpty (in *Alice in Wonderland),* we must let words know that we are the masters and that we decide what they will do for us. Anxiety is whatever we agree it is; we get into trouble when we can't agree on a definition. Such a problem has arisen, for instance, in the confusion about whether anxiety is a long-term personality characteristic—so that we can properly talk about an anxious person—or a short-term state in which any individual may find himself at one time or another. Psychologists frequently fail to make this distinction, but it is an important one. If anxiety is a long-term characteristic, then we should try to find out which people are anxious people and why they are that way. If it is a temporary state, into which anyone may fall occasionally, our focus should shift to the question of how person A or person B becomes anxious and why he stops being anxious and how he can learn to cope with his anxiety when it arises.

Charles Spielberger (1972), one of the leading students of anxiety behavior, has suggested a way out of this difficulty; he proposes that we use the terms *A-State* and *A-Trait* to refer to the short-term and the long-term phenomena, respectively. The *A-State* is a transitory phenomenon, usually brought on by a particular stimulus situation to which an individual responds in a characteristic fashion (I shall get more specific about these characteristic anxiety responses later in the chapter). The *A-Trait* is a relatively enduring personality characteristic that involves a tendency to see things or to react to them in ways characteristic of anxiety. In other words, the A-Trait person is one who finds himself in an A-State more frequently or more intensely or in response to a broader range of stimulus situations than a non-A-Trait person. The A-Trait may be thought of as a predisposition for anxiety states; and it is possible to identify people who are so predisposed. The A-State, however, can (and does) occur in anyone, and the state itself is no different for high-A-Trait people than it is for low-A-Trait people.

As teachers, we need to be alert to the fact that some learners are more likely than others to become anxious; we must also recognize that painful and often maladaptive anxiety states can occur in any learner, given the right set of circumstances. Throughout this chapter, the reader should keep in mind the distinction between A-State and A-Trait. For the most part, we shall be talking about A-States since this kind of anxiety has an immediate effect on learning behavior. At the same time, we shall want to know why some people fall into A-States so much more often than others—that is, why they are A-Trait people—and how we, as teachers, can help such individuals to deal with their anxieties.

## THE NATURE OF STATE ANXIETY

The most common description of anxiety is that it involves fear in the absence of a recognized fear source. That is, the anxious individual is afraid, but he doesn't know what he is afraid of. Spielberger says "Arousal of anxiety states involves a process or sequence of temporally ordered events initiated by either external or internal stimuli that are perceived to be dangerous or threatening by an individual. . . . Any internal stimulus which causes an individual to think about or anticipate a dangerous or frightening situation may evoke high levels of A-State. For example, a student who suddenly remembers that he has failed to prepare for an examination that is scheduled for the next class period would probably experience a sudden increase in A-State" (1972, p. 42). In this description, Spielberger does not specify the ambiguous nature of the fear, and I believe this is a serious omission. If I am walking down a country road and a vicious dog comes up to me growling and baring his teeth, this is certainly a dangerous and threatening situation; but my reaction is more likely to be fear than anxiety. However, if I am walking down that road and am reminded, in an only partly recognized way, of the possibility of being attacked by a vicious dog, I may experience true anxiety.

It is important to recognize that there are three separate and distinct parts to the anxiety experience, and only one of these parts is the A-State. First comes the stimulus situation, the set of perceptions (both external and internal) that lead to the anxiety reaction. Then, often for only a fleeting second or two, comes the A-State. Finally, and usually for a longer period of time, our coping mechanisms take over: we may still feel anxious, but the anxiety is no longer pure because we have added to it a whole set of (learned) reactions to deal with it and make it less uncomfortable. Both the nature of the stressful situation and the means of coping are appropriately a part of the study of anxiety, but they are not anxiety itself.

Spielberger points out that many kinds of situations are stressful or threatening to nearly everyone, but whether a particular situation arouses anxiety in a particular individual depends on how he perceives that situation. Even situations that most of us would agree are quite nonstressful may be perceived as dangerous or threatening by some people. This propensity to see situations as threatening defines the A-Trait: a high-A-Trait person sees more situations as threatening and thus finds himself in an A-State more often than does a low-A-Trait person.

Let's go back, for a moment, to Spielberger's example of the student who forgot to study for his exam. The situation is indeed threatening, and he is likely to feel anxious. But can't specific elements of this anxiety be identified? For one thing, he is uncertain: he doesn't know what the test will be like or whether he will be able to answer any of the questions or how a bad performance on this test will affect his final grade in the course. He feels helpless: here he is in this bad spot, and it's too late to do anything about it. And there is a characteristic time element in that the danger or threat is seen as a future thing, with unknown future implications. All these elements—uncertainty, helplessness, and future orientation—have been suggested as essential elements of the experience of anxiety.

*Uncertainty.* During anxiety there is uncertainty about one or all of several things: exactly what will happen, whether it will happen, when it will happen, and what can be done about it (Lazarus & Averill, 1972). If we see the anxiety of Spielberger's student as relating to his final grade in the course as well as to the immediately upcoming exam, then all these uncertainties are involved in his anxiety. He doesn't know exactly what effect this test will have on his final grade or when he will discover just how bad things are or what (if anything) he can do to redeem the situation.

Anxiety often occurs in social situations, and here again uncertainty is a central element. Social anxiety is most often related to not knowing how others will react to us or what they expect us to do. Kaczkowski and Owen (1972) suggest a reciprocal relationship between anxiety and anger: anxiety occurs when we don't know what others expect of us, and anger when others don't meet our expectations. Social anxiety may be further related to shame, the fear that we won't measure up to our own expectations for ourselves (often as reflected in the reactions of others). It is quite likely, I think, that these social anxieties, involving expectations of rejection or ridicule or shame, may have quite different concomitants and involve different coping mechanisms from anxieties revolving around threats to one's physical well-being. (It should go without saying that a given situation can involve a combination of social and physical anxiety.)

A slightly different quality of uncertainty is reflected in the question "What can (or should) I do?" Here the consequences are seen as determined, at least in part, by one's own actions, and the anxious person must take some responsibility for what happens to him. He is still helpless in that he doesn't know what behavior will be most helpful, but at the same time he feels that whatever happens will be partly his fault. The child with a history of school failure is a prime candidate for this variety of anxiety: he knows something is expected of him, but hasn't yet learned (with any certainty) how to produce it; and he has been made unmistakably aware that he will be blamed for his failure to meet expectations.

Thus far we have been discussing uncertainty in the context of the A-State. It is also possible to see a distaste for uncertainty as an element in the A-Trait. All of us must deal with some uncertainty in our lives; that is part of the human condition. But some individuals are more bothered by uncertainty than others, and they are the ones who are most likely to experience frequent anxiety. Shimkunas and Kime (1971) have devised a scale to measure uncertainty anxiety; in it they ask people to indicate how they react to a variety of ambiguous situations. Anxiety about uncertainties in one's life may be indicated by the avoidance of novel situations, by soliciting information to predict the possible outcome of future events, or by the experience of personal discomfort in ambiguous settings (Doster & Slaymaker, 1972). Such patterns of response tend to be relatively stable over time and may provide useful information about a given individual's A-Trait level.

*Helplessness.* It is difficult to separate the sense of helplessness from the sense of uncertainty in the A-State since uncertainty in effect denotes helplessness. When you don't know what will happen or what to do about it, you are helpless. If an event cannot be interpreted or given meaning, it cannot be dealt with; this leads to a sense of helplessness. It is primarily when we feel incapable and ineffective that we are apprehensive about the future (Lazarus & Averill, 1972). There is a dynamic quality about the helplessness of anxiety. It is not the "I can't do anything about it, so I'll just give up" feeling that often characterizes sadness or depression. Rather, the organism seems geared up to respond but can find no trustworthy responses to make. This stopped-action quality, the feeling of being poised and ready to act but not knowing what to do, is one of the characteristics that makes the sensation of anxiety so uncomfortable. Cattell (1972) describes it as a suspension of behavior combined with a heightening of readiness to behave, and goes on to point out that such a state implies an inability to cope with life. To the degree that a person is aware, then, of his own anxiety, it can feed on itself. I feel anxious and unable to decide what to do about it, and now I am anxious about my own anxiety. No wonder, says Cattell, that anxiety often carries with it feelings of lack of confidence, irritability, reduction of self-liking, and guilt; all these are reactions to a perceived inability to solve one's problems.

It is important to remember that the perception of helplessness, rather than an objectively helpless state, is a key element in anxiety. We may watch a child struggling to find a solution to a problem and realize that he is helpless to solve it; but until that child feels helpless—that is, until he perceives his own helplessness—that helplessness cannot contribute to his anxiety. Conversely, a person may find himself in a situation that he believes to be hopeless, even though external observers might see dozens of things he could do to make things better; here the feeling of helplessness can create anxiety regardless of whether he is, in fact, helpless. "In a state of arousal, the organism who has no behavior available to him, who continues to seek situationally or cognitively appropriate behavior, is 'helpless' and may also consider himself, in terms of the common language, as being in a state of anxiety. Thus helplessness is not defined by an objective situation, but by the organism and his repertory of behavior" (Mandler, 1972, p. 369).

The reasons for perceiving oneself as helpless may vary enormously from person to person and from situation to situation. In some circumstances a person is helpless to do much about his situation. In others he cannot think of an appropriate behavior through lack of problem-solving ability. Not infrequently, he may have a fairly good idea what he "ought" to do, but may not want to do it because he is afraid it may lead to worse consequences or because it would involve his giving up something else (or some other behavior) that he values (Costello & deKrasinski, 1972). Spielberger's student (poor fellow, he must be tired of sweating out that exam!), for example, has a full hour before his test; he could cut the intervening class and study like crazy. He may not want to do that because he doesn't want to miss the other class; or he may be afraid that even if he studied he would still fail, and studying now would make the failure more a reflection of his own ability. We have already seen how high fear-of-failure individuals often set unattainable goals, so that failing to reach them need not be seen as true failure ("it was too hard; nobody could have done it"). The helplessness of anxiety may involve some of the same dynamic pattern; for some people, it may be better to be anxious about failing and about one's own potential than to risk going through the certainty of the actual failure experience.

Phillips, Martin, and Meyers (1972) point out the relationship between anxiety helplessness and planfulness. Most human activity involves plans of one sort or another; frustration occurs when a plan is interrupted and we must shift to another behavior (which may be alternative goal setting). But when no alternative is available—when we can neither decide to try another route nor decide not to seek that goal after all—then we become anxious. Again, there is a stopped-action quality, a fly-on-flypaper-and-can't-even-struggle-to-get-away feeling that is characteristic of the anxiety experience.

*Future Orientation.* The anxious individual is not troubled so much by immediate and concrete dangers as by future possibilities. Hamlet, who made something of an art form of anxiety, was talking about this future orientation in his soliloquy: the dread of the unknown "makes us rather bear those ills we have than fly to others that we know not of." Again, it is hard to separate future orientation from uncertainty since the one usually implies the other; but both are important aspects of anxiety. Tomkins (1972) describes one common form of anxiety as a fear sequence stretched out in time, in which we ourselves have contributed to the temporal separation of present feeling and future consequences. "What we are afraid of right now we don't know. There is something we're afraid of, but we don't know it because that sequence has been pulled apart, and we intend to pull it apart and keep it apart as long as possible because even though we pay a price in present fear, or anxiety, what we are afraid of appears to be even worse" (p. 109).

It is possible that the pulled-apartness in time exists simply because anxiety takes a certain minimum amount of time to build up in an individual. Lazarus and Averill (1972) suggest that anxiety should require more time to grow than a simpler response such as fear or rage because anxiety is built on a series of relatively complex appraisals. They also suggest that as the time that one must wait (before coming face to face with whatever one is anxious about) increases, anxiety should increase too, at least until a workable means of coping is brought into play. As an example of the future orientation of anxiety, Lazarus and Averill use separation anxiety (the fear and dread of losing a loved one), which they relate to grief. The mature individual who suffers this sort of anxiety is not so much distressed about his deprivation right now as involved in projecting that distress into the future. "Will the separation continue?" he asks. "Will I continue to feel as bad about it as I do now? How will I ever manage to get along?" Again, we see in this form of anxiety the familiar mix of future orientation, uncertainty, and helplessness.

One last word before we move away from the question of time orientation: it is important to realize, in dealing with emotions, that our language is often only partially adequate to describe what happens in the realm of feelings. Feelings are a part of what Freud called the primary processes and as such are not bound by the ordinary rules of time and space and logic. Language, however, is (as it is generally used) very much a secondary process—a conscious-thought phenomenon—and it is bound by ordinary logic. As we usually think of things, something cannot be simultaneously in two places or two times; we progress from place to place and from time to time in a sequential fashion. But feelings may not be bound in this way. As Lazarus and Averill (1972, p. 249) put it, "Our common division of time into the future, present, and past is not always adequate to express phenomenal experience. If we consider anticipation not as apprehension of future happenings, but as a failure to comprehend events occurring now, then anxiety appraisals can belong to the present. It is, however, a present lacking structure and meaning and, hence, characterized by ominous foreboding. In a sense, then, present and future may coalesce during the experience of anxiety."

*Symbolization.* Just as language is sometimes inadequate to express the quality of our feelings, so it is often used to limit, to tie down, or to control those feelings. By constructing his world out of symbols, man gives it a set of meanings that he can understand and thus creates a sense of being able to cope with daily events. Anxiety occurs when these symbols begin to break down, when they no longer fit reality as one experiences it. We can see this breakdown clearly in the case of a psychotic reaction, where symbolization has broken away from reality as most of us agree on it; the psychotic lives in a world created by symbols quite different from those used by most people, symbols arrayed in a desperate—and often ineffective—attempt to control the pain of anxiety. But inadequate symbolization is a characteristic of the anxiety experience of "normal" people as well; we feel anxious when ideas, concepts, values, or goals to which we are heavily committed begin to lose their meaningfulness to us.

Since our symbols allow us to relate meaningfully to the world, a breakdown in symbolization is equivalent to a breakdown in our whole stance of self-in-the-world. Our sense of meaning is threatened; at its most extreme, the anxiety experience leaves us alone and defenseless in an angry whirlwind of alien experiences and stimuli. This is the ultimate helplessness: because it is our very coping skills that are being attacked, there is no way in which we can fight back. "The concrete nature and temporal characteristics of the harm cannot be clearly identified, [and] no rationally based action to dispel the danger can be potentiated. There is nothing concrete to change" (Lazarus & Averill, 1972, p. 250).

*Anxiety as a Combination.* We have seen that anxiety involves a number of feelings, of responses to perceived situations: uncertainty, helplessness, future orientation, disturbed symbolization. Does it make sense then to speak of anxiety as a single phenomenon? Or should we treat it as a complex of simpler reactions? Izard (1972) believes that there are nine "fundamental emotions" and that combinations of five of these are experienced as anxiety. The five anxiety emotions are fear, distress, shame (including shyness and guilt), anger, and interest excitement. Anxiety is experienced when an individual feels fear plus any two of the other four in some combination. Thus such different sorts of mixes as fear, shame, and interest excitement, or fear, distress, and anger, would create an experience that one would label as anxiety. Our only chance of understanding anxiety, Izard says, is to see it as a complex of emotions or emotion-related concepts; there is no such thing as a unitary phenomenon of anxiety.

Izard goes on to point out that "pure" anxiety, like any other "pure" emotion, is almost impossible to observe in an individual. The emotion is experienced for only a fleeting instant in a pure state; it immediately elicits other emotions and interacts with our cognitive processes. The first emotion elicited in the anxiety experience may be fear, but that is quickly followed by other emotions—so quickly that it is the combination of these others with the original fear that is recognized as anxiety.

One common way of studying emotion in the laboratory is through the use of facial expressions. Subjects are shown photographs or drawings of people with various expressions and are asked to indicate what the people in the pictures may be feeling. Through these and other experiments, researchers have determined that facial expression not only is a result of one's emotional state but is also a primary determinant of what one is feeling. If you cry while peeling an onion, you are almost sure to feel a fleeting sensation of sadness; and it is quite impossible to feel enraged while your facial muscles are in a state of relaxation. According to Izard (1972, p. 64), "innate programs" of facial activity are related to the fundamental emotions. "If the pattern combines elements of two or more innate programs or consists of two or more fundamental patterns in rapid sequence or alternation, the experience will consist of 'mixed emotion.' Such is the case with 'state anxiety.' It's a mix-up! It has no fixed neurophysiological structure. It has no characteristic face."

Yet, even though anxiety may result from combinations of different fundamental emotions, through a great deal of folk experience we have learned to recognize anxiety as an entity in itself. How is it that, say, fear, anger, and excitement can be experienced as the same sort of feeling as distress, guilt, and fear? I believe that it is the coming together of the qualities we have already enumerated—future orientation, helplessness, uncertainty, the falling apart of symbolization—that both characterizes and limits the anxiety state. When these qualities are present, regardless of which of the fundamental emotions may be predominant, and in what strength, the subjective experience is that of anxiety. The flavor of the anxiety, its direction, its intensity, and its relationship to external objects depend on the particular combination of fundamental emotions.

THAT LOOKS LIKE THE PUZZLED EXPRESSION OF SOMEONE WHO HAS JUST BEEN ASKED TO GUESS THE EMOTION BEHIND AN EXPRESSION IN A PICTURE.

## ANTECEDENTS OF ANXIETY

Having given some attention to just what anxiety is and what combination of elements constitute the anxiety experience, we can now turn to the question of where it comes from. Again, it is necessary to distinguish between the A-State and the A-Trait. The A-State arises as a response to a particular set of (external and/or internal) stimuli. It is always a result of a person's perception of what is or will be happening around or inside him. But some individuals respond with anxiety to a much broader range of stimulus possibilities than do others; this is the criterion for the A-Trait, or anxiety proneness. And it is the trait—the readiness to respond in an anxious fashion —that would seem to be an appropriate focus for an inquiry into antecedents. Just what in a given individual makes him so vulnerable to anxiety?

### Parents

As usual, it is the parents who first fall under suspicion. (Poor parents, they get blamed for everything.) They are the first socializing influence in a child's life and so must contribute in a fundamental way to his early response and coping patterns. The fact that anxiety does involve fear, helplessness, and uncertainty also suggests that the origins of this response may lie at a point where the child was in fact helpless and without the means of predicting what would happen to him next. Such helplessness and uncertainty would be most keenly experienced by a child in interaction with hostile, demanding, or indifferent parents. Spielberger (1972) points to parental nonreward as central in creating the A-Trait in children. The fact that high-A-Trait people blame themselves for failure and tend to devalue themselves under ego-involving conditions suggests that these people received excessive criticism and negative appraisals from their parents. Such criticisms may well have undermined their self-confidence and adversely influenced their self-concepts. In other words, the child who is not rewarded, praised, or otherwise made to feel adequate early in life will not be likely to develop a sense of himself as capable of interacting competently with the world around him. He will continue to feel helpless and uncertain and to expect the worst from any ambiguous situation.

Phillips and associates (1972) emphasize that any adult figure can arouse anxiety in children. Adults are bigger, stronger, more knowledgeable, and in control of more resources than are children. Moreover, adults do punish children; a large proportion of the negative consequences in a child's life are perceived by him as coming from adults. Teachers, too, share this appraisal. They are seen by students as evaluators and dispensers of reward and punishment. In fact, most adults in a child's life serve this function.

Overprotection—anxiety about the child's ability to function in one way or another—can also contribute to his trait anxiety. Parents who worry about their child teach that child to worry about himself. In a study of family therapy with highly anxious children, Lessing and Phillips (1971) found that parents of such children tended to be anxious about the children. Now, the obvious comment at this point is "Who wouldn't be?" And, of course, that's valid. Simply demonstrating that two things—in this case, parental anxiety and child's anxiety—occur together does not prove that one causes the other. Having a child become unhappy or disturbed enough to require psychotherapy is enough to make most people anxious, and it might well have been that the disturbed child caused the parents' anxiety rather than the other way around. However, Lessing and Phillips went a step further. Rather than working with the child's anxiety, they worked with the parents. They didn't try to reduce parental anxiety, but they did succeed in shifting its focus from the child to the parents themselves. That is, they helped the parents to express their anxiety in relation to their own behaviors rather than to the activities of the child. And in these families, the child's functioning improved, and the child's relationship to the parents became more comfortable. Whatever the origins of the anxiety pattern, the behavior of the parents clearly played an important part in maintaining it. When that behavior changed, the child's anxiety decreased.

*Failure Experiences*

It would be foolish, however, to attribute the totality of an individual's A-Trait level to his relationship with his parents or even with all the significant adults in his life. Every person experiences some successes and some failures in his interactions with the world; these successes and failures determine, in large part, his expectations about future interactions. The individual who has experienced failure or who has perceived the outcome of his efforts as failure is more likely to experience anxiety over future events than the successful individual. And the individual who has coped successfully with stress has a twofold advantage over his less successful peer: he not only has acquired an expectation for future success but has also developed a technique for coping with a stress situation. It follows that there must be an optimal range of stress situations within which children can learn to function. Too much stress leads to the experience and the expectation of failure, while too little stress precludes the development of effective coping responses. Either extreme is likely to produce an individual high in trait anxiety.

One bit of support for this line of reasoning comes from a study by Mann (1972), who investigated the residential history of college students. He found that students who had a history of high residential mobility (in garden-variety English, whose families moved around a lot) were lower in trait anxiety than less mobile students. The more mobile students seemed to experience stress in a different way; both their general reaction to the concept of stress and their responses to a particular stress situation were different. Mann concludes that the stressful experiences of frequent moving during childhood built up a tolerance for new and uncertain situations—that is, the children who went through a relatively large number of moves were able to acquire effective ways of handling the feelings of helplessness and uncertainty that those moves brought about.

Since a significant portion of most children's waking time is spent in school, one of the important questions for the student of anxiety (especially if he plans to become a teacher) is to what degree the school itself contributes to a child's anxiety. This question has arisen with particular force in the debate over ability streaming—that is, the practice of sorting children into fairly homogeneous ability groups in the classroom. Opponents of streaming contend that placing the child in a group labeled *low ability* (and the children always know which is the low-ability group, whether it's called "Dumbbells" or "Bluebirds") creates a continuing experience of negative evaluation, with consequent expectations of future failure and anxiety about failure. Gaudry and Spielberger (1971) carried out a study in an attempt to illuminate this issue. They argued that the very fact of being a low-ability child means that the child will have experienced failures many times in the past and that it is this history of past failures, rather than ability grouping, that is responsible for higher anxiety scores in low-ability-group children. To test this hypothesis, they divided children of the same ability level into two groups. All the children were given a test, and all thought that all the tests were the same; but in fact half the children were given impossibly difficult tests, and the others were given quite easy ones. The children then compared their scores with sets of "norms" that were displayed on the wall of the testing room. The children who had been given the difficult test and who had thus had a failure experience expressed significantly more anxiety than the "successful" children. The authors concluded that a single experience of failure can in fact cause an immediate rise in test anxiety and that it is reasonable to assume that the cumulative effects of failure will lead to higher levels of test anxiety. Furthermore, since children who fail are frequently placed in lower-level groups, it would be expected that members of such groups would have a higher mean level of test anxiety than would members of the higher-level groups. While these results are directed specifically to test anxiety (a special form of anxiety that we shall look at in detail later in this chapter), it seems reasonable to assume that they may be generalized to a variety of other anxiety responses.

### A Universal Human Response?

Overarching all our learning experiences, whether they relate to emotions or to anything else, is the pervasive influence of the culture within which we live. While this book is admittedly and deliberately chauvinistic in that it is written about and for Western people, we must still try to stop occasionally and peer around the edges of that cultural heritage. It may not be possible for us to understand how our culture has influenced the ways we behave, but we can at least recognize that such an influence is present and that it is to be expected that people from other cultures (and subcultures) may see and react to the world in different—and no less valid—ways. This is certainly true in the case of anxiety. While nearly all cultures provide members with the opportunity to experience helplessness or uncertainty or any of the other components of anxiety as we in the West know it, many have incorporated different responses to such feelings. Rather than feeling anxious about being helpless, for instance, one might be taught to welcome such a state since it means that one is no longer responsible for what happens. Also, different combinations of internal and external events may produce anxiety in different cultural settings. Izard (1972, p. 62) wraps it up: "cultural differences in attitudes toward certain emotions are incorporated during socialization and result in different relationships among the emotions and between the antecedents, concomitants, and consequences of a given emotion."

Beyond any possible cultural differences, though, is the likelihood that anxiety of some sort is a necessary aspect of humanness and that it arises from an internal struggle between essential aspects of the human personality. Freud believed that anxiety emerged out of the conflict between id and ego (the id is the original personality and contains one's primitive drives and needs, while the ego is that part of personality that has learned to accept and interact with reality), with the ego desperately trying to maintain control over the unacceptable impulses of the id. More recently, many psychologists have become interested in the existentialist view that anxiety is felt whenever one senses division within oneself—when one both desires and fears something. Kierkegaard, for example, says that the real terror in anxiety lies in the fact that each of us within himself is on both sides of the fight, and that "anxiety" is a desire for what one dreads. Some evidence for this contention can be seen in studies that compare the reactions of high-A-Trait people to threats to personal adequacy and to threats of physical danger. Anxiety-prone individuals tend to react much more strongly to threats to personal adequacy than to threats of physical danger; it is as if the strongest feelings of helplessness and distress arise when one is made aware of danger coming from within oneself rather than from external sources (Spielberger, 1972). Rollo May (1950) has commented that, in his own work in psychotherapy, anxiety seems to arise out of the patient's fear of his own powers and from the conflicts that such fear generates. External threats and/or deprivations, however strong or terrible they may be, still leave room to mobilize defenses, to somehow fight back. A certain amount of anxiety is "normal" in response to external threats; this kind of response occurs both in high-A-Trait and low-A-Trait individuals. But the high-A-Trait person is peculiarly sensitive to feelings of internal inadequacy, to the sense that he may somehow not measure up to himself, to the helplessness that comes through the loss of control of his own inner processes. Over years of interacting with and learning from his surroundings, he has come to suspect—or believe in—his own fundamental inadequacy. Such a belief is too distressing to be admitted consciously, but it continuously threatens to become conscious. In a very real sense, the high-A-Trait individual is afraid of fear; he is most anxious over the unthinkable prospect of experiencing his true anxiety.

## CONSEQUENCES OF ANXIETY

Everyone feels anxious some of the time, and some people feel anxious much more often than others. Well and good; but what does this mean in terms of how anxious people act? Let's take a look at some of the behavioral consequences of anxiety.

### Physiological Consequences

The most obvious consequence of anxiety is physiological arousal. Indeed, one of the major confusions in the study of anxiety has been the tendency to use arousal as a definition of anxiety. Changes in galvanic skin response (a highly sensitive indicator of sweat-gland activity), blood pressure, heart rate, and respiration have been used as direct indicators of the presence of an anxiety state (Auerbach & Spielberger, 1972). In fact, all emotional reactions involve physiological changes; measures of physiological arousal can indicate that a person is highly involved in some emotional state, but our understanding has not yet progressed far enough for us to be able to differentiate (with certainty) among various strong emotional responses purely on the basis of arousal patterns. It is likely that the notion of a one-to-one correlation between arousal and anxiety came about simply because anxiety is relatively easy to create in an experimental situation.

Izard (1972) suggests that adding striate-muscle-activity levels to the arousal pattern might give us a better picture of what happens physically during anxiety. Measures of such activity indicate the degree of muscle tension in a person; and this kind of tension seems to be an important consequence of anxiety. Izard further believes that since anxiety involves a combination of more fundamental emotional reactions, the anxious person's nervous system may be responding to conflicting or changing demands. The physiological pattern characteristic of shame may be quite different from that characteristic of fear, yet anxiety often involves both. "Components of two or more emotions may make simultaneous or rapidly alternating demands on neurophysiological mechanisms and on consciousness. Such a combination of the interacting and alternating components of different fundamental emotions could help account for the vagueness and undifferentiated character so frequently attributed to . . . anxiety" (Izard, 1972, p. 63).

There is a long tradition in psychology, beginning with William James, of argument over which comes first, the emotional experience or the physiological reaction. James suggested that the man who runs away from a bear is frightened because he runs, rather than the other way around. In other words, the body automatically mobilizes itself to deal with the situation, and this physical response is sensed by the brain and is labeled fear or joy or anxiety or what have you. The opposite point of view is that we recognize a situation and respond to it emotionally (in a kind of head trip), and then our body reacts accordingly. It seems likely that the truth lies somewhere between these two extremes: we sense both internal and external events in an ongoing interaction, a kind of running dialog between sensory input and cognitive creation. The experience of anxiety would be quite different—and perhaps impossible—in the absence of physiological arousal since anxiety and arousal build on each other. It may well be that anxiety can be triggered by either a cognitive or a physiological event; what is important is that anxiety is a kind of chain reaction involving both. In this sense, the physiological aspects of anxiety can be thought of as either cause or consequence.

## Social Consequences

One of the obvious questions to be asked about anxiety is the effect it has on one's social behavior. Does the anxious person prefer to be alone with his anxiety, or does he seek social supports? Does he reach out to others, or does he tend to close himself off? And how do others react to someone who is perceived to be experiencing anxiety? Early researchers in this area have generally concluded that, in answer to the first question, the experience of anxiety tends to make people want to be with others. A standard experimental technique is to tell experimental subjects that they are going to be given painful electric shocks as a part of the experimental procedure and then to give them a choice of waiting alone or with a group of other subjects until the experiment begins. Under these conditions, most subjects choose to wait with the group. This affiliative-preference effect has been linked with the ambiguity aspect of anxiety. When the situation is ambiguous, a person doesn't know how to evaluate his reactions. By seeking out others in a similar situation, he can compare his behavior and his feelings with the way those others are behaving and the way they seem to feel and thus obtain cues as to what responses are in fact appropriate (Navar & Helmreich, 1971).

As is so often the case with human behavior, though, such a simple explanation doesn't always work. There are many kinds of anxiety, as we have seen; and the affiliation-preference effect doesn't occur consistently in all of them. The classic study carried out by Sarnoff and Zimbardo (1961) demonstrated this clearly. Subjects were told to expect either physical pain or shame and embarrassment during the course of the experiment. Some subjects were told that the experiment would involve shock, and some were told that they would be required to suck on pacifiers or baby bottles (the control group was told that they would have to put balloons or whistles in their mouths). The results were clear: the pain-anxiety group (those led to expect shock) preferred to affiliate more than did the controls; but the shame-anxiety subjects (the baby-bottle and pacifier people) wanted to wait alone more than did the control-group subjects. Sarnoff and Zimbardo's shame-anxiety condition clearly created anxiety of a different kind than that aroused by threat of physical pain. We may interpret shame anxiety as a fear of the reactions of others (and of oneself) to one's looking silly or ridiculous, or we may relate it more psychoanalytically to latent sexual fears. In either case, shame anxiety clearly has to do with "what I might do or say or feel that would be socially wrong." Anxiety about social wrongness moves a person in the direction of social isolation, while other sorts of anxieties may move him to seek social support. Since many anxiety-producing situations involve combinations of social-wrongness anxiety with other anxieties, we may expect anxious people to be often in a state of social conflict: needing social support, yet driven away from such contact by their social anxiety.

If we look at descriptions of how high-anxiety children appear to others, the evidence suggests that the characteristics others see in them both contribute to and are consequences of social conflict. According to Gaudry and Spielberger (1971), high-anxiety children are self-disparaging, are unadventurous, possess negative personality characteristics, and have a strong tendency to indulge in daydreams. Their classmates appear to react unfavorably to them, and even their teachers tend to see them as possessing negative and unfavorable characteristics. Already responding with anxiety to a variety of situations, these children enter the school situation programmed for anxiety. They are likely to see themselves as incompetent and nonvaluable, to avoid danger or challenge (because such situations are threatening), and to retreat into the relative security of fantasy rather than face the social rejection that they both fear and expect. And these very behaviors make social rejection more probable.

The chain of events does not end with social rejection, however. Phillips and associates (1972) describe the further consequences. Isolated and rejected children first experience anxiety in social situations, and this anxiety is followed by either a slowing down of activity or by a heightened level of activity. These changes in activity affect both school work and non-school-related activities, and in many instances the activities (or lack of them) are classed as problem behavior by teachers and peers. Thus anticipation of social failure, and anxiety about it, becomes a self-fulfilling prophecy. The child's fear of failure makes it impossible for him to succeed; his anxiety makes him act in ways certain to make his peers reject or dislike him.

To cap it off, the anxiety reaction even interferes directly with therapeutic attempts at alleviation. Because the person (child or adult) has learned to expect pain in connection with social experiences, he communicates less readily. He expects relationships with others to be superficial and shallow, and he fears deep involvement with others. These attitudes make it extremely difficult for him to enter into a therapeutic relationship. Just as an animal that has been beaten may snarl at any new master, no matter how kind, so the socially rejected individual copes with his social anxiety by symbolically snarling at any offer of meaningful social interaction. He expects not only that the other person will eventually reject him, but also that his own attempts to relate will be so inadequate that these too will cause shame and pain. "The client's anticipation of discomfort, guardedness, or inadequate communication skills may likely inhibit steps toward first contact and create reservations about suitability for therapy or its success. Individuals who are more averse to uncertain or novel situations in their lives seem particularly prone to viewing therapy as a potentially unpleasant and low self-participating experience" (Doster & Slaymaker, 1972, p. 527).

Thus the highly anxious person defeats himself socially. He desperately needs social support, yet he cannot trust it—and rightly so, for people do, in fact, tend to reject him. Figure 10-1 indicates the circular nature of the reaction. The support-seeking aspects of anxiety make us want to be dependent, to conform to the behavior of others and thus gain their approval. At the same time, expectation of rejection makes for hostility and anger. The highly anxious individual's experience of this kind of conflict plus the reality of his social rejection plus the anxieties that began and that

*Figure 10-1.* The cycle of social anxiety.

undergird the whole cycle make up the world of psychic pain in which he must exist.

## Problem-Solving Consequences

In study after study of problem-solving behavior among anxious and nonanxious individuals, a curious discrepancy has emerged: for high-difficulty problems, anxiety tends to lower performance; but high-anxiety people tend to do better than low-anxiety people in solving easier problems. It has been hypothesized that, with easy tasks, low-anxiety people tend to become bored and thus perform badly, while the physiological arousal that accompanies anxiety tends to keep high-anxiety people working hard and thus performing at a higher level. A second possibility is that the high-anxiety person is so hungry for an experience of success or for the approval of others that this need alone keeps him working even at a nonchallenging task—indeed, the nonchallenging task may be the only sort of task he is willing to risk trying—while the low-anxiety person is able to find so many other sources of satisfaction that he doesn't need to demonstrate or experience success on easy problems. A third and still related possibility is that the task itself may create (in the case of hard problems) or allay (in the case of easy problems) anxiety, so that the A-State level is in fact a function of problem difficulty for high-A-Trait people but not for low-A-Trait people. Thurner and Wennehorst (1972) attempted to test this third hypothesis by giving high-anxiety and low-anxiety children different sets of tasks. One task set began with complex problems and progressed to simple ones, while in the other the order was reversed. The high-anxiety children (here high anxiety refers to A-Trait) did better than the low-anxiety children when they began with easy problems, while the low-anxiety children did better when the more complex problems came first. The authors concluded that the simple-to-complex problem set reassured the high-anxiety children and turned off the low-anxiety children, while starting with complex problems tended to elevate the anxiety level of the high-anxiety group much more than it elevated that of the low-anxiety group.

Complex tasks can be both difficult and emotionally arousing, and both these aspects should be taken into consideration (Sarason, 1960). Difficulty involves challenge and, by extension, danger; we have already seen that the anxious individual tends to avoid both. As for arousal, a low or intermediate level may be experienced as pleasant, while excessive amounts are unpleasant or distressing. An arousing task may elevate the arousal level of an initially nonaroused (nonanxious) person to a pleasantly stimulating level, but may elevate the already aroused (anxious) subject to a painful level. The implication seems clear: beginning with a reassuringly easy or simple problem and gradually increasing the level of complexity should facilitate the performance of an anxious child. Unfortunately, this procedure can have the opposite effect on his low-A-Trait peer.

One important part of the problem-solving process is data gathering. In order to arrive at an appropriate solution, the problem solver must have as much information as possible about the problem. Patton and Kotrick (1972) hypothesize that anxiety has a particularly harmful effect in the data-gathering phase of problem solving in that it reduces an individual's receptiveness to new information. Emotion reduces the number of inputs a person can deal with. Because his ability to process visual input is reduced, the anxious subject must scan the stimulus for a longer time before he has enough information to solve his problem or satisfy his curiosity. Even with a longer time available for gathering information, the anxious person is likely to miss important bits; high levels of emotion tend to narrow the focus of concentration, so that peripheral stimuli are ignored. Moreover, the anxious person must continually defend himself against hurt and danger, and this defensive stance by its very nature can act as a screen against potentially threatening (but possibly useful) information.

Patton and Kotrick's study was intended as an exploration of the curiosity behavior of anxious individuals. The general consensus of the literature has been that anxiety tends to decrease curiosity; this relationship has been demonstrated for infrahuman as well as for human subjects. Patton and Kotrick asked subjects to look at a series of photographs (of objectively nonthreatening scenic views) and recorded how long they spent looking at each picture. The anxious subjects spent significantly longer amounts of time looking at the pictures, leading Patton and Kotrick to conclude that they were more curious. There is, however, another possible explanation. These subjects were highly anxious people who knew that they were participating in a psychological experiment. They were seated in a room, alone with a slide projector and a set of slides, and given no instructions except that they were to look at the pictures. It seems quite reasonable to believe that the subjects would be suspicious and apprehensive about the purpose of such a procedure and might anticipate a whole variety of unpleasant next steps waiting for them when they finished their viewing. Under such circumstances, a common strategy is to proceed slowly and carefully. One searches for cues about what may happen next and tries to prepare for it (for instance, if I'm to be tested on these pictures, I'd better be sure I see everything there is to see); and one also puts off as long as possible whatever is scheduled to happen after the viewing is completed. Interpreted in this way, the longer viewing time of the anxious subjects reflects not curiosity about the pictures but a lack of curiosity (or at least of approach behavior) about the rest of the experiment.

Curiosity tends to enhance performance in novel problem areas, while it has little effect on or may even hurt performance of familiar tasks (as the problem solver becomes bored and looks for something more interesting to do or think about). If high-anxiety people are less curious than low-anxiety people, we should expect them to perform differently in novel and in familiar situations. Just as the high-anxiety person does poorly on difficult tasks but well on easy ones (relative to his low-anxiety peer), he should not perform well in a novel situation. A partial test of this hypothesis is provided by a study (Oros, Johnson, & Lewis, 1972) of children's performance on the Wechsler Intelligence Scale for Children (WISC). The WISC is divided into two subscales, a verbal scale and a performance scale. The verbal subscale consists of tasks that are, for the most part, quite familiar to school children: answering questions, solving arithmetic problems, defining words. The performance scale contains more unusual problems: the child must rearrange pictures to tell a story, put together odd shapes to make a picture, arrange colored blocks into specified designs, and code a sequence of numbers into nonnumerical symbols. In the Oros study, performance on the verbal subscale of the WISC was not affected by anxiety, but anxious subjects scored lower than nonanxious subjects on the performance subscale. While other characteristics of the two scales may have entered into this relationship, it seems reasonable that the amount of novelty was an important determinant of performance. Anxious individuals do not do well, relative to nonanxious individuals, in novel situations.

## CONSEQUENCES FOR LEARNING

In a general way, the relationship between anxiety and problem solving mirrors the relationship between anxiety and learning. This similarity should not be particularly surprising since learning can be viewed as a kind of problem solving. The literature on learning and anxiety gives us the same overall picture: anxiety tends to interfere with learning complex materials, but (in moderate degrees) does not hurt and may even facilitate learning simple things. There have also been studies of the interaction between anxiety and intelligence, and their combined effect on learning. One such study, by Hodges and Durham (1972), used both grade-point average in school and performance on a rote memory task as indices of learning ability. They found that higher levels of anxiety facilitated the performance (as measured by grade-point average) of the brighter students but hurt the performance of the duller ones. The same general result held for short-term learning as measured by the rote memory task; here, however, the bright subjects in the low-anxiety group learned less well than did the dull ones in that group.

It is easy to fall into the trap of assuming that anxiety is a "bad" thing and that the learning facilitator should try his best to reduce the anxiety levels of his students. This is probably true for many individuals—perhaps for most—but the person with an excessively low level of A-Trait is handicapped too. Hodges and Durham (1972), commenting on the finding that bright low-anxiety subjects did less well than dull low-anxiety subjects on a short-term memory task, say that we need to look particularly hard at what it means to be bright and low in anxiety. This is the plight of the student who has never had to study hard in order to succeed and, in addition, who does not have a high level of A-Trait that could serve as motivation to cope with various tasks. The bright, low-A-Trait student, when given a task that is irrelevant to him, does not apply himself to the task. In comparison, the dull, low-A-Trait student has had to develop ways of coping with academic situations and may well be better off as a result.

### Anxiety as a Drive

Results of this sort give strong support to the hypothesis that anxiety works like a drive, or motivator, in humans. Drive theory predicts that whenever there are many competing responses—that is, when the "correct"

response in a particular situation is not yet well learned—a strong drive will lead to making errors. The organism is pushed, or driven, into doing something, but the strength of the push often causes him to do the wrong thing. In contrast, in situations where there are few competing responses (where the task is easy or has been well learned in the past), a high drive level should lead to good performance. This is exactly the situation that exists with regard to anxiety: when anxiety is high, performance on difficult learning tasks goes down, but performance on easy tasks goes up.

Phillips and associates (1972) used the serial-position effect to provide a further test for this idea. The serial-position effect, as we learned in Chapter 5, has to do with learning a list—of words, of facts, of anything that must be committed to memory. In such a task, items at the beginning and at the end of the list are easier to learn than items in the middle. Learning psychologists believe that competing responses occur in the middle of the list more often than at either end; there is more likelihood of mixing up the responses when they are surrounded by other responses. If this is true, and if the notion of anxiety as a drive is valid, then anxious subjects should be particularly susceptible to the effect: the too-high-drive individual is less able to contend with response confusion. High-anxiety subjects, then, not only should make more errors in the middle of a list than at the ends, but should make more errors in the middle than do low-anxiety subjects learning the same list. This is exactly what Phillips and colleagues found.

In learning any set of material or doing any task, the early stages involve sorting through a relatively large number of incorrect responses to find and set in the correct ones. Later in the learning process, the incorrect responses begin to drop out, and the learner is engaged more in practicing the correct responses that he has already learned. Here, too, the drive theory of anxiety fits experimental observations of anxious subjects. "Generally, it is found that anxiety will debilitate performance early in learning, whereas later in learning anxiety is less likely to hinder performance, and it may even facilitate performance" (Phillips et al., 1972, p. 435). I shall have more to say later about the implications of such a finding for students and for teachers.

One of the most common strategies employed by teachers in trying to get students to do well on a learning task is to motivate them, to try to involve them in the task by telling them how important it is. This strategy often backfires with highly anxious students; they tend to clutch up in situations where the stakes are high and perform rather badly. The drive theory provides one explanation of this behavior. In motivating a student by convincing him that his performance is important, we raise his drive level. If he is anxious, however, his drive level is already high, and motivating instructions have the effect of raising that drive level still further—to a point where it interferes with performance. Moreover, anxious learners tend to emit a particular kind of interfering response in highly motivated or ego-involving situations: they become so preoccupied with assessing their ongoing performance that they can't attend fully to the learning task itself. The more threatened they are by the task, the more involved they become in this self-monitoring process. Telling a student that it is important that he learn something well or that he do well in a particular test carries with it an implied threat that something bad will happen if he doesn't do well; thus most "motivating" instructions are indeed threatening. They are especially so to the high-anxiety student, who is predisposed to react to situations as if they were dangerous. Thus, the more anxious a student tends to be, the more he is likely to be hurt by instructions that emphasize the importance of a particular task or the degree to which that task reflects his overall competence or learning potential (Sarason, 1960, p. 411).

## Task Difficulty

As we learn more and more about the effects of anxiety on learning, it becomes evident that we need to know also about the effects of various learning situations on anxiety itself. We need to know what sorts of circumstances are most likely to throw an A-Trait individual into an A-State. One factor that seems important in this regard is the difficulty level of the materials to be learned; as you would expect, the more difficult tasks tend to increase the level of A-State in high-A-Trait students. In a study by O'Neil (1972), stress (in the form of negative feedback) was added to easy and difficult learning tasks, with interesting results. The high-A-Trait students were more affected by stress than were the low-A-Trait students in that their A-State levels rose more. But their performance on the learning task was not differentially affected. In other words, even though these students became more immediately anxious when they were told that they were doing badly, their actual performance was not changed. Whether the difficulty of the material or the relatively novel experimental situation (they were working in a computer-assisted learning setting) had already raised their A-State level to a point where further increases could have little effect or whether some other aspect of the task or instructions tended to damp down the negative effects of increased anxiety is not known. Clearly, further work on the anxiety–bad performance–anxiety cycle is needed if we are to help students to deal effectively with their anxiety level.

One other finding is of particular interest to the classroom teacher. The further along in school a child is, the more his school-connected anxiety level tends to interfere with achievement. That is, negative correlations between anxiety and achievement increase in the higher grade levels (Gaudry & Spielberger, 1971). This negative relationship is particularly evident in mathematics and math-related subjects in the later grades; early-grade children feel the most anxiety over (and experience the greatest interference with performance in) learning to read.

Phillips and colleagues (1972) have provided us with a comprehensive list of the consequences of anxiety in learning (see Table 10-1). As you look

*Table 10-1.* Proximal and distal consequences of anxiety

1. Some proximal consequences
   a. Cautiousness, perseveration, rigidity, stereotyped thinking
   b. Dependency, direction seeking, conforming tendencies
   c. Reduced responsiveness to the environment
   d. Interference with a variety of cognitive and mediational processes
   e. Increased drive or motivational level
2. Some distal consequences
   a. Deterioration in complex intellectual, problem-solving, achievement, and learning activities
   b. Increased responsiveness to reinforcement
   c. Increased susceptibility to persuasion and the behavior of models
   d. Preoccupation with demands of self rather than the demands of learning situations, leading to reduced incidental learning, and so on
   e. Increased isolation from others, with heightened affiliation needs
   f. Enhanced learning of certain types of tasks

From "Intervention in Relation to Anxiety in School," by B. N. Phillips, R. P. Martin, and J. Meyers. In C. E. Spielberger (Ed.), *Anxiety: Current Trends in Theory & Research* (Vol. 2). Copyright 1972 by Academic Press. Reprinted by permission.

at these items, notice that not all of them are detrimental to the learning process. It may be that anxious individuals don't necessarily have more problems with learning than non- or less-anxious individuals, but just different kinds of problems.

## Test Anxiety

One of the particularly perplexing problems for teachers is the student who seems to do quite well on daily work but cannot perform well in a test situation. Many students fall victim to test anxiety; it occurs at all stages of the educational process, from elementary school through graduate work. Typically, the test-anxious individual reports that he knows the material well, but when confronted by the test he "forgets" everything or he "can't figure out how to say it." As soon as he leaves the testing situation, the "forgotten" material comes flooding back to him.

"A number of writers have viewed test anxiety as a proneness to emit self-centered, interfering responses when confronted with evaluative conditions. This [stimulus-response] interpretation typically has emphasized two response components. One is autonomic activity—sweating, accelerated heart rate, etc. The other concerns cognitive events, for example, saying to oneself while taking an entrance examination, 'I am stupid,'

'Maybe I won't pass' " (Sarason, 1972, p. 383). The test-anxious individual enters the testing situation viewing it as dangerous and threatening. From what we know of anxiety in general, we can assume that he is likely to see himself as relatively helpless in the situation. In response to these perceptions, his autonomic nervous system sets up defenses: he begins to sweat, and his heart starts to beat faster. Conscious awareness of this physical reaction makes him feel even more anxious. He worries about his own condition—particularly if he has been bothered by test anxiety before—to the point that he can no longer concentrate on the test itself, and thus the prophecy is self-fulfilled; "Maybe I won't be able to" becomes "I can't."

The test-anxious student is different from his more relaxed counterpart in two ways: what he attends to in his (internal and external) environment, and how he uses the information he gets. The test-anxious student attends to stimuli that have little or nothing to do with helping him pass his test; he focuses on the threatening aspects of the situation rather than on those things that he knows and can do well. He is *stimulus bound* as well: confronted with a question or problem that he can't handle, he tends to stay with that problem rather than to move on to others that might be easier for him. And he interprets selectively the information he does have; he attends primarily to those things that reinforce his prediction that he will do poorly.

A consistent theme among test-anxious individuals is the high degree of ego involvement they feel in the testing situation. Test-anxious students not only fear failure but believe that to fail is to demonstrate a fundamental kind of inadequacy. Along with this attitude toward failure runs a deep-seated distrust of their basic ability. The test-anxious student may say to his teacher "I really know this material well; I just can't handle the test"; but in fact his fear of failure and inadequacy is likely to extend far beyond test performance. And the more evidence there is that the test is in fact important, the more debilitating his anxiety is likely to be.

One obvious and immediate implication for the teacher is the doubt that findings about test anxiety throw on IQ test data—particularly IQ tests of the paper-and-pencil sort where no one-to-one interaction with the tester can be expected to reduce test anxiety. What kind of test could be more threatening, more ego involving, to the test-anxious individual than an intelligence test? It measures (or so many students believe) one's total competence, one's total intellectual worth; a low IQ score can be an ominous predictor of school failure, job dissatisfaction, and overall misery. We can hardly be surprised at studies that report that anxious subjects do less well than nonanxious subjects on tests labeled "intelligence tests" (Firetto, Walker, & Davey, 1972). Perhaps more interesting is the fact that careful measures of general A-Trait, as opposed to specific test anxiety, are not related to intelligence test scores (Sarason, 1960). In other words, intelligence (as a personality characteristic or enduring quality) does not seem to be related to one's proneness to become anxious. However, if we compare people who get anxious about tests with people who don't get anxious about tests, the test-anxious people look less intelligent. The appearance is almost certainly deceptive since the test anxiety is interfering with specific test performance rather than with general intellectual ability.

It would be easy to conclude, from what we know of anxiety in general and test anxiety in particular, that testing situations should be made as nonthreatening and as non-ego-involving as possible. Here again, though, we must hesitate: such a procedure would be helpful to the high-anxiety individual, but what would it do to the low-anxiety student? Achievement-orienting instructions may be the only way to get the low-anxiety student (particularly if he is bright) to perform up to potential. The motivational level of the low scorer may spurt when he is given reason to believe that a strong effort is needed or expected; it may fall when he is given information that suggests his level of performance is not of great interest or importance. The high-anxiety student is not always at the greatest disadvantage; too much drive may be preferable to too little. Even though test anxiety often hinders performance, under some circumstances it may help. "High have been found more responsive than low test-anxious subjects to reinforcements given in verbal conditioning experiments. . . . This would seem to suggest that when there are visible cues in the environment to problem solution, the high test-anxious person's vigilance pays off" (Sarason, 1972, p. 388). Rather than belittling the importance of a given test (which probably won't fool the test-anxious student anyhow), we should perhaps concentrate on helping him to focus on appropriate, task-relevant stimuli. In this way, his high drive level might turn to his advantage.

## Sex Differences

A number of studies have attempted to determine whether anxiety in general, as well as test anxiety, is more prevalent among girls or boys. According to Phillips and colleagues (1972), girls tend to score consistently higher than boys on measures of test anxiety, school anxiety, and general anxiety. This finding is supported by the work of Doyal and Forsyth (1972), who tested third-grade children under nonanxious conditions and then retested them in an anxiety-producing situation. The girls scored higher in the nonanxious situation, while the boys did better in the anxious condition. If we interpret these results according to drive theory, it appears that the girls were sufficiently anxious even in the low-anxiety condition so that they worked hard and did well, while the high-anxiety situation raised their drive level to the point where performance was hampered. The boys, however, started out at a very low drive level; low levels of anxiety did not motivate them, and it was not until they experienced high levels of anxiety that their performance was facilitated.

Other theorists, however, suggest that the sex/anxiety relationship is not as simple as it might appear at first glance. Most measures of both A-

State and A-Trait in children depend on self-report: the children answer questions about their feelings, and these answers are taken as indicators of the degree of anxiety the child experiences. There are, in our culture, important differences in the social acceptability of anxious feelings for boys and for girls. It is often considered acceptable or even desirable for a girl to feel upset, scared, or afraid, but boys are "supposed to" be brave, strong, and unafraid. Thus differences in scores on self-report measures may be merely a reflection of cultural stereotypes rather than indicators of true differences in feelings or responses. As Phillips and colleagues (1972) point out, sex differences in levels of anxiety and in relations between anxiety and functioning may be attributable to the boys' not wanting to admit the anxiety they feel. For boys, such admission would be socially disapproved as unmasculine; for girls, the admission or nonadmission of anxiety carries no similar implications regarding their femininity.

Carrying this line of reasoning a step further, we can hypothesize that the anxiety of boys may have more to do with their sex role than with questions of intellectual ability. Sex-role questions tend to be more salient for boys than for girls; tomboys are more easily tolerated in this culture than sissies. Phillips and his colleagues, in support of this hypothesis, found that boys who failed to adopt masculine behaviors between the ages of 3 and 10 were likely to have high sex anxiety as adults, but that sex-role behaviors of girls were not highly related to later sex anxiety.

Boys, then, may be in general just as anxious as girls, but their anxiety may relate to different kinds of behavior and/or situational threats. Mann (1972), who found that a history of residential mobility was a predictor of low anxiety levels in male college students but not in females, hypothesized that sex-role demands on females were relatively well defined and unchanging across many residential settings. Sex-role demands for boys, in contrast, may vary considerably from place to place. The boy whose family moves often must therefore deal with greater ambiguity (and anxiety) about his role as a consequence of the moves. Mann concludes that boys, through frequent changes of residence, develop better strategies for coping with uncertainty and anxiety than do girls, for whom residential changes do not imply role changes. There is, however, another way of looking at Mann's finding. Role expectations for boys in our culture tend to be relatively explicit. The boy may not like or be comfortable with these expectations, but there is little doubt as to what they are. If the expectations vary from place to place, he may, in moving from one place to another, sooner or later find a particular definition with which he is comfortable; this discovery should reduce his anxiety about himself in that sex role. Even if the male sex-role demands are fairly consistent in different residences, frequent moves give the boy a chance to start over without having to live down whatever mistakes he may have made in sex-role orientation in the past. For girls the situation is different: increasingly, sex-role expectations for women are vague, undefined, and conflicting. Women are portrayed, in the old stereotype, as dependent, fearful, suited only for homemaking and child rearing. This same stereotype condemns the professionally successful woman as unfeminine if not perverted. At the same time, the women's movement has been at least partially successful in breaking down the stereotype, in helping women (and men) to feel free to choose any career goal they wish and to view the professional woman as potentially both competent and feminine. These conflicting views make for a highly ambiguous set of sex-role expectations and self-perceptions for the young girl, and a change of residence is not likely to clarify things much. Residential mobility may allay boys' anxiety but not girls' anxiety simply because a new setting does not remove sex-role conflict for girls as it may for boys.

Anxiety about sex role, about academic achievement, about test taking, or about anything else arises in the context of past and present interactions with one's environment. We have already discussed the role of the parents and of other significant adults in contributing to the "habit" of anxiety in children. To the degree that boys and girls are treated differently and must respond to different sets of behavioral expectations, we can expect their anxiety patterns to be different. Particularly in the area of school achievement, different expectations have been placed on boys and girls. We are all familiar, for instance, with the notion that girls are not expected to do well in math and science. Not only in the academic arena but in other aspects of school life—classroom discussions, gym classes, playground activities—boys and girls receive consistently different sets of behavioral rewards. As a result of this differential treatment, it is highly likely that boys and girls, while displaying the same general relationship between anxiety and achievement, will differ greatly in the dynamics of those anxieties. The relationship varies "as a function of complex situational factors, such as the sex of the teacher or a teacher's value system. For example, in a classroom where there is a female teacher who allows girls to be dependent, and who sees high achievement as more important for boys than for girls, the negative relationship between anxiety and achievement may be stronger for boys than for girls" (Gaudry & Spielberger, 1971, p. 37). As our culture explores changing role patterns for men and women, we may expect the sex/anxiety relationship to continue to be unstable. In time, one hopes, we shall emerge from this period of change and growth with a healthier set of sex-role values for both men and women and a consequent decrease in sex-role anxiety. For the present, though, the question of "what is expected of me because I am a boy/girl" will continue to be a source of anxiety for many young people.

## COPING WITH ANXIETY

To the degree that anxiety interferes with the learning process, the teacher must be concerned with allaying it. As a human involved with the joy and pain of other humans who also happen to be students, the teacher will probably want to help those students to deal with their anxiety even when it does not seem to be interfering with learning. Many implications for anxiety reduction are inherent in the facts and the hypotheses that we have been looking at; in this section we shall consider some of those implications as well as some relatively new ideas.

### Conscious and Unconscious Processes

People—most people—learn to handle their anxieties without specific help from others. Aside from a few bits of folk wisdom (or unwisdom) such as "don't dwell on things" and "you'll feel better about it in the morning," most of us encounter little advice specifically designed to help us deal with anxiety. Yet we do somehow learn coping mechanisms that allow us to keep our anxiety at a bearable—and frequently unnoticeable—level. One group of investigators suggests that a major mechanism in the "natural" handling of anxiety may be dreaming. "Thinking about a stressful experience or discussing it with other people may facilitate adaptation, but anxious brooding, usually accompanied by sleep disturbance, indicates the limitations of conscious thinking as a mechanism of adaptation" (Greenberg, Pillard, & Pearlman, 1972, p. 261). According to these researchers, one's daily experience often arouses repressed conflicts or feelings; this arousal of old problems that have been repressed causes the feeling of anxiety. In dreaming, the repressed material interacts with the new perceptions, and defenses against anxiety are set up at an unconscious level. In order to test this hypothesis, Greenberg and his colleagues devised a Machiavellian experiment. They first exposed adult subjects to an anxiety-producing experience (they viewed a medical school film of an autopsy). Then half the subjects were not allowed to dream during the following night; they were awakened every time they entered the rapid-eye-movement stage that usually accompanies dreaming. The other half were allowed to dream, though they were awakened from nondreaming sleep occasionally so that they had about the same total amount of sleep as the experimental group. On the following day, both groups saw the autopsy film again; the nondreaming subjects, as predicted, experienced significantly higher anxiety levels than the subjects who had been allowed to dream. Perhaps "you'll feel better about it in the morning" is indeed a wise piece of advice! Unconscious processes are highly complex and manage to accomplish tasks that often surprise us. As we continue to learn more about these processes, we will likely develop more efficient ways of dealing with anxiety at an unconscious level—or of dealing with unconscious anxiety, which may amount to the same thing.

There is no clear dividing line between the conscious and the unconscious. Many of the activities of the unconscious have consciously observable effects; and the conscious mind is frequently able to influence or direct unconscious processes. One example of this influence is in relaxation. We are frequently unaware of being tense or tight; maintaining our musculature in this state of readiness is generally an unconscious process. Yet, when the tension is called to our attention, we can often relax it by a conscious effort. Since tension is an important part of the anxiety cycle (I am anxious, and this makes me tense, and the proprioceptive perception of my own tension adds to my feelings of anxiety), learning to relax physically is one way of coping with anxiety feelings. Such relaxation can be achieved by dealing with it directly, as in the systematic desensitization techniques of behavior therapy (here phobic subjects are taught to relax in the real or imagined presence of a feared object and thus are helped to lose the fear of it), or indirectly, by providing the anxious individual with other activities that help him to become less tense. As an example of a tension-reducing activity, Gaudry and Spielberger (1971) allowed students to write comments on their exam papers. Highly test-anxious students are quite tense, and giving them an opportunity to comment on the test itself, where it is clearly understood that the comments will not be evaluated, might make them less so. In Gaudry and Spielberger's experiment, the scores of anxious subjects did improve when comments were solicited. Moreover, the improvement showed up in response to questions subsequent to the one the comment was written about, suggesting that the relaxation may have a cumulative effect over time.

## Techniques

As we have noted previously, one of the basic cognitive aspects of anxiety is a feeling of helplessness. The anxious person feels threatened by an uncertain future and feels powerless to do anything about it. Helping him to change that self-perception of helplessness is probably the single most effective way to deal with anxiety. The basic approach is twofold. First, provision of knowledge regarding a stressful situation reduces a part of the threat that results from uncertainty. Second, providing help in the development of techniques for coping allows the anxious person to actively and constructively participate in the situation rather than to simply endure it. This channeling of stress into constructive avenues should also help to reduce anxiety (Phillips et al., 1972).

Coping techniques may involve ways of dealing with one's feelings as such, or they may involve ways of interacting with the external world and thus of handling the anxiety-producing situation. And it doesn't particularly matter whether the objectively real danger is in fact lessened by the interaction; it seems to be more the feeling of "I am doing something about it" that allows anxiety to subside. I know a woman who became disturbed about the continuing Arab-Israeli conflict. She was suddenly overwhelmed by a sense of personal vulnerability. If the conflict should precipitate global war, she and her family would die. They had no protection; there was nothing they could do. It was not so much the notion of being killed that bothered her, but rather the thought of sitting helplessly and waiting for it.

Shortly after she began to experience these feelings, she and her husband built a new home. In the basement they constructed a fallout shelter and stocked it with provisions. She reported that her anxiety disappeared as a result. She knew that the fallout shelter was not a real solution; that, even supposing it could save lives during an atomic war, the chances of later survival were low. But the fact of having done something—anything—to deal with the situation reduced her sense of helplessness and thus lowered her anxiety level.

Now, all of us can't afford to go out and build fallout shelters whenever we feel anxious. But we can construct behavior patterns—rituals, if you will—that serve as symbolic fallout shelters in dealing with damaging anxiety. Some students, for instance, make a practice of yawning several times before going in to an exam. Yawning relaxes the throat muscles and thus may have a direct effect on the physiological components of anxiety. More importantly, however, the student is not helpless in the face of his emotions: he has a way of coping, of dealing with them. Many kinds of behaviors, from blinking or yawning to complicated patterns of activities, can be used as anxiety reducers. Often we discover accidentally that a particular way of coping seems to work in an anxiety situation, and we deliberately use it again the next time we feel threatened. The reason why learned, organized behaviors are, in fact, inhibitors of distress or anxiety is that they provide the kind of completion or substitution pathway necessary to avoid the feeling of helplessness that comes from interruption and from the absence of relevant coping skills (Mandler, 1972).

### Classroom Strategies

Feelings of helplessness and threat tend to create anxiety. Learning situations can create such feelings, especially when the student is faced with new and (apparently) difficult materials. Most learning is harder at the beginning of the learning sequence than at later stages, so the anxiety-prone student is likely to be turned off by such new materials before he has a chance to wade in and discover for himself that he can handle them. Programmed-instruction methods would seem to be one way of dealing with this problem. In programmed instruction, new information is presented in small increments, with care being taken to provide the student with a relatively constant experience of success in mastering each step. High-anxiety students do seem to do better than low-anxiety students under programmed-instruction methods, in contrast with their performance under the more traditional teacher-directed methods (Gaudry & Spielberger, 1971). We might hypothesize that it is not only the experience of success and the reduction of threat that help the high-anxiety student in programmed instruction, but also his physical ability to relax more in this relatively noncompetitive situation. Also, as Phillips and his colleagues (1972) note, providing reinforcement and feedback helps reduce the ambiguity of the situation and thus counteracts the potentially debilitating effects of anxiety. Programmed instruction, providing feedback at every step, seems ideally suited to the learning needs of high-A-Trait students.

Short-term memory is adversely affected by anxiety. Anxious individuals have trouble memorizing things as well as retrieving things that have been memorized previously. Failures of memory, in turn, are threatening; again, the person is made even more anxious by the effects of his initial anxiety. Memory training is one way to break the anxiety cycle; by providing the anxious individual with techniques for improving memory, we can not only deal directly with that effect of anxiety but again give him a sense of his own effectiveness, his ability to cope. Comment Gaudry and Spielberger (1971, p. 29) "Mnemonic devices, diagrams and outlines, and detailed systems for organizing general ideas could all be quite useful in helping the high-anxious student perform up to his full potential." Providing external memory aids, too, can be helpful—giving an open-book exam, for instance, instead of insisting that students rely on their own memories for information. The highly test-anxious student may be gradually weaned from his anxiety; as he experiences success in the less threatening open-book situation, he becomes more and more able to face evaluation of other kinds without becoming anxious.

In a study reported by Sarason (1972), students were given a six-hour training program in techniques for attending to or concentrating on test materials rather than on their own personal reactions to the test. The treatment both reduced reported feelings of anxiety and improved the level of performance on several different tasks. Here again, we can see a dual effect: the intervention goes directly to one of the debilitating aspects of anxiety (in this case, inability to focus on test materials because of interference from self-oriented perceptions), and, in dealing with this aspect successfully, the student gains a sense of his ability to cope, of reduced helplessness.

Interventions and techniques of these sorts are not difficult to work out; the teacher should have little trouble in adapting such ideas or in using his understanding of anxiety to find other techniques for helping students to contend with their anxieties. It is important, though, that we not deal with "cures" to the neglect of prevention. By teaching coping skills to young children, who have not yet developed well-formed anxiety habits, we may be able to prevent such habits from ever developing. A child who does not develop painful anxiety reactions is preferable to a child who experiences painful anxiety but has learned to cope with it.

One last word of caution: we must remember that many of the techniques and interventions that are helpful for high-anxiety students may lead to reduced performance in low-anxiety students. Low-anxiety people do not perform as well in programmed learning, for instance, as they do in teacher-directed settings. Nor is their test performance improved (and indeed, it may be hurt) when they are encouraged to write comments about the test questions. In our zeal to help the anxious student, we must keep in mind that the low-A-Trait student has needs too. Identifying the anxiety-prone student and providing him with special helps or making such helps available to all students if they choose to make use of them would seem to be the best solution.

It is easy to label anxiety as bad, as a state that must be avoided whenever possible. Both researchers and philosophers, however, would seem to question such a position. The extremely low-anxiety individual has problems too; he has trouble motivating himself and finds it difficult to respond to positive feedback in constructive ways. Not to experience anxiety is not to experience growth since we learn and grow through overcoming our own helplessness. Snyder (in press), describing the philosophy of Rollo May, sums it up: "The positive aspects of selfhood develop as the individual confronts, moves through, and overcomes anxiety-creating experiences. If there is no working through or moving through anxiety, guilt, responsibility, the person gives up his freedom and constricts his autonomy and self awareness as well as his development." Or, at a more prosaic level, we might say that anxiety is like salt: too much of it can utterly ruin a meal, but a little is needed to give things flavor.

## QUESTIONS FOR UNDERSTANDING

1.  Discuss the elements of helplessness, uncertainty, future orientation, and symbolization breakdown as they enter into the following situations: (a) an only child on the first day of kindergarten; (b) a 13-year-old who is to play the lead in a major school play, the day before opening night; (c) a high school senior preparing to take a series of college entrance exams.
2.  You are a third-grade teacher in a small-town elementary school. The parents of one of your students, a tense and anxious boy, have asked you for advice in helping their son with his emotional problems. What will you ask/tell them?
3.  Recall the last time you felt really anxious. How did your feelings affect the way you interacted with people? The way they responded to you?
4.  As a teacher, it will be necessary for you to evaluate the progress of your students from time to time. How will you plan such evaluations so as to minimize the negative effects of anxiety?
5.  Describe a specific helping strategy that might be effective with each of the following individuals: (a) a second-grade boy who is constantly being teased about being a sissy and who is anxious about his sex-role behavior, (b) a student in an 11th-grade physical education class who complains that he does fine when practicing alone but falls apart whenever anyone watches him, (c) a bright but underachieving eighth grader who seems unwilling or unable to work on class assignments until it is too late to do a good job with them.

# Chapter 11

# Locus of Control

"Children get into trouble because their parents punish them too much."

"People's misfortunes result from the mistakes they make."

"Without the right breaks one cannot be an effective leader."

"The average citizen can have an influence in government decisions."

These statements (from Rotter, 1966) are the kind you would be asked to agree or disagree with if you were to take a test to determine your per-

ceived *locus of control.* If you look carefully at them, you can probably see what they have in common: each of them has to do with how much a person himself, as opposed to outside forces or influences, determines what happens to him. This is the essence of the locus-of-control concept—that each of us locates the controlling elements in our lives either inside ourselves or outside ourselves. The person who believes that he can decide for himself what he will do or be, that he is the "captain of his soul," locates his control internally; the person who believes that what happens to him is largely a matter of luck or who depends on the decisions of others is locating his control externally.

The notion of locus of control originated with J. B. Rotter, who wrote his original monograph on the subject in 1966. A number of psychologists were intrigued with the ideas that Rotter presented, and a great deal of research has been done and is still going on in this area. Rotter's original definition of internal and external control is worth quoting at the outset: "When a reinforcement is perceived by the subject as following some action of his own but not being entirely contingent on his action, then, in our culture, it is typically perceived as the result of luck, chance, fate, as under the control of powerful others, or as unpredictable because of the great complexity of the forces surrounding him. When the event is interpreted in this way by an individual, we have labeled this a belief in *external control.* If the person perceives that the event is contingent on his own behavior or his own relatively permanent characteristics, we have termed this a belief in *internal control*" (1966, p. 1). Notice that Rotter's definition does not deal directly with whether a person feels in control of his own behavior but with whether he believes he can control his reinforcements. Much of the more recent research in locus of control fails to make this distinction and defines internals and externals as we did in the opening paragraph. Now, if we are thoroughgoing behaviorists, we can say that reinforcements control behavior, and therefore having control over reinforcements is tantamount to controlling the behavior that precedes those reinforcements; the distinction will be a trivial one. Nevertheless, it is well to remember that the original concept, the original measurements, and the data supporting the validity and consistency of locus of control as a characteristic of human personality all dealt with control of reinforcements—control of what happened to one—rather than control of what one did.

A more serious error, and one often made by students, is to understand locus of control as having to do with whether a person is actually in control of his own behavior. Some of the research is written in a kind of shorthand jargon that contributes to this misconception; authors speak of externals and internals or, even more misleading, of externally and internally controlled individuals. Locus of control refers to what the individual believes about who is in charge, what he perceives to be the extent of his own power to control his life. It does not refer to what is actually true, or how much power an individual objectively has. Kings, dictators, and corporation executives can be (and have been) Externals; while prisoners, slaves, and paralytics can be (and have been) Internals. My locus of control depends on what I believe to be true and not necessarily on what *is* true about my power to influence or control my world.

Locus of control is of particular importance to educators because it bears on a host of other behaviors. A child's (or an adult's) perception of who is in control affects the way he deals with other people, the way he approaches his academic tasks, and the way he feels about himself as a human being. There is even some evidence that this variable may affect all other psychological research. Felton (1971) reports that experimenters who see themselves as Internally controlled are more likely to get significant results in their studies than those who are Externals, and that External subjects tend to yield data that agree with the experimenter's hypotheses! Of more direct concern to us as teachers is the relationship between Internality-Externality and learning. Rotter suggests that all research in learning should be evaluated according to the subjects' position on the Internal-External continuum. Internals respond to various learning conditions and contingencies differently from Externals, and the wise teacher or researcher takes these differences into account.

We might note, parenthetically, that the average position of students on the Internal-External continuum seems to be shifting toward an External orientation (J. M. Schneider, 1971; Ulan, 1971; Steger, Simmons, & Lavelle, 1973b). To be Internally oriented, to believe oneself capable and responsible for one's own behavior, is still seen as a socially desirable state (Joe, 1972), but the degree to which young people feel that way seems to be lessening. As we shall see in the next pages, such a shift may have serious implications for academic and interpersonal and general social behavior.

A number of researchers have questioned whether locus of control is too broad a term; they have suggested that it might be better (and more accurate) to break down the concepts Internal and External into component parts. Levenson (1973), for instance, maintains that Externals may be of two different sorts: people who believe the world is unordered (that things happen by chance) behave and think differently from people who believe the world is ordered but that powerful others are in control. This notion has led to the development of Powerful Others and Chance scales, which supposedly differentiate these two External orientations.

At the other end of the continuum, researchers have developed a test that distinguishes between the Internal who takes responsibility primarily for his successes (I+) and the Internal who blames himself for his failures (I-) (Crandall, Katkovsky, & Crandall, 1965). These two types have been shown to follow different developmental courses and to behave differently in the classroom (Buck & Austrin, 1971).

In spite of these possible subdivisions, most work on locus of control continues to address overall Internal-External differences. With regard to Internality, a study using responses of agreement or disagreement with familiar proverbs supported the notion that Internals did constitute a unitary group—that is, all the Internals responded in similar ways to the test proverbs. It would seem that while the concepts Internal and External can (and sometimes should) be broken down into meaningful subconcepts, there is still value in considering overall differences between the two. To use a crude analogy, meats can be broken down into beef, pork, lamb, and so on; and vegetables include such various things as potatoes and beans and rutabaga; but valid and useful comparisons can still be made between the two major categories. We shall concentrate, in this chapter, on the general Internal-External continuum and its importance to the learning process; but the reader should stop once in a while to remind himself that an occasional mashed rutabaga or lamb cutlet may not be quite the same as the other members of its general class.

## DEVELOPMENT OF A LOCUS OF CONTROL

### Age

The overall relationship between age and locus of control is clear and consistent: the older the child, the more Internal he is likely to be (Rotter, 1966; Distefano, Pryer, & Smith, 1971). This seems a logical enough reaction to the reality of the child's life situation. Small children do, in fact, have less control over their environment than older ones; they are less capable of influencing events, and they also are less able to understand why things happen as they do. As the child grows and matures, his area of control broadens. He learns to handle his own body; he begins to move about and manipulate his physical environment; gradually he develops skill in interacting with and influencing other people. He changes from a relatively helpless receiver to an active doer and initiator. It is not surprising, then, that his perception of being in control should reflect the objective truth of his growing abilities.

There is some evidence that exercise of competence and influence over others continues to increase the feeling of being in control well into adult life. A study of administrators in government departments (Harvey, 1971) indicates that the longer a man has been in an administrative position, the more Internal he is likely to be. We must note, however, that this result is confounded with age: men who have been in administrative jobs a long time are usually older than their less experienced counterparts. Internality scores may tend to increase with age well into adult life, given reasonably favorable experiences.

### Parent Influences

Age alone cannot account for all—or even most—differences in locus of control, for children within any age group show a broad range of Internal-External scores. We must look to other variables to help us understand how such differences come about. As might be expected, the kind of relationship a child has with his parents seems to be quite important here.

If one's perception of locus of control is based in part on external reality, we should expect that children of highly controlling, authoritarian parents would be more External than children reared in more permissive environments. A study by Pruitt (1971) lends some support to this notion; he found that black teenage boys who described their mothers as democratic tended to be more Internal than those who described their mothers as authoritarian. Moreover, a measure of the mothers' actual attitudes indicated that mothers of External boys valued techniques of authoritarian control more than did the Internal boys' mothers. A final interesting, though not surprising, finding of Pruitt's was that Internal-External scores of the boys and their mothers tended to correlate with each other; that is, External mothers tend to have External children. The parent who, as a child, was highly controlled and thus came to think of himself as relatively powerless, tends to use the same sorts of child-rearing techniques on his own children.

The similarity between parent and child Internal-External orientation is partly a matter of modeling: we learn how to be parents by imitating the ways in which our own parents behave. There is also, however, a direct influence of the parents' locus of control on the parents' own behavior. Internals, who believe that they can and do influence other people, tend to use "soft" influence techniques like praise or persuasion. Externals, in contrast, have less faith in their effectiveness as controllers, and their techniques tend to be harsher and more coercive (Goodstadt & Hjelle, 1973). If we put these contrasting techniques in the context of parent-child relations, it follows that parents who are themselves Externals tend to be harsher and more controlling in dealing with their children; and these very kinds of parental behaviors lead to Externality in the child. Thus External or Internal orientations are passed along from generation to generation.

Levenson (1973), differentiating between different kinds of Externality, also notes that belief in control by powerful others may be associated with kinds of parental control that are different from those associated with belief in chance. Individuals who score high on the Powerful Others scale describe their parents as demanding and punishing. The flavor of the way in which parents control these children is subtly different from the way in which parents control high Chance-scoring children; parents of high Chance-scoring children use what may be described as social-emotional punishments: social isolation and deprivation of emotional supports. Levenson speculates that using such personal punishments as not letting one be with friends and not letting one use favorite things may result in a child's withdrawing from close interpersonal relationships and his forming a view of the world as inconsistent and unreliable.

Parents of high Chance-scoring children punish their children by depriving them not only of their friends or their favorite things but also of the parents themselves. These parents do not comfort their children; they are often not available when the children need them. A parent who is preoccupied with other concerns, who only occasionally takes time for his children, or who vacillates between irritation and affection creates an environment in which the child sees himself as lucky when he is praised, cuddled, or attended to. From his point of view, there is no consistency or predictability in the relationship; whether a particular behavior will bring a cuff or a kiss is purely a matter of chance. Small wonder, then, that this sort of environment breeds Externals. Before he has had a chance to venture out of his home into a wider world, the child has learned very well that he is powerless to influence the single most important thing in his life—his parents' love.

It is possible for parents to use a kind of pseudoaffection as a means of controlling their children. The smother mother, who cannot allow her child to assume any responsibility, exemplifies this kind of parenting. Although smothering a child with affection is, in many ways, the opposite of ignoring him or being inconsistent in nurturing behaviors, a smothering nurturance also tends to produce External children. In a study by MacDonald (1971), External college students described their parents as being highly nurturant in the sense of overprotective and controlling. Internals, however, described their parents as warm and consistent and as encouraging them to be responsible for their own reinforcements. In general, then, parental nurturance tends to lead to Internality in children when the nurturance is consistent, is supportive, and encourages the child to move out on his own; it tends to lead to Externality when it is overprotective and controlling. Externality is also fostered when the parents are nonnurturant, either through ignoring the child or through being overly harsh and demanding. Joe (1971, p. 624), after an exhaustive review of locus-of-control literature, sums up the influence of style of parenting this way: "the parent who is warm, supportive, permissible, flexible, approving, consistent in discipline, and who expects early independence behaviors from his child is more likely to encourage his child's belief in internal control than is the parent who is rejecting, dominating, and critical."

To the extent that parents treat girl children differently from boy children, generalizations about parent attitudes and children's locus of control may not hold up. There is some evidence, for example, that girls who are only children are more External than girls who have brothers and sisters; but male only children tend to be more Internal than boys with brothers and sisters (Marks, 1972). Is this perhaps because the male only child is encouraged to go out and "make a success of himself" (to an even greater degree than would be the case if he had brothers to share the responsibility), while the female only child is more likely to be overprotected? This notion is partially supported by Levenson (1973), who found that males who were helped and taught by their mothers had higher Internal scores than did those who didn't get such help, but that girls who perceived that their mothers did not worry about them had significantly higher Internal scores than those who thought their mothers were protective. When the home environment is somewhat rejecting, says Levenson, the daughter may be forced to be more independent (Internal) to satisfy her needs.

Clearly, the relationships here are complex, and a great deal more information is needed before we can draw firm conclusions. We know—or at least have strong evidence to support our belief—that parents who encourage and support a child's efforts to be responsible for his own behaviors facilitate the development of Internal attitudes. But we are less certain about when that kind of encouragement and support (and by which parent, and toward which child) may be experienced as rejection or smothering or manipulative control—all of which tend to move the child in the opposite direction, toward an External locus of control.

Parents are only one of a number of influences on the growing child. Neighborhood, school, peer group, extended family—all these can help to create or to destroy a sense of personal effectiveness. In all, the same kinds of relationship seem to hold: environments that are harshly controlling or unpredictable and capricious tend to create Externals, while environments that are stable, dependable, and approving tend to create Internals. The inner-city environment is, on every count, a prime source of External influence. The crowded living quarters, the poverty, the complexity of relationships, and the harsh punishments often meted out for transgressions all make for a sense of personal helplessness. "Children in this situation . . . may perceive events as being unpredictable and beyond their control and may as a result feel helpless or powerless to do anything constructive about their condition" (Nowicki & Barnes, 1973, p. 247).

Even in these few pages, my own bias (which is shared with many researchers in this area) is apparent: I believe that an Internal locus of control is better than an External one. I believe that it is better in the sense that it is more adaptive; its holder is more able to deal effectively and constructively with his own life situation. Let's turn now to some of the evidence that bears directly on this value judgment. Just what does being an Internal or an External mean for a person? We shall look first at social behavior and how it is influenced by one's locus of control.

## SOCIAL BEHAVIOR

### Choice of Friends

Internals, according to Silverman and Shrauger (1971), both expect to be able to control other people and need to control other people. That is, their view of the world and themselves in the world demands that they be able to exert influence; they must act rather than be acted on. Given this kind of orientation, we might expect that Internals would seek out people who allowed themselves to be controlled, that they would prefer Externals for friends rather than other Internals. However, some evidence indicates that people generally tend to prefer the company of similar others; this finding would lead us to predict that Internals would seek out the friendship of other Internals rather than of Externals. Silverman and Shrauger were unable to demonstrate which of these two hypotheses was true; their data gave no consistent and significant correlations between Internal-External ratings and liking for similar or dissimilar people. However, the ratings suggested that Internals and Externals both liked to be with Internals. Externals seemed to be torn between being comfortable with other people who were similar to them and enjoying the company of "assertive, successful, intelligent, self-confident" people. We might ask whether these data are influenced by the factor of social desirability. In our culture, people are "supposed to be" intelligent, self-confident, and so forth. Moreover, we are "supposed to" like such people. It is likely that an External, even though he might feel more comfortable in the company of other Externals, would rather be seen (and see himself) as preferring friends whose descriptions fit this socially acceptable pattern.

Confusing the picture still further is the fact that we frequently do not assess the personality characterisitics of others accurately. Does one's own Internality or Externality affect the degree to which he sees others as Internal or External? According to Hannah (1973), it most definitely does. Hannah found that most of his Internal subjects rated others as more External than they themselves were, but that the Externals did not rate others as more Internal. These findings can be interpreted to mean that Internals, with a strong belief in personal responsibility, believe that others feel less responsible for their outcomes. Externals, however, with little felt personal responsibility, perceive others as having similar feelings. One catches an almost arrogant flavor in the Internal, as if his need to control and to feel in control demands that he see himself as slightly above (or at least apart from) the throngs of sheeplike others with whom he is surrounded. In contrast, the External does not see his lack of control as due to personal inadequacy; that's just the way the world is. The External does not see others as more Internal than himself (even if they are) because the possibility of Internality is not a part of his world picture. Internals are likely to feel drawn to, but also somewhat threatened by, other Internals (while somewhat irresponsible, they are at least less so than Externals). Externals seem to be drawn to Internals too, but they are less able to give the reasons for their attraction.

## Influence and Control

If Externals enjoy being around Internals, who can control them, we should expect to see in Externals a willingness to be controlled. Externals, we might expect, would tend to be conformers, followers rather than leaders. This prediction can be made simply on the basis of the nature of the

Internal-External dimension, without regard for social preferences: individuals who feel that events are manipulated mainly by external forces should be less likely to rely strongly on their own beliefs about a situation and thus be more likely to conform to the opinion of others or to the commonly accepted view of a phenomenon (Lotsof & Steinke, 1973). Research results tend to confirm such a hypothesis: in the laboratory situation, at least, Externals are more influenceable, more responsive to pressure, than Internals.

Rotter reported in his original monograph (1966) that Internals actively resist being conditioned or manipulated. A study by Biondo and MacDonald (1971) compared the responses of Internals and Externals under two levels of social pressure. When the pressure to conform was low, Externals went along with it more often than Internals, who tended not to change at all. Under high-pressure conditions, the Externals again yielded, but the Internals were often reactive—that is, they changed in the opposite direction from that of the pressure. A study by Doctor (1971) shows the same kind of reactivity among Internals in a conditioned learning situation. In Doctor's study, one group of subjects knew what the experimenter was trying to get them to do, while another group did not. Under both conditions, External subjects learned (were conditioned) more readily than Internals. But the greatest differences between Externals and Internals occurred in the "aware" condition. Here, the External subjects seemed to be trying to help the experimenter, to perform in such a way as to make his results come out as he wanted them to. The Internals, in contrast, were reactive; recognizing that the experimenter was trying to control their behavior, they tried to behave in just the opposite way from what was expected.

The Internal, who wants to control and believes he can control, resists influence and, indeed, tries to wrest it away from the person who he believes is trying to control him. The External does not believe he can ever be in control and thus is less likely to make such an effort. Goodstadt and Hjelle (1973) talk about the self-fulfilling prophecy inherent in these orientations; both Internals and Externals tend to act in ways that make their beliefs about themselves come true. If you don't think you can do something and so don't try to do it, you will never learn that you could have done it after all. And if you think you can and do try, you are bound to succeed at least occasionally. If Internals expect that they can seriously influence others, they are indeed influential. In contrast, Externals may expect that they cannot influence others, and they are, therefore, less powerful.

## Leadership

Goodstadt and Hjelle's theorizing led them into a highly interesting (and somewhat disturbing) area of Internal-External research. Given that Externals don't believe that they can influence people, they asked, what would happen if we placed Externals in a position of power, a position in which they were expected to control the behavior of others? To answer that question, they designed an experiment in which subjects acted as supervisors for an imaginary company. Each supervisor was told that he had a team working for him in an adjoining room; the workers' output consisted of simple coding exercises, putting pegs in boards, or the like. The supervisor never saw his workers (they were, in fact, imaginary too), but he did see their output; his job was to get them to increase that output by sending them written communications. He could use a number of techniques to accomplish this: he could praise them, give them suggestions about how to work faster, threaten them with demotion (making them work at a more boring job), threaten to fire them, and so on. Under these conditions, Externals and Internals behaved quite differently. Internals tended to use personal persuasion—gentle forms of influence—while Externals used the harsher, more coercive techniques. Internals, who believe that they can influence others, often try to do so quietly and constructively. Externals, having little faith in their persuasive powers, are more likely to threaten punishment of one sort or another. In light of the increasing shift toward Externality in the population as a whole (which I noted earlier), this finding of Goodstadt and Hjelle is particularly disquieting. Our complex and fragile world needs persuaders more than it needs punishers. This fact alone, I think, is sufficient justification for us as teachers to look for ways to help our students to become more Internal.

As we might expect, leadership tends to go with Internality. Politically active people are likely to fall toward the Internal end of the continuum (Rosen & Salling, 1971). Internals tend to be more committed to ideals or causes than Externals (Shimkunas & Kime, 1971) and to make decisions more readily than Externals (Higbee, 1972). In a study of small-group behavior, DeBolt, Liska, and Love (1973) found that Internals assumed leadership of the group more often than Externals. This result, however, was partially obscured by sex differences. The DeBolt subjects were students from a college psychology class, and the purpose of the groups was to prepare class projects, on which the students would be graded. In the mixed-sex groups, girls—no matter how Internal—did not often assume leadership. It would seem that, in spite of Women's Lib, the sex-role stereotypes of the assertive male and the submissive female are still alive and well among young adults.

## PERSONALITY AND LOCUS OF CONTROL

In view of the great interest that researchers have shown in the locus-of-control dimension and the large number of studies carried out to explore that dimension, it is not surprising that attempts have been made to link Internality or Externality with a wide variety of personality characteristics. In general, the evidence suggests that Internals are better adjusted, better able to cope with social and personal problems, than Externals. For example, a study by Warehime and Woodson (1971) concludes: "For males, internality was significantly related to feelings of personal freedom, satisfaction with present work, feelings of alertness and clarity of thought processes, acceptance and expression of own needs, and feelings of self-assurance and adequacy regarding one's capabilities. For females, internality was significantly related to general feelings of abundance and satisfaction in the life situation, calmness and freedom from anxiety, and feeling cheerful and free of depression" (p. 443). In this section, we shall take a closer look at the relationship between locus of control and a number of personal and emotional characteristics, trying to understand how this relationship may affect the behavior and the feelings of students in the classroom.

## Anxiety

One of the major concerns of the teacher in dealing with the emotional responses of students is anxiety. Anxiety, as we have seen, can interfere seriously with the learning process; if kept at a moderate level, however, it may not hamper and may even facilitate learning through increasing one's alertness and/or motivation. Do Externals and Internals differ in the degree to which they experience anxiety or in the ways in which they typically deal with it? The data would seem to indicate that they do. Joe (1971), summarizing the literature, concludes that Externals describe themselves as more anxious than Internals and as less able to show constructive responses in overcoming frustration. They tend to be more concerned with fear of failure than with achievement—that is, they focus on possible bad outcomes in the learning situation rather than on possible successes.

A study by Siegel and Mayfield (1973) found, in contrast with Joe's description, that Externals were less anxious after a failure experience than Internals. Siegel and Mayfield gave subjects an experimental task in which they could not themselves tell whether they had succeeded or failed; knowledge of success came from assessment by the experimenter. In this way, "success" and "failure" could be predetermined for each group of subjects. After the first series of tasks (which were described by the experimenter as being quite difficult), subjects were asked how anxious they felt about their ability to do well on the next series. Among subjects who had been told that they succeeded, both Internals and Externals reported moderate anxiety about their future performance. But among the "failures," the Internals were anxious about the next round, while the Externals were not. The authors suggest that the Externals, who do not usually think of themselves as able to control their own outcomes, did not in this case have to blame themselves for their initial "failure." How well they did on the task was a matter of luck, anyhow, so the prospect of failing again did not particularly bother them. "Internals may actually become more anxious in threatening situations than externals because they lack the external's belief that forces outside themselves are responsible for their fate and, therefore, cannot resign themselves to the situation as the externals presumably do" (Siegel & Mayfield, 1973, p. 1190).

Another suggestion comes from Stolorow (1971), who points to differences in the kinds of things that may cause anxiety in Internals and Externals. Internals, who value control over themselves and their environments, are distressed at the prospect of losing that control. Externals, however, are distressed over the loss of external supporting objects or people. In the Siegel and Mayfield study, neither success nor failure on the first set of tasks changed the fact that the tasks were difficult; Internals might be expected to feel some anxiety about doing well the next time around no matter how they had done initially. Externals who had succeeded probably experienced some pressure toward taking responsibility for their future performance—"I did it last time, and so it will be my fault if I don't do so well again." But initial failure allowed the Externals to disavow responsibility for the outcome— "The task is too hard; I can't really be expected to succeed." In some success situations, the External may feel as though external support is being removed, and he is being thrust into unwanted personal responsibility; failure reaffirms his belief that what he does or how hard he tries doesn't matter very much.

### Defensiveness

Anxiety and defensiveness are the "terrible twins" of the personality; one is seldom seen without the other. One of the classic ways of studying defensiveness is through the use of a tachistoscope—a machine that presents visual stimuli by throwing an image on a screen for only a fraction of a second. As the exposure time becomes shorter and shorter, it becomes more and more difficult to recognize the stimulus. Theoretically, this situation gives the defenses more of a chance to come into play; if the stimulus is a threatening one, the defensive subject can simply "fail to recognize" it. Sauber (1971) used a tachistoscope to present "taboo" words to Internals and Externals, and found that Externals failed to recognize the words significantly more often. Sauber concludes that an External has a greater need to deny the threatening stimuli when he perceives the task to be beyond his personal control. The External's defenses are essentially passive; he cannot move out—either physically or psychologically—to deal with external threat. His way of coping with anxiety, therefore, is to deny that the threat exists.

Externals use defensive denial to deal with their own behaviors as well as with outside threat. In situations where success is prized and generally thought to be a function of one's own ability and hard work (such as is the case with academic achievement), the experience of failure tends to make

Externals devalue success. Unlike the Internal, for whom failure can be a spur to greater effort, the External does not believe that working harder is likely to bring success. After all, he tells himself, it's a matter of luck anyhow. And since he has little control over whether he will get the reward— and past experience tells him the odds are against him—he denies the value of the reward. Like the fox who decided that the grapes were too sour after he found that he couldn't jump up and get them, the failing External tells himself that good grades are unimportant, that reading is for sissies, that going on to college is just a waste of time and money.

Defensiveness, and particularly denial, are ways of avoiding knowledge about what is happening—they are anti-information-seeking behaviors. Can we assume, then, that Internals are in general more likely to seek out information about themselves and their interactions with the world than are Externals? Rotter hypothesized that this would be the case: "the individual who has a strong belief that he can control his own destiny is likely to (a) be more alert to those aspects of the environment which provide useful information for his future behavior; (b) take steps to improve his environmental condition; (c) place greater value on skill or achievement reinforcements and generally be more concerned with his ability, particularly his failures; and (d) be resistive to subtle attempts to influence him" (Rotter, 1966, p. 25). Rotter seems to see the Internal as a highly alert individual, an individual in a state of readiness, constantly seeking cues that will help him to improve his mastery over his surroundings. Joe (1971) and Lefcourt and Telegdi (1971) also support this notion. Lefcourt and Telegdi suggest that the failure to explore and think about circumstances actively is a direct cause of the Externals' peculiar susceptibility to persuasion or manipulation.

## Depression

What if information about the environment is not readily obtainable? What if the environment yields confusing or contradictory cues? According to Korman (1971) such a situation makes for personal dissatisfaction and frustration. Satisfaction, he says, correlates positively with the extent to which the environment provides the opportunity to behave in a self-controlled, independent, nonsubmissive manner—in other words, to behave like an Internal. An environment that does not provide such opportunity forces people to behave, to think, and to feel like Externals. May we not say that it forces people to become Externals? And what is the result when an otherwise Internally oriented person is pushed into being an External? Prizing his ability to stand on his own feet, he is forced to admit that he can no longer do so. Having learned to trust his ability to handle himself, to exert control over his surroundings, he must now be controlled. According to Miller and Seligman (1973), it is precisely this state of affairs that leads to serious depression. Depression, they say, is caused by and equivalent to a distortion of the degree to which one sees oneself as able to affect or change one's environment (p. 62). Miller and Seligman gave depressed subjects a series of tasks in which individual skill was clearly the major determinant of success and asked them at intervals to estimate how well they expected to do in the next trial. Nondepressed people usually change their expectations depending on past performance—that is, if they have done well in the past, they expect to do well in the future. But the depressed subjects in the experiment did not become more optimistic after they had done well; they continued to attribute future performance to luck or chance, and their estimates stayed about where they were at the beginning. Like typical Externals, they were not receptive to cues from the world around them—cues that would help them to understand their interactions with that world.

Depression is exceedingly debilitating and painful. Unlike anxiety, which may facilitate certain behaviors if it is not too strong, depression facilitates nothing. If depression and Externality are linked in some way, and if Externals are (as Miller and Seligman suggest) more susceptible to depressed states, then to be an External is indeed a precarious and undesirable state. Yet here again, as with so many of the characteristics that we have looked at, the degree to which one is involved in his Externality seems a critical factor. It is the extreme External, the External who resists all pressures toward a more self-responsible orientation, who feels at the mercy of a hostile world and is a prime candidate for depression.

But extreme Internality, too, can lead to problems. Gurin, Lao, and Beattie (1969) point out that the highly Internal individual who fails in an important task is likely to fall prey to self-blame or guilt. Focusing on external forces, they say, may be motivationally healthy if it is the result of assessing one's chances for success against systematic and real external obstacles. In other words, an External orientation based on a realistic appraisal of the power of others is psychologically different from the "Nothing I do matters; it's just a question of luck" attitude. People who are in fact blocked from achieving their goals by circumstances beyond their control are better off if they can recognize what has happened than if they take full responsibility for the failure. "I will work harder" is not a useful philosophy if it leads one to ignore real limitations imposed by one's social or physical environment. Gurin and colleagues maintain that because of the potential for self-punishment inherent in an Internal orientation, people with extremely Internal scores, as well as those with extremely External scores, tend to be psychologically less well adjusted and healthy than people in a middle range.

You are probably aware that some psychologists scoff at the idea that an individual can control his behavior. Freud and Skinner, to name only two highly influential thinkers of this century, have insisted (for different reasons and coming from quite different sets of data) that self-control, or free will, is only an illusion, that man is in fact programmed by his past experiences in such a way that his behavior both follows rules and is potentially predictable. If this is true, is not an Internal orientation merely whistling in the dark, a self-deluding unwillingness to accept the unpleasant reality of one's real helplessness? The semantic and logical tangle that such a question involves us in suggests an important characteristic of human functioning: whether or not we do possess free will, it nevertheless feels as if we do. We feel as if we are making decisions as we go along and as if we could have made different choices if we had wanted to. Lefcourt (1973) believes that whether or not such a belief is objectively true, the belief itself is important in maintaining psychological health. "The sense of control, the illusion that one can exercise personal choice, has a definite and a positive role in sustaining life. The illusion of freedom is not to be easily dismissed without anticipating undesirable consequences" (p. 424). Personally, I am not convinced that my feelings of freedom are in fact merely an illusion; but such philosophical speculation is not important here. What is important is that a sense of personal power is essential to optimal human functioning. As we have seen, Internality must be tempered with realism lest it lead to self-blame and despair. But, on balance, a healthier personality seems to be associated with an Internal rather than an External orientation.

## ACADEMIC BEHAVIOR

After all that has already been said about the relationship of Internality to various other desirable aspects of human functioning, we might expect that Internals tend to do better academically than Externals. And so they do. Clifford and Cleary (1972) found significant correlations between academic performance and Internality among fourth-, fifth-, and sixth-grade children; Shipe (1971) maintains that "personality and motivation" account for about 50% of the variability in academic achievement; Felton (1971) has reviewed a number of studies of academic performance at various ages and concludes that failure to perceive and to internalize responsibility for one's own performance is one of the critical concomitants of low achievement.

When we move to the college level, however, the relationship is not so clear. Warehime (1972), testing more than 1700 university freshmen, found little or no relationship between Internal-External scores and grade-point average. "The [Internal-External] measure," he says, "has no practical utility for the prediction of academic achievement" (p. 314). To confuse the picture still further, Friedman and Manaster (1973) found that Externals appeared to have a greater chance of success in college than Internals. We might speculate that the highly Internal individual is more likely to rebel against the lock-step conformity often demanded in university classes and drop out of school, while the more passive External continues to plod along the academic route toward graduation; but such speculation is clearly born of our own biases. More information is needed here; until it is available, we can conclude only that the academic and social situation in which young adults find themselves is more complex and that the Internal-External variable does not have such clear implications for them as it does for younger students.

For younger children, there seem to be clear academic advantages in being an Internal. What, specifically, is there about Internals that makes them do better in public school than Externals do? The research points to at least three behavior differences that have a direct bearing on academic success. First, and most obvious, is the difference inherent in Rotter's original definition of Internal and External locus of control. The Internal believes that he can influence the strength and frequency of his rewards. He believes that what he does or tries to do makes a difference in what happens to him. Translating this definition into academic behavior, we can say that the Internal child, facing an academic challenge, studies hard because he believes that his effort will determine how well he performs and what will happen to him as a result of that performance. The External, in contrast, may believe that his score on the test depends on luck—whether the teacher happens to ask questions that he knows the answers to—or that scoring well on the test won't make much difference in the long run anyhow. The different kinds of behavior likely to result from these two sets of attitudes are obvious. Rotter, in a more recent discussion of the implications of locus of control, deals directly with learning behavior: "The important factors in learning were not only the strength and frequency of rewards and punishments, but also whether or not the person believed his behavior produced the reward or punishment" (Rotter, 1971, p. 37). Much of our educational system is based on rewards and punishments of one sort or another. That system, it would seem, may work only for the Internals. For the Externals, who see little or no connection between their behavior and its consequences, rewards and punishments are ineffective.

A second difference between Internals and Externals has to do with the kinds of strategies they typically use in a task situation. We know already that the External is less likely to try to succeed since he doubts that trying will make much difference. But even when he is trying, the External behaves differently from the Internal. Brown and Gordon (1971) involved Internals and Externals in an ambiguous task situation—a task in which the relationship between the subject's choices and his ultimate success was not easily determined. Internals performing that task used a skill strategy; that is, they set out to discover the relationship between their behavior and the task outcome, so that they could optimize their chances of being successful. Externals, however, used a chance strategy; they appeared to assume that the task payoffs were randomly determined and made their choices accordingly. For the young student, the learning situation often presents an ambiguous task, and the learner does not know how best to proceed. The Internal, working to discover a best way, moves away from the ambiguity much faster than does the External, who picks and chooses randomly.

A final achievement-related difference between Internals and Externals involves frequency of self-reward. Most teachers agree that externally administered rewards like gold stars and praise and good grades are at best only a temporary substitute for internally administered rewards. We want students to be self-directed and self-motivated, to learn because they want and need the information or skill rather than because parents or teachers reward them for acquiring it. The ability to reward oneself for one's performance, then, is a critical factor in learning, both in school and beyond. Heaton and Duerfeldt (1973) designed an experiment to compare the self-reward tendencies of Internals and Externals. Subjects were given the task of judging time intervals—that is, of indicating how long they thought a particular interval had lasted. They wrote their estimates on report forms, and they were also allowed to put check marks on the form if they thought they had done well. Significantly more checks were made by Internals than Externals. This result can be interpreted in two ways: either the Internals were more confident about their performance, or they took more pleasure in complimenting themselves for it (or both!). Either way, however, the greater number of checks made by Internals indicates a higher frequency of self-reward. Internals, it would seem, are better able to transfer from dependence on external rewards for learning to self-directed learning modes.

Before leaving the question of specific relationships between learning and locus of control, we should address ourselves to one last problem, that of sex differences. One of the puzzling aspects of the relationship between achievement and locus of control among young students has been that it shows up much more strongly and clearly among boys than among girls. Nowicki and Walker (1973) suggest that the real problem here is the relatively low social desirability of Internal responses for girls. Girls, beginning at a young age, are socialized in the United States to be nurturant, obedient, responsible, and dependent on others. The girl for whom social approval is important may conceal or disguise her Internal orientation in order to appear more "feminine." Nowicki and Walker differentiated girls high in social desirability—that is, for whom doing the "socially acceptable thing" was important—and girls low in social desirability; they found that for the girls low in social desirability there was a strong relationship between locus of control and achievement (in other words, these girls looked just like the boys). Interestingly, Nowicki and Walker's subjects were third graders; apparently the stereotype of the helpless female makes its appearance quite early in academic life.

## IMPLICATIONS FOR EDUCATION

It is difficult to organize or find a handle for a concept like locus of control because it cuts across so many different aspects of human functioning. Most of what children—or teachers—do in the classroom can be understood in the light of their locus of control. We have already talked about a number of behaviors that are quite relevant to the tasks of the teacher and the student; in this section, we shall consider some further implications and findings that have a direct bearing on teacher behavior.

### Identifying Internals and Externals

As practical people, one of the first things we must ask ourselves about any personality dimension is "How shall we react to it?" Given that I am convinced that Internals and Externals do differ in important ways, does that mean that I should treat them differently? If so, I should logically begin by sorting my students out, by deciding who is an Internal and who is an External.

Just talking to and observing children should, in most cases, provide the teacher with plenty of data that he can use to differentiate Internal and External children. One must keep in mind that most children, like most adults, do not fall at the extremes of the Internal-External continuum; most of us are somewhere in the middle, more this than that, but with a sizable dollop of both. For the teacher who is interested in pursuing Internal-External measurement more thoroughly, a short article by Stephens (1972) provides a list of Internal-External tests suitable for use with children.

### Structure and Feedback

But what about differential treatment? Identifying Internals and Externals is hardly worthwhile unless we intend to do something about them once they're identified. Some evidence suggests that, in certain situations, differential treatment of Internals and Externals is appropriate. External children respond well to structure and seem to be able to function better in a structured environment; Internals tend to be handicapped by too much structure (Golden, 1971). It has been suggested that since Internals tend to do better than Externals in the classroom, increasing the amount of structure there would tend to balance things out; I would prefer to see structure provided for those who want it (presumably Externals), but provided in such a way that those who don't want or need it could escape from it.

One aspect of structure is whether children are told what they should learn, what the "right" answers are, or whether they are allowed to discover this for themselves. Here again the evidence is consistent: Internals learn faster when they can discover for themselves whether they are right or

wrong, while Externals learn faster when they are told by the experimenter or teacher. Externals are more comfortable with the reassurance of a trusted authority who tells them that they are on the right track; Internals want—perhaps need—to find out for themselves.

Externals, being less convinced that they are responsible for the reinforcements they receive, are less encouraged by success; but by the same token they are less discouraged by failure than Internals. A study by Garrett and Willoughby (1972) used social reinforcement for a problem-solving task; Internal children (fifth graders) did better than Externals after an experience of success, but Externals outperformed Internals after an experience of failure. In providing structure, teachers are often careful to make their comments positive, to emphasize what the child is doing right rather than to point out what he is doing wrong. The response of Externals to failure experiences suggests that some of this concern may be unnecessary. The External child, who most needs feedback, can benefit from being told that he is wrong as well as from being told that he is right, while the Internal child may not need to be told at all but will find out for himself. In providing structure for the External child, honesty—rather than pussyfooting—would seem to be the best policy. Children are quick to spot phoniness in any adult, and the teacher who exudes a false or over-hearty "You're doing just fine!" will only add to the External's sense of powerlessness, of being unable to have any control over a bewildering and complex environment.

We are usually reluctant to give a child negative feedback because we don't want to discourage him or turn him off. The External child, paradoxically, is more likely to be the object of such concern than the Internal. "If only I could get him to try harder" the teacher complains. "He has a fine mind, but he just won't buckle down and use it." MacDonald (1972) warns that the assumption that a child is not motivated because he doesn't try may not always be justified. The External child may be highly motivated to succeed but convinced that trying will not help. After all, since external forces control his success or failure, hard work on his part will make little or no difference to the outcome. Indeed, trying hard may be a poor strategy, for it can cause him to get his hopes up; subsequent failure will then be even harder to bear. MacDonald points out that many programs in the public schools are designed to raise the motivational level of Externally oriented children. This may be a serious mistake because it may do little more than increase their sense of frustration. For these children, we might better focus on efforts designed to increase their sense of personal efficacy and power.

One word of caution is needed here, however—the teacher must not forget that his own Internal-External orientation is very much a part of the student-teacher interaction. Teachers, like everyone else, differ in their perceptions of how dependent people are, and these differences are a function of their own locus of control. The External teacher is likely to overestimate his students' need for reinforcement. If we are to be effective in using our understanding of Internal-External differences among students, we must first be clear about where we stand on the continuum. It is inevitable that we will view others through the filter of our own strengths and needs; but a conscious effort to recognize our biases can go a long way in helping us to overcome them. We are faced with a difficult—but not impossible—balancing act: we must understand the child's needs through putting ourselves in his place, but at the same time we must keep in mind that he may not see or react to things in just the way we do. Self-knowledge on the part of the teacher is the first step toward accurate empathy with the child, and accurate empathy is an important factor in the growth of the child's own self-knowledge.

### The School Environment

Social-interaction patterns, as we have seen, are both influenced by and have an influence on the child's growing sense of locus of control. What sort of overall social climate is best for the Internal or the External child? What sort of environment is most likely to facilitate the growth of an Internal orientation? A number of researchers have attempted to deal with these questions, particularly in the context of the continuing controversy over school integration. Perhaps the greatest springboard for debate in this area came from a summary statement in the Coleman *Report on Equality of*

*Educational Opportunity* (1966). Coleman concluded that there were some distinct disadvantages for the black child in being sent to an integrated school. A study by Harris and Phelan (1973) supports Coleman's conclusion in terms of the growth of a sense of control: black children in integrated schools, in the Harris and Phelan sample, appeared to be significantly more External than black children in segregated schools. The authors hypothesize that in an integrated school, blacks may feel at the mercy of the white power structure.

Other studies suggest that it is not so much the integration as the general attitudes embodied in the school climate that influence the development of locus of control. Gable and Minton (1971) tested junior high children from a "hard-core poverty" school (with 25% black students) and from an all-white "blue-collar" school. There were no significant differences between black and white children or between children of different economic levels when they were considered individually; but a grouping by schools produced higher External scores among the poverty group. If integration itself or the control of a white power structure were factors in the development of Externality, we would expect to see differences between poor and middle-class students and between blacks and whites within schools. Apparently the general attitude is more pervasive and affects all the children in the school, not just the less privileged ones. Bartel (1971) believes that attitudes and values of teachers and administrators toward their students are responsible for these between-school differences and that such attitudes show up in a variety of subtle ways. He cites a 1963 study that found that different textbooks were being used in schools serving higher socioeconomic neighborhoods than in schools where lower-economic-level children were enrolled. Textbooks used in the poorer neighborhoods emphasized an External orientation, while books used in the more well-to-do neighborhoods emphasized an Internal orientation. That the teachers and administrators in the lower-socioeconomic-level schools accepted these texts and were apparently unaware of the subtle messages that they conveyed suggests that they too may well have been contributing to the growing Externality of their students.

Finally, St. John (1971) also found that socioeconomic status was more important than racial mix in determining the locus of control of elementary school children. Being able to stand out in some way, says St. John, is important in developing a sense of Internal control; obviously, it is harder to be outstanding when one is competing against higher-socioeconomic-level children, who (presumably) enter the school situation with a head start. But the child who does not have a chance to compete with more privileged peers (whom he knows to exist) may not grow or become satisfied even if he does manage to excel in his own group. "For a sense of control it is important to be a big frog, but it is also important to be in a big pond" (St. John, 1971, p. 594). The message seems clear: it is not particularly helpful to the child to isolate him in a same-race or same-class setting.

He knows that the real world is out there and that he will have to enter it some day; being placed in a school setting obviously different from that real world can, in itself, contribute to a sense of powerlessness. But placing a minority or poverty-background child in a school environment in which he is told (subtly, by innuendo and unspoken assumption) that he is a powerless, useless, second-class citizen does not help him to assume responsibility for his own life.

### Changing the Child's Locus of Control

Apart from providing an environment in which children's sense of Internal control can develop naturally, can the teacher do anything specific to foster such growth? Before attempting to answer that question, we should perhaps consider whether fostering Internality is, in fact, always desirable. Ultimately, the relative superiority of Internal orientations may be a matter of personal values. Internals are likely to value Internal orientations in others, while such orientations may appear unrealistic or harmful to the successful External. I cannot deny that I value a sense of Internal control or that this value may bias my interpretation of the data. Insofar as I can be objective, however, it appears to me that the Internal child is better equipped for both academic and personal success than the External child. Internals suffer less from anxiety and depression, they are able to assess their own strengths and weaknesses more accurately (Steger et al., 1973a), and they are more likely to interact constructively with others (Goodstadt & Hjelle, 1973). In contrast, Externals like themselves less and feel that other people like them less than do Internals (Ryckman & Sherman, 1973; Bryant, 1972; Fish & Karabenick, 1971). Externals appear to know themselves less well than Internals, or at least to be less clear about just what kinds of people they think they are (Organ, 1973).

The Internal child, then, has a better chance of enjoying life both because he is happier with things as they are and because he is more able to change both himself and his environment for the better. "Learning to perceive an internal locus of responsibility facilities the learning of new and responsible behaviors" says Felton (1973, p. 1279). We do not want students to become so exclusively Internal that they are unable to recognize the reality of situations in which they must accept the power of other individuals or of circumstances, or that they become guilt ridden over their failures; but a tendency toward Internality rather than Externality appears to facilitate the development of a variety of skills and abilities.

Increasing the Internal-control orientation of most children is, then, a reasonable teaching goal. But, having made this decision, we often find it difficult to find specific ways to implement it. Providing success experiences for the External child is, as we have seen, not always effective; if such experiences are not provided with great care and are not linked clearly and specifically to the child's own efforts, they can strengthen rather than weaken his conviction that success or failure is a matter of luck. With older children or young adults, providing opportunities for self-exploration and discussion of feelings may be a useful technique; research data suggest that such discussions can increase the young person's sense of internal control. Felton (1973), for instance, included intensive group counseling as part of a training program for paraprofessionals in the mental-health field. The trainees filled out an Internal-External scale at the beginning and again at the end of their 11-month training period; their scores were significantly more Internal after training. Interestingly, their academic performance was also significantly better than that of a group of students from similar backgrounds who were not involved in the counseling. In another study, Diamond and Shapiro (1973) compared Internal-External changes among young adults involved in an 11-week encounter group. People who were involved in these encounter groups changed toward a more Internal locus of control, while no such change occurred in a group of control subjects. Moreover, the greatest amount of change occurred in groups with experienced leaders (as compared with student leaders). The authors conclude that the experienced leaders were themselves better models of an Internal locus of control.

The group-encounter or group-counseling approach may be necessary in dealing with the relatively well-established locus-of-control orientation of the older student. Younger children, who have not yet settled into a more or less permanent orientation pattern, may well respond more favorably to direct experiences of self-direction. One reason for preferring a more direct approach with younger children is that the kind of social-reinforcement patterns that develop in children's peer groups may work against, rather than for, the development of an Internal orientation. K. M. White (1972), studying groups of sixth-grade boys, found that they did not provide each other with the kind of social support that facilitated the growth of a sense of self-in-control. Peer evaluations in his study tended to be quite destructive, possibly because the individual child had little to do with setting the standards by which behavior was judged. Furthermore, the degree to which peers of this age are seen by each other as supporting and approving is probably not great. White found that encouraging these boys to evaluate their own performance (that is, to provide their own rewards) was most effective in raising their Internal-External scores. Teaching them to evaluate themselves allowed them to experience directly a kind of control over outcomes that were important to them.

Other researchers have approached the problem of shifting locus of control in an even more direct way. MacDonald (1972) reports on one successful effort in which the primary focus was on verbal behavior. Statements that reflected an External point of view were challenged, while Internal statements were rewarded. In addition, subjects were helped to recognize behavior contingencies—that is, the causal links between what they did and what happened to them. This straightforward behavior-modification approach resulted in a significant shift toward an Internal orientation among the children in the sample.

Ferster (1973) also sees reinforcement as critical in developing an Internal locus of control; in the child's earliest interactions, the right kind of reinforcement situation can sow the seeds of later self-direction. The first critical learning in this area, he says, occurs when the infant learns to respond to the body language of the mother. If he learns to anticipate what the mother will do and to act accordingly, he is well on the way to an Internal locus of control. But if he does not learn to interpret the body language correctly, he can't make the proper responses; he sees his mother (and, by extension, the whole world) as unresponsive to his behavior. This hypothesis has important implications for retraining: the learner must be provided with a new situation in which the reinforcement—like the old reinforcement pattern of mother to infant—is reliable, but still varies enough so that there are some circumstances where the performance is appropriate and others where it is not. The learning must be slow, but consistent. Too great a challenge, too much potential for failure, will drive the External further back into his Externality; he will tell himself that it's too difficult, that there's no way he could master it, and that running his own life is just an illusion after all. With too many rewards, the old, inappropriate behaviors and beliefs will never be exchanged for new ones.

The effectiveness of this here-and-now approach has been demonstrated in a number of studies. Dua (1970), for example, found that an action-oriented mode of counseling, in which clients were helped to work out specific ways in which they could change their patterns of behavior, was successful in shifting locus of control away from the External end of the continuum. Nowicki and Barnes (1973) provided a week-long structured camping experience to junior high–age inner-city boys and found a significant shift in Internal-External scores. They concluded that the camping experience made the youngsters feel more in control of events and better able to see the connection between their behavior and the results of their behavior (reinforcement). Finally, Hunt and Hardt (1971) found that while Internality does not automatically increase with age for disadvantaged high school youngsters, students involved in Upward Bound programs do show a significant increase.

It is not easy to change an individual's locus of control; the literature reports failures as well as successes, and doubtless many other attempts have failed and have never been published. Yet the research described here indicates that people can be helped to change. In spite of the differences in technique in the various successful efforts, all seem to share two common elements: a safe, structured environment, in which the learner can try out—very gradually—ways of controlling his own outcomes; and a reason to hope, a sense that things can be different from the way they have been. These two conditions may not be sufficient, in and of themselves, to cause change; but they do seem to be necessary. Making them a part of the classroom situation is a challenge to the teacher—a challenge that, if met successfully, could make important and long-range differences in the lives of many students.

## QUESTIONS FOR UNDERSTANDING

1. What kinds of classroom behaviors would you use as indicators of Internality and Externality in a group of second graders? Of fifth graders? Of high school seniors?
2. An I+ individual takes responsibility for his successes, while an I- person blames himself for failures. How might you expect these different orientations to show up in the behavior of a child who has just (a) earned a place on the basketball team, (b) been selected to perform in an all-city piano recital, (c) been asked to redo a carelessly written paper, (d) learned that he will be bused to a new school next year?
3. What would you expect to be the result of arranging for a highly External sixth-grade child to serve as chairman of a committee charged with organizing a class party?
4. You are a homeroom teacher in a newly integrated junior high school; your class is about half black and half white. What group activities might you plan to foster the development of healthy Internal growth for all your students?
5. How do you think the External-Internal development of a student might be affected by placing him in (a) a nonstructured open classroom; (b) a traditional, basics-oriented classroom; (c) a programmed-instruction setting?

# Chapter 12

# Conformity

Imagine yourself as one of a group of eight students seated in a room looking at sets of straight lines thrown on a screen by a projector. You and the other students, all strangers to you, have volunteered to be subjects in an experiment on perception; for each set of lines you are to decide which two are the same length. The procedure is always the same; after you have all had a chance to look at the lines, each person in the group calls out his answer. You understood what was required of you right away and expected that the task would be relatively easy, but something strange seems to be happening now. Because of the way you happened to seat yourself, you are always the seventh person in the group to announce your answer, and, on nearly every trial, all the other people in the group are giving answers that disagree with yours! You wonder whether you might have misunderstood the instructions. But no, they were perfectly clear. Maybe it is the angle that you're looking at the screen from; but then why do the people on either side of you agree with each other? Could you really be that wrong every time? Can this really be happening?

This is the situation into which Asch put student subjects in his classic study of conformity behavior (1956). If you aren't already familiar with the results of the study, you might stop here and ask yourself what the outcome probably was: did most people continue to give the answers that they thought were right, or did they go along with the group (all of whom were stooges, trained to agree with each other on the wrong answers)? Asch would have predicted wrong; he and his colleagues were quite surprised at the behavior of their experimental subjects. Fully three-fourths of them yielded to the majority to some degree, and more than a quarter of those Yielders went along with the group almost all the time.

Conformity wears many faces in our society and answers to many names. Verbal conformity—agreeing with others just for the sake of agreement—is known as *acquiescence.* Acquiescence has been studied primarily in the context of text-taking behavior; psychologists have been concerned with how valid personality test scores are when the test taker has an acquiescence response set—that is, when he is inclined to agree with whatever the test questions suggest. Conforming to the wishes or suggestions or commands of an authority figure comes under the heading of *obedience,* a quality frequently praised in children, demanded in the military, and yet looked down on when displayed to excess in adults. Long-term conformity to social rules and norms is *conventionality*—again, necessary to some extent if society is to function, yet deadening and even dehumanizing if carried too far. In order to have a common ground, so that we all know what is meant by the term, let's arbitrarily use Kiesler and Kiesler's (1969, p. 9) definition of conforming behavior: Conformity "involves an alteration of behavior and belief toward a group. It is not just any alteration—it is alteration that occurs as a result of some group pressure. If a person agrees with a group just by coincidence, we would not call this conformity." If I change my beliefs, my behavior, or both so as to make them agree with the beliefs and/ or behavior of a group, I am *conforming* to the standards of that group.

Even with this definition, though, important distinctions are still to be made. Asch, interviewing his subjects after the experiment was over, found that some of them were quite aware of having given in to group pressure. They thought that their original perceptions were correct, but had given the same answers as the majority in order not to look foolish or to seem differ-

ent. Such *public conforming* or *expedient conforming* is quite different from what happened to other subjects, who actually came to see the stimulus lines in the way the rest of the group seemed to see them. These latter subjects were unaware of how often they had yielded to group pressure; they believed that they had announced their own perceptions, even though they had been swayed by the majority opinion. This kind of internal-external distinction can be made with regard to conventionality, or conforming to social norms, as well: does one conform because one knows the rules, knows what is expected of one and behaves accordingly, or does one accept the norm as one's own preference? For example, imagine a hot afternoon on a crowded bus. At one stop, an obviously pregnant woman, with her arms full of packages, gets on the bus and stands near the front; all the seats but one in that area are occupied by women. The lone seated man gets up and offers the pregnant woman his place. Does he do so because this is expected of him, because he would rather stand than suffer the (probably silent) pressure of the group? Or has he *internalized* the norm, so that he is doing what he thinks is right? Obviously, the distinction between expedient, public conformity and internalized conformity is not always a clear one—more often than not, we behave on the basis of a combination of the two—but it is important to be aware of the difference. Expedient conformity changes as group pressures change; internalized conformity is more stable since the conformer believes that he is acting according to his own desires.

At the other end of the continuum of conformity behavior, an important distinction is to be made between nonconformity and counterconformity. If I am a nonconformer, I do what I want to, regardless of who says I should or should not behave that way. I act as if the group pressure were not there; I ignore the group demands. Counterconformers, in contrast, do not ignore group pressures—they actively resist them. The counterconformer responds to group pressure with stubbornness; he refuses to go along with the crowd even when the crowd is doing something that he might have wanted to do. The counterconformist not only resists having his judgments and actions move toward those of the group, but his judgments and actions tend to defy, to be the opposite of, the group norms. The cognitions and actions of the counterconformist are thus just as surely and predictably determined by the group as are those of the conformist (Crutchfield, 1963). And, like conformity, counterconformity may occur with or without the behaver's understanding why he is acting as he does; he may deliberately and consciously decide to do the opposite of whatever the group is doing, or he may honestly believe that he is following his own inclinations. One sometimes wonders how often a person is following the beat of his own drummer and how often he is simply staying out of cadence with the majority. Then, too, counterconformity or nonconformity to the majority can be at the same time conformity to a subgroup. The member of a religious sect who dresses in plain black clothes and refuses to own an automobile is clearly not in conformity with the larger culture, but he is conforming rigidly to the demands of his own group. As Kiesler and Kiesler (1969) point out, when we talk about conformity, we also must ask what or whom one is conforming to. In conforming to one set of rules, to the behavior of one group, we are often nonconforming to another. Rather than discuss the characteristics of conformers, they suggest, we should concern ourselves with the rules governing who conforms to whom, when, and why.

Such questions are clearly important; we do need to understand the situational variables that influence conforming behavior. Yet, equally clearly, some individuals are more vulnerable to conformity pressures than others. We should also be aware of the personality characteristics of such conformity-prone people and understand how these characteristics tend to contribute to conforming behavior. In this chapter, we shall deal with both these sets of questions. Before we do so, however, let us examine our own values with regard to conformity.

In general, our society pays a great deal of lip service to the values of independence. To be a conformist is somehow weak and wrong. Particularly, in the intellectual community, we set great store by "making up our own mind" and "being our own man." Asch's subjects demonstrated this value in the postexperiment interviews; when informed of what had been happening, "those who were independent expressed relief and joy, . . . while those who were caught by the majority were rueful but never proud" (Asch, 1956, p. 36). The events of recent history have underscored the dangers of unthinking obedience; we look at the activities of the 1972 Presidential campaign or at the tragedy of My Lai and wonder how intelligent people could possibly so give over responsibility for their own actions. Milgram, describing his well-known study of obedience (in which subjects believed they were giving painful and possibly harmful electric shocks to their peers at the request of the experimenter), comments "With numbing regularity good people were seen to knuckle under to the demands of authority and perform actions that were callous and severe. Men who are in everyday life responsible and decent were seduced by the trappings of authority, by the control of their perceptions, and by the uncritical acceptance of the experimenter's definition of the situation, into performing harsh acts" (Milgram, 1965, p. 74).

On a more personal level too, we have reason to be concerned about the effects of conformity. The habitual conformer runs a real danger of tuning himself so finely to the subtle influences of his group that he loses track of what he wants and believes and thus of who he is. Since in conforming he is careful not to do or say anything that rubs others the wrong way, the individual rough edges of his personality are rubbed away; in consequence, he becomes scarcely distinguishable from those whose approval he seeks (W. White, 1961). Riesman, in *The Lonely Crowd* (1950/1961), spends a great deal of time comparing the outlooks and attitudes of inner-directed and other-directed individuals. Inner-directed man, he says, acts according to his own internalized standards and thus has a certain freedom to fail according to the standards of others without having to see himself as a failure. Other-directed man (the compulsive conformer), in contrast, must go along with the group; when he cannot do so, both the group and he himself label him a failure. Moreover, the group—the cocktail party crowd, the TV ad men, the editors of slick fashion magazines—seems always to be saying that life is supposed to be fun, to be easy. Since it really isn't very easy for most people, the other-directed man is constantly aware of a niggling sense that things are not as they should be—that is, they are not the same for him as they are for others—and to that degree he will always see himself as a failure.

It is hard to argue with the statement that in this culture, at this time, independence is positively valued over conformity. Even the words we use to describe independence have value tones: strong, free, courageous. Yet, in accepting this value, are we in fact conforming (unthinkingly) to a cultural norm? Is conformity always so undesirable? I think not. Where does one acquire those independent values and standards that we praise so highly? The infant is not born with them. They are acquired from significant others—from parents, peer groups, religious authority, and the like—and internalized. We have, then, an interesting paradóx: in declaring proudly that I live according to my own (independent) standards, I am in fact announcing that at some time in the past I have unquestioningly accepted someone else's set of values or rules or norms about conformity.

At a more practical and immediate level, some conformity is necessary for any society to function. We simply could not relate to each other as human beings if we did not mutually conform to a minimum set of expectations about each other's behavior. These social rules allow us to condense large amounts of communication into a few words, a gesture, a simple action. They also allow us to experience the feeling of belonging, a feeling that most of us value highly. Social conformity is particularly important when one's group is threatened by outside danger. "Certain it is that when people feel themselves pressed into a dangerous corner, they do not want their fellows to ponder and consider, they want all to unite in conformity to repel the danger" (Mandelbaum, 1963, p. 242).

Perhaps the best word to describe the behavior of the individual who combines the best of both conformity and individuality is *autonomous*. The autonomous man is aware of his own beliefs and feelings, and sensitive to differences between himself and his groups. He is able, when appropriate, to take a stand quite different from that of the majority; he is also able to use the group as a reference, as a partial check on the validity of his own perceptions. He can conform when his own interests or those of others are best served by conformity, but he does so with full knowledge of what he is doing. Because he is aware of his own beliefs and perceptions, he can be more sensitive to the beliefs and perceptions of his fellows. Autonomous man is, first and foremost, a social creature; both his autonomy and his humanity emerge out of the interplay between independence and conformity.

All three of these stances—conformity, independence, and autonomy —can be considered as both causes and effects of other behaviors or behavioral attributes. As teachers, we are interested in both the causes and the effects. We need to know what sorts of events and/or characteristics are likely to lead to conforming or nonconforming behavior, just as we need to know what happens to people as a result of conforming or of not conforming. And, I believe—here my values are showing—we need to encourage our students and other clients to be neither rigidly independent nor slavishly conforming, but to strive toward an autonomous integration of the two extremes.

## THE DYNAMICS OF CONFORMITY

Often the simplest questions are the hardest to answer. The question "Why do people conform?" can be shrugged off with a careless "Why not?" or handled in a circular way with "Because they want to." But neither of these answers is particularly helpful in explaining just how conforming behaviors happen and why some people form habits of conforming while others do not.

### Reinforcement for Conformity

All behavior occurs because it works or because the behaver expects it to work—that is, he has formed opinions and beliefs about the outcomes of his behavior based on past observations and experiences. In previous chapters, we have spoken of such observations and experiences as *reinforcement;* a behavior, a response, that has led to pleasant consequences is said to be positively reinforced, and positive reinforcement makes that particular behavior more likely to occur again under similar conditions. Conforming behaviors are no exception to this rule. When the individual is presented with a conflict between his own perception of a situation and the apparently contradictory perceptions of others, his behavior is determined primarily by how often his own perceptions, relative to those of others, have been reinforced in the past (Elich, 1962). Embedded in this statement is a fundamental assumption about conformity: that an element of conflict is necessary in order for conformity to occur. Where there is no conflict between what the individual is inclined to do and what the group (or another individual) wants (or seems to want) him to do, conformity is not an issue. The conflict need not be a conscious one; we have seen that many conformers are not aware that they are conforming to anything. But at some point in the individual's history, either at the present moment of behavior or sometime in the past, there must have been a readjustment, a realigning of perception or intention, to fit more closely to the standards of others. By conforming to those standards, the individual reduces the conflict. Thus there is a double reinforcement: not only is the behavior itself reinforced (as it must be, if it is to continue), but also the very resolution of conflict is experienced as pleasant.

The effects of reinforcement are not confined to the specific behavior pattern that is reinforced; there is a general spread of effect to other similar situations. If I conform to group pressures in one kind of behavior, and this conformity is positively reinforced by subsequent events, I will be more likely to conform to that group in other ways as well. Let's imagine, for instance, that I am invited to a party. I had planned to dress up for the party, but I discover that several of the others who are going are all planning to wear old clothes. I conform and go to the party in a pair of jeans and a sweatshirt. When I arrive, I find that the party is a backyard picnic, with a wienie roast and a softball game. My choice of clothing is reinforced; my dress-up clothes would have been restrictive and uncomfortable. The likelihood of my conforming to the clothing style of other group members for the next party is increased; but also, I am somewhat more likely to conform to their behavior in other ways as well.

There is an insidious quality about this sort of conformity reinforcement. The person whose conforming behavior is reinforced is often unaware of why he looks to the group for direction—if, indeed, he is aware that he is looking. The choice of clothing is a good example; clothing preferences are more often than not a matter of conformity, though we don't usually think of them as such. Why do we wear bathing suits to go swimming? Certainly not for warmth or for comfort; rather, we wear them to conform to the standards of the group. We may have internalized these standards, so that we would feel uncomfortable without the swim suit (or we express some sort of "moral" opposition to nudity), but even so the preference originated in conformity to pressure from peers or authority figures. As one implicitly learns the ways of society, learns how to recognize and meet its requirements, one invariably experiences some restrictions in one's freedom to perceive and select among alternative behaviors (Albert, 1967). As we learn to behave in certain ways, through consistent social reinforcement, we stop noticing other possibilities. It simply doesn't occur to us that we are conforming because we don't realize that we might want to behave otherwise. Why do we greet friends on the street? Eat eggs or cereal for breakfast? Drive our cars on the right side of the road? Refrain from staring into a person's eyes all the time he is talking to us (try it sometime; you will both be uncomfortable!)? These are social customs to which we conform because of years of consistent reinforcement.

Reinforcement for conformity begins with parents. Conformity here is often of the obedience variety, and punishment for disobedience (nonconformity) is swift and sure. When the child is very young, a certain amount of disobedience is tolerated on the grounds of his inability to understand the demands made of him; as he grows older, he is expected not only to obey specific commands but to anticipate parental expectations and comply with them even before they are voiced. How paradoxical, really, the philosophy of the modern "progressive" parent: "I insist that my children be independent!" No parent who cares for his child can avoid demanding a certain amount of obedience/compliance/conformity; the child's physical and social survival depends on his learning to respond appropriately to some rules of behavior. We don't lay our hands on hot stoves; we walk across the street when the light is green; we thank Aunt Mary nicely for the birthday present (if we want another one next year).

In the same way, peer pressures provide strong early reinforcement for conforming behavior. The child who refrains from kicking his next-door neighbor is more likely to be invited over for soda and cookies; the child who spends recess talking with an imaginary playmate may be teased and tormented. With peer-to-peer behavior, though, we enter the realm of another sort of conflict: To whom shall I conform? Shall I be polite, as Mother and Daddy insist, and earn the scorn of my friends? Or shall I join in shouting dirty words at police cars and be punished by my parents? The kinds of reinforcements a child has received for various behaviors, his understanding of the relationships between the behaviors and the reinforcements, and the relative importance of different reinforcers all help to determine the kind and degree of conformity he exhibits.

## Information Seeking

People conform when and if they expect that conforming will work. But when is that likely to be the case? Often, the relationship is quite simple and straightforward: we conform when we ourselves aren't sure of what to do, and we believe that other people may know. When I am in a situation about which I know relatively little, or when I am with people whom I believe to be more expert or experienced than I, I may reasonably believe their opinions or beliefs or reactions to be more valid than my own; in that situation, it makes logical sense to bow to their superior knowledge. This line of reasoning can be converted into a predictive statement: the greater the perceived ambiguity of the stimulus and the greater the perceived prestige of those who hold a conflicting view, the more likely the individual will be to shift his judgment to coincide with that of others (Elich, 1962).

Translating this general statement into classroom behaviors, we may expect conformity to increase when a child is unsure of what is expected of him by teacher and/or peers. Not only is the individual more likely to change his behavior under these conditions, but also he is more likely to actively seek out the opinions and reactions of others. One of the criticisms of experiments that use Asch's method (that is, placing the subject in a group of disagreeing peers) is that this method doesn't fit what happens to people in a real-world conformity situation. As Crawford and Haaland

(1972) point out, when an individual faces a decision between two or more alternatives, people don't approach him and say "do this" or "do that." Rather, the individual seeks out the opinions of others before making his decision. In other words, the decision maker places himself in a position to be influenced. To the degree that a child feels uncertain about what he should do, he exposes himself to the ideas of others whom he respects— that is, of others who have status (for him). We can extrapolate one step further and predict that information seeking and conformity will be positively correlated: the more one seeks out the opinions of others, the more likely he is to be swayed by those opinions.

Information seeking is related to conformity when the potential conformer is aware that he is making a decision and, if he does conform, will be aware that he has done so. The relationship is less certain in the case of unconscious conformity; here, the conformer seldom has to ask others what behavior is appropriate because they are already exerting subtle (and sometimes not so subtle) pressures on him to behave in socially acceptable ways. Elich (1962) subjected children to an Asch-type situation and found that even though there was a great deal of conformity behavior, nearly all the children were unaware of the degree to which the group had influenced their judgments. Conformity had occurred, unconsciously; but there was no explicit information seeking on the part of the conformers. It seems to me that, particularly for children and adolescents, there is often a great deal of unsolicited group pressure; people do in fact approach children and say "do this" or "do that." Parents and teachers, particularly, make explicit and implicit demands for conformity, as do peers. A child seldom goes to his parents and asks whether it is all right to wear a dirty shirt to school; rather, he wonders whether they will notice what he has done and what will happen to him if they do. The teen-ager doesn't have to ask his friends whether they think he should participate in a beer-drinking party; they make it abundantly clear to him what they will think of him if he refuses. By the time a person reaches adulthood, he has had plenty of opportunity to find out what other people will think about a whole range of possible behaviors and to form and internalize evaluations based on the reactions of those others. While conscious conformity often involves information seeking, conformity based on the expectations of others' reactions or on the internalized evaluations of others seldom does.

## The Comfort of Conformity

Both conscious and unconscious conformity, though, do have one aspect in common: both help the individual to feel more secure about what he is doing. We seek information and opinions from others in order to make a "better" decision—that is, to be more sure that what we are doing is right. And the unconscious conformer gains a sense of certainty from doing what he has learned "should" be done. Were he to abandon those internalized yardsticks of performance, he would be unsure and uncomfortable. We acquire these yardsticks originally not only from being told directly but also from just watching how others behave. How people verbally define the meaning of an event, what they do in response, and what they tell others to do may all communicate their expectations to a person of what he should do (Staub, 1972). We all would like to be sure that we are right—that we have made the right decisions, hold valid opinions, respond to situations appropriately. Conformity to others, at either a conscious or an unconscious level, helps us to feel that kind of certainty. Conformity tends to make us comfortable.

Conforming to respected or high-status others helps one to be sure one is doing the right thing. It also leads to another sort of comfort. The more one conforms to the behavior of a respected individual or group, the more one feels *like* them. Moreover, by conforming to the behavior of attractive others, one can feel less like the unattractive others from whom one wants to dissociate oneself. "Holding opinions similar to positive others and dissimilar from negative others is one way to define the self positively. Changing one's attitudes and opinions so that they are more like positive others and more unlike negative others enhances one's self-view" (Kiesler & Kiesler, 1969, p. 67). As I sit in my office writing these words, I am smoking a cigarette. Smoking today is, in many groups, a nonconforming behavior; there is group pressure not to smoke, and going ahead and doing it anyhow often makes me feel rather uncomfortable. But what a different situation years ago, when I first began to smoke! Every time I sat with a lit cigarette between my fingers or took a puff and casually blew out the smoke, I felt terribly sophisticated—this was a truly adult behavior; this was the big time. Nobody gets physical pleasure from smoking when he first starts; the only possible reason that I can see for beginning to smoke is that of conformity. Either one bows to group pressure (to avoid being thought of as a "chicken" or "just a kid") or one gains comfort and security from seeing oneself as like the respected others. Or both.

One of our implicit assumptions in this discussion is that people conform in order to gain acceptance from the group—the group will reject them (or, at least, that is their expectation) if they do not conform. The Asch subjects expressed this fear directly; many of them felt that the other group members were focused on their wrongness and that by giving what they thought were correct answers (but with which the group disagreed), they were making fools of themselves. Elich, who used grade school children in a similar setting, quotes one of his subjects as describing his feelings after the experiment was over: "I felt kind of funny when I saw the other guys' answers. I guess I felt kind of embarrassed. I couldn't decide whether I should do what the other guys wanted me to do or what I thought I should do" (Elich, 1962, p. 59). Elich notes that this interpretation is particularly interesting in that nothing in the instructions implied that group agreement was desirable. Pressure for conformity seems to grow naturally out of group interaction.

What, in fact, does happen to the group member who refuses to conform? It is clear that he expects rejection or ridicule, but is this expectation a valid one? Kiesler and Kiesler report an experiment that was designed to find out. Schachter, the experimenter, included three stooges in his experimental groups, one of whom was instructed to be a deviate. Whatever the group seemed to agree about he was to take a different position on. Here is what happened: "As the experimental hour progressed, more and more communication was directed towards the deviate. However, towards the end of the experimental hour, this communication dropped off, suggesting that the group had first tried to induce the deviate to change his opinion, and when this failed, decided to ignore him. . . . The consequences of deviation appear to be quite clear. First, one can expect a great deal of pressure put upon the deviate to change his opinions towards the greater accord of the group. If this fails, one can expect rejection" (Kiesler & Kiesler, 1969, p. 43).

Rejection and the fear of rejection create anxiety. Conformity, then, is one way to avoid or reduce anxiety. The anxiety-reducing effects of conforming behavior have been demonstrated at a physiological level, in an interesting study carried out at Duke Medical Center. The researcher took measures of the level of plasma-free fatty acid in subjects' blood during a group-interaction situation. Plasma-free fatty acid is an indicator of central nervous system activity or arousal and thus is one of the physiological accompaniments of anxiety. As the amount of pressure in the group increased, fatty-acid levels increased for all subjects. But the levels decreased rapidly for those who reached agreement (who conformed with the group), while it stayed high for the nonconformers (reported in Crutchfield, 1963, p. 221). Not only do subjects report feeling anxious when they disagree with the group, but this anxiety shows up physiologically as well.

### The Camel's Nose Effect

One last observation about the dynamics of conformity behavior before we move on: this has to do with what I call the camel's nose effect, from the old Arab warning about not letting the camel get its nose inside the tent because once it is that far it will surely come in the rest of the way. (I could just as easily call it the foot-in-the-door effect, but camel's nose sounds much more exotic!) At any rate, the camel's nose effect predicts that if a person conforms in a small and relatively insignificant way, he is much more likely to conform later in major and significant ways. Moreover, once having begun to conform, he finds it very difficult to shift over to an independent or nonconforming mode.

Asch discovered the camel's nose effect among his subjects: the Yielders tended to yield on the first or second trial, and almost no one began as an Independent and became a Yielder late in the series of trials. Asch's typical subject "adopted a course of action toward the entire experimental situation which decided his over-all responses. He arrived at what is analogous to a decision to oppose or follow the majority, which imposed a single direction upon his judgments, thus obscuring some distinctions that might otherwise emerge" (Asch, 1956, p. 16). Milgram made a similar observation about the subjects in his obedience studies. Having once obeyed the instructions to shock their confederate at a low voltage, they found it almost impossible to stop obeying even when they were afraid of injuring the confederate. Comments Milgram "Somehow, the subject becomes implicated in a situation from which he cannot disengage himself" (Milgram, 1965, p. 72). Salesmen and fund raisers are well aware of this phenomenon and use it to their advantage: getting the prospect to let you into his home is the first step toward getting him to buy or support your product. Teachers, too, make use of it. "You don't have to read the story, Sammy, but why not open the book and just look at the pictures?" "Go ahead and prepare the outline, and then you'll have a better idea whether or not you really want to junk the whole project." The camel's nose effect is a powerful one and, as you can see, can be used in a highly manipulative way. As might be expected, it also works in reverse: when one has taken a stand not to conform to the group, further resistance is less difficult. In the Asch study, early independence somehow conferred immunity from group pressure. Whatever stand one has taken toward conforming in a given situation tends to be continued in later behavior.

## CHARACTERISTICS OF CONFORMERS

As I mentioned earlier in this chapter, some students of conformity believe that talking about the characteristics of conforming people is a waste of time since conforming is not a well-defined or clear-cut phenomenon. Yet some individuals seem more susceptible than others to group pressure; they are less inclined or able to take an independent position in the face of group opposition. These individuals are likely to behave in a conformist way in a wide range of situations; and they do seem to share some personality and/or behavioral characteristics. The evidence, though, is by no means clear; in fact there are some highly interesting contradictions or suggestions of contradictions among the many studies that have attempted to discover what the "typical" conformer is like.

### Self-Esteem

A number of researchers have concentrated on the degree of self-esteem or self-confidence exhibited by an individual as an index of how strongly he is likely to conform to group pressure. Hochbaum (1954), for instance, measured subjects' perceived expertise in dealing with an issue—how well informed they felt they were or how competent in that area—and found this measure to correlate negatively with conformity to group opinion on that issue. The less a person felt he knew about something, the more likely he was to go along with what others said or believed about it. At a more general level of self-esteem, Janis (1954) found that people who described feelings of social inadequacy were more persuadable than those who did not describe such feelings. His study, like Hochbaum's, used relatively neutral or nonthreatening issues: whether a cure would be found soon for the common cold, what would happen to movie theaters in the next few years, and whether world meat supplies would continue to be adequate. Crutchfield (1963, p. 225) supplies a sweeping description of the typical conformer: he has "a disposition toward pronounced *feelings of personal inferiority and inadequacy,* a self-conception of lack of confidence, of helplessness, and the like. Coupled with this, the extreme conformist exhibits an intense preoccupation with other people." Studies of birth order suggest that first-born children tend to conform more strongly or easily than later-born children. This phenomenon may also relate to self-esteem; parents tend to expect more of their first-born child than of later children, creating a perceived inability to measure up and thus a low sense of self-esteem (Gould, 1969).

However, a study by Savell (1971) created a situation that might be expected to raise self-esteem and that also increased conformity. He showed children a series of pictures and asked them to indicate which pictures they preferred. After the child had indicated his preference, the experimenter either agreed with him or disagreed with him. In a second series of pictures, the experimenter gave his choice first; children who had originally been agreed with tended to conform more to the experimenter's choice than children who had been disagreed with. Having a high-status adult agree with one's own preferences might be expected to raise one's confidence about the "rightness" of one's opinions; why, then, did this group conform more than the others in the second part of the experiment? Possibly the agree-with condition created an artificial bond between experimenter and child, a feeling of "us against the world." Or, the child may have so enjoyed the experience of agreeing with the experimenter that he wanted to continue in that mode. The camel's nose effect may be occurring here: even though the initial agreement or disagreement was forced by the experimental conditions, the subjects did experience either conformity or nonconformity during the first part of the experiment, and that initial position may have been well enough established to have continued during the second part.

Zellner (1970) offers a theoretical explanation of the way in which self-esteem may interact with conformity in a variety of situations. He suggests that both very high and very low self-esteem may interfere with conformity. In order to conform, one must first perceive what the group (or the other individual) is saying and then decide to go along with it. The person whose self-esteem is very low may be so focused on his own inadequacy that he doesn't receive the message from the group, or he may receive it in a distorted fashion; the person who has very high self-esteem is likely to hear the message clearly but is less likely to yield to it. It follows that the most clearly observable conformity behavior should be found among people whose self-esteem lies in an intermediate range. This formulation has not been tested experimentally; more research is needed before we can fully accept Zellner's ideas. The absolute level of self-esteem (that is, one's overall and generalized opinion about oneself) and a person's self-confidence relative to the particular group (or individual) with whom he is confronted and the area of information or behavior with which he is dealing are probably both factors in determining the degree of conformity he will exhibit.

## Emotional Responses

Self-blame is closely related to self-esteem; the more one tends to blame oneself for what happens (either to oneself or to others), the lower one's self-esteem. A study by Costanzo (1970) demonstrated that blaming oneself for a minor accident correlated significantly with overall conformity to group pressure; this was true for all the age groups Costanzo studied, from 7 to 21 years old. Similarly, McMillen (1970) found that a person who had transgressed (lied, hurt, or cheated) against other individuals was more likely to yield to their wishes later on. Self-blame implies guilt, stress, emotionality; carried to an extreme, it frequently interferes with one's ability to function adequately. Does responding to stress in a generally inappropriate or ineffective way tend to be associated with conformity? According to Crutchfield (1963, p. 224) it does: "individuals high in conformity-proneness are characterized by a generalized *incapacity to cope effectively under stress,* a tendency to panic when placed under the pressure of conflicting forces, of uncertainty, of danger." Logically, this association of emotionality with conformity makes a good deal of sense. If I tend to fall apart under pressure, it is just good strategy to follow the lead of someone else who seems to be functioning better than I am. Moreover, blaming myself when things go wrong is uncomfortable; if I go along with the group, then the responsibility can be shared. Emotional upset tends to be accompanied by general disorganization of one's thinking processes, by general inability to see things clearly; under such conditions, resistance to group pressures might be expected to be low. Thus the highly emotional person is both less able to resist what he might otherwise know to be wrong or inappropriate and is also more inclined to follow the guidance of the group in situations where he doesn't know what to do.

Crutchfield describes the high conformer as having basically disturbed and distrustful attitudes toward other people. He is a poor judge of others and is generally less socially adequate. In other words, he tends to be alienated from his interpersonal surroundings. A study by Gould (1969) confirms this description: here high conformers (in an Asch-type study) gave self-descriptions implying distrust, pessimism, cynicism, apathy, and emotional distance from others. Further confirmation comes from a study of college women (Toder & Marcia, 1973) in which the greatest amount of conformity was found among students who had a diffuse and unclear sense of their own identity. The high conformer feels isolated and different from his peers; he uses conformity as a way to conceal or overcome this isolation. And, of course, it doesn't work; in conforming he denies even further his own value and validity, and thus increases his feeling of being an outsider, a misfit.

## Healthy and Unhealthy Conformity

I have been describing here a kind of pathology of conformity—the side of conforming behavior that is inappropriate and that springs from deep feelings of personal inadequacy. It is important to recognize that these descriptions apply to extreme conformers, to those individuals who conform compulsively because they feel they have no other choice. As we noted earlier, much conforming behavior is not pathological; on the contrary, it is necessary if society is to function at all. And the line between socially useful conformity and pathological conformity is not at all a clear one; the two tend to blend together in a murky gray area. In the Asch studies, for instance, there was no particular social usefulness in conforming; on the contrary, conforming meant abandoning what one knew to be right and going along with what one knew (consciously or unconsciously) to be wrong. Yet the Yielders were not just social misfits, emotionally upset or disturbed individuals—they constituted three-quarters of the total sample. Moreover, according to a study by Barron (1952), who worked with Asch's original data, the Yielders strongly valued ease and helpfulness in interpersonal relations, personal effectiveness and planfulness, and personal stability and healthy-mindedness. Obviously, just because one values something does not mean that he possesses it. But a comparison of the Yielders and the Independents strongly suggests that the Yielders were, for the most part, quite socially adequate and indeed may have been more interpersonally sensitive and concerned about others than the Independents.

Conformers want to be right—right not only with their fellows but also in an abstract sense of correctness. The conformer uses his group in an informational sense, as a source of information, a perception check. His conforming behavior is likely to increase as his need to be right increases, since he believes that everyone else also wants to be right and that they, being many, are better able to find right answers than he is. "Though the individual is strongly seeking to get the right answer, he also assumes that each other group member is trying equally hard to get the right answer; thus he is led to ascribe added validity to the judgements given by the others" (Crutchfield, 1963, p. 220). Alker and Wohl (1972) divide high achievement-oriented students into two groups, those who tend to seek achievement through conformity and those who tend to seek achievement through independence. As can be seen in Figure 12-1, the high-conformity-

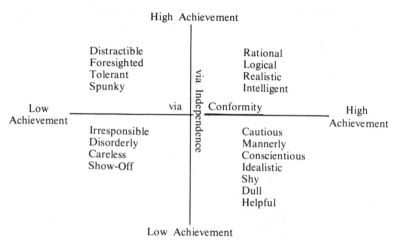

*Figure 12-1.* Relationship of achievement-motivation characteristics to conformity and independence (Alker & Wohl, 1972).

low-independence individual is a caricature of the organization man; he does his job, steps on no toes, holds to conventional values, and is often dreadfully dull. The high-independence–low-conformity person is more interesting, but has his own problems: he often doesn't finish what he has started and may be unnecessarily argumentative. The individual who combines high independence with high conformity (a seeming contradiction, but necessitated by Alker and Wohl's model) appears to have the advantage over the other three types: he can utilize either mode of striving when appropriate and is trapped by neither.

In one sense, Kiesler and Kiesler are right: it is not particularly helpful to describe the characteristics of the conformer. It does seem possible, however, to generalize about healthy conformity and unhealthy conformity. The unhealthy conformer conforms because he has no choice; conformity is the only way he knows to feel related to others or to feel confident about his own behavior. The healthy conformer uses his groups as a source of information. He may be swayed into making wrong judgments, into yielding to the group when his original inclination would have been better;

but overall his is a conformity that affirms and underscores his own related-ness, the social reality of his existence.

### Development of Conformity

Not surprisingly, studies of the relationship between age and confor-mity behavior present a rather confusing picture. A number of experiments with school-age children (Costanzo, 1970; Hamm & Hoving, 1969) have demonstrated substantial increases in conforming as the child moves through early childhood into preadolescence. Other researchers (Allen & Newtson, 1972; Elich, 1962) cite evidence that children become more and more independent of group pressure as they move through the school years. Hamm and Hoving suggest that part of this confusion may lie in the choice of stimulus materials for the experiments: children respond differ-ently (in conformity behavior) to ambiguous and nonambiguous situ-ations. As the child grows older, he places greater value on giving "right" answers. When the stimulus is ambiguous, as in questions involving what one "ought to do" in social situations, his odds of being right are better if he agrees with the group. But in less ambiguous tasks, such as the Asch-type experiment, conforming means choosing an answer that he knows to be wrong; here conformity should decrease with age.

Weinheimer (1972) points out that conformity is related to egocentric-ity. The egocentric child, in Piaget's terminology, is unable to understand that others may see the world differently from the way he does. With matu-rity, he loses this egocentric bias; he realizes, for instance, that to someone sitting on the other side of the room a visual stimulus may look different from the way it looks to him. Conformity, then, is different in the egocen-tric and in the nonegocentric individual, since it cannot be a consciously mediated behavior for an egocentric. Although the external behavior may look the same, the act of conforming or being independent is governed by different internal processes in an egocentric child and in a nonegocentric adult. The shift from egocentric to nonegocentric functioning usually begins around or just before the beginning of the school years, but the pro-cess is a gradual one; some of the apparent contradictions in the age-conformity studies may be due to differences in egocentricity among the children being studied.

Albert (1967) points out another possible source of inconsistency in this area: children feel a need to conform for different reasons, and the need may be greater or less, depending on the reason. Some conformity, particu-larly conformity to adults, is based on a need for physical survival or well-being; other kinds of conformity relate to social or psychological comfort. As the child grows older, his biological well-being is progressively less threatened by deviance, but his psychological well-being becomes increas-ingly dependent on conformity. We might conjecture further that as he grows older still, the message with regard to psychological well-being begins to be conflicting. From the teacher and from his parents, he hears "Do as you are told" and "Think for yourself." From his peers, depending on the situations he finds himself in and the ways he may have reacted to them, he may have experienced rewards for being a good leader or for being a good follower. We are, in the United States at least, going through a period of social upheaval in which many of the "good old values" are being questioned. Depending on the particular family constellation, the particular neighborhood, the particular school situation in which a child finds himself, the pattern of conformity or independence development may vary tremendously from one person to the next.

As I mentioned in earlier chapters, a major area of cultural conflict and change today is that of women's roles. Not only are women's roles and role values changing, but these changes are accompanied by the most emotion-laden and agonizing conflicts, between women and men and among women themselves. Changing values have themselves had an effect on conformity behavior among women. As the "right" way for a woman to act becomes less and less agreed on within the society, women have fewer safe role models to conform to. Women today—young and old—cannot simply conform, because no matter what they do they will be violating some group's values. Thus, many women who might have wished to adopt a more passive, conforming behavior are forced to choose among highly value-charged alternatives. And, to a lesser degree, similar changes seem to be occurring for men.

It seems likely that the pressure to make independent choices of life-style and career is more difficult for women (in general) to cope with than for men. Conformity patterns have traditionally been different for men and for women, and research has consistently verified that these differences are in fact real and lasting: girls tend to be more conforming than boys, and women to be more conforming than men. Chabassol (1973, pp. 249-250) sums up the possible reasons underlying this finding: "If it can be accepted that girls are kept under closer scrutiny in our society than boys, the possibility exists that such adult vigilance has made for more permanent dependency needs in females than in males. . . . Or again, it may be that the female is not under pressure to be independent to the same extent as is the male, so that she can, without feeling threatened in her role, admit to fairly high WS needs [needs for structure] even in later adolescence." Both these causal conditions seem to be changing in our culture today. While boys are probably still less closely supervised than girls (at least during adolescence), the amount of adult vigilance expended on girls is decreasing drastically. And again, although there is still great pressure on girls to choose a role as homemaker, child rearer, and helpmate for a man, there is also increasing acceptance of the validity of independent career goals for women. If this trend continues, we may expect to see fewer differences between boys and girls in conformity behavior in the future. Indeed, some evidence of such a trend already exists: it has been shown that girls who accept the conventional notions of female roles are consistently more conforming than girls who reject such roles. While this statement is admittedly circular—since accepting those conventional roles is in itself a kind of conformity—it nevertheless points toward a trend that I believe will become increasingly pronounced.

## SITUATIONAL FACTORS

Throughout the last section, we found that it was difficult to generalize about conformers because whether one conforms depenos to a great degree on the situation. Two main clusters of situational factors affect conformity, one having to do with the nature of the individuals or group to which one may conform and the other having to do with the nature of the conforming activity. Let's consider each of these in turn.

### The Group

The more one values a group, the more likely one is to conform to its standards of behavior. This statement goes directly to the issue of "Conformity to whom?", which we mentioned earlier. In conforming to one individual or group, we inevitably fail to conform to another individual or group. Other things being equal, we conform to that person or group that we value the most. There are several reasons for this pattern, and most of

them are just a matter of common sense. The more we value someone, the more we want him to value or like us. A common way of getting someone to like you—or at least avoiding his dislike—is to conform to his ideas and behaviors. The sycophant, or yes man, is a caricature of this behavior; he agrees with his superior in every regard in hopes of gaining favor. Also, as I have pointed out, conforming to someone else's behavior is one way to feel that you are like him. The more we like a person or want to be a part of a group, the more we want to see ourselves as similar to that person or the people in that group. Conformity is a means to that end. Finally, the more attracted I am to someone, the more likely it is that I believe he will be "right"—that he will hold the "right" opinions, do the "right" things. It follows that the more I conform to him, the more "right" I will be. The stronger the individual's identification with his peer group, the greater the probability that he will value the peer group's attributes and behaviors more positively than his own. Further, the more strongly one identifies with one's peer group, the more negative is his evaluation of deviation from or transgression against the group and its members (Costanzo, 1970).

It seems reasonable to assume that members of cooperative groups will like each other better or will at least feel more friendly toward each other than members of competitive groups do; perhaps this is one reason cooperative groups have been found to exhibit more conforming behavior than competitive groups do (Crawford & Haaland, 1972). Also, the very nature of cooperation implies a degree of trust among group members that probably enhances conformity. If I am in competition with someone, I don't expect him to give away things that I can use (conform to), and I may suspect that he will throw out false cues so that conforming to him or imitating him may lessen my chances of winning. Cooperation requires a kind of togetherness in which members go along with each other for the sake of group unity, and to some degree this may make independent thinking more difficult or unlikely on the part of individual members. Cooperative groups tend to be more cohesive; members like each other better than they do in competitive groups. Again, this factor tends to increase conforming behavior (Elich, 1962).

With regard to the element of cohesiveness, however, we must be careful about drawing conclusions too quickly. Manipulating group cohesiveness in the laboratory setting is difficult to do. Frequently, the experimenter chooses subjects from a natural setting, such as a classroom, by asking people to indicate whom they would like to be with in a small group. This procedure yields a kind of sociometric chart, from which the experimenter can select groups of subjects who chose each other (the cohesive groups) and groups who did not choose each other. But almost inevitably the chosen individuals are chosen by many of their classmates, while the nonchosen group members are nonchosen not only by their comembers but by almost everyone else. In other words, the cohesive groups tend to contain the better-liked members of the class, while the noncohesive groups tend to be composed of the people who are rejected or ignored in the natural group (Moursund, 1963). Results that seem to relate to cohesiveness, then, may actually be related to or caused by differences in the kinds of people who are popular and unpopular in their social settings.

The size of the group to which one conforms helps to determine the amount of conforming behavior, but only up to a point. As the number of people to whom one feels pressure to conform increases, conformity does increase, but only up to about four or five people. Increasing the size beyond this relatively small number has little or no effect. And the influence of group size can be completely canceled out if there is one dissenting member—that is, one other person in the group with whom the nonconformer can agree. A dissident opinion, if expressed loudly and clearly, can have a tremendous effect in strengthening the independence of like-minded people (Crutchfield, 1963). A single nonconformer is a rebel, an outcast; but two dissenters form a group of their own. The person who agrees with me against the majority gives me information—since there are two of us, it is more likely that we are, in fact, correct—and also serves as an indicator that it is "all right" to disagree.

This latter notion—that disagreement with a majority position serves as support for disagreement in general—is related to studies of risky-shift behavior. It has been demonstrated many times that after discussing an issue openly in the group, members tend to become more willing to express ideas that may turn out to be wrong or to diverge from the group consensus. The shift from safe, conservative expressions to risky ones probably comes about as the more conservative group members see others taking chances. They learn that it is all right to voice hypothetical ideas, ideas that they may have to discard later (Wallach & Mabli, 1970). In the same way, the lone dissenting member in the conformity studies signals to other group members that it is all right to disagree, to be a nonconformer.

We can summarize the group characteristics affecting conformity, then, as follows: Conformity tends to increase as the group increases in size (up to a point) and as the group is valued by the potential conformer. It tends to decrease as the amount of cooperation within the group decreases and as the amount of support for a dissenting view increases.

## The Activity

The more ambiguous the task that must be performed or the decision that must be made, the more likely an individual is to conform to the group. Since difficult tasks are usually more ambiguous than simple ones—that is, the "correct" answer is less obvious—it follows that there will be more conforming behavior when the activity is difficult or complex (Trickett, 1971). In Asch's study and others that used the same experimental situation, conformity increased as the differences between the lengths of the lines shown to the subjects were made smaller; when the discrepancy between what the majority were saying and what the subject saw on the screen was great, conformity decreased. Nemeth and Markowski (1972) investigated this element of discrepancy in some detail and related it to the informational versus the normative influence of the group. When the discrepancies are low— that is, when the subject may have some doubt about whether his own perception is correct—the group provides information about what the objectively right answer may be. When the discrepancy is high, the subject finds it more difficult to doubt the accuracy of his perception; in this case, the pressure of the group becomes a *normative* influence, pushing him toward conformity for conformity's sake rather than conformity as a means of getting the right answer.

Nemeth and Markowski measured both public and private conformity in their experiment: that is, they asked some subjects to announce their choices out loud, while others recorded them privately. For all levels of discrepancy, public conformity was greater than private conformity (a finding that has been replicated by other experimenters and that was reported in the original Asch study). But the difference between private and public conformity was much greater at moderately high levels of discrepancy than at low levels of discrepancy. As the amount of discrepancy increased, subjects who were allowed to record their answers privately saw the information contained in the group's responses as less and less useful; they were able to disregard the normative pressure of the group because nobody in the group saw or heard their responses. When the answers were public, though, conformity increased as discrepancy increased. Pressure to go along outwardly became greater as evidence mounted that they and the group were seeing (or at least saying) different things. Finally, at extreme levels of discrepancy, both public and private conformity dropped to almost zero. With regard to private conformity, Nemeth and Markowski conclude that subjects may show conformity at low discrepancy levels, whereas at high discrepancy levels they may show no influence or even polarization—that is, they may become counterconformers.

Summarizing the factors relating to the conforming activity, then: Conformity depends on the informational and the normative influence of the group. Private conformity is more influenced by informational influences and thus tends to increase as the difficulty or ambiguity of the activity increases. Public conformity depends on both informational and normative aspects of group behavior—that is, on both social pressure to do the "right" thing and the use of the group as an information source—but as the difference increases between what one believes one should do and what the group is doing, normative influences become predominant. Up to a point, public conformity increases with this shift to normative group pressure; beyond that point, little or no conformity will occur. Where the shift will take place—how much disagreement an individual will go along with—is probably a function of the variables we mentioned in our discussion of group factors as well as of the personal characteristics of the potential conformer.

## THE TASK OF THE TEACHER

As teachers, we can have a significant impact on the conformity behavior of our students. In fact, we will have such an impact whether we want to or not; we cannot avoid encouraging some behaviors and discouraging others, as well as serving as role models for students. As a first step in clarifying our task, then, we should decide where we ourselves stand with regard to conformity. This is a value judgment, not one that can be decided on simply by weighing the facts (although knowledge of facts must surely enter in). Some educators value independence of thought and behavior as the only road to intellectual and creative growth; others see a certain amount of social conformity as the lubrication that allows the wheels of social interaction to continue to turn; still others value group cooperation and agreement and/or obedience above all else. None of these positions can be proven "right" or "wrong"; but we are morally and professionally obligated to decide for ourselves what we believe so that we can be open rather than covert in passing on those beliefs to our students.

I shall, therefore, pause here and try to make explicit my own values regarding conformity. I value highly the ability to think clearly and accurately; I hold this ability as a goal for both myself and my students. But I do not believe that acquiring such an ability implies that one must never conform. On the contrary, knowing—or sensing—when and how much to conform is for me an important part of the thinking process. Appropriate conformity is, I believe, an affirmation of one's humanity. Never to conform (and I mean here conforming in the sense of yielding to group pressure, not just coming to the same conclusion as the rest of the group) is to deny one's essential relatedness to others, to deny that feelings with and about others can and should enter into one's thinking. But there is a delicate balance here; too far in the direction of conformity and one endangers one's ability to think for oneself. I stand, therefore, in a position of compromise: valuing both conformity and independence, I should like to strive for the ability to know what I am doing or intend to do and why; with this knowledge, I can attempt to use either independence or conformity (or both) to serve the best interests of myself and others.

Self-knowledge is the essential ingredient in achieving an optimal mix of conformity and independence, and it is with self-knowledge that the teacher must begin. Riesman (1950/1961), in the midst of despair at the other-directedness (conformity) of society, saw understanding of one's own processes as a path toward more autonomous functioning. "The autonomous man growing up under conditions that encourage self-consciousness can disentangle himself from the adjusted others only by a further move toward even greater self-consciousness. His autonomy depends not upon the ease with which he may deny or disguise his emotions but, on the contrary, upon the success of his effort to recognize and respect his own feelings, his own potentialities, his own limitations" (p. 259). By respecting and valuing the student's feelings, as well as his intellectual productions, the teacher can lead him to respect and value those feelings himself; through respect and value of the feelings of which he is now aware, the student can become sensitive to broad ranges of feelings previously hidden from awareness. If knowledge is power, then self-knowledge is the most powerful power of all—especially in the area of understanding one's conformity.

But other knowledge is power too. "First and foremost, " says Crutchfield (1963, p. 227), "the individual needs to be educated as broadly and as deeply as possible. Armed with knowledge in many areas, he is . . . less vulnerable to conformity pressures that feed on ignorance." Blind conformity increases as ambiguity increases; and the best antidote for ambiguity is information. The better informed a person is, the less likely he will be to fall back on conformity as a substitute for thought.

It is incumbent on the teacher to be alert for ways to engage students in the search for, and appreciation of, knowledge. It is not necessary, or even likely, that these methods will exclude demands for some classroom conformity. Working for grades or other external reinforcers may enhance conformity behavior (Alker & Wohl, 1972), but it may also provide an opening wedge into a world of intellectual stimulation. Like the farmer who never beat his animals, but frequently hit his mule on the head with a hammer just to get its attention, the teacher may find grades or other coercive techniques to be useful in drawing the student's attention to new lines of thought. Demanding compliance (or conformity) can be the first step toward developing independence.

The teacher must never forget the subtle pressure that he exerts on his students simply as a function of being in the classroom and interacting with them. By virtue of the role he is in, the teacher is invested with an aura of authority, of power, of "rightness." And the better the teacher is at his job, the stronger this witch-doctor effect becomes; as the student learns to trust and respect and like the teacher, he is increasingly inclined to emulate him (to conform to him) in a variety of ways.

One of the dangers of the modern or progressive school format is that the teacher, in trying to escape from the old-fashioned lock-step conformity of predetermined assignments and examinations and so forth, will unwittingly set up a new and even more pervasive kind of conformity pressure. Instead of conforming to an authority figure, many modern school children are learning to conform to peers, and the classroom teacher is all too often the greatest proponent of such conformity. "She conveys to the children that what matters is not their industry or learning as such but their adjustment in the group, their cooperation, their (carefully stylized and limited) initiative and leadership" (Riesman, 1950/1961, p. 63). Again, we see the need for balance: total conformity to the group sounds the death knell for creativity and independence; but total independence leads to social isolation and chaos.

It is not enough to teach the child how to think for himself or how to be sensitive to the opinions and needs and feelings of others or even how to find a balance between the two. If one is to engage in such behaviors after he leaves the immediate learning environment, he must be convinced of their usefulness—he must learn to value them. One does not become an independent thinker or an "appropriate" conformer or a fully functioning interactor at some point and then continue to operate in that mode forever. Optimal functioning is a process, a quality one always approaches but never acquires. Albert (1967), who places the highest value on independent thinking, says that maintaining independence is not something one can do halfheartedly; if one is going to operate consistently independently one does it as a central part of his life-style and personality. So it is with the appropriate conformity that arises from sensitivity to self and others; one has to work at it, like any other skill, or it gets rusty. And rustiness implies falling back into older and easier habits of unthinking conformity or of automatic nonconformity or arrogant independence. Only a strong conviction as to the value and virtue of finding the best balance point between independence and conformity will keep a person at the difficult task of trying to maintain such a balance.

It is difficult, indeed, but I am convinced that the outcome can be well worth the effort. I hope to be the kind of teacher who can hold up for myself as well as for my students the goal of freedom: the sensitivity to others that underscores and emphasizes our individuality, and the independence that leaves us free to conform when we wish to.

## QUESTIONS FOR UNDERSTANDING

1. Both modeling, as a mode of learning, and locus of control, as a personality characteristic, have implications for conformity behavior. Discuss the relationships that may exist among these three concepts.

2. How are you, as a classroom teacher, likely to react to the conformity-independence continuum when you are dealing with (a) a child who consistently disrupts the group activities of the class; (b) a child who gets his assignments done well and on time, is consistently obedient to adult demands, but who has almost no friends his own age; (c) the leader of a street-corner gang of (pre)delinquent youths?

3. How might you best facilitate the development of healthy attitudes toward conformity and independence in a social studies class that is focusing on changing roles for women?
4. Discuss the advantages and disadvantages of conforming and nonconforming behavior in traditional academic achievement.
5. What sorts of classroom activities are most likely to move children in the direction of conformity? In the direction of independence? Discuss these activities as they might be specifically planned for the age group you intend to work with.

# Chapter 13

# Humor

There was once a South American scientist who was fascinated with the problem of longevity. He determined to spend his life trying to find ways of increasing the life span; while he was interested primarily in human life, he found himself forced to work with lower animals because of the possible side effects involved in his experiments. He worked with a number of different species, but finally settled on porpoises because of their similarity to humans iñ mental abilities. Finally, he hit on what seemed to be a perfect way of extending life: he found that feeding the porpoises a diet of freshly hatched sea gulls prevented them from aging. He presented his findings to the dictator of the country in which he lived—it was, like many South American countries, more or less a police state—and was provided money to set up an elaborate research facility. At one location on the coast he established a porpoise castle, where his experimental animals were housed. A few miles away he established the sea gull hatchery. Newly hatched sea gulls were delivered from the hatchery, in special vans, several times daily. All went well until one day when a tired old lion escaped from the state zoo and wandered off toward the coast. It grew sleepy and finally lay down to rest right in the middle of the road leading from the hatchery to the porpoise castle. One of the delivery vans, in great haste to deliver the sea gulls fresh, ran over the lion and killed it. Whereupon the police came, arrested the scientist, tried him, and bundled him off to jail. The charge: transporting gulls across a state lion for immortal porpoises.

That sort of joke is more often greeted with groans than with laughter, yet many people would agree that it is, indeed, funny. But why? What makes it funny? Or, perhaps more to the point, what is it in you that makes you respond to it with feelings of amusement? There are a number of theories about why people laugh or why they are amused by certain things. In this chapter, we shall discuss some of those theories. We shall also talk about the functions served by humor and about how a sense of humor develops in a person. Finally, we shall look at humor specifically as it relates to learning, particularly classroom learning. Although we shall leave this specific relationship until last, it may be well to point out a fundamental assumption at the outset: humor is (as far as we know) a uniquely human attribute. It adds a whole new dimension to the way in which we view and deal with the world. The ability to react humorously—to be amused—is a highly valuable quality; its growth is something the teacher should be sensitive to and should try to encourage. In addition to its value for its own sake, humor can serve a number of other functions: like a hot shower on a cold day, it not only feels good but also is useful. Awareness of the ways in which humor can be used can make the job of both the teacher and the student easier—as well as a lot more fun.

## WHY ARE THINGS FUNNY?

The problem of explaining the nature of humor presents a challenge that has intrigued psychologists and philosophers for years. Humor is like quicksilver; the moment you think you have it captured, you find it isn't there any more. It melts away at the first touch. Few things are as unfunny as the explanation of a joke, and the quickest way to destroy the humor in a situation is to try to tell someone else why you think it is funny. Yet, though it seems to defy analysis, humor is always recognizable to the person experiencing it. "Humor is unique in the sense that it can hardly be mistaken for anything else. Nobody is ever in any doubt about whether a joke is funny to him. Its humor can hardly be confused with any other quality. Anybody can usually pinpoint without hesitation what it is about a joke that amuses him, although it is often hard to explain why it is amusing" (Keith-Spiegel, 1972, p. 44). Yet attempts have been made, and while they often seem to fall short, to be partly right but to miss an essential aspect, they do provide some insights for each of us into a process that may be unique and specific to the individual.

More likely—and certainly more parsimonious—than the notion that each person responds to potential humor in a different way is the suggestion made by Davis and Farina (1970): humor is an umbrella term that refers to a number of different processes. An explanation or description may fit one class of humorous events well and another not at all. Humor may thus be a composite of different behaviors rather than a single one, and any attempt to explain them equally will probably only partially explain an individual one. As we look at some of the better-known theories about the mechanisms underlying humor, we would do well to remind ourselves that a single explanation need not fit every instance of humor, any more than a single item of clothing need be appropriate for all occasions in order to be a useful garment.

## Humor and Aggression

Freud made one of the first attempts to deal with humor as an important aspect of human behavior. In his 1916 book, *Wit and Its Relation to the Unconscious* (1938), Freud distinguished between harmless wit and tendency wit. *Harmless wit* results from condensation of meaning of one sort or another and is funny (or pleasurable) because of the cleverness with which the witty person economizes in expressing what he is trying to say. Freud's analysis of harmless wit has received less attention than that of tendency wit, however: *tendency wit* allows one to express taboo or unacceptable ideas in a disguised form. These ideas are always based on either aggressive or sexual impulses. That humor can reduce aggressive and sexual drives is the most widely tested hypothesis in the field of humor research, according to Goldstein, Suls, and Anthony (1972). The relationship between humor and aggression, in particular, has been the subject of much study.

Nearly any joke or humorous situation can be related in some way to aggressive and/or sexual fantasy. The story about the scientist and the porpoises, for instance, involves driving over an animal with a truck and also throwing someone into jail—both fairly aggressive activities. And the punch line of that joke is obviously sexual in its allusion. To be amused simply by the idea of violence against animals or people or by thoughts of prostitution is socially unacceptable; the joke allows us to experience pleasure in such ideas. At the same time, the punch line displays the element of condensation that, according to Freud, is fundamental to humor: it neatly packages two different notions into one sentence.

The chief source of pleasure in wit, according to Grotjahn (1966), is the release of inhibition or of repression. Modern humorists such as Don Rickles and Godfrey Cambridge have built their whole style on the aggressive content of humor—often, in their routines, the hostility is hardly disguised at all; but the hostility can be tolerated because it is presented (and accepted by the audience) as something funny, something to be laughed at.

If some things are funny because they allow us to express aggressiveness in socially acceptable ways, does it follow that aggressive people respond more favorably to hostile humor than do nonaggressive people? A study by Heatherington and Wray (1966) suggests that this is true. They measured the aggressiveness of a group of college students by means of a self-description personality test and then asked them to indicate how much they liked a set of cartoons. The high-aggressive subjects preferred aggressive cartoons to nonsense cartoons, while the low-aggressive subjects liked the nonsense cartoons better.

The person who is able to describe himself on a questionnaire as having aggressive characteristics is not likely to be anxious or defensive about his aggression; he is quite willing to admit to it. But what about the person who is defensive? If I don't like my aggressiveness—if I'm afraid or ashamed of it—then being reminded of it will probably make me feel anxious. A self-description personality scale should do just that; as I read the items and try to decide whether they apply to me, I become anxious about the aggressiveness that I don't want to admit to. Doris and Fierman (1956) asked their subjects to take a personality questionnaire and then to rate cartoons, but they scored the questionnaires on the basis of anxiety. The high-anxious subjects did not like aggressive humor as much as the low-anxious subjects did. Aggressive humor, then, is likely to be funny to the person who is openly aggressive or is accepting of his own aggressiveness; it is likely to be threatening to the person who is bothered by his own aggressiveness.

Since many humorous situations combine aggressive content with other aspects of humor (which we'll discuss later), the aggressive and the nonaggressive person may both laugh at the same joke but for different reasons. Anger, according to Dworkin and Efran (1967), does not make people more appreciative of humor in general; rather, it appears to lead the individual to respond selectively to hostile humor. In other words, people respond more strongly to humor stimuli that in some way parallel or relate to their current feelings and beliefs. The opportunity to release angry or hostile feelings is an important part of humor when it speaks to the condition of the angry or hostile individual.

## Humor and Arousal

The idea that a joke may have sexual as well as aggressive content is certainly nothing new to most of us; we've all heard (and frequently enjoyed) dirty jokes. Following the line of reasoning established in the previous section, though, can we assume that sexually oriented jokes are funnier to the sexually aroused individual, just as aggressive humor seems to be funnier to the aggressive person? Studies by Lamb (1968) and by Davis and Farina (1970) confirm this hypothesis: they found that sexually aroused subjects found sexual cartoons funnier than did nonaroused subjects, but there were no differences between the two in their reaction to other sorts of humor. Reactions to humor are often highly complex, and the dirty joke is no exception. How often have you heard someone say "I like a dirty joke if it's funny, but not if it's just dirty for the sake of being dirty"? That sort of statement brings us back to the original question; the speaker would probably find it quite difficult to say what there is about some dirty jokes that makes them funny while others are not. Even in this day and age we tend to be defensive about our sexuality or about certain aspects of it; the sexual joke that touches on a sensitive area may not seem funny to us at all. Also, reactions to sexual humor are complicated by a number of other factors, such as the sex of the person telling the joke (Doris & Fierman, 1956) and the sex of the audience (O'Connell, 1960). The number of other people listening to a joke can influence our reaction to it, as can our expectations as to whether the others will think it funny or will think it vulgar of us to be amused.

General physiological arousal, as contrasted with sexual arousal, has been suggested as another possible underlying factor in the humor response. Berlyne (1972) hypothesizes two arousal patterns that can contribute to experiencing a situation as funny. One of these, the *arousal boost,* involves a moderate increase in arousal that can be experienced as pleasant all by itself. The other, which Berlyne calls an *arousal jag,* occurs when the arousal level goes too high to be pleasant any more; pleasure is felt when the level falls off again. Both arousal patterns can occur in the same situation: the arousal level rises a bit, which feels good, and a subsequent reduction in arousal also is pleasant. This boost-jag pattern is possibly the most common one in a joke-telling situation. The joke begins by arousing our interest, our curiosity, or our expectation of being amused by the promised story; the punch line "solves" the problem in a novel way and allows the arousal level to be reduced. The rise and fall in arousal, according to Berlyne, is at the root of what we call amusement or mirth. Shellberg, in a paper reported by Langevin and Day (1972), expands on this theory. According to her, the relaxed person (low arousal level) responds to a joke or cartoon with a moderate boost in arousal and thus finds the situation amusing. The moderately aroused person adds the arousal from the joke to the arousal already present from other sources; he experiences a higher arousal level and a greater drop in arousal at the end of the joke, and thus finds it funnier. In contrast, the highly aroused person is already experiencing an uncomfortable level of stimulation, and adding arousal from a comic stimulus raises it still further; thus he either ignores the humor stimulus or finds it unpleasant. The teacher who tells a joke during an ordinary class session may find the students receptive and amused, but the same joke told just before an important exam may meet with a quite different response.

Physiological arousal is more easily and reliably measured than many of the variables important to human behavior, so it is not surprising that a number of researchers have attempted to test directly the relationship between arousal and humor. Langevin and Day (1972), for instance, found that galvanic skin response (a measure of the conductivity of the skin, which is directly affected by the activity of the sweat glands) in their subjects was positively correlated with humor appreciation. One of the best known studies of arousal and humor was carried out by Schachter and Wheeler in the early 1960s. They administered doses of epinephrine (an arouser), chloropromazine (a depressant), or a sterile water placebo to subjects and then asked them to watch a humorous movie. All of the subjects thought they were getting harmless "vitamin shots," but some were told that there might be a few short-term physiological side effects from the shots. The epinephrine subjects found the movie much funnier than the chloropromazine subjects; the placebo subjects were between the two extremes. The authors conclude that the subjects' reactions to the film involved both their physiological state and their understanding of what was happening. "Given a state of physiological arousal for which an individual has no immediate explanation, he will 'label' this state and describe his feelings in terms of the cognitions available to him" (Schachter & Wheeler, 1962, p. 127). Schachter and Wheeler also found that epinephrine subjects who were not told that they would experience side effects from the "vitamin shot" found the movie much more amusing than those who were told that they would feel high or euphoric. In other words, if they could attribute their physical condition to the drug, they were not as likely to think it was the film that was causing their response, and so they didn't need to label it particularly funny. Even when the source of the arousal is known, however, it can still contribute to amusement. Substances that affect body chemistry are frequently used both to help an individual enjoy a situation more and to explain his "overreaction"—alcohol and marijuana are common examples.

## Expectancy Violation

I have now mentioned a physiological (arousal) and an emotional (impulse-release) theory of humor; the third major theory deals with cognitive behavior. According to this theory, humor is based on *expectancy violation*—the abrupt shift in perspective or implication that accompanies the punch line of a joke. The punch line of the porpoise story, for example, involves using five words in a totally different sense from the way they were used before. This sudden change, the feeling of being yanked into a quite different context, is what makes the joke funny. Zijderveld (1968) sees this expectancy violation as a kind of social unmasking, in which we are allowed (or forced) to look at our social customs or institutions or meanings in a different light. A socially accepted or traditional meaning structure is exposed to a totally different meaning structure; and the traditional meaning is then seen in the context of the new structure. McGhee (1972) suggests that such an interpretation of humor be considered a minitheory; it explains only one possible aspect of humor. He goes on to point out that enjoying humor based on expectancy violation requires a certain degree of cognitive mastery—that is, a person must be able to form an expectancy based on understanding of the real world in order to get the joke. The child who has not yet formed a stable expectancy about the subject matter of the joke is likely to try to *reality assimilate* its content. He tries to understand it in a literal sense and does not experience it as funny. An expectancy violation, in contrast, involves *fantasy assimilation:* the joke content need not be fitted into reality as the listener understands reality but can be enjoyed as fantasy.

In this context, we should note that the timing of the joke is important.

Whether it is the punch line of a funny story or a bit of stage business of a comedian or a quite unintentionally humorous remark, the expectancy violation must be sudden in order to be experienced as funny. The speed with which the shift takes place can be related to arousal theory as well; here, too, it is a quick change rather than a gradual one that accompanies the feeling of amusement. "Whatever processes produce humor, including any perceptual or intellectual processing and any shifts in arousal level, are generally abrupt and over within a few seconds" (Keith-Spiegel, 1972).

### Identification

Do we need to feel personal involvement—that is, identification—with a story or situation in order to find it funny? Or does such involvement at least enhance the funniness? Here again the complex nature of the humor response makes the question hard to answer in a simple yes-or-no way. Williams and Cole (1964) used an experimental treatment that made some of their subjects feel inadequate—or at least feel that the experimenter thought they were inadequate. They then asked the subjects to rate the funniness of a series of jokes in which the humor involved someone else's inadequacy. As the authors expected, subjects who had been made to feel inadequate found such jokes funnier than subjects who had not experienced such treatment. Hammes and Wiggins (1962), however, found that the intensity of the feeling that formed the basis for identification was an important factor. Their subjects rated *Peanuts* cartoons for funniness; males, who were better able to identify with the male characters in the cartoons, found them funnier than did females. But high-anxiety males, who probably experienced many of the same kinds of problems that *Peanuts* cartoons so often spoof, did not find the cartoons particularly amusing.

Most jokes have either a hero or a victim; many have both. It is possible to identify with either or even with both at the same time. Or we may form a *counteridentification,* in which we see an unpleasant character as unlike ourselves. In this situation, we are likely to enjoy the counteridentified character's discomfiture; the joke is funny because the victim gets what he deserves in some way or another. Cantor and Zillman (1973) found that counteridentification alone was enough to enhance the funniness of a situation. Resentment toward the victim facilitated enjoyment, whether or not the subject identified with the punishing or ridiculing agent. Yet here again feelings can be too strong for humor; when the victim in Cantor and Zillman's cartoons was severely punished, subjects saw the situations as less funny. These findings, then, relate to Shellberg's hypothesis regarding arousal. A certain amount of identification helps us to enjoy a joke in that it contributes to our arousal level. But too much identification means too much arousal, and the joke is no longer funny. It reminds us too directly of our own personal needs, it hits too close to home; and our response is, like Queen Victoria's, "We are not amused."

### The Social Nature of Humor

One final comment about the nature of humor: humor and its appreciation are essentially social phenomena. It is difficult, if not impossible, to imagine a humorous situation that does not involve at least the potential of social interaction. We may smile at something when we are alone, but laughter is enjoyed in the company of others. Laughter occurs—or is expected to occur—only within patterns of interaction. This seemingly most spontaneous means of individual release and self-expression is not expected to be used by a person who is alone. Laughter must be shared; it is socially defined as a prime part of the interactive process, of the give and take of social life (Coser, 1959). Laughter invites laughter; hearing someone else laugh may, all by itself, initiate a laughter response in us. The film *Mary Poppins* has a delightful scene in which the old uncle of Bert, the chimney sweep, laughs so hard that he floats up to the ceiling and can't get down. Bert, Mary Poppins, and the children come to help him and are so caught up in the contagion of his laughter that they, too, rise to the ceiling and bob there helplessly. This episode illustrates not only how infectious laughter can be for the characters of the movie, but how the audience as well cannot help laughing along with the giggles, snickers, and guffaws coming from the screen.

Humor as a kind of social contagion—humor as impulse release—humor as changes in arousal level—humor as a response to cognitive shifts

—which are we to accept as the valid explanation? Fortunately, we need not choose; there is no reason to believe that there must be only one determinant of humor. A given situation may involve any combination of these four elements, and the same situation may involve different elements for different people. Understanding some of the basic determinants of humor can help us to explain why one person may find something funny while another does not; it may point to the reasons why one kind of humor is more effective with youngsters than another; it may (perhaps most importantly of all) give us some insights into our own reasons for laughing or not laughing at ourselves or others. Knowing why something is funny or when it is likely to be funny is the first step toward using humor effectively in facilitating learning. Let's go on now to the next major step: understanding what humor and laughter do for us.

## THE FUNCTION OF HUMOR

Humor is "the ego's victorious assertion of its own invulnerability. It refuses to be hurt by the arrows of reality or to be compelled to suffer. It insists that it is impervious to wounds dealt by the outside world, in fact, that these are merely occasions for affording it pleasure" (Freud, 1928/ 1959, p. 217). Freud made a fundamental distinction between humor and wit; the purpose of wit, he said, is simply to afford gratification or, in so doing, to provide an outlet for aggressive tendencies. Humor, for Freud, has a loftier nature; it has an almost sublime quality of defying reality, affording pleasure, and yet maintaining sanity and reason. How does such a remarkable thing come to happen? How does humor—or rather, how does man, using humor—manage to attain such an end?

Humor serves a number of functions, no one of which taken alone could account for Freud's "victorious assertion." Yet all these functions taken together may do just that. We shall examine some aspects of the humor experience one at a time, but we should keep in mind that each of these is part of a larger picture; we do not experience them one at a time but rather all together, and that total experience is what humor is all about.

Let us start with a truism: it feels good to laugh. However we may ultimately break that statement down or analyze the components of feeling good, there is a basic and irreducible truth right here. Laughing, being amused, is pleasant, just as eating a good meal when you are hungry or relaxing in a hot tub when you are tired is pleasant. My 3-year-old daughter, when she is being tickled, squirms and tries to escape; but as soon as she is released, she demands "Do it again!" It is not the physical sensation of being tickled that she enjoys, but rather her own laughter. As we grow older, that which causes us to laugh is less likely to be tickling and more likely to be a social-cognitive event, but the feeling is the same: it is pleasant to be amused and to laugh. "It is hard to imagine anybody finding something humorous and not enjoying it. He might very well be left indifferent by somebody's attempt at humor. But if he does not derive pleasure from it himself, it is certainly not humorous for him" (Keith-Spiegel, 1972, p. 44). While humor undoubtedly serves other functions as well, the importance of this simple, indivisible pleasure response should not be overlooked. Laughing, like scratching an itch, feels good because it feels good; it would need to do nothing else for us in order to be valuable.

### Avoidance and Catharsis

But humor does do something more, as many theorists have asserted. One function, as we have already seen in Freud's remarks, is allowing us to escape or deny reality. McGhee (1972) points out that reality assimilation —that is, perceiving reality accurately and dealing with it effectively—is often a difficult and tiring necessity from which we all need an occasional vacation. Humor offers an easy and socially acceptable means of accomplishing this escape; and perhaps that is why humor is so frequent and important in everyday behavior. From this point of view, humor's value lies not so much in what it gives us as in what it allows us to avoid.

In extremely stressful situations, we can often find humor being used deliberately and consciously as a means of avoiding reality. I remember clearly my first experiences working in a mental hospital, back in the pre-tranquilizer days when patients often did and said quite bizarre things. I was shocked by the way in which staff members laughed at such patients—after all, we were there to help them, and laughing at them seemed hurtful and cruel. I soon found, however, that laughing at patients was one way—and sometimes the only way—to keep from being overcome by the real tragedy of their circumstances. "It's better to laugh at them than to cry for them" said one staff psychologist; for his professional survival, he was undoubtedly right. Grotjahn (1966, p. 63) makes much the same comment about the cynic: "A cynic keeps himself from becoming depressed through his callous show of aggressiveness. A cynical remark keeps the tears away, as any newspaper man or ambulance attendant assigned to cover a disaster will vouch for."

Humor allows us not only to avoid feeling bad but also to convert unpleasant feelings into pleasant ones. Laughter, says Berlyne (1972), functions as a discharge, as a means of relief. People may very well be extremely wrought up and uncomfortable before laughing, but they usually feel markedly better for at least a short while afterward. The release from tension through an emotional outburst is known as *catharsis,* and the outburst can be one of tears, anger, or laughter. Cathartic outbursts of anger or grief seldom occur until one's emotional tension has grown very great, and the outburst is usually equally intense. Laughter, in contrast, can reduce tension at lower levels, without the feelings of upheaval and exhaustion that typically follow other kinds of cathartic release. Using humor in this way is clearly a part of the folk wisdom of our culture and probably of others as well. We tell a funny story to someone who seems depressed in order to cheer him up, or we try to make a child smile or laugh to help him get over a disappointment. We use humor catharsis on ourselves as well; the laughter in the teacher's lounge or the staff dining room is often the result of an anecdote that, when it first occurred, elicited feelings of anger or distress. By retelling the story, by laughing at ourselves and encouraging others to laugh too, we relieve the distress and replace it (at least temporarily) by pleasure.

Even situations involving extreme personal distress and pain are sometimes relieved by humor. Hysterical laughter is an example of the distress-to-humor reaction in a highly uncontrolled form. Inappropriate laughter oftens betrays internal tension; we have all seen children giggle when they are facing a frightening ordeal such as a public appearance, and many of us have experienced as adults that almost uncontrollable urge to laugh in stressful interpersonal situations where to do so would invite social disaster. Zijderveld (1968, p. 302) talks about the "coincidentia oppositorium," or merging of opposites, common in emotional jokes. "An example of this is the current, often rather crude joking after burial of a loved person: the emotions of grief change into their opposite and become stimuli for laughter. Through this, relief from emotional tensions is accomplished."

Relief of anger through humor has been a favorite subject for experimental study, perhaps because anger is created more easily in an experimental situation than many other kinds of emotional response. Landy and Mettee (1969) asked their experimenters to treat subjects in nasty and frustrating ways. When the subjects were thoroughly angry with the experimenters, they were divided into two groups: one group worked on a cartoon-rating task, in which they judged how funny a series of cartoons were, while others looked at photographs of people. As the theory predicted, subjects who looked at cartoons reported less anger at the end of the experiment than did those who just looked at photographs. Even under highly frustrating conditions, humor tends to defuse anger. R. E. Smith (1973) reports a case history in which the anger-reduction characteristics of humor were deliberately used in psychotherapy. A 22-year-old woman suffered from extreme anger, which she was unable to control and which did not respond to conventional psychotherapeutic treatment. The therapist taught her to fantasize a humorous situation whenever she found herself getting angry; the humor response to the fantasy reduced her anger and also allowed her to gain new insights into the anger-eliciting situations.

## Communication

We have already seen that laughter and humor are primarily social activities. As such, they have important functions in establishing and maintaining social relationships. Zijderveld (1968) comments that jokes are essentially empty forms that can be filled up with totally different meanings, depending on the specific people and the specific situations. The funniness of a joke depends not only on the intention of the joker but also on the audience's definition of the joke situation. Both the joker—and this refers not only to the teller of a formally defined joke but also to the person making a witty comment or pointing out the humorous element of a social situation—and the listener help to determine whether a joke will be experienced as funny, and both participate in the social benefits of the joke.

A major social function of humor is communication. The joke or joke situation involves a condensation of meaning; it conveys a great deal more than it says explicitly. The subtleties of meaning in a joke allow a kind of tentative communication, in which the joker can make a comment without completely committing himself to it. If he senses that his communication is not received as he had hoped—if it is not understood or if it is disapproved—he can pretend that he never intended to say that in the first place; he was "only joking." The listener, too, takes part in this tentative communication. His smile or laughter signifies initial approval, but he can always fall back into a pretense of having misunderstood the underlying message or of having been amused by some other, less threatening aspect of the joke situation.

Such joking allows people to explore gradually each other's beliefs and attitudes without having to make these beliefs so explicit that they need stand in the way of further communications if disagreement occurs. Much of this social reconnaissance goes on at an unconscious or preconscious level. Both speaker and listener may be relatively unaware of the nature of their communication; indeed, such unawareness is necessary if the possibility of not understanding is to be maintained. Yet mutual appraisal is undeniably present in many joking situations, particularly when the participants are not well acquainted. One of the reasons that we like people who laugh at our jokes or who say things that make us laugh is that we tend to share their attitudes and values. Joking and laughter first define these shared areas and later continue to confirm them. "The 'little jokes' and humorous banter so often observed in everyday interactions and when first acquaintances are made are ways of revealing friendship, approval, and a sharing of sentiment, and relieving a somewhat awkward situation. More specifically, the function of humor is to initiate and facilitate communication and development of social relationships: through humor, consensus is achieved and social distance is reduced" (Martineau, 1972, pp. 116–117).

To laugh or to cause others to laugh by using humor and wit is to invite those present to come close (Coser, 1959). Like an invitation to a party, such an invitation can be the prelude to enjoyable interaction, to the forming and strengthening of group bonds, to the establishment of intimate and meaningful relationships. As with other invitations, though, there is the potential for social embarrassment: inviting you to my party means that you must invite me to yours, and I must try to come. It is difficult to maintain distance once one has been close, and the intimacy of shared laughter is a destroyer of status and role distance.

## Group Effects

One consequence of the social-communication effect of humor is the facilitation of other group activities. If I know, through shared laughter, that I am an accepted and valued member of a group, I am more likely to work harder toward group goals. Also, when group members disagree about how to proceed in their activity, the person who feels secure is better able to make a risky suggestion; he is not afraid that disapproval of the suggestion will lead to his rejection by the group. Groups who laugh together can argue with each other productively because the disagreement is more likely to be confined to its own appropriate area; it doesn't spill over into generalized interpretations of "They disagree with me so therefore they are rejecting me as a person." Goodchilds (1972) describes humor that has this kind of communicative function as healing humor. Group humor does help heal the breaches in group solidarity; but, more importantly, it works to prevent those breaches from opening in the first place.

Humor that emphasizes us as a group laughing at him or them, the outsiders, unifies and solidifies the group. In a more general sense, any shared laughter increases cohesiveness among those who laugh: people who laugh together tend to like each other. Cohesiveness is especially enhanced, however, when there is a reason why we can laugh at the joke but nobody else can. The in joke, which uses special vocabulary or depends for its humorous effect on an incident known only to group members, is a good example. Laughing at an in joke increases my feeling of belonging to the group and thus brings me closer to its individual members.

Similarly, a joking remark that calls attention to a shared experience can go a long way toward creating a group out of a collection of individuals. Coser (1959), who observed the joking behavior of hospital patients, was particularly interested in the group-making function of jocular griping. Unlike the complainer, the patient who invited others to laugh with him created or strengthened the feeling of equality. Jocular griping brought about a social relationship in its purest form: that of reciprocity. The jocular gripe is based on shared experience. More than that, however, it is based on experience shared by equals. When a person of lower status attempts a jocular gripe to a higher-status individual, he is often rejected; sharing the joke would imply equality, which the listener is unwilling to confer. Teachers can and do gripe to each other about the aberrations of their principal, but sharing such gripes with students is often considered inappropriate. The doctor who exchanges jocular gripes with his hospitalized patient or the teacher who does so with his student is saying "Look, we're both under their thumbs; we share in being forced to submit to the unreasonable restrictions that they place on us." Both doctor and teacher need (for a variety of reasons) to present themselves at times as being allied with the "them" of this communication; to share in the jocular gripe creates a realignment that may seriously interfere with meeting this need.

We saw earlier that humor releases tension and helps the individual to temporarily deny unpleasant realities. It serves the same function in group relationships. "Humor is a 'safety valve,' i.e., it provides institutionalized outlets for hostilities and for discontent ordinarily suppressed by the group" (Coser, 1959, p. 180). Anger at a comember of the group, openly expressed, breaks down cohesiveness; anger expressed in humor can dissipate itself in laughter or can pave the way to better understanding and acceptance. Laughing together at an outside threat is one way of denying the seriousness of the threat. It allows the members to fall back and regroup, to draw on mutual strength with which to meet the danger. Humor can be a compensatory device, making the fear and tragedy of the moment seem perhaps only temporary. Humor therefore serves as a means of controlling the behavior of those who share the burden (Martineau, 1972). Joking about objectively real danger or pain is a way of telling the group that one is not ready to deal with that danger on a reality basis and of asking for support for the denial; laughter provides the support and also promises the threatened individual that he will not have to face the danger alone.

## Disapproval Humor

Humor can be used to express disapproval as well as approval. We have all seen political cartoons that are savagely destructive. To be laughed with is delightful; to be laughed at can be devastating. Children's humor often seems especially cruel in this respect; but I suspect that it appears so to us adults only because we have grown accustomed to disguising the same kind of humor when we use it ourselves. A knife is no less sharp when it stabs someone from behind a veil. The child who chants "Sammy wears fun-nee clothes" and the newspaper columnist who satirizes the administration are both using the same kind of weapon. The difference is that the child is open and unsubtle, while the columnist makes use of highly skillful techniques that allow us to laugh without admitting to ourselves how cruel or destructive that laughter is.

Not all disapproval humor, though, is destructive. Humor is used to express grievances or can be directed at someone in the group who either has not learned or has violated the norms of the group. Humor can be a subtle way of warning the deviant and at the same time of providing him with an opportunity to accept the humorous definition of the situation, to acknowledge that his behavior was out of line and to correct it, and then to rejoin the group without losing face (Martineau, 1972). Gentle humor can correct and admonish without confronting, without forcing the offender to admit openly that he is wrong. It also allows the admonisher to retreat if he is wrong—again, he can claim that he was only joking. In the movie *Anatomy of a Murder,* James Stewart played a lawyer who loved to go fishing. Eve Arden, his secretary, was annoyed because the office refrigerator was full of fish that would probably never be eaten. "If this refrigerator gets any more fish in it," she commented, "it's going to have to swim upstream and spawn." The remark was a gentle rebuke that demanded no open acknowledgement. Its disapproval was clear, but either party could choose to deny the underlying message.

In summary, then, humor can serve both positive and negative social functions. It can draw group members closer together, and it can exclude people from the group. It can encourage, or it can disapprove. It can invite, or it can reject. Martineau (1972, p. 103) says:

> We advocate that humor be viewed from the sociological perspective as a "lubricant" and an "abrasive" in social interaction—especially in such common everyday interaction that constitutes the basis of the social order and makes the routine flow of social life possible. By this we mean, to use an analogy, that on the one hand, the interjection of the humorous serves as oil pumped from an oil can. . . . On the other hand, but not mutually exclusive from the former, humor may serve as an abrasive. Rather than oiling the workings of social interaction, it constitutes a measure of sand. The consequence of such abrasive humor is interpersonal friction and a juncture in the communication process which may modify the character of the interaction.

Whether as oil or as sand, humor communicates feelings and subtleties of meaning that cannot be expressed directly. It is an important tool for social interaction; even when expressed as nonsense or as a "trivial" witticism, it is highly meaningful.

## THE DEVELOPMENT OF ADULT HUMOR

It is extraordinarily difficult to describe or understand the development of humor in children simply because we as adults cannot readily escape from our own frame of reference. Children don't laugh at many things that are funny to adults; does that mean that their sense of humor is less well developed? They do laugh, however, at many things that seem quite unfunny to you or me; and we, in true heads-I-win-tails-you-lose fashion, point to this fact as another indication of their immaturity. Humor can, at best, be defined only subjectively. When we talk about the development of a child's sense of humor, then, what we mean is the way his sense of humor comes to conform to our own. There is at least a minimal consensus as to the kinds of things that are, or ought to be, funny among adults; and we can try to discover the process by which a child becomes a part of this consensus. But we should take care to recognize what we are doing. The child's sense of humor is different from that of most adults, and few adults can share or understand it. Through a gradual metamorphosis, children's humor becomes adult humor. It is that process, the shift from one kind of humor to another, rather than the "growth" of humor, that we shall explore in this section.

*Infant Behavior.* If we cannot understand children's humor or appreciate it subjectively, how do we know when it is present? One simple answer is to look for its correlates, smiling and laughter. While this criterion is not a terribly accurate one (among adults, at least, laughter and smiling can occur in the absence of humor, and humor can sometimes be produced and/or appreciated in the absence of smiles or laughter), it seems to be the best we have. You may argue that best simply isn't good enough—that babies smile and gurgle and laugh just because they feel good and not because they find something funny. But perhaps that argument is a semantic trap: what, after all, differentiates feeling good from being amused? Is the distinction perhaps not a part of the very thing we are trying to look at —the transformation of children's humor into adult humor? The question, of course, is unanswerable, again because we cannot get out of our own frame of reference to examine it. We shall have to leave it (and ourselves) dangling and move on to studies that have in fact dealt with smiling and laughter in children.

In 1946, Spitz published an extensive account of smiling responses in infants. He found that very young infants smiled most often in response to a human or humanoid (that is, with eyes, nose, and mouth in standard position) face. The full face was necessary to elicit a smile—a profile would not do—and smiling and nodding helped. Although it cannot be substantiated, one can speculate that the infant's smile is, in this case at least, a rudimentary form of interaction; the necessity that the stimulus face be turned toward the infant suggests that the two are looking at each other, which in turn seems to imply communication of a sort.

Smiling behavior as described by Spitz begins around the sixth week of life. Laughter comes later, although it is well established by the end of the first year. At first, laughter is directly connected to body movement as the child is dandled, bounced, or swung about by adults. As he learns to control his own movements, physical accomplishments are often accompanied by laughter. "While laughter appears to accompany a sheer joy of bodily movement in most infants, the mastery of motor skills through play probably plays an important role in . . . superiority laughter" (McGhee, 1971b, p. 329). Something new has entered the picture here; "I can do it" has a different flavor from the simple "It feels good" or the "You are here" smile of the small infant. It implies a contrast—"I can do it now" contrasts with "I couldn't do it before." As mastery grows, the "I can do it" experience is a confirmation of that mastery. We saw earlier in this chapter that one element of adult humor is expectancy disconfirmation, in which things don't turn out as we expect them to. Is it possible that the pleasure derived from disconfirmation is an outgrowth and reversal of the infant's delight in confirmation, of the establishment of expectancies? If so, the child's laugh of delight when he manages to stack one block on another and his happy crow at a game of peek-a-boo are both aspects of the same process: the building up and confirming of expectations about how the world around him (and he himself as a part of that world) will behave.

*Humor in Young Children.* In addition to confirming one's expectations, the experience of mastery relates directly to the competence motive. As was discussed in Chapter 8, a number of theorists have suggested that the exercise of competence is a basic drive among humans (and other species as well). Satisfaction of that drive, like any other, feels good: the good feeling may be sufficient in itself to elicit laughter in a child. This is McGhee's position: "Young children appear to show very early a need to master or deal competently with their environment, both cognitively and physically. Immense pleasure seems to be derived from the child's initial understanding of some previously unmastered physical task. The acknowledgement of the inaccurate depiction of that event may serve to remind [the child] of his own high level of mastery of the event and consequently reinitiate the original pleasure in mastery. This pleasure is manifest in the form of a smile or laugh" (McGhee, 1972, p. 71). McGhee, then, relates the laughter of children to the infant's initial pleasure in mastery. Jokes, cartoons, or situations are funny if they remind the child of his own triumphs over the physical world.

Experiencing mastery can have another meaning for the child; it is a disconfirmation of his helplessness and as such is a means of allaying his anxiety about being small and defenseless in a dangerous world. If the world is orderly, then he has a chance of coping with it; and if he can cope with it, then he need not be helpless and dependent on others. Just as the exercise of mastery declares his ability to cope, so the nonsense joke of the child is a reaffirmation of the orderliness and dependability of the world. "See," the joke is saying, "we can mix things all up in words and create a fantasy world where everything is topsy-turvy, but the real world—a world that I can cope with and where I don't feel helpless—will still be there when we are done."

Freud took a quite different view of humor in childhood: he denied that there could be such a thing. Young children's laughter, he believed, represented a naturally nonanxious state; the humor of adults is in essence an attempt to return somehow to the prehumor joy of childhood. "The euphoria which we are thus striving to obtain is nothing but the state of a bygone time, in which we were wont to defray our psychic work with slight expenditure. It is the state of our childhood, in which we did not know the comic, were incapable of wit, and did not need humor to make us happy"

(1905/1960). Perhaps the euphoria described by Freud does indeed exist in very young children, but I find it difficult to believe that blissful ignorance can persist for long in the face of the frustrations that children must experience. Childhood is, from one point of view, an endless series of inexplicable want-but-can't-haves. The older one grows, the more one is expected to understand and even anticipate and agree with these prohibitions, and thus anxiety is added to frustration: "I'm going to want it, and I shan't be allowed to have it; and it may even be bad of me to want it in the first place." Wolfenstein (1954) suggests that the child's need to free himself from such impossible and often forbidden desires underlies many of his early attempts at humor. He goes on to say that by the age of 6, most children also use jokes as a way of disguising their unacceptable ideas. Just as in adult humor, the joke of the school-age child creates an area of ambiguity between what may and what may not be said. The "indecent" thought may creep, disguised, past both internal and external censors and be openly enjoyed.

For the very young child, the physical world is complicated and confusing. The understanding and anticipating of events occupies a great deal of his time, and most information that comes his way is stored as a conceptual notion of "This is the way things are." According to McGhee (1971b), the child at this stage of development may smile or laugh at pictures in which objects are distorted so that they don't conform with reality, but he does not experience true humor. Humor, being based on expectancy violation (this is McGhee's definition of humor), can occur only when the child has formed firm conceptions of the world. Until then, he accepts the distorted stimulus as an interesting, if puzzling, example of the great variability of the world he is trying to understand. He will perceive expectancy violations as being funny only when he has acquired a stable enough conceptual grasp of the real world that he can assimilate the disconfirmed expectancy as being only a play on reality.

Just as conceptual mastery must precede the appreciation of visual humor, so verbal humor depends on language mastery. "While the sense of the comic and laughter develop with physical and especially with anal mastery, the enjoyment of wit is a sign of beginning intellectual growth and mastery of language" (Grotjahn, 1966, p. 77). Amusement and delight in the sounds and rhythms of language, with little or no concern for meanings, are among the first kinds of verbal humor to appear. Young children, for instance, are often delighted by strings of rhyming words and chant them over and over—"Betsy, wetsy, letsy, detsy. . . ." Later, a statement contrary to known fact can be hysterically funny: reversing the sex of siblings around the dining table can send children into gales of laughter. As language mastery increases, the child's humor becomes more subtle; that is, it comes to be more like our own. I am not amused by "Betsy, wetsy, detsy . . ." or by the statement that "Andy is a girl, Jenny is a boy. . . ." I can smile at the story of the man who took a ladder to bed because he wanted to get up in the morning, and I find myself inexplicably amused by the riddle "What lies in the grass and goes 'ding-dong, ding-dong'?" "A wounded Avon lady." I believe these four "jokes" represent a continuum of language use, from no meaning at all, to a simple reversal of fact, to a play on words, and finally to a full-fledged verbal expectancy disconfirmation. I realize, however, that I see the jokes through my own linguistic and emotional screen; I too am judging other people's sense of humor by my own.

*Later Childhood.* The statement that children's humor does change as the child gains conceptual and linguistic mastery, however, is not a subjective evaluation; it is an objective fact. McGhee (1971a, 1971b) points out that expectancy violations undergo a gradual transformation in the growing child's humor. Early expectancy violations involve discrepancies in sensory input—the man with a horse's head, the car with wings, and so forth. In later years, however, a child who has learned to think logically may find humor in the logical discrepancies of an idea that makes perfect visual sense. This ability to see something funny in a logical mismatch, according to McGhee, marks the beginning of adult humor. Keith-Spiegel (1972), too, points out the growing intellectual element in children's humor as the child matures; in addition, she points out that both the production and the appreciation of humor become more controlled and less spontaneous as the child grows older.

As the child gains mastery over various aspects of his internal and external environment, he also gains the capacity to enjoy new kinds of humor. Jokes and cartoons involving sex-role inappropriate behavior, for instance, are funny to the child only when he has begun to feel secure in his own sex-role identification (McGhee & Grodzitsky, 1973). Increasing interpersonal competence helps him to tell whether a particular communication is intended as a joke or as a serious statement; cues of this sort continue to be important in humor enjoyment all through adulthood.

*Adolescence.* The humor of the adolescent often reflects the social and physiological stress of this period of growth. Sensitive to, and often frightened by, the changes in his own body, he may use crudely obscene humor as a way of defending against sexual anxiety. Or he may take refuge in asceticism, refusing to be amused by or even to understand sexual humor. Aggression is a favorite content in the humor of children of all ages—one has only to watch the Saturday morning cartoons to be convinced of this— but in adolescence aggression can take on a quality of deliberate cruelty. Goodchilds (1972) noted the hostility of the jokes told and acted out by Eastern prep school boys; and we are all familiar with stories of hazing or of initiations carried to the point of inflicting serious pain.

Another kind of humor typical of adolescence is the *sick joke,* the joke that finds its humor in violations of social taboos or in portraying human suffering as laughable. J. Levine (1963) suggests that the adolescent uses the sick joke as a means of attacking authority and breaking with parental control. It is a kind of safe rebellion: "Look, I am saying these horrible things and you can't punish me for it because I am telling a joke." A more analytic approach would point out the highly aggressive nature of the sick joke and see it in relationship to the adolescent's need to control his reawakening sexuality.

If, as we have said, humor development in children depends on the acquisition of various kinds of mastery, then where does intelligence fit in? Should we expect the more intelligent child to have a better—or at least a more adultlike—sense of humor? Surprisingly, researchers have not been able to demonstrate in any convincing fashion that such a relationship holds among normal children (Flugel, 1954; Smith & White, 1965; Cunningham, 1962; Hauck & Thomas, 1972). In order to understand this statement, we must realize that intelligence scores are adjusted for age; that is, an 8-year-old with an IQ score of 100 is considerably more intellectually able than a 5-year-old with an IQ score of 100. Sense of humor does correlate with age, insofar as it shifts to more and more adult patterns as the child grows older. And, therefore, it must correlate to some degree with intellectual ability. But investigators have not been able to establish that, within a given age grouping, bright children react to humor differently from the way less bright children do. This lack of a relationship suggests that intellectual ability is only a general and underlying factor and that other psychological and social variables play a more immediate role in influencing humor behavior.

## EDUCATIONAL IMPLICATIONS

We have now made our way through a great deal of research and speculation about the nature and development of humor, and many of you may be wondering what all this has to do with your professional role. "This is all very interesting," you may be saying, "but what am I, as a teacher, supposed to do about it?" The answer to that question is "quite a lot." Encouraging a child to appreciate humor and to be sensitive to the humorous aspects of his life situations is an important—if often overlooked—goal for the classroom teacher.

### The Need for Humor

Why should we regard the development of a sense of humor as an educational goal? We have already addressed that question indirectly, but let's look directly now at the humor response as an aspect of mature personal and social functioning. One's response to humor is an integral part of one's overall personality. It serves as a defense against anxiety and as a way of expressing hostility and aggression in a nondestructive fashion. Moreover, it colors and enriches one's whole experience of being-in-world. "To have a sense of humor implies . . . that the individual does not take the situation too seriously and is able to approach it with some detachment and playfulness. It suggests that the individual can accept the incongruous and the ridiculous without being disturbed by it" (J. Levine, 1963, p. 788). The exercise of humor helps one to tolerate frustration, to accept one's own failings; it is a source of strength, both for the person and for those around him. Just as the dash of salt in an apple pie enhances the flavor of the other ingredients, so humor enhances and highlights the emotional and cognitive meaningfulness of one's daily interactions with the world.

As teachers, we are told that our concern should be for the whole child. We are committed to facilitating not only his intellectual growth but his personal and social development as well. We want to teach him facts, but we also want to teach him skills—skills in interacting with others, in setting goals, in using all the facets of his developing selfhood in a constructive and satisfying way. Humor can be an important, perhaps essential, integrative factor in this process, particularly if it can be directed at oneself. Humor is closely related to personal insight. Epstein and Smith (1956) looked specifically at this relationship between insight and humor; they concluded that the two are related only when humor involves an ability to accept the self as its object. Presumably the person who is able to laugh at his limitations should be low in defensiveness and accordingly should be insightful. A study by O'Connell (1960) also confirmed the relationship between humor and personal adjustment. Psychologists do not know whether being able to laugh facilitates adjustment or whether personal adjustment makes it possible for the individual to laugh; quite possibly the causal arrangement is a circular one, with humor and personality integration enhancing each other. Clearly, however, the ability to laugh and to foster laughter in others is a valuable characteristic.

As we saw earlier, wit and humor can be facilitative of group processes and thus are highly desirable classroom ingredients. Students who can produce constructive and appropriate humor can help their classroom groups to function more effectively. Goodchilds (1972), for instance, reports that groups containing witty people were more efficient in solving a group arithmetic problem, were less defensive, and were higher in satisfaction than groups not containing wits or in which there was less joking. The implications of this sort of finding for the classroom are clear. Joking and clowning around are not necessarily interruptive of the overall educational process (though they may interrupt a smaller segment); rather, they tend to facilitate that process in that they make it easier for individuals to work together and to enjoy each other.

## Negative Aspects of Humor

A word of caution is needed here: we must keep in mind that there are different kinds of humor and different kinds of humorists. Some humor is adaptive, helpful, and growth producing; other sorts are destructive and cruel. Constructive humor is a creative behavior that tends to facilitate both personal and interpersonal processes. O'Connell reports that the group member who says amusing things to motivate others to laugh is seen by his peers as outstanding in other behaviors as well; he is accepted and influential and does not use conformity as a means of obtaining approval. In contrast, the sarcastic wit uses his humor in a clashing and attention-seeking way. His nonconformity seems to be based less on self-confidence than on defiance, and he tends to impede rather than facilitate group inter-action. Humor is rather like a walking stick: it can be used as an aid in get-ting somewhere or as an aggressive weapon. The child who seems to be developing the aggressive tendency is not using his humor optimally; the habitual use of sarcastic, hostile wit may hinder rather than aid the devel-opment of self-actualization.

Another maladaptive use of humor can be seen in the behavior of the fool—the individual who encourages others to laugh at, rather than with, him. His actions seem to proclaim "I can never be as good as others, but maybe if they can laugh at my failure, they will accept me anyhow." In adopting this attitude, the fool cuts himself off from eventual mastery: he has to fail because social acceptance depends on his appearing foolish and incompetent. According to Daniels and Daniels (1964), social settings in which rules are rigid and inflexible tend to foster the appearance of this kind of role behavior. Other group members encourage and appreciate the foolish behavior of a peer as an indirect expression of their own frustration; because of his incompetence, he can get away with things that the others would like to do but don't dare to try. When rules are rigidly enforced, then, the group creates a kind of social pressure for the emergence of a fool who can serve as a vicarious satisfier of the group's desire to rebel. Such a situation is helpful neither to the fool himself nor to the other group mem-bers, who tend to develop a callous insensitivity to the pain their laughter inflicts.

## The Teacher's Role in Developing Humor

The person most influential in determining the humor climate of the classroom is the teacher. Not only does he set and enforce the limits of per-missible behavior but he also serves as a role model. If he uses humor con-structively and responds to it spontaneously, his students are likely to do the same. Some years ago, Brumbaugh carried out observations of humor behavior and laughter in a number of large-city classrooms. Her findings, while they emphasized the importance of the teacher's behavior in encour-aging or limiting classroom humor, cast some doubt on the teacher's ability to do so constructively. In describing the teacher's humor behavior, Brumbaugh says "Her remarks were the most potent in causing laughter and the data indicated that anecdotes were much less frequent than unkind remarks. Exasperated teachers not only relieved their tension by making wounding remarks but resorted to 'calling names' and ridicule." However,

some teachers did seem to have mastered the art of constructive humor: "Those teachers who retained the playful spirit of childhood, and who had an aptitude for seeing the funny side of life, used laughter as a solvent for many difficult situations. Friction was dissipated by light remarks made to the class, who responded to the 'mental tickle' with gaiety" (Brumbaugh, 1940, p. 408). We may hope that thirty-plus years of evolution in education have resulted in teachers who are more like the latter than the former.

The teacher who takes advantage of his higher status in the classroom to joke at the expense of his students is engaging in an activity common in many structured societies and described by sociologists and anthropologists as *joking down*. Many primitive societies have institutionalized joking-down relationships, setting up strict rules (usually based on kinship structure) about who may joke down with whom. A higher-status person may make jokes at the expense of a lower-status person, and this relationship helps maintain the overall structure of the society; joking-down relationships are often paternalistic devices to keep the lower ranks in their place. Joking down is accepted in a social setting only as long as the members of the group accept the status ranking implied by that joking down. As long as the situation is taken for granted, joking with inferiors is experienced as good-naturedness or just funny behavior. But any form of emancipation is a fatal blow to this sort of joking. In the United States, the joking of the white man, once accepted, is now a source of violence and conflict (Zijderveld, 1968, pp. 298–299). In the classroom, joking down is acceptable only when the student is viewed—and views himself—as inferior in a fundamental way to the teacher. If the student is to participate as a partner in the educational process, taking responsibility for his own learning, then joking down by the teacher not only is inappropriate but also deters real learning. The teacher cannot say to the student, on the one hand, "You are here to learn to participate maturely and responsibly in your own learning" and, on the other hand, "I am superior to you and can therefore make you the butt of my jokes." Joking down, in short, has no place in the modern classroom.

Providing a role model for the constructive use of humor and avoiding its destructive uses are two ways in which the teacher can facilitate the development of healthy humor in his students. But the teacher can also work toward this goal in other, more direct ways. Particularly in working with younger students, the teacher can provide a variety of opportunities to interact with and experience real-world situations in order to form a solid ground on which humor responses can be built. As McGhee (1972) says, children who experience a highly stimulating and diverse environment should acquire a broader range of knowledge and expectations than children who know only a more deprived environment. This increased breadth and depth of knowledge should allow the child to react with enjoyment and humor to (to fantasy assimilate) many of the expectancy violations he encounters. McGhee also stresses the importance of consistency in the child's experiences. While experiences should encompass a broad range of circumstances and situations, children need the reassurance of being shown or being helped to construct for themselves consistent patterns with which to handle these experiences. Application of such patterns or principles then helps the child to determine whether a new input should be reality assimilated (that is, treated as an objective fact) or fantasy assimilated (enjoyed as humor).

A number of writers (McGhee, 1971a, 1971b; Brumbaugh, 1940) have stressed the importance of participation in humor. Humor is not a spectator sport; to enjoy humor thoroughly one must be an active participant. "In truth, people sometimes read humor; they sometimes watch humor; but most often they participate in humor. It is a phenomenon preeminently interactive, immanent, impromptu" (Goodchilds, 1972, p. 176). A child need not be center stage in order to participate in humor activity; he may be straight man, aider and abettor, or appreciative audience. But unless he learns to participate actively in some way, his humor potential does not develop fully. We may note, too, that learning to participate actively in humorous exchanges may give the child confidence to participate more in other classroom activities. This is only one of the ways in which spontaneous humor may lead to broader skill development; other examples include the facilitation of creative ability and the facilitation of memory through the use of humor as a mnemonic device.

With regard to creative development, we must note that there seems to be little or no relationship between the ability to create humor and the ability to appreciate it (O'Connell, 1969). Participating in humor as active audience does not necessarily facilitate creative development. Nor does the amount of spontaneous humor in a group relate directly to the quality of its creative productions. Creating humor and creating humorously are not the same, and success at one does not imply success at the other (Goodchilds, 1972). Different approaches to humor and different ways of enjoying and participating in it spill over into a variety of other cognitive and social activities; it would be a mistake to generalize too broadly as to the facilitative potential of any single facet of humor activity. We must look at each child as an individual, assessing carefully the way in which his particular approach to humor can strengthen his learning in other areas.

To understand and analyze the child's reaction to and utilization of humor is an important prerequisite to helping him use it constructively. Yet, as we have seen, too much analysis can destroy the essence of humor. Perhaps this is one of the many areas of teacher functioning in which art must combine with science: the teacher must blend his intuitive and empathic understanding of the child's personality with the application of scientific principles of learning, personality development, and social interaction. Through sensitive application of his art and his skill, the teacher can help the child to integrate humor into his overall functioning. For both teacher and child, the goal is the happy state of affairs described by Grotjahn: "The sense of humor as a character trait comes to full flower . . . later, after the sense of the comic and the enjoyment of jokes has been established. A sense of humor signifies emotional maturity. When social relationships are mastered, when the individual has mastered—or come close to mastering—a peaceful relationship to himself, then he has this cherished characteristic, the sense of humor. He can be good, tolerant, and accepting of himself and therefore of other people too. Humor is the final integration of all stages" (1966, p. 81).

## QUESTIONS FOR UNDERSTANDING

1. Think back to the last time you laughed really hard about something. Why was it funny to you? Would it have been funny to a junior high student? What differences would you expect between you and that student in the things that make you laugh?
2. You are a fifth-grade teacher, and one of your students seems to be developing a pattern of playing the role of fool in class interactions. What can you do about it?
3. Riding across the playground on his bicycle, a student slips and falls into a mud puddle. He is not hurt but is wet and angry. What reaction

to this incident would you expect from (a) a first grader, (b) a sixth grader, (c) a high school senior?

4. At Hi-Dee-Ho Elementary School, a student council meets regularly with staff members to discuss policy issues and implementation. In what ways might humor facilitate the working of this group?

5. How can a classroom teacher best encourage active participation in humor on the part of all students?

# Epilog

We have come a long way in these pages. We have looked at simple stimulus-response learning and at creativity, at brain chemistry and at group interaction, at laughter and fear and rote memory. Indeed, there is little in the life of the learner that we have not touched on in one way or another.

Throughout all our discussions, we have taken pains to be "scientific." We have made use of research findings and have tried to understand how psychological theory relates to the way children learn and teachers teach. But we have laced our science with common sense; we have seen that both folk wisdom and our own experiences and feelings can help us to understand the learning process.

I think it important that we recognize that some answers may emerge from other than scientific or experimental data. Throughout our academic and professional careers, we may expect to be bombarded with information, with hypotheses, with the pronouncements of "experts." It is and will be all too easy to forget that we ourselves are also information sources, that artists and writers and just plain people know something about learning and teaching too. In our eagerness to learn from the specialists, we should be careful not to sell short our own insights, our own growing knowledge.

As an antidote to the spreading disease of "scientists know everything," I would like to end this volume with some words from a quite non-scientific source, words that seem to me to have a great deal of relevance for both the teacher and the learner. They sum up, rather beautifully, a goal for the educated person, the wise person, the learner whose learning is a way of life, unfinished, and unfinishable. They were found in Old Saint Paul's Church, in Baltimore, dated 1692:

Go placidly amid the noise and haste, and remember what peace there may be in silence. As far as possible without surrender be on good terms with all persons. Speak your truth quietly and clearly; and listen to others, even the dull and ignorant; they too have their story. Avoid loud and aggressive persons, they are vexations to the spirit. If you compare yourself with others, you may become vain and bitter; for always there will be greater and lesser persons than yourself. Enjoy your achievements as well as your plans. Keep interested in your own career, however humble; it is a real possession in the changing fortunes of time. Exercise caution in your business affairs; for the world is full of trickery. But let this not blind you to what virtue there is; many persons strive for high ideals; and everywhere life is full of heroism. Be yourself. Especially, do not feign affection. Neither be cynical about love; for in the face of all aridity and disenchantment it is perennial as the grass. Take kindly the counsel of the years, gracefully surrendering the things of youth. Nurture strength of spirit to shield you in sudden misfortune. But do not distress yourself with imaginings. Many fears are born of fatigue and loneliness. Beyond a wholesome discipline, be gentle with yourself. You are a child of the universe, no less than the trees and the stars; you have a right to be here. And whether or not it is clear to you, no doubt the universe is unfolding as it should. Therefore be at peace with God, whatever you conceive Him to be, and whatever your labors and aspirations, in the noisy confusion of life keep peace with your soul. With all its sham, drudgery and broken dreams, it is still a beautiful world. Be careful. Strive to be happy.

# Bibliography

Acker, L. E., Acker, M. A., & Pearson, D. Generalized imitative affection: Relationship to prior kinds of imitation training. *Journal of Experimental Child Psychology*, 1973, *16*, 111-125.

Ackerman, P. D. Formulations regarding an experimental analysis of covert impulse and depression responses as mediators of consummatory S-R sequences. *Psychological Record*, 1973, *23*, 477-486.

Akamatsu, T. J., & Thelen, M. H. A review of the literature on observer characteristics and imitation. *Developmental Psychology*, 1974, *10*, 38-47.

Albert, R. S. The influence of patterns of conformity and general reasoning ability on subjects' responses to an inconclusive message: A preliminary study. *Journal of Social Psychology*, 1967, *73*, 241-251.

Alker, H. A., & Wohl, J. Personality and achievement in a suburban and an inner city school. *Journal of Social Issues*, 1972, *28*(4), 101-113.

Allen, V. L., & Newtson, D. Development of conformity and independence. *Journal of Personality and Social Psychology*, 1972, *22*, 18-30.

Allik, J. P., & Siegel, A. W. Facilitation of sequential short-term memory with pictorial stimuli. *Journal of Experimental Psychology*, 1974, *103*, 567-573.

Altmann, H. A., & Conklin, R. C. Further correlates of the Barron complexity scale. *Perceptual and Motor Skills*, 1972, *34*, 83-86.

Anastasi, A., & Schaefer, C. E. Biographical correlates of artistic and literary creativity in adolescent girls. *Journal of Applied Psychology*, 1969, *53*, 267-273.

Anastasiow, N. J., & Hanes, M. L. Cognitive development and the acquisition of language in three subcultural groups. *Developmental Psychology*, 1974, *10*, 703-709.

Anderson, J. R. Retrieval of propositional information from long-term memory. *Cognitive Psychology*, 1974, *6*, 451-474.

Andrews, F. M., & Farris, G. F. Time pressure and performance of scientists and engineers: A five-year panel study. *Organizational Behavior and Human Performance*, 1972, *8*, 185-200.

Anwar, M. P., & Child, I. L. Personality and esthetic sensitivity in an Islamic culture. *Journal of Social Psychology*, 1972, *87*, 21-28.

Apter, M. J. Free information-structuring and the investigation of cognitive style. *Psychological Reports*, 1971, *29*, 1250.

Ardrey, R. *African genesis*. New York: Atheneum, 1961.

Asch, S. E. Studies of independence and conformity: I. A minority of one against a unanimous majority. *Psychological Monographs*, 1956, *70* (Whole No. 9).

Attneave, F. How do you know? *American Psychologist*, 1974, *29*, 493-499.

Auerbach, S. M., & Spielberger, C. D. The assessment of state and trait anxiety with the Rorschach test. *Journal of Personality Assessment*, 1972, *36*, 314-335.

Ausubel, D. P. The use of advance organizers in the learning and retention of meaningful verbal material. *Journal of Educational Psychology*, 1960, *51*, 267-272.

Ausubel, D. P. Creativity, general creative abilities, and the creative individual. *Psychology in the Schools*, 1964, *1*, 344-347.

Bahrick, H. P., Clark, S., & Bahrick, P. Generalization gradients as indicants of learning and retention of a recognition task. *Journal of Experimental Psychology*, 1967, *75*, 464-471.

Bailey, K. G., Hartnett, J. J., & Glover, H. W. Modeling and personal space behavior in children. *Journal of Psychology*, 1973, *85*, 143-150.

Baird, R. L., & Bee, H. L. Modification of conceptual style preference by differential reinforcement. *Child Development*, 1969, *40*, 903-910.

Bandura, A. Analysis of modeling processes. In A. Bandura (Ed.), *Psychological modeling*. Chicago: Aldine, 1971. (a)

Bandura, A. Influence of models' reinforcement contingencies on the acquisition of imitative responses. In A. Bandura (Ed.), *Psychological modeling*. Chicago: Aldine, 1971. (b)

Bandura, A., & Perloff, B. Relative efficacy of self-monitored and externally imposed reinforcement systems. *Journal of Personality and Social Psychology*, 1967, *7*, 111-116.

Bandura, A., Ross, D., & Ross, S. A. A comparative test of the status envy, social power, and secondary reinforcement theories of identificatory learning. In A. Bandura (Ed.), *Psychological modeling*. Chicago: Aldine, 1971.

Baron, J. Semantic components and conceptual development. *Cognition*, 1973, *2*, 299-317.

Baron, R. M., & Ganz, R. L. Effects of locus of control on the task performance of lower-class black children. *Journal of Personality and Social Psychology*, 1971, *21*, 124-130.

Barron, F. Some personality correlates of independence of judgement. *Journal of Personality*, 1952, *21*, 287-297.

Bartel, N. R. Locus of control and achievement in middle- and lower-class children. *Child Development*, 1971, *42*, 1099-1107.

Bartlett, F. C. *Remembering*. New York: Macmillan, 1932.

Bateson, G. *Steps to an ecology of mind*. New York: Ballantine Books, 1972.

Bauer, R., & Gillies, J. Cognitive style and influence of success and failure on future time-perspective. *Perceptual and Motor Skills*, 1972, *34*, 79-82.

Bauer, R., & Snyder, R. Ego identity and motivation: An empirical study of achievement and affiliation in Erickson's theory. *Psychological Reports*, 1972, *30*, 951-955.

Becker, W. C. Applications of behavior principles in typical classrooms. In C. E.

Thoresen (Ed.), *Behavior modification in education.* Chicago: University of Chicago Press, 1973.

Beloff, H. Two forms of social conformity: Acquiescence and conventionality. *Journal of Abnormal and Social Psychology,* 1958, *56,* 99–104.

Bereiter, C., & Engleman, S. *Teaching disadvantaged children in the preschool.* Englewood Cliffs, N.J.: Prentice-Hall, 1966.

Berkowitz, L. The contagion of violence. In W. J. Arnold & M. M. Page (Eds.), *Nebraska symposium on motivation* (Vol. 18). Lincoln: University of Nebraska Press, 1970.

Berlyne, D. E. Humor and its kin. In J. H. Goldstein & P. E. McGhee (Eds.), *The psychology of humor.* New York: Academic Press, 1972.

Bernstein, B. *Class, codes and control* (Vol. 1). London: Routledge & Kegan Paul, 1971.

Berzonsky, M. D. Component abilities of children's causal reasoning. *Developmental Psychology,* 1975, *11,* 111.

Bindra, D. Drive and incentive-motivation. In D. Bindra & J. Stewart (Eds.), *Motivation.* Harmondsworth, Middlesex, England: Penguin Books, 1971.

Binet, A., & Simon, T. *The intelligence of the feeble-minded.* Baltimore: Williams & Wilkins, 1916.

Biondo, J., & MacDonald, A. P., Jr. Internal-external locus of control and response to influence attempts. *Journal of Personality,* 1971, *39,* 407–419.

Bjork, R. A. Theoretical implications of directed forgetting. In A. W. Melton & E. Martin (Eds.), *Coding processes in human memory.* Washington, D.C.: Winston, 1972.

Black, R. W. Theories of reward. In D. Bindra & J. Stewart (Eds.), *Motivation.* Harmondsworth, Middlesex, England: Penguin Books, 1971.

Black, R. W. Some problems with incentive motivation to learn. In C. E. Thoresen (Ed.), *Behavior modification in education.* Chicago: University of Chicago Press, 1973.

Blackburn, R. Dimensions of hostility and aggression in abnormal offenders. *Journal of Consulting and Clinical Psychology,* 1972, *38,* 20–26.

Blank, M. Cognitive functions of language in the preschool years. *Developmental Psychology,* 1974, *10,* 229–245.

Blocher, D. H. Education: An enterprise in motivation. In M. C. Reynolds (Ed.), *Proceedings of the conference on psychology and the process of schooling in the next decade.* Minneapolis: University of Minnesota, Audio-Visual Extension, 1973.

Bloom, R. D. Learning to read: An operant perspective. *Reading Research Quarterly,* 1973, *8,* 147–166.

Boismer, J. D. Comments on "Sex differences in cognitive style." *Perceptual and Motor Skills,* 1971, *33,* 966.

Booth, D. A. Protein synthesis and memory. In J. A. Deutsch (Ed.), *The Physiological basis of memory.* New York: Academic Press, 1973.

Boring, E. G. Where is human behavior predetermined? *Scientific Monthly,* 1957, *84,* 1–85.

Botterberg, E. H. The cognitive style of field-dependence: Field independence and the modus of temporal experience. *Psychologie und Praxis,* 1971, *15,* 138–141.

Bourne, L. E., Jr. An inference model for conceptual rule learning. In R. L. Solso (Ed.), *Theories in cognitive psychology: The Loyola symposium.* New York: Wiley, 1974.

Bower, G. H. Stimulus-sampling theory of encoding variability. In A. W. Melton &

E. Martin (Eds.), *Coding processes in human memory.* Washington, D. C.: Winston, 1972.

Bower, G. H., & Karlin, M. B. Depth of processing pictures of faces and recognition memory. *Journal of Experimental Psychology,* 1974, *103,* 751-757.

Brown, A. S. Examination of the hypothesis-sampling theory. *Psychological Bulletin,* 1974, *81,* 773-790.

Brown, E. R., & Gordon, R. Internal versus external control as related to performance in two-choice probability learning. *Organizational Behavior and Human Performance,* 1971, *6,* 200-214.

Brown, S. R., & Hendrick, C. Introversion, extraversion and social perception. *British Journal of Social and Clinical Psychology,* 1971, *10,* 313-319.

Brumbaugh, F. The place of humor in the curriculum. *Journal of Experimental Education,* 1940, *8,* 403-409.

Bruner, J. S. On cognitive growth. In J. S. Bruner, R. Olver, & P. Greenfield (Eds.), *Studies in cognitive growth.* New York: Wiley, 1966. (a)

Bruner, J. S. On cognitive growth II. In J. S. Bruner, R. Olver, & P. Greenfield (Eds.), *Studies in cognitive growth.* New York: Wiley, 1966. (b)

Bruner, J. S. An overview. In J. S. Bruner, R. Olver, & P. Greenfield (Eds.), *Studies in cognitive growth.* New York: Wiley, 1966.

Bruner, J. S., Goodnow, J., & Austin, G. *A study of thinking.* New York: Wiley, 1956.

Bryant, B. K. Student-teacher relationships as related to internal-external locus of control. *Proceedings of the 80th Annual Convention of the American Psychological Association,* 1972, *7,* 567-568.

Buchanan, L. J., Jr., & Lindgren, H. C. Brainstorming in large groups as a facilitator of children's creative responses. *Journal of Psychology,* 1973, *83,* 117-122.

Bucher, B., & Schneider, R. E. Acquisition and generalization of conservation by pre-schoolers, using operant training. *Journal of Experimental Child Psychology,* 1973, *16,* 187-204.

Buck, M. R., & Austrin, H. R. Factors related to school achievement in an economically disadvantaged group. *Child Development,* 1971, *42,* 1813-1826.

Bucky, S. F., Banta, T. J., & Gross, R. B. Development of motor impulse control and reflectivity. *Perceptual and Motor Skills,* 1972, *34,* 813-814.

Buhler, C. The developmental structure of goal setting in group and individual studies. In C. Buhler & F. Massarik (Eds.), *The course of human life.* New York: Springer, 1968. (a)

Buhler, C. The general structure of the human life cycle. In C. Buhler & F. Massarik (Eds.), *The course of human life.* New York: Springer, 1968. (b)

Buhler, C., & Marschak, M. Basic tendencies of human life. In C. Buhler & F. Massarik (Eds.), *The course of human life.* New York: Springer, 1968.

Buhler, C., & Massarik, F. (Eds.). *The course of human life.* New York: Springer, 1968.

Calfee, R. C., Lindamood, P., & Lindamood, C. Acoustic-phonetic skills and reading—kindergarten through twelfth grade. *Journal of Educational Psychology,* 1973, *64,* 293-298.

Campbell, D. T. Blind variation and selective retention in creative thought as in other knowledge processes. *Psychological Review,* 1960, *67,* 380-400.

Cantor, J. R., & Zillman, D. Resentment toward victimized protagonists and severity of misfortunes they suffer as factors in humor appreciation. *Journal of Experimental Research in Personality,* 1973, *6,* 321-329.

Cantril, H., Crutchfield, R. S., & May, R. R. The organization of freedom. In S. M. Farber & R. H. L. Wilson (Eds.), *Man and civilization: Conflict and creativity.* New York: McGraw-Hill, 1963.

Carroll, J. B. Language development. In A. Bar-Adon & W. Leopold (Eds.), *Child language.* Englewood Cliffs, N.J.: Prentice-Hall, 1971.

Catiana, A. C. Elicitation, reinforcement, and stimulus control. In C. E. Thoresen (Ed.), *Behavior modification in education.* Chicago: University of Chicago Press, 1973.

Cattell, R. B. The dynamic calculus. In G. Lindzey (Ed.), *Assessment of human motives.* New York: Holt, Rinehart and Winston, 1958.

Cattell, R. B. The nature and genesis of mood status: A theoretical model with experimental measurements concerning anxiety, depression, arousal, and other mood states. In C. E. Spielberger (Ed.), *Anxiety* (Vol. 1). New York: Academic Press, 1972.

Cazden, C. B. *Child language and education.* New York: Holt, Rinehart and Winston, 1972.

Cazden, C. B. Problems for education: Language as curriculum content and learning environment. *Daedalus,* 1973, *102*(3), 135-148.

Chabassol, D. J. The measurement of some aspects of structure in adolescence. *Journal of Educational Research,* 1973, *66,* 247-250.

Chapouthier, G. Behavioral studies of the molecular basis of memory. In J. A. Deutsch (Ed.), *The physiological basis of memory.* New York: Academic Press, 1973.

Chomsky, N. Language and the mind. In A. Bar-Adon & W. Leopold (Eds.), *Child language.* Englewood Cliffs, N.J.: Prentice-Hall, 1971.

Clifford, M. M., & Cleary, T. A. The relationship between children's academic performance and achievement accountability. *Child Development,* 1972, *43,* 647-655.

Cohen, S. An examination of autonomous and heteronomous instructional-motivational contingencies on children's exploratory task performance. *Psychology,* 1971, *8*(4), 3-12.

Cole, M., & Bruner, J. S. Cultural differences and inferences about psychological processes. *American Psychologist,* 1971, *26,* 867-876.

Coleman, J. S. *Equality of educational opportunity.* Washington, D.C.: National Center for Educational Statistics, 1966.

Collins, J. K., & Thomas, N. T. Age and susceptibility to same-sex peer pressure. *British Journal of Educational Psychology,* 1972, *42,* 83-85.

Coltheart, M., Lea, C. D., & Thompson, K. In defense of ikonic memory. *Quarterly Journal of Experimental Psychology,* 1974, *26,* 633-641.

Cook, H., & Smothergill, D. W. Racial and sex determinants of imitative performance and knowledge in young children. *Journal of Educational Psychology,* 1973, *65,* 211-215.

Coser, R. L. Some social functions of laughter. *Human Relations,* 1959, *12,* 171-182.

Costanzo, P. R. Conformity development as a function of self-blame. *Journal of Personality and Social Psychology,* 1970, *14,* 366-374.

Costello, C. G., & deKrasinski, M. Recognizability of behaviors popularly associated with different emotions. *Psychological Record,* 1972, *22,* 559-568.

Craik, F. I. M., & Lockhart, R. S. Levels of processing: A framework for memory research. *Journal of Verbal Learning and Verbal Behavior,* 1972, *11,* 671-684.

Crandall, V. C., Katkovsky, W., & Crandall, V. J. Children's beliefs in their own control of reinforcements in intellectual-academic achievement situations. *Child Development*, 1965, *36*, 91–109.

Crane, V., & Ballif, B. L. Effects of adult modeling and rule structure on responses to moral situations of children in fifth grade classrooms. *Journal of Experimental Education*, 1973, *41*(3), 49–52.

Crawford, J. L., & Haaland, G. A. Predecisional information seeking and subsequent conformity in the social influence process. *Journal of Personality and Social Psychology*, 1972, *23*, 112–119.

Creber, J. W. *Lost for words*. Baltimore: Penguin Books, 1972.

Cronbach, L. J. Intelligence? Creativity? A parsimonious reinterpretation of the Wallach-Kogan data. *American Educational Research Journal*, 1968, *5*, 491–511.

Cronbach, L. J. Beyond the two disciplines of scientific psychology. *American Psychologist*, 1975, *30*, 116–128. (a)

Cronbach, L. J. Five decades of public controversy over mental testing. *American Psychologist*, 1975, *30*, 1–15. (b)

Crutchfield, R. S. Independent thought in a conformist world. In S. M. Farber & R. H. L. Wilson (Eds.), *Man and civilization: Conflict and creativity*. New York: McGraw-Hill, 1963.

Cunningham, A. Relation of sense of humor to intelligence. *Journal of Social Psychology*, 1962, *57*, 143–147.

Daniels, A. K., & Daniels, R. R. The social function of the career fool. *Psychiatry*, 1964, *27*, 219–229.

Davis, A. J. Cognitive style: Methodological and developmental considerations. *Child Development*, 1971, *42*, 1447–1459.

Davis, J. M., & Farina, A. Humor appreciation as social communication. *Journal of Personality and Social Psychology*, 1970, *15*, 175–178.

Davis, W. L., & Davis, D. E. Internal-external control and attribution of responsibility for success and failure. *Journal of Personality*, 1972, *40*, 123–136.

Dawson, J. L. Effects of sex hormones on cognitive style in rats and men. *Behavior Genetics*, 1972, *2*, 21–42.

Dawson, M. E., & Biferno, M. A. Concurrent measurement of awareness and electrodermal classical conditioning. *Journal of Experimental Psychology*, 1973, *101*, 55–62.

Dawson, R. G., & McGaugh, J. L. Drug facilitation of learning and memory. In J. A. Deutsch (Ed.), *The physiological basis of memory*. New York: Academic Press, 1973.

Day, D. E. Language instruction for young children. *Interchange*, 1974, *5*(1), 59–72.

Day, H. A curious approach to creativity. *Canadian Psychologist*, 1968, *9*, 485–497.

DeBolt, J. W., Liska, A. E., Love, W., & Stahlman, R. W. Status-role consequences of internal-external control of reinforcement. *Psychological Reports*, 1973, *32*, 307–311.

Deetz, S. Words without things. Toward a social phenomenology of language. *Quarterly Journal of Speech*, 1973, *59*, 40–51.

Dellas, M., & Gaier, E. L. Identification of creativity: The individual. *Psychological Bulletin*, 1970, *73*, 55–73.

Denney, D. R. The assessment of differences in conceptual style. *Child Study Journal,* 1971, *1,* 142–155.

Denney, D. R. Modeling and eliciting effects upon conceptual strategies. *Child Development,* 1972, *43,* 810–823. (a)

Denney, D. R. Modeling effects upon conceptual style and cognitive tempo. *Child Development,* 1972, *43,* 105–119. (b)

DeRussy, E. A., & Futch, E. Field dependence-independence as related to college curricula. *Perceptual and Motor Skills,* 1971, *33,* 1235–1237.

DeStefano, J. S. Linguistics and logical reasoning. *Theory into Practice,* 1973, *12,* 272–277.

Deutsch, J. A. The cholinergic synapse and the site of memory. In J. A. Deutsch (Ed.), *The physiological basis of memory.* New York: Academic Press, 1973.

Deutsch, M., & Gerard, H. B. A study of normative and informational social influences upon individual judgement. *Journal of Abnormal and Social Psychology,* 1955, *51,* 629–636.

Diamond, M. J., & Shapiro, J. L. Changes in locus of control as a function of encounter group experiences. *Journal of Abnormal Psychology,* 1973, *82,* 514–518.

Distefano, M. K., Jr., Pryer, M. W., & Smith, C. E. Comparisons of normal adolescents, psychiatric patients, and adults on internal-external control. *Journal of Clinical Psychology,* 1971, *27,* 343–345.

Dittman, A. T. Developmental factors in conversational behavior. *Journal of Communication,* 1972, *22,* 404–423.

Doctor, R. M. Locus of control of reinforcement and responsiveness to social influence. *Journal of Personality,* 1971, *39,* 542–551.

Dollard, J., & Miller, N. E. Learned drive and learned reinforcement. In D. Bindra & J. Stewart (Eds.), *Motivation.* Harmondsworth, Middlesex, England: Penguin Books, 1971.

Dominowski, R. L. How do people discover concepts? In R. L. Solso (Ed.), *Theories in cognitive psychology: The Loyola symposium.* New York: Wiley, 1974.

Doris, J., & Fierman, E. Humor and anxiety. *Journal of Abnormal and Social Psychology,* 1956, *53,* 59–62.

Doster, J. A., & Slaymaker, J. Need approval, uncertainty anxiety, and expectancies of interview behavior. *Journal of Counseling Psychology,* 1972, *19,* 522–528.

Doyal, G. T., & Forsyth, R. A. The effect of test anxiety, intelligence, and sex on children's problem solving ability. *Journal of Experimental Education,* 1972, *41* (2), 23–26.

Dua, P. S. Comparison of the effects of behaviorally oriented action and psychotherapy reeducation on introversion-extraversion, emotionality, and internal-external control. *Journal of Counseling Psychology,* 1970, *17,* 567–572.

Dubner, M. A. P. The effect of modeling and vicarious reinforcement upon the subsequent imitation of a socially approved response. *Journal of School Psychology,* 1973, *11,* 132–138.

Dudek, S. Z. A longitudinal study of Piaget's developmental stages and the concept of regression II. *Journal of Personality Assessment,* 1972, *36,* 468–478.

Dudek, S. Z., & Dyer, G. B. A longitudinal study of Piaget's developmental stages and the concept of regression I. *Journal of Personality Assessment,* 1972, *36,* 380–389.

Duffy, O. B., Clair, T. N., Egeland, B., & Dinello, M. Relationship of intelligence, visual-motor skills, and psycholinguistic abilities with achievement in the third, fourth, and fifth grades: A follow-up study. *Journal of Educational Psychology,* 1972, *63,* 358-362.

Duncker, K. On problem solving. *Psychological Monographs,* 1945, *58* (Whole No. 270).

Durrell, D. E., & Weisberg, P. Imitative play behavior of children. *Journal of Experimental Child Psychology,* 1973, *16,* 23-31.

Dworkin, E. S., & Efran, J. S. The angered: Their susceptibility to varieties of humor. *Journal of Personality and Social Psychology,* 1967, *6,* 233-236.

Eiduson, B. T. Infancy and goal-setting behavior. In C. Buhler & F. Massarik (Eds.), *The course of human life.* New York: Springer, 1968.

Eisner, D. A. Developmental relationships between field independence and fixity-mobility. *Perceptual and Motor Skills,* 1972, *34,* 767-770.

Elich, P. J. *The modification of children's judgements.* Unpublished doctoral dissertation, University of Oregon, 1962.

Elliott, R., & Vasta, R. The modeling of sharing: Effects associated with vicarious reinforcement, symbolization, age, and generalization. *Journal of Experimental Child Psychology,* 1970, *10,* 8-15.

Epstein, S. The nature of anxiety with emphasis upon its relationship to expectancy. In C. E. Spielberger (Ed.), *Anxiety* (Vol. 2). New York: Academic Press, 1972.

Epstein, S. The self-concept revisited. *American Psychologist,* 1973, *28,* 404-416.

Epstein, S., & Smith, R. Repression and insight as related to reaction to cartoons. *Journal of Consulting Psychology,* 1956, *20,* 391-395.

Estes, W. K. Reward in human learning: Theoretical issues and strategic choice points. In R. Glazer (Ed.), *The nature of reinforcement.* New York: Academic Press, 1971.

Eysenck, H. J. *Uses and abuses of psychology.* Baltimore: Penguin Books, 1953.

Eysenck, H. J. Hysterical personality and sexual adjustment, attitudes and behavior. *Journal of Sexual Research,* 1971, *7,* 272-281. (a)

Eysenck, H. J. *The IQ argument.* La Salle, Ill.: Open Court, 1971. (b)

Fajnsztejn-Pollack, G. A developmental study of decay rate in long-term memory. *Journal of Experimental Child Psychology,* 1973, *16,* 225-235.

Fein, G. G. The effect of chronological age and model reward on imitative behavior. *Developmental Psychology,* 1973, *9,* 283-289.

Felton, G. S. The experimenter expectancy effect examined as a function of task ambiguity and internal-external control. *Journal of Experimental Research in Personality,* 1971, *5,* 286-294.

Felton, G. S. Teaching internalization to middle-level mental health workers in training. *Psychological Reports,* 1973, *32,* 1279-1282.

Ferster, C. B. A functional analysis of depression. *American Psychologist,* 1973, *28,* 857-870.

Finch, A. J., Lloyd, A., Frerking, R. A., & Rickard, H. C. Model's competency, vicarious reinforcement, and subject's strategy in imitative performance. *Psychological Reports,* 1973, *32,* 442.

Firetto, A. C., Walker, R. E., & Davey, H. Digit symbol performance and self-report of anxiety. *Perceptual and Motor Skills,* 1972, *35,* 382.

Fish, B., & Karabenick, S. A. Relationship between self-esteem and locus of control. *Psychological Reports,* 1971, *29,* 784.

Flanders, J. P. A review of research on imitative behavior. *Psychological Bulletin,* 1968, *69,* 316–337.

Flavell, J. H. *The development psychology of Jean Piaget.* New York: Van Nostrand Reinhold, 1963.

Flavell, J. H. First discussant's comments: What is memory development the development of? *Human Development,* 1971, *14,* 272–278.

Fleck, J. R. Cognitive styles in children and performance on Piagetian conservation tasks. *Perceptual and Motor Skills,* 1972, *35,* 747–756.

Fleming, J. D. The state of the apes. *Psychology Today,* 1974, 7(8), 31–38, 43–50.

Flugel, J. C. Humor and laughter. In G. Lindzey (Ed.), *Handbook of social psychology* (Vol. 2). Reading, Mass.: Addison-Wesley, 1954.

Forehand, R., & Gardner, H. L. An examination of verbal imitative performance in young children. *Journal of Psychology,* 1973, *85,* 323–328.

Fowler, H. Implications of sensory reinforcement. In C. E. Thoresen (Ed.), *Behavior modification in education.* Chicago: University of Chicago Press, 1973.

Francis, H. Children's experience of reading and notions of units in language. *British Journal of Educational Psychology,* 1973, *43,* 17–23.

Freud, S. Wit and its relation to the unconscious. In A. A. Brill (Ed.), *The basic writings of Sigmund Freud.* New York: Random House, 1938. (Originally published, 1916.)

Freud, S. Humor. In J. Strachey (Ed.), *Collected papers.* New York: Basic Books, 1959. (Originally published, 1928.)

Freud, S. Jokes and their relation to the unconscious. In J. Strachey (Ed.), *Complete works.* London: Hogarth, 1960. (Originally published, 1905.)

Freud, S. *A general introduction to psychoanalysis.* New York: Simon & Schuster, 1969. (Originally published, 1917.)

Friedman, S. T., & Manaster, G. J. Internal-external control: Studied through the use of proverbs. *Psychological Reports,* 1973, *33,* 611–615.

Gable, R. K., & Minton, H. L. Social class, race, and junior high school students' belief in personal control. *Psychological Reports,* 1971, *29,* 1188–1190.

Gagné, R. M. *The conditions of learning.* New York: Holt, Rinehart and Winston, 1965.

Gagné, R. M. *Essentials of learning for instruction.* Hinsdale, Ill.: Dryden Press, 1974.

Gardner, H. Metaphors and modalities: How children project polar adjectives onto diverse domains. *Child Development,* 1974, *45,* 84–91.

Garrett, A. M., & Willoughby, R. H. Personal orientation and reactions to success and failure in urban black children. *Developmental Psychology,* 1972, *7,* 92.

Gattegno, C. Comment in discussion of papers. In M. C. Reynolds (Ed.), *Proceedings of the conference on psychology and the process of schooling in the next decade.* Minneapolis: University of Minnesota, Audio-Visual Extension, 1971.

Gaudia, G. Piaget's theory and psychometric intelligence. *Elementary School Journal,* 1972, *73,* 37–43.

Gaudry, E., & Spielberger, C. D. *Anxiety and educational achievement.* New York: Wiley, 1971.

Gieselman, R. E. Positive forgetting of sentence material. *Memory and Cognition,* 1974, *2,* 677–682.

Gillies, J., & Bauer, R. Cognitive style and perception of success and failure. *Perceptual and Motor Skills,* 1971, *33,* 839–842.

Goldberg, R. W. *Cognitive flexibility: Its relationship to personality style and its generality as a thought process.* Unpublished doctoral dissertation, University of Michigan, 1971.

Golden, C. J. S. *Concept formation as a function of locus of control and method of presentation among some disadvantaged and advantaged 5th grade students.* Unpublished doctoral dissertation, Pennsylvania State University, 1971.

Golden, M., & Birns, B. Social class, intelligence, and cognitive style in infancy. *Child Development,* 1971, *42,* 2114-2116.

Goldman-Eisler, F. Discussion and further comments. In E. H. Lenneberg (Ed.), *New directions in the study of language.* Cambridge: M.I.T. Press, 1964.

Goldstein, A. M., & Reznikoff, M. Suicide in chronic hemodialysis patients from an external locus of control framework. *American Journal of Psychiatry,* 1971, *127,* 1204-1207.

Goldstein, J. H. Humor appreciation and time to respond. *Psychological Reports,* 1970, *27,* 445-446.

Goldstein, J. H., Suls, J. M., & Anthony, S. Enjoyment of specific types of humor content: Motivation or salience. In J. H. Goldstein & P. E. McGhee (Eds.), *The psychology of humor.* New York: Academic Press, 1972.

Goodchilds, J. D. On being witty: Causes, correlates, and consequences. In J. H. Goldstein & P. E. McGhee (Eds.), *The psychology of humor.* New York: Academic Press, 1972.

Goodstadt, B. E., & Hjelle, L. A. Power to the powerless: Locus of control and the use of power. *Journal of Personality and Social Psychology,* 1973, *27,* 190-196.

Gough, H. G., & Olton, R. M. Field independence as related to nonverbal measures of perceptual performance and cognitive ability. *Journal of Counseling and Clinical Psychology,* 1972, *38,* 338-342.

Gould, L. J. Conformity and marginality: Two faces of alienation. *Journal of Social Issues,* 1969, *25*(2), 39-63.

Graham, D. R. The maturational factor in humor. *Journal of Clinical Psychology,* 1958, *14,* 326-328.

Greenberg, R., Pillard, R., & Pearlman, C. The effect of dream (stage REM) deprivation on adaptation to stress. *Psychosomatic Medicine,* 1972, *34,* 257-262.

Greeno, J. G. The structures of memory and the process of solving problems. In R. L. Solso (Ed.), *Theories in cognitive psychology: The Loyola symposium.* New York: Wiley, 1974.

Grimberg, L. (Chair). Panel on creativity. *International Journal of Psychoanalysis,* 1972, *53,* 21-30.

Groninger, L. D. The role of images within the memory system. *Journal of Experimental Psychology,* 1974, *103,* 178-180.

Grotjahn, M. *Beyond laughter: Humor and the subconscious.* New York: McGraw-Hill, 1966.

Guilford, J. P. Creativity. *American Psychologist,* 1950, *5,* 444-454.

Guilford, J. P. Three faces of intellect. *American Psychologist,* 1959, *14,* 469-479.

Gurin, G. Lao, R. C., & Beattie, M. Internal-external control in the motivational dynamics of Negro youth. *Journal of Social Issues,* 1969, *25*(3), 29-54.

Guthrie, E. R. An S-R contiguity theory of learning. In E. Stolurow (Ed.), *Readings in learning.* Englewood Cliffs, N.J.: Prentice-Hall, 1953. (Originally published, 1930.)

Gutman, J., & Priest, R. F. When is aggression funny? *Journal of Personality and Social Psychology,* 1969, *12,* 60-65.

Hall, C. S., & Lindzey, G. *Theories of personality.* New York: Wiley, 1957.

Hall, J. W., & Pierce, J. W. Recognition and recall by children and adults as a function of variations in memory coding instructions. *Memory and Cognition,* 1974, *2,* 585–590.

Hall, V. C., & Turner, R. R. The validity of the "different language explanation" for poor scholastic performance by black students. *Review of Educational Research,* 1974, *44,* 69–81.

Hamm, N. H., & Hoving, K. L. Conformity of children in an ambiguous perceptual situation. *Child Development,* 1969, *40,* 773–784.

Hammes, J. S., & Wiggins, S. L. Manifest anxiety and appreciation of humor involving emotional content. *Perceptual and Motor Skills,* 1962, *14,* 291–294.

Hannah, T. E. Perception of internal-external control as a function of one's own I-E score. *Perceptual and Motor Skills,* 1973, *37,* 119–122.

Harlow, H. F. The formation of learning sets. *Psychological Review,* 1949, *56,* 51–65.

Harlow, H. F. The nature of love. *American Psychologist,* 1958, *13,* 673–685.

Harlow, H. F. Mice, monkeys, men and motives. In D. Bindra & J. Stewart (Eds.), *Motivation.* Harmondsworth, Middlesex, England: Penguin Books, 1971.

Harris, H. F., & Phelan, J. G. Beliefs in internal-external control of reinforcement among blacks in integrated and segregated high schools. *Psychological Reports,* 1973, *32,* 40–42.

Harris, M. B., & Fisher, J. L. Modeling and flexibility in problem-solving. *Psychological Reports,* 1973, *33,* 19–23.

Harris, S. L., & Nathan, P. E. Parents' locus of control and perception of cause of children's problems. *Journal of Clinical Psychology,* 1973, *29,* 182–184.

Harrison, A., & Nadelman, L. Conceptual tempo and inhibition of movement in black preschool children. *Child Development,* 1972, *43,* 657–668.

Harvey, J. M. Locus of control shift in administrators. *Perceptual and Motor Skills,* 1971, *33,* 980–982.

Hauck, W. E., & Thomas, J. W. The relationship of humor to intelligence, creativity, and intentional and incidental learning. *Journal of Experimental Education,* 1972, *40*(4), 52–55.

Heatherington, M., & Wray, N. Effects of need aggression, stress, and aggressive behavior on humor preferences. *Journal of Personality and Social Psychology,* 1966, *4,* 229–233.

Heaton, R. C., & Duerfeldt, P. H. The relationship between self-esteem, self-reinforcement, and the internal-external personality dimension. *Journal of Genetic Psychology,* 1973, *123,* 3–13.

Hebb, D. O. Drives and the CNS (Conceptual Nervous System). In D. Bindra & J. Stewart (Eds.), *Motivation.* Harmondsworth, Middlesex, England: Penguin Books, 1971.

Henderson, R. W., & Garcia, A. B. The effects of parent training program on the question-asking behavior of Mexican-American children. *American Educational Research Journal,* 1973, *10,* 193–201.

Hendrick, C., & Brown, S. R. Introversion, extraversion, and interpersonal attraction. *Journal of Personality and Social Psychology,* 1971, *20,* 31–35.

Henle, M. Fishing for ideas. *American Psychologist,* 1975, *30,* 795–799.

Henry, G. H., & Brown, J. A. An inquiry into the nature of concept development within the on-going classroom situation. United States Office of Education Cooperative Research Project #1487, n.d.

Heron, W. The pathology of boredom. *Scientific American,* 1957, *196*(1), 52–56.

Hertzig, M. E. Aspects of cognition and cognitive style in young children of differing social and ethnic backgrounds. In J. Hellmuth (Ed.), *Cognitive studies II: Deficits in cognition.* New York: Brunner/Mazel, 1971.

Higbee, K. L. Perceived control and military riskiness. *Perceptual and Motor Skills,* 1972, *34,* 95–100.

Hilaael, T. M. *Perceived parental-cognitive control and the development of locus of control modalities in children.* Unpublished doctoral dissertation, Case Western Reserve University, 1972.

Hinde, R. A. Critique of energy models of motivation. In D. Bindra & J. Stewart (Eds.), *Motivation.* Harmondsworth, Middlesex, England: Penguin Books, 1971.

Hirsch, J. Genetics and competence: Do heritability indices predict educability? In J. McV. Hunt (Ed.), *Human intelligence.* New Brunswick, N.J.: Transaction Books, 1972.

Hochbaum, G. M. The relation between group members' self-confidence and their reactions to group pressures to uniformity. *American Sociological Review,* 1954, *19,* 678–687.

Hochman, S. H. Field independence and Stroop color-word performance. *Perceptual and Motor Skills,* 1971, *33,* 782.

Hodges, W. F., & Durham, R. L. Anxiety, ability, and digit span performance. *Journal of Personality and Social Psychology,* 1972, *24,* 401–406.

Hoffman, L. W. Early childhood experiences and women's achievement motives. *Journal of Social Issues,* 1972, *28*(2), 129–155.

Hohmuth, A. V., & Ramos, R. A. Locus of control, achievement, and failure among disadvantaged college students. *Psychological Reports,* 1973,*33,* 573–574.

Holmes, D. S. Pupillary response, conditioning, and personality. *Journal of Personality and Social Psychology,* 1967, *5,* 98–103.

Homme, L. E. Perspectives in psychology: XXIV. Control of coverants, the operants of the mind. *Psychological Record,* 1965, *15,* 501–511.

Horn, J. L. Intelligence: Why it grows, why it declines. In J. McV. Hunt (Ed.), *Human intelligence.* New Brunswick, N.J.: Transaction Books, 1972.

Horner, M. S. Toward an understanding of achievement-related conflicts in women. *Journal of Social Issues,* 1972, *28*(2), 157–175.

Houston, S. H. Syntactic complexity and information transmission in first-graders: A cross-cultural study. *Journal of Psycholinguistic Research,* 1973, *2,* 99–114.

Hughes, M. P., Jr. *An attempt to modify locus of control.* Unpublished doctoral dissertation, University of Nebraska, 1971.

Hunt, D. E., & Hardt, R. H. The effect of upward bound programs on the attitudes, motivation, and academic achievement of Negro students. *Journal of Social Issues,* 1969, *25*(3), 117–129.

Hunt, J. McV. Experience and the development of motivation: Some reinterpretations. *Child Development,* 1960, *31,* 489–504.

Hunt, J. McV. *The challenge of incompetence and poverty.* Urbana: University of Illinois Press, 1969.

Hunt, J. McV. The role of experience in the development of competence. In J. McV. Hunt (Ed.), *Human intelligence.* New Brunswick, N.J.: Transaction Books, 1972.

Iversen, S. D. Brain lesions and memory in animals. In J. A. Deutsch (Ed.), *The physiological basis of memory.* New York: Academic Press, 1973.

Izard, C. E. Anxiety: A variable combination of interacting fundamental emotions.

In C. E. Spielberger (Ed.), *Anxiety* (Vol. 1). New York: Academic Press, 1972.

Jackson, P. W., & Messick, S. The person, the product, and the response: Conceptual problems in the assessment of creativity. *Journal of Personality*, 1965, *33*, 309-329.

Jacobs, P. I., & Vandeventer, M. Evaluating the teaching of intelligence. *Educational and Psychological Measurement*, 1972, *32*, 235-248.

Jacobson, L. I., Berger, S. E., Bergman, R. L., Millham, J., & Greeson, L. E. Effects of age, sex, systematic conceptual learning, acquisition of learning sets, and programmed social interaction on the intellectual and conceptual development of preschool children from poverty backgrounds. *Child Development*, 1971, *42*, 1399-1415.

Janis, I. R. Personality correlates of susceptibility to persuasion. *Journal of Personality*, 1954, *22*, 504-518.

Jenkins, J. J. Remember that old theory of memory? Well, forget it! *American Psychologist*, 1974, *29*, 785-795.

Jensen, A. The differences are real. *Psychology Today*, 1973, *7*(7), 80-86.

Joe, V. C. Review of the internal-external control construct as a personality variable. *Psychological Reports*, 1971, *28*, 619-640.

Joe, V. C. Social desirability and the IE scale. *Psychological Reports*, 1972, *30*, 44-46.

Johnson, J. H. Memory and personality: An information processing approach. *Journal of Research in Personality*, 1974, *8*, 1-32.

Johnson, N. F. Higher order encoding: Process or state? *Memory and Cognition*, 1973, *1*, 491-494.

Joslin, D., Coates, B., & McKown, A. Age of child and rewardingness of adult model in observational learning. *Child Study Journal*, 1973, *3*, 115-124.

Kaczkowski, H., & Owen, K. Anxiety and anger in adolescent girls. *Psychological Reports*, 1972, *31*, 281-282.

Kagan, J. Preschool enrichment and learning. *Interchange*, 1971, *2*(2), 12-22.

Kagan, J., Rosman, B. L., Day, D., Albert, J., & Phillips, W. Information processing in the child. *Psychological Monographs*, 1964, *78* (Whole No. 578).

Kanfer, F. H. Behavior modification—An overview. In C. E. Thoresen (Ed.), *Behavior modification in education*. Chicago: University of Chicago Press, 1973.

Katz, J. M. Cognitive tempo and discrimination skill on color-form sorting tasks. *Perceptual and Motor Skills*, 1972, *35*, 359-362.

Keith-Spiegel, P. Early conceptions of humor: Varieties and issues. In J. H. Goldstein & P. E. McGhee (Eds.), *The psychology of humor*. New York: Academic Press, 1972.

Kelly, G. A. Man's construction of his alternatives. In G. Lindzey (Ed.), *Assessment of human motives*. New York: Holt, Rinehart and Winston, 1958.

Kendler, H. H., Kendler, T. S., & Ward, J. W. An ontogenetic analysis of optional intradimensional and extradimensional shifts. *Journal of Experimental Psychology*, 1972, *95*, 102-109.

Keppel, G., & Underwood, B. J. Proactive inhibition in short-term recognition of single items. *Journal of Verbal Learning and Verbal Behavior*, 1962, *1*, 153-161.

Kiesler, C. A., & Keisler, S. B. *Conformity*. Reading, Mass.: Addison-Wesley, 1969.

Klausmeyer, H., & Goodwin, W. *Learning and human abilities* (2nd ed.). New York: Harper & Row, 1966.

Klein, G. S. Cognitive control and motivation. In G. Lindzey (Ed.), *Assessment of human motives*. New York: Holt, Rinehart and Winston, 1958.

Klonoff, H. IQ constancy and age. *Perceptual and Motor Skills*, 1972, *35*, 527-534.

Knapp, R. H., & Garbutt, J. T. Variation in time descriptions and n achievement. *Journal of Social Psychology,* 1965, *67,* 269-272.

Kniveton, B. H. The effect of rehearsal delay on long-term imitation of filmed aggression. *British Journal of Psychology,* 1973, *64,* 259-265.

Kodroff, J. K., & Roberge, J. J. Development analysis of the conditional reasoning abilities of primary-grade children. *Developmental Psychology,* 1975, *11,* 21-28.

Koppen-Thulesius, L. K., & Teichmann, H. Accelerative trends in intellectual development. *British Journal of Social and Clinical Psychology,* 1972, *11,* 284-294.

Korman, A. K. Environmental ambiguity and locus of control as interactive influences on satisfaction. *Journal of Applied Psychology,* 1971, *55,* 339-342.

Lamb, C. W. Personality correlates of humor enjoyment following motivational arousal. *Journal of Personality and Social Psychology,* 1968, *9,* 237-241.

Landers, D. M., & Landers, D. M. Teacher versus peer models: Effects of model's presence and performance level on motor behavior. *Journal of Motor Behavior,* 1973, *5,* 129-139.

Landy, D., & Mettee, D. Evaluation of an aggressor as a function of exposure to cartoon humor. *Journal of Personality and Social Psychology,* 1969, *12,* 66-71.

Langevin, R., & Day, H. I. Physiological correlates of humor. In J. H. Goldstein & P. E. McGhee (Eds.), *The psychology of humor.* New York: Academic Press, 1972.

Lawton, F. G., & Busse, T. V. Residential mobility and creative thinking among eighth-grade students. *Journal of Genetic Psychology,* 1972, *121,* 325-326.

Lazarus, R. S., & Averill, J. R. Emotion and cognition: With special reference to anxiety. In C. E. Spielberger (Ed.), *Anxiety* (Vol. 2). New York: Academic Press, 1972.

Lefcourt, H. M. The function of the illusions of control and freedom. *American Psychologist,* 1973, *28,* 417-425.

Lefcourt, H. M., & Telegdi, M. S. Perceived locus of control and field dependence as predictors of cognitive activity. *Journal of Consulting and Clinical Psychology,* 1971, *37,* 53-56.

Lessing, E. E., & Phillips, R. L. Reduction of children's symptomatology through reduction of parental, child-focused anxiety: An exploratory study. *Psychotherapy: Theory, Research, & Practice,* 1971, *8,* 158-164.

Levenson, H. Distinctions within the concept of internal-external control: Development of a new scale. *Proceedings of the 80th Annual Convention of the American Psychological Association,* 1972, *7,* 261-262.

Levenson, H. Perceived parental antecedents of internal powerful others, and chance locus of control orientations. *Developmental Psychology,* 1973, *9,* 260-265.

Levine, J. Humor and mental health. In A. Deutsch & H. Fishman (Eds.), *The encyclopedia of mental health.* New York: Franklin Watts, 1963.

Levine, M. A transfer hypothesis, whereby learning-to-learn, einstellung, the prereversal-nonreversal shifts, and other curiosities are elucidated. In R. L. Solso (Ed.), *Theories in cognitive psychology: The Loyola symposium.* New York: Wiley, 1974.

Levinson, E. J. The modification of intelligence by training in the verbalization of word definitions and simple concepts. *Child Development,* 1971, *42,* 1361-1380.

Lewis, M. Sex differences in cognitive style: A rejoinder. *Perceptual and Motor Skills,* 1971, *33,* 1006.

Loftus, E. F., & Palmer, J. C. Reconstruction of automobile destruction: An example of the interaction between language and memory. *Journal of Verbal Learning and Verbal Behavior,* 1974, *13,* 585=589.
Logan, F. A. Incentive theory, reinforcement and education. In R. Glazer (Ed.), *The nature of reinforcement.* New York: Academic Press, 1971.
Lotsof, E. J., & Steinke, J. Internal-external control, divergent thinking and levels of abstractness. *Psychological Reports,* 1973, *32,* 1035-1041.
Lowry, D. The effects of mnemonic learning strategies on transfer, interference, and 48-hour retention. *Journal of Experimental Psychology,* 1974, *103,* 16-20.
Lubow, R. E. Latent inhibition. *Psychological Bulletin,* 1973, *79,* 398-407.
Luchins, A. S. Mechanization in problem solving. *Psychological Monographs,* 1942, *54* (Whole No. 248).
Lunnenborg, P. W., & Lunnenborg, C. E. Sex differences in aptitude maturation in a noncollege sample. *Journal of Counseling Psychology,* 1972, *19,* 529-536.
Luria, A. R. The directive function of speech in development and dissolution. In A. Bar-Adon & W. Leopold (Eds.), *Child language.* Englewood Cliffs, N.J.: Prentice-Hall, 1971.
Luria, A. R., & Yudovich, F. I. *Speech and the development of mental processes in the child.* London: Staples Press, 1959.
MacDonald, A. P. Internal-external locus of control: Parental antecedents. *Journal of Consulting and Clinical Psychology,* 1971, *37,* 141-147.
MacDonald, A. P. Internal-external locus of control change-technics. *Rehabilitation Literature,* 1972, *33,* 44-47.
MacKinnon, D. D. Personality and the realization of creative potential. *American Psychiatrist,* 1965, *20,* 273-281.
Malpass, L. F., & Fitzpatrick, E. D. Social facilitation as a factor in reaction to humor. *Journal of Social Psychology,* 1959, *50,* 295-303.
Mandelbaum, D. G. The interplay of conformity and diversity. In S. M. Farber & R. H. L. Wilson (Eds.), *Man and civilization: Conflict and creativity.* New York: McGraw-Hill, 1963.
Mandler, G. Helplessness: Theory and research in anxiety. In C. E. Spielberger (Ed.), *Anxiety* (Vol. 2). New York: Academic Press, 1972.
Mann, P. A. Residential mobility as an adaptive experience. *Journal of Consulting and Clinical Psychology,* 1972, *39,* 37-42.
Marks, E. Sex, birth order, and beliefs about personal power. *Developmental Psychology,* 1972, *6,* 184.
Martineau, W. H. A model of the social functions of humor. In J. H. Goldstein & P. E. McGhee (Eds.), *The psychology of humor.* New York: Academic Press, 1972.
Martorella, P. H. *Concept learning.* New York: Intext Educational Publishers, 1972.
Matti, S. R. Motivational aspects of creativity. *Journal of Personality,* 1965, *33,* 330-347.
May, R. *The meaning of anxiety.* New York: Ronald Press, 1950.
Mayer, R. E. Acquisition processes and resilience under varying testing conditions for structurally different problem-solving procedures. *Journal of Educational Psychology,* 1974, *66,* 644-656.
McCarthy, D. Language development. In A. Bar-Adon & W. Leopold (Eds.), *Child language.* Englewood Cliffs, N.J.: Prentice-Hall, 1971.
McDougal, W. On the nature of instinct. In D. Bindra & J. Stewart (Eds.), *Motivation.* Harmondsworth, Middlesex, England: Penguin Books, 1971.

McGhee, P. E. Cognitive development and children's comprehension of humor. *Child Development*, 1971, *42*, 123-138. (a)

McGhee, P. E. Development of the humor response. *Psychological Bulletin*, 1971, *76*, 328-348. (b)

McGhee, P. E. On the cognitive origins of incongruity humor: Fantasy assimilation versus reality assimilation. In J. H. Goldstein & P. E. McGhee (Eds.), *The psychology of humor*. New York: Academic Press, 1972.

McGhee, P. E., & Grodzitsky, P. Sex-role identification and humor among preschool children. *Journal of Psychology*, 1973, *84*, 189-193.

McLauren, W. A., Bishop, G., & Bell, J. Otis IQ and information-processing rate in a work-paced and self-paced task. *Perceptual and Motor Skills*, 1972, *35*, 883-886.

McMillen, D. L. Transgression, fate control, and compliant behavior. *Psychonomic Science*, 1970, *21*, 103-104.

McNemar, Q. Lost: Our intelligence? Why? *American Psychologist*, 1964, *19*, 871-882.

Mednick, S. A. The associative basis of the creative process. *Psychological Review*, 1962, *69*, 220-232.

Meehl, P. E. Second-order relevance. *American Psychologist*, 1972, *27*, 932-940.

Melnick, G. I. A mechanism for transition of concrete to abstract cognitive processes. *Child Development*, 1973, *44*, 599-605.

Meyer, D. E. Correlated operations in searching stored semantic categories. *Journal of Experimental Psychology*, 1973, *99*, 124-133.

Meyer, M. M. The development of healthy and unhealthy goal setting. In C. Buhler & F. Massarik (Eds.), *The course of human life*. New York: Springer, 1968.

Milgram, S. Some conditions of obedience and disobedience to authority. *Human Relations*, 1965, *18*, 57-76.

Milgram, S. The frozen world of the familiar stranger. *Psychology Today*, 1974, *8* (1), 71-80.

Miller, A. G., Gillen, B., Shenker, C., & Radlove, S. The prediction and perception of obedience to authority. *Journal of Personality*, 1974, *42*, 23-42.

Miller, G. A. The magic number seven, plus or minus two. *Psychological Review*, 1956, *63*, 81-97.

Miller, G. A. Language and psychology. In E. H. Lenneberg (Ed.), *New directions in the study of language*. Cambridge: M.I.T. Press, 1966.

Miller, G. A., Galanter, E., & Pribram, K. H. *Plans and the structure of behavior*. New York: Holt, Rinehart and Winston, 1960.

Miller, W. R., & Seligman, M. E. P. Depression and the perception of reinforcement. *Journal of Abnormal Psychology*, 1973, *82*, 62-73.

Moerk, E. L. Specific cognitive antecedents of structures and functions involved in language acquisition. *Child Study Journal*, 1973, *3*(2), 77-90.

Moore, J. W., Hauck, W. E., Biddle, W. B., & Houtz, J. C. The effect of risk on concept acquisition. *Journal of Experimental Education*, 1973, *42*, 51-58.

Mosher, F. A., & Hornsby, J. R. On asking questions. In J. S. Bruner, R. Olver, & P. Greenfield (Eds.), *Studies in cognitive growth*. New York: Wiley, 1966.

Moulton, W. G. The nature of language. *Daedalus*, 1973, *102*(3), 17-35.

Moursund, J. *Small group interaction and individual growth: Academic, social, and personal*. Unpublished doctoral dissertation, University of Wisconsin, 1963.

Murray, H. A. Drive, time, strategy, measurement, and our way of life. In G. Lindzey (Ed.), *Assessment of human motives*. New York: Holt, Rinehart and Winston, 1958.

Navar, I., & Helmreich, R. Prior social setting, type of arousal, and birth order as determinants of affiliative preference for a working situation. *Representative Research in Social Psychology*, 1971, 2(2), 32–42.

Neal, W. R., Jr. The effect of environmental deprivation on speech and language development. *Child Care Quarterly*, 1972, 1, 157–166.

Nelson, D. L., Wheeler, J. W., Borden, R. C., & Brooks, D. H. Levels of processing and cueing. *Journal of Experimental Psychology*, 1974, 103, 971–977.

Nelson, T. O., & Hill, C. C. Multiple retrieval paths and long-term retention. *Journal of Experimental Psychology*, 1974, 103, 185–187.

Nemeth, C., & Markowski, J. Conformity and discrepancy of position. *Sociometry*, 1972, 35, 562–575.

Newell, A., Shaw, J. C., & Simon, H. A. Elements of a theory of human problem solving. *Psychological Review*, 1958, 65, 151–166.

Newmeyer, F. J. Linguistic theory, language teaching, sociolinguistics: Can they be interrelated? *Modern Language Journal*, 1973, 57, 405–410.

Nicholls, J. G. Creativity in the person who will never produce anything original and useful. *American Psychologist*, 1972, 27, 717–727.

Nigl, A. J., & Fishbein, H. D. Perception and conception in coordination of perspectives. *Developmental Psychology*, 1974, 10, 858–866.

Nilsson, L. Further evidence for organization by modality in immediate free recall. *Journal of Experimental Psychology*, 1974, 103, 948–957.

Nolan, J. D. Conceptual and rote learning in children. *Teachers College Record*, 1973, 75, 251–258.

Norman, D. A. What have the animal experiments taught us about human memory? In J. A. Deutsch (Ed.), *The physiological basis of memory*. New York: Academic Press, 1973.

Nowicki, S., Jr., & Barnes, J. Effects of a structured camp experience on locus of control orientation. *Journal of Genetic Psychology*, 1973, 122, 247–252.

Nowicki, S., Jr., & Walker, C. Achievement in relation to locus of control: Identification of a new source of variance. *Journal of Genetic Psychology*, 1973, 123, 63–67.

Nunney, D. N., & Hill, J. E. Personalized educational programs. *Audio-visual Instruction*, 1972, 17(2), 10–15.

Nystedt, L. A modified lens model: A study of the interaction between the individual and the ecology. *Perceptual and Motor Skills*, 1972, 34, 479–498.

O'Connell, W. E. The adaptive functions of wit and humor. *Journal of Abnormal and Social Psychology*, 1960, 61, 263–270.

O'Connell, W. E. The social aspects of wit and humor. *Journal of Social Psychology*, 1969, 79, 183–187.

Odom, R. D., & Corbin, D. W. Perceptual salience and children's multidimensional problem solving. *Child Development*, 1973, 44, 425–432.

Offenbach, S. I. A developmental study of hypothesis testing and cue selection strategies. *Developmental Psychology*, 1974, 10, 484–490.

Olds, J. Self-stimulation experiments and differentiated reward systems. In D. Bindra & J. Stewart (Eds.), *Motivation*. Harmondsworth, Middlesex, England: Penguin Books, 1971.

Olive, H. The relationship of divergent thinking to intelligence, social class, and achievement in high school students. *Journal of Genetic Psychology*, 1972, 12, 179–186.

Olson, D. R. On conceptual strategies. In J. S. Bruner, R. Olver, & P. Greenfield (Eds.), *Studies in cognitive growth*. New York: Wiley, 1966.

Olson, D. R. Language and thought: Aspects of a cognitive theory of semantics. *Psychological Review*, 1970, *77*, 257-273.

Olver, R., & Hornsby, J. On equivalence. In J. S. Bruner, R. Olver, & P. Greenfield (Eds.), *Studies in cognitive growth*. New York: Wiley, 1966.

O'Neil, H. F., Jr. Effects of stress on state anxiety and performance in computer-assisted learning. *Journal of Educational Psychology*, 1972, *63*, 473-481.

Organ, D. W. Locus of control and clarity of self concept. *Perceptual and Motor Skills*, 1973, *37*, 100-102.

Ornstein, P. A., Trabasso, T., & Johnson-Laird, P. N. To organize is to remember. *Journal of Experimental Psychology*, 1974, *103*, 1014-1018.

Oros, J. A., Johnson, J. J., & Lewis, M. L. The effect of induced anxiety on the Wechsler Intelligence Scale for Children. *Psychology in the Schools*, 1972, *9*, 388-392.

Paivio, A. *Imagery and verbal processes*. New York: Holt, Rinehart and Winston, 1971.

Paivio, A. Spacing of repetitions in the incidental and intentional free recall of pictures and words. *Journal of Verbal Learning and Verbal Behavior*, 1974, *13*, 497-511.

Palmer, R. D. Parental perception and perceived locus of control in psychopathology. *Journal of Personality*, 1971, *39*, 420-431.

Patton, G. W. R., & Kotrick, C. A. Visual exploratory behavior as a function of manifest anxiety. *Journal of Psychology*, 1972, *82*, 349-353.

Pedhazur, L., & Wheeler, L. Locus of perceived control and need achievement. *Perceptual and Motor Skills*, 1971, *33*, 1281-1282.

Pennscott, W. W., & Brown, D. F. Anxiety and empathy in a counseling and guidance institute. *Counselor Education and Supervision*, 1972, *11*, 257-261.

Percy. W. Toward a triadic theory of meaning. *Psychiatry*, 1972, *35*, 1-19.

Persely, G., & Leventhal, D. B. The effects of therapeutically oriented instructions and of the pairing of anxiety imagery and relaxation in systematic desensitization. *Behavior Therapy*, 1972, *3*, 417-424.

Peters, J. T., Hammond, K. R., & Summers, D. A. A note on intuitive vs. analytic thinking. *Organizational Behavior and Human Performance*, 1974, *12*, 125-131.

Pezzullo, T. R., Thorsen, E. E., and Madaus, G. F. The heritability of Jensen's level I and II and divergent thinking. *American Educational Research Journal*, 1972, *9*, 539-546.

Phares, E. J. Internal-external control and the reduction of reinforcement value after failure. *Journal of Consulting and Clinical Psychology*, 1971, *37*, 386-390.

Phillips, B. N., Martin, R. P., & Meyers, J. Interventions in relation to anxiety in school. In C. E. Spielberger (Ed.), *Anxiety* (Vol. 2). New York: Academic Press, 1972.

Piaget, J. *The thought and language of the child*. London: Kegan Paul, 1926.

Piaget, J. *The origins of intelligence in children*. New York: International Universities Press, 1952.

Piaget, J. *The construction of reality in the child*. New York: Basic Books, 1954.

Posner, M. I., & Warren, R. E. Traces, concepts, and conscious constructions. In A. W. Melton & E. Martin (Eds.), *Coding processes in human memory*. Washington, D.C.: Winston, 1972.

Potter, M. C. On perceptual recognition. In J. S. Bruner, R. Olver, & P. Greenfield (Eds.), *Studies in cognitive growth*. New York: Wiley, 1966.

Powell, A., & Gable, P. Adult locus of control and self-righteous attitudes. *Psychological Reports*, 1973, *32*, 302.

Premack, D. Reinforcement theory. In D. Levine (Ed.), *Nebraska symposium on motivation* (Vol. 13). Lincoln: University of Nebraska Press, 1965.

Premack, D. Catching up with common sense or two sides of a generalization: Reinforcement and punishment. In C. E. Thoresen (Ed.), *Behavior modification in education.* Chicago: University of Chicago Press, 1973.

Pribram, K. H. Education: An enterprise in language learning. In M. C. Reynolds (Ed.), *Proceedings of the conference on psychology and the process of schooling in the next decade.* Minneapolis: University of Minnesota, Audio-Visual Extension, 1971. (a)

Pribram, K. H. Oral presentation. In M. C. Reynolds (Ed.), *Proceedings of the conference on psychology and the process of schooling in the next decade.* Minneapolis: University of Minnesota, Audio-Visual Extension, 1971. (b)

Pruitt, J. H. *Maternal attitudes, internal-external expectancy and academic achievement in inner-city adolescents.* Unpublished doctoral dissertation, Case Western Reserve University, 1971.

Quay, L. C. Negro dialect and Binet performance in severely disadvantaged black four-year-olds. *Child Development,* 1972, *43,* 245–250.

Randolph, D. L., & Wallin, K. R. A comparison of behavioral consultation and behavioral consultation with model-reinforcement group counseling for children who are consistently off-task. *Journal of Educational Research,* 1973, *67,* 103–107.

Rao, N. C. S. *Strategy in concept learning as a function of certain personality and cognitive variables.* India: Indian International Publications, 1971.

Renner, V. Effects of modification of cognitive style on creative behavior. *Journal of Personality and Social Psychology,* 1970, *14,* 257–262.

Renner, V., & Renner, J. Effects of a creativity training program on stimulus preferences. *Perceptual and Motor Skills,* 1971, *33,* 872–874.

Riccio, D. C., & Silvestri, R. Extinction of avoidance behavior and the problem of residual fear. *Behavior Research and Therapy,* 1973, *11,* 1–9.

Richardson, L., & Soucar, E. Comparison of cognitive complexity with achievement and adjustment: A convergent-discriminant study. *Psychological Reports,* 1971, *29,* 1087–1090.

Riesman, D. *The lonely crowd.* New Haven, Conn.: Yale University Press, 1961. (Originally published, 1950.)

Ritter, K., Kaprove, B. H., Fitch, J. P., & Flavell, J. H. The development of retrieval strategies in young children. *Cognitive Psychology,* 1973, *5,* 310–321.

Ritter, W., & Burche, H. Free, forced, and restricted recall in verbal learning. *Journal of Experimental Psychology,* 1974, *103,* 1204–1207.

Roberts, G. C. Effect of achievement motivation and social environment on performance of a motor task. *Journal of Motor Behavior,* 1972, *4,* 37–46.

Rosekrans, M. Imitation in children as a factor of perceived similarity to a social model and vicarious reinforcement. *Journal of Personal and Social Psychology,* 1967, *7,* 307–315.

Rosen, B., & Salling, R. Political participation as a function of internal-external locus of control. *Psychological Reports,* 1971, *29,* 880–882.

Rosenthal, T. L., Alford, G. S., & Rasp, L. M. Concept attainment, generalization, and retention through observation and verbal coding. *Journal of Experimental Child Psychology,* 1972, *13,* 183–194.

Rosenthal, T. L., & Zimmerman, B. J. Organization, observation, and guided practice in concept attainment and generalization. *Child Development,* 1973, *44,* 606–613.

Rotter, J. B. Generalized expectancies for internal versus external control of reinforcement. *Psychological Monographs*, 1966, *80* (Whole No. 609).

Rotter, J. B. External control and internal control. *Psychology Today*, 1971, *5*(1), 37–42; 58–59.

Ruble, D. N., & Nakamura, C. D. Task orientation vs. social orientation in young children and their attention to relevant social cues. *Child Development*, 1972, *43*, 471–480.

Ryan, E. D., & Lakie, W. L. Competitive and noncompetitive performance in relation to achievement motive and manifest anxiety. *Journal of Personality and Social Psychology*, 1965, *1*, 342–345.

Ryckman, R. M., Rodda, W. C., & Stone, W. F. Performance time as a function of sex, locus of control, and task requirements. *Journal of Social Psychology*, 1971, *85*, 299–305.

Ryckman, R. M., & Sherman, M. F. Relationship between self-esteem and internal-external control for men and women. *Psychological Reports*, 1973, *32*, 1106.

Rystrom, R. Language patterns and the primary child. *Reading Teacher*, 1972, *26*, 149–152.

Sadler, T. G., & Mefferd, R. B., Jr. The interaction of extraversion and neuroticism in human operant behavior. *Journal of Experimental Research in Personality*, 1971, *5*(4), 278–285.

Salthouse, T. A. Using selective interference to investigate spatial memory representations. *Memory and Cognition*, 1974, *2*, 749–757.

Sarason, I. G. Empirical findings and theoretical problems in the use of anxiety scales. *Psychological Bulletin*, 1960, *57*, 403–415.

Sarason, I. G. Experimental approaches to test anxiety: Attention and the uses of information. In C. E. Spielberger (Ed.), *Anxiety* (Vol. 2). New York: Academic Press, 1972.

Sarason, I. G., Peterson, A. M., & Nyman, B. Test anxiety and the observation of models. *Journal of Personality*, 1968, *36*, 493–511.

Sarnoff, I., & Zimbardo, P. G. Anxiety, fear, and social affiliation. *Journal of Abnormal and Social Psychology*, 1961, *62*, 356–363.

Sauber, S. R. Locus of control and task categorization: A study using the perceptual defense paradigm. *Journal of Social Psychology*, 1971, *85*, 311–312.

Savell, J. M. Generalization of the effects of prior agreement and disagreement. *Journal of Personality and Social Psychology*, 1970, *15*, 94–100.

Savell, J. M. Prior agreement and conformity: An extension of the generalization phenomenon. *Psychonomic Science*, 1971, *25*, 327–328.

Schacter, S., & Wheeler, L. Epinephrine, chloropromazine, and amusement. *Journal of Abnormal and Social Psychology*, 1962, *65*, 121–128.

Schneider, F. W. Conforming behavior of black and white children. *Journal of Personality and Social Psychology*, 1970, *16*, 466–471.

Schneider, J. M. College students' beliefs in personal control, 1966–1970. *Journal of Individual Psychology*, 1971, *27*, 188.

Seligman, M. E. P. Fall into helplessness. *Psychology Today*, 1973, *7*(1), 43–48.

Shimkunas, A. M., & Kime, R. G. Personality correlates of student commitment to social action. *Journal of Personality Assessment*, 1971, *35*, 561–568.

Shipe, D. Impulsivity and locus of control as predictors of achievement and adjustment in mildly retarded and borderline youth. *American Journal of Mental Deficiency*, 1971, *76*, 12–22.

Shouksmith, G. *Intelligence, creativity, and cognitive style.* London: Batsford, 1970.

Shugart, B. J., Souder, M. A., & Bunker, L. K. Relationship between vertical space perception and a dynamic non-locomotor balance task. *Perceptual and Motor Skills,* 1972, *34,* 43-46.

Shultz, T. R., & Pilon, R. Development of the ability to detect linguistic ambiguity. *Child Development,* 1973, *44,* 728-733.

Siegel, J. M., & Mayfield, R. Internal-external control and anxiety following success and failure. *Psychological Reports,* 1973, *32,* 1189-1190.

Silverman, R. E., & Shrauger, J. S. Locus of control and correlates of attraction toward others. *Journal of Social Psychology,* 1971, *84,* 207-213.

Singer, D. L., & Berkowitz, L. Differing "creativities" in the wit and the clown. *Perceptual and Motor Skills,* 1972, *35,* 3-6.

Skinner, B. F. *Contingencies of reinforcement.* New York: Appleton-Century-Crofts, 1969.

Slobin, D. I. Seven questions about language development. In P. C. Dodwell (Ed.), *New horizons in psychology 2.* Baltimore: Penguin Books, 1972.

Smith, E. E., & White, H. L. Wit, creativity and sarcasm. *Journal of Applied Psychology,* 1965, *49,* 131-134.

Smith, K. A note on the possibility of a reinforcement theory of cognitive learning. *Bulletin of the Psychonomic Society,* 1974, *4,* 161-163.

Smith, R. E. The use of humor in the counterconditioning of anger responses: A case study. *Behavior Therapy,* 1973, *4,* 576-580.

Snyder, R. Self psychologies. In A. Warmoth (Ed.), *The art and science of psychology.* Monterey, Calif.: Brooks/Cole, in press.

Solso, R. L. *Contemporary issues in cognitive psychology: The Loyola symposium.* Washington, D.C.: Winston, 1973.

Spielberger, C. E. Anxiety as an emotional state. In C. E. Spielberger (Ed.), *Anxiety* (Vol. 1). New York: Academic Press, 1972.

Spitz, R. The smiling responses: A contribution to the ontogenesis of social relations. *Genetic Psychology Monographs,* 1946, *34,* 57-125.

Staub, E. Instigation to goodness: The role of social norms and interpersonal influence. *Journal of Social Issues,* 1972, *28*(3), 131-150.

Steger, J. A., Simmons, W. L., and Lavelle, S. Accuracy of prediction of own performance as a function of locus of control. *Psychological Reports,* 1973, *33,* 59-62. (a)

Steger, J. A., Simmons, W. L., & Lavelle, S. Reply to Wolfe and Egelston. *Psychological Reports,* 1973, *33,* 312. (b)

Stephens, M. W. Dimensions of locus of control: Impact of early educational experiences. *Proceedings of the 80th Annual Convention of the American Psychological Association,* 1972, *7,* 137-138.

Stephens, M. W., & Delys, P. A locus of control measure for preschool children. *Developmental Psychology,* 1973, *9,* 55-65.

St. John, N. The elementary classroom as a frog pond: Self-concept, sense of control and social context. *Social Forces,* 1971, *49,* 581-595.

Stolorow, R. D. Causality-interpretation and the precipitation of distress. *Journal of Personality Assessment,* 1971, *35,* 122-127.

Stratton, R. P., & Brown, R. Improving creative thinking by training in the production and/or judgement of solutions. *Journal of Educational Psychology,* 1972, *63,* 390-397.

Stromnes, F. J., & Nyman, J. Immediate and long-term retention of connected concrete discourse as a function of mnemonic picture-type sequence and context. *Scandinavian Journal of Psychology*, 1974, *15*, 197–202.

Sulin, R. A., & Dooling, D. J. Intrusion of a thematic idea in the retention of prose. *Journal of Experimental Psychology*, 1974, *103*, 255–262.

Sullivan, S. J. *An attempt to modify external locus of control*. Unpublished doctoral dissertation, Catholic University of America, 1971.

Tarrance, D. G., & Davis, J. K. The relationship of cognitive style and method of instruction to performance in 9th grade geography. *Journal of Educational Research*, 1971, *65*, 137–141.

Thacker, B. T., & Rosenbluth, E. S. Creativity as a reflection of teacher-pupil relationships. *Psychology*, 1972, *9*(1), 23–26.

Thelen, M. H., & Fryrear, J. L. Effect of observer and model race on the imitation of standards of self-reward. *Developmental Psychology*, 1971, *5*, 133–135.

Thomas, D. L., & Weigert, A. J. Socialization and adolescent conformity to significant others: A cross-national analysis. *American Sociological Review*, 1971, *36*, 835–847.

Thomas, S. A. Violent content in television: The effect of cognitive style and age in mediating children's aggressive responses. *Proceedings of the 80th Annual Convention of the American Psychological Association*, 1972, *7*, 97–98.

Thompson, D. M. Context effects in recognition memory. *Journal of Verbal Learning and Verbal Behavior*, 1972, *11*, 497–511.

Thoresen, C. E. Behavioral humanism. In C. E. Thoresen (Ed.), *Behavior modification in education*. Chicago: University of Chicago Press, 1973.

Thorndike, E. L. *An experimental study of rewards*. New York: Columbia University, Teachers College, Bureau of Publications, 1933.

Thorndike, E. L. Connectionism. In E. Stolurow (Ed.), *Readings in learning*. Englewood Cliffs, N.J.: Prentice-Hall, 1953.

Thorndike, E. L. The law of effect. In D. Bindra & J. Stewart (Eds.), *Motivation*. Harmondsworth, Middlesex, England: Penguin Books, 1971.

Thurner, F., & Wennehorst, L. Can anxiety facilitate problem solving? *Psychologische Rundschau*, 1972, *23*, 115–126.

Tinbergen, N. Hierarchical organization of instinctive actions. In D. Bindra & J. Stewart (Eds.), *Motivation*. Harmondsworth, Middlesex, England: Penguin Books, 1971.

Toder, N. L., & Marcia, J. E. Ego identity status and response to conformity pressure in college women. *Journal of Personality and Social Psychology*, 1973, *26*, 287–294.

Tolman, E. C. There is more than one kind of learning. In E. Stolurow (Ed.), *Readings in learning*. Englewood Cliffs, N.J.: Prentice-Hall, 1953.

Tolor, A., & LeBlanc, R. F. Personality correlates of alienation. *Journal of Consulting and Clinical Psychology*, 1971, *37*, 444.

Tomkins, S. S. Comments on Dr. Izard's paper. In C. E. Spielberger (Ed.), *Anxiety* (Vol. 1). New York: Academic Press, 1972.

Torrance, E. P. Factors affecting creative thinking in children: An interim research report. *Merrill Palmer Quarterly*, 1961, *7*, 171–180.

Torrance, E. P. Career patterns and peak creative achievements of creative high school students 12 years later. *Gifted Child Quarterly*, 1972, *16*, 75–88.

Trickett, E. The interaction of achievement motivation, task difficulty, and confidence-enhancing information in producing conformity behavior. *Journal of Social Psychology,* 1971, *84,* 233-242.

Tulving, E., & Watkins, M. J. Continuity between recall and recognition. *American Journal of Psychology,* 1973, *86,* 739-748.

Tunnell, G. B., & Falkenberg, P. R. Effect of context on transfer of information from short- to long-term memory. *Perceptual and Motor Skills,* 1974, *38,* 495-501.

Ulan, H. C. *Locus of control and response to situations varying in novelty.* Unpublished doctoral dissertation, Northwestern University, 1971.

Underwood, B. J. Attributes of memory. *Psychological Review,* 1969, *76,* 559-573.

Underwood, B. J. Are we overloading memory? In A. W. Melton & E. Martin (Eds.), *Coding processes in human memory.* Washington, D.C.: Winston, 1972.

VanDuyne, H. J. Age and intelligence factors as predictors of the development of verbal control of nonverbal behavior. *Journal of Genetic Psychology,* 1974, *124,* 321-331.

Vardy, M., & Greenstein, M. Perceptual field-dependence and psychopathology: Replication and critique. *Perceptual and Motor Skills,* 1972, *34,* 635-642.

Wachtel, P. L. Cognitive style and style of adaptation. *Perceptual and Motor Skills,* 1972, *35,* 779-785. (a)

Wachtel, P. L. Field dependence and psychological differentiation: Reexamination. *Perceptual and Motor Skills,* 1972, *35,* 179-189. (b)

Walker, E. E. *Conditioning and instrumental learning.* Monterey, Calif.: Brooks/ Cole, 1968.

Wallace, J. G. *Stages and transition in conceptual development.* London: National Foundation for Educational Research, 1972.

Wallach, M. A., & Kogan, N. Creativity and intelligence in children. In J. McV. Hunt (Ed.), *Human intelligence.* New Brunswick, N.J.: Transaction Books, 1972.

Wallach, M. A., & Mabli, J. Information versus conformity in the effects of group discussion on risk taking. *Journal of Personality and Social Psychology,* 1970, *14,* 149-156.

Walters, R. H., & Parke, R. D. Influence of response consequences to a social model on resistance to deviation. In A. Bandura (Ed.), *Psychological modeling.* Chicago: Aldine, 1971.

Warehime, R. G. Generalized expectancy for locus of control and academic performance. *Psychological Reports,* 1972, *30,* 314.

Warehime, R. G., & Foulds, M. L. Perceived locus of control and personal adjustment. *Journal of Consulting and Clinical Psychology,* 1971, *37,* 250-252.

Warehime, R. G., & Woodson, S. G. Locus of control and immediate affect states. *Journal of Clinical Psychology,* 1971, *27,* 443-444.

Warrington, E. K., & Weiskrantz, L. An analysis of short-term and long-term memory defects in man. In J. A. Deutsch (Ed.), *The physiological basis of memory.* New York: Academic Press, 1973.

Watkins, M. J. Concept and measurement of primary memory. *Psychological Bulletin,* 1974, *81,* 695-711.

Wechsler, D. Intelligence defined and undefined: A relativistic appraisal. *American Psychologist,* 1975, *30,* 135-140.

Weiner, B. Achievement motivation and task recall in competitive situations. *Journal of Personality and Social Psychology,* 1966, *3,* 693-696.

Weiner, B. Attribution theory, achievement motivation, and the educational process. *Review of Educational Research*, 1972, *42*, 203-215.

Weinheimer, S. Egocentrism and social influence in children. *Child Development*, 1972, *43*, 567-578.

White, K. M. Conceptual style and conceptual ability in kindergarten through the eighth grade. *Child Development*, 1971, *42*, 1652-1656.

White, K. M. The effect of source of evaluation on the development of internal control among young boys. *Psychology in the Schools*, 1972, *9*, 56-61.

White, R. M. Hypothesis behavior as a function of amount of pretraining. *Journal of Experimental Psychology*, 1974, *102*, 1053-1060.

White, R. T. The validation of a learning hierarchy. *American Educational Research Journal*, 1974, *11*, 121-136.

White, R. W. Motivation reconsidered: The concept of competence. *Psychological Review*, 1959, *66*, 297-333.

White, W. *Beyond conformity*. New York: Free Press, 1961.

Whitehurst, G. J., & Novak, G. Modeling, imitation training, and the acquisition of sentence phrases. *Journal of Experimental Child Psychology*, 1973, *16*, 332-345.

Wickelgren, W. A. Single-trace fragility theory of memory dynamics. *Memory and Cognition*, 1974, *2*, 775-780.

Wickens, D. D. Encoding categories of words. *Psychological Review*, 1970, *77*, 1-15.

Wickens, D. D. Characteristics of word encoding. In A. W. Melton & E. Martin (Eds.), *Coding processes in human memory*. Washington, D.C.: Winston, 1972.

Wickens, D. D. Temporal limits of human information processing. *Psychological Bulletin*, 1974, *81*, 739-755.

Wickersham, P. H. *Classroom interaction patterns: Differential effects and relationships between 6th grade children's self-concepts and locus of control of reinforcements*. Unpublished doctoral dissertation, University of Illinois, 1970.

Wilcox, B., Meddock, T. D., & Steinman, W. M. "Generalized imitation" on a non-imitative task: Effects of modeling and task history. *Journal of Experimental Child Psychology*, 1973, *15*, 381-393.

Willerman, L., & Stafford, R. E. Material effects on intellectual functioning. *Behavior Genetics*, 1972, *2*, 321-325.

Williams, C., & Cole, D. L. The influence of experimentally induced inadequacy feelings upon the appreciation of humor. *Journal of Social Psychology*, 1964, *64*, 113-117.

Witkin, H. A., Dyk, R. B., Faterson, H. F., Goodenough, D. R., & Karp, S. A. *Psychological differentiation*. New York: Wiley, 1962.

Wolf, T. M. Effects of live-modeled sex-inappropriate play behavior in a naturalistic setting. *Developmental Psychology*, 1973, *9*, 120-123.

Wolfe, R. N. Perceived locus of control and prediction of own academic performance. *Journal of Consulting and Clinical Psychology*, 1972, *38*, 80-83.

Wolfenstein, M. *Children's humor*. New York: Free Press, 1954.

Wright, P. The harassed decision-maker. *Journal of Applied Psychology*, 1974, *59*, 555-561.

Young, P. T. Affective processes and motivation. In D. Bindra & J. Stewart (Eds.), *Motivation*. Harmondsworth, Middlesex, England: Penguin Books, 1971.

Zellner, M. Self-esteem, reception, and influenceability. *Journal of Personality and Social Psychology*, 1970, *15*, 87-93.

Zelnicker, T., Jeffrey, W. E., Ault, R., & Parsons, J. Analysis and modification of search strategies of impulsive and reflective children on the Matching Familiar Figures Test. *Child Development,* 1972, *43,* 321-335.

Zigler, E. Research on personality structure in the retardate. In N. Ellis (Ed.), *International review of research in mental retardation* (Vol. 1). New York: Academic Press, 1966.

Zijderveld, A. C. Jokes and their relation to social reality. *Social Research,* 1968, *35,* 286-311.

Zimmerman, B. J., & Dialessi, F. Modeling influences on children's creative behavior. *Journal of Educational Psychology,* 1973, *65,* 127-135.

Zimmerman, B. J., & Pike, E. O. Effects of modeling and reinforcement on the acquisition and generalization of question-asking behavior. *Child Development,* 1972, *43,* 892-907.

Zimmerman, B. J., & Rosenthal, T. L. Observational learning of rule-governed behavior by children. *Psychological Bulletin,* 1974, *81,* 29-42.

# Name Index

# Subject Index